# CURRICULUM-BASED EVALUATION

# EVALUATION

*Teaching and Decision Making*

THIRD EDITION

## Kenneth W. Howell

Western Washington University

## Victor Nolet

Western Washington University

**Wadsworth**
Thomson Learning™

*Australia • Canada • Denmark • Japan • Mexico • New Zealand • Philippines*
*Puerto Rico • Singapore • South Africa • Spain • United Kingdom • United States*

Education Editor: Dianne Lindsay
Assistant Editor: Tangelique Williams
Editorial Assistant: Keynia Johnson
Marketing Manager: Becky Tollerson
Publisher: Peter Marshall
Project Editor: Trudy Brown
Print Buyer: Barbara Britton
Permissions Editor: Susan Walters
Production: Hockett Editorial Service

Designer: Rita Naughton Book Design
Photo Research: Linda Sykes
Copy Editor: Rus VanWestervelt
Illustrator: MacArt Design
Cover Design: Ellen Kwan
Cover Image: David Young-Wolff; PhotoEdit
Compositor: GAC/Indianapolis
Printer: Webcom Limited

Printed in Canada
4  5  6  7  03

For permission to use material from this text, contact us:
  Web: www.thomsonrights.com
  Fax: 1-800-730-2215
  Phone: 1-800-730-2214

**Library of Congress Cataloging-in-Publication Data**
Howell, Kenneth W.
  Curriculum-based evaluation : teaching and decision making / Kenneth W. Howell, Victor Nolet. — 3rd ed.
      p. cm.
  Includes bibliographical references (p.     ) and indexes.
  ISBN 0-534-34370-8
  1. Curriculum-based assessment—United States. 2. Educational tests and measurements—United States.
I. Nolet, Victor. II. Title.
LB3060.32.C74H68 1999
371.26'4—dc21                      99-17563

**For more information, contact**
**Wadsworth/Thomson Learning**
**10 Davis Drive**
**Belmont, CA 94002-3098**
**USA**
**www.wadsworth.com**

**International Headquarters**
Thomson Learning
290 Harbor Drive, 2nd Floor
Stamford, CT 06902-7477
USA

**UK/Europe/Middle East**
Thomson Learning
Berkshire House
168-173 High Holborn
London WC1V 7AA
United Kingdom

**Asia**
Thomson Learning
60 Albert Street #15-01
Albert Complex
Singapore 189969

**Canada**
Nelson/Thomson Learning
1120 Birchmount Road
Scarborough, Ontario M1K 5G4
Canada

 This book is printed on acid-free recycled paper.

*This book is dedicated to Kathy Lorson-Howell and Geneva M. Blake.*

# Contents

## *Chapter 4*  **Thinking About Instruction**  67

## Chapter 9    Decoding   247

## Chapter 10    Language   289

## Chapter 11    Written Expression    325

## Chapter 14   Task-Related Behaviors   431

# Preface

This text represents an expansion and revision of several previous works on the topic of evaluation and teaching. Throughout this sequence, we have become increasingly aware of two things: the need to emphasize decision making over measurement, and the need to unite the functions of evaluation and instruction. Both are reflected in this volume.

The current literature is filled with the business of assessment. For example: journal articles with baseline and intervention data; task analyses; statistical operations of all sorts; and critiques of one or another of the hundreds of tests used to identify, label, place, or program for children who need help in school. In addition, every school must now contend with mandated assessments derived from political agendas and legislative mandates pertaining to accountability. But mechanisms for distilling and coordinating this inventory of techniques and evaluation initiatives are seldom provided. As a result, common classroom action often seems to continue in the same unproductive direction without regard for improved practice.

This text was written in an attempt to break through the inertia of common practice by integrating the basic concepts of evaluation and instruction with the best current knowledge. Not surprisingly, the goal of generating productive tools for classroom use has dictated the plan of this book. Part One consists of chapters that focus on the thought processes of teachers and the basic models of evaluation and teaching. Part Two illustrates the application of material from the first part across academic and social-skills content. This part includes extensive material on the things teachers teach. It also provides exact directions for deciding which of these to teach a particular student. In a very real way Part Two is more an assessment manual than a textbook.

Because assessment involves collecting and summarizing behavior, you will need various status sheets, tests, and forms to carry it out. Some of these materials are provided in the exhibits and appendices of this text. In an effort to add flexibility to the total Curriculum-Based Evaluation package, however, many more can be found in *Resources for Implementing Curriculum-Based Evaluation* (Howell et al., 2000a).

This companion book, which complements the text, is not a supplement. It contains concrete, serviceable, and handy information to help the reader carry out the actions presented in this text. It is aligned with Part Two of this text and it contains testing and interpretation materials as well as quick (and, we hope, understandable) guides to the statistical, monitoring, and instructional content referenced in the chapters.

## *Rationale for Our Approach*

The majority of remedial students (sometimes including, within special education, those called mildly disabled) require help because of their failure to learn the academic or social curriculum presented in school. The "exceptional" services these students require may range from small instructional accommodations provided by the general education teachers—to service modifications carried out by specialists in separate programs and settings. The special programs developed to combat student failure (not only remedial education and special education programs but also migrant education, bilingual education, and those for students disadvantaged by their living conditions) have many commonalties. For example, each program's primary goal is to raise students' level of curricular performance. Students who are behind in the curriculum are given exceptional programs and those who catch up are removed from them. Therefore, by its very nature, special/remedial education is curriculum-based.

Functional, classroom-based evaluation draws much of its strength from the principle of alignment. This principle states that greater learning will occur when evaluation and instruction complement each other. The essential ingredient for alignment is the curriculum (i.e., the body of things a student is expected to learn). In other words, students will learn more if teachers use materials and activities that target needed portions of the curriculum and make decisions from measures that concentrate on those portions of the curriculum. This "evaluate what you teach" and "teach what you evaluate" orientation makes common sense. And it is effective.

Curriculum-based evaluation is not new (Carroll, 1963). However, in the past it has lost the competition for coverage in journals and texts in special education and educational psychology. While the rest of education has been acutely interested in curriculum-based issues (such as mastery learning, outcome-based instruction, essential learnings, alignment, and teacher effectiveness), special/remedial education has often shown more interest in trying to map the supposedly impaired learning characteristics of its students. It is this failure to focus on curriculum and instruction, not the absence of functional measurement technology, that has led to the torpor that clogs much of current practice. In short, we are where we are today because a lot of us have made mistakes in *thinking*. Such mistakes are not corrected by writing new tests. They are corrected by promoting new ways to solve problems.

The most easily recognized label for the thought processes and techniques we will present in this text is "curriculum-based evaluation"; however, other terms such as "functional evaluation," "practical evaluation," "situation-centered evaluation," and even "direct evaluation" are all descriptive. Whatever the terminology, this approach to evaluation is no less complex, theoretical, or sophisticated than approaches that focus on the incapacities of students. While it does involve some different procedures and techniques, its main distinction is one of focus. It concentrates on what teachers and evaluators do—not on whom they do it to.

Evaluation is a difficult, time-consuming business. The authors recognize that the efforts of schools and teachers are often vandalized by social failures beyond the scope of this text. Still, while we'd like to claim that our techniques will solve those problems while saving you time and effort, they probably won't. But we do offer you a chance to see to it that you are never prevented from using quality practice because you don't know how!

## Notes on the Text

1. References to the gender of students and teachers are reversed in each chapter of this text. Therefore, in one chapter all references to teachers are male and in the next they are female. This pattern does not hold when specific case studies are provided. In those instances, references to the gender of the actual student or teacher involved are not changed.

2. To facilitate referral, all figures and tables in this text are simply called "exhibits." This makes Part Two of the text easier to use. A number of these exhibits also appear in *Resources for Implementing Curriculum-Based Evaluation*. We grant you permission to duplicate those exhibits for the purpose of working with students.

3. Throughout the text, notations like these appear: (see Chapter 1, pages **4–5**). These notations are provided to help you find related information without having to refer to the index. In some cases, when the coverage of a topic is infused throughout a chapter, page numbers are not supplied.

4. Each chapter begins with a quote.

5. Sometimes we refer to our clients as students, and at other times we refer to them—as we do in our everyday conversations—as "kids." However, many of the practices explained in this text have utility for anyone, regardless of age. Please do not assume that the use of "kid" is intended to preclude adult learners.

## Acknowledgments

So many people who have contributed to this text in so many different ways that we can't list them all without adding a new Appendix. But here are a few.

First, much of the material presented here is drawn directly from the invaluable work of Joe Kaplan. Dr. Kaplan's conceptualization of evaluative practice are as much a part of this work as those of the current authors, and we thank him for his continued contributions of ideas and support. Similarly, the ideas and products of the people working with Randy Allison at the Heartland Area Education Agency 11 in Iowa, particularly Sharon Kurns, can be found throughout this text.

We thank Pam Hamilton for her unrestricted assistance. In addition, we owe much to Julie Schmitke for her extraordinary skill and temperament, Kim "Merch" Fricke for her perseverance, as well as Karna "Catfish" Nelson and Kris Slentz for their provision of friendship and reality checks. In addition, we are grateful to Gina Lockman, Dana Brown, Kevin Candela, Aumony Dahl, Jennifer Woods, and Susan "Alacrity" Bigelow for their efforts in preparing and organizing this manuscript.

Thanks and gratitude go to Chuck Atkinson and the entire special education faculty at WWU for their tolerance and good humor.

We would also like to acknowledge the assistance of the following reviewers: Nancy Cooke, University of North Carolina, Charlotte; Harry Dangel, Georgia State University; Leonard Haines, University of Saskatchewan, Saskatoon; Deborah Hammond, Arizona State University; Cregg Ingram, Brigham Young University; Louise LaFontaine, Northeastern University; Sarah Lang, Norfolk State University; Tom

Lovitt, University of Washington; K. C. Sacca, Buffalo State College; Linda Meloy, Western Illinois University; Donna Montgomery, East Tennessee State University; Stephen Wagner, California State University, San Bernardino; Lori Marks, East Tennessee State University; Sharon Raimondi, State University of New York, Buffalo; Richard Towne; and Gregory Williams, Pacific Lutheran University.

Our thanks also go to the staff at Wadsworth Publishing Company—Dianne Lindsay, our editor; Tangelique Williams, assistant editor; and Trudy Brown, the project editor. We are grateful to Rus VanWestervelt, for his great help in copyediting, and to Rachel Youngman at Hockett Editorial Service, for shepherding the book through production.

# *Part One*

# THINGS TO THINK ABOUT

# Chapter 1

# Educational Decision Making

*Situations, or tasks, rather than people, should be the basic units of analysis.*
—E. Brunswick (1943)

## What Is Evaluation and Why Do It?

**Evaluation** is the process of making a decision or reaching a conclusion. In schools, evaluation usually involves decision making about student **performance** based on information obtained from an assessment process. Assessment is the process of *collecting* information by reviewing the products of student work, interviewing, observing, or testing. Evaluation is the process of *using* information that is collected through assessment. The ultimate purpose of *any* evaluation process that takes place in schools should be to improve student learning. However, in actuality, there are so many reasons to examine what goes on in classrooms and schools that clarification of the specific purpose of evaluation must be the initial step of the evaluation process. The various purposes for engaging in evaluation are important to understand because confusing them can lead to wasted resources, the selection of ineffective measures, and flawed instructional decisions. Furthermore, the *purpose* of an evaluation process must be distinguished from the *procedures* used to collect the information that will be analyzed. With alarming frequency, educators are guilty of collecting the wrong data and making the wrong comparisons for the decisions they are attempting to make.

There are two categories of purposes for engaging in evaluation in schools: those purposes that originate and are made *outside* of the classroom and those purposes that originate and are made *inside* the classroom. Although the measurements employed to collect data used to accomplish *either* purpose may be taken inside the classroom, the decision making and interpretation for purposes that originate *outside* the classroom occur outside. These data typically are collected after instruction is finished and are aggregated by classes and schools. This means that

**Exhibit 1.1    *Examples of Outside and Inside Evaluation Purposes.***

| Examples of Outside Purposes | Examples of Inside purposes |
| --- | --- |
| • Measurement-driven exercises of school, school district, and state accountability<br><br>• Determination if students are entitled to categorical funding<br><br>• Certification of student accomplishments to outside audiences (e.g., through grading, granting of certificates, or the issuing of statements of mastery) | • Screening for students who need to be taught particular skills<br><br>• Collecting data to inform instructional decisions<br><br>• Selection of goals and the choosing of instructional procedures and materials that will be utilized to accomplish these goals<br><br>• Monitoring to check the results of classroom efforts |

the information collected for outside evaluation is of limited use for instructional decision making. The measurements used to accomplish *inside* purposes typically employ direct samples of the skills and knowledge being taught. In addition, they may involve frequent measurement, which occurs within the flow of instruction, with data summarized for each individual. Thus, the information is of great use for informing instructional decision making but of little use for outside purposes. Exhibit 1.1 shows some examples of "outside" and "inside" evaluation purposes. Think about other reasons for educational assessment that are not included here and decide whether they are for "outside" or "inside" purposes.

This book focuses primarily on procedures associated with evaluation *inside* the classroom. However, educators often fail to adequately distinguish inside from outside evaluation purposes, and this confusion has been exacerbated by recent efforts to link assessment of student performance to school reform. Therefore, the notion of "outside" evaluation merits some discussion here.

Outside evaluation can serve as a powerful lever to bring about change in practice at the classroom and school levels. At the time this text was being prepared, measurement-driven, standards-based reform efforts were under way in 48 states in the United States (CCSSO, 1996). The premise

of this movement is that when schools are held accountable for helping all students meet high academic standards, improvements will occur in the overall quality of education. According to a National Academy of Science report (McDonnell & McLaughlin, 1997), reform efforts at the national, state, and local levels have four elements in common:

1. Student achievement is the primary measure of school success.

2. Rigorous standards are established that specify the knowledge and skills students should acquire as well as criteria for mastery.

3. All students, including those for whom expectations traditionally have been low, are expected to meet the standards.

4. Tests of student achievement are used to monitor the success of schools in meeting reform goals.

The rationale for such measurement-driven reform goes something like this:

• dissatisfaction with schools is widespread and well documented (Berliner, 1993);

• one solution to this dissatisfaction is to "reform" the way schools work (Elmore, 1995);

• this reform should be linked to high standards for learning (Nitko, 1995; Stallings, 1995);

- assessment that is based on those standards can be used to find out if students are meeting the outcomes (Kane, 1994);
- schools can be persuaded to improve when it is mandated that students reach proficiency on these standards (Howe, 1994) and that sanctions will be imposed on those schools that fail to bring students to a high level of performance.

It is noteworthy that few models of program evaluation and reform outside of education are based solely on the measurement of outcomes. More often, such efforts include measurement of the resources available to the programs and the processes employed to use those resources (Gilbert, 1978; Laufer, 1997). This philosophy is a "carrot and stick" approach in which schools are provided sufficient resources to engage in meaningful reform, and only those that fail to make progress are subject to sanctions. However, the primary source of federal dollars for school reform, Goals 2000 funding, is extremely limited, and few states have engaged in meaningful allocation of new funds or reallocation of existing monies to pay for the expected reform of schools (McDonnell & McLaughlin, 1997). Therefore, most of the costs of school reform are being borne at the district or school level. At the same time, numerous states have enacted or are implementing various accountability measures for students (e.g., assessments required for graduation from high school) and for schools (e.g., cash rewards, reporting of test results at the school level, or reassignment of administrative personnel). As a result, efforts at standards-based reform generally are viewed by educators as the stick without the carrot, and for many students and teachers, the stakes associated with measurement-driven reform efforts are perceived as very high. This situation is roughly equivalent to telling a student that he will be punished if he doesn't do well on a test while failing to provide that student with the instruction he needs to improve. At the very least, it produces a tense student.

In such a climate, it is not surprising that the goals of evaluation often are confused, nor is it surprising that assessment has come to be disliked and distrusted among many educators. Indeed, the assessment procedures that are implemented in high stakes accountability testing often *are* intended to serve both the outside purpose of school reform and the inside-the-classroom purpose of informing teachers about the performance of their students on the standards. However, a growing body of research suggests that simply mandating high stakes testing will not be sufficient to improve outcomes for all students (Cohen, 1996; Editors, 1999; Noble & Smith, 1994; Shepard et al., 1995). We believe any effort at school improvement should result in the improvement of student learning and that student learning, ultimately, depends on the quality of teacher thought (Freire, 1993) and classroom practice (Good & Brophy, 1994). These include the making of good decisions about *what* and *how* to teach. That is the primary reason that this text deals almost exclusively with *inside* evaluation purposes.

### The Curriculum and Student Progress

Formal education is planned and carried out by our society at great public expense with the intent of benefiting both individual students and society. Because education is a social undertaking, discussions of it often become political (Boulding, 1972; Darling-Hammond, 1996). However, for most teachers, the ultimate purpose of education is to prepare students to be socially competent. They try to do this by teaching the things students need to know. Unfortunately, not all students learn these "things" as quickly or as well as we—or they—would like.

When students have problems learning, it is up to teachers to help solve those problems. Sometimes, problem solving is carried out by individuals; at other times, it is carried out through collaboration by groups of professionals and parents. But no matter who has the problem or who is trying to solve it, the problem will be solved more effectively if the process is informed by data that are aligned with the curriculum.

The term "curriculum" can refer to a variety of things, including the courses taught in a school or program, the document that lists the courses taught, a set of teaching materials that are organized in some sequence or framework, or a framework for selecting and organizing learning experiences. In this text, we will refer to **curriculum** as a structured set of learning outcomes (objectives) that are expected to result from instruction (Johnson, 1967; Sands et al., 1995).

The curriculum is pivotal to all instructional activities, including evaluation, because it defines *what* students are expected to learn. Because all of the things in the curriculum cannot be taught at the same time, the curriculum is often subdivided so that different outcomes can be assigned to different grades, classes, and times of the year (for example, most school districts expect students to have learned multiplication facts by the end of third grade). For any given student, the clarity of these expectations hinges upon how formally the curriculum in a school has been developed and how closely the teachers follow it. In some schools, the outcomes may be highly defined and very formal; in others, they may not be well defined at all.

This phenomenon has lead to the tradition of thinking of curricula as having three dimensions. The *intended* curriculum is the formally recommended or adopted curriculum. Other terms that could refer to the intended curriculum are "expected," "official," "explicit," or "sanctioned." This is the curriculum that administrators, parents, and teachers believe is being taught in the classroom. In many schools, the curricular frameworks that form the basis for statewide accountability tests are increasingly becoming the intended curriculum. Individual Education Plans (IEPs) developed for students who have disabilities also constitute an intended curriculum. The *taught* curriculum is the one that is actually implemented in the classroom and is directly based on what teachers do and use. The taught curriculum is influenced by the instructional methods, materials, and expectations that a teacher brings to the classroom. It may be either closely aligned or only loosely linked with the intended curriculum. Other terms that could refer to the taught curriculum include "implemented," "operationalized," or "implicit." Finally, the *learned* curriculum is what students actually learn as a

result of being in a classroom. The learned curriculum may include things teachers and parents want students to learn or it could include unexpected or unintended outcomes such as misconceptions, learned helplessness, or ineffective learning strategies.

It is important to realize that learning expectations, whether formally or informally defined, *do exist*. As a result, disappointment surrounding the acquisition of the outcomes also exists when the curriculum that students learn is not aligned with the intended curriculum. This means it is natural to try and fix blame when desired learning does not occur. Unfortunately, students who fail to meet expectations are often treated as if *they* are the problems.

Exhibit 1.2 shows a line of **expected student progress**. This line is determined by noting the intersections of time spent in school and various levels of anticipated curriculum acquisition. The line in Exhibit 1.2 indicates that a student is expected to have learned 1 year's worth of curriculum in 1 year's time. Students whose progress is above the line are working above their **expected level**; students whose progress falls below the line are below expectation.

For various reasons, many students have trouble moving through the curriculum at the expected rate. Often, these students end up in remedial and special education programs. For example, the student shown in Exhibit 1.2 is only progressing at 50% of the expected rate. He has only learned about 2.5 years' worth of curriculum in 5 years' time. This failure to progress typically prompts teachers or parents to seek special support for their students. The aim of this support is to move the student through the curriculum faster to catch him up. To get additional support, a decision-making process must be set in motion. This process will be most effective if it focuses on things teachers can control rather than variables over which the teacher has no influence.

### How Do Students Who Need Extra Help Get It?

This text will teach you how to make decisions about teaching—*what* to teach, *how* to teach it, and even *when* to teach it. Furthermore, we will

**Exhibit 1.2 (a) Expected Course of Student Learning. (b) Actual Course of Special Student.**

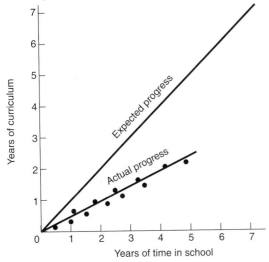

focus almost entirely on the needs of students like the one illustrated in Exhibit 1.2, whose educational progress (including social behavior) is not meeting expectations. These students can be found in all classrooms at all grade levels. However, *some* students will need support designed to help them progress adequately in school. This support often comes through specialized programs that are subsidized by federal (and/or state) funds and have very specific eligibility requirements. Such programs include various remedial programs, English as second language classes, and special education. These programs often are referred to as **entitlements**.

Because it is hard to imagine a book dealing with the needs of students who are not making progress in school that doesn't spend some time addressing the topic of **entitlement**, particularly as it applies to special and remedial education, we will do so here. Entitlements are legislative-funded mandates for service. They are typically created to provide benefits to specific groups of individuals. In schools, the students targeted by these programs fall roughly into two types: those with a disability and those who are members of a group that is thought to be "at risk" because of cultural, linguistic, or economic characteristics that lower their probability of school success. Entitlement programs are designed to "level the playing field" for individuals who, because of circumstances beyond their control, are unable to take advantage of services that are widely available to the rest of the students.

The largest and probably most controversial of entitlement programs in schools is special education. In the United States, Public Law 105-17, the Individuals with Disabilities Education Act (or IDEA), mandates that children between the ages of 3 and 22 who have a disability in one of the categories specified in the law and *need* special education because that disability adversely affects their educational progress are entitled to a free, appropriate public education. This special education legislation had its genesis in the civil rights movement of the 1950s, and most notably the landmark United States Supreme Court decision *Brown v. Board of Education*. The *Brown* decision stipulated that under the provisions of the Fourteenth Amendment to the Constitution, states must provide equal protection to people within their jurisdiction. Specifically, if a state provides a free education for some of it citizens, it must do so for all of its citizens (Yell, 1998). With the 1975 enactment of PL 94-142, the provisions of *Brown* were extended to include individuals with disabilities. This law has been regularly updated during the last 25 years, and provisions of the most recent amendments are completely consistent with the original legislation. For a complete history and analysis of legal issues associated with special education, readers are encouraged to refer to Yell (1998) and Bateman & Linden (1997).

Notice that IDEA requires schools to establish eligibility by substantiating two things (Bateman & Linden, 1997). First, the school must determine that the child has one of the categories of disability specified in the law; second, the student must be in *need* of special education. This means that if a student has a disability, but is doing fine in general education, that student is *not* eligible for special education. At the same time, a student who is not progressing adequately in school but does not have one of the categories of disability specified in IDEA also is not eligible for

*We learned how to teach but when do we learn how to think?*

special education. Therefore, in terms of entitlement for special education services, recognition and delineation of "need" is as important as the recognition of a disability.

This book will *not* teach you how to decide whether a student has a disabilities under one of the categories specified in IDEA or any other law. We will *not* talk about the characteristics of mental retardation or learning disability or any of the other categories of disability specified in IDEA or any other entitlement program. This book *will* teach you how to decide what help a student needs to progress adequately in school. It is important not to confuse entitlement with need. It is our job to find ways to respond to *all* students who need effective educational services, regardless of funding procedures and administrative regulations.

Sometimes, educators' efforts are impaired by misunderstandings about why entitlement decisions are made and what tools must be used to make them. Historically, the focus of entitlement decision making has been on establishing the existence of a disability through the use of highly questionable measures devised to correspond to equally uncertain ideas about human ability. For example, many so-called evaluation specialists (who should know better) persist in trying to establish the existence of a learning disability by searching for apparent discrepancies between a student's score on an intelligence test and his score on an achievement test. In addition to being ludicrous for a variety of technical and theoretical reasons that we won't go into here (Kavale & Forness, 1987; Shinn et al., 1998), this practice is expensive, time consuming, and instructionally irrelevant. Yet, this and many other questionable assessment practices continue because so many administrators, school psychologists, and teachers confuse assessment aimed at making the narrowly defined determination of "disability" with the more important decision about what a student *needs*. Entitlement is meaningless if it doesn't lead to development of an effective plan to help the student succeed.

Despite wording in federal law (IDEA Reg. 300.533) that clearly *prohibits* basing teaching plans on a student's label, it has been found that the labels given to students during entitlement processes often influence teaching plans (Bateman & Linden, 1997). Why does this happen?

Here are reasons why labels inappropriately influence teaching.

*Saying Too Little* The main problem with labeling is that, once the label is applied, it blocks consideration of the individual (this is usually called *stereotyping*). For example, all First Nations Students do not need to be taught the same things, just as all children of migratory workers do not learn the same way. However, some people seem to think they do.

*Saying Too Much* When a term is used in many different ways, a person who hears it may not know how to interpret it. Therefore, labels may lack meaning or have more meaning than they should. The term *retardation* (or *retarded*) nicely illustrates how a term may have surplus meaning because the term has various professional and everyday definitions. The traditional professional meaning includes ideas like *permanent limitation*, *limited intellectual capacity*, and *central nervous system damage*. But it also means "delayed." This can cause confusion. For example, a school psychologist once wrote that a child under review was "retarded in the area of reading." By using that phrase the psychologist was trying to say that the student's skills in reading were delayed. However, the parent took it as an accusation of incurable mental deficiency. When the parent and school psychologist got together to discuss the report, it was not a friendly meeting.

*Costing Too Much* Traditional entitlement evaluations utilize significant economic and human resources. Although estimates vary, the cost of determining eligibility is often said to be somewhere between $3000 and $5000 and 40–60 hours of student time. This time and money is **not** spent helping anyone; it is spent deciding if a person *qualifies* for help. If the resources could be used to help people and determine if they are entitled to receive help, it would, obviously, be a big improvement. (When one considers that most students are referred for poor reading skills, one wonders if many problems couldn't be solved more efficiently by taking the money allocated to eligibility and telling the student "I'll give you $3000 if you'll learn to read.")

## Is There Another Way to Think About Assessment?

Evaluation is a thoughtful process. It involves inquiry and the comparison of the way things are to the way they should be. It also requires the use of judgment and the making of decisions. Evaluation requires good measures, but it also requires good thinking. Traditionally, educators have viewed learning problems as resulting from some intrinsic characteristic of the individual. In this text, we will teach you how to use curriculum-based evaluation (CBE). This is a problem-solving strategy in which learning difficulties are viewed as the result of a *mismatch* between expectancy and performance.

Inherent in this view to problem solving is the idea that learning problems children experience in schools are multidimensional and may result from interference between setting demands and the student characteristics. Such a view leads to examination of a wide range of variables that may exist outside of the child, including curriculum, instructional approaches, and allocation of time and resources within a school.

For many people who work in schools, particularly those who spend most of their time engaged in assessment and evaluation activities, this is a new way to think about assessment. Rather than focusing assessment activities on identification of *student characteristics* that might explain poor performance, evaluation entails collection and use of information that will help solve a problem construed as existing at least partly—if not wholly—in the *learning environment*. Assessment activities, therefore, are not tied to the kind of decision being made (e.g., entitlement), but to the need for information that will be used to make teaching decisions.

Although categorical entitlement programs such as special education often are hailed as positive forces because of the good they can do for the students served in them, think about what entitlement programs say about the current state of our public schools and the larger society that sponsors them. Entitlement programs are a way to allocate scarce resources. After all, if the services provided in these programs weren't scarce, we wouldn't need Federal mandates to decide who gets in and who doesn't. Is it really true that effective instruction aimed at meeting the needs of each student who comes through the front door is a *rare commodity* in schools today? Probably not, given that the vast majority of students who attend public schools succeed. However, the authors of this text believe that an effective educational program should not be a scarce resource for even the smallest minority of students. Therefore, in this book, we will focus our attention on making the resource less scarce rather than trying to figure out who is or isn't entitled to it.

## How Are Teaching Decisions Different from Entitlement Decisions?

Effective teachers know when and how to make changes to meet the needs of students who are not progressing. These teachers know that they must *do* something *different*, or *exceptional*, to help children who are having difficulty in catching up. Being effective means modifying instruction by applying exceptional evaluation and teaching techniques. This means *deciding* which of many paths to take when selecting objectives, settings, facilities, groupings, materials, social settings, and staff. When teachers use good judgment, make the correct decisions, and carry them out effectively, student performance improves. Remember, the purpose of educational evaluation is to improve

student performance. We need to apply this test *whenever* we use assessment, including those times when we are making outside evaluation decisions associated with entitlement programs.

Look at Exhibit 1.3. This figure shows the progress of a student before and after effective educational decision making was employed. Before the decision was made, the student was not progressing adequately; after the decision was made (and implemented), his rate of progress increased.

It is important to know (and to believe strongly) that decision making and teaching can have this kind of positive effect on student learning (Good & Brophy, 1994).

Teaching decisions deal with two things: *what* will be taught and *how* it will be taught. Teaching decisions are based on different information than are entitlement decisions. For that reason, it is best to keep entitlement and teaching clearly separated in our thought and practice. The eligibility criteria developed to move students through the school system, and to hold the entire system accountable, reflect policies that vary from year to year and from place to place. These criteria are often determined as much by funding, political, and administrative trends as they are by sound educational practice.

In contrast, the proficiency criteria for task performance and the prerequisite skills students must master to succeed in their work are determined, to a large extent, by the tasks making up the curriculum. In general, these tasks (e.g., reading, problem solving, getting along with others) are the same in all schools. A child found eligible for support services in Iowa may not be found eligible in California, but a child who knows her math facts in Iowa will still know her math facts when she gets to California.

There are many possible learning objectives that may be relevant for a student, and there are many types of instruction that can be used to teach those objectives. Although effective teachers must be good at working with kids and good at delivering instruction, they must also be good at deciding what to teach and how to teach it. Such decisions, when based on good evaluative information and a good decision-making model, will increase student progress.

**Exhibit 1.3   *Effect of Decision Making on Educational Progress.***

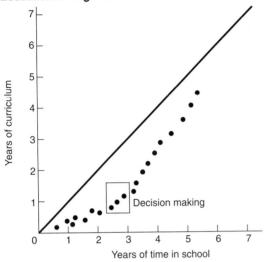

The things teachers *do* that influence learning produce what Bloom (1976) referred to as the quality of instruction. For example, an extensive body of research over the last two decades has shown that effective teachers engage in specific instructional behaviors that include lesson preview, explanation, guided practice, correction, and independent practice. However, although it does seem possible to recognize the *actions* that effective teachers take, it is simplistic to suppose that just getting someone to engage in these actions will make her an effective teacher. It is more likely that teacher *thought processes* determine teacher actions and that the thought processes of effective teachers differ from those of ineffective teachers (Berliner, 1989; Carter et al., 1988; Clark & Peterson, 1986; Gersten, 1990; Price & Nelson, 1999; Shavelson, 1983; Shavelson & Stern, 1981; Udvari-Solner, 1996; Wassermann, 1999).

For example, Lipman (1997) illustrated how the standard motto "Success for all" may be interpreted completely differently by teachers holding different ideas about the purposes of education and characteristics of students. She found, among other things, that when teachers are preoccupied with the "deficits" of students, this preoccupation often encourages them to avoid examination of their own teaching techniques. Bennett et al. (1997) found similar differences between the thinking of teachers and parents.

## How Do Teachers Who Use CBE Think?

Because CBE accentuates the role of teacher thought, it is appropriate to spend some pages covering what it is teachers think about. This link must be established now so that, as you read, you will interpret the material in subsequent chapters in terms of evaluation *as well as* teaching. This doesn't mean you should work to ignore any instructional implications that might come along; it means that teaching and evaluation should be closely linked, both in the actions that take place in the classroom *and* in your thinking processes. What a person thinks about teaching, curriculum, and learning will influence the way he or she evaluates.

We believe teachers should view themselves as active problem solvers. By some estimates, teachers may make as many as one critical decision every two minutes (Clark & Peterson, 1986), which is more than the Chief Executive Officers of some corporations make in a day. Each of these decisions are determined by the way a teacher thinks about learning, students, teaching, and subject matter.

### Learning

What teachers believe about learning in general affects the way they teach (Ball & Cohen, 1996; Fuchs et al., 1992; Pugach & Johnson, 1988; Shulman, 1986). In addition, what teachers think about the individual learning characteristics of their own students can also have a profound impact on the way they interact with those students in class (Lipman, 1997). This has been shown within the specific content of student evaluation (Cadwell & Jenkins, 1986; Good & Brophy, 1994; Hemingway et al., 1987) and the broader context of teacher expectation (Good & Brophy, 1986; Teddlie et al., 1989).

Given the major changes that have occurred in the field of learning theory in the last two decades, particularly with respect to problem learners (Harris & Graham, 1996b; Wang & Peverly, 1987), it can be expected that not all teachers share a common view of the learning process (Gersten, 1990). Yet, the problem-solving skills of teachers, like everyone else, are limited by their own knowledge and values (Shavelson & Stern, 1981). Teachers' judgments hinge as much on their own theories of learning as they do on observations of individual students. This is particularly obvious in relation to what Bloom (1980) called alterable variables.

A **variable** is an environmental or student characteristic ("student height" and "intensity of room lighting" are variables). **Alterable variables** are things that teachers can change *through reasonable instructional efforts*. Because we are talking about instructional efforts here, something is considered unalterable if it can't be changed through reasonable classroom work. This topic is covered in depth in Chapter 2.

### Students

Teachers also base decisions on beliefs about individual students (Ball & Cohen, 1996). One of the strongest findings in the literature about teacher thoughts is that when they hold high expectations for a student, that student is much more likely to learn (Good & Brophy, 1994). Similarly, when teachers have low expectations and write off a student, that student won't learn. Sometimes this happens because they are making the mistake of over-generalizing the impact of unalterable variables on student learning. In other cases, it happens because they have worked with the student to the point of despondency. And, unfortunately, sometimes it happens because the expectation that learning will occur is blocked by the bias introduced through gossip, disability labels, and even racial or ethnic stereotypes. When teachers write off students, their problem-solving efforts stop.

When working with students who have learning problems, we often have difficulty remembering the idealism of the first day on the job. This can be true even when there are reminders. For example, in the entryway of a school that one of the authors visited, there was a plaque that read *"At our school we believe all students can learn."* However, in a meeting that day, many of the teachers seemed to be spending time

trying to convince the visitor that a student named Rocko *couldn't* learn. The talk about this student was so negative and the thinking of the teachers was so closed that nothing recommended to help Rocko even seemed to be considered. Rocko had been written off. Finally, in a desperate effort to get Rocko back into the picture, the author made a sign that said *"except Rocko"* and taped it under the entryway plaque where every visiting parent and civic leader would see it. No one seemed amused by this juxtaposition of school philosophy and teacher expectation (except maybe Rocko), and none of the staff really wanted to agree with a sign that read *"At our school we believe all students can learn—except Rocko."*

### Teaching

Leinhardt and Greeno (1986) say that teaching skill resides within two systems: knowledge of the lesson structure and knowledge of the subject matter being taught. A skilled teacher's knowledge of lesson structure is composed in large part of routines that allow the teacher to carry common classroom tasks efficiently while allocating most of their attention and energy to important goals.

Knowledge of lesson structure includes certain teacher actions, or functions, that have been found to be necessary for effective instruction (Good & Brophy, 1994; Price & Nelson, 1999; Rosenshine & Stevens, 1986; Ysseldyke & Christenson, 1996). These include lesson preview, explanation, demonstration, guided practice, correction, and independent practice.

### Subject Matter

It seems obvious that what teachers believe about the task being taught interacts with how they teach it (Stodolsky & Grossman, 1995). Still, Peterson et al. (1989) cite Shulman's observation (1986) that the failure to consider a teacher's knowledge of the content being taught is a major blind spot in investigations of teaching.

Teachers vary widely in their beliefs about content. The endless debates about the importance of phonics in reading (McGee & Lomax, 1990; Schickedanz, 1990; Stahl, 1990) are examples of the kind of disagreements often found in our profession. We know that different categories of teachers have significantly different beliefs about what they teach. For example, teachers of math tend to believe that their content is clearly defined and sequential, whereas teachers of high school English do not. Stodolsky & Grossman (1995) found these differences to be so great that they referred to "subcultures of teachers" defined by differing views on the static, sequential, and coordinated nature of the curriculum they teach. The existence of these subcultures is of particular interest to those who advocate for integrated educational programs as well as collaborative efforts at problem solv-ing (Baker & Zigmond, 1990; Nowacek, 1992; Ysseldyke et al., 1992).

### Is Decision Making the Same as Judgment?

Maybe the first thing to figure out is whether these two terms are redundant. Certainly the two terms are sometimes used interchangeably. In an effort to clarify the distinction between these two terms, the authors turned to the Classics and found Cherlyte. Cherlyte said, "Wherever there can be contention, there judgment should exist" (that certainly cleared it up for us!).

Deciding is an act (i.e., something one does), whereas judgment is a quality (i.e., how well something is done). It is possible to make a decision without illustrating good judgment. For example, Leader (1983) reported on an incident that happened during World War II. Admiral Karel Doorman of the Royal Netherlands Navy decided to engage a stronger force of the Japanese Navy. Upon encountering the enemy, he signaled "follow me" to his ships and got half of them destroyed, himself killed, and didn't sink a single enemy vessel. Doorman was decisive (and brave), but in retrospect his judgment has been questioned.

In general, if the contention gets resolved to our own satisfaction, we think it was done with good judgment. If the resolution does not seem positive, then the judgment seems bad.

It is easy to outline the steps for decision making (Arkes & Hammond, 1986), but the steps to good judgment are not as easily outlined, and according to Edwards and Newman (1986), there are at least three reasons for this:

1. judgment makes use of data, which can be seen, to draw conclusions about things that can't be seen (because they are absent or in the future);

2. the conclusions drawn in situations requiring judgment only have a *probability* of being correct (when there is no risk of error, judgment is not necessary); and

3. the correctness of a judgment is defined by how well it matches the setting and, in addition, how well it works. (Joking about your boss in front of your boss's best friend is probably never good judgment—even when nothing goes wrong. It is clearly bad judgment when something does go wrong.)

The word *probability* is a critical one for this discussion (and for this entire text). Some of the synonyms for probability are "chance," "likeliness," and even "odds." It is important to understand that, in teaching, few actions lead to absolute and predictable outcomes. Therefore, decisions based on the best possible judgment don't always work. This truth results from the fact that outcomes often depend on more than our decisions. Consider Admiral Doorman's unfortunate naval battle. Was it bad judgment that the admiral went after 17 Japanese ships with only 15 allied ships? In 1797 Horatio Nelson violated British battle protocol and took on 18 enemy ships with his *single* ship. He captured two Spanish vessels, turned back the enemy fleet, and as a result was promoted to admiral (Leader, 1983). Yet on the surface, Nelson's decision seems like worse judgment than Doorman's.

The definition of good judgment, then, does not hinge on good results. However, the *probability* of good results should increase whenever good judgment is used. Good judgment diminishes the risk of failure, but it does not guarantee success.

### Summary

Expert evaluative techniques are usually acquired by finding out how someone who is already an expert works (not *what* they accomplish but *how* they work). It may also be accomplished by reflecting on professional literature and research (which is the formalized experience of others) as well as personal experience. This is the way most things are learned. When teaching a student to solve problems, teachers, acting as experts, first demonstrate and explain how one should go about solving the problem and then ask the student to practice by using feedback. This is the format that will be used later in this text to teach you to make teaching decisions.

The goal of this text is to teach you to be an expert at educational problem solving. Although this involves discussing good classroom practice, it also involves descriptions of bad practice so that you will avoid errors when you make teaching decisions about students. In the chapters that follow, we present specific procedures and strategies that you can use to make instructional decisions for students who are not progressing through the curriculum. You will be given explanations and guidelines that will show how expert teachers would go about collecting information, developing assumed causes for problems, and making decisions. This chapter presented an introduction to the kind of decision making that will be the focus of the rest of the book. Here are the main points we discussed in this chapter.

- The quality and process of any evaluation is tied to its purposes.
- There are different reasons to evaluate.
- Some evaluation occurs for reasons that originate inside the classroom, whereas others occur for outside reasons.
- The focus of this text is inside evaluation.
- Inside evaluation is carried out by following a predetermined format of scientific inquiry.
- A curriculum-based evaluation is carried out by employing certain assumptions about curriculum, understandings about measurement, rules for developing hypotheses, and guidelines for making decisions.
- All of these can be carried out with greater, or lesser, levels of quality.
- Expert teachers influence the quality of their work by using good judgment when they make decisions.
- The use of good judgment depends on knowledge (of curriculum, students, learning, and instruction).
- Good judgment also depends on freedom from certain threats and on the availability of quality options.
- This expert decision-making skill can be learned.

## STUDY QUESTIONS

1. Why is entitlement determination considered an "outside" decision?

2. How would you determine whether the curriculum a student learns is the same one you intended to teach?

3. Mr. Marshall is a fourth-grade teacher who uses curriculum-based evaluation to make instructional decisions. Juanita is a student in his class. Exhibit 1.4 shows Juanita's progress in math during the last 6 weeks. The *solid line* shows Mr. Marshall's expectations about the rate with which Juanita will progress through the curriculum. The *black dots* show the number of items Juanita got correct on each weekly math test.

**Exhibit 1.4    *Progress in Math in a 6-Week Period.***

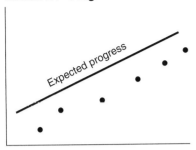

Decide which of the following statements you believe would best reflect Mr. Marshall's thoughts during the last 6 weeks. Tell why you made that choice.

- Juanita seems to be having trouble with multistep problem solving. Her learning style probably is incompatible with the task. She may not be able to do sequential activities. I think she has been doing better lately because her development has caught up with the curriculum.
- Juanita is not learning multistep problem solving as quickly as I hoped she would. She must not have learned some key information that I assumed she already knew. If I find out what prior knowledge she is missing and teach it to her, I think she will improve.

What are the fundamental decisions that underlie each of the components of curriculum-based evaluation?

# Chapter 2

# Thinking About Learning

*Alterable variables can be changed through instruction and are the result of a student's previous learning.*

—Snow & Lohman (1984)

What teachers do is influenced by what they think (Ball & Cohen, 1996; Clark & Peterson, 1986; Shavelson, 1983). One of the things that the literature on decision making, as well as the literature on learning, has shown is that what a person already knows affects how she learns (Boorstin, 1983; Nisbett & Ross, 1980). Prior knowledge is important to learning and thinking. Unfortunately, the things many of us think we know about learning are not completely true. Myth, folklore, and misconceptions about learning abound in our profession, and the persistence of these half-truths is a destructive force.

## What Are Some Examples of Educational Misconceptions?

Erroneous prior knowledge interferes with teaching because it constrains decision making and limits effective problem solving. Here are some examples of common misconceptions many people hold about learning.

### Overreliance on Practice

This idea comes from the belief that learning occurs gradually (the way muscles are built). Learning doesn't occur gradually, it occurs almost instantaneously (when new information is linked to prior information). Therefore, learning is best assisted through explanation or demonstration that builds connections between what is already known and what is about to be learned.

You can only practice what you *already* know. **Proficiency** (how well you use what you've learned) does build gradually; therefore, improved proficiency requires lots of practice. So, practice is appropriate at the right point in the instructional sequence.

### Enabling

It is often thought that motivation can be developed by giving students easy things to do. Many people confuse the idea of successful completion of a task, even an easy or trivial task, with the idea of *accomplishing* a goal. However, motivation does not come with success alone; it comes with the sense of control and accomplishment. Motivation is promoted by the student's adaptive interpretation of *both* successes and failures. Such adaptive interpretations are themselves promoted by the way teachers and parents respond to and *explain* the victories and failures in students' lives (Giangreco et al., 1997).

### Attempts to Measure and Teach to Learning Styles

There is a common belief that each individual's approach to learning is unique and constant over time. In this **learning-style** view, learning problems are often conceptualized as the result of the student's "unique learning style." Many people also believe that these preferences can be identified through testing and used to enhance individualized instruction. It is this second belief, that styles of learning can be accurately measured and then used as the basis for selecting how to teach, that seems to cause problems.

To remedy learning problems, advocates of learning-style instruction (LSI) recommend testing students to map out their cognitive and/or perceptual styles so that instructional techniques, which are thought to complement those preferences, can be selected (Carbo, 1992; Chan, 1996; Tobias, 1994). However, for decades LSI has been refuted by authors such as Waugh (1975), Arter and Jenkins (1979), Kavale (1981), Glass (1983), Lakin (1983), Lloyd (1984), Ulman and Rosenberg (1986), and Snider (1992). The scientific fact is that there is very little truth to the myth of learning styles.

LSI is *not* to be confused with selecting different objectives for students at different skill levels or with assuming that some treatments are more efficient than other treatments. Those beliefs are accurate. But when educators test for an individual's *fixed strengths and weaknesses* and use the results to make long-range predictions about how they should be taught, they are making a mistake.

### Homogeneous Grouping

Homogeneous grouping, which is closely aligned with assumptions about learning styles, is education's *Holy Grail*. This belief has led us into an exhausting, and often fruitless, search for educationally relevant ways to group students. It stems from the belief that students who are *the same* are best taught together. This belief has led to a focus on ways to reduce the variability in classrooms by trying to group students and then attempting to separate the groups through techniques like tracking, leveling, pull-out, and referral to compensatory programs. The belief may also have promoted resistance to techniques that might help teachers *accommodate* student variability (such as peer tutoring and cooperative learning). With the exception of short-term skill groupings, which are based on highly specific objectives, these efforts at grouping have not worked.

Just to clarify, we are not necessarily advocating that all students, regardless of the severity of their difficulties, should be left in the same classes, the notion that underlies **full inclusion** (Fox & Ysseldyke, 1997; Giangreco et al., 1997). We are not actually talking about class placement at all (that is, general, resource, or self contained). We are talking about the idea that all students at a certain skill level can be taught effectively with a common "instructional approach." This idea has a long history of failure. As for physical placements, students should be placed in the least restrictive environment that is most likely to provide educational benefit. For most students, that is the general classroom. If a student fails to make adequate progress, then a range of options should be considered, including the addition of resources within the current placement *or* movement to another, perhaps more restrictive placement.

### Fixed Ability

It is commonly assumed that the speed and eventual extent of most learning is determined by a student's fixed ability. This idea, which is obviously true in extreme circumstances (that is, lowering a student's ability to zero by ending his life), can have negative implications when it is applied at the level of individual goals or lessons. If a teacher is working under the assumption that he already knows what the student is capable of learning, he may continue to treat the student according to this preconception. As a result, the teacher may hold inappropriately low expectations for the student or fail to attend to displays of competence that exceed what has been predicted. These displays may even be labeled **overachievement** and disregarded as some sort of fluke.

A teacher who believes that a student's *capacity* to learn is fixed and nonalterable may interpret that student's failure to learn as evidence that the student has reached the limits of her potential. As a result, when a student starts having trouble, the teacher may give up trying to teach her (Greenwood, 1991; Teddlie et al., 1989). Worse, he may inadvertently teach the student to take the same view.

One of the main goals of this chapter is to convince you that students who haven't learned in the past *can* learn in the future. This is important because without that belief, the role of remedial and special educators may revert to the status it held in the past when it was sometimes thought of as nothing more than baby-sitting to supply custodial care for hopelessly "defective" children. The idea that things like capacity, potential, ability, or intelligence are fixed is inconsistent with current learning theory (Anderson et al., 1996; Sfard, 1998). In fact, as will be pointed out shortly, *students learn how to learn.*

## How Do Misconceptions Influence Teaching?

Teachers' misconceptions about learning can have disastrous impact on their effectiveness. A teacher who believes the myth of practice may drill students when he should be explaining things to them. A teacher who accepts the myth of enabling may not allow students to experience the personal satisfaction of overcoming challenge. A teacher who believes the myth of learning styles may avoid assignments he thinks

conflict with the student's preferred **mode** of learning. A teacher who believes the myth of homogeneous grouping may try to sort students instead of teach them. A teacher who believes that the failure to learn is the result of an unalterable lack of intelligence, motivation, attention, or memory may simply give up.

## How Does Learning Occur?

Learning is interactive. It arises from the interchange of many factors that can be grouped under the headings of student, curriculum, and instruction. If one of these factors is out of balance with the others, the interaction may fall apart. A teacher with no material to present or no student will not produce learning, just as a student without instruction (of some sort) will not learn. Similarly, a student's reading problem cannot be identified if she is not given something to read, and the kind of reading problem she seems to have will depend in large part on the kind of material we ask her to read.

The failure to learn can result in missing knowledge, and that same missing knowledge can cause other failures to learn (just as someone who has failed to learn to read would have trouble learning the material in this book). Failure at a skill can also result from missed opportunities to learn. Missing skills and missing opportunities, while reciprocal, can also occur independently. You may want to take a moment and think about curriculum, instruction, and student tasks. What is meant by *instruction*? Although it is obviously the job of teachers to provide instruction, these opportunities are also influenced by parents, communities, and schools. Whereas the focus of this text will be almost exclusively on those things teachers can directly control, the existence of these other factors must also be acknowledged (Miller et al., 1999).

When learning occurs in the classroom, we must be willing to give some credit to each of these three elements: instruction (evaluation, teaching, and materials), curriculum (learning outcomes and expectations), and student. Similarly, when learning fails to occur, we must consider each element along with the other factors that define the opportunity to learn. Most

*Learning is a complex (and often puzzling process involving the connection of prior knowledge with new information.*

important, we must consider each element not in isolation but in *interaction* with the others. All of us have encountered a task in a curriculum that was easy to learn but proved difficult for someone else—or teachers under whose instruction we seemed to learn effortlessly while the person next to us sweated out the course in near despair. These illustrations of the interactive nature of learning point out the truism that evaluations designed to guide instruction must focus on the learning interaction, not on individual components of the interaction (Eisner, 1982).

The point is simple. Remember, this book is about decision making. Decisions about a student's failure to learn cannot be made by just looking at the child. It is critical that this be understood because the traditional procedure for evaluating special/remedial students has been, and unfortunately continues to be, to focus almost exclusively on student characteristics such as **IQ**, learning style, cerebral dominance, perceptual ability, preferred mode of information processing, and family/home situation. What is particularly problematic about this narrow focus on kids is that many of the variables that have enjoyed our attention are things that we, as teachers, can do almost nothing about. Despite this, as Ysseldyke et al. (1992) point out, some studies have found that only 5% of teachers blame themselves or the schools for the widespread occurrence of student failure. The rest of the teachers seem to attribute failure to factors that cannot be routinely influenced by instruction.

## Why Do Some Students Experience Failure in School?

Obviously, we are proposing a shift away from this preoccupation with unalterable student

**Exhibit 2.1    Effects of Early Decision Making on Progress of Students.**

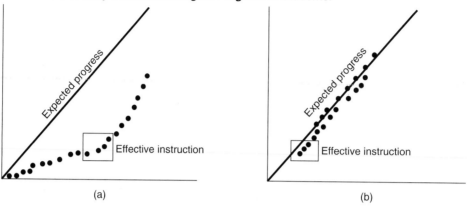

(a)                                        (b)

characteristics as an explanation for school fail-ure. Although this is hardly a new proposal (Howell et al., 1979), it remains timely. Consider the following example, which is a logical exten-sion of the discussion of progress and decision making. In Exhibit 1.2, data were presented showing the learning of a student who was falling behind in school. Now look at Exhibit 2.1a. This student is moving across time but is functioning below expected levels. As a result of the decision making, the student begins to get more effective instruction and progresses faster. Exhibit 2.1a shows that instruction can alter the rate at which students learn (which is the basic premise behind the entire teaching profession).

Exhibit 2.1b is only slightly different. In this case, the student has received effective instruc-tion all along and, as a result, has never fallen be-hind. This illustration is not intended to build a case for early intervention (although that is often a good idea). Instead, it is intended to make the point that if a student *can catch up* with effective instruction, then the lack of effective instruction must explain why that student fell behind in the first place.

Although educators must consider that there is truth to the old saying "if the pupil has not learned, the teacher has not taught," it is interest-ing to note that talking about "more effective in-struction" tends to alienate some teachers much faster than talking about "ineffective learners." This is because it sounds like an accusation. But

"inappropriate instruction" is not synonymous with bad teaching. Inappropriate instruction is instruction that didn't work. It means that, for some reason, the arrangements made to influ-ence learning were not to a student's benefit. These arrangements may work great for a differ-ent student.

## Learning Theory

### If Learning Difficulty Is Not Caused by Low Fixed Ability, What Causes It?

Students with learning difficulties often exhibit two problems. One of these is their lack of partic-ular skills; the other is their apparent difficulty in learning. Both kinds of learning problems reside in missing, or erroneous, **prior knowledge**.

Learning is influenced by the quality of teaching, the nature of tasks, and student charac-teristics. The student characteristics of greatest importance to a teacher are those that are alter-able (Bloom, 1980). These are the skills, strate-gies, perceptions, expectations, and beliefs that students learn. All of these are lumped under the heading *prior knowledge*. A student's prior knowl-edge (what she already knows) is the primary personal limitation on her learning.

Understanding the functional and concep-tual role of prior knowledge is sometimes diffi-cult because it has implications that seem counterintuitive. For example, consider the idea of **task difficulty**. To most of us, driving a car is no harder than fixing lunch, and reading this page is no harder than cleaning up after lunch. That is because we are adequately skilled to do all of these things. However, not every one is. Tasks become difficult when we don't have adequate prior knowledge and skill to do them. Because we all have different prior knowledge, tasks that are hard for one person may be easy for another. In general, tasks are difficult if they have ambiguous cues, missing information, and a lack of predictability (Fisher & Hiebert, 1990; Kotovsky & Simon, 1990; Nelson et al., 1994; Nolet & Tindal, 1995). However, as you probably have discovered, the things that seem ambiguous to a novice are often quite clear to an expert.

Task difficulty does not reside in the task, it resides in the interaction of the task and the learner's prior knowledge. This means that the students with the fewest skills have the hardest time in school. On the face of it, this seems pretty obvious. Unfortunately, as has already been pointed out, many people attribute difficulty in school to deficits in a student's fixed capacity to learn—not to missing prior knowledge. Therefore, when faced with a student who is not learning, these people begin trying to solve the problem by considering ability deficits. That is a mistake. When a student has trouble learning, teachers should check to find out what the student does and does not know. To do this well, a teacher must understand that there are different types of knowledge.

### What Types of Knowledge Do Students Need?

As will be explained in Chapter 3, knowledge can be categorized. In this text, it will be divided into two broad headings: **task-specific** knowledge and **task-related** knowledge. Task-specific knowledge refers to the academic and social subject matter most teachers think they are employed to teach. These include things like reading, spelling, making friends, and doing math. Task-related knowledge refers to those skills required to learn. These include attention, motivation, and problem-solving skills. Task-related skills are learned, and many of them are learned from teachers. However, not all teachers think that it is their job to teach such skills, and some do not even realize when they are doing so.

A student's knowledge about how they think, and their awareness and control over their own reasoning and studying, is called **metacognitive knowledge**. The prefix "meta" derives from ancient Greek and usually means "about" or "pertaining to." Metacognitive knowledge, or **metacognition**, is "knowledge about cognition." However, metacognition is not simply knowledge about learning, it is knowledge about how to use learning. For example, suppose a student knows that summarizing passages is a good way to aid recall and comprehension and that the student realizes through self-monitoring that her comprehension of a passage is limited. If the student *thinks* about the problem and *decides* to write summary statements as a solution, she has used metacognition.

Just as it is important for teachers to know about how students learn, it is important for students to know and use knowledge about their own thinking. This is most obvious when the student seems to be making thinking errors. It seems that students with learning problems have trouble in several areas of metacognition (Tindal & Nolet, 1996). These areas include (but are not limited to) the analysis of task demands and the selection of strategies for task completion. Without skills in these two critical areas, a student faced with a new learning goal may have little understanding of the effort required to meet the goal or of procedures for studying. Students can learn without adaptive metacognitive skills, but to do so requires extremely structured instruction and tremendous teacher energy. That is why teachers working with students who have "learning problems" should build information about how to learn into their lessons. By doing so, teachers can accomplish three important things. First, they can teach the student the content (reading, math, or language) that the student has failed to learn. Second, they can teach the student about learning and how to use that knowledge to learn more effectively. Finally, they can transfer responsibility for future learning directly to the student. In other words, by teaching task-related and metacognitive skills, the teacher teaches the student how to learn.

*Exhibit 2.2    The Functions of Executive Control.*

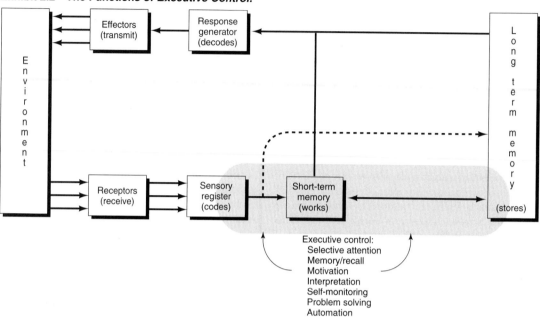

## Information Processing

To understand how prior knowledge works, it is important to know something about the way learning seems to occur. According to current theory, the brain does not simply store new information, it processes and amplifies it by linking it to prior knowledge through elaborate networks of organization (Reid, 1992). This is accomplished by the **information-processing** system illustrated in Exhibit 2.2.

Here is what happens within this system:

- new information is received by **receptors**

- new information is coded by the **sensory register**

- both new and old information are worked on by **short-term memory**

- information is stored by **long-term memory**

- information is decoded by the **response generator**

- information is transmitted to the environment by the **effectors**.

Each of these functions, and the model component said to carry out that work, is represented in Exhibit 2.2. Let's run a bit of information through that model to see how the components work.

Suppose a teacher holds up a flashcard and asks a student "What is $6 \times 8$?" That information comes into the system through the receiving sensory organs (eyes, ears). Once it has arrived, it is translated from its sensory language (light waves bouncing from the flashcard and sound waves coming from the teacher) into an electrochemical code the rest of the system can understand (we'll call this language "brainese"). The coding is necessary because light and sound cannot exist within the brain (just as your memories of a trip to Australia don't mean that there are real kangaroos inside of your head). Instead, it is a brainese **analog** that flows through the system. This is something like a song on a CD. There is no music on the CD—only a digital representation of music that must be uncoded to be returned to sound waves.

In the "old days" (still being experienced in some classrooms), it was widely believed that messages maintained their sensory definition by staying in separate channels. These sensory channels (or modalities) were named according to the source of the information they handled (auditory mode, visual mode, tactile mode). That is why some people still refer to things like "visual memory" or "auditory attention deficits." But according to current theory, there is only one long-term memory, and it handles information from all sources (although it may not handle them equally well).

Once the environmental stimuli have been coded into brainese, the message goes into the network of short-term memory and long-term memory. The component we call **long-term memory** apparently lasts longer than we do (that is, people often die of old age before their memories erode). Once something is in there, it's usually there for good.

Short-term memory, however, is very limited. It can only hold a few items (six or seven) for a few seconds. It isn't just short, it is sort of narrow too. The length of stay in short-term memory is generally described in terms of milliseconds or seconds—at most a couple of minutes. When someone says "I told her the answer yesterday, but she missed the item today; she has a short-term memory problem," he is actually referring to long-term recall, not short-term memory. Short-term memory is typically described as **working memory**. We are only aware, or conscious, of things that are currently in short-term memory.

Notice that in Exhibit 2.2 the *arrow* connecting the long-term and short-term memory has two heads. This means information may move back and forth between these components—a critical point about the learning process. For learning to occur, short-term memory must have access to information from two directions: new information from the environment and prior knowledge from long-term memory.

Because short-term memory is so important and so limited, it must work very efficiently. Short-term memory is protected by something called the **executive control**. Many of the most important functions of the information-processing system reside within executive control, as listed here:

- Selective attention
- Memory/recall
- Motivation
- Interpretation
- Self-monitoring
- Problem solving
- Automation

These executive functions are different from the other functions of the information-processing system that have been discussed so far. Executive control regulates how information is processed by influencing the way it flows through the other components (such as sensory register or long-term memory). In this sense—and this is a risky metaphor—the mind works like a school. It has a principal. Although principals seldom collect milk money, develop class lessons, teach students, or type tests, they do influence how these things are done. They monitor activity, allocate resources, evaluate outcomes, and tell people what to do. Those are the functions of executives. But some executives are more effective than others. Therefore, whereas two principals may have equivalent faculties (no pun intended) and budgets to work with, they may not be equally effective.

## What Do These Executive Functions Do?

Reading comprehension will be used as the example content for purposes of explaining the executive-control functions. This is necessary because executive-control functions do not exist in the absence of a task. For example, without something to attend to, there isn't any attention, and the way a student attends to one thing will differ from the way that student attends to another.

### Selective Attention

Selective attention functions like a screen, allowing only certain environmental input inside for processing while keeping other stuff out. The reading strategy that best illustrates this phenomenon is the use of prereading questions. Students who are given questions about a passage before they read it are more apt to find the answers than those who aren't (Reynolds & Anderson, 1982). That is because they are searching for particular information when they read. Therefore, teaching students to develop their own **prereading questions** is an excellent way to get them to focus on the important aspects of a passage (Gillespie, 1991; Ryder, 1991). (Are you using prereading questions as you read the sections of this text?)

The key term here is focus. Attention, as we are using the term, refers to the selective allocation of processing. The successful student focuses on what is important and ignores what is not. Of course, to do this while reading, a student must categorize the messages in the passage as "important" or "non-important." As Carnine (1990, p. 372) put it, "Categorization and recategorization might be viewed as the overriding activity of the brain." Teachers who review important ideas and ask students prereading questions make it easy for them to categorize by providing criteria for judging the relevance of different parts of a passage. Without selective attention, the student wishing to remember something wouldn't be able to figure out what to remember or what to ignore. This would leave her in the position of trying to remember everything; as a result, her information processing would be overloaded.

### Recall

When we think of memory, there is a tendency to conceptualize it as storage. But memory includes the recall of what has been stored. Our long-term memory is like a file cabinet. We have stuff in there, but we can't use it until we open the drawer, find the file, and take it out. (It's like income tax preparation—it doesn't matter that you *kept* the receipt from last September, what matters is that you can *find* it by April 15th.) Both storage and recall can be facilitated through the use of strategies. Lets go back to the example of reading.

Effective readers utilize a variety of strategies to help them remember and recall what they read. For example, students who score high on comprehension tests are more likely to underline, highlight, write notes in the margin, or write summaries. They also actively review and organize what they have read (Bakken et al., 1998; Chan, 1996; Duffy & Zeidler, 1996). Teaching students to engage in these activities will improve their recall of the information they have marked, summarized, and organized.

The storage and recall of new knowledge is thought to be controlled, in part, by the individual's use of **schema**. Schema are most conveniently conceptualized as webs, or nets, that link separate nodes of information. According to schema theory, once a sufficient number of defining nodes have been activated, the executive-control function will recall the complete net of information. This has the effect of making all information about the topic immediately available. Schema activation allows for highly efficient access to large bodies of information by eliminating the executive's need to search out each separate bit (node). The popular technique of producing semantic webs is a reading comprehension approach that is based on schema theory.

### Motivation

Interestingly, it is very hard for some teachers to accept that motivation is learned. To these teachers, selective attention and memory may seem alterable, but motivation is a different story. This may be because some people associate motivation with "wanting to learn." In fact, there are many students who want to learn but fail because they have acquired nonadaptive motivational strategies. Probably, there are just as many students with effective motivational strategies who learn easily despite limited interest in the topic.

To understand motivation, we need to define it. Motivation can be operationally defined as perseverance (Dweck, 1986; Katzell & Thompson, 1990). The student who works on something the longest, particularly in the face of difficulty or negative feedback, seems the most motivated. Some students work harder in the face of difficulty, whereas others with equal skills give up. Why?

Many researchers believe that some skilled students fail to persevere because they suffer from **learned helplessness**. According to motivation theory, learned helplessness is rooted in mistaken beliefs about success and failure. Students who have been taught that positive outcomes are the result of external factors like luck, easy assignments, or pampering teachers don't become motivated. Neither do students who believe success is the result of unalterable, internal factors like high intelligence (Dweck, 1986; Landfried, 1989; Schunk, 1996; Seligman, 1990).

How effectively a person works is determined in part by her beliefs about herself, her skills, and the assignments on which she is working. These beliefs, which reside with the executive-control function, may be motivationally adaptive or destructive. When a student believes that things she can't control cause failure, the onset of difficulty becomes a signal to quit working. In contrast, a student who believes that success is related to things she can control (for example, how much effort she puts into work) views the same difficulty as a cue to work harder. On reading-comprehension assignments, a student who believes she is helpless will skip over a passage that is difficult to understand. Conversely, a student who believes she has control over her own success, upon encountering a difficult passage, will slow her reading rate, reread the passage, or consult needed resources.

There are many possible nonadaptive motivational patterns. One of these centers on the student's personal definitions of success and failure. For example, some students believe that completing assignments is more important than learning. This is interesting because, whereas all teachers want students to feel successful, many teachers do not understand that students may define success in different ways. Dweck (1986) draws a distinction between *learning* and *performance* definitions of success. According to her theory, a student with a **learning orientation** believes that success comes with progress toward learning goals and a student with a **performance orientation** believes success comes with completing work.

A learning orientation is adaptive because it allows students to find success in challenging work as long as they improve, even when they don't correctly complete it (Schunk, 1996). In distinction, the performance orientation may lead a student to develop techniques for finishing assignments regardless of learning (that is, by turning them in with errors or copying from other students). This maladaptive motivational pattern may be fostered when teachers instruct students to "get this assignment done by recess," rather than instructing them to "use this assignment to learn new vocabulary skills."

### Interpretation

People seem to have a basic need to explain and understand things. When we don't know why something is happening we are uncomfortable. Not knowing why something is happening may even feel so awkward that we will accept an incorrect explanation over no explanation. Gazzaniga and associates (1989) have conducted a series of studies that seem to document the existence of a specialized cognitive subsystem for unifying prior knowledge and current experience. This interpretation function "explains" what is happening to the rest of the information-processing system, which then stores the explanation and/or acts upon it. This is true even though the explanation may not have come into the system through the receptors.

We use interpretation strategies to explain things and to attribute them to certain causes. We may even develop routine sets of explanations that we tend to rely on unless forced to think beyond them. The *performance* and *learning orientations* just discussed could be examples of such sets. Pervasive attitudes of pessimism or cheerfulness are other examples. Such patterns of interpretation, although difficult to define, are commonly observed.

As the world flows toward us, our information-processing function tries to "make sense" of it by fitting new information into previously developed categories. If data are found to be inconsistent with the categories that already exist, we may develop new schemes for categorizing it. In some cases, to explain a new experience we may even recategorize previously stored information. We call that "changing our mind."

Because of the interpretation function, information that comes to us only has potential. What it ultimately means to us is determined by the connections established between that new experience and our prior knowledge. This is one reason why two people reading the same passage may disagree sharply about what the passage means. They are interpreting the passage in terms of their unique histories and behaving, not in direct response to the written page but in response to their explanations of it (Kaplan, 1996; Mahoney, 1977). Their reactions and interpretations can be changed if a teacher explains the passage or provides them with a set of guidelines for critical reading.

### Self-Monitoring

One main focus of this text is problem solving. However, the use of any problem-solving approach hinges on the recognition of problems. If we think there is nothing wrong, we don't work to improve things. Or, if everything is fine but we think there is a problem, we may mess up something that is working well. It is the self-monitoring function of executive control that tells us when and when not to employ other executive-control functions.

According to Rigney (1980), a competent learner is always confronting questions like these:

What is the problem?

What should I do about it?

How am I doing so far?

Am I finished yet?

Although we don't consciously ask ourselves these questions, we do get alarmed if we can't answer one or more of them. During reading comprehension, for example, a student must monitor the meaning of a passage to recognize when selective attention, problem solving, recall, or motivational strategies should be applied (Gillespie, 1991; Ryder, 1991). Self-monitoring alerts students to the need for extra effort or the application of problem-solving strategies.

### Problem Solving

Numerous researchers have noted that students who experience academic or social skill difficulties in school are poor at solving problems (Ellis & Lenz, 1990; Paris & Winograd, 1990). However, this isn't too surprising because *everyone* has trouble solving some types of problems. The kinds of errors people make in problem solving are fairly predictable. Some of these mistakes are listed in Exhibit 2.3.

Think about the last time you were unsuccessful at solving a difficult problem. Maybe you were trying to get a noisy class to quiet down, find an address in a part of town with which you were unfamiliar, or fix a leaky faucet. How many of the rules in Exhibit 2.4 did you make?

A set of general problem-solving steps, when followed correctly, can help students succeed. Such a list is outlined in Exhibit 2.4. That list includes things like recognizing problems, generating options, developing plans, and checking work. Although the steps in this exhibit can never take the place of task-specific strategies (such as the long-division algorithm), they do provide a way to deal with general problems.

Note that the first step listed in the problem-solving sequence is recognition of the problem. Problem recognition is particularly important as it relates to self-monitoring, and this is an area in which students who have learning problems, as a group, experience difficulty (Lloyd et al., 1991).

### Automation

The short-term memory function allows us to solve problems with consideration and intent; it allows us to work. However, it is so limited that we can't consciously work on too many things at one time or even on one thing for too long. Therefore, to protect the space in our working memory, we must keep routine activities out of it. As you can see from the *arrows* in Exhibit 2.2, information can get into, and out of, long-term memory without going through short-term memory. This is accomplished by raising proficiency on routine activities to automaticity. Automation is the process of making responses so routine that we can do them without the use of short-term memory.

Before a response can become automatic, it must first be learned, and that requires working memory. For example, when you first learned to drive a vehicle, you occupied your short-term memory with the work of driving. You may even have talked to yourself as a device for recalling what to do when you got in difficult situations. Hopefully, you don't do that now because driving has become automatic. (When a stop light turns red, you automatically put on the brake. You don't "think" about it.) Achieving auto-

**Exhibit 2.3    Threats to Judgment.**

| Threat | Explanation/Example |
|---|---|
| Data characterization (selective attention) | Seeing what you expect or want to see. Two people watching the same event don't agree about what they saw. |
| Lack of the knowledge needed to make a judgment | Working on things you don't know about (trying to teach about the role of minority cultures in United States history when that wasn't taught to you when you were in school). |
| Stereotyping (overgeneralization) | Working with someone's label and not their characteristics (ignoring Ralph and only attending to the fact that he is labeled LD). |
| Failure to define the problem | Not knowing what it is you are trying to do (deciding to have students work lessons without giving them a pretest). |
| Defining the problem too trivially or narrowly | Concentrating on a trivial aspect of a larger problem (thinking about the haircut of a student who has no friends). |
| Lack of perspective | Only seeing things one way (not seeing the problem from the parents' point of view). |
| Fear | Of failure, risk, notoriety, success, responsibility, or nearly anything else. |
| Premature resolution | Stopping work too early; failing to be comprehensive (picking the first solution recommended). |
| Insensitivity to probabilities | Not considering that some things are already more or less likely to work (adopting specialized reading materials when the general-education class materials haven't been tried). |
| Sample size | Drawing conclusions from too few experiences or examples (concluding a student can add because he works four problems correctly). |
| Misconceptions of chance | Thinking that unrelated events can affect each other (believing that flipping three heads in a row somehow alters the 50/50 chance of flipping a head with a fourth coin—it doesn't). |
| Unwarranted confidence | Deciding to do something on the basis of evidence, or advocacy, that doesn't have anything to do with the problem at hand (deciding a student will have trouble in math because she is bad at reading). |
| Selective or incomplete search | Only considering one category of options (only considering the use of teaching methods advocated by your friends). |
| Mistaking a correlational relationship for cause and effect | Just because two things happen at the same time doesn't mean one causes the other (thinking that a student threw up in class for attention because everyone looked at her when she did). |
| Lack of a supportive environment | Not having a chance to observe others use good judgment or have that use encouraged (working in a school where everyone routinely makes all of these errors). |

*Exhibit 2.4    Rules for Good Educational Judgment.*

| Rule | Example/Explanation |
|---|---|
| Work with others to define the problem | If possible, collaborate. Decide if there even is a problem and if it seems to be related to the curriculum, instruction, environment, or student. |
| Focus on solutions not problems | Shift the discussion from what the student is doing wrong to what you want the student to do right. |
| Focus on alterable variables and the curriculum | Think about what the student needs to be taught and what things you can control through instruction. |
| Decide what the student will be doing once the problem is fixed | Operationally define success. Have a clear vision of success and get agreement so that everyone (including the kid) understands what they are working to achieve. |
| Decide if the problem is a priority | Consider the problem in relation to other needs. |
| Isolate the parts | See if there are portions of the problem that can already be solved or that will be easier to solve than others. Get those out of the way first. |
| Look for simple solutions | Do not assume that big difficulties always indicate complex problems. There may simply be a missing step or piece of information. |
| Act quickly | The sooner you start working on the problem, the sooner you will get feedback on the quality of your solution. You will also get more information on the problem. Besides, the student is behind already. |
| Reconfigure | If the solution involves several individuals, include a mechanism for them to meet and discuss progress. |
| Monitor | Monitoring reduces the need for "front-loaded" certainty. If you have good monitoring data and are flexible, you can arrive at the best solution by improving the one with which you started. |

maticity allows us to employ strategies without allocating any of our awareness to them.

The shift from automaticity to problem solving is illustrated with a reading example in Exhibit 2.5. In this exhibit (based on a model by Holdaway, 1979) the boxes are words labeled "E" for easy or "H" for hard. Actually, the difficulty of any word is related to the person's background, so what is hard for one person may be easy for another. The reader in Exhibit 2.5 is represented by the *dotted line*. She is doing fine (not thinking about reading) until she hits the first "hard" word. At that point, self-monitoring says that meaning has been lost. As a result, the reader drops out of automatic reading and into

**a zone of problem solving**. In the zone of problem solving, the reader has to think (be aware) of the act of reading. It is here that the reader may think about the context of the story to try to guess the word, or even think to raise her hand for help from a teacher. Once the problem is solved, the kid returns to the **automatic zone** until the next hard word comes along.

Automaticity at word recognition is necessary so that the student does not have to allocate short-term memory to the routine act of decoding. This frees the short-term memory for other activities such as comprehension and enjoyment of the passage. For readers with limited prior knowledge of a topic, or of word recognition it-

*Exhibit 2.5* **Task Difficulty and Information Processing.**

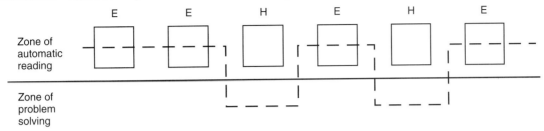

self, many words seem difficult. Thus, much of their awareness must be allocated to the problems of code rather than to the meanings of a passage. These students will understand little of what they read. Incidentally, another equally disabling problem occurs when a student's self-monitoring skills are so poor that she fails to notice the loss of meaning and simply misreads difficult words without recognizing the need to solve the problems they present. Students who lack skills *and* don't recognize when to use them may be thought of as working in the *ozone*.

The model of task performance presented in Exhibit 2.5 is a reasonable analogy for many assignments. The *squares* can represent arithmetic problems, social situations, road conditions, ideas to verbalize, or words to spell. In each case, success depends on the proficient use of skills. High levels of proficiency are necessary for students to achieve automaticity. A person who works automatically must maintain accuracy even when they are working fluently and in the presence of distracters. Teachers need to be cognizant of the extent to which tasks can become automatic because many students have become automatic at doing things wrong. How can someone be automatic at making mistakes?

Have you ever switched off the lights when someone else was still in the room? Have you ever underlined a passage in a book you borrowed? How about automatically locking your house when your keys were inside? In each of these cases, automaticity was actually working against you. Similarly, some students will automatically read passages they don't comprehend, or they'll resort to violence when it isn't needed. In such cases, the students are failing to be

mindful of their behavior. Self-monitoring must always be emphasized when attempting to build a student's automaticity because, from an information-processing view, it is just as easy to become automatic at doing things wrong as it is to become automatic at doing them right (Spiro et al., 1988). In fact, that is exactly what has happened to many special and remedial students.

## Do Successful and Unsuccessful Students Process Information Differently?

### Executive-Control Strategies (ECS)

Strategic use of executive control is part of a student's prior knowledge. It is considered strategic knowledge because it relates specifically to the way things are done. Strategies are rules or procedures for working (Marzano et al., 1988). Therefore, a "memory strategy" is a way to go about recalling information (it is not the information to be recalled). Research has shown us that remedial students and students with mild disabilities don't use executive-control strategies effectively (Mastropieri & Scruggs, 1996; Pressley, 1995, 1996). This doesn't mean they don't use strategies; it means they don't use adaptive strategies. There are rules and procedures that, if followed, can cause one to make mistakes. This is one of the big reasons some students do not learn. However, adaptive ECS can be learned (Brown, 1987; Graham, 1997; Palincsar, 1990; Paris & Winograd, 1990; Wong, 1991a, 1991b), which means that they need to be taught. Let's consider an example.

### Carl Teaches His Name

A researcher, Carl, takes an *average-OK-general-education 6-year-old* and tells her "Hi! My name is Carl. In 5 minutes I'm going to ask you what my name is. If you remember my name I'll give you a Porsche. If you forget it, I'll break your legs." (That is a joke, of course.) The *average-OK-general-education 6-year-old* will immediately begin to do something. She will start saying "Carl, Carl, Carl" over and over. This is called *rehearsal*, and it is an executive-control memory strategy for holding something in short-term memory by simply updating the memory every second or two. It is efficient as long as the person using it doesn't want to think about anything else. Therefore, 5 minutes later, the student will tell the researcher that his name is Carl and will get a new sports car. (This is one reason research is so expensive!)

Next, the researcher selects an *at-risk LD-remedial 6-year-old* and gives her the same directions. But the *at-risk LD-remedial 6-year-old* just looks at the researcher, smiles, and says "OK." She does not use rehearsal and will not remember the researcher's name. (We hope she has a ride home.)

Now for the important part of this example. Suppose the researcher selects another *at-risk LD-remedial 6-year-old* and says "Hi! My name is Carl. I want you to say my name to yourself over and over for 5 minutes." The 6-year-old will start saying "Carl, Carl, Carl," and 5 minutes later will remember the name.

The punch line here is that, if the original difference in memory between the general-education kid and the remedial kid were a matter of fixed ability (for example, if the general-education kid was born with ten pounds of memory but the remedial kid was only born with three), the use of the rehearsal strategy would not have helped. But it did!

### How Are Cognition and Behavior Linked?

The information-processing model and descriptions of executive-control strategies that have been presented here form the basis for the remainder of the text. Everything else you read in this text is premised on the idea that students fail to learn because they are missing information—not because they are lacking in fixed ability. However, there are several cautions that need to be applied to the theory illustrated in Exhibit 2.2.

1. We must remember that theories are temporary, and, like the modality theory that preceded it, this one will be modified.

2. Theories have multiple purposes. Primarily, they are developed and presented to help people understand things as well as to coordinate investigations of them. Although they may be helpful for guiding practice, they need not, and will not always, have immediate instructional implications. Remember, it is better to judge the quality of teaching by the positive effect it has on a student than by its congruence with a theory.

3. The only things in Exhibit 2.2 that have any *physical* reality (or specific location) are the receptors and effectors. You can be poked in the eye. You cannot be poked in the short-term memory. The rest is the product of carefully and tenuously assembled supposition.

4. The shapes and lines in the exhibit are better thought of as functions than parts. These are things our minds get done, not pieces of our minds. They cannot be isolated from each other physically or through testing. As you may have noticed when going through the examples above, the different functions often blend together. For example, it is clear that one must selectively attend to something to recall it. Short-term memory, whatever it is, cannot exist on its own. Therefore, it is unlikely that it can have anything wrong with it.

5. Even though it has often been described as one, it is probably better *not* to insist on conceptualizing the information-processing system as a computer, because that encourages us to think of job-specific components and permanent circuits. Human thinking is more fluid than that.

*Exhibit 2.6   Applied Behavior Analysis of Ellen's Hitting Behavior.*

| Antecedents $S^1$ | Behavior R | Consequences $S^2$ |
|---|---|---|
| a. Classroom | Ellen hits peer | a. Peer runs away |
| b. Free time | | b. Negative comments to stop |
| c. Morning | | c. Teacher puts Ellen in time-out |
| d. Low structure | | |
| e. Peers make negative comments | | |

## What About Behavior?

First this chapter questioned traditionally held views of ability, then it moved on to discuss the importance of prior knowledge and acquired patterns of problem-solving skills. With all of this discussion of thought processes, one might wonder whatever happened to behavior. Just as there have been shifts in our understanding of cognition, there have been shifts in our understanding of the relationship of thought to behavior. Today's understanding of information processing is different from traditional **psychodynamic** and **medical** views of ability and thought. Similarly, today's views of **operant** behavior and **environmental contingencies** are very different. These shifts are difficult to present without doing a complete history of both "camps," but it is also hard to pass off concepts as "traditional" and "new" without providing some context concerning the past.

The view of learning presented in traditional psychology held that behaviors largely were the result of personal characteristics (traits) such as intelligence and personality. These traits were often viewed as unalterable. Behavioral psychology modified this view by attributing behavior to a person's current context. As the behavioral orientation gained influence, the focus of assessment shifted from attempts to map the personality traits of students to attempts to link student behavior to the environment through assessment that focused on the antecedent and consequential stimuli that surround the student. In the strictly operant camp, behaviors were overt. It was recognized that a behavior occurring in the presence of one set of stimuli may not occur as often in a setting where these stimuli are absent. Therefore, the best way to explain either the presence or absence of a behavior (academic or social) is to analyze the environment by mapping out the stimuli (Zirpoli & Melloy, 1997). This point is illustrated with the **applied behavior analysis** (ABA) example of Ellen in Exhibit 2.6.

In very abbreviated terms ABA refers to the process of examining a behavior in the context of its antecedent and consequent stimuli. The exhibit shows the antecedent to and consequences of Ellen hitting a peer. The behavior took place in the classroom during unstructured free time. The consequences of Ellen's hitting behavior were that her peers made negative comments, her teacher told her to stop, and then she was put in time-out.

The ABA procedure can be extremely informative if one is looking for information about how to change behavior in a specific setting. However, it has some limitations, the main one being that it only makes sense if students respond *directly* to the environment. There is major evidence, however, that humans *don't* respond directly to the environment—or at least to what traditional operant literature described as the environment (one's tangible and physical surroundings). That evidence is the fact that all students don't act the same way in the same class.

Today, psychologists are apt to agree that neither children nor adults respond to the environment itself but to their cognitive representations of the environment (Kaplan, 1996). Stated another way, people don't behave according to what is going on but according to what they *think* is going on. These covert thoughts and feelings are the result of executive-control activity and the **interpreter** function's explanations of *physical* (for example, geographic) environmental stimuli. They may also be the result of learned *rules* that can take precedence over current external stimuli to control behavior (Malott et al., 1997). These rules, perceptions, expectations, and beliefs are stored in memory and used to interpret what is happening. Because the physical environment is experienced through a filter of prior learning, it is *interpretation* and the *expectation* of consequence that causes us to behave differently from each other. People have learned different things—their behavior is partially the result of their learning—so they behave in different ways.

Think about how attention, a covert and cognitive abstraction, can affect overt behavior. To select an option, a student must first attend to it. As already explained, attention works like a template between our awareness and the outside world. It protects short-term memory by allowing people to notice only those things that prior experience has taught are worth consciousness and to disregard those things they have been taught to ignore. But many students have learned to ignore options others see as important. One explanation for this can be found in the so-called **availability heuristic** (Tversky & Kahneman, 1973).

According to the availability paradigm, people are most apt to select options that are easy for them to recall (Shrum, 1996). This ease of recall is thought to be a function of experience or practice. If in the past a person has experienced one type of option frequently (or dramatically), regardless of how successful or pleasant the event was, that is the type of option she will most easily recall and select. Aggressive behavior is a good example of this. If a student has seen force applied frequently or dramatically to solve problems (even if it didn't work), then she is best prepared to recognize (perceive) forceful solutions to new problems. Because of learning she fails to "see" non-forceful options, has fewer choices to make, and therefore has less freedom to act.

If a student does class work for extra recess, she carries out the work in the *expectation* that the recess will be received. This expectation (or contingency) is the result of experiences in which recess was actually received after work. In the past, the teacher followed work with a pleasant stimulus, so now the student has an expectation that more work will lead to additional pleasant stimuli. The work then is the result of the learned expectation, not the actual consequence that follows the work. The work will still be done, even if the teacher reneges on the recess.

Compare the two parts of Exhibit 2.7. In the top part of the figure, the strict operant model (S-R-S) is illustrated. If we take this operant model and insert perceptions and expectations, the model looks like the lower portion. According to this amended model, behaviors are chosen from among the perceived available responses. The selection is also based on the consequences that are expected to follow choosing any of the perceived responses (Malott et al., 1997; Rotter, 1982). Therefore, our relationship to the environment is *mediated* by past learning.

Behavior and ABA have not gone away. They have, however, been modified to include the covert mediator that we call prior knowledge.

### Can Student Thinking Be Altered?

Throughout this chapter, we have talked about the functions involved in thinking and learning. The purpose of presenting this information here is to emphasize that the cognitive functions students employ in learning are not static or permanent but can be directly improved through instruction. Student cognition is an **alterable variable**. What are alterable variables? "Alterable" variables are those that a teacher can be reasonably expected to change through the process of instruction. They are sometimes called "proximal variables" as they are close to the learning event and have been shown to directly and immediately affect the quality of learning. Some examples of proximal variables are the student's prior knowledge of the lesson, the sequence and structure of the lesson, and the classroom management skills of the teacher. All of these can be changed through instruction and

**Exhibit 2.7    *The Cognitive-Behavior Model.***

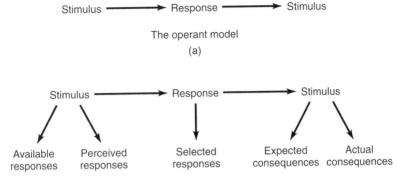

Stimulus ⟶ Response ⟶ Stimulus

The operant model

(a)

Stimulus ⟶ Response ⟶ Stimulus

| Available responses | Perceived responses | Selected responses | Expected consequences | Actual consequences |

The operant model including perceptions and expectations

(b)

are the result of a student's or teacher's previous learning. These are the things that teachers need to think about because these are the things that they can do something about.

"Unalterable" variables are those that a teacher cannot be reasonably expected to change through the process of instruction. They are sometimes called **distal variables** because, although they affect the probability that learning will occur, they do not have a direct and immediate impact on the quality of lessons. Here are some variables that, in this sense, are considered to be *unalterable*: race, gender, family poverty, parental drug use, ethnicity, teachers' education, teachers' caring, class size, birth order, school funding, various student abilities (that is, cerebral dominance, innate potential to learn), and student disability label. Although these are considered to be unalterable, they *are* important; they are simply beyond the influence of effective instruction. Certainly school funding, class size, and family poverty can be changed—and they should be! But that alteration won't come about through a few weeks of classroom instruction (it is more likely to occur in the voting booth). That is why, despite their importance, they are called unalterable.

Unfortunately, it has been found that when asked to explain why a student is having trouble in class, many teachers report that the problem is the result of unalterable variables (Ysseldyke et al., 1992). This error in thinking effectively stops the teacher from engaging in productive decision making. However, teacher thoughts about teaching (like student thoughts about addition) are learned. And that means that they also can be changed.

## *Summary*

Learning is the result of an interaction occurring among the characteristics of the student, the curriculum the student is expected to learn, and the instruction the student receives. When learning occurs, the student combines the new information provided during the lesson with her existing knowledge to arrive at new understandings and skills.

- According to current learning theory, some students fail to learn because they lack the prior knowledge required to succeed. They do not fail because they lack the capacity, or ability, to learn.

- The single best predictor of how well a student will learn in any given lesson is the student's knowledge of the task prior to the start of the lesson. This includes task-specific knowledge (such as how to read words or multiply fractions) and task-related knowledge (such as how to recognize critical information or deal with failure).

- The next best predictor of learning is the teacher's skill at managing proximal variables in a way that productively matches the new information of the lesson with the student's existing knowledge. An effective teacher structures lessons so that new information is presented in a way that harmonizes with what the student already knows.

- Successful instruction does not depend upon the attention, memory, and motivation of the student—the attention memory and motivation of the student depend on successful instruction.

## STUDY QUESTIONS

1. Here are some learning tasks. Decide which component(s) of the information-processing system is most important for each task and describe the teaching activities you think would best facilitate learning.

   Memorize the names of the students in your class.
   Take notes on a chapter in this book.
   Decide if you need to study some more for the test you will take tomorrow.
   Read the actual wording of a Supreme Court decision in a law book.

   Read the following scenario and answer questions 2–4 below.

---

It is seventh period, which is "activity period" at the Millervale Middle School. Students who aren't involved with activities such as band, yearbook, or sports stay in their homerooms for an unstructured study period. Jessica, Hunter, and Brittany are sixth-grade students working in your homeroom. Jessica is working on her math homework. Hunter walks past Jessica's desk and flips her book closed. Jessica looks up and shouts "Keep your frigging hands to yourself you stupid jerk," opens her book, and resumes working. At this point, Brittany, who is sitting two rows away, begins crying and says "I wish I didn't have to go to school here" and runs from the room without asking for permission. Hunter returns to his seat and begins tapping his desk loudly with a pencil.

---

2. Given the information here, conduct an ABA analysis of the scenario.

3. What are three things you would do immediately in this situation?

4. What steps would you take to prevent future events such as this in your homeroom?

5. Brenda is a student in your third-grade class who is having difficulty making the transition from printing to cursive. Her cursive writing is nearly illegible, and lately she has been failing her weekly spelling tests. Brenda's mother believes Brenda is an auditory learner and wants you to allow Brenda to complete her reading journal assignments at home on the family computer. What are you going to do?

# Chapter 3

# Thinking About the Curriculum

*Anyone who has had occasion to visit a country in which he does not know the language must have discovered that a good deal of human discourse can be handled using no more than a grammarless handful of nouns and verbs, supplemented by shrugs, points, facial expressions, etc. Language apparently developed because human beings had something more to say to each other. The most striking candidate for the "something more" is that human groups thrived that were able to explicitly plan and coordinate activities tailored to novel contingencies.*

—H. Margolis (1987)

*The key insight uncovered by the study of complex systems in recent years is this: The only way for a system to evolve into something new is to have a flexible structure.*

—K. Kelley (1997)

## What Is the Curriculum and What Is It Good For?

Chapter 1 described learning as an interactive phenomenon (involving the student, instruction, and the curriculum), and it briefly explained how decision making can improve learning. Chapter 2 illustrated how learning occurs and made the point that prior knowledge is critical to learning. In this chapter, we will elaborate on the idea of knowledge and show how it can be organized and taught.

This chapter is about curriculum. A curriculum is a structured set of learning outcomes, or tasks, that educators usually call goals or objectives (Howell & Evans, 1995; Johnson, 1967; Sands et al., 1995). Students are expected to learn the information specified in the curriculum so that they will have the skills needed to transition from childhood into adult life. Curriculum is intended to prepare students to succeed in society. It is the "something more" to which Margolis refers in the quote above. Consequently, the material in the curriculum comes from someone's analysis of what society requires for success (Wraga, 1999).

Learning outcomes based on society's requirements are written into curriculum guides before the student even shows up for class. These include not only static bits of skill and knowledge but also the dynamic principles of how to learn. The sequence of the curriculum may be shuffled, its tasks may be broken into small pieces or combined into larger ones, its organizational structure may be altered, it may be reassigned to different instructors, and it may be taught in different ways. But the *substance* of the curriculum should not be changed as long as we believe that *all* students deserve a competitive shot at success in life (Burstein et al., 1995; Johnson & Immerwahr, 1994).

Curriculum is not the same thing as *instruction*. Unfortunately, they are commonly confused. You can tell this is happening when you ask a teacher *what* she is teaching and she responds with the name of a program or instructional approach (that is, Direct Instruction, Whole Language, Spalding, SRA, Merrill, or Addison-Wesley) rather than a skill (such as saying vowel sounds, solving multiplication problems, writing prime factors, or comparing economic systems). However, it is a mistake to confuse curriculum with instruction because there is often more debate and confusion about *how* to teach than there is about *what* to teach.

Knowledge of the curriculum is an absolute for successful assessment, evaluation, decision making, and teaching (Howell, 1986; Nitko, 1995; Shulman, 1986). For example, one can't evaluate a student's reading without first deciding what reading entails and what aspects of it are essential. The primary thing to understand about curriculum is that, without a curriculum component (for example, something to be taught), there is no need for teacher-directed instruction and, therefore, no lesson. Deciding which of the curriculum tasks a student should be taught—and which instructional approach will allow us to teach it—best requires the use of evaluative procedures that are themselves sensitive to a student's prior knowledge of the curriculum.

## How Is Curriculum Conceptualized?

Look at Exhibit 3.1. This figure presents a representation of the main elements of school curriculum. This representation goes beyond traditional notions of curriculum as academic content. As you examine the illustration in Exhibit 3.1, remember that in the first two chapters of the book, we emphasized that students' learning problems are the result of missing prior knowledge. The model presented in Exhibit 3.1 breaks prior knowledge into two categories: Knowledge of Literacy and Task-Related Knowledge.

### What Is Literacy?

This area includes the academics and social skills that most people think of when they think of school outcomes. When a student is missing one or more of these skills, they may be unable to do well in school or life. A student could be missing one of these skills because he was gone the week (or month) it was taught, moved to a new district where the skill had already been taught, or had ineffective instruction. A student who is missing a skill has what is usually called a **performance deficit**. This doesn't necessarily mean the student has trouble learning, but it does mean there are things he doesn't know.

### What Is Task-Related Knowledge?

This area includes study skills and basic learning skills. These are the skills that a student needs to learn in a typical class. A student who is missing these skills will fall behind in the curriculum and may end up with one or more performance deficits. However, the underlying cause of these performance deficits is his **progress deficit**. Such a student has not learned how to learn. As a result, if a teacher corrects his performance deficits and moves him to an acceptable level of literacy, he may just fall behind again as other students continue to progress.

*Exhibit 3.1    An Expanded View of Curriculum.*

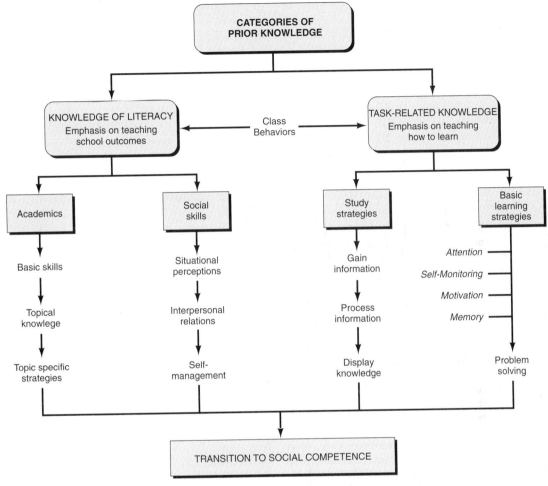

It is the student's failure to progress that results in performance discrepancies. So, whenever a student is making inadequate progress in school (for example, there is a discrepancy between the expected and actual rate of progress through the curriculum), attention should be paid to the task-related domain.

### What About Class Behavior?

How the student behaves in class can have an impact on either of the two main categories in

Exhibit 3.1 For example, *careful treatment of equipment* might be a part of learning about chemistry. Similarly, class behavior is related to task-related skills because *talking too much*, *fighting*, or *failing to arrive at class* will all probably slow down the student's learning rate.

### How Is Literacy Best Represented?

Literacy is the efficient exchange of messages within a particular cultural context. Literate communication and language are the means by which we engage in extended thinking. They also let us label our wants and needs, express our feelings and emotions, and form our social interactions. Literate communication also can refer to use of numbers and symbols. In this text, we will use the term literacy to refer to the entire range of literate and numerate behaviors.

Children's success in school and life depends on acquisition of literacy skills. Literacy is at the heart of any socially relevant curriculum. The failure to develop literacy may prove devastating and isolating. An illiterate child, or adult, will have difficulty gaining information, have problems displaying what he knows, and often may not be sufficiently skilled to express needs for help. That is why literacy is the main focus of instruction in schools.

Literacy implies proficiency of use and communication. To clarify the nature of literacy, let's consider a couple of examples. First, imagine that you have spent years learning to speak Spanish and are now fluent. You have a friend, also a teacher, who is just as fluent at speaking Pohnpeian (used to conduct government business in the Federated States of Micronesia). You and your friend are certified to teach in both elementary education and special education. You have decided to apply for jobs in California. In that state there are many thousands of Spanish-speaking students and relatively few who speak Pohnpeian. Which one, you or your friend, is most likely to get a job?

Let's try another example. This one was suggested by Langer (1991). You are touring a local junior high school. First, you go to a social studies class where students are working on an assignment. They have silently read a passage about life in the Middle East and are answering questions at the end of the unit. As you walk around the room you note that the students are quiet, all answering correctly, and that their spelling and handwriting is excellent.

After leaving the social studies class, you walk by the room used for in-school suspension of problem students. When you walk in you find the students engaged in an argument. You are surprised to find that the argument is also about the Middle East. It was sparked by a TV show that two of the students watched the night

before. Much of what the students are saying is poorly worded, but their ideas seem considered and they are trying hard to get the rest of the students to understand the dispute presented in the broadcast. The other students seem to be trying especially hard to understand.

Now the question: In which setting, the social studies class or the detention class, did you find students engaging in the most literate exercise? More direct to this illustration, in which class did the students seem to be learning important curricular skills?

Dictionaries typically define a literate person as one who is "cultured." This means that the form and quality of literacy are linked to the cultural context in which it occurs (Valencia et al., 1992). What is literate behavior in one setting may be less than literate in another. Similarly, illiteracy may be a function of misalignment, not inaccuracy. Your Pohnpeian-speaking friend, although technically skilled, may seem less cultured to a class of Latino students in Modesto, California, than will you, the Spanish speaker. The key term here may not even be literacy—or culture; it may be communication.

To understand literacy one has to understand the ways individuals communicate within a cultural context and how social context modifies the definition of literacy. For example, someone who is considered "computer literate" is proficient at using a computer. However, computer work that was worthy of University credits a decade ago is now common in many elementary schools. As a result, a person who has maintained stable computer skills over the last decade may have slipped from the *literate* to the *illiterate* category as those around him advanced.

Literacy is "enabled" by underlying skills (Valencia et al., 1992). If students do not have those enabling skills, they cannot efficiently employ the complex operations we associate with literate communication. Similarly, if they have the enabling skills but lack the knowledge for using them, they will not behave in a literate fashion.

The relationship between enabling skills and literacy strategies is easiest to see in terms of transcribing and recognizing. As the Margolis quote implies, a person can have a wonderful vocabulary but have nothing to say. Therefore, vocabulary enables—but does not assure—literate transcription and recognition of messages. Skills, like vocabulary usage, that enable literate behavior are sometimes called **prerequisites** or **subtasks**.

## How Can Teachers Work with the Curriculum?

Teachers make decisions about the curriculum whenever they make decisions involving what should be taught. Traditionally curricular decisions are made according to the calendar. Fixed periods of time are allocated to teach particular objectives (for example, 4 weeks to work on "developing story outlines"). At the end of the scheduled time, the teacher stops instruction on that task and moves on, regardless of student performance. In this approach, the number of sessions is fixed but the learning of the students in class is not. Therefore, when time runs out, some students will have learned all they need to know and others won't. Planning based on the calendar is easy to understand because in group instruction many decisions must be based on ideas about how to teach the most people the best things in the easiest way. But, for almost every student there comes a time when that kind of group decision making doesn't work. That is when "individualized" instruction is required.

When a teacher uses individualized instruction, she must be willing to vary the type, length, and the number of sessions to guarantee that all students learn what they need to learn. Therefore, the variability in student learning is replaced with variability in instruction. This is one of the basic principles of mastery learning (Engelmann, 1997; Kulik et al., 1990) and the Carroll Model (Clark, 1987). It is safe to say that, if teachers are unwilling to be flexible according to student needs, all other discussions of program or method superiority are silly.

One of the first steps in individualization is selection of an appropriate goal for instruction. This step requires the teacher to pick goals from the mass of expected learnings. This process begins with **task analysis**. Task analysis is the

process of defining all of the essential components of a task (Bateman, 1998). The idea behind task analysis is that a student must learn the prior knowledge required by a task to learn the task. Teachers using task analysis attempt to identify the prior knowledge and to test the student's knowledge of it to decide which skills need to be taught to the student. Incidentally, this need to exactly specify subcomponents does *not* mean that the components must be taught in isolation.

In this text, we use the terms **task** and **objectives** to mean roughly the same thing. Any job or activity that a student learns to do during the school day may be referred to as a task. Any behavior, or set of behaviors, in which a child must engage to demonstrate skill or knowledge is a task.

Subtasks are simply smaller, or more elementary, tasks required for the performance of an objective. Subtasks and tasks are exactly the same except for their relative positions in some skill sequence. If counting is required for addition, then counting is a subtask of addition. If addition is required for multiplication, then addition is a subtask of multiplication. (Maybe this means that one task's subtask is another subtask's task—bet that cleared it up for you!) Subtasks can be viewed as the stuff (strategies, concepts, facts, vocabulary, skills) students use whenever they try to do something.

Earlier, we used the term *individualize*. Let's discuss what individualization is and what it is not.

- Individualization is *not* one-to-one teaching.
- Individualization is *not* unique instructional objectives.
- Individualization is *not* necessarily different instruction.
- Individualization *is* a flexible process of decision making.

Task analysis often is at the center of effective individualization, however, individualization is a thought process, not a product. Picture this. Chip is a special education teacher. He overhears Norma being praised for the fantastic objectives she wrote for her student. Chip borrows Norma's objectives, copies them, and puts them in his student's plan. Then, Chip is shocked when he is criticized for writing terrible objectives. What happened? Chip didn't individualize; he mistakenly believed that the product of someone else's efforts was more important than going through the process of identifying objectives for his particular student. The best plan is the one resulting from the most careful consideration of the individual student.

When we individualize, we look at the curriculum, decide what the student already knows [The Present Level of Educational Performance (PLEP)], what he needs to know, and what he is ready to learn. For example, Exhibit 3.2 demonstrates an analysis of critical reading (Carnine et al., 1997) and a student's status on each of the subskills, if the skill is to recognize author bias through critical reading.

Given this task analysis and the information about the student's skills, the teacher can see which critical reading tasks the student can already perform and which he can't. Therefore, *judge quality of evidence* and *judge author's expertise* will become instructional objectives for the student.

## How Can Curriculum Be Organized?

Tasks (instructional objectives) often are categorized in an effort to coordinate the curriculum. Curricular tasks typically are categorized by content. For example, one might refer to "language tasks" or "reading objectives." Curricular tasks also may be grouped according to the type of information they involve, such as facts, concepts, rules, or strategies. Indeed, many middle and high school curriculum materials are extremely dense with facts but contain only a few key concepts or unifying rule relationships (Jitendra et al., in press). Recently, curriculum design has begun to focus on "big ideas" that subsume concepts and principles and cut across multiple strands of content. For example, in a synthesis of 5 years of research into the pedagogical and curriculum demands of schools, Kameenui and Carnine (1998) identified instruction around big ideas as one of the

**Exhibit 3.2 Analysis of Critical Reading and Student Status.**

| Subskill | Student's status |
|---|---|
| Recognize author's purpose | Knows how to do this |
| Distinguish evidence from opinion | Knows how to do this |
| Judge quality of evidence | Does not know how to do this |
| Judge author's expertise | Does not know how to do this |

key features of high quality educational tools for diverse learners.

Curriculum also may be categorized according to the complexity of the intellectual activity involved. For example, curriculum tasks may require students to "synthesize," "evaluate," or "apply." Categorization according to intellectual complexity is closely aligned with the notion of curriculum "levels." For example, it is common to find subsets of curriculum described as "higher level" or "lower level." In such cases, tasks may be referred to by titles like "meaningful," "abstract," "concrete," "rational," "symbolic," "rule-governed," "synthetic," "cognitive," or "affective" (Simmons & Kameenui, 1990). The idea of levels implies some mechanism for scaling the cognitive demands of learning so that lessons can be organized into a meaningful progression. Such designations imply gradations in the cognitive quality (for example, sophistication or complexity) of the curriculum segments. To support these subdivisions, some authors employ *taxonomies* based on beliefs about the various shades of thinking involved in the use of content. Likely the most influential of these taxonomies is the one articulated by Bloom et al. (1956).

Bloom's taxonomy was originally developed as a tool for teachers to use in specifying the expected outcomes of instruction, and although it has served as a useful heuristic for thinking about the intellectual demands of curriculum tasks, the various "levels" of Bloom's taxonomy have not held up as discrete points along a continuous scale (Krathwohl, 1994; Miller et al., 1979). In part, this is because it is hard to distinguish a thought requiring higher level thinking from a *bigger* thought—that is, one that has more bits of information. For example, although it may seem that world governance is more sophisticated than city government, it may also be true that both can be understood exactly the same way; it is just that, in world government, it is carried out on a larger scale. Much of what we see as cognitively complex is actually simple; there is just a lot of it.

The idea of conceptualizing curriculum tasks according to cognitive levels recently has enjoyed renewed popularity because so much of the rhetoric associated with the standards-based reform movement focuses on notions of so-called "higher order thinking." Unfortunately, there is relatively little empirical support for organizing curriculum tasks according to some underlying scale of sophistication. It *is* possible to describe observable sets of behaviors that can be given labels such as "illustration" or "evaluation" and then obtain high rates of agreement among observers that those behaviors have actually been displayed (Nolet & Tindal, 1994; Williams & Haladyna, 1982). However, interobserver agreement about the existence of a phenomenon implies nothing about the relationship of that particular phenomenon to other events. Although all those conspiracy theorists on late-night talk-radio seem to be not the least bit troubled by this bit of logic, teachers interested in making effective decisions about instruction must be. For example, there is no reason to believe that a set of behaviors associated with *critical thinking* (for example, "make a choice and support it with a rationale") is more or less cognitively difficult than a set of behaviors associated with *analysis* (for example, "decide what circumstances or events resulted in an observed outcome").

In practice, most curriculum progressions still are an artifact of the calendar or some other pragmatic consideration. For example, we sometimes teach government first at the local level and then the state, nation, region, and world. Once again, this isn't necessarily because government at the local level is inherently less sophisticated or complex, it is because one cannot teach everything at once and it seems logical to start with topics about which students may have some preexisting familiarity.

So what does this all mean? It means that we can fairly easily divide curriculum by content headings. However, it is harder to successfully divide it by level of thinking. As Hoeg (1994) points out, ". . . In all of the history of the world, no code of practice has ever existed for the assessment of complex phenomena. . . . If no code exists for determining if something is good or bad, why do people talk as though it does?" (p. 90). Good question. Given the problem of defining levels of thinking, the alternative option is to scrap ideas about cognitive difficulty and focus on finding functional task sequences. These do not require us to speculate about what is easy to think about and what is hard to think about, but to simply ask what is best to think about first and what is best to think about second. Such an approach to *levels* frees us from the theoretical considerations of cognition and leaves us with comparatively simple questions about the hierarchical relationships imposed by application. And many of these can, and have been, empirically illustrated. For example, it is faster to learn to spell words if one first learns the sounds letters make. Does that mean spelling is more cognitively demanding than learning letter sounds? Who knows? But it is still a good idea to start a lesson on spelling words by introducing, or reviewing, the sounds of the letters (or combinations of letters) that will be in the words.

In this text, an effort will be made to organize the presentation of curriculum so that what should be taught first can be distinguished from what should be taught next. In cases where lists or tables are employed, the first things taught will be at the bottom of the page and the last things will be at the top—this will explained in the section on **Tables of Specifications**. An effort will also be made to acknowledge when a clear sequence has not yet been established (which is often the case). When this happens, we may step back and organize the curriculum according to some functional or logical scheme.

Here are the key things to remember about how curricula are organized.

- Curriculum organizational strategies are useful for imposing order on large bodies of information so it can be taught in an efficient sequence.
- Curriculum tasks can often be organized according to the specific content, the type of information they involve, or their cognitive complexity.
- The organizational scheme we recommend in this text is based on task analysis; enabling subtasks must be learned before more encompassing skills can be mastered.
- When a student lacks prior knowledge, the organization and sequencing of curriculum tasks should be examined to pinpoint what is missing.

## What Goes into a Curriculum?

So far we have talked about what curriculum *is* (an organized set of learning outcomes) and we have talked about a process for *organizing* curriculum (task analysis), but we have not discussed the actual substance of curriculum. Clearly, curriculum involves some body of information that represents what it is the student is expected to learn. However, analysis of the specific content of *every* curricular domain taught in school would be a daunting task that is certainly beyond the scope of this text (and it probably would have little merit). It turns out that curriculum content can be characterized according to the *form* that the information takes. Furthermore, when a teacher knows the form of the information they want to teach, instruction becomes fairly straightforward, thanks to nearly 40 years of research in instructional design (Simmons & Kameenui, 1990).

In general, information in curriculum can take the form of *facts, concepts, rules,* or *strategies.* However, as we have emphasized repeatedly in this text, any task a learner is expected to master subsumes *all* component subtasks. This point has two implications for curriculum content. First,

task demands do not reside exclusively within the tasks themselves but within the linkage of the task to the prior knowledge and thought processes of the learner. Therefore, curriculum tasks should be thought of as amalgamations of facts, concepts, rules, or strategies. No task is purely factual, conceptual, or strategic. We will return to this point in a little while.

The second implication is that information contained in curriculum does not become knowledge until it is incorporated into the student's cognitive repertoire or schema. The importance of using teaching to transform the *potential* information in curriculum into knowledge that a student can directly access in long-term memory is paramount. This issue is particularly salient given the extent to which *materials* often drive instruction in classrooms.

In this text, when we refer to "curriculum," we are not referring to "materials." Most materials commonly found in classrooms contain lots of information that potentially may be useful for some students to learn, depending on what the students already know and what they will be expected to do with the information. These same materials also contain a great deal of information that, for some students, is nothing more than useless drivel. It is the teacher's job to engage in a thoughtful selection process to identify the information that is most relevant, given the student's current level of performance.

Curriculum materials serve an important function in schools because they eliminate the need for teachers to "start from scratch" in deciding what to teach to meet district, state, and societal expectations. However, curriculum materials should be thought of as the parts list rather than the blueprint for designing instruction. Some of the "parts" contained in materials can be used right off the shelf. Other information contained in curriculum materials may need to be modified to make it accessible for a particular student. Let's look more closely at the types of curriculum content.

### What Is Factual Information?

Facts represent a simple one-to-one association between a stimulus and a response. Factual

*Teachers must select the correct level of expected performance, as well as the content to be taught.*

knowledge is sometimes called rote or declarative knowledge (Marzano et al., 1988). Here are some examples of facts: "6 times 8 is 48," "James A. Garfield was the 20th president of the United States," and "the atomic weight of helium is 4.0026." Here is another fact (just in case you are in need of motivation right now) "the average salary for college graduates is about $1800 a month higher than the average salary of high school graduates" (Bassuk et al., 1996). Facts are discrete bits of information that stand alone. For example, knowing that the capital of Indiana is Indianapolis does not lead one to know that the capital of Switzerland is Bern.

Facts are things a person can know without knowing how to figure them out or what they mean. Learning facts entails memorization, and instruction designed to teach facts must focus on moving the information from short-term memory to long-term memory through repeated rehearsal distributed over time (Simmons & Kameenui, 1990).

## What Is Conceptual Information?

Concepts are objects, events, actions, or situations that share a set of defining characteristics. Any concept belongs to a category that has a rule for defining the relevant features of all members of the category. The rule provides the basis for organizing the attributes of the concept and for distinguishing between examples and nonexamples of the concept. Conceptual information permits a student to grasp the implications and underlying ideas associated with an idea. For example "6 × 8 = 48" means the same thing as counting by 8 six times.

Concepts are best taught through presentation of examples and nonexamples that illustrate the full range of the concept class. For example, to teach the concept "metal," a range of elements that qualify as metals would be presented as positive examples, whereas transition or metalloid elements might be presented as minimally different nonexamples. Some concepts are difficult to teach and learn because they are made complex by conditional or nested attributes (or the examples have membership in multiple categories). Consider for example, the concept "boat" defined as "a small watercraft." Examples could include "canoe," "rowboat," "rowing shell," and "sailboat." However, larger craft often are referred to as "boats" too, so something as big as an automobile ferry or a tug boat seems to qualify as a "boat." If you were interested in finding out whether a particular student was lacking prior knowledge about boats, you might first need to specify what you mean by "boat." This idea seems somewhat confusing when thinking about noun concepts like "boat," and it becomes more difficult when the concept under consideration is "correct spelling," "two-step problem solving," or "appropriate talk."

## What Are Rule Relationships?

A rule usually represents an if-then, cause-effect, or covariant relationship among different facts or concepts. A rule generally involves applications in which the fundamental relationship is constant across virtually all examples. For example, the law of supply and demand may be taught as the principle "when supply goes up, demand goes down," with comparable applications found in the context of Medieval European city states, a child's lemonade stand, and the 1929 Stock Market Crash. Explicit rule relationships are found frequently in science and social studies classes, but more implicit rules often form the basis for literacy-enabling skills. Here are some examples: "'i' before 'e' except after 'c'"; "when you subtract, you get a smaller number"; "if there is a silent 'e' at the end of the word, say the long sound for the vowel."

Learning rules requires a student to attend to both parts of the rule and then discriminate the relationship that connects them. Instruction entails presentation of a wide range of instances of

the rule in which one of the parts of the relationship is provided and the student predicts the contingent part ("If the 'e' is silent, then what sound will the vowel make?").

## What Is Strategic Knowledge?

The term "strategy" currently is very trendy in the educational literature. Although it has yet to be clearly defined (de Bettencourt, 1987; Harris & Graham, 1996b; Pressley, 1996), it seems the term is used most widely to characterize the process of work, as opposed to its products (Marzano et al., 1988; Weinstein & Mayer, 1983). The term "strategy" often is used in a military context to refer to the timely deployment of troops or weapons to achieve maximum benefit in a battle. The same idea applies in the context of thinking and problem solving. Strategic knowledge involves the timely deployment of facts, concepts, and rules to achieve maximum benefit to solve a problem or achieve a goal. Strategies are the procedures students follow to combine subtasks into larger tasks. There can be several different strategies for combining the same set of subtasks because there is often more than one way to do something correctly (and there are definitely many ways to do something incorrectly). If two students with the same subskill competency follow different strategies, one may succeed at the task whereas the other might fail. For example, think about how you would solve this problem:

$$14(27 - x) = 56$$

First, you would divide both sides by 14. You'd get:

$$27 - x = 4$$

Next, you'd subtract 4 from both sides. You'd get:

$$23 - x = 0$$

Finally, you'd add $x$ to both sides. You'd get:

$$23 = x$$

Here is the information you probably used to arrive at this solution.

1. This problem requires me to solve for the unknown.

*Exhibit 3.3* *Task Analysis of Fractions.*

| Task | Example |
|---|---|
| Add or subtract fractions without common denominators that *do not* have common factors between denominators. Convert to simplest form. | $2/7 + 3/4 = 1\ 1/28$ |
| **Task Strategy**<br><br>— (a) Decide if denominators are the same<br>— (b) Find the least common denominator<br>— (c) Produce the equivalent fractions<br>— (d) Decide what operation (add or subtract) is called for<br>— (e) Carry out the operation<br>— (f) Decide if the answer is in simplest form. If it isn't,<br>— (g) Convert it | |
| **Essential Subtasks**<br><br>—5. Converting fractions to simplest form<br>—4. Adding and subtracting fractions that do have common factors<br>—3. Multiplication and division facts<br><br>—2. Finding least common denominators<br>—1. Addition facts | $29/28 = 1\ 1/28$<br>$8/28 + 21/28 = 29/28$<br>$7/28 = 4 \quad 4 \times 2 = 8$<br>$4/28 = 7 \quad 7 \times 3 = 21$<br>$7, 14, 21, 28$<br>$2 + 3 = 5$ |

2. If I isolate the unknown ($x$) on one side of the equation, I can solve for it.

3. If I do something to one side of the equation, I need to do it to the other side.

4. If I subtract a number from itself, I get 0.

Notice that the steps used for solving the problem involve a series of rules and that nested within these rules are various concepts (that is, "unknown" and "equation") and facts (such as "56 divided by 14 equals 4" and "23 − 23 = 0"). The strategic knowledge you employed informed you of *what* to do and *when* to do it. You might not have been consciously aware of all of the steps you followed to solve the problem if all of the component information is part of your background knowledge. However, if you were missing *any* of the key pieces of information, you might not have been able to solve the problem.

This point is further illustrated in the example shown in Exhibit 3.3.

Look at the fraction example in Exhibit 3.3, where the task (adding 2/7 + 3/4) is presented at the top and the subtasks are presented at the bottom. The strategy for combining the subtasks is also presented. As you read the strategy, you will notice that it isn't particularly sophisticated; it simply tells what to do first, second, third, and so on. Now suppose you have a student named Glen. As you can see, if Glen can't multiply and divide accurately (subtask 3), he will be unable to succeed at this task even if he has memorized the strategy and writes it on the board 50 times every day. Glen would need to work on multiplication and division (Graham & Harris, 1994; Kameenui & Carnine, 1998).

Sticking with the problem in Exhibit 3.3, imagine that another student, Loren, who can multiply and divide just fine, writes the following answer:

$$2/7 + 3/4 = 29/28$$

This answer is wrong because it is not converted to its simplest form. This doesn't necessarily mean Loren can't convert fractions (subskill 5). It could mean he forgot the last step in the strategy (step g). If that is the case, having Loren memorize the strategy might be a good instructional technique (but *not* by writing it 50 times a day). Working on multiplication would be a waste of his time.

Errors are not always the result of a flawed strategy. Rather, they are often the result of a correct strategy incorrectly applied. We all attempt to solve new problems by using a strategy that has worked in the past. For example, a student who writes $2/7 + 3/4 = 5/11$ has not gotten the "add-unlike-fractions strategy" wrong, he hasn't used it at all. In the $2/7 + 3/4$ example, the student applied the addition strategy for whole numbers to a fraction problem. In one sense, what the student did was right (added correctly). Unfortunately, that wasn't what was needed. A common type of strategic error is to apply strategies already learned to new tasks where they don't apply.

There may be several different strategies for any one task. The fraction strategy presented in Exhibit 3.3 is one way to arrive at the answer; another way is to ask the teacher. The first strategy (adding fractions without a common denominator) is specific to fractions. The second strategy (seeking assistance) is a general strategy and may be used in many situations.

**Specific strategies** apply to only a limited range of tasks, whereas **general strategies** may be used across several content domains (Frederiksen, 1984; Rigney, 1980; Wagner & Sternberg, 1984). The fraction algorithm in Exhibit 3.3 is a specific strategy that is good for solving only one type of fraction problem. It won't help you do long division, it won't help you get a date, and it won't help you find words in a dictionary. Asking for assistance, in contrast, is a strategy that may help you succeed at all of those tasks and many more. Exhibit 3.4 shows the steps of a general strategy and how it might be applied to

three different problems: solving the division problem 27 divided by 84, arranging a date, and defining the term "strategy."

## How Can Strategies Fit into the Curriculum?

The belief that problem learners lack the basic capacity or ability to learn has been replaced by a belief that these students do not have the knowledge they need to make effective use of the capacity they have. The importance of this change lies in the idea that use of cognitive strategies, unlike cognitive capacity, can be altered through instruction. The characterization of mildly disabled students as "strategy deficient" has been followed by the recommendation that strategies be taught (Derry & Murphy, 1986; Herrmann, 1988; Swanson & Hoskyn, 1998). As is often the case, such calls for change in instructional practice have not been accompanied by complementary calls for change in the practice of curriculum development and evaluation. This isn't good.

Calls to include strategies in instruction are, by implication, calls to include them in the curriculum. Exactly how this inclusion should take place is not clear, although at least two alternatives are available. In one approach, general thinking skills could be taught as a new area within the content curriculum. Unfortunately, the research evidence for teaching general thinking skills to special/remedial students, although interesting, isn't setting the world on fire (Brown & Duguid, 1996; McKeachie, 1987a, 1987b). This may be because the general thinking skills are not being generalized to specific academic and social tasks, or it may mean the instruction is simply not effective. In any case, we believe that teaching thinking skills is not a bad idea, it simply isn't sufficient.

The second approach is to include strategies as part of existing objectives (Palincsar & Brown, 1987). This has been referred to as Embedded Strategy Training (Derry & Murphy, 1986). At present, this idea of embedding strategies within the existing curriculum holds the most promise for students who are experiencing difficulty in schools. In an embedded strategy curriculum, the outcomes (objectives) are not simply

**Exhibit 3.4    General Strategy Applied to Three Problems.**

| General Strategy | Problem | | |
|---|---|---|---|
| | 27/84 | Arrange a Date | Define "Strategy" |
| Recognize a problem | I have to figure this out and I don't know the answer. | If I don't get a date I'll end up watching reruns of *Seinfeld* Saturday night. | I still don't know what a strategy is. |
| Generate options | I could use a calculator. I could copy off Rodger. I could ask the teacher. I could look for help in my math book. | I could ask Rodger or Chuck to go to a movie, to dinner, or skiing. | I could look it up in the dictionary. I could reread this chapter. I could check the glossary. |
| Consider resources | I don't have a calculator, Rodger is worse at math than I am, I can't read the math book, and I hate the teacher. | Chuck has a girlfriend who knows karate. I don't know how to ski. | I've read this chapter already and don't have time to waste. |
| Anticipate consequences | If I do copy off Rodger I'll owe him a favor and that's the *last* thing I want. | If I ask Rodger he'll owe me a favor. If I ask Chuck he'll say no or his girlfriend will kill me. | The dictionary and glossary will be too simplified for my needs. |
| Solve problem | I'll ask the teacher for help. | I think I'll ask Rodger. | I'll check the index to see if there is more information on strategies somewhere else in the text. |
| Check work | Asking worked out OK and the teacher put me in a work group with Chuck. | It didn't work. Rodger was busy Saturday. I hope I've only seen this episode ten times. | There is a lot of stuff on strategies in Chapters 2, 7, and 8. |

conceptualized as things a person will do; the objectives also specify how the student will do them. An embedded strategy objective, therefore, combines orthodox product statements ("student will write the answers to multiplication fact problems with 100% accuracy") with process statements ("count by the larger number as many times as indicated by the small number"). This would yield instructional objectives that sound like this: "The student will write the answers to multiplication fact problems with 100%

accuracy by counting by the larger number as many times as the smaller number indicates." A student who recalls these facts by rote, copies them from the child across the aisle, or uses a calculator would not have met this objective even if every answer was right.

Because an objective like the one above is longer, it would take more time to write. Fortunately, as most teachers are not awash with extra time, writing an objective like that would only be necessary if a student was having extraordinary trouble learning a particular way to multiply. In most cases, the strategy should just be assumed as part of the learning process implied when one writes a traditional objective. However, it is still a good idea for teachers to consider how they want students to work a task. This helps the teacher plan what to say during the lesson and helps prevent the student from inventing his own ways of doing things (some of which may not be effective or acceptable).

### How Is Curriculum Integrated with Instruction?

The next chapter deals with instruction and will present different ways to teach the types of information described here (facts, concepts, rules, and strategies). However, at this time it may be a good idea to reinforce a point made above. Each of these types of information should be taught within the boundaries of any given lesson (but that *doesn't* mean they need to all be taught at the same instant). Here is an example of how these types of information could be integrated in a lesson designed to teach how living things interact within an ecosystem.

1. The lesson would start with a review of key information assumed to be already part of the students' prior knowledge. This information might include meanings of words (such as "organism" and "respiration") or key cause-effect relationships (such as the phases of the water cycle).

2. Next, the lesson could branch into instruction pertaining to new concepts such as "ecosystem" and "interdependence."

3. Then, the lesson could present a three-step strategy for observing interdependence within an ecosystem and provide students an opportunity to use this strategy while describing various ecosystems (the aquarium in the back of the classroom, a computer-simulated ecosystem, or an ecosystem they see out their window).

4. Finally, students would summarize the results of their observations in a brief written or oral report to the class, using the vocabulary that was already part of their

prior knowledge and that was learned during this lesson.

### What About Goals and Objectives?

Up until now, this discussion of curriculum has been fairly esoteric. We have covered categories of prior knowledge (literacy and task-related), types of information contained in curriculum materials (facts, concepts, rules, and strategies), tasks, and task analysis. Some subdivisions have also been covered. These included things like enabling skills, subtasks, specific strategies, and general strategies. Now the presentation will be more applied.

Some students have trouble in school. They fall behind in the curriculum. The curriculum is operationally defined as a set of goals and objectives. For most students, instructional goals and objectives are not individually selected. They are the same goals being taught to everyone else in the class. But when students need to be taught things that the rest of the students are not currently working on, it is necessary that we select goals and objectives specifically for them.

There are a number of very good reasons for specifying goals and instructional objectives for students in special/remedial education.

1. *To maintain curriculum focus.* Without specific goals and objectives, curriculum and instruction can drift away from what the student needs.

2. *To meet the requirements of the law.* Specification of instructional goals and objectives has been a requirement of special education law for over 25 years now and also is required in various other legislation such as Section 504 of the Rehabilitation Act.

3. *To be accountable.* We have a professional obligation to provide students with learning problems the best possible education. To advance this aim, we must demonstrate that students are benefiting from our instruction. This accountability is accomplished by clearly describing the student's present

levels of performance and developing goals and objectives that detail where he needs to go.

4. *To monitor.* The selection of instructional programs, methods, and materials always involves an element of guesswork. Without goals and objectives, there is nothing against which progress can be judged and, therefore, no basis for evaluating the impact of instruction.

5. *To motivate.* Establishing goals and objectives that allow us to be accountable to students and their parents and to monitor progress also facilitates motivation. Students, particularly those who have trouble in school, learn more when sequences of curriculum are specified (Gleason et al., 1991; Kulik et al., 1990); progress through the sequence is monitored, and teachers are able to feel a sense of competence when they see their students reach these goals (Sulzer-Azaroff & Mayer, 1991).

## What Are Criteria?

It is not easy to say what makes a goal or objective good, but there are some areas we can examine to get an idea about their quality. Here are the most important criteria for writing effective goals and objectives:

- Syntactic correctness
- Compliance with legal requirements
- The "stranger test"
- Both knowledge and behavior are addressed
- The "so-what test"
- Individualization
- Common sense

### Are They "Syntactically" Correct?

One of the first ways people think of to tell if an object is good is to look at it to see if it has all of its parts. But this isn't always the best indicator of quality. That is because the writing of goals and objectives is often presented like a grammar lesson. As a result of such lessons, some teachers end up paying more attention to the form of the objectives than to the utility (that is, when asked to write an objective, most teachers will always start it with the word "given"). Still, instructional objectives do have certain elements that most people agree need to be included (or at least logically assumed) in the wording. These are as follows:

- Content: what the student learns;
- Behavior: what the student does to indicate that he has learned;
- Criterion: how well the student needs to do the behavior; and
- Conditions: the circumstances under which the student will work.

Each of these elements must be in the objective, or logically inferred from it, for the objective to be "correct" (Price & Nelson, 1999). However, it is possible to have a correct, but stupid, objective. For example,

"When handed a squirrel (the condition) the student will correctly (the criterion) put her index finger in the squirrel's left ear (the behavior) upon hearing a cow bell (the content)."

This objective is meaningless, but it goes back to the point of the Margolis quote at the beginning of this chapter that something can be said correctly even if it isn't worth saying. By the way, just in case you think no one would ever write a silly objective, some examples of real ones found in actual IEPs will be included in this section.

### Do They Comply with the Law?

Here are some general guidelines about goals and objectives from the federal government (such as the Office of Special Education and Rehabilitation Services, Education, Pt. 300, App. C).

1. There should be a direct relationship between the annual goals and the student's present levels of educational performance.

2. The annual goals should describe what a child can reasonably be expected to accomplish within a 12-month period *given appropriate instructional resources.*

3. Short-term instructional objectives should be stated so clearly that it is obvious how one would measure to see if the objective is met.

4. The objectives should describe a sequence of intermediate steps between a child's present levels of educational performance and the annual goals that are established for the child. In this way, they can serve as milestones for measuring progress toward meeting the goals.

5. For a child with disabilities, there should be a direct relationship between the student's daily instruction and the goals and objectives written in his **Individual Education Plan** (IEP).

6. The goals and objectives should help both parents and school personnel check on a child's progress.

### Do They Pass the "Stranger Test"?

Goals and instructional objectives must be measurable so that their status can be monitored. This does not mean that they need to be derived from, or linked to, published tests. However, basic measurement principles such as reliability do apply. Probably the simplest way to judge if a goal or objective can be reliably measured is to apply the **stranger test** (Kaplan, 1995).

If the goals and instructional objectives pass the stranger test, someone not involved in developing the statements—a stranger—could still use them to write appropriate instructional plans and evaluate student progress. Obviously, a stranger could not reliably do so unless the goals and objectives were written in a sufficiently observable and specific form. The secret to stating something in observable form is using behaviors. *"Knowing* the answer" is hard to measure (because *knowing* is not directly observable), but *"writing* the answer" is easy to measure because *writing* is a behavior.

### Do They Address Knowledge as Well as Behavior?

The stranger test and the need to specify instructional objectives in terms that are measurable raise an issue that has proven to be disconcerting to many educators. It is the confusion of knowledge and behavior. This confusion seems to arise because, although it is knowledge that we are most often trying to transmit, we need to see behaviors to know if we have succeeded.

The statement of behavior must be in an objective to provide a measurable indicator of learning. But it is the learning, not the behavior, that is of primary importance to most teachers. Therefore, when they compose an objective that calls for the student to ". . . write the correct spelling of science vocabulary . . ." they are *not* teaching the student to *write*, they are trying to increase knowledge of spelling. Although it is true that the student must do something (like "write") for us to know if the knowledge has increased, it is a mistake to focus only on the behavior. In fact, it would be a mistake to produce an objective that requires writing for a student who can't write, unless your goal is to produce writing.

Consider another example. A typical objective for addition might call for the student to ". . . say that $5 + 3 = 8$." But, simply saying "$5 + 3 = 8$" is not the same as adding (we could teach a parrot to say it), so getting students to say "8" is not really our purpose. But what is?

This section of the chapter is about writing *instructional* objectives. Although it is possible to have objectives that only target overt behaviors, that is not the kind of objective that this text and chapter are about. This is not a behavior management book. It is a book about teaching, and it is implicit within the idea of teaching that educators are trying to improve the knowledge of students. Therefore, the specification of an instructional objective implies that the teacher will teach the student (not control or coerce the student) with the goal of improving his knowledge so that ultimately he will "behave" like a more educated person. So the definition of our objectives is actually tied to our definition of instruction. If we direct our instruction at the domain of addition knowledge, we can assume that saying "$5 + 3 = 8$" indicates that knowledge. If we direct our efforts at getting a student to *say* "$5 + 3 = 8$" we cannot make that assumption. Changed behavior only indicates changed knowledge when the behavior is changed by instruction focused at the domain of knowledge itself. Instruction should not focus on the individual items that are sometimes specified in instructional objectives or included on tests. The point of all this is that by teaching to knowledge, not simply trying to manipulate behavior, teachers have the most extensive impact. This is an important point and it should not be lost within the need for behavioral specificity.

Teaching is actually an excellent way to change behavior. That is because instruction targeting a domain can lead to changes in many more behaviors than might efficiently be changed if each were addressed individually. The dictionary defines a **domain** as a distinctly marked territory. Some synonyms for domain on the authors' word processor are zone, area, sphere, jurisdiction, and province. A domain, therefore, has boundaries; something consolidates it or ties it together. Knowledge domains are often consolidated by concepts and/or strategy components. When this is the case, learning within a domain is facilitated because the solution for one item often points the way to solving others. For example, if a domain is sufficiently consolidated by strategies, a student may learn how to solve problems in it without ever actually being asked to do so before seeing them on a test. It is completely possible that you have never faced the division problem 10101/333333, but you can work it (relax, you don't have to) because you have learned the strategy for dealing with items in the domain—division—from which it was drawn.

### Do They Pass the "So-What" Test?

Here is an objective found on an actual IEP: "Student will decrease sleeping in class from 80% of the time to 30%." That one doesn't win the Proactive Education Award and it doesn't pass the so-what test. The so-what test speaks to validity. Because the purpose of education is to prepare people to be socially competent, the so-what test asks whether the goals and instructional objectives are important. This is a more difficult test than the stranger test because it involves value judgments about the curriculum and speculation about the child's long-term

needs (but as difficult as it is to tell, the squirrel objective is still a loser).

Try this one. "He will improve his behavior in school so as not to draw any undue attention to himself." Aside from the fact that "undo attention" fails the stranger test, good objectives specify outcomes that will benefit students by teaching them things that are socially significant (Ensminger & Dangel, 1992) and not simply make life easier for parents and teachers (although these are not always mutually exclusive). To pass the **so-what** test, an objective should act to develop, rather than to suppress, behavior. In cases where behaviors need to be suppressed (because they are dangerous), goals or objectives should include alternate positive behaviors (Kaplan, 2000; Martin & Pear, 1996; Sulzer-Azaroff & Mayer, 1991).

### Are They Aligned (That Is, Individual)?

Imagine you have a student named Randy. Is this objective a good one for him?

"When they are pointed out by his teacher, Randy will write the correct answer for all addition errors he makes on homework assignments."

It is measurable. Addition is important. It has all the parts ("When they are pointed out by his teacher (conditions), Randy will write (behavior) the correct answer for all (100% accuracy criterion implied) addition (content) errors he makes on homework assignments."). But, there is no way to tell if this objective is appropriate because you don't know anything about Randy. What if he is 2 years old? What if he is 8 years old and mastered addition last year? Appropriate goals and instructional objectives are derived from assessment data. They must be *aligned* with the student's present level of educational performance (PLEP) and the student's goal.

Here is an example of an appropriate goal, and corresponding objectives, written for one area of need identified in this PLEP for a fourth-grade student named Kim. This goal and corresponding objectives pertain to addition with regrouping. Other goals and objectives could also be required for other areas of concern.

---

### Present Levels of Educational Performance Statement

Kim is a fourth-grade girl with good attendance and appropriate social skills who is having difficulty in math. She indicated a good understanding of how to tell time and of metric measurement, but she does not understand money value or computations in addition or subtraction when problems yield answers greater than ten. This level of math performance is usually associated with students in the second grade. Through testing and teacher interview, it was determined that her skills in other academic areas are average or above. Her vision, hearing, speech, and health are normal according to records.

---

*Goal*: Kim will improve her accuracy and rate at writing answers to addition problems.
   *Objectives:*

1. Kim will write answers to addition fact problems with sums 11 to 18 (for example, 6 + 5) on a worksheet with 100% accuracy.

2. Kim will write answers to addition fact problems with sums from 1 to 20 (for example, 1 + 0 or 14 + 4) on a worksheet at a rate of 40 problems correct per minute with no errors.

3. Kim will write answers to two-digit plus one-digit, *without regrouping*, addition problems on a worksheet with 100% accuracy.

4. Kim will write answers to two-digit plus one-digit, *with regrouping*, addition problems on a worksheet with 100% accuracy.

5. Kim will write answers to two-digit plus two-digit, *with or without regrouping*, addition problems on a worksheet with 100% accuracy.

6. Kim will work two-digit addition problems in the context of a checkbook with 100% accuracy.

### What Is a Nonexample of an Objective?

The following statements, also drawn from Kim's present level of performance statement, are not appropriate goals or objectives. The reasons they are inappropriate are presented in brackets.

*Goal 1*: Kim will draw the geometric shapes: line, circle, square, triangle, and rectangle when the shape name is given. [unrelated to PLEP statement]
   *Objectives:*

1. Kim will recognize geometric shapes on paper when the shape name is given. [no behavior (so it doesn't pass the stranger test) and no criteria]

2. Kim will point to geometric shapes in the classroom when the shape names are given. [no criteria; also, both objectives 1 and 2 call for *identification* responses, whereas the goal calls for *production*]

*Goal 2*: Kim will write answers to subtraction fact problems 10/20 with 80% accuracy. [criteria too low]
   *Objective*: Kim will say answers to subtraction fact problems when shown flash cards. [no criteria, only one objective for the goal (remember that instructional objectives must describe the entire path from the PLEP to the annual goal); also fails to comply with the regulations calling for "objectives" (for example, more than one)]

*Goal 3*: Kim will understand the importance of doing homework. [too vague (stranger test)]
   *Objective*: Kim will write down her homework assignments with 100% accuracy. [no condition specified; only one objective for goal].

### Do They Make Common Sense?

Sometimes it is hard to write instructional objectives that meet all of the quality requirements

*Exhibit 3.5    Checklist for Goals and Objectives.*

| Status | | Question |
|---|---|---|
| Yes | No | |
| | | 1. Do the goals and/or objectives represent an important learning outcome that is a priority for this student? |
| | | 2. Is there a goal written for each area of need stated in the present levels of performance? |
| | | 3. Are the goals realistic 1-year accomplishments? |
| | | 4. Are the goals and objectives easily measured? |
| | | 5. Are there multiple objectives representing intermediate steps to each goal? |
| | | 6. Are the goals and instructional objectives appropriately calibrated (sliced neither too broadly nor too narrowly)? |
| | | 7. Are the goals and instructional objectives useful for planning and evaluating instructional programs? |

and still fit into one sentence. Well, guess what. Instructional objectives don't have to fit into one sentence, and trying to make them do so can be very confusing. Here is an example taken from a real IEP: "As a yearly process on appointed days and times, when instructed to do so he will participate in taking math notes/blurbs from the overhead in a copying mode in his designated math notebook with a C (10-79%) or above grade as monitored in a grading period by the special and/or regular education teacher-note-taking-checklist."

If something can logically be assumed it need not be stated in the objective. For example "... on appointed days and times when instructed to do so ... ," "in a copying mode," or "... in his designated math notebook ..." (can you imagine a kid grabbing a "non-designated notebook" and taking math blurbs?). Don't write things like that! But if you must, use periods.

Are you worried that someone might not know what the teacher-note-taking-checklist looks like? If so, don't describe it in the objective. Staple it to the page.

How about this? "Student will correctly write answers to the questions in each end-of-unit quiz." It may not seem to meet the syntax test but, if you use the idea that it isn't necessary to specify things that can logically be inferred it does. Here is how: "Student will correctly (If there are any errors the objective is not met; criterion is 100%) write (behavior) answers to the questions (content) in each end-of-unit quiz (condition)."

Now look at these: "Improve math computation to at least 80% accuracy in addition, subtraction, multiplication, and division of fractions" or "By next year, given a situation in which he behaves inappropriately, 10% of the time he will acknowledge his misbehavior within 30-45 minutes." These were both written, and neither wins the Most Likely to Succeed Award. They both specify trivial growth (a student who is 80% accurate at adding fractions would never be skilled enough to multiply fractions).

Here are two final examples for the common sense category: "The class aide will escort him to class" and "She will finish Book 3 in the reading series." These kinds of statements are fairly common. However, they are not objectives, they are treatment statements. We must always remember not to confuse objectives with instruction. Objectives tell what the student will learn. They are not descriptions of what the teacher will do, or what process the student will follow to learn.

Goals and objectives are statements of curricular expectation. They tell us what students will do after instruction has taken place. Therefore, they must reflect the tasks, skills, content, behaviors, and thought processes that make up curriculum domains; they must also match the student's needs. A series of guidelines, in the form of questions, can be found in the checklist in Exhibit 3.5. These are the questions one might ask when attempting to discriminate between examples and nonexamples of appropriate goals and instructional objectives.

### How Can Goals and Instructional Objectives Be Generated Through Unit Planning?

#### Why Is Quality a Problem?

Few teachers will ever need to develop curriculum from scratch. However, to engage in curriculum-based evaluation and problem solving, it is necessary that one understands how curriculum should be developed and how it can be modified. It is easiest to explain this in the context of developing a unit of instruction.

The curriculum is composed of goals and objectives. Objectives contain the four elements (content, behavior, conditions, and criteria). When a unit is planned, these elements are manipulated to create different objectives. Examine the following objective as it is modified in (1) content, (2) behavior, (3) conditions, and (4) criteria.

*Original objective*: Pam will write the answers to addition facts on a worksheet at a rate of 40 correct per minute.

*Content modification*: Pam will write the answers to subtraction facts on a worksheet at a rate of 40 correct per minute.

*Modification of behavior*: Pam will say the answers to addition facts on a worksheet at a rate of 40 correct per minute.

*Condition modification*: Pam will write the answers to addition facts in a checkbook at a rate of 40 correct per minute.

*Criteria modification*: Pam will write the answers to addition facts on a worksheet with 100% accuracy.

Unit planning is based on decisions about each of the four objective elements. We'll elaborate.

#### What Is Content?

We aren't going to spend much time on the content element because it is the most familiar and the most obvious. An objective covering "multiplication" is clearly different than one covering "context-dependent vocabulary" or "dressing oneself." You will see many content sequences in this text, and they typically look like this:

6. Passages

5. Words

4. Blending

3. Sound/letter correspondence

2. Letter sounds

1. Letter recognition

Content can be categorized in a variety of ways. One way it is routinely categorized is by the kind of information that it seems to reflect (facts, concepts, rules, and strategies).

#### What Is Behavior?

The behavior statement is put in an objective for two reasons. First, it is there because it makes the objective more reliably measurable (that is, so it will pass the stranger test). Second, different types of behavior can indicate different levels of competence. Two familiar behavior domains that seem to do this are *"identify"* and *"produce."*

We can test a student's knowledge of vocabulary by asking him to identify pictures of the objects we name or by asking him to produce the names of objects in pictures that we show. As a domain, identifying (recognition) is typically easier for the student than producing (recall). If asked to name all of the states and capitals, you might have trouble. But if given a list of states and capitals and asked to match them, you'd probably get them right. If a student is tested on his identification skill (pointing, circling, crossing out), we can't leap to the conclusion that he can produce (say, write). Sometimes it is important that the student be able to identify before we ask him to produce; sometimes it isn't. It depends on the task. If a student can't produce answers, practice at identifying them may not even be a useful instructional activity.

The critical thing to remember is that identification and production are different domains of behavior and that "write the correct answer" is a different objective than "circle the correct answer," no matter what the content of the objective.

### What Are Conditions?

There are many conditions under which students may work. They may work in small groups or large groups, on worksheets or at the board, with assistance or on their own. Two condition domains that are useful for individualizing are *"in isolation"* and *"in context."* Something done in isolation is separated from all contextual clues and distractions. Something done in context is embedded within a larger frame of reference.

If a student needs to learn to read words that consist of a consonant, a vowel, and a consonant (CVC) such as "dog" and "top," we have to decide whether he needs to be taught it in isolation first (such as on flashcards), or in context (for example, within sentences). Ordinarily, doing a task in context is preferable because it will have more meaning and involve more realistic, or authentic, application. Typically, teachers need only isolate specific skills if the student is just starting to learn the task or if his skills are so limited that the context will only distract him.

In many cases, particularly with social behavior and language skills, instructional objectives can be written to specify movement along a sequence of conditions rather than of content.

For example:

1. Initiate contact with strangers in unfamiliar situations
2. Initiate contact with strangers in familiar situations
3. Initiate contact with peers in unstructured activities
4. Initiate contact with peers during role playing

The conditions specified in the objective have direct implications for assessment. The need for alignment, for example, dictates that objective 4 must be assessed outside the classroom.

### Assistance

One classroom condition that is extremely important to student performance is the level of assistance the student receives from the teacher or from peers. The subtasks and strategies introduced by various materials and classroom techniques need to be examined carefully and probably deserve the same attention we typically give to content (Gersten et al., 1986; Lloyd & Loper, 1986; Shulman, 1986).

When generating goals and objectives for students who have learning problems remember that they may need to learn task-related skills to benefit from different types of instruction. This means we must consider what a student must know to benefit from particular lessons and, if he is lacking those skills, we must specify objectives to teach them. These objectives may target study skills and knowledge of other tasks imposed by the correction routines, mode, and *pace* of the presentation in his class. As a teacher, you must remember that some students may learn more efficiently if you provide different levels of instructional assistance (by accommodating for different task-related skills).

It is remarkable how many hours teachers have spent analyzing the demands of tasks like spelling and multiplication without paying similar attention to the demands imposed, and the assistance provided, by their own instructional approach. A task analysis of "how to learn in my class" would represent time well spent by any teacher, as it would be relevant to *all* areas of the curriculum.

It has been argued that mapping out the level of assistance (sometimes called the "zone of proximal development") (Berk & Winsler, 1995) required for a student to learn is critical to recognizing those students who need special educational interventions. This process is often called **assisted assessment**, and it will be discussed in some detail in Chapter 7.

To carry out assisted assessment, an evaluator must:

1. Establish a sequence of learning outcomes;
2. Establish a sequence of instructional assistance;
3. Find outcomes the student cannot perform;
4. Retest performance on those outcomes under varying levels of assistance; and
5. Summarize the assistance level required for the student to learn.

Obviously, to carry out this process one must know how to establish meaningful sequences of classroom assistance. An example of such a sequence is shown in Exhibit 3.6.

In this example, a student who can name body parts at assistance level 1 would be seen as needing less instructional help than a student needing assistance at level 3. If Maria can only name body parts at level 3, then that is considered her PLEP; her objectives would include "Naming body parts with prompts plus demonstrations (level 2)" and then "Naming body parts with prompts (level 1)."

The next chapter will present considerable information on instruction including guidelines for developing sequences of instructional assistance. For now, try to hold the idea of "assisted assessment" in your long-term memory and remember that, when different teaching techniques impose different conditions on student performance, we have two choices. We can change the instruction to provide greater assistance or we can teach the student the task-related skills he needs to learn from it.

## How Are Criteria Defined?

A criterion is a *standard*. It is how well the student will be expected to do the objective. Like the behavior element, criteria are needed in instructional objectives to allow for evaluation to take place. Criterion statements also are in objectives to specify different levels of competence, or proficiency. Three commonly utilized proficiency levels are *accuracy*, *mastery*, and *automaticity*. Look back at the section where we talked about two types of performance in objectives: to identify and to produce. We can further subdivide these instructional objectives by specifying the proficiency levels at which we want students to identify or produce. For example, we could say that a student needs to produce answers to addition fact problems with 100% accuracy. We can add another dimension by saying that the student will produce answers to addition fact problems with 100% accuracy at a rate of 40 per minute. Doing a task accurately and quickly represents a higher level of knowledge and is called mastery (fluency). The third level of proficiency involves doing a task accurately, quickly, and in context. For example, "Student will produce answers to addition fact problems within a

**Exhibit 3.6   Levels of Classroom Assistance.**

| Outcome | Assistance Level | | |
|---------|---------|---------|---------|
| | Level 1 | Level 2 | Level 3 |
| Student will name body parts | With prompt | With prompt plus demonstration | With prompt plus demonstration and explanation |

checkbook" or "at the grocery store when buying ingredients for a recipe that needs to be quadrupled." This is called automaticity. Identification tasks, because they typically indicate low levels of proficiency, often only include accuracy, not rate, criteria.

Most people are familiar with the idea of accuracy and appreciate the need to facilitate application by raising skills to automaticity. However, the idea of specifying fluency (rate) criteria is hard for others to accept. Consider this story. A parent came in to a special education classroom and complained to the teacher, Linda Levett, "Why are you always testing my child with stopwatches and telling him to work faster?" Linda looked at the parent a moment and replied "Do you remember why your child is in this class? He's a slow learner. The cure for slow is fast."

Rate has functional implications. If two firefighters both put on their uniforms with 100% accuracy, but one does it in 1 minute and the other does it in 10 minutes, which one do you want working in your neighborhood? If students disregard space dimensions, like height or width, they will walk into walls. Similarly, students who are not prepared to work within certain time constraints will not be able to function in the real world. For example, slower workers are less proficient workers because rate is a proficiency dimension, just like accuracy. That is why slower workers get fired.

Rate is also related to generalization, and automaticity, in that it is hard to complete a complex response if you are slow at all the pieces. Without automaticity, our thoughts would be so crowded with minutia that our thinking would become paralyzed.

So, it is important that we not establish proficiency levels or standards arbitrarily. Establishing a standard of 80% accuracy, for every objective, which is common practice, is not appropriate. Would a standard of 80% accuracy on multiplication facts mean that we think $8 \times 7$ or $4 \times 5$ is not particularly important or useful? Will we hope that quadrupling that recipe will not require knowing $4 \times 5$? Appropriate fluency levels are very important too. The chances are slim of getting through a page of long-division problems if your rate on multiplication facts is only five

per minute. Appropriate standards of accuracy and fluency for basic skills in reading, writing, and math are available in various research studies and in the topical chapters of this text.

The distracters we include in automatic level objectives should be relevant—that they have a real world application. We shouldn't write an objective that says "Student will read sight words while standing on her head." More appropriate might be ". . . reading sight words in job notices at the crowded and noisy Employment Security Office."

## What Is a Table of Specifications?

If you need to teach or test in an area you know little about, you should begin by organizing the curriculum. The best way to do this is to develop a table of specifications. Exhibit 3.7 presents part of what is called a **table of specifications**. Tables of specifications can be used to plan tests and units of instruction (Gronlund, 1973; Guskey, 1997). In Exhibit 3.7 there are four columns and two content rows. Each square in the grid represents a separate objective. If the expected outcome is to have the student balance her checkbook using two-place addition without regrouping (square D.1 in the grid), then objectives A.1, B.1, and C.1 represent a sequence of reasonable enabling objectives leading to that goal.

A table is made by following these steps:

1. Describe the target task;

2. Recognize the content to be taught and/or tested;

3. Sequence the content;

4. Select a behavior and/or condition sequence;

5. Arrange the content, behavior, conditions, into a table of specifications;

6. Examine the grid to see if there are objectives that you do not want to teach and put an "X" in them;

7. Examine the grid to see if there are objectives that you want to emphasize and put a small plus (+) sign in them;

**Exhibit 3.7    Table of Specifications for Addition with and without Regrouping.**

| | Behavior | | | |
| --- | --- | --- | --- | --- |
| | Identify Accuracy | Produce Accuracy | Produce Mastery | Produce Automatic |
| Two digit to two digit **with** regrouping | <A.1><br>"Point to the answer for this problem":<br>15<br>+17<br><br>a) 16<br>b) 32<br>c) 11<br>d) 25 | <B.1><br>"Write the answers to two-place addition problems **with** re-grouping accurately." | <C.1><br>"Write the answers to two place addition problems **with** re-grouping at a rate of 20 problems per minute." | <D.1><br>"Quickly balance a checkbook and make no errors in two-place addition **with** regrouping." |
| One digit to two digit addition **without** regrouping | <A.2><br>"Point to the answer for this problem":<br>10<br>+ 1<br><br>a) 6<br>b) 7<br>c) 11<br>d) 15 | <B.2><br>"Write the answers to two-place addition problems **without** regrouping accurately." | <C.2><br>"Write the answers to two-place addition problems **without** regrouping at a rate of 20 problems per minute." | <D.2><br>"Quickly balance a checkbook and make no errors in two-place addition **without** regrouping." |

8. Locate or establish criteria; and

9. Write instructional objectives.

Following these steps, and the numerous substeps that follow, is a long process but a valuable one. You can't expect to write objectives and teach in an area that is a mystery. Today, this type of work is needed most of all at the high-school level and in the areas of transition, social, and task-related behaviors. But you may also want to do it in a familiar area if you teach and test it frequently. The hardest part of the whole process is probably the first step.

### Step 1: Describe the Target Task

Content clarification begins by describing what will be taught. Once this image is available, you have something to analyze. Start by finding authorities, in the form of people or research, that talk functionally about what you are going to teach. If during this review you find that the curriculum is already well-organized and sequenced, you can skip this step. When the curriculum is not organized, you need to employ the process of task analysis. Here is what you'll need to do.

### Focus on the Target

The **target behavior** is what you want the student to know how to do. The target isn't what the student is doing wrong. That is called the **maladaptive behavior**. Often the referral, or errors on a test, will lead you to focus on maladaptive performance. This is a mistake. It should be assumed the student engages in maladaptive

**Exhibit 3.8    Targets Incompatible with the Error.**

| Maladaptive | Target |
|---|---|
| Misreads multisyllabic words | Reads multisyllabic words accurately |
| Avoids other children | Approaches other children |
| Omits operation signs | Includes operation signs |
| Vaguely expresses message | Clearly expresses message |

behavior because she lacks the essential prerequisite skills of appropriate (correct) behavior. To find these prerequisites you must identify and focus on a target that is incompatible with the error (Kaplan, 2000). Some examples are given in Exhibit 3.8.

Note that these examples have both content ("multisyllabic words," "other children," "operation signs," and "messages") and behavior components ("reads," "avoids," "includes," "expresses"). There are even a couple of criteria words included ("correctly," "vaguely").

### Behaviorally Define the Target Performance

Task analysis will be easiest and most useful if the target product (what the student will do after the unit or lesson has been finished) can be described very clearly in behavioral terms. At the very least, the statement must include the elements of content, behavior, conditions, and criteria. Often it is helpful to find an exemplary sample, or description of, acceptable student work. Then you can say "My goal is to get the students to do work just like this." For example, "at recess the student will approach (walk within a radius of 5 feet) other children. This will occur at least four times per recess."

### Identify Attributes of the Target Performance

This process lets you examine the behavioral description you just developed and find its critical attributes. This process also has a set of steps to follow.

1. Find or produce several clearly correct instances (exemplars) of the target behavior or product.

2. Find or produce several clearly incorrect instances (non-examples) of the target behavior or product.

3. Identify attributes (characteristics) that are present in *all* instances of the target performance.

4. Identify attributes that, if present, will change an example of target performance into a non-example (a square can never have a curved side).

5. List the attributes found in steps 3 and 4 as *critical (essential) attributes*. These are the things that define the target performance and that students should include (or exclude) in their performance.

6. List attributes that are found in some instances but not in others as **non-critical** (not essential). These can be used later as distracters for instruction when teaching generalization of the lesson. They also make good distracters if you want to make an end-of-unit multiple choice test.

### Identify Required Prerequisite Knowledge

This is what a student must know to include, or exclude, all of the critical aspects of performance. To find them, you can do the following:

1. Ask "What must a student do and know to complete this task?"

2. State each subtask in the same behavioral format used for the main task.

3. Keep the distance between subtasks small. As a rule, if the subtasks you list will take more than a week or two to learn, you are dealing with oversized chunks of material. Units that take several weeks to teach are better called "classes" and should be broken up.

4. List subtasks close to the target performance. This is very important. If you find yourself listing subtasks that underpin many tasks (not just the targeted main task), you may want to consider that the main task

is stated too generally or that you have failed to focus specifically on it.

5. Only list motivation, attention, memory, or other information-processing skills as subtasks if you can see how they can be taught within the context of the unit lessons.

### Identify Strategies

1. Determine rules for task completion.

2. State the simplest procedure for completing the target product or performance (the simplest procedure is the one with the fewest steps).

3. Determine if a formal algorithm (widely agreed upon step-by-step procedure) is commonly employed by experts for completion of this task.

4. Consider that a general study or test-taking strategy may be required. General strategies often include:

   - Deciding what needs to be done;
   - Evaluating resources;
   - Selecting a procedure to follow;
   - Carrying out all steps in a procedure;
   - Monitoring work;
   - Checking work; and
   - Self-correcting work.

5. Anticipate common errors to recognize where a procedural step is needed for accurate performance.

### Terminate

1. Do not overanalyze, as there is some risk of becoming trivial. A good curriculum writer constantly balances the need for specificity against the need for authenticity. Most skills are learned best in context.

2. Initially recognize no more than five subtasks or attributes close to the main task.

3. If testing indicates that the student can handle (learn) the least complex of these

subtasks, then the analysis has been sufficient and can be terminated.

## Step 2: Recognize Content

### Review Task Analysis

Analyze and underline the content statements in each subtask. (For example, "At recess the student will <u>approach</u> (walk within a radius of 5 feet) <u>other children</u>. This will occur at least four times per recess.")

### Decide Whether Content Is Part of a Larger Class of Content

If this is the case, you should reexamine the literature on that topic to see if a sequence has already been identified. Also, look for rules for sequencing content. For example, when developing the *Read Well* program, M. Sprick et al. (1998) developed the sequence of letters and sounds according to these rules:

- Separation of letter/sound relationships that sound or look alike;
- Access to sounds needed to read high frequency words; and
- Access to sounds needed to write stories.

## Step 3: Sequence the Content

Once you have recognized the content for the unit, list it down the left side of a grid or spreadsheet. You may want to bracket the original content with simpler and more complex tasks. By convention, put the last, usually the most complex, task to be taught at the top and the simplest at the bottom.

## Step 4: Select a Behavior and/or Condition Sequence

Now that you have defined and sequenced what content you want the student to know, decide what he will do to display that knowledge. Look at the original task analysis and content sequence and decide on a succession of behaviors that complements the content. For example, the

**Exhibit 3.9   *Objective Overlays for Types of Knowledge.***

| Factual Knowledge | | | | |
|---|---|---|---|---|
| **Identify Answer**<br>(underline, circle, point to,<br>highlight) | **Produce Answer**<br>(write, say, construct an example) | | | |
| Accuracy | Accuracy | Mastery/Fluency | | Automatic |
| <2 + 2 = ><br><3><br>\|4\|<br>5<br>6 | 2 + 2 =<br>(*untimed*) | 2 + 2 =<br>(*at rate*) | | 2 + 2 =<br>(*in check<br>book*) |

| Conceptual Knowledge | | | | | |
|---|---|---|---|---|---|
| **Sort Examples<br>from Nonexamples**<br>(place, mark, label) | | **Specify Attributes**<br>(list, mark, name) | **Define Concept**<br>(state, write,<br>illustrate) | **Contrast/Modify**<br>(list similarities,<br>state differences,<br>change attributes) | **Explain/Imply**<br>(state implications,<br>predict or estimate<br>select strategy) |
| Far<br>Examples | Near<br>Examples | Noncritical | "A Square has<br>four straight<br>sides and<br>90-degree<br>corners." | "Squares have equal<br>sides, rectangles<br>don't." | "To draw a<br>square I'll need<br>something to<br>measure the<br>sides." |
| Squares<br>and<br>circles | Squares<br>and<br>rectangles | Color,<br>size,<br>location | Critical<br>Four sides,<br>straight<br>sides | | |

| Strategic/Procedural Knowledge | | | | |
|---|---|---|---|---|
| **Identify when to<br>Use Process**<br>(sort examples,<br>say label, circle) | **Specify Process**<br>(say, write, outline, diagram) | | | **Apply Process**<br>(say, write, do<br>(construct product)) |
| | List Steps | List Rules | | |
| "This would be a good<br>time to use self-<br>management." | Set goal;<br>find alternatives;<br>anticipate<br>consequences;<br>make a plan | Problem must be<br>mine;<br>it must be worth<br>the effort;<br>it must be what<br>others want | | Use self-management<br>to negotiate getting<br>in the ball game<br>at recess. |

identify/produce and the accuracy/mastery/automatic sequences shown in Exhibit 3.7 are often very good for basic skills. In distinction, sequences of context, or teacher support, are often good for social behavior and language. Exhibit 3.9 shows three objective overlays you might select to generate objectives that are factual, conceptual, or procedural. Example objectives are written in *italics* for each column.

## Step 5: Arrange the Content, Behavior, and Condition Sequences into a Table of Specifications

By placing the content down the side of a grid and the behavior/conditions across the top, you form a set of intersections. These intersections, because they are defined by the elements of instructional objectives, each represent a potential objective for your unit. Therefore, making the table generates the objectives for you. If you are able to sequence the content by difficulty and the behaviors by difficulty, the squares in the grid will automatically be sequenced.

Exhibit 3.10 is a table of specifications for multiplication. Below the table, the accuracy production objectives have been written out. Like most tables, this one is a grid defined by content, behavior, and proficiency dimensions. Exhibit 3.11 shows the key to a test composed of items from the accuracy column of the multiplication table. The number in parentheses above each item can be found in the table of specifications in Exhibit 3.10. The full objective is found below the table. This clear cross-referencing of each item to an objective is called alignment. It allows teachers to see immediately in which domains of content or behavior an error has occurred and to select an appropriate objective for the student.

### Step 6: Examine the Grid to See if There Are Objectives That You Do Not Want to Teach or That You Want to Emphasize

A big advantage of tables is that they allow you to visualize the actual defining elements of the curriculum without getting bogged down trying to read a huge list of instructional objectives. Therefore, they are a useful tool for picking and choosing content or behaviors that you want or don't want to emphasize. Simply cross out (or write N.A.) in squares you aren't going to teach. Put a plus (+) sign in those you want to emphasize. By cutting up the tables it is also easy to assign objectives to different teachers.

### Step 7: Locate or Establish Criteria

The final defining element of an objective is the criterion. Criteria are established through a process that will be discussed in Chapter 6.

### Step 8: Write Instructional Objectives

As you can see in Exhibit 3.10, once the table of specifications is developed, it is easy to write the objectives. All you need to do is recognize the

elements for a square in the grid and string them together according to the rules of syntax. So, if the content is "historic figures of Alaskan history," the behavior is "write in the correct name," the conditions are "on a weekly test," and the criterion is "correctly," then the objective is "On the weekly test the student will correctly write the names of historic Alaskan figures."

### How Short Is a Short-Term Objective?

Part of curriculum development in any school involves apportioning lessons. Typically, this is handled by designating which topics will be covered, at what depth, at each grade level. After this grade-level allocation has occurred, individual teachers will also plan to cover particular lessons at particular times. In most classrooms, these planning decisions are based on ideas about the expected progress of students. This process of lesson and time allocation is different in special/remedial education programs because, whereas the character of the objectives remains the same, the amount of material covered per time unit (day, week, month) is adjusted to match the ambitious individual progress expectations of each student.

### What Is Calibration?

Calibration is a technical term referring to the process of setting values, gradations, positions, and segments. Starlin (1982) pointed out, for example, that the material in lessons on written communication could be "sliced" to target any of the following outcomes:

- Write a letter or theme
- Write a paragraph
- Write a sentence
- Write a phrase
- Write a word

When it comes to the topics of goals and instructional objectives, two of the most confusing questions are "Just exactly how long is a long-term goal?" and "How short are short-term instructional objectives?" These are calibration

Exhibit 3.10    Table of Specifications for Multiplication.

| | Identify | Accuracy | Mastery | Automatic | MASA curriculum level | Local curriculum level |
|---|---|---|---|---|---|---|
| Placement test<br>Mixed multiplication problems | | | | 9p | | |
| Squaring<br>Squares of numbers (0–12) | 8i | 8a | 8m | 9p | 8 | |
| Regrouping and no regrouping<br>Two or more digits by<br>two or more digits | | 7a | | 9p | 4–5 | |
| Two-digit numbers by a<br>two-digit number | | 4a | 4m | 9p | 4 | |
| Place value<br>Multidigit problems with zeros | | 6a | | 9p | 4 | |
| Multiply by 1, 10, 100, 1000 | | 5 | | 9p | 5 | |
| Regrouping<br>Two-digit number by a<br>one-digit number | | 3a | 3m | 9p | 4 | |
| No regrouping<br>Two-digit number by a<br>one-digit number | | 2a | 2m | 9p | 4 | |
| Facts<br>Multiplication facts (0–10) | 1i | 1a | 1m | 9p | 4 | |

Accuracy Production Objectives

| 8a—Squaring | Produce squares of numbers (0–12). Accuracy CAP 100%. |
|---|---|
| 7a—Regrouping and<br>no regrouping | Multiply a number containing two or more digits by another number containing two or more digits with or without regrouping. Accuracy CAP 100%. |
| 6a—Place value | Multiply multidigit problems with zeros as place holders. Accuracy CAP 100%. |
| 5a—Place value | Multiply 1, 10, 100, 1000. Accuracy CAP 100%. |
| 4a—Regrouping and<br>no regrouping | Multiply a two-digit number by a two-digit number with or without regrouping. Accuracy CAP 100%. |
| 3a—Regrouping | Multiply a two-digit number by a one-digit number with regrouping. Accuracy CAP 100%. |
| 2a—No regrouping | Multiply a two-digit number by a one-digit number without regrouping. Accuracy CAP 100%. |
| 1a—Facts | Multiplication facts (0–10). Accuracy CAP 100%. |

Source: Howell, K. W., Zucker, S. H. & Morehead, M. K. (2000b). Multilevel Academic Skills Inventory. Bellingham, WA: Applied Research And Development Center. To order contact the Student Co-op Bookstore, Western Washington University. Fax (360) 650-2888. Phone (360) 650-3656. Reprinted with permission.

*Exhibit 3.11   Test Key: Multiplication Accuracy Production.*

| 1. (1a) | 2. (1a) | 3. (1a) | 4.  (2a) | 5.  (2a) |
|---|---|---|---|---|
| 2 | 9 | 8 | 64 | 24 |
| $\times\,6$ | $\times\,5$ | $\times\,3$ | $\times\,7$ | $\times\,3$ |
| 12 | 45 | 24 | 448 | 72 |
| 6. (2a) | 7. (3a) | 8. (4a) | 9.  (4a) | 10. (5a) |
| 91 | 18 | 22 | 85 | $194 \times 10 = 1940$ |
| $\times\,1$ | $\times\,9$ | $\times\,86$ | $\times\,63$ | |
| 91 | 162 | 1892 | 5355 | |
| 11. (5a) | 12. (5a) | 13. (6a) | 14.  (6a) | 15. (6a) |
| $3 \times 1000 = 3000$ | $100 \times 74 = 7400$ | 102 | 40 | 7005 |
| | | $\times\,20$ | $\times\,31$ | $\times\,26$ |
| | | 2040 | 1240 | 182130 |
| 16. (7a) | 17. (7a) | 18. (7a) | 19.  (8a) | 20. (8a) |
| 87 | 215 | 5684 | $5^2 = 25$ | $12^2 = 144$ |
| $\times\,25$ | $\times\,48$ | $\times\,39$ | | |
| 2175 | 10320 | 221676 | | |

*Source:* Howell, K. W., Zucker, S. H. & Morehead, M. K. (2000b). *Multilevel Academic Skills Inventory.* Bellingham, WA: *Applied Research And Development Center.* To order contact the Student Co-op Bookstore, Western Washington University. Fax (360) 650-2888. Phone (360) 650-3656. Reprinted with permission.

questions and, although not as imposing as the so-what test, they are equally problematic.

There is considerable controversy about how detailed goals and objectives should be. Strickland and Turnbull (1990) state that it is very important that each teacher and planning committee resolve this question. The secret, it seems, is to keep the needs of the individual student in mind when gauging progress expectations and to err in the direction of specificity. There are a couple of reasons for this. First, although many teachers complain that they do not have time to develop specific objectives, once they have been written they don't need to be written again (they can be stored on a list or computer disk so that they can be selected later if another student with similar needs comes along). Second, if teachers find that annual goals and instructional objectives in IEPs or curriculum manuals are too broad to be helpful in planning, these objectives will come to be seen as unrelated to teaching, and teachers will stick them in a file drawer

somewhere. Finally, it is easier to see when specific objectives are met because they clearly specify the intended outcome of instruction. This means that students, parents, and teachers get to have the satisfaction of checking off learned objectives. When objectives are broadly defined, they may never seem to be met.

Probably the hardest thing for many teachers to accept is that the timeline for meeting goals and objectives for students with learning problems often needs to be *more* ambitious than those for other students. This means the number of instructional objectives to be covered with a given time must be ambitious. The reason for this is simple. As was explained in Chapter 1, students with learning problems are behind in the curriculum. The only way to catch them up is to move them through it at a faster pace. As will be explained in Chapter 4, this can be accomplished by providing the students with more effective instruction and, in some cases, more program resources. We don't individualize by leaving out important content or lowering standards (student will cross busy street with 80% accuracy) but by setting realistic goals and instructional objectives and teaching effectively.

### Is This Trip Necessary?

OK. Now we have goals, objectives, content, behavior, conditions, criteria, facts, concepts, rules, strategies, accuracy, fluency, automaticity, legal requirements, common sense, tables of specifications, and who knows what else. These are all derived from two simple ideas:

✓ That one should know what she wants the student to do at the end of instruction, before instruction starts; and

✓ That assessment and curriculum should be aligned with instruction.

But what if there is an easier way? What if, as Good (1999) and others have pointed out, we could replace all of this front-end planning with a set of general outcome measures.

This idea is that, in reality, most students only have problems in one, or more, of four areas: reading, expression (written or oral), math, and/or behavior. Knowing this, why not allow teachers to do whatever they want in terms of curriculum design, materials selection, and instruction but impose a general outcome measure (for example, oral reading) and require that the measure be used frequently to monitor improvement. This would allow us to dump much of the "documentation" that fills teachers' time (the ideas of outcomes and alignment would still be there) and replace it with an unyielding focus on the demonstration of improved learning.

The current approach to remedial education is to prescribe (as we have explained above) the process a teacher, or team, must go through. However, learning is not required by any law or policy. It may be better to drop the process— and cut straight to the product (measurable improvement in reading, expression (written or oral), math, and/or behavior). In this scenario, accountability would be shifted from the teacher's adherence to processes of preassessment and alignment during planning, to forma-

tive evaluation, innovation while teaching, and accountability for learning. Of course, goals would still need to be established in the areas of need and aligned measures located. But much of the pretense of individualization (which gave of the award-winning objectives presented earlier) would be dropped in recognition of the fact that most special/remedial students need instruction in the same things.

Think about it a bit. None of the things we have presented in this chapter would go away. They would remain as the basis for alignment and assessment. But the system would be recalibrated and the focus of accountability would be shifted from planning to learning. Who might have the most to win, or lose, from this kind of change?

### Summary

This has been a crowded chapter, and a final review is definitely in order. The curriculum is an ordered set of learning outcomes. Typically, these outcomes are called instructional objectives or tasks. Instructional objectives are derived from an analysis of the demand for literacy that society places on its members. Literacy, which can be viewed as communication within a cultural context, demands the use of effective strategies for sending and receiving messages. These literacy strategies in turn depend on the use of numerous enabling skills.

Tasks have subtask and strategy components. Subtasks (like tasks) are composed of elements of content, behavior, conditions, and criteria. Each of these elements must be present or the task has not been truly defined. If a change is made in any of the four elements, a new objective is produced. By systematically varying the four elements, a sequence of objectives or tasks can be produced for the purpose of planning instruction or evaluation.

Content sequences should be relevant, complete, free of trivial material, composed of necessary material, and free of redundancy.

Behavior sequences should correspond to the real-world demands of tasks and allow the designation of meaningful proficiency levels.

- Conditions should also reflect the real world.
- Criteria must meet functional levels of performance.
- The format of the information to be learned needs to be reflected in instructional objectives: factual, conceptual, rule relationships, and strategic. All of these are important.

Although they probably can't exist independently of each other, different instructional and measurement procedures are used to address facts, concepts, rules, and strategies.

There are two kinds of strategies: task-specific and general. Task-specific strategies apply to a particular domain. General strategies apply to many domains. Strategy use depends on prior knowledge, self-monitoring, and problem solving.

Task analysis is a process applied to well-defined tasks. Through task analysis, the essential components of the task can be identified. When a student is unable to work a task, the student should be taught any missing subtask and/or strategy components.

## STUDY QUESTIONS

1. Write one long-term goal and short-term objective, based on **the Present Level of Performance Statement** below for Joline.

   Joline is a third-grade girl with good attendance and appropriate social skills who is having difficulty in reading. She is able to read material from the first-grade curriculum fluently (70 words correct in 1 minute) but does not read fluently in second grade material (42 words correct in 1 minute) or in third grade material (18 words correct in 1 minute). She does not use context cues to develop meaning from passages and has a small sight vocabulary. Through testing and teacher interview, it was determined that her skills in other academic areas are average or above. Her vision, hearing, speech, and health are normal according to records.

2. Identify the content component of each of the following subtasks:
   - Jeremy will read aloud from his reading book for 1 minute when instructed to by his teacher.
   - Saundra will place her math homework in the basket beside the teacher's desk within 1 minute of arriving in the classroom at the beginning of math class.
   - Hector will copy the list of weekly spelling words from the board into his notebook before lunch on Mondays.

3. Analyze each of the following objects. Decide whether each is acceptable as written or needs to be "fixed up." If an objective is not acceptable, tell what is wrong with it and rewrite it to fix any errors.
   - Juanita will read aloud for 1 minute.
   - Jackie will obtain 100% accuracy on the weekly spelling pretest.
   - Michael will refrain from hitting or inappropriately interacting with other children on the playground.

# Chapter 4

# Thinking About Instruction

*Education is about opportunity and enfranchisement. It is about knowledge, economic potential, self-determination, perspective, and power. Education is inherently political. However, the political issues are those of how committed one is to education and for whom. Given full commitment, questions of how best to achieve it are issues that belong, not to politics, but to science and pedagogy.*

—M. J. Adams (1991)

In the last chapter, we defined curriculum as a structured set of learning outcomes, or tasks that students are expected to learn. Curriculum is the "what" of teaching. This chapter is about instruction—the "how" of teaching. Instruction refers to the things a teacher does that help students learn the information contained in curriculum. Instruction can include a wide variety of events and activities that a teacher plans and implements. Instruction can entail very specific teacher behaviors or very general categories of activities. Coming to terms with what instruction is, and is not, is one of the most controversial issues in our profession today. As you will see in this chapter, the reason instruction is so controversial is it is impossible to decide *how to teach* without confronting some of your most cherished beliefs about the teaching and learning process.

## Which Instructional Approaches Are Most Effective?

When talking about instruction, it is necessary to use terms like *type, approach, program, method, style, orientation,* and even *philosophy*. These are used to differentiate among various ways of teaching. There seems to be an almost endless debate about the relative superiority of these different ways to teach. One reason these debates are so bewildering is that it is often impossible to tell if the contestants are arguing about *what* should be taught (that is, curriculum) or about *how* it should be taught (such as instruction). Although it is unlikely that this chapter is going to put these quarrels to rest, it is important to mention them to make the instructional recommendations in this book easier to understand.

When the debate finally does come down to two methods, the main contestants usually end up being the **supplantive** approach and the **generative** approach. The supplantive approach is popularly referred to as "direct instruction" (Adams & Engelmann, 1996), and the generative approach is often referred to as "constructivist" or "developmental."

The two approaches are contrasted in Exhibit 4.1. The problem with comparisons like the one in Exhibit 4.1 is that they are so binary that they prohibit compromise. So, they always misrepresent someone and leave something out. Besides, the two approaches frequently seem to differ more in explanation than in practice. For example, many supplantive teachers purposefully plan portions of the day for students to explore and experiment with their own learning. Similarly, many constructivist teachers give explicit directions to students who have failed to discover needed information.

Proponents from both "camps" have been guilty of heated and at times silly rhetoric during the past decade. Unfortunately, much of the so-called "debate" has been philosophical rather than scientific. However, the crux of the difference between the two approaches comes down to two issues: (1) the role of the teacher in the teaching and learning process and (2) the timing for presentation of information.

With a supplantive approach, the teacher attempts to promote learning by providing explicit directions and explanations regarding how to do a task. The teacher assumes primary responsibility for linking new information with the student's prior knowledge and, ultimately, what the student learns. Consequently, with a supplantive approach, information usually is presented in an ordered sequence in which component subskills are taught directly as a foundation for later tasks. In this respect, a supplantive approach to instruction is highly teacher-directed.

With a generative approach, the teacher functions as a facilitator who takes a less central role

in a learning process that is student directed (Ensminger & Dangel, 1992). The teacher provides opportunities for the student to make her own linkages to prior knowledge and to devise her own strategies for work. Generative instruction is "constructivist" because much of its emphasis is on helping students to construct their own educational goals and experiences as well as the knowledge that results. With this approach, information usually is presented on a schedule determined by student interests and goals. With generative instruction, subskills may not be taught explicitly. Prerequisites for more complex information are expected to be learned as a consequence of the larger understandings students would be guided to construct.

With the generative approach to instruction, learning is assumed to be socially constructed out of the interaction between the student's innate tendencies and predisposition (following the student's own timeline) and the social context in which the student lives (Stone, 1996). But advocates of the generative approach sometimes take a restrictive view of social context. Often, they do not seem to view teachers and classrooms as part of the social context. Therefore, they see intentional instruction by teachers (or parents for that matter) as "unnatural" and "meaningless." However, as Stone (1996) puts it, "Developmentalism . . . fails to recognize the extent to which valued social, emotional, and cognitive attributes may be induced and sustained (not merely facilitated) by the purposeful actions of teachers and parents" (p. 20). A bad-tempered interpretation of the generative position on development is that it is condescending to teachers because it diminishes their role in student learning as well as the importance of their teaching skills. It can be argued that teachers who adopt this approach have abrogated their responsibility for teaching by turning instructional decision making over to the student.

Proponents of the supplantive approach also can be accused of being condescending to teachers to the extent that instruction may seem formulaic or contrived. For example, the DISTAR reading materials, originally developed for use by untrained paraprofessionals working in the early Head Start programs, were based on a direct in-

*Exhibit 4.1 A Comparison of Teaching Approaches.*

| Attribute | Generative Approach | Supplantive Approach |
|---|---|---|
| Buzz words used by proponent | • Constructivist<br>• Developmental<br>• Top down<br>• Holistic<br>• Authentic<br>• Meaning based | • Direct instruction<br>• Teacher-directed<br>• Mastery learning<br>• Task analytic<br>• Competency-based<br>• Effective teaching |
| What proponents call the other | • Romantics<br>• Fuzzy<br>• Postmodernist<br>• Unrealistic | • Reductionist<br>• Drill-and-kill<br>• Dogmatic<br>• Unauthentic |
| Underlying beliefs about what is taught | • Students construct their own understandings<br><br>• When learning is contextualized, students will identify what they are ready to learn | • The skills that students need to learn can be derived from an analysis of the social demands placed on them |
| Underlying beliefs about how learning occurs | • Learning is "socially constructed"; students link new information to prior knowledge when provided opportunities to observe or experience<br><br>• Learning is developmental and occurs much the way early language is acquired | • Learning can be induced through instruction that builds explicit links between new information and prior knowledge<br><br>• When learning does not occur, it can be facilitated by building it from the "bottom up" through teaching of prerequisite subskills |
| Underlying beliefs about how to teach | • Teachers take a "hands-off" approach and seek to provide a meaningful context in which learning will occur naturally | • Teachers take a "hands-on" approach by structuring lessons and providing explicit direction |
| Common error made by proponents | • Creating interesting classroom activities but failure to link these activities to learning outcomes<br><br>• Too much emphasis on larger ideas, not enough emphasis on the components | • By focusing on specific learning outcomes, they may fail to attend to other equally important interests and topics<br><br>• Too much emphasis on the components, not enough emphasis on the larger ideas |

struction approach (Adams & Engelmann, 1996; Carnine et al., 1997). These materials were designed to be "teacher proof" with scripted lessons and procedures that teachers were expected to follow verbatim. For many, these so-called "Teacher-proof" materials have come to epitomize a direct approach to instruction. This perception is inaccurate and unfortunate because it perpetuates the confusion of curriculum materials with instructional approach. Clearly, a teacher who turns all responsibility for decision making over to the curriculum materials also is guilty of abrogating their responsibility for teaching.

The idea that lessons should be situated in a larger context is closely tied to the generative view of meaning. This view, quite correctly, holds that items are best learned if they are meaningful and that meaning is promoted by presenting an item in its "natural" context. Generativists have long complained that instruction in content area classes such as social studies or science often is decontextualized and heavily fact-laden. Indeed, some of these complaints are legitimate. For example, it probably makes little sense to require students to memorize state capitals in isolation from the larger context of government and geography.

### Which Approach Is Better for Students Who Have Learning Problems?

One problem with a generative approach is that students with very limited skills may not be sufficiently knowledgeable about the context to see the linkages that would make a "situated" presentation meaningful. For example, whereas everyone would agree that letter sounds are ideally learned within the context of words, some students may have such limited knowledge of the concepts of print and sound that the presentation of multiple letters would simply confuse them. To address this problem, a supplantive teacher may isolate initial sounds and teach them out of the context of words. He may also compensate for the resulting loss in contextual meaning by producing a temporary context of verbal praise, or even tangible rewards, to keep the student motivated and to make the lesson meaningful (Geary, 1995; Dev, 1997).

This move to isolated skill presentation has been called *reductionist* by supporters of the generative view. Once again, the problem between the two camps seems to be related to the idea that the actions of teachers may be "unnatural." Their efforts to clarify lessons by isolating salient features and introducing rewards that the student already recognizes seem artificial and at odds with the developmental philosophy. What is often missed in this categorization of teaching actions is that the steps of isolation and introducing known rewards are always meant to be temporary. The goal of the supplantative teacher always should be to combine isolated skills and remove introduced rewards as soon as the student has sufficient skills to work with the context without the additional support.

The issue of timing also comes into play here. The question is "when should a generative approach be used and when should a supplantive approach be used?" In teaching, as with all things in life, there is a time and a place for everything. A teacher who *only* knows how to use a generative approach is as poorly equipped to meet the needs of his students as a teacher who *only* knows how to use a supplantive approach.

Because this book is about working with students who have limited skills, much of the emphasis is on teacher-directed, or "hands-on," instruction. This sort of instruction is curriculum-based, meaning that the teacher intentionally aligns instruction with the intended outcomes of the lesson (Deno & Markell, 1997; Palincsar, 1990; Spady, 1988). You might want to go back and take a look at Chapter 1 for support of this position. In that chapter, it was asserted that the primary defining characteristic of students requiring individual help in classes is their failure to progress through the curriculum. This argues strongly for the need to facilitate the movement of these students and, by implication, the need for teacher direction. The debate about the relative merits of telling students answers versus having them discover answers is interesting. However, if the kid has failed to discover what she needs to know for so long that the system is about to call her "disabled," the situation requires that teachers give her a break and tell her what she needs to know. Advocating *appropriate* use of hands-on approach to teaching does not mean one is a proponent of "nonmeaning-based," "half-language," and "noninteractive rote" instruction.

Similarly, *appropriate* use of a generative approach to teaching does not mean one is guilty of "academic child abuse" or should be sued for malpractice. Although the authors often advocate use of teacher-directed approaches in this book, we acknowledge that despite the best efforts of highly skilled teachers, some students progress through the curriculum at a slower rate than others and may arrive at middle and high school without having mastered the enabling skills that may be required to use textbooks or complete assignments. If we wait until these students are "ready" to learn content by virtue of having sufficient skills at reading, writing, or computation, "ready" may mean "never." Some of these students would benefit from instruction in content classes, such as social studies and the sciences, that is structured around "big ideas" situated in meaningful contexts.

It is the responsibility of a skilled teacher to make an informed, reasoned decision about which instructional approach is appropriate for a particular student at a particular time. If you are not willing to retain responsibility for this decision or if you would rather turn this decision over to your students or to a curriculum publisher, you might as well close this book now and start looking in the want ads for a new job because you are in the wrong profession.

### How Do I Know Which Instructional Approach to Use?

Instructional quality is the focus of a substantial portion of the current research that deals with teaching and learning (Nowacek et al., 1990; Rosenshine, 1997; Stodolsky & Grossman, 1995; Swanson & Hoskyn, 1998; Wang et al., 1990). Just as beliefs about learning have changed, so have beliefs about teaching—and the shifts in these beliefs have been intriguingly similar. Early research on teaching focused almost exclusively on the personal characteristics of teachers. These characteristics included things like their form of dress, gender, sense of humor, race, and voice. The assumption driving this research was that certain types of people make good teachers. The

results were kind of silly and easier to understand in terms of public relations than instruction. In addition, because the things being studied were almost impossible to alter, the research results were nearly useless to teacher trainers (Bloom, 1980).

Beginning in the mid-1970s, research on teaching changed dramatically as it shifted from an emphasis on the personal characteristics of teachers to the quality of their teaching. Using simple methods of observation and testing, researchers began to map out relationships between certain teacher actions and student learning. This research identified sets of teacher actions that tend to promote student learning and have come to be called "effective teaching" (Gersten & Brengelman, 1996; Good & Brophy, 1994; Rosenshine & Stevens, 1986; Lloyd et al., 1998; Swanson & Hoskyn, 1998; Ysseldyke & Christenson, 1996). Effective teaching includes variables such as how teachers use questions, review previous lessons, or explain new material.

This information is of obvious importance to teachers interested in helping students with learning problems, and much of the support for use of supplantive instruction with these students comes out of this research. The emphasis we place in this text on use of supplantive instructional methods is not based on philosophy but rather on research findings that show that students who are behind in the curriculum benefit from instruction that teaches missing prior knowledge directly. Much of what constitutes a supplantive approach to instruction employs the findings of the effective-teaching research.

Students requiring a hands-on/supplantive approach are those who are experiencing difficulty and are working on critical skills. They also may be lacking adaptive motivational skills and have little instructional time left (because they have fallen behind and need to learn more information per lesson to catch up). The **minimum/maximum rule** applies to such students. That rule says that the students with the least skills, who are making the least progress, need the most instructional support. In other words, *minimum skill = maximum teaching*. The teacher-effectiveness literature defines the qualities of maximum teaching (Gersten & Brengelman, 1996).

*Exhibit 4.2    Guidelines for Selecting an Instructional Approach.*

|  | Select the Generative Approach When: | Select the Supplantive Approach When: |
|---|---|---|
| *The student* | • Has considerable prior knowledge of the task<br>• Has adaptive motivational patterns<br>• Experiences consistent success on the task | • Has little prior knowledge of the task<br>• Has nonadaptive motivational patterns<br>• Experiences repeated failure on the task |
| *The task* | • Is simple for the student<br>• Is well-defined<br>• Can be completed using a general problem-solving strategy<br>• Is to understand, but not necessarily apply, what is learned | • Is complex<br>• Is ill-defined<br>• Has missing information<br>• Requires the use of a task-specific strategy<br>• Is pivotal to the learning of subsequent tasks<br>• Must be used with a high level of proficiency |
| *The setting* | • Allows plenty of time to accomplish outcomes<br>• Places priority on experiences and activities | • Time allowed to accomplish outcomes is limited<br>• Places priority on task mastery |

One implication of the minimum/maximum rule is that the way a teacher teaches may need to be adjusted according to the learning needs of his student. Because of this idea, the generative and supplantive methods can never be in strict opposition. Instead, a teacher must be prepared to use the salient features of different instructional techniques. This means teachers working with students who have learning problems cannot have a *favorite way to teach.* Again, the real issue is never *whether* or not a teacher should use an approach but *when* (Gersten & Dimino, 1993; Smith, 1992; Stahl & Kuhn, 1995). Some guidelines for deciding which approach (generative or supplantive) may be best for any particular student are shown

in Exhibit 4.2. Many of the descriptors in that exhibit are explained elsewhere in this book.

When learning does not occur, it is the instruction that should be changed. Just as a good amplifier allows someone to adjust bass with one control and treble with another, a good teacher can fine-tune instruction by adding a splash of support without overriding the student's interest in inquiry or joy of discovery. Constructivist instruction, as we are defining it, does not have an exclusive claim to concern about literacy or recognition of the student's role in learning. These things are always necessary. However, the generative philosophy, if applied incorrectly, can promote failure to focus the lesson. And, under the minimum/maximum rule, a lack of alignment is difficult to justify when the student is lost.

### What Is the Difference Between Intrinsic and Extrinsic Knowledge?

In Chapter 2, as you recall, the statement was made that task difficulty does not reside in the task but in task demands and their interaction with the prior knowledge of the student. In the case of instruction, the required level of structure and teacher direction also is determined, in part, by the characteristics of the student. Some instructional interventions involve the use of teacher actions that seem to be more excessively hands-on and explicit than others. But, when examining a lesson according to its surface appearance, opinions about *excess* must always be taken as superficial. That is because lesson quality is always determined, in part, by the individual student's needs. This is as true of lessons that seem to be too structured as it is of those that seem to be too unstructured.

In many discussions of learning and student performance, terms like **external** and **internal** are used to describe the location of a lesson's control (external referring to teacher control and internal referring to student control). These terms bring us close to the perpetual instructional and behavior management debates about the relative superiority of **intrinsic** and **extrinsic** kinds of knowledge (regardless of the academic, motivational, or social nature of the content). Here, in brief, is our take on that debate. In the dictionary, intrinsic is defined as *innate* or *inbred*. That means it refers to things that were wired in at birth. Knowledge of a particular skill is only *intrinsic* if it is *instinctual*.

Students are not born knowing that $6 \times 8 = 48$. So why would we think they were born knowing that screaming is an inappropriate way to solve problems or that "listening attentively to Mrs. McCorcal" (an indicator of motivation) is more interesting than "listening to Mr. Das"? Such things are unlikely to be biologically native to any student. But if something is in a student's mind, how else could it get in there? The answer, of course, is through learning.

During the process of learning, information from external sources is combined with prior knowledge (most of which was also learned) to become part of the internal body of knowledge. So, whereas something may be *internal* (that is, in a child's mind), this does not mean it is, or ever was, *intrinsic*. In most of the cases with which this text deals (that is, academic and social literacy), things got to be internal after there was an external learning event of some sort. This means if a student exercises self-control skills, the likelihood is that those skills were originally learned from an outside source (or assembled internally by the student from information taken previously from external sources). External experiences precede internal learnings. If a child doesn't have self-control skills, then the likelihood is that those skills need to be taught.

Why is this an issue? Because, by conceptualizing a particular behavior (or lack of behavior) as *intrinsic*, the teacher may really be viewing it as *instinctual*. If this is the case, the teacher is putting the behavior outside of the realm of instruction. The risk, therefore, is that he may write the student off as being beyond help.

### What Happens During Good Teaching?

In Chapter 2, the terms "proximal" and "distal" variables were introduced. These terms were used in conjunction with the idea that a student's learning is influenced by her opportunities to learn. Proximal variables are those that have been found to be immediately and causally related to learning, whereas distal variables are more remotely related and are often correlational and not causal. Proximal variables, because they are primarily under the direct control of teachers, are the focus of this text. However, there will be times when teachers will want to consider, and possibly attempt to influence, distal variables. When teaching a lesson, a good instructor considers proximal factors. The research on effective teaching mentioned earlier in this chapter showed that three categories of variables in particular can be manipulated by teachers to improve the learning outcomes for students. These categories are time, assignments, and teacher actions.

## How Can Teachers Manipulate Time?

Haynes and Jenkins (1986) studied the reading instruction given to students with reading problems. Students in one class they observed received an average of 57.79 minutes of reading instruction a day. Students in another class only received an average 16.67 minutes a day. They also found that (and this will be a big surprise) students in the 57.79-minute class learned more about reading than students in the 16.67-minute class.

Time, and how it is spent in classrooms, is important. How much time a person works greatly influences how good they become at whatever it is they are working on. This fact, for all its intuitive clarity, has managed to allude authors in search of the best approach to teaching. As it turns out, many of the findings that are routinely attributed to the power of an instructional approach, or to the influence of an ability variable like student intelligence, can actually be traced to the role of time.

## What Happens to Students Who Need More Time to Learn?

One of the most interesting ideas discussed in the educational literature in the last decade is a phenomenon called the *Matthew Effect* (Stanovich, 1986). The term is based on a quote from the Bible that says *"For unto every one that hath shall be given, and he shall have abundance: but from him that hath not shall be taken away even that which he hath"* (XXV:29). The translation into education is simple. Students who have a lot of skills do better in school and learn more. Students with limited skills don't do well in school and fall further behind. Stanovich (1996) reviewed an extensive body of literature and wrote what is probably the most comprehensive review of the Matthew Effect on slow learners. He was focusing on reading acquisition, but the conclusions apply to students trying to learn any skill. They also are clearly related to the minimum/maximum rule.

Stanovich showed that the "rich-get-richer" problem can explain much of the variability in student learning, which is commonly attributed to differences in instructional approach and/or fixed student ability. He cites the finding that, in one study, total words read in first grade reading lessons ranged from a high of 1,933 words per week for a student in a high reading group to a low of 16 words per week for a student in a low reading group. The obvious cumulative impact in this disparity in reading experience can, according to Stanovich, result in high achieving students having read from 10 to 50 million words by the middle grades, whereas lower achieving students may only have read 1 million words in the same time frame. That means that students who are initially successful at reading may read 50 times more than students who are having trouble. These are massive experiential differences that increase proportionally as students advance through the grades. They literally dwarf the differences in learning that one might attribute to instructional approach.

## How Can Time Be Increased?

Simply increasing the length of the school day will not guarantee improved learning. Perfect attendance at an ineffective school is not valuable. In recognition of this, researchers have defined different types of classroom time.

One type of time is "engaged time." This is that portion of the day during which a student is working. We know that the larger the proportion of engaged time in a class, the more students will learn. We know that students are more engaged when teachers are using **hands-on instruction** (Kameenui & Carnine, 1998; Murphy et al., 1986; Rosenshine, 1997). Unfortunately, we also know that a student can be intensely engaged in activities that have nothing to do with what she needs to learn. Teachers can employ classroom activities that are fun, entertaining, and filled with intense student engagement. But if the lesson does not emphasize what the student needs to learn, the student's learning needs will not be met. So, if the answer isn't length of school day or amount of engaged time, what is it?

Academic Learning Time (ALT) is that time when a student is working on something dir-ectly related to what she needs to learn (Berliner, 1987; Walberg, 1988). Like engaged time, ALT contributes to learning and increases with teacher direction (Cohen, 1987). But ALT is also increased by assuring that the curriculum and instruction are aligned. One way to do this is to make sure that instructional decisions are not driven by assignment giving. Instructional decisions need to be based on curriculum need (Jones et al., 1998).

### Where Does All the Time Go?

One of the biggest threats to ALT is the belief that the core of teaching is assignment giving. Working within this erroneous belief system, a teacher may make decisions about the number and kind of assignments a student should do, not what the student needs to learn. In some classes, students spend from 50% to 70% of the time allocated to instruction doing independent, non-teacher-directed (hands-off) activities (Adams, 1990; Borg, 1980; Doyle & Carter, 1987). This finding has been noted in elementary, secondary, and special education classrooms (Muyskens & Ysseldyke, 1998). This isn't good because ALT decreases when students are working on assignments that are unrelated to what they are supposed to learn. In addition, inappropriate classroom behaviors increase under these conditions.

Unless teachers have specific information about student skill levels and take steps to align instructional activities with those levels, students may spend time working on tasks that are interesting and enjoyable but educationally inappropriate. Such tasks may be irrelevant, too hard, or too easy. As a result, even if engagement were to be high, ALT would be low. Unfortunately, many teachers apparently do not accurately match students to activities (Anderson, 1985; Bennett & Desforges, 1988; Bennett et al., 1987; McIntyre et al., 1983). Worse yet (from the perspective of this text), they do the poorest job with low-achieving students (Baumman & Ivy, 1997).

There are several possible explanations for the failure of teachers to select appropriate assignments. One of these explanations is that the teacher becomes so committed to designing activities that are stimulating and interesting that they forget the purpose of having the activity in the first place. For example, a teacher might use an activity during reading instruction that, while pleasing to the students, is not linked to reading.

In some cases, the teacher actually seems to forget the need for the alignment and in others the teacher may believe that it is the student's role to find the link.

Another possible explanation is that teachers select inappropriate assignments because they do not engage in a systematic decision process. Many teachers simply give the same assignment to everyone (Borko et al., 1990). Often, teachers give an assignment because it is the next lesson in whatever published series they are using. For example, they assign lesson 27 because they are 27 days into the year.

In such classes, decision making is driven by the need to finish lessons—not the need to learn—and that constitutes bad judgment. It also represents the ultimate in hands-off instruction, because the teacher relinquishes all delivery of information, selection of curriculum, and placement of students to the published materials. Teachers may even convey this emphasis on completing work to their students.

### What Do Students Think About Assignments?

Learning is more important than completing assignments. However, when teachers emphasize assignment completion over learning, students come to believe that the purpose of doing assignments is to get them done—not to learn anything from them. This misunderstanding is supported in part by the teacher's talk and in part by the general confusion most low-achieving students experience in school. Therefore, the students who can least afford to misunderstand the purpose of an assignment are the ones who are most apt to misunderstand (Bennett & Desforges, 1988). When asked why they are doing assignments, these low-achieving students report that their teachers "want the assignments done" (Anderson, 1984; Doyle, 1983; Englert, 1987). Often, they will even add "by recess" to their explanations. In classes where assignment completion is stressed, special/remedial students tend to develop strategies for finishing assignments (such as copying from other students), not for understanding them. Although they realize they don't understand what they are doing, they see no reason to change. That's because they don't think

*Exhibit 4.3    Categories of Teaching Functions.*

| | | Teacher Actions | | | | | |
|---|---|---|---|---|---|---|---|
| | | Prepare for Instruction (B.2.1) | Deliver Information (B.2.2) | Ask Questions (B.2.3) | Respond to Efforts (B.2.4) | Conduct Activities (B.2.5) | Evaluate for Instruction (B.2.6) |
| **Type of Information** | Facts | 1 | 2 | 3 | 4 | 5 | 6 |
| | Concepts and rules | 7 | 8 | 9 | 10 | 11 | 12 |
| | Strategies | 13 | 14 | 15 | 16 | 17 | 18 |
| **Proficiency Level** | Accuracy | 19 | 20 | 21 | 22 | 23 | 24 |
| | Mastery | 25 | 26 | 27 | 28 | 29 | 30 |
| | Automaticity | 31 | 32 | 33 | 34 | 35 | 36 |

understanding has anything to do with the assignment.

How can such misunderstandings occur? Often, it's simply that the assignment is meaningless to remedial students. In such a case, getting the work finished to make it to recess reflects good judgment. But students also think about what teachers talk about. And some teacher talk is compatible with the "getting it done" mentality. Teachers often comment about how busy students are, not how accurately they are working (Anderson, 1982, 1984; Doyle, 1986; Mergendoller et al., 1988). These teachers literally say "Here is your math worksheet; get it done by the end of the period." It would be much better if they would say "Here is your math worksheet; I don't care if you finish it as long as you use it to learn about place value (Wellington & Martinek, 1995)."

There is a saying, often attributed to George Santayana, that goes "It isn't important what happens, but it is important how you handle it." This is probably good advice relative to classroom assignments. The actual nature of the activity is not as important as what the teacher says and does during the activity. One of the biggest errors a teacher can make is to convey the message that assignment completion is more important than learning. Assignments do not need to get done. Students need to learn.

## What Can a Teacher Do to Ensure Learning?

Learning is ensured by explanation, demonstration, guided practice, timely correction, and task-specific feedback. If these are aligned with objectives, they make up the substance of effective teaching. The effective-teaching literature has clarified a set of teacher actions used during instruction (Rosenshine, 1997). These are generic, meaning they can be applied across content, types of students, and approaches to instruction. Because these actions are not method-specific, any teacher should be able to accommodate most of them within his teaching.

Look at Exhibit 4.3. This exhibit outlines some of the factors that influence how a lesson is delivered. They include the type of information being taught, the targeted proficiency level, and the teacher actions used to address this information and achieve these outcomes. There are six categories of teacher action listed across the top of Exhibit 4.3: *planning for instruction, delivery of information, asking questions, responding to efforts, conducting activities, and evaluating for instruction.* These actions must be aligned with the objectives of the lesson. This means that the teacher thinks about the objectives while planning the lesson, delivers information about the objectives, asks questions about that information, uses activities to emphasize or practice using the information, responds to the student's work with objective-specific feedback and praise, and evaluates the outcome.

The numbers in the grid represent functions that teachers often need to fulfill during teaching. These are *things* that must get done, not necessarily *ways* to teach. It is important to understand the variables listed along each axis and how they interact with each other as they define the nature of each of the 36 separate functions.

Because most of Chapter 3 dealt with planning and almost all of the rest of the book deals with evaluation, this chapter will focus on the four actions in the center of Exhibit 4.3: *delivery of information, asking questions, responding to student efforts,* and *conducting activities.*

Information about specific proximal (teacher actions) and alterable distal variables are found in Appendices A.13 and A.14 and in Howell et al., 2000a. The content listed there was drawn directly from the TIES-2 (Ysseldyke & Christenson, 1996). The content in TIES-2 was itself drawn from a comprehensive review of teacher-effectiveness literature. As a group, the exhibits in this chapter and the appendix information define "opportunity to learn." They supply a set of guidelines for effective teaching and, as such, may be used for purposes of evaluating classroom instruction.

To cross-reference the TIES-2 content directly to this chapter, we have listed most of Ysseldyke and Christenson's TIES components under the six headings used in Exhibit 4.3. Turn to Appendices A.13 and A.14 and Howell et al., 2000a and examine the TIES-2 components. They present a vivid impression of exemplary teaching. Alterable proximal variables also are listed.

### How Are Different Types of Information Taught?

Four different kinds of information were presented in Chapter 3 (factual, conceptual, rules, and strategic). As indicated in Exhibit 4.3, each of these types of information is taught using different lesson formats. The topical chapters (8-14) will include evaluation procedures and objectives that target each of the kinds of knowledge, so it is important to understand what they are and how to teach them. Guidelines for teaching each of these types of information are summarized in Howell et al., 2000a. You will want to refer to the information presented there as you read the next few sections.

### How Should Factual Information Be Taught?

Facts (sometimes called "literal information") are the least complex form of information students are expected to learn (Simmons & Kameenui, 1990). This is good news and bad news when it comes to designing instruction. The good news is that facts can be taught with a fairly straightforward instructional format that requires relatively little class time. The bad news is that fact learning places a heavy load on student's memory and recall skills. Therefore, instruction designed to teach facts must assist the student to store and retrieve information efficiently. The teacher must consider how many facts to teach and how often they should be rehearsed.

Fact learning may break down when instruction fails to address two critical executive functions: selective attention and recall. These functions were described in Chapter 2. Instruction should be brisk, to the point, and focused on the critical association being taught. A student's attention may wander if the instructional presentation is too cluttered with unnecessary chatter or irrelevant stimuli. When teaching facts, effective teachers generally use some form of signal to consistently communicate the requirements of the task and the key association to be learned. Here is an example in which Mrs. Ferris, a second-grade teacher, teaches her class the fact "7 plus 2 is 9":

Mrs. Ferris:  OK everyone, eyes on me. Listen. We are going to learn a new addition fact. What are we going to learn?

Students:  A new addition fact.

Mrs. Ferris:  Yes that's right. Listen. 7 plus 2 is 9. 7 plus 2 is 9. Now say it with me.

Students and Mrs. Ferris:  7 plus 2 is 9.

Mrs. Ferris:  Again.

Students and Mrs. Ferris:  7 plus 2 is 9.

Mrs. Ferris:  Nice work. 7 plus 2 is 9. Now you say it.

Students:  7 plus 2 is 9.

Mrs. Ferris:  Good job. What is 7 plus 2?

Students:  9.

Mrs. Ferris:  Yes. 7 plus 2 is 9.

Mrs. Ferris:  Once more. What is 7 plus 2?

Students:  9

Notice in this example that Mrs. Ferris focused her students' attention on the key fact to be learned and eliminated any superfluous talk not related to that fact. Notice also, that she used a model-lead-test format to teach the fact. First, she modeled the fact, then lead the students through recitation of the fact, and finally tested their acquisition of the fact.

This is only the initial teaching sequence for this fact. At this point, Mrs. Ferris's students have placed the fact in short-term memory, but they have not actually "learned" the fact yet because it is not stored and readily accessible in long-term memory. To help her students move the fact from short-term to long-term memory and to increase ease of recall, Mrs. Ferris needs to schedule additional practice sessions throughout the day and subsequent weeks (for example, "OK. What is 7 plus 2?"). Assuming Mrs. Ferris is an effective teacher, she probably would test her students on this fact every 10 minutes or so during the next 2 hours, three times during the hour after that, and at least four more times before the students go home that day. By the end of that day, Mrs. Ferris's students would have practiced the fact 15-20 times. The next day, Mrs. Ferris would schedule an additional 8-10 practices distributed throughout the day (mixed in with other facts also being taught) and then an additional 3-5 sessions each day for the next week.

If Mrs. Ferris found that her students were not readily recalling the fact from long-term memory, she would repeat the initial teaching sequence illustrated above and then increase the density of practice sessions until her students were able to recall the fact, on demand. Of course, as we have emphasized in this text, all students do not learn at the same pace when given the same instruction, so some students *will* need more practice than others to become proficient at recalling the fact.

The next requirement for teaching facts is to ensure that the learner accurately discriminates the new fact from previously learned facts. This discrimination teaching phase is critical because it is often here that students' skills break down. The goal is for the student to recall the appropriate fact from long-term memory when it is needed. If you have any doubts about the importance of this phase, think about how frustrated you were the last time an automatic teller machine retained your ATM card after you repeatedly entered the wrong PIN. Discrimination teaching entails juxtaposition of previously mastered facts with newly learned ones. Initially, the new fact would be juxtaposed with previously learned ones that are very different. Then, over time, finer discriminations would be required.

Here is how Mrs. Ferris would teach her students to discriminate among addition facts. After she was sure her students have learned that $7 + 2 = 9$, she would include in the practice sessions very dissimilar facts that were previously learned (that is, $5 + 1 = 6$; $4 + 3 = 7$). Gradually, she would bring in more similar facts (that is, $6 + 2 = 7$; $7 + 3 = 10$, etc.) until her students can accurately recall that 7 plus 2 is 9, even when the question is asked in the context of other information.

Finally, because Mrs. Ferris is a truly effective teacher, she would have a task-specific error correction procedure that is designed to prevent students practicing incorrect facts to mastery. As soon as she hears a student make a mistake, she corrects the student by providing the correct fact. She would eliminate superfluous chatter from the instructional sequence and focus student attention on the correct response rather than the incorrect response. For example, if a student responds that "$7 + 2$ is 8", Mrs. Ferris would simply say, "No. $7 + 2$ is 9. What is $7 + 2$?"

## How Should Conceptual Information Be Taught?

A concept is an object, event, action, or situation that is part of a class of objects, events, or situations. Concepts may range from concrete (that is, "triangle," "mountain," or "table") to abstract (that is, "freedom," "integer," or "thought"). Concepts allow students to categorize things. For example, if a student understands the concept of *fairness,* she will be able to sort examples of behavior into *fair* and *unfair* categories. As explained in Chapter 3, this sorting is possible if the student knows about the **attributes** of the concept. *Relevant* (or critical) attributes are those that are present (or always missing) in *all* examples of the concept. *Irrelevant* (non-critical) attributes may or may not be present.

Teaching functions associated with concept instruction are shown in Howell et al., 2000a. As we discussed in Chapter 3, concept teaching involves presentation of examples and non-examples that help the student accurately discriminate members and non-members of the concept class by attending to relevant attributes. The challenge is to present examples that do not accidentally teach misconceptions. For example, to teach the concept "square," a teacher would present squares that vary in dimensions such as color, size, material, and texture. If the teacher only used yellow paper squares to teach the concept, a student might learn the misconception that something is only a square if it is yellow and paper.

Of course, with a concrete concept like "square," correcting this misconception is pretty easy. However, more abstract concepts are highly susceptible to misconception and require more extensive instruction incorporating a wide range of examples and nonexamples over an extended period of time. Unfortunately, some of the most socially relevant concepts are also the most abstract. For example, academically relevant but abstract concepts such as "multiplication," "topic sentence," or "verb tense" may be highly susceptible to misconception. Similarly, concepts associated with self-management or social behavior (such as "appropriate," "polite," "quickly," etc.) may need to be taught explicitly using carefully chosen examples. For example, some students need to be taught directly the salient attributes of the concept "working quietly" to distinguish this concept from "sitting quietly" or "free time" or "wandering aimlessly around the room."

Strategies for teaching concepts have been well researched and documented over the last 30 years (compare with Gagne et al., 1988; Markel, 1975; Simmons & Kameenui, 1998). Here are some general considerations for teaching concepts from that research.

1. Select examples and non-examples based on the abstractness of the concept and the prior knowledge the student brings to the learning situation. A greater number and range of examples will be required for abstract concepts or when the student lacks sufficient prior knowledge.

2. Separate instruction on concepts that are easily confused (because they are either similar or otherwise linked). For example, contrary to common practice, opposites should be taught at different times (that is, left/right, up/down; reptiles/amphibians; verbs/gerunds; etc.).

3. When a student has learned a misconception, reteach the concept using examples and nonexamples with which the student is already familiar.

4. Provide sufficient practice during concept attainment and then systematically teach generalization through introduction of clearly different positive examples.

5. After the student has initially attained the concept, provide opportunities for the student to recognize examples of the concept, given its attributes. Also, ask her to provide the attributes, given the concept name. For example, when learning the concept "insect," the student would be asked to tell "what kind of creature has six legs?" and "what are the characteristics of an insect?"

6. Provide discrimination practice only after the student has mastered the concept in isolation. Teach discrimination by juxtaposing similar nonexamples. The greater number of relevant attributes nonexamples share, the finer the discrimination that will be required. When a student confuses similar concepts, reteach each separately and then reintroduce discrimination practice.

## How Should Rule Relationships Be Taught?

A rule is a proposition that specifies a connection between at least two facts or concepts. By knowing the relationship specified in a rule, the student can detect that relationship in examples that contain facts or concepts specified by the rule. Rules are stated as "if/then" or "when/then" relationships and can be found in beginning literacy skills as well as advanced content areas (you'll see a lot of them in the second part of this text). For example, in spelling, a student might be taught the rule "When there is a 'y' at the end of a word, then the plural is often spelled 'ies.'"

Teaching functions associated with rule relationships are summarized in Howell et al., 2000a. Because rules generally are composed of facts or concepts, instruction to teach rules is consistent with the formats discussed above. The general way to teach rule relationships includes the following steps:

1. Teach rules using positive and negative examples that are carefully selected and sequenced.

2. Identify the component information in the rule (facts, concepts).

3. Determine if the student knows the component information that comprises the rule. If this information has not been mastered, it must be taught *before* the rule can be taught.

4. Break the rule into two parts and identify the parts explicitly. The rule specifies the *connectedness* of the two parts where the first part is used to predict the second part. Present a range of examples of the first part of the rule and ask the student to predict the second part.

Here is an example of a teaching sequence for the rule "When you add two numbers together, (then) you can change their order but the sum doesn't change."

Teacher:  Listen. This is a rule about adding numbers. If you change the order of two numbers you are adding together, then you still get the same answer. Now look (teacher writes problem on the board). 3 plus 5 is 8. If I change the order of the numbers so that the problem is 5 plus 3, will I get the same answer?

Student:  Yes.

Teacher:  How do you know?

Student:  If you change the order of two numbers being added together, then you still get the same answer.

Teacher:  Yes. That's right. Now look. 4 plus 12 is 16. If I change the order so that the problem is 12 plus 4, will I get the same answer?

Student:  Yes.

Teacher:  How do you know?

Student:  All you did was change the order of the numbers you are adding together. The answer will still be 16.

Teacher:  Yes that's right. If you change the order of two numbers being added together, then you still get the same answer.

Notice the features this instructional sequence has in common with the one shown earlier for facts teaching. The teacher focuses the student's attention on the key relationship to be taught and, after stating the rule, quickly provides a set of examples. If the student failed to discern the connection between the two parts of the rule (that is, "changing the order of two numbers being added" and "the sum is the same"), the teacher would restate the rule and provide another test example. If the student still did not discern the rule, the teacher could then check to make sure the student had sufficient prior knowledge. For example, the teacher might need to reteach the concept of addition or of number order.

## How Should Strategic Information Be Taught?

Having strategic knowledge allows a student to direct her actions and to solve problems (Marzano et al., 1988). Through strategy instruction, the student is taught procedures for using previously learned skills. Therefore, it is essential that a teacher check to make sure these skills have in fact been learned. For example, telling a student how to critically read a passage won't work if the student has not been taught the vocabulary in the passage. Teaching functions associated with strategy instruction are summarized in Howell et al., 2000a.

Here are some important points about strategy instruction.

- Strategy instruction does not teach answers, it teaches how to arrive at answers;

- Emphasis is on the process of doing the task, not on the product that is completed;

- Feedback targets the strategy (for example, in a lesson teaching the repeat-addition strategy of multiplication, feedback might include a statement like "Good, you remembered to add the largest number to itself as many times as the smaller number indicated.");

- Teachers teach strategies by making them visible to the student. This is most effectively accomplished by demonstrating (actually carrying out) while talking through the act of problem solving in front of the students (as opposed to showing a model of a problem that is already completed);

- The best demonstrations show the effort, procedures, and even the revision of work;

- In strategy demonstrations, the teacher talks through the process aloud (this is called "making your thought process public" (Englert et al., 1991));

- Teachers also have students talk through a solution while carrying out the steps (Gerber, 1987). This is called verbal mediation; and

- Strategy instruction seems to be most successful in classrooms where the teacher promotes a "strategic environment" (Edmunds, 1999).

One way to maintain a strategic environment is to accentuate personal accountability in the form of self-monitoring. For example, in a strategic classroom when students turn in math pages with errors, the teacher does not mark the errors. Instead he says "I see a mistake on this page, see if you can find it and fix it." This requires the student to self-check her work and holds her accountable for doing so. Similarly, whenever a teacher finds many students asking the same question over and over, he should teach the students a strategy for finding the answer on their own.

Sometimes this emphasis on self-monitoring and accountability may seem harsh. There is a teacher named Karla in western Washington State who works with students who have fairly severe skill deficits. It rains a lot in western Washington, and before recess Karla's students always used to ask her if they needed to wear a coat. Often the same student would ask that same question several times a day. This made the issue a good candidate for strategy instruction. So Karla taught her students to open the window, touch the window, or look at the sky to decide for themselves if they needed coats. Occasionally a student made a wrong decision and went outside without a coat when it was cold, wet, or both. The first couple of times this happened, other teachers returned the kid and asked for a coat. When Karla refused, saying "He decided he didn't need one," the other teachers probably thought Karla wasn't all that nice. But her students quickly learned to make decisions and dress appropriately on their own.

### How Can All of This Learning Occur at Once?

Humans rarely learn new things in one attempt. Rather, learning occurs in **phases.** The initial phase of learning is **acquisition,** when the learner first is exposed to the new skill or knowledge and begins to move it from short-term to long-term memory. At the beginning of this phase, the learner makes many errors, and use of the information or skill requires conscious effort. As the learner moves through the acquisition phase, accuracy improves. The next phase of learning is **fluency.** During this phase, the learner begins to build speed and efficiency in use of the skill or knowledge. By the end of this phase, the student is able to use the skill or knowledge with a high rate of accuracy and at an appropriate rate. The final phase is **automaticity/generalization,** when

**Exhibit 4.4    Teaching for Accuracy, Mastery, and Automaticity.**

| Phase of Learning | Prior Knowledge or Skill Required | Goal of Instruction | Deliver Information | Ask Questions | Respond to Student Efforts | Teaching Activities |
|---|---|---|---|---|---|---|
| Acquisition | None | Accurate use of knowledge or skill | • Extensive explanation<br><br>• Modeling and demonstration | • Ask about strategies and concepts<br><br>• Do not emphasize answers | • Praise accurate responses<br><br>• Use elaborate correction procedures | • Use only guided and controlled practice<br><br>• Student completes partially worked items |
| Fluency | Accurate use of knowledge or skill | Mastery of subskills | • Review | • Emphasize answers<br><br>• Ask many questions | • Praise fluent work<br><br>• Do not use correction procedures | • Drill and practice<br><br>• Independent practice |
| Generalization and transfer | Mastery of subskills | Automaticity | • Explain how existing skills can be generalized<br><br>• Teach related vocabulary | • Ask how existing skills can be modified | • Use elaborate corrections when generalization or transfer fails to occur | • Use "real world" examples<br><br>• Deemphasize classroom-specific tasks |

the student generalizes the skill or knowledge to novel contexts and as prior knowledge for learning new information. At the end of this phase, use of the skill or knowledge is automatic and effortless. Effective teaching entails designing instruction that is aimed at maximizing student learning at each phase. Each phase has a different target outcome and requires the teacher to use different instructional strategies (Rosenshine, 1997; Shuell, 1990).

Exhibit 4.4 shows instructional considerations for each phase of learning. A more detailed discussion of the instruction required by each phase is presented here.

## How Can Teachers Facilitate Learning During Acquisition?

Lessons designed for this phase of learning teach the student to be accurate. They are designed to take a student through the novice phases of task performance. Because students in this phase make frequent errors, they should never be allowed to work without carefully arranged monitoring and feedback procedures. These initial lessons are characterized by elaborate explanations, extensive use of models, correction procedures that focus on accuracy and deemphasize rate, and reinforcement for accurate performance.

Because it is designed to promote accuracy, feedback and error correction are important parts of the acquisition phase. During acquisition, it is sometimes best to introduce a lesson and its key strategies briefly, get the child working immediately, and then use elaborate correction procedures.

To do this, certain preconditions must be met:

• The student must not view an error as a failure, and

- The student must know when a correction is taking place.

Because a correction procedure relates to a past event (the production of the error), it can easily confuse a student. The way to handle this is to use consistent correction techniques, including physical or verbal cues to signal when a correction begins and ends. Here is an extreme example of this confusion.

A common language-correction procedure involves "expansion" by the teacher of an incorrect utterance. So if a student were to say "She gonna sleep there?" the teacher would expand and say "Is she going to sleep there?"

The first author once saw a child ask "I go ba-eroom," to which the teacher replied "Can I go to the bathroom?" After the teacher's response, the student stood in obvious confusion and eventually shrugged and nodded at the teacher as if she were an idiot. The kid was thinking "Of course *you* can go to the bathroom; you're the teacher. But what about *my* problem?"

Such confusion can be avoided if the teacher precedes all corrections with a cue (that is, a hand on the shoulder of a younger child) and follows the correction by responding to the meaning of the incorrect utterance. Then the whole exchange might go like this:

Student: "I go ba-eroom."

Teacher: (placing hand on child's shoulder) "May I go to the bathroom?" (Removing hand): "Yes, you may."

The need for correction is obvious if the student makes important errors, but it is also justified when a student seems to be accurate but is very slow. Students who are extremely slow are often inaccurate, though they don't display their errors. These students may avoid errors by skipping items or using functional but inefficient strategies (such as counting on their fingers or repeating the whole alphabet in sequence to recall a particular letter).

If you find a student who is inaccurate, you should check less complex skills (the subtasks) to find out what accounts for the current failure. When a point is reached at which the student is inaccurate at a task, but accurate at its subtasks, stop testing and teach for acquisition of the task strategy.

### How Can Teachers Facilitate Fluency?

Lessons designed for this phase of learning take accurate students and add speed to their performance. Fluency formats are characterized by drill and practice, repetition, minimal teacher talk, heavy external reinforcement (if needed), and feedback without correction. No correction is needed because the student is already accurate and errors are viewed as rate-induced. During this phase, feedback should prompt the student to employ what was learned during acquisition. The need for fluency building is indicated when the student is accurate but slow at the task. How accurate a student has to be at something before moving into rate-building instruction is debatable, but estimates range from 80% to 100%, with most authors settling for something around 90% (Berliner, 1984; Liberty et al., 1980; Rosenshine, 1997; White, 1986). As you can imagine, placing a student who is inaccurate into a fluency format without any feedback and correction procedures would be a mistake because it would allow the student to practice (and become "better" at) being inaccurate. Incidentally, some computer programs offer nothing more than electronic worksheets. Some may provide feedback whereas others may give feedback and corrections. Clearly, teachers must choose instructional materials and software according to the phase of learning at which they will be used.

Many worksheets, of the type given during independent seat work (and most homework assignments), are designed as fluency-building activities. After all, independent seat work and homework, by definition, are assignments that students do without feedback. You can see it is a bad idea to assign these activities if the student is not at about 90% accuracy on the task.

### How Can Teachers Facilitate Generalization and Automaticity?

Lessons designed for this phase of learning teach students to apply skills in a larger context. They involve presentations of novel situations (those including distractions as well as the transfer and modification of knowledge) and an emphasis on self-regulation and adaptive task-related beliefs. They may also include the use of **distractions.** Realistic distractions are those imposed by the context in which a skill would normally be used. For example, suppose you are testing a student's skill at driving a car. You could test this skill in an empty parking lot or on a freeway in the middle of high-speed traffic. The freeway is a good test of automaticity at driving as it supplies realistic distracters (in any case we'd always advise seat belts). Testing a student's recall of history vocabulary in the middle of a freeway would *not* provide a good test of automaticity for vocabulary (but seatbelts would *really* be needed). The same distracters—speeding trucks and occasional highway-patrol cars—that provide realistic distractions for the driving test do not provide realistic distractions for testing historical vocabulary.

It is also important to make sure that students maintain the information they have learned. Maintenance lessons do not involve any active teaching and are usually limited to periodic reviews and monitoring. Materials designed for maintenance are very appropriate for independent seat work or homework.

## Some Other Issues Related to Instruction

### How Can Teachers Accommodate Variability in the Classroom?

There is an old joke in education that says if you ask any teacher what he thinks is the perfect class size he will reply "The number of students I have right now minus one—that kid over there!" But today the shift is away from efforts to reduce the range of students in the general education classroom by sending them out to special programs. Today, the emphasis is on increasing accommodation in the general education class (King-Sears, 1998; Richardson, 1994).

The accommodation of students with varying skill levels depends on a number of system modifications that, although beyond the scope of this text, are clearly needed in education.

These include programs of teacher consultation and prereferral (Fisher et al., 1995; Fuchs et al., 1992; Johnson & Pugach, 1991; Nolet, 1999). However, accommodation also depends on the wide-scale adoption, by general education, of effective procedures for group instruction. These include teacher-assistance teams (Carter & Sugai, 1989; Nolet et al., 1992), direct instruction (Gersten, 1992), peer tutoring (Jenkins & Jenkins, 1988; Warner, 1992), cooperative learning (Antil et al., 1998; Tateyama-Sniezek, 1990), cognitive strategy instruction (Harris & Pressley, 1991), instruction in task-related behavior, curriculum-based measurement (Shinn & Hubbard, 1992; Ysseldyke, 1987), and use of computer technology.

Although it is common to contrast various delivery models (resource room, self-contained, pull-out, transition class, tracking, and consultation), student learning hinges most directly on the teacher's use of the actions shown in Howell et al., 2000a. Therefore, a special education pull-out teacher working 1:1 who fails to employ these actions will facilitate less learning than a whole class general class teacher who does. The question is "Can a general education teacher do all that stuff in a room with 30 students?" The answer is "yes." It isn't necessarily easy, but it can be done.

First of all, remember that none of the supports mentioned in this text would ever be supplied all of the time to all 30 of the general class students. However, it may need to be supplied to as many as 10 of them. Regardless of the number, however, it is likely that the teacher will need some sort of support to provide the service while maintaining sanity (Kauffman & Hallahan, 1997).

Many schools currently provide support to classroom teachers through the use of a multi-level problem-solving model in which the amount of assistance provided in the classroom is matched to the instructional needs of the student and the expertise of the teacher (Howell, 1997). We will discuss such a model in some detail in Chapter 7.

The exact nature of user-friendly instruction varies according to the age of the students and the content being taught. However, peer-mediated instruction (peer tutoring), cooperative learning, and computer-assisted instruction are

**The most important step in teaching may be planning how to teach.**

three of the most commonly employed ways of increasing the range of general education class instruction (Stevens & Salisbury, 1997).

The provision of in-depth coverage on cooperative learning, computers, and peer tutoring is well beyond the scope of this chapter. However, at the end of this chapter, we can provide what we believe to be excellent direction for readers interested in pursuing these topics, along with another topic of particular concern these days: instruction of remedial students at the middle and high school levels.

### Isolation and Meaning

It is safe to say that the more meaning a student perceives in a task the easier it will be for her to learn it. This is largely because meaning tends to

motivate and activate the storage and retrieval functions of memory, as well as promote early application and generalization of skills (Paris & Winograd, 1990; Torgesen & Kail, 1980). These advantages justify an initial bias toward teaching all skills within a context that seems to make them meaningful. As mentioned earlier, information seems to be meaningful as a function of its context. For example, snorkels have more meaning by the pool than they do on a ski slope (don't confuse novelty with meaning). But what if someone who knows nothing about them finds a snorkel by the pool?

The sentiment that meaning resides in "real" or "authentic" tasks is commonly voiced (Terwilliger, 1998), but there is an alternative idea. That is the idea that the student's skills make the context meaningful (Stanovich, 1986). In this view, students would need to have a potentially meaningful situation *and* the skills necessary to gain access to it to reap the learning benefits that come with a meaningful lesson. Let's put this another way. Ignorance can isolate a person. Regardless of the contextual contours of the lesson, *low-achieving students often are forced to work in isolation.*

The decision to purposefully teach a skill in isolation (for example to teach letter sounds outside of the context of words or spelling outside of the context of written expression) is commonly based on assessment data indicating that the student can't handle the demands imposed by the context. There are cases where students are so unskilled that they can't even appreciate the context. Here, isolation has the advantage of focusing all attention on a particular skill, but it has the disadvantages of inhibiting generalization and making the skill seem meaningless.

The idea that some tasks are more *meaningful* than others is something like the idea that some tasks are harder than others. As you may recall, the idea of *task difficulty* was explained in Chapter 2. In that presentation, the point was made that a task only seems difficult if the learner does not have sufficient prior knowledge to understand it. Similarly, a task may seem meaningless to a student who lacks the skills to decode its meaning. Because lessons from advanced segments of the curriculum require greater prior knowledge to understand, they are more apt to seem meaningless to low-achieving students. Such tasks also tend to have more ambiguous cues, missing information, and a lack of predictability. Furthermore, some tasks seem more meaningful than others, only because they are immediately useful or useful in a variety of contexts.

For a student who understands English and knows how to order at a restaurant, learning key phrases for ordering dinner in French is a good example of a task best approached from an applied and contextual orientation. This means it will probably be more efficiently taught by going to a French restaurant to use the obvious and familiar cues associated with ordering dinner. In contrast, learning the specific names of the powers and limitations assigned to the various branches of the federal government probably won't be any easier to learn in the state capital than it will be at home. Going to the capital and watching government workers may raise your interest, but it is unlikely that you will observe anything in the day-to-day operations of the state capital that will provide clues to the specific powers and limitations upon which a democratic government is based. That is because those structures, like many examples associated with highly evolved and/or abstract bodies of information, are seldom directly labeled or observed in one place. Governing is complex, ambiguous, and requires considerable prior knowledge to understand. So, the next time you need to know the powers and limitations of government for a test, save the cost of driving to the capital and just put the money on flash cards.

When a student cannot gain access to context (either because the context is obscure or the student has limited skills), intense isolated practice may be justified. In these cases, it is natural to reduce the demands of the lesson in the hope that the student will learn more easily (Adams & Engelmann, 1996; Engelmann, 1997). However, whenever a task is removed from its context the teacher must be sure to eventually add the context back into the lessons as the student becomes more skilled. For many special and remedial students, it is *the demands of the setting* that they need to learn to handle. This is obvious within the domain of social behavior when, presented with a student who has difficulty communicating appropriately in a typical general education fourth grade (if there is such a thing), we remove the student to a smaller special class. Then, after teaching her to communicate in that setting we later find that she still can't communicate within the larger general classroom context. The significant contextual attributes of the general class must now be fed back into the communication lessons to assure generalization. During this process, it is possible for a teacher to use praise and encouragement to make the task meaningful to the student without losing the focus, which may be required to teach an important skill.

### How Can Teachers Compensate for Students' Missing Prior Knowledge?

As just pointed out, it "makes sense" to teach something in isolation until the student gains sufficient knowledge of the context to draw meaning from it. In these cases, which usually occur very early in a sequence of instruction (but chronologically late for students who are behind), the teacher should take extra steps to make the exercise seem meaningful and to provide motivation. This is done until the skill can be gradually shifted from isolation into its functional context. This approach to motivation may be handled through efforts to link the task to favorite activities, point systems, or other rewards. It may also be accomplished by using what the student already knows about a related task to make up for what she doesn't know about the targeted task. For example, the teacher can read the words in a sentence that the student doesn't know, then pause and cue the student to read the words she is currently studying. Through this process, the teacher is temporarily supporting the student as she reads the book by using her own skills. As the student's skills increase, the teacher gradually relinquishes her support by expecting the student to take a larger role in reading the passage (Weed et al., 1990). The idea is called scaffolding (Carnine et al., 1997; Rosenshine, 1997).

The scaffolds with which most of us are familiar are the temporary structures assembled to support workers as they construct buildings. These are usually formed from prefabricated metal tubes and wooden planks that can be easily assembled, moved, and removed during the building process. Learning scaffolds work the same way. Teachers build them from what the student already knows and then take them away when they are no longer needed. Of course, this requires the teacher to have a very clear idea about what the student already knows. This is the sort of information a functional evaluation should supply. Here is an illustration of scaffolding.

Suppose you are about to get on an airplane in Seattle. While waiting for the flight you sit staring out the window at low clouds, fog, and drizzle. Given that it is hard for you to see the airplane, let alone the runway, you start worrying about the flight. Just as the worrying increases it is sharply aggravated when a woman dressed as a pilot walks up to the window, looks outside, and says "What an awful day!"

"Are you a pilot?" you ask.

"Yes," the woman replies, "I'm about to go to Phoenix."

"That's my flight," you say.

"Oh, good—then I'll be your captain. My name is Stewart." You shake hands.

"So, Captain Stewart," you venture, "I was sort of wondering. How can you find Phoenix when you can't see the end of the runway? And for that matter, how can you avoid hitting the flight coming *from* Phoenix when they can't see you?"

Captain Stewart smiles, as she has been trained to do, and explains.

"We do it the same way you drove to the terminal. We follow roads and make sure we are in the correct lanes. The difference is that these roads are defined by a navigational network. The roads (we call them airways) are laid out all across the nation. For example, on part of our trip we will follow a route called "Vector 562" to Prescott then turn right onto V 105-257 and follow it to Phoenix. We have a map—just like a road map—that shows us all the airways and tells us how to get from one to another. We even have traffic signals, speed limits, and one-way streets to keep us from running into each other. The only real difference is that we also have assigned altitudes, speeds, and distances from each other."

As Captain Stewart turns to leave you notice that you feel less concerned about the flight (you also notice that airline captains always say "we" instead of "I"). This sense of relief might not have been as great if the captain had told you exactly the same thing in these words.

"We have to go IFR. I filed a flight plan, but because we'll be under positive control there's no telling where we'll get sent, or at what altitude. I expect that the trip will take us outbound on the 119-degree radial from 112.0 down V 562 to Drake, then 145 degrees from 114.1 to Rio Salado, the Papago NDB, and a back course ILS. We'll assume center is guaranteeing separation."

The second explanation presupposes you know about instrument flight, whereas the first explanation allows you to gain understanding by temporarily using what you know about driving and road maps to explain the trip. In this explanation, Captain Stewart was assisting you by constructing a scaffold. This was done by assembling the temporary road-map metaphor and using it to bridge the gaps in your existing understanding of the topic of flight.

Now consider this. Just as the second explanation would have confused you (assuming you aren't a pilot), the first explanation would have confused a person who had never experienced driving or road maps. That is because such a person, a young child or a citizen of a remote society, would not have been able to construct the scaffold even with Captain Stewart's assistance. Such a person would not have the prefabricated scaffolding materials—the prior knowledge.

Special and remedial students, because they are deficient in literacy strategies and/or enabling skills, miss much of what is taught in schools. Consequently, they may end up not being able to read and not knowing the stuff one learns about in books. As they move into higher and higher grades, the lack of general knowledge compounds until a student may literally not know enough to learn. (Because this is more apt to occur for those subjects acquired in school, the same student may seem "street-wise" and "intelligent" outside of school while appearing "stupid" and "slow" in class.)

The distinction between "topical knowledge" and "prerequisite prior knowledge" is fairly arbitrary, in that the same information could fit into either category (the road-map reference would be topical in a driver's education class).

Expert teachers recognize the degree to which a student can succeed at a learning task by comparing the demands of that task to what they know about the student's existing skills. When the student is missing necessary skills, the teacher may then take steps to reduce the demands of the task. Strategies for reducing task demand include breaking it into smaller chunks, isolating it from context that is confusing to the student, or by providing increased instructional support (possibly in the form of a scaffold). These modifications require the teacher to be fully aware of the student's skills and the demands placed on the student by the task that is being taught or the instructional procedure that is being used. This last point is especially important.

Often, when a teacher uses a scaffold, it is not required to learn the content of the lesson, it is required to learn that content in the way the lesson is being presented. This point takes us back to the contrast of teaching approaches and the requirements referred to in Exhibit 4.1. In Chapter 3, we talked about ways to recognize essential subtasks or strategies for the topics we teach in school. But sometimes learning to do something requires different knowledge than doing it once learned (Howell, 1983). This means that learning in one instructional program, in one teacher's class, is a different task from learning in another program or class. For example, we are all familiar with non-reading students who fail subject-area courses because they cannot read history or science books. Yet, reading is not a subskill of knowing the causes of the Civil War. However, if the instruction a student receives from the history teacher involves reading assignments, then reading has become a subskill of *learning* to know the causes of the Civil War in that teacher's classroom.

The subtasks and strategies introduced by various materials and classroom techniques need to be examined carefully and probably deserve the same attention we typically give to content (Gersten et al., 1986; Lloyd & Loper, 1986; Shulman, 1986). It is remarkable how many hours teachers have spent analyzing the demands of tasks like spelling and multiplication without paying similar attention to the demands imposed by their own instructional approach. A task analysis of "how to learn in my class" would represent time well spent by any teacher. Effective teachers carefully consider what a student needs to be able to do to benefit from the lesson they are giving. If the student is missing the needed vocabulary, basic skills, study skills, knowledge of contextual demands, or other tasks imposed by the teacher's presentation, the teacher may change the presentation (possibly by providing a scaffold) or teach the student the missing skills they need to learn in the class.

### How Can Teachers Reduce Uncertainty in the Classroom?

Expert teachers use fixed **routines** for carrying out common classroom functions (Borko et al., 1990; Schumaker et al., 1991; Udvari-Solner, 1996). There are many advantages to developing such routines. They decrease student uncertainty, save instructional time, and support academic focus. However, their primary advantage is that, by adopting and practicing routines, students and teachers are able to deal with recurring instructional demands automatically. Automaticity frees students and teachers to think about the curriculum. Expert teachers use fixed routines for carrying out common classroom functions.

Schumaker and colleagues (1991) list five criteria for useful instructional routines:

- They must be straightforward and easy to master;
- They must be practical and easy to use;
- They must be effective with typical and hard-to-teach students;
- They must improve student performance; and
- They must complement current teaching practices.

Here is an example of a routine for monitoring students that seems to meet these five criteria. It was developed by Kaplan (1972) as part of a peer-tutoring program and can be used whenever students are expected to follow along while another student reads. We'll call it the "point-to-place routine."

To use the point-to-place routine, a teacher teaches students that he will occasionally tap them on the shoulder. When this happens, the student who has been tapped is expected to point in the book to the word currently being read. This simple routine replaces a lot of coaxing and dramatically increases the participation of the class.

Routines must be taught to students—and practiced. They must also be periodically reviewed. Expert teachers set aside time early in the school year to teach routines so that active learning time will be increased later.

## How Do All of These Instructional Techniques Fit Together?

Take another look at Exhibit 4.3. All of the headings in that cube imply boundaries that can't

exist on their own. They are more a convenience of text writing than they are a representation of instruction. This means that eventually a teacher must take all of the actions, promote all of the thought processes, and utilize all of the formats.

The following section provides a description of a typical "hands-on" lesson. The word **[marker]**, accompanied by a number, will be inserted throughout this description for later use debriefing the lesson. The room we will visit is providing services to students with learning problems. However, this doesn't mean the actions of the teacher should only be carried out with problem learners.

### A Visit to Room 38

When you enter the room, the teacher, Chris Peterson, is working with a group of six students clustered in front of the board. Two students are working alone at their desks, while four others work with an aide. The board says:

**Want**
**Water**
**Wall**
**Wasp**
**Watch**
**Wash**
**Wand**
**Walrus**

**Kathie would-**
**play with him.**
**teach him tricks.**
**eat with him.**
**give him a name.**
**give him a home.**
**buy him a fish.**

**Walrus**
   **soft body**
   **silly face**

**Ad ver tise ⟶ commercial**
**Advertisement**   **try to sell something**

In the corner is a sign that says, "Be friendly with classmates." The room has five clusters of tables. Student folders sit on each table. There are fabric-covered room dividers and a large set of free-standing bookshelves to break up the space. Signs hang from the ceiling with words like *exit* and *tomorrow* printed on them. Everything is covered with posters, signs, and student art work. The space above your head is busy with the gently rotating signs.

Chris is introducing vocabulary for an upcoming story.

**[marker 1]** "Before we read I want to make sure everyone is familiar with some of the words in this story. Why should I care about that Mark?"

"Well, if we don't know what the words mean it's not going to make any sense."

**[marker 2]** "That's right. Vocabulary is important for comprehension."

She writes "**Plan.**" on the board. "Who can give me a sentence?" **[marker 3]**

"I have a plan," dictates a girl with pink yarn bows in her hair. Chris writes it out and underlines the target word.

"What's the underlined word?" she asks.

"**Plan,**" they all respond at once.

"Everyone read the sentence."

They read aloud in unison. No one misses a beat. **[marker 4]**

Chris writes **Plum** on the board below **Plan.**

"Who can give me a sentence?"

John, a thin boy, replies, "I have a plum on my thumb," with a smile to the side of his face.

She hesitates. "On my thumb? Can you have a plum on your thumb?" She glances at you and then at the ceiling. "I guess?"

"Stuck in my thumb," John reminds.

"Oh!" she comments to herself. "Good sentence. It just took Ms. Peterson a second to realize what it meant. You have to know what the sentence means to know what each word means." **[marker 5]** Chris finishes the activity, then tells the students to open their books.

"I want you to read the first paragraph to yourselves and tell me what Dad was going to do." As they read, she clears off the board. When they've finished, Chris asks "Who can tell me?" **[marker 6]**

Someone raises a hand and tells the group, "He was going to dig a pit next to the kitchen."

Chris looks around the group and gets nods of agreement. She writes **Dig a pit next to the kitchen** on the board. She is left-handed and writes with her right hand on her hip.

"What was he going to do with the pit?" she asks. No one knows. "OK—read the next paragraph and find out." **[marker 7]**

The lesson goes in steps. Each reading is preceded by questioning and is followed by the answer and an extension of the answer into a question for the next paragraph. Each answer is written on the board so that by the end, an outline of the story has been recorded. Chris uses the outline to summarize. It's a nice, tight lesson. It has clear purpose, is easy to understand, consistent, and has a natural summary. Lots of teachers don't summarize well, you realize. **[marker 8]**

Other students are working alone at their desks. They get up and move around to get new materials out of a yellow box, turn in assignments to a blue box, and get Kleenex or pencils. They get their work and materials without asking permission. They are on-task and well behaved without any attention or direction from Chris or her aide. **[marker 9]** You sit at a table and sneak a look at someone's folder. It's a basic plastic spiral folder with pockets in the front and back. An assignment calendar is taped to the inside cover. The front pocket holds work that needs to be done, while the back one has stuff that's finished. **[marker 10]** The student's name is on the spine and it's been personalized with stickers of animals and hearts.

Some of the pages seem to have schedules or directions for working on them, as opposed to actual work. For example, there is a page of spelling with dittoed directions and spelling words handwritten. It looks like this: **[marker 11]**

## *Words to learn*

*1. sand*

*2. band*

*3. flags*

*4. play*

*5. ask*

*6. land*

*7. rake*

*8. slat*

*9. aunt*

*10. want*

**Monday—read words, define, make up sentences, copy words**
**Tuesday—write each word** *five* **times**
**Wednesday—write a sentence with each word**
**Thursday—trial test: write misspelled words** *ten* **times each**
**Friday—final test**

A bell rings, and there is a brief buzz of excitement as the girls line up and leave with the aide.

"Every spring the girls get to go see a movie on menstruation," Chris explains to your quizzical glance. "It's a real big deal." **[marker 12]**

With the girls and the aide gone, the room seems empty. Chris takes three boys to a table and begins to work with them. You examine one wall and find photos of a field trip and drawings of each student's family. All characters are labeled.

There are also pictures. One of them shows a catlike dog with empty, pointed ears surrounded by birds. Under the picture some printing explains:

My dog. She eats birds. She eats food. She is big, too. She is a good dog. Sometimes she jumps on people. She has a cage, too, she sleeps in a big box sometimes. Her name is Ginger.

Along the shelves you find organized workbooks, a puzzle of the United States, a school menu, *Multiplication Self-teaching Flash Cards*, and two books, *Stellaluna* and *Desert Voices*. There is a bulletin board titled *Responsibilities* that has *sink, shelves, dust, chairs, chalkboard, tables*, and *materials* listed on it. Next to each responsibility are tacked cut-out hands with student names. There are bright birds and fish proceeding up one wall.

Chris is sitting with three boys: John, Manuel, and Bill. All three are working on math but are doing different assignments. Bill works almost exclusively by himself on a worksheet requiring him to identify ones, tens, and hundreds places in multidigit numbers while adding and subtracting. Chris glances at his work. He is adding 224 to 432.

"What did you just do?" she asks.

"Added 4 plus 2."

"When you add tens and ones, which column do you add first?"

"Ones."

"Very good. Point to the ones column." He points. "That's the ones column." She says. **[marker 13]** "Tell me what you do first." She asks for a rule. **[marker 14]**

"Add the numbers in the ones column," he replies. **[marker 15]**

Manuel has worked a sheet of problems and submits it for her approval. She looks at it and informs him "I can see mistakes. If you don't know how to find an answer, what are you going to do?"

"Ask?" he wonders.

"That's right," she nods, "and to find out if you don't know the answer, you must work the problem, then check it twice. **[marker 16]** I can see errors in the very first row. I want you to check all the problems on this page." She hands it back to Manuel and turns to John. **[marker 17]**

John is subtracting 4 from 7. He's gotten 11 for an answer. "You started with what, John?"

"Seven."

"And then?"

"Plussed it to 4."

"Look at the problem and read it to me." She leans back and quickly writes **7 [minus] 4 =** on the board.

Chris points to the 7 as John says "Seven," then to the subtraction sign as he hesitates and says, "Take away 4."

"First you must always decide what to do," she reminds. "What are you doing in this problem?" **[marker 18]**

"Subtracting."

"When you do a take-away, do the numbers get bigger or smaller?" **[marker 19]**

"Smaller."

"Good for you. Now try again."

Turning back to Manuel she says, "After you write an answer, check it, then check it again. What are you going to do?"

"Check it twice."

"Excellent. That's the way to take care of yourself." **[marker 20]**

Her hand drifts across the table toward Bill as if to let him know she is aware of his continued work while she returns to John, who's looking really confused.

Chris produces a set of seven blocks and has him take four away. "Did the number get smaller?"

"Yes."

"Now show me what you did with your fingers."

He holds up his hands and quickly counts out seven fingers. When he has them identified to his satisfaction, he folds down four. As he folds them down, he says "one-two-three-four." Then he counts the leftovers, "one-two-three" and says "Three?" with a mix of confusion and what looks like welcome resolution. **[marker 21]**

John's confusion is suddenly obvious. He is subtracting. Subtraction is the inverse of addition. Addition is counting forward; therefore, subtraction should be counting backward. Given seven fingers, he should be folding four of them down and saying, "Seven-six-five-four." But he isn't. As he tries to solve the subtraction problem, he employs the exact technique he uses on addition—counting forward. **[marker 22]**

The girls come back in the room and, with the boys, move quickly to their business. Several of them group around Susan, the aide, and work on an alphabetizing drill. Other students work quietly in teams using their folders. **[marker 23]** Susan corrects and praises the students' fluency with exactly the same phrases and inflection that Chris uses. She also periodically arranges for the students working independently to check each other. **[marker 24]**

Back at the table, one girl has joined the group. Chris is repeating the subtraction strategy once more as a summary of the lesson. "When you do 'take-away,' do the numbers get bigger or smaller?" **[marker 25]**

"Smaller."

Chris turns to Manual, who has been diligently checking his work. Manual has taken an extra sheet of paper and used it to mask his previous answers. This is a strategy Chris had taught him earlier.

"Good, Manual. Covering up the old answers, that's a good idea." It *is* a good idea. **[marker 26]**

### Reviewing Chris's Lesson

Now let's look at the lesson for evidence that Chris seems to be using effective instruction. There are markers scattered throughout the description, and we'll explain them in sequence. These tell you which of the teacher actions in Exhibit 4.3 are illustrated at that point.

*Marker 1*   Chris is giving the purpose for the lesson, explaining what she will be doing, and activating the student's prior knowledge gained in earlier lessons **[2, 8, 14]**. Her question is conceptual **[9]** after she has asked the question and paused to be sure all students are thinking about it **[21]**.

*Marker 2*   Here, Chris gives feedback on the accuracy of Mark's answer **[22]**. The feedback supplies a critical attribute of comprehension. This is a conceptual follow-up to her conceptual question **[10]**.

*Marker 3*   Generating sentences for each word is a vocabulary-building activity. Reviewing the sentences builds automaticity and promotes generalization **[35]**. From a decoding perspective, the words are being taught as facts (Chris shows each word and tells what it is **[2]**), but this lesson isn't really about decoding.

*Marker 4*　Choral responses are an excellent way to increase the active participation of a small group. By training the students to respond simultaneously, the risk of mimicking answers is removed, and it is easy to hear errors. This increases ALT for the whole class **[4, 10, 16, 22, 28, 34]**.

*Marker 5*　Nice recovery! She took her own confusion and converted it into a scaffold of the strategy for figuring out context-dependent vocabulary **[14]**. She also made her thought processes public and, therefore, modeled use of self-monitoring and the context-vocabulary strategy **[14]**.

*Marker 6*　This is another strategic exercise. Asking questions about the story before reading is an excellent technique for enhancing reading comprehension **[15, 17]**. Many published programs seem to expect the student to read the story and incidentally remember all of it to answer questions at the end. This assumes that the student thinks that what the author (teacher) believes to be important is worth remembering. The technique Chris is using develops the students' search skills by telling them what she thinks is important. It causes them to become active readers who must judge the relevance or irrelevance of the passage components by comparing them with the given question **[11, 17]**. By using it on various passages, she is building mastery and ultimately automaticity **[29, 35]**.

*Marker 7*　Delivery of information about the strategy for finding answers **[14]**.

*Marker 8*　Chris is leaving a tangible model of the process she is demonstrating **[2, 8, 14, 20]**. Additionally, her instruction is sequenced and consistent.

*Marker 9*　This means that the students have been taught *routines* for managing their common needs on their own. This leaves more time to teach **everything.**

*Marker 10*　Whereas the group exercises are building accuracy on various strategies **[14, 20]**, the independent practice is designed to promote mastery **[17, 29]**. Therefore, the aide is reinforcing rate **[27]**.

*Marker 11*　This serves three purposes: (1) it teaches spelling **[14]**; (2) it is a routine that relieves the teacher of the time-consuming task of explaining to each student what he is to do each day; and (3) it teaches the students a strategy for studying **task-related skills.**

*Marker 12*　This is a good example of how society's current reliance on schools creates competition for student time. The girls are going to an important lesson, but their departure reduces their **ALT** relative to Chris's content. (Unfortunately, it is safe to say that you will never see a teacher get credit for this time. You may read that reading scores are below expectation, but you'll never hear that the students score at grade level in "understanding of menstruation.")

*Marker 13*　Chris is giving content-specific feedback **[22, 24]**.

*Marker 14*　Throughout all of her lessons, Chris is consistently teaching problem-solving strategies and procedures for learning **task-related skills [14]**, in addition to isolated bits of information **[2]**. By teaching the strategies, Chris teaches the students how to learn and how to take control over their own learning. Additionally, the strategies tend to tie together bits of material that may seem unrelated and nonsensical to a student who is experiencing problems.

*Marker 15*　Notice that, throughout her lessons, Chris does not merely say things to the student. She expects the student to be able to say them back **verbal mediation.** Once the students are able to verbalize the procedure, they are able to literally talk their way through a situation to its solution.

*Marker 16*　This is a nice, clear accuracy format response to Manuel's efforts **[22]**.

*Marker 17*   Chris is creating a strategic environment by emphasizing **self-monitoring.** Watch as she continues in the next few exchanges with Manuel [14, 15, 16, 17].

*Marker 18*   Here, Chris is teaching a **general problem-solving** strategy.

*Marker 19*   Here, she is checking for understanding of the conceptual aspects of the problem [12] by having John sort problems into those yielding answers that are bigger or smaller.

*Marker 20*   Task-specific feedback on **self-management.**

*Marker 21*   Chris has an excellent correction procedure. She begins by having John say the strategy that he will follow to arrive at the answer [16]. Next, he works it concretely with blocks, then with his fingers, and eventually in writing. Each time, he repeats the strategy aloud as he works **verbal mediation,** but he lacks one subskill necessary to carry out the strategy (how to count backward).

*Marker 22*   Error correction is often the most sophisticated portion of a lesson [4, 10, 16, 22, 28, 34].

*Marker 23*   The students wouldn't be working quietly if they didn't know how to do that and where to find their folders. These behavioral expectations and logistical needs were handled by teaching the students **routines.**

*Marker 24*   By using student checkers, the seat work is made interactive and becomes much more effective [5, 11, 17]. One way to handle this is to pair students, with one of the students having answers to all even-numbered items while the other has answers to all odd-numbered items [24, 30, 36]. Then, both students work problems and check each other [4, 10, 16, 22, 27, 34].

*Marker 25*   Again, this is a straightforward concept-building exercise. Chris is having the student sort problems into two categories [11].

*Marker 26*   Manual has been checking his own work and learning how to take care of himself. He has even figured out his own strategy for keeping his work in order.

Years ago, this room might have looked very different. At that time, the analysis of curriculum tasks, problem-solving strategies, subskills, correction procedures, routines, scaffolding, and verbal mediators were almost unheard of. More frequent was the analysis of fixed abilities, learning styles, and perceptual/intellectual function. In those days, students would have been working alone on worksheets, and there would have been little demonstration and explanation by the teacher.

You realize that in your whole visit you haven't heard a single reprimand and that you haven't heard Chris talking about what assignments to do or when to get them done. You have heard her talk about how to do things and why it is important to work hard at learning. The students have been on task and ALT has been high.

During your visit, you may have noticed that there is a student in Chris's class who has Down's syndrome. But that student reads, spells, and does math and social studies as the other students do. The reason is that Chris's focus is on reading, spelling, math, and social studies. The girl with Down's syndrome has just returned from watching a film on menstruation with the other girls in the school.

Manuel is correct. It's a good idea to cover up the old answers, so we don't drag yesterday's errors into today.

## Summary

Instruction, no matter where it occurs, is a complex activity that requires teachers to use a variety of actions to accomplish a variety of functions. However, as we saw in Chris's lessons, these functions and actions need not necessarily be allocated to different time periods. They come in and out according to the flow of the lesson. In the context of a daily lesson, a teacher can cover a topic in many ways. The teacher may utilize routines for explanation, demonstration, and correction that provide drill and independent practice. A complete lesson should never be all explanation or all activities. During a lesson, each action should be utilized and each thought process addressed. This chapter provides in-depth explanations of the sort of instruction that can be used to promote learning of various kinds of information.

# STUDY QUESTIONS

It is the first week of the school year and Audrey Wheeler is sorting the 22 children in her third-grade class into four reading groups. She has administered a standardized test to the entire class and rank-ordered the students according to their scores on the test. Students with higher scores are placed in more advanced curriculum materials. Here is her grouping arrangement. Exhibit 4.5 shows the number ($N$) of students in each group, the level of the curriculum materials each group will use, the number of minutes each day that each group will work directly with her, the number of minutes each group will work with Marcus Miller, a paraprofessional, and the number of minutes each group will be engaged in independent seat work or other self-directed reading activities

**Exhibit 4.5   *Grouping Arrangement Summary.***

| | | | Minutes of Instruction | | |
|---|---|---|---|---|---|
| **Group** | **N** | **Curriculum Level** | Wheeler | Miller | Seat work |
| Tigers | 3 | Grade 4, Book 1 | 15 | 20 | 35 |
| Wolves | 6 | Grade 3, Book 2 | 20 | 25 | 25 |
| Falcons | 10 | Grade 3, Book 1 | 25 | 25 | 20 |
| Bears | 3 | Grade 2, Book 2 | 35 | 25 | 10 |

1. What strategy did Ms. Wheeler use to arrive at her grouping and time allocation arrangement?

2. What instructional approach should Ms. Wheeler use with the Bears? Why?

3. Tell which group(s) would likely benefit *most* from each of the following assignments. More than one group may be selected.

   _____ Explicit instruction that models a strategy for comprehension monitoring.

   _____ Drill and practice with vocabulary words introduced at the beginning of third grade.

   _____ Reading comprehension tasks selected from *USA Today.*

   _____ Explicit instruction with error correction in vocabulary taught at the beginning of third grade.

   _____ Review of vocabulary and decoding skills students are expected to master in the second grade.

4. The first chapter in the book used by the Falcons discusses different types of weather and presents the following new vocabulary words: *sleet, hail, blizzard,* and

*downpour.* Describe the most important activities associated with each of the following teaching functions that Ms. Wheeler should use to teach these new vocabulary words:

- Delivering information
- Asking questions
- Responding to student efforts
- Conducting activities

# SUPPLEMENTAL READINGS

### Peer Tutoring

Fuchs, L. S. (1996). Models of classroom instruction: Implications for children with learning disabilities. In D. L. Speece & B. K. Keogh (Eds.), *Research on Classroom Ecologies: Implications for Inclusion of Children with Learning Disabilities* (pp. 81-90). Mahwah, NJ: Lawrence Erlbaum.

Jenkins, J.R., & Jenkins, L.M. (1988). *Cross-Age and Peer Tutoring: Help for Children with Learning Problems.* Reston, VA: The Council for Exceptional Children.

Meyen, E.L., Vergason, G.A., & Whelan, R.J. (1998). *Educating Students with Mild Disabilities: Strategies and Methods* (2nd ed.). Denver: Love Publishing.

Olson, J.L., & Platt, J.M. (1996). *Teaching Children and Adolescents with Special Needs* (2nd ed.). New Jersey: Prentice-Hall.

Warger, C.L. (1992). *Peer Tutoring: When Working Together Is Better than Working Alone.* Reston, VA: The Council for Exceptional Children.

### Cooperative Learning

Salend, S.J. (1994). *Effective Mainstreaming* (2nd Ed.). New York: Macmillan.

Vernon, D.S., Schumacker, J.B., & Deshler, D.D. (1993). *The SCORE Skills: Social Skills for Cooperative Groups.* Lawrence, KS: Edge Enterprises.

### Teaching Older Students

Lovitt, T., & Horton, S.V. (1991). Adapting textbooks for mildly handicapped adolescents. In G. Stoner, M. Shinn, & H. Walker (Eds.), *Interventions for Achievement and Behavior Problems* (pp. 43-72). National Association of School Psychologists. Washington, D.C.

Sabornie, E.J., & deBettencourt, L.U. (1997). *Teaching Students with Mild Disabilities at the Secondary Level.* New Jersey: Prentice-Hall.

Vogel, S.A., & Adelman, P.B. (1993). *Success for College Students with Learning Disabilities.* New York: Springer-Verlag.

### Computer-Assisted Instruction

Male, M. (1994). *Technology for Inclusion: Meeting the Needs of All Students.* Boston: Allyn and Bacon.

Ray, J., & Warden, K. M. (1995). *Technology, Computers, and the Special Needs Learner.* Albany, NY: Delmar.

# Chapter 5

# *Fundamentals of Evaluation*

*When it's said that something means something, what's meant by that?*
— R. M. Pirsig (1974)

*The guarantee of validity is not in experience itself.*
— B. Brehmer (1986)

Good judgment requires access to good information. Chapters 5–7 cover technical aspects of defining and collecting useful information. These chapters detail how to go about conducting evaluations. Some additional material, particularly the discussion of statistics, are available in the Resource Guide that accompanies this text (Howell et al., 2000a). If you're not current on basic statistics, we encourage you to read this material, as the tools associated with measurement and comparison are central to an understanding of informed decision making. Also, just to make your reading easier, from this point on, the terms **evaluator** and **teacher** will be used to refer to the same people (people like you). That is because, as a teacher, you should carry out *both* the act of evaluating and the act of teaching. The activities may be different, but that doesn't mean that different people are always needed to carry them out.

## Why Evaluate?

The central assumption underlying this entire text is that, when a student is not learning, a teacher or group of teachers working in collaboration must do something to fix the student's learning problem. This process of "fixing the problem" generally is referred to as **programming.** Unfortunately, the term "programming" recently has acquired a somewhat negative connotation, implying something that would be done *to* a student to compel them to behave in a certain way. For example, computers are *programmed* to perform various functions, and cult members must be *deprogrammed* to remove the influences of a charismatic leader. When we use the term *program,* we are **not** referring to something that is done *to* a student to compel them to behave differently. Rather, we are referring to the services and interventions that are provided for a student who is experiencing learning problems. Programming refers to systematic manipulation of pertinent variables in the student's learning environment for the purpose of improving student learning. These variables include all of those discussed in the previous chapters, such as curriculum, instruction, and student prior knowledge.

The actions that need to be taken when developing a student's program, and the thought processes that determine how those actions are carried out, are presented in Exhibit 5.1 (Howell & Davidson, 1997). You may want to use this exhibit to consolidate your understanding of the material presented in Chapters 5, 6, and 7. As you can see, many of the actions in the exhibit require the evaluation of curriculum, student knowledge, and quality of instruction.

## How Does Evaluation Lead to Programming?

Evaluation is the process of making a decision, or reaching a conclusion about student performance, based on information obtained from an assessment, testing, or measurement process. Where assessment is the process of <u>collecting</u> information, evaluation is the process of <u>using</u> information. In this respect, students are not evaluated; rather, data about their performance (scores, results, ratings, etc.) are evaluated. The reason we engage in evaluation is to collect information that will help us make better decisions about what our students need to learn and how we will go about helping them learn it. If we make effective decisions, we will develop effective programs that help students learn what we want them to learn. This idea seems pretty straightforward but, in fact, is fraught with difficulty.

Think about all of the things that could go wrong (and, therefore, *not* result in an effective program). We might collect the wrong information. We might collect inaccurate or misleading information. We might collect the right information but make the wrong decision. We might collect the right information and make correct decisions, but we might not collect enough information or make enough decisions. Or, we might collect too much information and make too many decisions. (That about covers it doesn't it?) In any of these instances, we would likely fail in our attempt to develop an effective program for a student who is not succeeding. In the next few sections of this chapter, we will address some of the considerations that underlie the process in making decisions.

## Is There More to Evaluation Than Measurement?

Evaluation entails a reasoning process that is based on **inference.** Inference is the process of arriving at a logical conclusion from a body of evidence. Inference usually refers to the process of developing a conclusion on the basis of some phenomenon that is not experienced or observed directly by the person drawing the inference. Consider the following example. Imagine you have just whiled away a lazy Saturday afternoon at your favorite bookstore, browsing the travel section and sipping cappuccino. Alas, it is time to go home and catch up on all that work you've been ignoring for the last 3 hours. You wonder if it has started to rain while you have been so pleasantly occupied. How will you find out? You could walk to the front door, step outside, and look up at the sky. If you see raindrops coming down, and you find yourself getting very wet, you might conclude it is raining. Given that this conclusion is based on your own direct observations, it is very likely that you are correct.

On the other hand, you could stay in the travel section and look around at people who have recently come into the store. If most of them seem to have what look like raindrops on their heads and shoulders, you might also conclude it is raining. This inference is not based on your direct observation of raindrops falling from the sky but on indirect evidence you have collected. You

*Exhibit 5.1    Steps in Developing Effective Programs.*

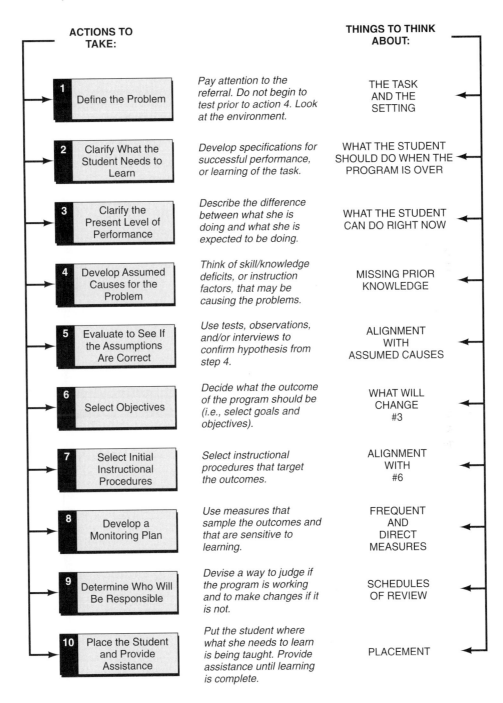

| ACTIONS TO TAKE: | | THINGS TO THINK ABOUT: |
|---|---|---|
| **1** Define the Problem | Pay attention to the referral. Do not begin to test prior to action 4. Look at the environment. | THE TASK AND THE SETTING |
| **2** Clarify What the Student Needs to Learn | Develop specifications for successful performance, or learning of the task. | WHAT THE STUDENT SHOULD DO WHEN THE PROGRAM IS OVER |
| **3** Clarify the Present Level of Performance | Describe the difference between what she is doing and what she is expected to be doing. | WHAT THE STUDENT CAN DO RIGHT NOW |
| **4** Develop Assumed Causes for the Problem | Think of skill/knowledge deficits, or instruction factors, that may be causing the problems. | MISSING PRIOR KNOWLEDGE |
| **5** Evaluate to See If the Assumptions Are Correct | Use tests, observations, and/or interviews to confirm hypothesis from step 4. | ALIGNMENT WITH ASSUMED CAUSES |
| **6** Select Objectives | Decide what the outcome of the program should be (i.e., select goals and objectives). | WHAT WILL CHANGE #3 |
| **7** Select Initial Instructional Procedures | Select instructional procedures that target the outcomes. | ALIGNMENT WITH #6 |
| **8** Develop a Monitoring Plan | Use measures that sample the outcomes and that are sensitive to learning. | FREQUENT AND DIRECT MEASURES |
| **9** Determine Who Will Be Responsible | Devise a way to judge if the program is working and to make changes if it is not. | SCHEDULES OF REVIEW |
| **10** Place the Student and Provide Assistance | Put the student where what she needs to learn is being taught. Provide assistance until learning is complete. | PLACEMENT |

could be wrong. These people may simply have walked under a sprinkler on their way into the store. You could increase your confidence in your inference by collecting more information. For example, you could check your own prior knowledge for additional information to support or refute your inference. You might suddenly remember that you are in Phoenix in July and decide that it is unlikely that it is raining, and, therefore, these people probably walked by a sprinkler; or, you might be in Seattle in February, and the odds are pretty good that it is raining. Finally, you could ask someone "Is it raining out?"

In educational evaluation, we are always concerned with the accuracy of our inferences. We want to make inferences that have a high likelihood of reflecting the true state of affairs. Here are some things to remember about drawing accurate inferences.

1. Inferences based on direct observations are more likely to be accurate than inferences based on indirect evidence.

2. The accuracy of an inference is dependent on the quality of the evidence collected. Remember the old computer-programming adage "garbage in, garbage out." If you base your inferences on silly or irrelevant information, plan to be wrong.

3. The accuracy of an inference is dependent on the *quantity* of evidence collected. In the previous example, when we based our conclusion that "it's raining" on indirect evidence, our confidence in the accuracy of that inference grew with the addition of each new piece of evidence (observe drops of water on other customers, review prior knowledge, ask someone).

4. The greater the costs associated with being wrong, the greater the need for sufficient information of high quality. If the consequences of being wrong aren't too severe, you can afford to collect a little information or use information of questionable quality. On the other hand, if the cost of being wrong is great, you need to collect multiple forms of evidence and use information that is of high quality. Clearly, if

you had worn your favorite $400 wool sweater to the book store, you might be more concerned about getting all wet than if you had worn a raincoat and brought an umbrella.

As with all human endeavors, the quality of people's inferences varies greatly (Nisbett & Ross, 1980) both within and between individuals. Someone might be very good at reasoning in one domain but very poor at reasoning in another. (If you doubt this, think about all those skilled politicians who become embroiled in embarrassing sex scandals.) Similarly, in a particular situation, two people given the same evidence might arrive at very different conclusions. This variation in quality may be introduced by the limitations of measurement tools or by interpretations of evaluators. In the context of educational and psychological evaluation, these two issues are not distinct because the selection of measurement tools also reflects the professional judgment of the individuals doing the evaluation.

Judgment and inference are closely linked. One of the interesting things about judgment is that both good and bad examples of it are based on the same mechanism. That mechanism is the prior knowledge of the person making the inference. This point is illustrated by the example of evaluators *A* and *B* in Exhibit 5.2.

Two different evaluators are presented with the same situation: a student whose reading is slow and inaccurate. Evaluator *A* thought of different things than evaluator *B* because she knew about and believed in different things before the evaluation even started. What one believes before one starts evaluating will affect the inferences she makes as surely as will the student's behavior on assessments. Curriculum-based evaluation (CBE) depends on the evaluator thinking in ways that are consistent with the information presented in those earlier chapters.

The use of good judgment influences the **probability** that the consequences of evaluation and problem solving will be beneficial. It is always important to remember probability. Some factors in students' lives (such as family divorce, moving frequently, drug use, and poor teaching) lower the *probability* that they will learn and get

*Exhibit 5.2    Thought Processes of Two Evaluators.*

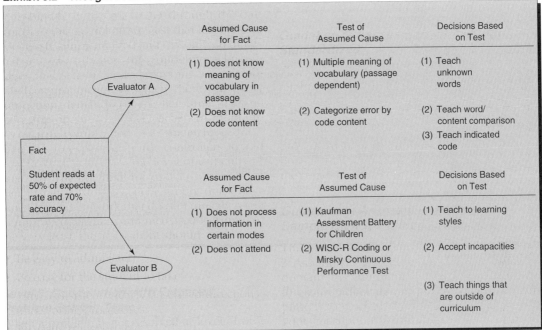

| | Assumed Cause for Fact | Test of Assumed Cause | Decisions Based on Test |
|---|---|---|---|
| **Evaluator A** | (1) Does not know meaning of vocabulary in passage | (1) Multiple meaning of vocabulary (passage dependent) | (1) Teach unknown words |
| | (2) Does not know code content | (2) Categorize error by code content | (2) Teach word/ content comparison |
| | | | (3) Teach indicated code |
| **Fact** | Assumed Cause for Fact | Test of Assumed Cause | Decisions Based on Test |
| Student reads at 50% of expected rate and 70% accuracy | (1) Does not process information in certain modes | (1) Kaufman Assessment Battery for Children | (1) Teach to learning styles |
| | (2) Does not attend | (2) WISC-R Coding or Mirsky Continuous Performance Test | (2) Accept incapacities |
| **Evaluator B** | | | (3) Teach things that are outside of curriculum |

along with others. These factors do not assure student failure, they simply make the odds of failure greater (there are plenty of people reading this book who came from a divorced background, moved around as kids, used drugs, and had poor teachers—but still learned). In a sense, all CBE does is allow teachers and psychologists to introduce new factors into the student's life that *raise* the probability of learning.

One of the most severe limitations affecting the quality of decision making is that humans tend to make consistent and somewhat predictable errors of judgment (Kelley, 1994; Nisbett & Ross, 1980). Because these errors are predictable, we can exercise caution in our decision making to avoid them. Because they are avoidable, we should think of these common errors of judgments as *threats* to inference. Some of these threats are listed in Exhibit 7.4. Look ahead at that exhibit now. As you read the list, think about times your own judgment may have fallen prey to some of the errors of thinking listed.

## Once Again, What Are the Reasons to Evaluate?

**Assessment** is the process of *collecting* a behavior sample. It can be accomplished through review, interview, observation, and/or testing. Evaluation is the process of *using* that information to make a reasoned decision. **Evaluation** is a thoughtful process. We use it to help us understand things. Evaluation has been defined in a variety of ways, all of which have at their core the idea of *comparison*. When we evaluate, we make comparisons between things, note any differences, summarize our findings, and draw conclusions about our results.

A basic model can be used to represent the evaluation process. This model is shown in Exhibit 5.3. In the model, a sample of student behavior is compared with a performance standard, and the discrepancy (difference) between the two is noted (Deno & Mirkin, 1977; Yavorsky, 1977). The behavior represents what the student is doing; the discrepancy represents how much the student's behavior must change to match the performance standard. If, for example, a student is expected to read 140 words per minute in material selected from his reading curriculum, but only reads 35 words per minute, there is a 105-word-per-minute discrepancy in reading behavior. Progress standards, such as "the student will improve by 25% per week" also can be specified.

Three primary reasons for making comparisons will be discussed in this book: screening, problem solving, and monitoring.

**Screening** is a kind of evaluation used to recognize the potential existence of problems or to sort students into instructional groupings. Screening usually entails brief sampling of many students to identify those that are widely discrepant from the rest on some dimension. For example, a teacher might ask all of her third-grade students to read aloud for 1 minute from a passage selected from the reading curriculum. Based on the number of words each student reads correct, the teacher would sort students into instructional groups and also identify those whose performance was so discrepant as to warrant further investigation.

**Problem-solving evaluation** is conducted to inform decision making about what and how to teach. Problem-solving evaluations typically include two types of assessment, survey and specific, as well as a variety of decision-making steps. Survey-level assessment is roughly analogous to screening, except that instead of testing many students on a single behavior, the evaluator tests a single student on many related behaviors. The result is identification of those behaviors that may or may not require further investigation. Specific-level assessment involves in-depth analysis of a narrow range of behaviors in a particular domain.

**Monitoring** is conducted to see if the solutions generated through problem solving are successful. Monitoring involves the collection of information on a repeated basis over time to see if the student is showing adequate growth toward a particular goal. Both monitoring and screening can, and should, be carried out through the use of General Outcome Measures (GOM).

**Exhibit 5.3    The Comparison Model.**

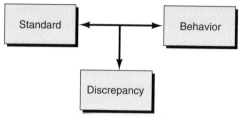

Here is an example that shows the general differences among these three evaluations.

Ms. Williams is a fourth-grade teacher. In September, she conducts a reading screening by asking all of her students to read aloud for 1 minute from a passage selected from the reading book typically used by the middle reading group at the beginning of the year. All students read the same passage under the same testing conditions. She then sorts students into groups based on the number of words each student reads aloud. Those students who read very few words correct in the passage are identified for further examination.

Next, Ms. Williams conducts a survey-level assessment with each of these students by asking them to read several more passages from other levels in the curriculum. She also asks them to complete a test of reading comprehension that requires students to read a passage from the curriculum in which every fifth word is replaced by a blank and the student must select the correct word to fill in the blank (from among three choices). Based on an analysis of the errors and correct answers exhibited on the survey-level assessment, Ms. Williams conducts a more in-depth, specific-level assessment with each child to identify areas of prior reading knowledge that may be missing and, therefore, contributing to the child's reading difficulty. For some students, this specific-level assessment may focus on decoding knowledge; for others, it may focus on vocabulary or strategic knowledge. Specific assessment procedures are selected for each child, based on Ms. Williams's hypothesis about what may be causing the child to have reading problems.

From the results of the specific-level assessment, Ms. Williams selects annual goals for each of her low-performing readers and designs programs intended to help each student reach individual goals. On a weekly basis, Ms. Williams monitors the progress of each student. She asks each student to read aloud for 1 minute from a passage that reflects the student's annual goal. If the student consistently reads more words correct (is making progress), Ms. Williams decides that his instructional program is effective. If the student is not making adequate progress, Ms. Williams decides to adjust the program.

## How Is the Adequacy of Scores Evaluated?

It is not enough to derive scores. We must know how to determine if the scores are adequate. To make this determination, we must compare the individual's status to a legitimate performance or progress standard. These standards are extremely important because an inappropriate standard can lead to inappropriate decisions. Just as a test that inaccurately represents a student's knowledge is of limited value, a standard that inaccurately represents what that knowledge *should be* also is of limited value. Because of this, whenever someone tells you that they know of a kid who is unusual, or special, you should get in the habit of responding "As compared to what?"

Most of us are familiar with two types of standards: *norms* and *performance criteria.* Normative standards are used when we are interested in the way a student's score compares with other students (above average, below average, way below average). Performance criteria are used when we are interested in the way a student's status compares with the requirements of a particular task (can he read the directions well enough to assemble the class's new computer?). These standards define the criteria for acceptable performance (CAP). Once a student meets CAP, instruction is no longer needed.

In the previous example, Ms. Williams used a normative standard during screening to sort students into groups and to identify those whose oral reading fluency was very discrepant from their peers. Ms. Williams used performance criteria during specific-level and survey-level assessment

to decide whether her low-performing readers needed individualized programming.

Norm-referenced samples (NRS) and criterion-referenced samples (CRS) compare (reference) scores with either norms or criteria. If norms or criteria are not available, there is nothing to which the scores can be referenced, so the scores are essentially meaningless. In such a case, evaluation is impossible. Norms and criteria must be formally established and their relationship to decision making validated for them to be useful. This process is called **standardization.**

The term *standardized* test can have two meanings. One is that the test was developed to be administered in a standard fashion. This means a manual with administration guidelines must be available. The second meaning is that standards have been established following some type of standardization activity. In this case, technical information must be available describing the procedures followed to set the standards. There is a tendency to use the term *standardized test* as if it were synonymous with published or norm-referenced tests. This is a mistake. Criterion-referenced samples also need to be **standardized.**

To use an NRS to determine how a student compares with his peers, you obviously need a measure of the peers' behavior. The way to obtain these measures is to gather a representative group of the student's peers and review, interview, observe, or test to get a sample and summarize the performance of the group. This group is called the standardization sample. This process of assessing and summarizing group scores is called **norming.** Given this summary of the group's behavior, you can see how any individual's performance compares with the group. In discussions of sampling, the key concept is representative because it is the selection of the standardization sample that, by definition, separates NRS and CRS.

A representative sample used in the standardization of an NRS should include a relatively large number of individuals at each age or grade level. To ensure that the sample is representative, it may be carefully controlled to include the appropriate proportions of male/female, majority/minority, high/low socioeconomic status, and urban/rural students. These individuals are selected with no attention paid to their skill or knowledge in the domain being tested. Indeed, the standardization group for an NRS should be chosen at random from the population to *ensure* an even distribution of skills. Ideally, the standardization group for the NRS would include people who represent the entire range of skills or knowledge being tested from having "none at all" to having "as much as possible." For example, if you wanted to standardize a math test for use with students applying to a college of education, you would not go to the Massachusetts Institute of Technology for your norming sample. Average MIT freshmen might have superior interest and training in math. If your test were standardized on this group, it would have limited value because the norms would describe people who did not apply to a college of education.

In direct contrast, the criterion-referenced sample need only include a small number of individuals with no attention to minority status, socioeconomic status, or home setting. These individuals may differ widely according to age or grade. However, they all would have one thing in common—the very thing the NRS tried to avoid. All the people in the CRS sample should have the skill or knowledge being tested. This is important, because a CRS is used to assess whether a student has a particular skill. A random sample can't be used here because students picked by chance might not have the skill. For example, if we wanted to find out how well a student must know the steps to writing an essay, we would construct an essay measure and then give it to a group of students skilled at essays. The middle (median) score of this skilled standardization group would become the criterion for acceptable performance. This CAP is the standard, or criterion, for a CRS. If we chose students at random, we would probably include some who do not do well on essays. Therefore their performance on the essay exam would lower the group score.

Notice the difference between the standardization samples in the two types of measures. On the norm-referenced math test for college applicants, we didn't want to pick a select group of successful math students. We were looking for

the typical applicants. On the criterion-referenced essay writing test, we wanted to pick a select group of students who had the skill being measured. This is the essential difference between the two types of assessments: NRS assessments reference student behavior to norms for the purpose of comparison with a group, whereas CRS assessments reference student behavior to behavioral criteria to guide teaching. Obviously, a criterion-referenced test is worthless if the criterion is arbitrarily established or completely missing. Unfortunately, this is the case for many published tests that claim to be *criterion-referenced*. Assessments that are only keyed to content should be called content-referenced, not criterion-referenced.

## What About Individual Comparisons?

There is one last type of standard that is particularly important in special/remedial education. However, this type of standard is so unfamiliar to most people it doesn't even have a widely accepted name. We're going to call it the **idiosyncratic** standard. The term "idiosyncratic," as it is used here, does not mean peculiar or quirky; it means individual. Whereas norms compare students with groups and CAP with tasks, the idiosyncratic standard compares a student with himself. Exhibit 1.3 presented idiosyncratic data illustrating a student's progress while learning a task. These kind of data can be used to decide if one approach to instruction is superior to another because the student's progress under one teaching technique can be compared with his progress under different teaching. In this case, the comparison is not "student versus group" or "student versus task." Rather, it is student versus himself. Exhibit 5.4 also shows an example of an idiosyncratic standard. However, in this case, an additional comparison is being made. The student's current performance is being compared with previous performance to see if he is showing growth. In addition, his performance is being compared with an aimline that represents a goal rate and level of performance. When his performance is below this line, he is not on target to meet his long-term goal, and an instructional change must be considered.

Return again to our previous example of Ms. Williams, the fourth-grade teacher. She used idiosyncratic standards to evaluate whether each of her low-performing reading students were making progress toward their particular annual goal. The data she collected during this monitoring process would resemble those shown in Exhibit 1.3 and in Exhibit 5.4.

## Some Measurement Fundamentals

The comparison of a student's behavior with a standard is central to the process of evaluation. There are many ways to make such comparisons, but they all require that the behavior be **operationally** defined through measurement. **Measurement** is the assignment of numerical values to objects or events according to rules (Campbell, 1940). Measurement is a tool used to summarize a student's behavior, or products of behavior, in manageable terms (scores) so that comparison can take place. The characteristics of measurement are critical to evaluation. Before looking closely at the measurement process, here is a *brief* review of some central measurement concepts and terms that will be referred to throughout the remainder of the text.

An **overlay** procedure is one that can be applied to nearly any content area. Overlays are simply measurement rules. Overlay procedures don't include materials as these rules can be used on any sample of tasks related to the instructional goal.

**Curriculum-based measurement** (CBM) is a specific set of overlay procedures for collecting and evaluating student performance using the student's own curriculum materials. CBM employs short, direct measures of student behavior that usually are interpreted using rate or fluency scores. CBM overlay procedures have been extensively researched and are a very effective means for monitoring student growth toward long-term goals.

**Curriculum-based evaluation** (CBE) is a set of comparison and decision-making rules grounded in an awareness, and analysis, of the

**Exhibit 5.4   A Student's Progress Compared with His Aim.**

things the student is expected to learn. CBE is carried out to increase the learning of students by improving teaching decisions. CBE often depends upon the use of CBM to collect the data required for decisions. These data are then used in conjunction with a set of "rules" that are based on the assumptions about learning, curriculum, and instruction that were presented in Chapters 1–4 of this text.

**Knowledge** and the **display of knowledge** are two different things. Often, students know something but can't display their knowledge through a particular assessment procedure. When we conduct an assessment, we are trying to find out what the student *knows*, not just what he can *display.* **Behavior** and **products** are not knowledge. Educational evaluators are primarily interested in measuring children's prior knowledge (skills, thought processes, and attitudes). Although none of these is directly observable, we can draw inferences about them from the way students behave and the products they produce.

Many behaviors are **overt** (observable) and are assumed to be brought about by thought processes that are **covert** (not readily observable). Because we depend on observed behavior to make inferences about thought processes, our conclusions will always be threatened by the imperfect correspondence between the overt (behavior), the covert (actual knowledge), and the occasional reluctance of students to display what they know.

The **critical effect** is the product left after a behavior has occurred. "Problems completed" is the critical effect of the overt behavior "writes answers." In some cases, the critical effect of a student's behavior may actually include someone else's behavior. For example, the grade a student earns on an assignment, or the rank he is given on a rubric, reflects the behavior and thought process of the teacher who did the grading. Similarly, a detention note for inappropriate behavior, while not created by the student, may show up in a review of records.

**Sampling** is the act of selecting a few behaviors, products, or times from a domain of interest. Some domains of knowledge, ability, or attitude are so large that it is impossible to measure every item. Therefore, we must sample and draw inferences from the items selected.

A **score** is a numerical summation of the student's overt behavior, covert behavior, state, or product. A score is not the same as a grade. Grades often are highly subjective, reflective of very broad categories of behavior, and often tell more about teacher attitudes and opinions than student performance. Grades and grade-equivalent scores are almost useless as a measurement tool. Whereas other scores also may be derived through a somewhat subjective process, if they are more narrowly focused on a specific sample of behavior they will result in more measurement, not opinion.

**Standards** are expectations. As explained above, they provide benchmarks against which the quality of a person's performance or progress can be judged. The data collected through reviews, interviews, observations, and tests must be compared with standards before they can be interpreted. **Criteria** are standards that specify the level of acceptable task performance.

**Tests** are sets of circumstances arranged to promote particular behaviors (you know what tests are).

**Observations** are time intervals set aside to watch for particular behaviors.

A **probe** is an interview, test, or observation procedure. It is the material or time interval used to sample a very specific behavior or area of knowledge. In this text, the term probe will often be used to refer to any criterion-referenced sampling procedure.

**Portfolios** are samples of student behavior collected over time rather than during a single testing situation. In this respect, portfolios involve some element of repeated measurement. Portfolios usually sample tasks regularly performed in class. Data in portfolios are generated

from multiple procedures, under a variety of stimulus and response conditions, all of which sample a single domain. Portfolios should contain at least two different "levels" of data: raw data and summarizing data (Valencia, 1990). Therefore, different inferences may be valid for each type of data, and the evaluation standard must be specified. Usually, material is selected for inclusion in the portfolio through a process that involves at least some degree of student participation.

**Status sheets** are lists of skills. They are used to summarize what is currently known about the student to avoid unneeded testing and observation. By using the lists to mark skills that the student clearly does—or does not—have, the teacher reduces the number of things that must be assessed.

Finally, **rubrics** are a lot like status sheets. They are generally lists of content accompanied by a rating scale that the teacher uses to mark off, or rate, what a student knows.

## What Exactly Is Measurement?

**Measurement** is limited to the *characteristics* of things. People, and the products they produce, have physical and behavioral characteristics that can be observed and measured. However, you should never assume that scores based on even the most thorough measurement procedure can actually summarize the total person. The results of every measurement should be interpreted not only in terms of what is summarized but also in terms of what is *not* summarized.

This point can be observed by noting that many different outwardly observable behaviors may indicate the same thought process. For example, Exhibit 5.5 shows that a student's knowledge of addition may be indicated by several behaviors. Whereas a student who can only perform one of these responses is assumed to know less than a student who can carry out all four, the student who performs any one of the responses has still demonstrated *some* knowledge of addition.

Just as many behaviors and critical effects can indicate the same thought process, many

*Exhibit 5.5    Various Item Formats.*

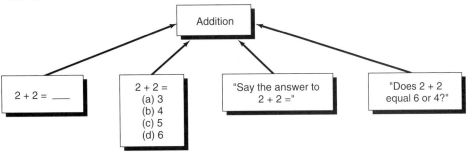

different thought processes can result in the same behavior. This means that there is more than one way to get a correct or incorrect answer. For example, suppose a test requires two students to solve this problem:

$$50$$
$$+\ 43$$

One student might work the problem by following the standard addition algorithm (0 + 3 = 3, 5 + 4 = 9). The other, realizing that both numbers together will approach 100, could solve it this way: 43 is 7 less than 50, 50 + 50 = 100, 100 − 7 = 93. These two students will both write "93," but they have arrived at the answer by applying very different computation strategies. Although both students probably know the addition algorithm, we might assume that only the second student knows how to solve problems by rounding and subtracting. However, this is a hypothesis that would need to be checked.

### How Are Large Domains Sampled?

Some domains have so many elements that any attempt to test all of them would take so long that the student would die of old age before the measurement was complete. For this reason, it is necessary to use a sampling process. Sampling involves systematic selection of items from a domain to ensure that a measurement procedure fairly represents it. For example, if we were interested in finding out whether a child could read the entire list of 500 words that occur most frequently in third-grade reading curricula, we could present that list to a child and keep track of

how many words the child was skilled enough to read aloud. This would be an exhaustive but time-consuming measurement process. Instead, we could randomly choose a sample of 25 words from the list, ask the child to read them aloud, and then make an inference about the likelihood that he could read the other 475 words on the list, based on his accuracy in reading our 25-word sample.

The procedure used to select the items, products, or times included in a sample influences the usefulness of a measure and the quality of our inferences. Although several items may indicate knowledge in an area, some are better indicators of that knowledge than others. For example, supplying the names of coins and selecting objects of equal value are both indicators of knowing about money. However, "selecting objects of equal value" is probably a more meaningful behavior than supplying names.

If a student does well on a sample, the evaluator infers that the student will do well within the domain from which the sample was taken. In Exhibit 5.6, four items have been sampled, and an eighth-grade student has passed only two. This leads to the inference that the student knows only half of what he should know about math. But to accept that this conclusion, based on four items, applies to the thousands of math items an eighth-grader is expected to have learned is to place great faith in those four items. However, educators do this sort of thing all of the time when they interpret scores from achievement tests that include only a few items at each grade level.

*Exhibit 5.6    Sampling.*

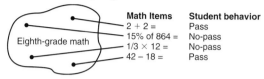

Items may also be memorized. Once, Dr. Howell was giving a popular achievement test to some students in a correctional institution. When he paused too long between spelling words, one of the students in the group supplied the next word—and the exact sample sentence in the manual—from memory!

If your purpose is to use the results of a sample to make teaching decisions, the number of items (remember these are not just written test items, they may also be interview questions and observation intervals) required to adequately represent a domain depends in part on the cohesiveness, or *consolidation,* of the domain from which the sample is taken. If the domain is composed of items that are very dissimilar from one another (for example, capital cities of states), the student's response on one item will say little about his likely response on another; therefore, *every* item of importance should be tested. If the domain is too large to allow testing of every item, *randomly* select a number large enough to allow generalization from the sample to the domain.

If the items in the domain share many stimulus and response properties, or if the domain is *consolidated* by a common set of underlying strategies or rules, generalizations are easier to draw. Therefore, fewer items are needed as a basis for making an inference.

### How Does Item Sampling Relate to Scoring?

The size and definition of the units reflected by any individual score will vary according to the **scoring rules** employed to obtain it. This is important because it controls how much meaningful information can be ascertained through a single measurement and conveyed by a single score. You never want to use scoring rules that

yield scores that are insensitive to learning. Such data will have limited utility. Sensitivity is required if the scores are to be used to make precise and timely decisions. This sensitivity is obtained by finding assessment procedures and scoring rules that complement what you are teaching.

To be functional, scoring rules must have certain characteristics. For example, they must:

- assign scores to "units" of student behavior that are known to represent units of knowledge;

- be sensitive enough to reflect any *educationally important* differences in the quality of knowledge (among students, between a student and CAP, or between previous and current measurements of the same student); and

- be easy to use.

Remember, with curriculum-based measures, you may be working with measurement concepts with which you are unfamiliar. For example, most of us are used to the idea that the behavior-sampling technique and the scoring rules used to summarize how well someone does on that technique are permanently linked (in other words, you always score the same test the same way). But that may not be the case. It is possible to use any number of scoring rules to summarize the same student behavior. Which one you choose depends on your purpose and on the nature of the decision you are trying to make.

Dr. Howell was once talking with a group of teachers about the evaluation of written expression, and Dr. Jerry Tindal was sitting in on the presentation. The group had covered many of the standard scoring rules presented in Chapter 11 of this text, but there was some concern that we had not yet hit upon a scoring process that provided good information about selecting objectives to improve the way students managed the ideas, or themes, of their writing. So, during the discussion, Dr. Tindal created a new set of rules for scoring a writing sample.

In this case, the assessment had consisted of an assignment to write about ". . . a moment I'll never forget." One particular student had responded to this prompt by writing about an ice-skating incident. In the passage, she had used 18 transition words ("one day," "when," "after that"), 19 words about an ice-skating incident ("practice," "ice," "tripped"), and 8 words that dealt with memory ("so embarrassed," "never again"). Tindal's simple scoring rule and the student's scores are shown in Exhibit 5.7.

An examination of these scores led to some obvious conclusions about the passage. First, it was well structured and organized (18 of the total words written had been allocated to that). But the student had failed to address the assignment adequately because she got sidetracked and wrote more words (19) on the incident that prompted the memory than she wrote on the topic of forgetting and memory itself (8 words). The passage told the reader plenty about what had been remembered but not much about why that event was memorable. It was a nicely organized passage with lots of "reporting" but showed little "insight." The conclusion of the group was that this student should be taught to maintain focus on her central ideas and decrease her coverage of examples.

That same writing sample could have been scored for other dimensions of writing such as punctuation, grammar, letter formation, syntactic errors, or "use of words from this week's vocabulary lesson." Each of these alternatives would have changed the *definition* of the scores. The writing sample also could have been scored using a different-sized unit of writing such as letters, words, phrases, or paragraphs. This would have changed the *sensitivity* of the scores. Each variation of a scoring rule would yield different information and probably would have lead to different opinions about what a student needs to be taught.

Inherent in the use of scores is the idea that something can be represented by a number value. The notion that measurement summarizes behavior is obviously true of pencil-and-paper tests, but many other types of behavior, skills, or knowledge also can be summarized by scores. For example, the intricacy and expression of ice-skating routines are reduced to scores by Olympic judges. Remember that measurement

**Exhibit 5.7 Tindal's Simple Scoring Rules and Student Scores.**

| Tindal's Scoring Rule | Example from the "Moment I'll Never Forget" Assignment |
|---|---|
| Count total words then decide how many pertain to— | 158 words |
| • Transition and sequence | 18 words (11%) |
| • The assigned main idea (memory and forgetting) | 8 words (5%) |
| • The incident being remembered | 19 words (12%) |

**Exhibit 5.8 Two Scoring Procedures.**

Item Scoring

(a)   3
     + 2
      5

(b)   838
    +282
    1120

Score=<u>2</u>

Addition Scoring

(a)   3
     + 2
      5

(b)   838
    + 282
    1120

Score=<u>6</u>

involves assigning numerals to objects and events according to rules.

It is critical to understand that scores don't just reflect information about the student, they also reflect the measurement rules used to derive the scores. As stated above, different rules applied to the same event can produce different scores. For example, two addition problems scored according to two different rules are shown in Exhibit 5.8.

Using the *item-scoring* rule, if a student gets both problems correct, he gets a score of 2, although in reality, problem (b) contains five times as much addition behavior as problem (a). Using the *addition-scoring* rule, a point is given each time the student correctly adds one number to another. The resulting score of 6 describes the student's addition behavior better than a score of 2.

On a pretest, using the item-scoring rule, a student saying that the answer to problem (b) is 9 would get a score of −1 for that item. If later he retook the test and gave an answer of 2110, he would still get −1 even though that answer shows considerable improvement in addition. Therefore, the *item-scoring* rule is less sensitive to learning. Because learning is operationally defined as change, measurement rules that are sensitive to change are the best rules to use. This sensitivity is usually obtained by assigning a number to the smallest educationally meaningful unit of behavior that is to be changed during instruction. For example, as seen above, if one is teaching addition, the number is better assigned to *acts of addition* than to the *number of problems* completed. However, this does not mean that instruction needs to target small and isolated units. Remember, most things are best taught in a larger context.

## What Makes a Good Measure?

Whenever we select a tool we are interested in its quality. If we buy a car we want to know about its safety features and fuel economy; if we buy a radio we want to know about its reception and sound; if we select a measure of student behavior we want to know about its reliability and validity. In measurement terms, **reliability** means consistency. Knowing that a test is reliable means knowing that it will work the same way every time it is given or on every student to whom it is given. In distinction, **validity** has to do with the quality of the decisions we make that are based on the measure. If a test actually provides the kind of information we think it is supposed to provide, the validity of our inferences is increased. It is possible for a measure to be reliable but not result in valid decision making. However, if a measure is unreliable, we can never be sure the decisions we make that are based on that measure are valid. Therefore, reliability is necessary but not sufficient for validity.

**Exhibit 5.9    The Effect of Error.**

|        | True Score | Error Score |   | Truth in Obtained Score |
|--------|------------|-------------|---|-------------------------|
| Test A | .75        | .25         | = | .50–.75                 |
| Test B | .60        | .40         | = | .20–.60                 |

Reliability is easier to document. Proving reliability only requires showing that something is consistent, not good. An automobile that never starts is reliable. It may not take you anywhere but you can depend on how it will function. Documenting validity, however, requires establishing a relationship between the assessment and some other indicator of reality. This "reality," of course, is difficult to pin down. Validating a test can be like interviewing people leaving an Arnold Schwarzenegger movie. Opinions vary.

To understand reliability and validity, you must understand the thing that makes an assessment unreliable or invalid. That thing is **error.** Error can be the result of imprecise measurement or imperfect inference. Because all measurement requires some level of inference and contains some degree of imprecision, it is unreasonable to expect any measure to be 100% error-free.

All obtained scores (what you get after the test, review, interview, or observation is done) are composed of two components: truth and error. We can illustrate the relationship of truth and error in the form of two equations, as shown in Exhibit 5.9.

Adding error to a true score is like adding a negative number. For the equations to balance, any increase in error must be offset by a decrease in our vision of truth. Therefore, 25 points of error may decrease the truth in the obtained score by as much as 25 points.

Error is anything that affects a score other than the quality targeted for measurement. Error may arise from many sources, but labeling a thing as error does not mean it is bad or even unimportant. It only means it is not what the item in question was designed to measure. For

example, suppose a teacher has designed a history test that includes the following item:
Circle the correct letter:
1. The first man on the moon was

    a. John Glenn

    b. Glenn Ford

    c. Neil Bush

    d. Neil Armstrong

This item would seem to be a valid measure of the student's recall of history. However, it also measures the student's skill at reading, following directions, and drawing circles. To the extent that a student does not perform these tasks, requiring their use during measurement becomes a potential source of error. Does a student need to know how to read to display his knowledge of the first man to touch the moon? No. Therefore, even though reading is an important skill, the dependence of this history test item on reading is a possible source of error.

An assessment procedure is sufficiently valid if it correctly describes reality well enough for us to accomplish our purpose. As already indicated, validity may be hard to establish when opinions about "truth" vary. Validity is even harder to establish when truth itself varies. (What is happening can change, just as our opinions about what is happening can change.) When reality fluctuates rapidly because of changes in the targeted domain, learning, fatigue, or the intrusion of observers, validity is very hard to pin down. This is frequently the case when educators are attempting to get a look at a student's status on a short-term instructional objective. A student's skill and knowledge may change quickly in the presence of instruction. This is one reason it is good to shift to progress data when trying to illustrate learning.

### Must All Tests Be Reliable and Valid?

People talk about the "reliability and validity of assessments" as if those things are characteristics of the instruments themselves. When you hear things like "the test is valid" or "the test-retest reliability is 0.89," you can almost imagine that at some critical point in the publishing process

someone yells "OK, bring in the validity" and in response someone else (probably a reliable worker) comes running in from the next room with a bucket of validity and pours it into the ink. *But it isn't in the test.*

Both reliability and validity are determined by having students or experts interact with the assessments. Reliability, for example, may be established by having a group of students take the same test twice to see if they get the same score both times (this type of reliability is known as *test-retest reliability*). Validity may be established by asking experts to examine the test to see if it is measuring important material. Therefore, our impressions of reliability and validity also come from how these students or experts behave. The important point (often forgotten) is that the resulting statements about reliability and validity say as much about those people as they say about the tests. The results of a validation study done on 8-year-old students may have little similarity to the results of a study using the same test on 18-year-old students. Always remember that conclusions about reliability and validity cannot be safely generalized (applied) to populations that differ along important variables from those populations used in the validation studies. Some of the population variables to be aware of are disability, age, gender, language status, socioeconomic status, geographic location, and especially differences in educational background that may have influenced prior knowledge of the task.

### Are There Different Types of Reliability and Validity?

Although many discussions of reliability and validity list various types (content validity, concurrent validity, predictive validity, construct validity, alternative form reliability, test-retest reliability, and internal consistency), there is only one quality of reliability, and that is *consistency*. Similarly, there is only one quality of validity, and that is *goodness*. All of the other "types" are actually derived from the purpose of the assessment (Messick, 1995). If the purpose of the test is to predict, then "predictive validity" seems of interest. If the purpose is to see if the trait being measured is stable over time, then "test-retest reliability" seems important. Everything in evaluation depends on a thorough understanding of purpose.

In the absence of validity data (or even in their presence), a teacher/evaluator should sit down with the assessment and carefully review it in terms of the purpose for which it will be used. Some guidelines for judging an assessment's quality will be given in a minute. But ultimately you must look at the items and ask yourself, "Does this assessment do what I need it to do?"

When reviewing a measure, one must rely on data and not on tradition or marketing influences. That is because there is one "type" of validity that seems unrelated to goodness. This is *cash* validity. Tests that sell well have high cash validity (Dick & Hagerty, 1971). Apparently, it is possible to have high cash validity in the absence of goodness because best-selling tests are not necessarily the most useful (Reschly et al., 1986). It is important, as consumers, for educators to critically examine the specifications of the tools they use. (Cash validity, by the way, is the only kind that can exist in the absence of reliability.)

## What Assessment Procedures Do Evaluators Commonly Use?

Exhibit 5.10 shows a matrix produced by overlapping common assessment procedures with domains of information. This matrix was developed by the Heartland Education Agency, (1998) and is presented for a couple of reasons. First, it introduces the various ways evaluators collect information and the various sources of information they target. Second, the matrix gives a good impression of "comprehensive" evaluation. This second point is particularly important because it is a mistake to think that the process of evaluation depends solely on giving tests to students. As you can see in the matrix, there are multiple assessment procedures and multiple domains to sample.

The four categories of **assessment procedures** most commonly applied in education and psychology are listed across the top of the matrix. These are sometimes referred to by the acronym

**RIOT:** *Review* products, records, and history; *Interview* teachers, parents, and students; *Observe* the setting, instruction, and student; and *Test* the student's prior knowledge and fixed abilities.

Just as assessment procedures are not limited to testing, **assessment domains** are not limited to the student. As you can see in Exhibit 5.10, a comprehensive evaluation is based on an analysis of multiple domains of information. These include *Instruction; Curriculum;* learning *Environment;* and the *Learner.*

## How Does the Timing of an Evaluation Affect Decision Making?

There are two general evaluation strategies that educators can use to guide decision making: **summative** and **formative** (Bloom et al., 1981). All of the ideas about inference, measurement, and comparison apply equally to both, and many of the same assessments can be used with either approach. However, the traditional measures we are most familiar with (classroom achievement and aptitude tests) are used almost exclusively for summative evaluation. Here are the key distinctions between these two approaches to evaluation.

- Summative evaluation occurs *after* teaching and learning have taken place. Summative evaluation is employed to measure the end result (product) of instruction (in classrooms, summative evaluation is typically carried out to grade students). Summative evaluation is useful for deciding *what* to teach.

- Formative evaluation is used to illustrate the process of learning. Formative evaluation is useful for making decisions about how to teach. Formative evaluation attempts to examine learning *as skills are being formed.*

Have you ever had trouble learning something in school? (If not, keep it to yourself.) If so, who noticed the problem first—you or the teacher? That question has been asked of hundreds of adults and children. In almost every case, the answer was that they, as the student, were aware of the problem long before the teacher. That is because students are aware of

Exhibit 5.10    R.I.O.T. Assessment Matrix.

| Domains | R (Review) | I (Interview) | O (Observe) | T (Test) |
|---|---|---|---|---|
| **I** Instruction | Permanent products (written pieces, tests, worksheets, projects) | Teachers' thoughts about their use of effective teaching and evaluation practices, such as checklists | Effective teaching practices, teacher expectations, antecedent conditions, consequences | Classroom environment scales, checklists and questionnaires; student opinions about instruction and teacher |
| **C** Curriculum | Permanent products (books, worksheets, materials, curriculum guides, scope & sequences) | Teacher & relevant personnel regarding philosophy (generative vs. supplantive), district implementation and expectations | Classroom work, alignment of assignments (curriculum materials) with goals and objectives (curriculum); alignment of teacher talk with curriculum | Level of assignment and curriculum material difficulty; opportunity to learn; student opinions about what is being taught |
| **E** Environment | School rules and policies | Ask relevant personnel, students & parents about behavior management plans, class rules, class routines | Student, peers and instruction; interactions and causal relationships; distractions and health/safety violations | Classroom environment scales, checklists and questionnaires; student opinions about instruction, peers, and teacher |
| **L** Learner | District records Health records Error analysis Records for: educational history, onset & duration of the problem, teacher perceptions of the problem, pattern of behavior problems, etc. | Relevant personnel, parents, peers, & students (what do they think they are supposed to do; how do they perceive the problem?) | Target behaviors— dimensions and nature of the problem | Student performance; find the discrepancy between setting demands (instructions, curriculum, and environment) and student performance |

learning on a daily basis, whereas the teacher often only becomes informed after giving a test in a summative evaluation process. Students have a formative view of their own learning.

When teachers gather formative information during the teaching/learning process, growth patterns are visible to the teacher as well as to the student. Formative evaluation is critical to evaluation in special/remedial education. Information about how to do formative evaluation will be presented throughout the text. However, we are going to provide the rationale for its use here.

Recall that in Chapter 1 we presented a description of students who have learning problems. These students were described as having lower rates of learning, or progress, through the curriculum (as illustrated in Exhibit 5.4). If a student's problem is inadequate progress, then instructional interventions that improve progress should solve that problem. Because student progress through the curriculum is directly determined by the instruction received, timely information about progress, and the impact of various program modifications on it, is essential to the teacher. This information is provided by formative evaluation. The procedures for collecting this information are more easily understood if the distinction between performance and progress is clear.

**Performance** refers to how well a person does something. A person's current performance on a task can be shown by her position on the vertical (behavior) axis of charts like the ones shown in Exhibit 5.11.

A performance level can be determined with as little as one summative measurement of the target behavior. The performance level is noted by simply giving a test (or taking an observation) and recording the student's score. For example, in Exhibit 5.11, the score reported is 40. (Note that the vertical axis always represents descriptions of skill or behavior, whereas the horizontal axis always represents the passage of time.)

Now look at Exhibit 5.12. As seen in Exhibit 5.12, if a performance standard (CAP) is 80 correct per minute, and the student works at a rate of 40 per minute, there is a discrepancy between the performance and the standard that can be summed up by saying "The student is only

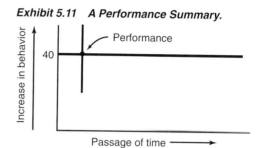

Exhibit 5.11    A Performance Summary.

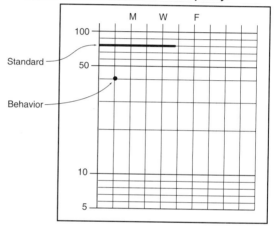

Exhibit 5.12    A Performance Discrepancy.

doing half what he should be doing and needs to move along the behavioral axis by going from 40 to 80." That's a summative statement.

A performance discrepancy tells both where the student is (40) and where he should be (80). Unfortunately, this sort of summative statement gives no information about where the student is actually going, so an evaluator can't tell by looking at Exhibit 5.12 if the student is getting better, worse, or staying the same. Performance data can only tell us that instruction is needed (so they are useful for deciding what to teach). For this reason, performance data are sometimes referred to as **static** data, meaning they do not show movement. These are the kinds of data with which educators are most familiar, as they are derived from single administrations of a test, usually after instruction already has taken place.

Learning **progress** can be displayed by simultaneously summarizing changes along both the vertical (behavior) and horizontal (time) axes of a chart. It is not possible to note progress without also noting performance because progress is a change in performance over time. Therefore, progress cannot be determined with a single datum. Several data points are needed to determine progress adequately and, although no fixed number is required, the validity of progress statements increases with both the number and quality of the data points upon which they are based.

Exhibit 5.13 shows several data points. Each data point represents a performance score obtained by giving the same (or equivalent) measure at different times. If identical, or equivalent, curriculum-based assessments were repeated daily; the differences in performance from day to day can be attributed to learning. As seen in Exhibit 5.13, there is clearly acceleration up the chart. This progression in a particular direction (it could be up, down, or flat) is called **trend.** Trend has more stability than the individual data points used to establish trend because over time, day-to-day variability will average out. Two different students with two different trends would be thought of as learning (progressing) at different rates.

Progress data also have little meaning without an aim or standard. If the standard is an increase of 40 per minute in 1 week (five instructional days) and the student only increases 20, then he is progressing at a lower rate than desired. As seen in Exhibit 5.13, this unacceptable rate of progress produces a performance deficit of 20 per minute in only 1 week. If the student's behavior remains at 40 for the entire week, no progress (change in behavior) is noted. If the student's behavior decreases, then he is "progressing" away (decelerating) from the standard. In this context, progress only means change; it does not necessarily mean improvement.

Because learning is indicated by a change in behavior across time, it can be seen in the progress of the student toward a performance objective. This is formative information, and it is important because progress data are uniquely suited to deciding how to teach. Progress data tell you where the student is and, more important, where

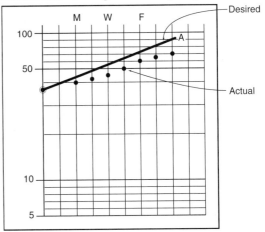

**Exhibit 5.13   A Progress Discrepancy.**

he is going. This type of information is fluid, or **dynamic,** showing both the direction and magnitude of change.

All formative approaches share certain common attributes:

- Use of direct measures of the thing being taught (CBM)
- Use of measures that are sensitive to learning
- Frequent use of assessment
- Use of visual display (charting or graphing) of assessment results
- Determination of expected progress
- Determination of the trend in actual progress
- Decision making (CBE) based on review of the trend in terms of the expectation.

## Is Teaching to Learning Styles the Same as Individualizing?

Educators have long acknowledged the idiographic (individual) nature of learning. The problem is finding the best way to teach individuals. As explained in Chapter 4, there are many different approaches, programs, techniques, and methods available for presenting any objective. Therefore, teachers must make selections.

Curriculum-based formative evaluation is used to recognize which instructional techniques

*Evaluation is more than assessment and assessment is more than testing.*

are most effective for particular students. Formative evaluation procedures can make your teaching many times more effective (Fuchs et al., 1985b; White, 1986). Formative procedures, most notably data-based program modification (DBPM) (Deno & Mirkin, 1977), and assisted assessment (Campione & Brown, 1985), provide the most promising solutions to the problem of selecting effective treatments for students. But these are not always the most popular techniques.

Many educators have elected to base teaching selections on summative measures of student abilities or aptitudes. Historically, the line of research associated with these efforts has been called **aptitude treatment interaction** (Bracht, 1970; Cronbach, 1957; Lloyd, 1984). This research deals with attempts to use various cognitive or perceptual aptitude measures, to find types of learners, and to match these types to complementary instructional programs. Today, this is more commonly called **learning styles instruction** (LSI) (Carbo, 1992). It is one of the most popular approaches to individualizing instruction. However, as popular as the idea of LSI may be, it has been invalidated (Erbaum et al., 1999; Snider, 1992). The LSI approach to treatment selection isn't simply ineffective—it is dangerous. Here are some reasons why.

1. It is based on the use of cognitive/perceptual measures that are (1) time consuming to give, (2) poorly validated, (3) generally unreliable, and (4) not curriculum-based;

2. By emphasizing summative measures, LSI encourages teachers to label students and commit to predictions about "best" ways to teach the label. This makes programming inflexible, discourages monitoring, and promotes "write-offs";

3. LSI advocates disregarding easily altered factors that cause treatments to vary in effectiveness, such as the teacher's actions and the student's prior knowledge. Instead, LSI tends to conceptualize student characteristics as fixed and focus on relatively unalterable variables such as disability label (for example, attention deficit disorder) or "type of intelligence";

4. LSI ignores the existence of task-related behavior and is inconsistent with the idea that students should be taught "how to learn" in a variety of ways; and

5. LSI doesn't work (Arter & Jenkins, 1979; Kavale & Forness, 1987; Snider, 1992).

The ultimate problem with LSI is that it is a **"front-loaded"** summative procedure. Efforts to identify student learning styles have always been tied to the administration of some sort of test or questionnaire, the results of which are used to make predictive statements about the student's future response to instruction. For LSI to work, these measures would need to have *spectacular* predictive strength, yet no summative test has ever demonstrated such strength (Fuchs et al., 1987; Ysseldyke et al., 1983). Summative evaluation, at its best, only tells us what a student can—or can't—do *now*. That's it. It may be powerful enough to predict outcomes for large groups of students on globally defined tasks, but those of us interested in selecting treatments for individ-

uals will always be disappointed by a strictly summative approach.

## How Can LSI Be Dangerous?

LSI is "dangerous" because it often requires time-consuming assessments and leads teachers to think about unalterable (distal) student characteristics. At present, the best way to decide how to teach is to pick one technique and use it. This initial selection should be based on empirical support for the technique (Gersten & Brengelman, 1996). That is, place the student in it, and see how he does. In the past, this technique was not used because the tools were not available to quickly evaluate the effectiveness of the intervention. The risk of misplacing a student for months or even weeks wasn't acceptable. But owing to advances in formative evaluation, applied behavioral analysis, and curriculum-based measurement, this is no longer the case. It is now possible to place a student in a program and evaluate the validity of the placement in a matter of days. The result is a movement away from attempts to measure and define abilities and toward the exact measurement of student behavior, tasks, and teaching (Deno & Espin, 1991).

## How Does Formative Evaluation Work?

Formative evaluation is sort of like peer tutoring; it gets rediscovered every few years and every few years it is found to be effective. Research clearly demonstrates that teachers who periodically review formative data and base treatment decisions on this review are more effective (Fuchs et al., 1985a; Shinn & Hubbard, 1992; White, 1986). Twenty years ago, Liberty et al. (1980) found that a group of teachers using formative data were 2.2 times more successful at selecting appropriate teaching modifications. Fuchs and Fuchs (1986), in a meta-analysis, reviewed 21 studies and concluded that cumulative effects are obtained when formative data display, decision rules, and behavior modification are combined during teaching. In this case,

---

### Exhibit 5.14    The Curriculum-Based Evaluation Process.

**Step 1. Define Your Purpose**

Decide why you are doing the evaluation and what decision you plan to make.

**Step 2. Define The Thing To Be Measured**

Specify the content, behavior, conditions, and proficiency levels you wish to examine.

**Step 3. Devise A Way To Make The Thing In Step 2 Observable**

Construct or select behavior samples, then administer them appropriately.

**Step 4. Conduct Assessment**

Collect information.

**Step 5. Use The CBE Process Of Inquiry**

Follow the steps of the CBE format.

**Step 6. Summarize**

Derive scores, make comparisons, and report or display results.

**Step 7. Make Decisions**

Use the data to decide what and how to teach.

---

the average performance of students receiving data display, decision rules, and behavior modification was 37% higher than controls. That study looked at 3835 student programs, 83% of which involved learners with disabilities.

There is little doubt that formative evaluation is one of the most powerful tools currently available to teachers. It would be nice to say that formative evaluation provides a quick and easy way to individualize, but in education, just as in any other field, the hardest problems necessitate the greatest effort. You will see the theme of formative evaluation woven throughout the rest of this text.

### How Can All of These Aspects of Evaluation Be Combined?

Our discussion is going to change from general information about the topic of functional curriculum-based evaluation to more specific information about how to carry out an evaluation. The process that will be described contains seven major steps that are detailed in Exhibit 5.14. To follow these steps, one must sometimes carry out multiple actions and ask numerous questions.

It is important to follow these steps. Evaluation should never be piecemeal, nor should it subject all students to a standard battery of tests regardless of their needs. (That is not evaluation—it is called fishing or, worse, child abuse.)

Exhibit 5.14 is presented to summarize and clarify the CBE process. This sort of organizer may be important to you because the steps of the CBE process are described over several chapters. Steps 1–2 will be explained in this chapter, steps 3–5 will be explained in Chapter 6, and steps 6–7 will be explained in Chapter 7.

Exhibit 5.15 is a **flow chart.** There will be several flow charts in the book, and they will all use the following conventions:

*circles*  are questions;

*simple rectangles* are things the evaluator may do; decisions (evaluation summaries and teaching recommendations) are given in *numbered rectangles;* and in this flow chart the seven major steps of the evaluation process are presented in double-sided rectangles.

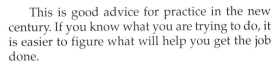

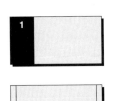

This is good advice for practice in the new century. If you know what you are trying to do, it is easier to figure what will help you get the job done.

---

**The Curriculum-Based Evaluation Process**

## Step 1. Define Your Purpose

Step 2. Define The Thing To Be Measured

Step 3. Devise A Way To Make The Thing In Step 2 Observable

Step 4. Conduct Assessment

Step 5. Use The CBE Process of Inquiry

Step 6. Summarize

Step 7. Make Decisions

---

Flow charts seem to drive some people out of their minds. However, they help other people (Sugai, 1997). If you suffer from the dreaded "disflowchartia," just ignore the images and focus on the words that accompany them.

Take a look back at Exhibit 5.1. As you can see, the first action in the programming process is "Define the Problem." Defining the problem and deciding what you want to do about it are basic steps to evaluation and then eventually to programming. In Chapter 1, a distinction was made between **inside** and **outside** purposes for evaluation. As described in that chapter, outside purposes were generally related to political activities such as school reform and funding entitlement. This text is not about those things. It is about the teacher's need, inside the classroom, to make decisions about what and how to teach.

Over a decade ago, the Joint Committee on Testing Practices (1988) said the following:

Before you make any decision, you should review your options. For inside evaluation you will be making *what to teach* and *how to teach* decisions. What materials you use will depend on which of these decisions you will be making and where you are in the decision-making process. There are three types of assessment from which to choose depending on the stage of decision making at which you are working. They are described in Exhibit 5.16.

Because your purpose will vary with the kind of decision you are trying to make and your current stage in decision making, it is not always easy to decide exactly why you are giving an assessment. That is one reason many people give more of them than they need. Here is some advice.

*First,* decide if you are making a *what to teach* or *how to teach* decision. You decide **what to teach** by using CBM and then comparing the student's

---

| Test Developers Should: | | Test Users Should: | |
|---|---|---|---|
| Define what each test measures and *what the test should be used for* [emphasis added]. | Describe the population(s) for which the test is appropriate. | First define the *purpose for testing* [emphasis added] and the population to be tested. | Then select a test for that purpose and that population based on a thorough review of the available information. |

*Exhibit 5.15    Flow Chart of Step 5 in the CBE Process.*

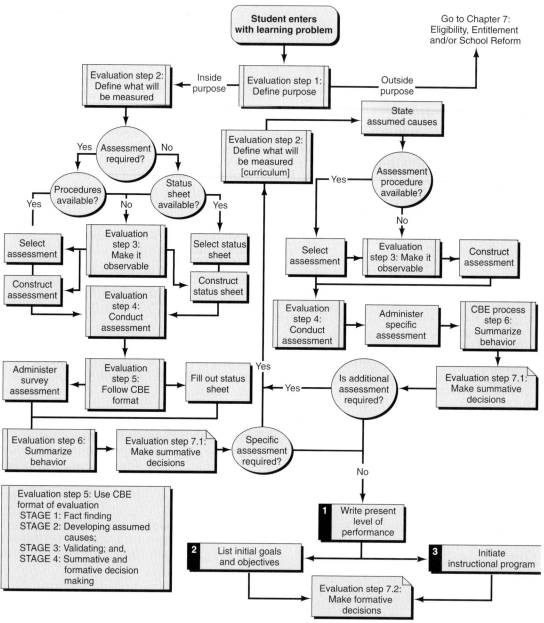

knowledge with the things the student needs to know. When you find something that the student needs to know, check his prior knowledge; if he has the required pre-requisite knowledge, pick that thing as a goal. This can be completed with summative (performance) data. To program, you must also make **how to teach** decisions. This requires formative (progress) data.

*Exhibit 5.16   Types of Assessments Used for Various Decisions.*

| Reason For Assessment | Type of Assessment | Typical Materials: | Example: |
|---|---|---|---|
| **To Find Problems** | *Screening* | Must indicate skill in an area. Must be quick and easy to give to large numbers of students. The results need only rank the students so that those who are doing poorly may be identified. | • One minute timed reading from class text. <br> • Teacher ranking of students on peer relations. <br> • Two minute outline for the answer to an essay test item. |
| **To Get Facts About The Student's Current Skills** | *Survey assessment* | Survey, or *broad band,* assessments are similar to screening techniques but they collect a larger sample of behavior in order to allow the evaluator to make judgments about what domains seem to be causing the student problems. | • Multiple reading samples across levels of difficulty. <br> • A review of student records and interviews with teachers and parents. <br> • A review of essay responses the student has written in several classes. |
| **To Get The Information Needed to Solve That Problem** | *Specific assessment* | Must give specific (narrow band) information about the student's knowledge. Must focus on samples of the student's work which are instructionally relevant. They are usually "criterion" or "domain" "referenced." | • Extensive oral reading sample and analysis of specific errors. <br> • Interview with student about the steps she would follow while trying to enter into a game at recess. <br> • Ask student to explain process for answering on essay item. |
| **To See If The Resulting Solution Is Effective** | *Monitoring* | Must be very sensitive to learning (so that they can be used for formative evaluation). They must be quick and easy to use over and over again. They also must accurately and immediately reflect the impact of instructional efforts. | • Charting of one minute timed readings from class text. <br> • Interval observation of student's interactions with students during recess. <br> • Periodic review of student's grades on tests. |

Summative data can be collected during a single assessment session, but formative data must be collected over time. Therefore, if you are making "How" or "What" decisions has immediate implications for the sort of assessments you will use and the data you will collect.

*Next*, decide where you are in the decision-making process. Look at Exhibit 5.16. It shows what sort of assessment procedure you might use depending on how far you have progressed through the process. By first deciding if you are asking a "what" or "how" question, you can determine what assessment processes you need to use. For example, if you are just trying to recognize students who are not progressing in a lesson (to decide if they need modified instruction), you would want to *screen* students by using formative data collection.

---

**The Curriculum-Based Evaluation Process**

Step 1. Define Your Purpose

# Step 2. Define The Thing To Be Measured

Step 3. Devise A Way To Make The Thing In Step 2 Observable

Step 4. Conduct Assessment

Step 5. Use The CBE Process of Inquiry

Step 6. Summarize

Step 7. Make Decisions

---

Curriculum was discussed in great detail in Chapter 3. Among other points, it was stressed that a task is more than a statement of content. Therefore, to assure **alignment** between evaluation and the curriculum, you must use assessments that sample the sorts of conditions and behaviors specified in goals and objectives. All of this assumes that the goals and objectives exist.

In CBE, this means you must define what will be measured in terms of the curriculum (by specifying the knowledge the student needs to have to be successful). As you can see in Exhibit 5.15, this step comes before assessments can be selected or administered.

Curriculum development, or at this stage, *problem definition,* is always a difficult task. There are reasons for this. One of them is that the process requires activities that are both **divergent** and **convergent.** Exhibit 5.17 demonstrates two ways of thinking that are often placed in opposition but actually can be complementary.

The divergent stage generally precedes the convergent stage. However, if you (or the group you are working with) have trouble producing the products of the convergent stage, that often means you need to go back and work in the divergent stage a while. Too often, when people try to solve problems, they move to the convergent stage too soon (some of us simply start there) or stick to it too long. For good problem solving and curriculum definition, it is important to consciously shift between the stages as needed.

Once the curriculum is defined, assessments are often fairly easy to develop. To assure that these assessments remain aligned with the curriculum, make sure that scores on items or subtests are directly keyed to goals and objectives. For example, if a student scores low on the addition subtest of a math inventory, it might be interesting to know that several of the items missed involved addition of fractions and decimals. Without that knowledge, a teacher could erroneously conclude that the student wasn't skilled in addition when the real problem was fractions. The point isn't that fractions don't belong; however, their presence should be clearly identified.

Exhibit 5.18 presents a specific criterion-reference test (CRT) designed to measure a student's rate at addition with regrouping. In this case, the diagonal lines, which would not appear on the student's copy, are used to point out items that have the same content. The diagonal grouping technique shown in Exhibit 5.18 allowed an even distribution of items by difficulty, with item types (problems with eights, addition of a number to itself, regrouping) identified to allow easy recognition of subtasks that are troubling the student. The diagonal pattern also has the advantage of being hard to figure out, so that the test can be used to collect formative data. As you can see, a teacher would have no trouble using this test to decide what skills a student does or doesn't have. That is because the addition curriculum was clearly examined and defined before the test was constructed.

All objectives in a curriculum should be numbered, and all test items that measure those objectives should be given the same numbers. In this way, the curriculum-test match (alignment) is assured. It would be even better if applicable instructional materials could also be labeled with the same numbers. There are many ways to define the curriculum, and one that was presented in Chapter 3 is particularly effective. That is the use of tables of specifications. You may want to go back to that chapter and take a second look at Exhibits 3.10 and 3.11. They illustrate how the tables can be used and are accompanied by a description of how to develop tables of specifications. This process of definition is essential for the next step in the CBE process, described in the next chapter.

*Exhibit 5.17   Problem Identification.*

| Problem Identification | | | |
|---|---|---|---|
| Divergent Stage | | Convergent Stage | |
| Process | Outcomes | Process | Outcomes |
| • No boundaries are placed on the discussion<br>• All options are viewed as preliminary<br>• Early resolution is avoided<br>• Efforts are made to assure comprehensive and wide input<br>• Options and opinions are presented without judgment | • Options are reviewed<br>• The general parameters of the domain are defined<br>• Tentative goal statements are drafted | • Rigorous analysis is applied<br>• Options and opinions are judged<br>• Strict rules are developed<br>• Proof of accuracy is demanded<br>• Attempts are made to reduce the range of options<br>• Priorities are set | • Specific descriptions of the domain are developed<br>• Objectives (including standards) are developed and written<br>• A plan for teaching the objectives is designed |

## Summary

This has been a chapter crowded with information that you will need to recall in the chapters to follow. That is why text illustrations and exhibits have been provided for many of the main points. Here are some of the main points from the chapter:

- Evaluation is not the same as assessment

- Assessment is simply collecting a sample of behavior

- Evaluation involves the use of measurement to obtain samples of a student's knowledge

and to compare those samples with some sort of standards, or expectations, for what is acceptable. The results of this comparison can then be used to inform decision making.

There are seven steps to the CBE process, and they are presented with some elaboration in Exhibit 5.15. The first of these, defining purpose and curriculum, has been discussed in previous chapters. Finally, the structure of an evaluation is determined by the type of decision to be made, the nature of the measure to be employed, and the type of standard to be applied to the measurement results.

## STUDY QUESTIONS

1. Examine each of the situations presented below and decide what reference standard is being used (norm, criterion, individual).

**Exhibit 5.18   An Addition Probe Sheet.**

| Objective: Student will write answers to addition problems having one-digit addend to two digits with regrouping. CAP: 70 digits correct per minute. | | | Practice Items | | 45 <br> + 7 <br> 52 | 28 <br> + 6 <br> 34 | 94 <br> + 8 <br> 102 | 76 <br> + 4 <br> 80 | |

| 28 <br> + 4 <br> 32 | 53 <br> + 9 <br> 62 | 16 <br> + 8 <br> 24 | 94 <br> + 8 <br> 102 | 87 <br> + 7 <br> 94 | 63 <br> + 9 <br> 72 | 60 <br> + 8 <br> 68 | 32 <br> + 9 <br> 41 | 42 <br> + 2 <br> 44 | 51 <br> + 9 <br> 60 | Digit Count |
|---|---|---|---|---|---|---|---|---|---|---|
| | | | | | | | | | | 1s       (21) |
| 31 <br> + 5 <br> 36 | 58 <br> + 2 <br> 60 | 13 <br> + 7 <br> 20 | 26 <br> + 4 <br> 30 | 74 <br> + 7 <br> 81 | 69 <br> + 9 <br> 78 | 83 <br> + 7 <br> 90 | 49 <br> + 0 <br> 49 | 22 <br> + 8 <br> 30 | 93 <br> + 3 <br> 96 | Non-instance   (41) |
| 39 <br> + 9 <br> 48 | 62 <br> + 4 <br> 66 | 78 <br> + 3 <br> 81 | 43 <br> + 8 <br> 51 | 56 <br> + 5 <br> 61 | 24 <br> + 9 <br> 33 | 18 <br> + 8 <br> 26 | 71 <br> + 8 <br> 81 | 83 <br> + 5 <br> 88 | 92 <br> + 9 <br> 101 | |
| | | | | | | | | | | 2s       (62) |
| 28 <br> + 1 <br> 29 | 49 <br> + 6 <br> 55 | 93 <br> + 6 <br> 99 | 98 <br> + 5 <br> 103 | 15 <br> + 7 <br> 22 | 85 <br> + 9 <br> 94 | 34 <br> + 6 <br> 40 | 45 <br> + 5 <br> 50 | 63 <br> + 9 <br> 72 | 71 <br> + 4 <br> 75 | Non-instance   (83) |
| 31 <br> + 9 <br> 40 | 97 <br> + 2 <br> 99 | 19 <br> + 5 <br> 24 | 70 <br> + 9 <br> 79 | 48 <br> + 8 <br> 56 | 65 <br> + 8 <br> 73 | 95 <br> + 6 <br> 101 | 84 <br> + 8 <br> 92 | 36 <br> + 6 <br> 42 | 83 <br> + 8 <br> 91 | |
| 1s | Non-instance | 9s | Non-instance | 8s | 3s 5s | 6s 5s | 4s | Number added to itself | 3s | (104) |

Source: Howell, K. W., Zucker, S. H. & Morehead, M. K. (2000b). *Multilevel Academic Skills Inventory.* Bellingham, WA: Applied Research and Development Center. To order contact the Student Co-op Bookstore, Western Washington University. Fax (360) 650-2888. Phone (360) 650-3656. Reprinted with permission.

- A teacher wants to find out how her students compare with other students in the country in the area of math computation. She administers a published standardized math test and records each child's z score.
- A group of teachers is trying to decide whether a particular student needs extra help in writing. They look at the work samples in his portfolio.
- A teacher is meeting Merton's parents to discuss his reading performance. On a box plot displaying the oral reading fluency of fourth-grade students, the teacher makes a mark just below the bottom line of the box to show Merton's score when he read the fourth-grade passage aloud.
- Arliss can perform two-digit columnar addition. She decides that the next thing Arliss needs to work on is adding three-digit and two-digit numbers.

2. Decide whether each of the following situations is an example of formative or summative evaluation.

- Melissa must obtain a score of 70% on her spelling test to be able to receive a passing grade for the quarter.

- Each week, students in Mrs. Willburn's fifth-grade class write a narrative essay under standardized conditions. The students then record the percent of words spelled correctly on their essay on a chart they each keep in their portfolios.
- Based on his scores on a reading test that accompanies the curriculum, Herb's teacher decides to place him into the middle reading group.

3. A group of teachers is trying to decide what to do for a student who has been having difficulty in math. The teachers are trying to come up with some assumed causes for the student's problems. Tell whether you think they are engaged in divergent or convergent thinking at this point. Why?

4. Decide whether you agree or disagree with this statement. Tell why.

*You can still make valid decisions about a student's performance even if the testing procedures you use are not reliable.*

# Chapter 6

# Tools for Assessment

*This comparison of worth yields a measure of potential for the improvement of performance. . . There are great differences in what people accomplish, but small differences in their repertoires of behavior.*

—T. F. Gilbert (1978)

## Where Are We Now?

Chapter 5 contained considerable information about measurement and how evaluation fits in the process of programming. It also presented guidelines for following the first two steps in CBE. Now we are up to Step 3. The steps of CBE are considerably easier to carry out than to explain. As you go through the topical chapters (8–14), the process will become not only clear but also intuitive. However, it is important to explain each step in Chapters 5, 6, and 7 so that the later chapters will have minimal redundancy. This presentation goes into great detail describing actions that, in practice, will take only seconds to complete. So try to focus on the flow of the process so that you can learn how the various skills of evaluation fit with one another. It may help to go back and look over Exhibit 5.15. We are now up to Step 3, in which you make observable whatever it is you will be measuring.

In practice, Steps 3 and 4 blend into a process called the *CBE Format of Inquiry* (Step 5). However, to facilitate the rationale and procedures for each, this discussion will separate the steps (at least for a while).

---

**The Curriculum-Based Evaluation Process**

Step 1. Define Your Purpose
Step 2. Define The Thing To Be Measured
### Step 3. Devise A Way To Make The Thing In Step 2 Observable
Step 4. Conduct Assessment
Step 5. Use The CBE Process of Inquiry
Step 6. Summarize
Step 7. Make Decisions

---

## How Is Curriculum-Based Measurement Used in the CBE Process?

Every attempt at observation involves ethical as well as measurement issues. In the following discussion, we will address both. Recall that measurement has been defined as "the assignments of numerals to objects or events according to rules" (Campbell, 1940). Any useful measurement procedure has four components: the definition of the quantity to be measured, a device for making that quantity observable, a mechanism (rule) for assigning different numerals to different magnitudes of the targeted quantity, and a mechanism (numerical or visual) for summarizing the whole activity (Thorndike & Hagan, 1969). All assessments, including the four assessment procedures from the matrix in Exhibit 5.10, must share these four essential components.

To make student performance observable, curriculum-based evaluation makes use of a particular type of measurement technology called curriculum-based measurement (CBM). Curriculum-based measurement was developed in the early 1980s at the Minnesota Institute for Research on Learning Disabilities as a tool for teachers to use in formative evaluation of the effectiveness of their instruction (Deno, 1985). Unlike traditional educational and psychological measures, CBM is not typically linked to a particular set of materials. Instead, it employs local curriculum materials and a general set of measurement and scoring rules. These measurement rules are known as *overlay* techniques because they can be superimposed on a variety of materials and/or content.

Usually, CBM is used in the so-called basic skills areas of reading, written expression, math computation, and spelling, although recently, applications of CBM have been devised for use in middle and high school content areas (Espin & Foegen, 1996). Curriculum-based measurement employs brief, standardized measures that directly sample from the local curriculum. For example, in reading, students read aloud from a passage sampled from the local curriculum for 1 minute, and their score is the total number of words read correctly. In math, students would complete 2- to 3-minute tests that contain problems similar to those at a particular grade level in the curriculum. The technical characteristics (for example, reliability and validity) of CBM have been documented extensively. CBM is highly correlated with more expensive, less instructionally relevant measures, and when used in conjunction with decision rules results in improved learning of students who are experiencing learning difficulties (Fuchs & Deno, 1991). Because CBM is not tied to a particular set of materials, it is not marketed by test publishers and is not well known outside of special education. However, it is widely used in many school districts around the country.

Recall that in the last chapter, we discussed three reasons for evaluation: screening, problem solving, and monitoring. There are two approaches to using CBM that pertain directly to these evaluation purposes. One approach entails development of local norms that can be used to establish expectations about what constitutes "typical performance" in the curriculum used in a particular school or district. This approach to CBM is useful for making screening decisions. All students in a particular grade level in a school or district complete the same task, under the same conditions, and their scores are rank ordered. The performance of an individual student can then be compared with this rank ordering.

In larger districts, or when resources are limited, a norming group can be created by randomly selecting a representative sample of the children in the district. For example, if there are 10,000 third-grade students in a district, a norm group of 2,500 third graders can be created by selecting every fourth student from the third-grade roster. Usually, a school or district creates such local norms in the fall, winter, and spring. After an initial base period of 3 years, schools can collect norms every other or every third year as long as curriculum adoptions are systematic and infrequent and student mobility is stable. Whenever new curriculum materials are adopted or if there are significant changes in the size or characteristics of the student population in a district, new norms should be collected.

In the other approach to CBM, a student would take alternate forms of a test each week, and her progress would be noted over time. The test would be constructed, administered, and scored in exactly the same manner as in normative use of CBM. Each test would consist of materials that would be sampled from the local curriculum, it would be administered under standardized conditions, and the same scoring rules would be used to summarize the student's performance each time. Scores could be compared with a goal level or rate of progress, using an aimline, or with an idiosyncratic standard (described in the last chapter). This approach to using CBM also is known as "individual-referenced" decision-making because the individual's previous performance establishes the comparison standard. This approach to using CBM is most useful for making monitoring decisions or evaluating the effects of an intervention for a particular student.

The distinction between these two uses of CBM and their applicability to our current discussion is illustrated in Exhibits 6.1 and 6.2.

Exhibit 6.1a shows spring norms in oral reading fluency for five grades in a school district. Each child in grades 1–5 read for 1 minute from a passage reflecting the curriculum used by the middle reading group at their grade at the time of the norming. For example, all third-grade students would read aloud for 1 minute from a passage reflecting the reading curriculum in use by the middle reading group in third grade. All students at a grade level read the same passage, and all reading samples were administered and scored using the same procedures.

These data are illustrated using graphs known as box plots. Exhibit 6.1b shows how to interpret box plots. Box plots display percentile ranks on the basis of the actual scores students receive. As shown in Exhibit 6.1b, the top of the box indicates the 75th percentile and the bottom of the box indicates the 25th percentile. Approximately 75% of the people who took the test got a score lower than the one indicated by the top of the box, and approximately 75% of the people who took the test got a score higher than the one indicated by the bottom of the box. The middle line in a box plot indicates the 50th percentile, or median. This is the middle score of the distribution. The T-shaped lines above and below the box

**Exhibit 6.1    (a) CBM Box Plots. (b) Interpreting Box Plots.**

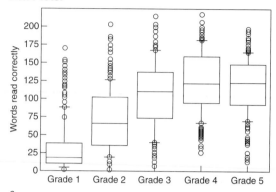

a.

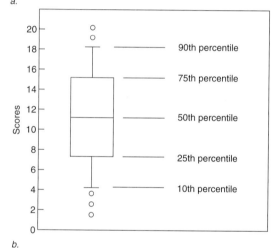

b.

**Exhibit 6.2    Individual Referenced Data.**

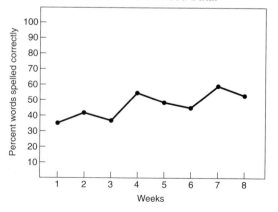

indicate the score at the 90th and 10th percentiles. The circles above and below the box plot represent individuals who got scores above or below the 90th or 10th percentile.

In Exhibit 6.1a, the median score for third graders is about 100 words correct. Approximately 25% of the third graders read more than 140 words correct in a minute, and approximately 25% of third graders read fewer than 75 words correct in a minute. Take a moment and compare the performance of third-grade students with fourth-grade students. What score would be considered "typical" performance in the fourth grade?

Exhibit 6.2 illustrates the second approach to using CBM. The graph shows written expression data collected over a period of 8 weeks for Jenna, a fourth-grade student. Each week, under standardized conditions, Jenna was presented with alternate forms of a story starter such as "One day my friend and I were walking to school and the strangest thing happened. . . ". She then wrote a story in response to the story starter. At the end of 3 minutes, Jenna's teacher instructed her to put a star beside the last word written and then continue writing to finish the story. The scores plotted on the graph represent the percent of words spelled correctly in these first 3 minutes. The percent of words spelled correctly is a reasonably accurate predictor of more global indicators of written expression and is a relatively easy score to collect from student writing samples (Parker et al., 1991). In week 1, Jenna spelled 35% of the words in her essay correctly. In week 4, she spelled 55% of the words correctly, and in week 8, Jenna spelled 52% of the words correctly. Examine Exhibit 6.2 and decide whether you think Jenna is making sufficient progress in writing. What course of action do you think her teacher should follow?

Exhibit 6.3 shows an example of a report card that can be used to communicate the results of district norming to parents. The front page of the report card in Exhibit 6.3 shows the actual performance of Aurora Franklin, a third-grade student, recorded on the examiner's copy of a CBM oral reading fluency probe. On the first of the two passages administered, Aurora read 110 words correctly in 1 minute; on the second pas-

sage, she read 120 words correctly in 1 minute. The last word Aurora read or attempted to read on each passage is indicated by a bracket (]). On the first passage, that word was "persnickety." The back page of the report card (Exhibit 6.3b) shows box plots that present winter oral reading fluency norms for each grade in Aurora's school. To help parents interpret these box plots, an interpretive guide also is included. Finally, the back page of the report card shows Aurora's progress in reading over the last 8 weeks. With this sort of report card, a parent can easily understand what his or her child is actually doing in reading.

## How Does CBM Fit into the CBE Process?

In the last chapter, we introduced you to the R.I.O.T. assessment matrix. In this chapter, we will discuss each of the components of the matrix as they apply to Steps 3 and 4 of the CBE process. CBM overlays can be used in each of these components. As you go through the following descriptions of the R.I.O.T. procedures, you will be shown examples of tests, status sheets, interview forms, and observation summaries to help explain and illustrate the decision-making process.

*Review*   Frequently, the best indicators of student knowledge are not collected through testing or observation but through the analysis of existing permanent products. Although these products are not actual behavior, they are the **critical effects** of behavior. They may range from grades on report cards to much smaller artifacts. For example, one of the authors once heard about a teacher who, when he left his classroom, would put tape over the outside edge of the door. If the tape was broken when he returned, he knew that someone had left a seat to peek down the hall. The broken tape was the critical effect of "getting out of seat."

The sources of review information and the sorts of data that may result from reviews are illustrated in Exhibit 6.4.

A tremendous amount of information is routinely collected about students. School atten-

**Exhibit 6.3   CBM Report Card: (a) Front Page; (b) Back Page.**

CURRICULUM-BASED MEASUREMENT PERFORMANCE REPORT

**Student:** Aurora Franklin | **Grade:** 3 | **Teacher:** Otis Holden | **Date of Testing:** 2/18/99

On February 18, 1999, every child in the school district was tested in the area of reading. Each child read aloud for one minute from each of two passages selected from the reading curriculum used by the middle reading group at their grade level. Each child's score was the average number of words read correctly on these two passages. Aurora's performance on these passages is shown here. A comparison of Aurora's performance with other children in her grade is shown on the other side of this page.

**Student:** Aurora Franklin

| Words Read 110 | Fall Grade: 3 | Winter | Spring |
| --- | --- | --- | --- |
| Miss/Subt. / | Omission ◯ | Reversal ∼ | Hesitation H |

**Student:** Aurora Franklin

| Words Read 120 | Fall Grade: 3 | Winter | Spring |
| --- | --- | --- | --- |
| Miss/Subt. / | Omission ◯ | Reversal ∼ | Hesitation H |

### Fly High, Fly Low

In the beautiful city of San Francisco, a city famous for its frogs and 14
flowers, cable cars and towers, there once stood an electric-light sign on 26
top of a tall building, and inside the letter B of this sign there lived a 42
pigeon. 43

Before choosing to make his home here this proud gray pigeon had tried 56
living in many other letters of the alphabet. Just why he liked the lower 70
loop of the letter B, now one yet knew. 79

During the day the wide side walks kept the wind away, and at night 94
the bright light kept him warm and cozy. 101

The pigeons who roosted along the ledges of the building across the 113
street thought he was a pretty persnickety pigeon to live where he did. 126
"He's too choosy! He's too choosy!" they would coo. 135

The only one who never made fun of him was a white-feathered dove. 148
She felt sure he must have a good reason for wanting to live in that letter. 164
Every morning as soon as the sun came up, these two met in mid-air 178
and together they swerved and swooped down into Union Square Park, 189
where they pecked up their breakfast. Mr. Hi Lee was certain to be there, 203
throwing out crumbs from his large paper sack. He would always greet 215
them by saying, "Good Morning, Sid and Midge. How are my two early 228
birds?" 229

All the birds in the city regarded Mr. Hi Lee as their best friend, and he 245
had nicknames for many of them. 251

### Aunt Flossie's Hats (and crab cakes later)

On Sunday afternoons, Sarah and I go to see Great-great-aunt Flossie. 11
Sarah and I love Aunt Flossie's house. It is crowded full of stuff and 25
things. Books and pictures and lamps and pillows...Plates and trays and 36
old dried flowers...And boxes and boxes of HATS! 46

On Sunday afternoon when Sarah and I go to see Aunt Flossie, she 59
says, "Come in, Susan. Come in Sarah. Have some tea. Have some 71
cookies. Later we can get some crab cakes!" 79

We sip our tea and eat our cookies, and then Aunt Flossie lets us look 95
in her hatboxes. 97

We pick out hats and try them on. Aunt Flossie says they are her 111
memories, and each hat has its story. 118

Hats, hats, hats, hats! A stiff black one with bright red ribbons. A soft 132
brown one with silver buttons. Thin floppy hats that hide our eyes. 145
Green or blue or purple. Some have fur and some have feathers. Look! 159
This hat is just one smooth soft rose, but here's one with a trillion flow- 173
ers! Aunt Flossie has so many hats! 178

One Sunday afternoon, I picked out a wooly winter hat, sort of green, 191
maybe. Aunt Flossie thought a minute. Aunt Flossie almost always 202
thinks a minute before she starts a hat story. Then she sniffed the wooly 216
hat. "Just a little smoky smell now," she said. 224

Sarah and I sniffed the hat, too. "Smoky smell, Aunt Flossie?" 235

"The big fire," Aunt Flossie said. "The big fire in Baltimore. Everything 247
251

Your child's performance is shown on the box plot for his grade level below left. Aurora read an average of 115 words correct on the two passages shown on the opposite side of this page. Each week for the last two months, Aurora has read aloud from a passage selected from her reading curriculum and the number of words she read was recorded. Her progress on this task is shown in the graph below left.

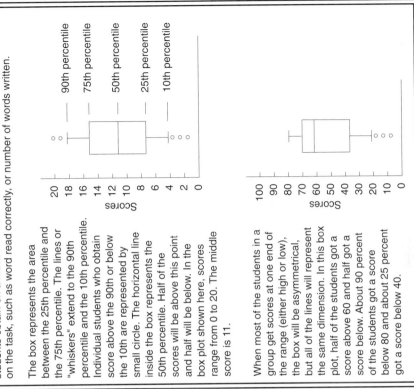

## Interpreting Box Plots

Box plots graphically display percentile data referenced to the actual scores students obtain on a measure. The vertical axis contains the range of score on the task, such as word read correctly, or number of words written.

The box represents the area between the 25th percentile and the 75th percentile. The lines or "whiskers" extend to the 90th percentile and the 10th percentile. Individual students who obtain score above the 90th or below the 10th are represented by small circle. The horizontal line inside the box represents the 50th percentile. Half of the scores will be above this point and half will be below. In the box plot shown here, scores range from 0 to 20. The middle score is 11.

When most of the students in a group get scores at one end of the range (either high or low), the box will be asymmetrical, but all of the lines will represent the same dimension. In this box plot, half of the students got a score above 60 and half got a score below. About 90 percent of the students got a score below 80 and about 25 percent got a score below 40.

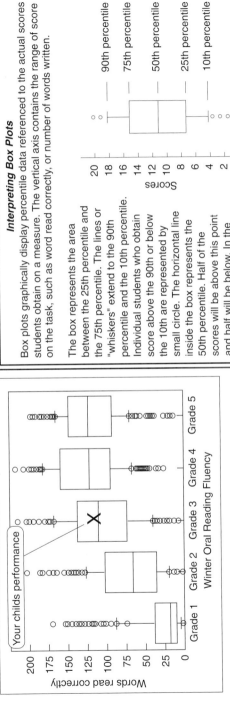

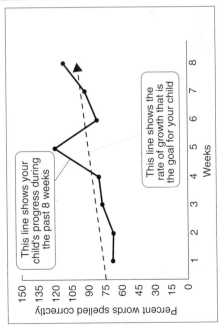

*Exhibit 6.4   Sources of Review Information.*

| Domains | Source | Data Outcomes |
|---|---|---|
| **I**<br>Instruction | • Permanent products (paper-pencil tasks)<br>• Classroom work (style demands of the task, difficulty levels, skill requirements)<br>• Class schedules<br>• Attendance records<br>• Lesson plans (IEPs) | • Nature of instructional demands<br>• Instructional approaches, pacing, difficulty, prerequisite skills,<br>• Allocated time |
| **C**<br>Curriculum | • Permanent student products<br>• Lists of scope and sequence of lessons<br>• Curriculum materials (books, worksheets, curriculum guides, etc.) | • Nature of instructional demands reflected in curricular materials (instructional approaches, pacing, difficulty, prerequisite skills)<br>• Scope and sequence of instructions |
| **E**<br>Environment | Reports or statements about:<br>• School rules<br>• Class sizes<br>• Policy on disruptive behavior<br>• Permanent products<br>• Peers' work | • Policies/procedures that define what is deemed as "situationally appropriate"<br>• Standard of performance of peers |
|  | Cumulative records:<br>• Grades<br>• Attendance<br>• Discipline reports | • Patterns of behavior<br>• Onset and duration of the problem<br>• Interference with personal, interpersonal, and academic adjustment<br>• Settings or content where behavior of concern has occurred |
| **L**<br>Learner | Health records | • Existence of health, vision, and/or hearing problems potentially related to the behavior of concern<br>• Medications |
|  | Permanent products:<br>• Student work<br>• Portfolios | • Patterns of performance errors reflecting skill deficits<br>• Failure to profit from general education instruction<br>• Consistent skill and/or performance problems over time<br>• Settings where behavior of concern is evident |
|  | Teacher's grade book | • Student performance in relationship to setting demands (teacher expectations, task demands) |
|  | • Records of meetings held about the student<br>• Teacher intervention records | • Response to interventions as reflected in "action plans" and progress monitoring |

Based on Heartland, 1998

dance, for example, may be of particular interest if the student is not making adequate progress (you wouldn't want to redesign a child's program if she hasn't been attending often enough to benefit from the existing one). Attendance, grades, and discipline records are all excellent products to use when monitoring the effectiveness of task-related and social interventions.

**Portfolios** In addition to the routine institutional records collected in schools and classes, many students will have portfolios containing important work assignments. Work samples collected in portfolios can provide direct evidence about student skills, and often it makes more sense to review and analyze the contents of a student's portfolio than to have the student spend instructional time producing new samples in the context of a test. As we described in the last chapter, when using portfolio assessment, teachers collect samples of student work on a routine basis in the classroom. The teacher periodically organizes, analyzes, and summarizes these data to assess student learning. Often the student evaluates her own work using guidelines provided by the teacher. These work samples can be examined and compared across time to support decisions about skills and progress (Hall & Tindal, 1991). One particular advantage of the portfolio approach is that it "grounds" the evaluation procedures to the classroom by replacing externally developed assessments with classroom-generated work samples (Fuchs & Deno, 1991). Indeed, portfolios can be a convenient vehicle for integrating CBM data with other forms of classroom work samples (Nolet, 1992).

For portfolio review to have utility, it must meet the same standards of fidelity, sampling, scoring, and comparison that any assessment procedure must meet. In terms of sampling, this can become a major issue as different teachers take different approaches to the maintenance of portfolios. Some routinely replace products with newer samples that are thought to represent the student's "best work," whereas others collect a more random sample across time. If you do collect samples over time, a great activity is to mix up the samples and then ask the student to put them back into chronological order. This often is a simple task, and it illustrates the student's improvement in a personal way.

**Record Analysis** Many forms of school records are available for examination by teachers who are working directly with a student, and these can be reviewed when decisions about a student's educational program are being made. However, policies on records and laws regarding access vary tremendously between states and school districts. Obviously, professionals working in schools need to check out local policies and to use common sense. Part of common sense, as it pertains to records, is to never talk about a student to anyone who does not need to know the information (while being sure to provide the information to those who do). Also, only supply the impressions you gained from examining the records; never supply exact quotes. Confidentiality issues include consideration of teacher confidentiality as well as the student's.

When reviewing records, remember that some of the information contained in them may have become outdated. Behavior or learning patterns that were observed when a child was in first grade may not reflect the student's performance by the time the child reaches second grade. This applies to previous evidence that the student *was* having learning or social skills problems as well as to evidence that he or she *was not.*

Also, when reviewing records, do not be unduly influenced by information provided by so-called "experts." Often, the observations of a teacher who sees a student perform on a day-in, day-out interactive basis are much more accurate and useful than the observations of someone who may have worked with the student for less than 2 hours while administering a highly structured intelligence or achievement battery.

Also, don't be misled by the presence of meaningless or uninformative labels. Diagnostic labels go in and out of style with about the same frequency as clothing fashions, popular music, and fancy kitchen gadgets. For example, the diagnosis "attention-deficit disorder" (ADD) was fashionable in the late 1990s. The label now crops up on psychological reports that have become part of too many children's permanent school records. Although it has received considerable attention in clinical and school psychology literature, ADD is not currently recognized as a category of disability under IDEA and is a highly controversial diagnosis in the educational community. Many students do have a constellation of behavior and learning problems that is characterized by the label ADD, but others with the same problems do not deserve the label. Unfortunately, there are plenty of snake-oil salesmen who (usually for a fee) blithely generate reports that have lasting and in some cases harmful consequences. Before you attach too much meaning to a diagnostic label contained in a student's school records, remember that the labels "imbecile," "idiot," "low-grade," "moron," and even "negro" all were considered legitimate diagnostic categories at some time during the 20th century.

### Product Analysis

Review of assignments can be useful because incorrect procedures will eventually lead to incorrect products. Patterns in these incorrect products may reveal the flawed processes that produced them. (The diagonal item pattern illustrated in Exhibit 5.18 is one device a teacher might use to recognize error patterns.) This is known as **error analysis** or *rule assessment* (Siegler, 1983). The idea that product analysis can be used to determine what to teach is common. In reading, it is sometimes called *miscue analysis.* One disadvantage of product analysis (that is, a problem with all review assessment) is that some products won't occur if you don't happen to promote them. A student who has trouble spelling words with double consonants won't ever display that problem if you don't put double-consonant words on the spelling test. Similarly, a student who doesn't use past tense could speak correctly throughout an entire conversation conducted in the present tense. Unfortunately, error analysis is hard to do on many survey tests, especially the ones that use multiple-choice items. Another problem with error analysis is that things can be analyzed beyond the point of instructional utility. Also, processes like "running records" are too time consuming for students with minor problems.

### Does This Mean I Shouldn't Do Error Analysis?

If you do error analysis, be careful. Use the *minimum/maximum* rule. That is, use the most intensive analysis (the *maximum*) with those students

who have *minimum* skills. To analyze errors during product reviews, follow these steps.

1. Select an assessment or product that provided an opportunity for a variety of errors to occur;
2. Encourage the student to attempt everything and to show all work;
3. Try to get as many examples of meaningful errors as possible (by reviewing products on which the student was only partially correct or those that illustrate her best efforts);
4. Try to gain insight into the student's processes by noting patterns, or thought consistencies, in the errors;
5. Try to categorize errors or corrects by content, behavior, condition, or thought process (fact, concept, rule, strategy);
6. Note and categorize skills that were not displayed;
7. Ask yourself (or the student) "How did you arrive at this answer?"; and
8. Once you think you have found an error pattern, see if you can confirm it by predicting the sort of mistake a student will make and then giving a specific assessment to see if the pattern occurs.

### Interview

Sources of information and the data that can result from interviews are illustrated in Exhibit 6.5. Structured and formal interviewing is probably used to collect data more often than any other assessment procedure. Not only are interviews used to decide who to hire for jobs or to gather opinions about national policy, but they are the main sources of treatment-related information in mental health and social services. Yet, somehow interviewing doesn't seem to have found a place in educational assessment.

Interviews have several advantages. For students these include the reflection of the student's opinion and the opportunity to contrast what the student thinks with what others (teachers, parents) think.

Interviews can take the form of personal conversations or questionnaires/checklists. In either case they are important because many of the

**Exhibit 6.5 Assessment by Interview.**

| Domains | Source | Data Outcomes |
|---|---|---|
| I<br>Instruction | • Teachers<br>• Students | • Expectations<br>• Teachers' philosophical orientation (generative vs. supplantive; hands-on vs. hands-off)<br>• Preferred instructional practices<br>• Alignment of materials and curriculum |
| C<br>Curriculum | • Teachers (at current, previous, and next grade levels) and relevant personnel (curriculum directors, principals, etc.)<br>• District policy regarding adoption and use of curriculum materials | • Philosophical orientation of the curriculum (generative vs. supplantive)<br>• Organization and structure<br>• Expectations for pacing and coverage of the curriculum<br>• Alignment of materials and curriculum |
| E<br>Environment | • Teachers<br>• Other personnel<br>• Parents<br>• Peers<br>• Student | • Classroom instructional routines, rules, behavior management plans<br>• Reflected definition of "situationally appropriate" instruction<br>• Expectations<br>• Perception of support<br>• View of class as "considerate" and "user friendly" |
| L<br>Learner | • Teachers<br>• Other relevant personnel<br>• Student<br>• Parents<br>• Behavior rating scales, checklists<br>• Status sheets | • Interviewees' perceptions of the problem—its nature and intensity<br>• The significance to the student and to peers<br>• Patterns of behavior<br>• Settings in which behavior is viewed as problematic<br>• Significance of behavior<br>• Current levels of skill and knowledge |

Based on Heartland, 1998

variables that effect student achievement, and determine the quality of the instruction students receive, are cognitive and not easily observed. As explained in Chapter 2, teacher and student behavior is not always the result of what is going on in a class. It may be the result of what the person *thinks* is going on in the class. It has also been pointed out that teachers and students may hold widely different beliefs about learning, curriculum, and instruction (Stodolsky & Grossman, 1995).

Exhibit 6.5 presents some of the topics one might want to address in an interview. However, in an educational interview, the targets of inquiry are determined by the concerns about the student (these are sometimes articulated in a formal referral for help), demands of the task, and the student's skills. Here are some topics of general importance that should be covered when interviewing students, teachers, and parents.

**Student's thoughts about . . .**

- The particular problem that has led to the interview
- The reason for the interview
- History related to the problem
- Assignments affected by the problem
- Instructional approaches that seem acceptable and effective
- Opinions about teacher expectations
- Class rules and routines
- Skill proficiency
- Self-efficacy and attributions
- Instructional needs

**Teacher's thoughts about . . .**

- The particular problem that has led to the interview
- Teaching
- Student learning
- The reason for the interview
- History related to the problem
- The content of the lesson
- Accommodating diverse learning needs
- The student's existing knowledge
- Evaluation of student progress

**Parent's thoughts about . . .**

- The particular problem that has led to the interview
- Expectations for the student
- Involvement with school
- The reason for the interview
- History related to the problem
- Responsibility for, and attributions about, student learning
- Fixed and alterable variables

Many of the topics listed above are taken from McConaughy (1996) and Ysseldyke & Christenson (1996). They are aligned with the TIES materials written by Ysseldyke & Christenson and discussed in Chapter 4. The full TIES contains interview formats and other procedures for gathering data about students and teaching environments (see Appendices A.13 and A.14 and Howell et al., 2000a).

When conducting an interview, it is especially important to establish rapport (as will be discussed shortly) and to approach the activity with honesty and empathy. When we normally think of rapport, it is in terms of student comfort. However, in the case of an interview, rapport becomes important to both the interviewer and the interviewee. During an interview, there is no test or observation form to provide you with the protection of anonymity or to protect the student from the biases and prior beliefs you may bring to her answers. As many questions will focus on someone's thoughts about other people, it is also important to remember the need for professionalism and confidentiality.

### How Should I Conduct an Interview?

General information about working with students during assessments will be given under Step 4 below. The primary rule for a good curriculum-based interview is to be sure the discussion is aligned with the curriculum. The discussion of curriculum alignment in the last chapter provided information that can help you maintain this focus. In addition, McConaughy (1996) recommends that you:

- Avoid judgmental comments;
- Follow the student's lead by letting her control the direction or sequence of the interview;
- Limit the length of questions and interviewer talk (particularly with younger students);
- Ask the student to describe things and avoid phrasing prompts as questions; and
- Avoid rhetorical questions.

**Status Sheets**    Teachers and other school personnel are also good sources of information.

Status sheets are excellent devices for focusing these interviews. These sheets list the necessary prior knowledge for success at tasks. Therefore, they can serve as the foundation for questions. There will be several status sheets presented in the following chapters. The sheets are best used by getting people who have task-specific experience with the student together (this may include parents, previous teachers, or the student). The group can then go down the list of required skills, discuss each one in terms of the key topics listed above ("things to talk about"), and mark those that need instruction and those that do not. Notes should be taken on the topics discussed, and skills on which there is little agreement should be marked for additional assessment.

Status sheets, if they have appropriate content listed on them, are valuable tools for streamlining the evaluation process. By acknowledging that much is often known about the student, they reduce the need for assessment. (Unfortunately, they are of little use if the student has just moved into town and her previous teachers can't be contacted.)

**Observe**    Observation is an excellent way to collect information about student behavior, but it has some limitations. The biggest limitations are as follows.

- Observations aren't good for behaviors that don't occur spontaneously, frequently, or visibly.

- Observations of the student are meaningless without including observations of the environmental context in which behaviors occur (test items and interview questions provide context, but observing that a student is "out of seat" without also noting if the behavior occurred during history class or swimming is nonsense).

- The limitation above is compounded by the reality that geographic environments often have less to do with student behavior than the student's personal cognitive environment (remember, as explained in Chapter 2, we don't behave according to what is going on around us but rather according to what we *think* is going on).

- When we observe things we change them. This doesn't just mean we interpret an event in some novel way or misrepresent it in our summary (though that happens too). It means once the observer enters the scene, things are changed. This line of discussion quickly gets metaphysical (if a child miscues in the forest where no one can hear, is there an error?).

- Most observations take samples of time intervals as well as particular behaviors. If these time intervals are not representative, the usefulness of the observation is decreased. For example, think about times during your typical day and imagine the different conclusions an evaluator might reach if you were observed for a 10-minute period at 1 P.M. or 1 A.M. (such misalignment could be corrected by lengthening the observational interval or by breaking the interval into ten 1-minute samples taken at different times throughout the day).

An overview of the main issues to remember in making observations is provided in Exhibit 6.6.

The first thing to do when planning an observation is the first thing to do in any educational assessment activity: define what will be measured by finding or writing an objective. A basic rule for observation is that "to count anything you must be able to recognize its beginning and end" (White & Haring, 1982). For example, the behavior "writes digit" begins when the student puts pencil to paper and ends when the student stops writing the digit required. The status, or state, of "in seat" begins when the kid's rear hits the seat of the chair and ends when it leaves (most teachers don't think standing on the chair qualifies as "in seat"). These starting and stopping points must be recognizable if something is to be counted.

### Things to Observe

When conducting observations, we may collect data from one of four categories: overt behavior, covert behavior, state, and/or critical effect (product). These four observation targets represent different approximations of our main focus,

*Exhibit 6.6   Assessment by Observation.*

| Domains | Source | Data Outcomes |
| --- | --- | --- |
| I<br>Instruction | • Systematic observation<br>• Setting analysis (TIES)<br>• Anecdotal recording<br>• Checklists | • Effective teaching practices<br>• Evidence of teacher expectations<br>• Evidence of differential treatment of students<br>• Modifications in materials<br>• Classroom routines and behavior management |
| C<br>Curriculum | • Use of mandated curriculum materials<br>• Use of modified materials<br>• Teacher talk<br>• Assignments<br>• Assessments | • Alignment of materials with curriculum<br>• Task-related skills required to learn from lesson<br>• Task-related skills required to display learning |
| E<br>Environment | Systematic observation for:<br>• Academic focus<br>• Opportunity to learn<br>• Use of work groups<br>• Availability of technology<br>• Distractions<br>• Physical or health risks<br>• Demographics of peer group | • Physical environment (seating arrangement, equipment, lighting, furniture, temperature, noise levels)<br>• Classroom routines and behavior management<br>• Interaction patterns<br>• Class standard of "situationally and developmentally appropriate behavior" |
| L<br>Learner | Systematic observations with anecdotal recording, checklists, and status sheets. Focus on:<br>• Nature and dimensions (frequency, duration, latency, intensity) of target behaviors<br>• Response to interventions<br>• Knowledge of curriculum and task-related behavior<br>• Interaction patterns | • Present levels of performance<br>• Targets for instruction<br>• Nature of the behavior of concern<br>• Interaction patterns of behavior and concern<br>• Response to interventions as reflected in progress monitoring<br>• Evidence of student's instructional preferences |

Based on Heartland, 1998

which is always the student's skill or knowledge. In some cases, one of these categories may be more convenient to use or may seem more clearly aligned with the essential nature of the knowledge we are after.

### Overt Behaviors

Overt behaviors involve muscular movement. Overt behaviors are things like "say name" or "throw ball." They are best measured through

*Exhibit 6.7   Examples of the Dead-Man and Repeatability Tests.*

| Example | Dead-Man Test | Repeatability Test | Conclusion |
|---|---|---|---|
| "Student will not interrupt." | Can a dead man do it? Yes. They seldom bother anyone. | Is it repeatable? Not clearly. | It's not a movement cycle as it lacks movement and fails the dead man test. It can't be counted. |
| "Out of seat." | Can a dead man be out of seat? Yes. | Is it repeatable? Yes. | It's not a movement cycle because it has no movement. It can't be counted. |
| "Get out of seat." | Can a dead man do it? No. | Is it repeatable? Yes. (It starts when the student's rear no longer touches the seat.) | It is a movement cycle. It can be counted. |
| "Raises hand." | Can a dead man do it? No. | Is it repeatable? Yes. | It is a movement cycle. It can be counted. |

frequency counts (a mark is made every time the behavior occurs) to determine their rate (frequency of occurrence, divided by time in minutes) or to get the average occurrence per minute within a time interval. Counting overt behaviors is made easier by applying the concept of a "movement cycle" (White, 1986). In traditional behavioral or operant circles, concepts such as the movement cycle are considered to be absolute. This means that if it doesn't move (start and stop), it can't be counted. Two tests are applied to decide if something can be counted: the **dead-man test** and the **repeatability test.**

The dead-man test asks the question 'Can a dead man do it?' If the answer is "yes," it isn't a movement cycle. For example, could a dead man 'sit quietly in his seat?' The answer is "yes." A dead man could accomplish this with no effort at all, so "sitting quietly in his seat" would not be considered a movement cycle.

The repeatability test asks the question 'Can you tell when the behavior starts and stops?' If you cannot, the behavior does not pass the repeatability test. For example, "listen to teacher directions" would not pass the repeatability test because it would be very difficult to tell when the behavior begins or ends. A student could look directly at a teacher, gazing intently as though rapt with attention, but in fact be thinking about the lyrics of the latest hit by her favorite musical group. It would be impossible to tell if she was actually "listening" to the teacher.

Other examples that illustrate these two tests are shown in Exhibit 6.7.

The advantage of overt behavior is that it can be "seen." However, what people see is determined totally by what they have learned to see and are able to see. Suppose a student *leaves her seat,* but the observer has been looking out the window. Does that mean that, because the student could not be observed, the behavior didn't occur? Of course not. The point is that what one can see is influenced by one's observational equipment.

### Covert Behaviors

Covert behaviors are thoughts and feelings. They are called *covert* because they can't be directly observed. Examples include such things as "thoughts about food," "concern about failure," or "feeling happy." Covert responses can be self-

**Exhibit 6.8    Interval-Sampling Formats.**

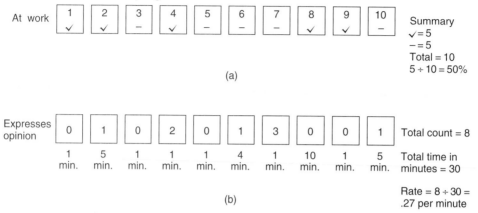

(a)

(b)

recorded by students because they (and only they) are in a position to "see" and record them. The rest of us draw inferences about coverts by observing overt behaviors that we think indicate the internal status of the student (just as we infer from test answers that the student has "knowledge" of the topic tested). When collecting self-reported data, it is helpful to explain both the *dead-man test* and the *repeatability test* to the student. Obviously, counting covert behaviors raises a variety of measurement issues.

**State**    The state of a person is her condition or location. It is the condition (physical or psychological) in which the person resides. "In seat" is a *state* like "at work" or "in love." "Getting in seat," "going to the beach," and "hugging a friend" are behaviors. We may target overt states (in seat, paying attention, asleep, on time for class) or covert states (happy, angry, depressed, compliant) for observation.

We must monitor coverts by drawing inferences from overt behavior (for example, constant frowning indicates the student is unhappy). When observing states, it is a good idea to develop a clear definition of the state and to share that definition with the student. For example, "at work" might always mean "no talk, work materials out, appearance of attention to task."

To take data on someone's state, it is best to use **duration** (length of time in condition) data. It is also possible to check at various intervals and

to summarize the proportion of intervals the student is in the targeted state.

## Data Collection

Data can be collected continuously or at intervals. If a behavior is very disruptive and overt ("throws chair through window"), you might as well count it continuously because you're going to know about it every time it happens. If it is a more subtle behavior (makes eye contact with peer) or a state, you will want to set aside a time (or times) to watch so you don't have to try to observe the student's eyes all day. This is called **interval sampling.** Two interval sampling examples are shown in Exhibit 6.8. In the first case, the "at work" state of the student is observed when the signal from a kitchen timer goes off. If the student is in the target state, the teacher records a check; if not, a dash is recorded. In this example, the measurement rule being used is that a check is made only if the student is in the target state at the instant the timer signals the teacher to look up. In other cases, the measurement rule might be to make a check if the student maintained the state throughout the interval. Both cases would be examples of interval sampling, though different scoring rules are used. This procedure is often called **time sampling** (Kaplan, 1995).

In the second example in Exhibit 6.8, "expresses opinion" is counted every time it occurs during the time the evaluator watches for it. In this example, the observer has watched for a total of 30 minutes over ten separate intervals. During the 30 minutes of actual observation, the behavior occurred eight times for a rate of 0.26 (8 ÷ 30) times per minute. The conversion to rate per minute puts the score on a common scale, so that we can compare rates across days even if a different amount of observation time was used. Converting the "at work" data into a percentage (occurrence/opportunity) accomplishes the same thing. Of course, as is the nature of sampling, the percentage listed is the percentage of intervals and not necessarily the actual percentage of time the student works.

### Recording Interactions

Observation tends to be used for language, classroom, and social behaviors, all of which are highly sensitive to changes in context. To capture the context in which a behavior occurs, it is sometimes necessary to take data on the student's behavior and the behavior of others around her. This is done to try to find things that prompt or support the targeted behavior. The most important people will be the teacher, close friends, and archenemies.

### How Does Observing the Context Differ from Observing the Student?

When you are observing context, you can quickly find yourself on shaky ground. Some teachers who refer a student for evaluation won't take kindly to it if they think you're evaluating them. Collecting data on interactions raises ethical concerns. Primary among these is the idea of consent. If an evaluator must obtain parental permission to observe a student, shouldn't they also obtain teacher permission to observe a teacher? Teachers may not necessarily believe they have agreed to be observed simply by accepting their job. Unfortunately, if you explain what you are doing and why, some teachers may change their teaching behavior when you're in the room. This is a real problem, as nothing will imperil your observation as quickly as the suspicion that you are an undercover agent for the administration.

Exhibit 6.9 shows a recording device in which the student's behavior is compared with the teacher's response. Every time the student says something, it is coded as + (on-task) or △ (off-task) and **T** (to teacher) or **P** (to peer). The teacher's responses are coded as + (positive), − (negative), or 0 (ignore). Positive and negative responses are coded as **S** (to student) or **P** (to peer). The data in Exhibit 6.9 show a pattern in which off-task student talk is preceded and followed by negative teacher comments to the student. Additionally, on-task student talk is always ignored (observations 4, 5, and 8). The implications of these data for teaching (encourage the teacher to attend positively to on-task student talk) would be completely missing if the only data available were on the student. There are many systems for observing interactions. For more examples see Kaplan (2000).

### Spot Observations

Spot observation (Rogoff, 1978) is a sort of time-sampling procedure. With it the observer takes a mental snapshot of a moment in the classroom and later follows up on the snapshot with interview questions. The spot observation begins as the observer briefly notes an event, being sure to include the surrounding circumstances and people. He then turns away and writes down everything he can think of to explain what was seen. Sometimes this is done by "framing" the moment with a brief description of its antecedents and consequences. Here is a single frame:

| Antecedents | Events | Consequences |
|---|---|---|
| History lesson— large group—on Civil War. Many other students confused; Pam asking lots of advanced questions. Teacher responding to all questions. | Pam asks the teacher a question and the other students make fun of her. | Teacher ignores the reaction of the other students and answers Pam's question. |

***Exhibit 6.9   Recording Interactions.***

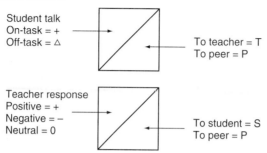

Student talk
On-task = +
Off-task = △

To teacher = T
To peer = P

Teacher response
Positive = +
Negative = −
Neutral = 0

To student = S
To peer = P

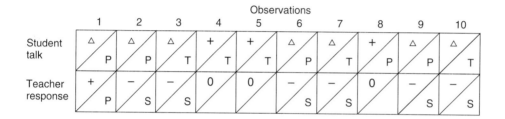

It is hard to reach many conclusions from one frame (the sample is too small), but if several are used a better image of the class interaction may become clear. As a rule, it is better to observe for several short periods spread over the day than for one long period. Although this procedure requires the observer to compile somewhat wordy notes, it allows the observer to capture a moment so thoroughly that he can later ask the participants (teacher, student, peers) questions about it. This combined observation and interview approach allows the evaluator to compare what appeared to be going on with what the participants thought was going on. The differences in perceptions of the event (as may be illuminated by asking "Why did Pam ask questions?") can provide useful information about **maladaptive** covert behaviors.

## Some Final Advice About Observations

Nothing is more obvious than an unfamiliar adult lurking around the back of a classroom trying to observe a student. If the student targeted for observation isn't one of your students,

you may want to prepare the least bothersome observation system you can and then try to get the student's regular teacher to use it. If that doesn't work, walk boldly into the room and get to know everyone (not just the target student). This is better than trying to be sneaky.

Sometimes, concerns about observation seem to be more in the minds of adults than children. Dr. Howell once asked a teacher what a target student was wearing so he'd be able to spot him from a distance at recess. Howell then went out the back way and walked around the building to make a casual approach from the parking lot (not always the best idea these days). As soon as he leaned against the flagpole and started making notes, one of the other students yelled "Hey, Brian! Someone's watching you!" Everybody on the playground froze as Brian (an 8-year-old) walked timidly over and asked "Why are you watching me?"

Howell replied "It's OK, I'm paid to do it."

Satisfied with that, Brian shrugged and went back to "punching others" apparently unconcerned with being observed.

One-way mirrors have their pluses and minuses, depending on which side you are on.

Videotaping is excellent after the class has had a day or so to get used to the camera. When videotaping, be sure to leave the TV monitor turned off. One favorite technique for unobtrusive counting is to fill one pocket with coins and then shift a coin to an empty pocket every time the behavior occurs. At the end of the day you just count the coins shifted and mark the number in your records. (Of course, with some behaviors, some students, and some teacher salaries, this technique will be impractical.)

The real secret to conducting a classroom observation is to *not* be an outsider. Obviously, this is not a problem if you are the classroom teacher, and it isn't a problem if you work in a collaborative context (Jenkins & Leicester, 1992). However, the tone of partnership needed to support collaboration isn't developed quickly and can only be established through active administrative support (Nolet, 1999). Therefore, if you already have a collaborative environment, use it. If you don't, you must still proceed in your attempts to help the student.

Finally, it is our position that a teacher who refers a student for help, particularly in classroom, social, or language areas, is referring the whole room—including himself. However, it would be best to advertise this policy *before* pushing the issue.

## Test

To carry out Step 3 in the evaluation process, one must use reviewing, interviewing, observing, or testing. Testing is reviewed in Exhibit 6.10. It is the last of the R.I.O.T. procedures but is probably the most familiar to you.

When a teacher is interested in a student's knowledge of the Civil War, for example, he might observe the student for some time before the student happens to start spontaneously chatting with friends about the Dred Scott decision. If the teacher couldn't wait for that inspired conversation, he would probably be forced to elicit a display of knowledge. The process of manipulating the environment to elicit behaviors at particular times, or under particular conditions, is called **testing** (which can include role playing and use of simulations).

### What Kind of Test Is Best?

Assessments are constructed according to the purposes for which they are designed. Criterion-referenced tests (CRT) collect samples of behavior to compare them with behavioral standards. In contrast, norm-referenced tests (NRT) collect behavior to be compared with the performance of other people. The behaviors of these other people are summarized in **norms** (see the section on statistics in Howell et al., 2000a). Because norm-referenced assessments are used to determine how one student compares with age-mates (or in some cases grade-mates), it is important that they sample items from across a wide range of curricula. This broad-band sampling assures variability (some high and some low) in the scores that students obtain. Obviously, if every student who took an NRT got the same score, it would be impossible to decide who was above average or below average.

Exhibit 6.11 provides an example of the types of progressively difficult items found on typical NRTs. Suppose you give this test to Lisbeth, a third-grade student. Although there are a few items in Exhibit 6.11 for an "average" third-grader (items 6 and 7), most of the items—probably as many as 80% of them—are either too hard or too easy. Therefore, although the test *will* show how she compares with other third-graders, it *won't* show much about her skill at third-grade math. The normed achievement test was designed to measure a student's academic functioning in relation to peers—not to summarize actual skill.

The criterion-referenced test, in contrast, is designed to measure a narrow band of curriculum. It is composed of items that are all at about the same level. Because this results in less variation in performance, you would not use a CRT to see how Lisbeth's performance compares with her age-mates. The CRT includes only those items that measure the skill or knowledge in question. Students either have a sufficient amount of the skill or knowledge being measured or they do not. Recall that in the last chapter, Exhibit 5.18 provided an example of a

**Exhibit 6.10    Assessment by Test.**

| Domains | Source | Data Outcomes |
|---|---|---|
| I<br>Instruction | • Aggregated peer performance on class assessments<br>• Class standing on district or schoolwide testing<br>• Classroom environment scales, checklists, and questionnaires<br>• Student opinions about instruction and teacher | • Teacher standing in content area (strong or weak in area)<br>• Position of the student relative to class peers |
| C<br>Curriculum | • Aggregated peer performance on class assessments<br>• Level of assignment and curriculum material difficulty<br>• Student opinions about what is being taught | • Difficulty levels of curriculum materials as indicated by student test scores |
| E<br>Environment | • Aggregated peer performance on class assessments<br>• Classroom environment scales (TIES)<br>• Opportunity to learn | • Opportunity to learn<br>• Adequacy of learning environment as indicated by student test scores |
| L<br>Learner | • Curriculum-based measurement (CBM) | • Student performance on curriculum-specific tasks<br>• Accuracy and fluency in oral reading, math computation, and written expression<br>• Resistance to intervention as illustrated through (systematic progress monitoring)<br>• Student academic performance identifying skill strengths and weaknesses |
|  | • Classroom tests | • Student academic performance on classroom measures of achievement<br>• Failure to profit from general instruction<br>• Resistance to intervention (informal progress monitoring) |
|  | • Norm-referenced (individual and group) | • Student academic performance in relationship to a norm group—as a performance standard<br>• Personal trait data in relationship to a norm group |
|  | • Self-reports (checklists, inventories, rating scales, etc.) | • Personal trait data reflecting student perception of the problem the situation and his or her personal adjustment |

Based on Heartland, 1998

**Exhibit 6.11   Computation Survey.**

| 1. (A1,1) | 2. (S1,1) | 3. (A3,2) | 4. (A5,2) | 5. (S2,2) | 6. (S6,3) |
|---|---|---|---|---|---|
| 2 | 8 | 3 | 39 | 46 | 51 |
| +3 | −6 | 6 | +4 | −3 | −28 |
| 5 | 2 | +2 | 43 | 43 | 23 |
|   |   | 11 |   |   |   |

| 7. (A8,3) | 8. (S7,4) | 9. (M1,4) | 10. (M3,4) | 11. (D2,4) | 12. (D3,4) |
|---|---|---|---|---|---|
| 601 | 9062 | 8 | 47 | 6 | .63 |
| 39 | −4185 | ×9 | ×5 | 4$\overline{)24}$ | 4r5 |
| 1 427 | 4877 | 72 | 235 |   | 8$\overline{)37}$ |
| 1067 |   |   |   |   |   |

| 13. (M7,5) | 14. (D6,5) | 15. (DR% 11,5) | 16. (F11,5) | 17. (F16,6) | 18. (F20,6) |
|---|---|---|---|---|---|
| 3075 | .36 | $\frac{4}{20} = \frac{1}{5}$ | $\frac{3}{11} + \frac{2}{11} = \frac{5}{11}$ | $\frac{1}{2} - \frac{5}{18} = \frac{2}{9}$ | $2\frac{3}{4} \times 2\frac{1}{3} = 14\frac{2}{3}$ |
| ×   62 | 41r27 |   |   |   |   |
| 190650 | 74$\overline{)3061}$ |   |   |   |   |

| 19. (F24,6) | 20. (DR% 8,7) | 21. (DR% 9,7) | 22. (M8,8) | 23. (D7,8) | 24. (DR% 6,8) |
|---|---|---|---|---|---|
| $6\frac{3}{4} + 3\frac{1}{6} = 2\frac{5}{38}$ | 2.43 | 16.26 | $7^2 = 49$ | 12 | $\frac{7}{8} =$ 87.5% |
|   | ×2.5 | 1.5$\overline{)24.39}$ |   | $\sqrt{144}$ |   |
|   | 6.075 |   |   |   |   |

*Source:* Howell, K. W., Zucker, S. H. & Morehead, M. K. (2000b). *Multilevel Academic Skills Inventory.* Bellingham, WA: Applied Research and Development Center. To order contact the Student Co-op Bookstore, Western Washington University. Fax (360) 650-2888. Phone (360) 650-3656. Reprinted with permission.

CRT covering addition problems involving one- and two-digit numbers. This happens to be first-grade material. If a student passes this test (sometimes called a probe sheet), it doesn't necessarily mean that she is working on a first-grade level in arithmetic. There are many other math objectives in first grade not represented on this CRT. It does tell us, however, that she has learned the band of skill being measured. Although CRTs are not generally useful for comparing the relative *performance* of students with each other, they can be used to compare their relative *progress*. Whereas NRTs are designed to reveal performance variability during a single testing session, CRTs lend themselves to repeated use. Therefore, a student's progress toward an objective can be monitored with the CRT, and a trend can be established. Although it is almost never done, it is possible to establish progress norms and to use CRTs to find students who are learning at relatively slower or faster rates. In this process, the variability of interest is not in performance but in the time it takes a student to reach a particular performance level (that's called progress).

## What Does a CRT Look Like?

A criterion-referenced test is composed of two things: (1) a behavioral objective and (2) the materials and time necessary to sample knowledge of the objective. Of course, these objectives must have statements of content, behavior, conditions, and criterion of acceptable performance (CAP). The standard (CAP) for CRTs can be determined several ways. Most commonly it is determined by guessing. This is the worst way. For some reason, teachers often guess 80% accuracy. If asked to write any objective, many teachers will write "Given, _____, the student will _____, with 80% accuracy." We're not sure, but we think 80% became popular because Gronlund (1973) used it as an example in one of the first books on the subject. It is a nice enough number, but it cannot be equally relevant to all areas of curriculum: 80% add facts, 80% spell words, 80% adjust brakes, 80% merge onto freeway? Howell once read an objective for a high school math student that said "The student will write and read checks with 80% accuracy." That is not a reasonable criterion! Anything less than 100% accuracy in checking can have a profound impact on one's standard of living. (Just look up the term "check kiting" in your state's criminal code.)

CRTs should be based on short-term instructional objectives. These objectives are either obtained directly from the school district's or state's curriculum or from a task analysis of an objective found in the curriculum. This issue was discussed in Chapter 3. Obviously, if the results of the test are to be used to guide instruction, there should be no difference between the elements measured and those that will be taught. This assures alignment between testing and teaching. The CRT objective and the instructional objective are one and the same. The more specific and behavioral the objective is, the more clearly it defines some quantity of the concept, rule, strategy, or fact it represents, thereby making the knowledge more "observable."

### Item Format

Lisa was a third-grader. After taking a norm-referenced achievement test, she scored at the third-grade, 6-month level in spelling. At first glance, there was nothing unusual about this, except that every Friday she brought home an "F" on her spelling paper because she had failed every spelling test given by the teacher that year. When her parents heard about the achievement scores, they were dumbfounded at first and then became angry. They complained to the principal about Lisa's teacher. However, the behavior expected on the spelling section of the achievement test was different from the behavior expected on the Friday quizzes.

As part of the achievement test, Lisa was given a page with rows of four words, one of which was spelled correctly. Lisa looked at each of the four words and underlined the one she thought was correct. Sometimes she actually recognized the correct word and sometimes she just guessed. This test format was in marked contrast to the format of the Friday class quiz, when the teacher dictated a word and Lisa had to write it from memory. Essentially, the teacher was testing spelling while the achievement test was testing proofreading. These are two different tasks that, while sampling "spelling," employed two very

different testing formats. Needless to say, this disparity in format caused a great deal of confusion, not to mention friction.

Although the target content of two items may be the same, the format or conditions imposed by the items may vary. Here are two items with different formats for four domains of content.

| Addition | | Geometry | |
|---|---|---|---|
| (a)  2<br>$+\,2$ | (b) 2 + 2 = | (a) Define<br>the term<br>*triangle.* | (b) Which of<br>the<br>following<br>is *not* a<br>triangle? |
| Spelling | | Phonics | |
| (a) Spell the<br>word<br>*analytical.* | (b) Circle<br>the mis-<br>spelled<br>word:<br>• analitical<br>• sequence<br>• computation<br>• components | (a) What<br>sound<br>do<br>these<br>letters<br>make?<br><u>oo</u> | (b) Circle<br>the<br>word<br>that<br>rhymes<br>with <u>oo</u>:<br>• dome<br>• run<br>• some<br>• tune |

It is hard to say which of these formats is best, but usually the best item formats are those that are most realistic. They don't just sample what a person knows, they sample it the way a person will use it in real life. Therefore, sticking with Lisa, item **a** is the best spelling item in the group.

### If Tests Are So Complex, Should Teachers Construct Their Own?

Many teachers think they don't have the time to produce tests that will yield valid inferences about the performance of their students. There is some logic to this thinking. If there already is a test available that will suit your purposes, it is foolish to spend time writing another. However, there may come a time when you need a test that doesn't exist. The steps to test construction are as follows.

1. Examine the curriculum to select the slice of material to be covered.

2. Plan the test by recognizing content, behaviors, and conditions.

3. Sequence the content, behaviors, and conditions and arrange them into a table of specifications (test plan).

4. Once the table has been developed examine the grids to see which ones you want to use for objectives (you don't have to use them all). Those are the squares for which you will need to write items. If you are interviewing, you can also develop questions according to the table.

5. You may "weight" a column, row, or square by writing additional items for that part of the table.

6. Decide on the item format you are going to use and then select or write items for the squares you identified in the table of specifications. Remember that the number of items and their format (identify or produce) may be different for different kinds of proficiency (accuracy or fluency) or content. Remember, the format will be different if you are going to use the test for formative evaluation.

7. Establish CAP by standardizing the test through a search of the professional literature or by conducting your own sampling study with skilled students.

Many school administrators and classroom teachers prefer published assessments over teacher-made instruments or simple classroom observation. These educators seem to have more faith in published material than in anything they could design themselves (after all, don't we always call published assessments "formal" and teacher-made ones "informal"?). The reasoning may not be logical.

Regardless of other characteristics, published tests are on the market because they make money. It isn't illegal to publish a bad test.

If you need to select an assessment, choose a good one. All tests are not created equal. Get rid of the notion that being copyrighted, published, and marketed automatically makes something good (remember *cash validity?*). Educators must become better consumers. Although it is popular to criticize test publishers, keep in mind that they sell only what educators continue to buy. Years ago, Postman and Weingartner (1969) stated that schools should prepare students to become experts at "crap" detecting. One way teachers can do this is to start detecting some themselves. This can be accomplished by assuring that the ten guidelines in Exhibit 6.12 are met. Each of these guidelines is briefly described below.

### Guideline 1: Assessment and Curriculum Must Be Aligned

The single most important aspect of any assessment used for CBE is that it be aligned with the curriculum. This means it must test the knowledge the teacher is teaching and that the student should be asked to display that knowledge the way she is asked to display it in class. If what she is expected to know (or how she is expected to display her knowledge) is unimportant or irrelevant, that is a curriculum development problem—not an assessment problem. As you recall from Chapter 3, curriculum follows from an analysis of the important goals. When you teach what you intend the student to learn and the student is learning what you teach, you have achieved a critical element of curriculum alignment. But you will only know whether or not the student is learning what you want her to learn when assessment also is aligned with curriculum.

In CBE curriculum, instruction and evaluation become so tightly meshed that they are difficult to separate, and that's the way it should be. Assessment that shows a student is *not* making sufficient progress means a change in instruction is needed. Instruction continues until assessment shows the student *is* making adequate progress. Adequate progress is indicated when a student successfully completes curriculum-based measures with greater accuracy and/or fluency.

### Guideline 2: Assessments Must Be Easy to Use

Assessment must be easy to use or it won't get used. This fact of life is not an indication that

**Exhibit 6.12    A Checklist for Selecting and Constructing Assessments.**

| Status | Guidelines | Explanation |
|---|---|---|
| YES  NO | 1. Assessments must be aligned with the curriculum. | Select or construct assessments that cover the same content, behaviors, and conditions as those taught in class. |
| YES  NO | 2. Assessments must be easy to use. | Make sure there are directions and scoring procedures. Make the assessment easy to follow. |
| YES  NO | 3. Assessments must have clearly defined purposes. | Know the purpose and limitations of the instrument being used. Determine whether it is an entitlement or a treatment assessment and whether it is a norm- or criterion-referenced assessment. |
| YES  NO | 4. Assessments should be standardized. | Be sure the appropriate type of data (accuracy or rate) for the content is being assessed. Standards should be set by reviewing the literature, asking experts, or sampling a standardization population. |
| YES  NO | 5. Assessment should sample clearly defined content domains. | Be able to cross-reference items and procedures to content and behavioral domains. |
| YES  NO | 6. They should assess relevant types of knowledge. | Decide if fact and concept evaluation is sufficient. If not, devise a way to make the strategy observable. |
| YES  NO | 7. Some assessments should collect rate data. | Design assessments that do not inhibit rate by assuring the random distribution of difficulty, adequate sample size, and opportunity to respond. Score fluency. |
| YES  NO | 8. Assessments should collect an adequate sample. | Decide how consolidated the content is. Write adequate items (usually 10) for each strategic element of highly consolidated content or for each attribute of a concept. |
| YES  NO | 9. Assessments should use appropriate scoring rules. | Use measurement rules that assign points to the smallest educationally relevant units. |
| YES  NO | 10. Some assessments should be complex and interactive. | Try to include the most "authentic" items you can without losing sensitivity to learning or alignment. |

teachers are a slothful lot who will do only what is absolutely necessary to get through the day. Nor does this guideline suggest that teachers are hopelessly simpleminded and can only do things that are easy. Rather, this guideline acknowledges that schools and classrooms are complicated environments in which there are many competing demands on teacher time. It is no more appropriate to expect teachers to adopt unnecessarily complicated assessment procedures than it is to expect air-traffic controllers to add new tasks that increase the level of difficulty of their job. The potential for disaster is real in either instance. Most teachers simply don't have time to spend on work that doesn't directly result in improved teaching and increased learning. At the very least, the assessment should:

- Be easy to administer;
- Be easy for the student to take;
- Have consistent, clearly described directions and scoring procedures;
- Be easily transportable;
- Be easy to interpret; and
- Make the trouble of giving it and taking it worthwhile by providing reliable and valid results that can be used to make educationally relevant decisions.

Concerns about ease of use must be balanced against the principle of maximum effort for minimum skills, meaning that it is just plain *harder* to evaluate the educational needs of the most problematic students. You have to be prepared to spend more time and effort with more complex instruments if you intend to help the students that need the most help.

### Guideline 3: Assessments Must Have Clearly Defined Purposes

This issue has been discussed extensively throughout this book. It can be distilled to the following three rules:

1. If you don't know why you are testing, don't test.
2. When in doubt, teach. Teaching is more important than testing.

3. If you don't know what to teach, test.

### Guideline 4: Assessments Should Be Standardized

As we already have discussed, standardization refers to both administration/scoring and comparison. Use consistent administration and scoring procedure to ensure that you don't introduce error (see Howell et al., 2000a) into the testing process. Also, find or develop legitimate expectations so that a comparison can be made between the standard and the student's behavior.

### Guideline 5: Assessments Should Sample Clearly Defined Domains

This guideline is actually a corollary of guideline 3. Assessment procedures must sample whatever domain it is you think you are testing. The way to ensure adequate and effective domain sampling is to be clear about what the domain is. If your conception of the domain is too narrow, your assessment procedures will be too narrow. Similarly, if your conception of the domain is too broad or fuzzy, it will be impossible to devise (or select) efficient, direct assessments. For example, if it is difficult for you to say what "reading comprehension" entails, it is going to be difficult for you to devise an assessment procedure to test a student's reading comprehension. If you think reading comprehension is simply reading a story and answering questions, you may not test use of context clues, text structure, or decoding. On the other hand, if you think "reading comprehension" entails students choosing their reading material, completing reading logs, and correcting miscues, your reading assessment may be too vague or multidimensional to be of much use.

### Guideline 6: Assessments Should Sample Relevant Types of Information

Chapters 3 and 4 presented the idea that different kinds of information might be applied to the same task. These kinds of information included facts, concepts, rules, and strategies. It follows that different evaluative procedures should be used to collect information about them. Recall the discussions in Chapters 3 and 4 concerning the nature and teaching of various kinds of information. Also, the instructional guidelines presented in Howell et al., 2000a provide guidance for evaluating student learning on various types of information.

When constructing assessment tasks that are intended to sample various information types, recall that the tasks must reflect the characteristics of the information and the manner in which it must be learned.

*Facts* are simple associations of a stimulus with a response. Students learn facts by memorizing them. To test them, we check to see if the student has stored the fact accurately and can recall it on demand. For example, if $2 + 2 = 4$, then you show the student $2 + 2$ and ask "What does this equal?" It is easy to both test and teach factual knowledge.

*Concepts* are objects, events, actions, or situations that share a set of defining characteristics. As we discussed in Chapters 3 and 4, concepts are best taught through presentation of examples and nonexamples that illustrate the full range of the concept and its defining attributes. Any concept belongs to a category that has a rule for defining the relevant features of all members of the category. The definition provides the basis for organizing the attributes of the concept and for distinguishing between examples and nonexamples of the concept. Assessment, then, must focus on the student's skill to distinguish examples from nonexamples of the concept. As we discussed in Chapter 4, teaching concepts involves juxtaposition of increasingly similar nonexamples so that the student makes finer and finer discriminations on the basis of the defining characteristics of the concept. Conceptual knowledge is most conveniently evaluated by using categorization activities. These formats require the student to sort items into "example" and "nonexample" groupings or "always," "sometimes," and "never." As demonstrated in Exhibit 6.13, easy conceptual items ask the student to sort between obvious examples and nonexamples of attributes, whereas difficult items require fine discriminations.

During an interview, it is often convenient to directly ask students about the relevant ("always" or "never") attributes of a concept. For example,

**Exhibit 6.13    Items Testing: Conceptual Knowledge.**

| Easy Item | Difficult Item |
|---|---|
| Which of the following is most clearly a "type of information"? | Which of the following is most clearly a "type of information"? |
| (a) red | (a) understanding |
| (b) fish | (b) relevant formats |
| (c) conceptual | (c) conceptual |
| (d) eating | (d) evaluation |

"What are the characteristics of a professional?" (It may also be appropriate to ask them to role-play the concept; for example, "Act like a professional.") You can also ask the student to define the concept. The answers for characteristics and definitions should be the same, although asking for characteristics is more apt to avoid the possibility of a rote (factual) response. Look again at Exhibit 5.18. Notice that although the objective of the test is "Add one-digit addend to two-digit with regrouping," some items (labeled "noninstances") do not require regrouping. This is to test the student's skill at deciding what to do as well as her skill at doing it. Deciding what to do is one step in all problem-solving exercises, and it hinges on conceptual knowledge (categorizing types of "problems").

Have you ever seen a student borrow when it wasn't necessary, convert a vowel to the long or short sound without reason, or raise a hand for permission to speak when the situation was informal? Those students knew what to do but they didn't know when to do it. The inclusion of noninstances (items of a different type than the type being tested) on assessments allows the evaluator to know when students do not have the conceptual knowledge needed to recognize when a particular strategy should be used.

A *rule* usually represents an if-then or cause-effect relationship. Learning rules requires a student to attend to both parts of the rule and discriminate the relationship that connects them. Instruction entails presentation of a wide range of instances of the rule in which one of the parts of the relationship is provided and the student predicts the contingent part. Assessment, then,

*Exhibit 6.14   Test of Mathematics Strategies.*

There are 40 students. 25% of the students have blue eyes. How many have blue eyes?

(a)
$$\begin{array}{r} 40 \\ + .25 \\ \hline \end{array}$$

(b)   (.25)40

(c)
$$\begin{array}{r} 40 \\ - 25 \\ \hline \end{array}$$

(d)
$$\begin{array}{r} 40 \\ \times .25 \\ \hline \end{array}$$

2% of the students were absent on Tuesday. 20% of those present brought a sack lunch and 75% of those present bought a hot lunch. The rest of the students fixed a lunch in their classroom. What percent of the students in school fixed a lunch in their classroom?

(a)
$$\begin{array}{r} 20\% \\ + 75\% \\ \hline \end{array} \qquad \begin{array}{r} 100\% \\ - 95\% \\ \hline \end{array}$$

(b)
$$\begin{array}{r} 2\% \\ 20\% \\ + 75\% \\ \hline \end{array} \qquad \begin{array}{r} 100\% \\ - 97\% \\ \hline \end{array}$$

(c)
$$\begin{array}{r} .20 \\ \times .02 \\ \hline \end{array} \qquad \begin{array}{r} .20 \\ \times .75 \\ \hline \end{array}$$

(d)
$$\begin{array}{r} 75\% \\ \times 20\% \\ \hline \end{array} \qquad \begin{array}{r} 100\% \\ - 15\% \\ \hline \end{array}$$

should employ a similar format. A student might be asked to predict an outcome, given the first part of a rule, or to describe the events that lead to a particular outcome. For example, suppose you wanted to find out if a student has learned a rule about making words that end in "y" plural: "Change the 'y' to 'i' and add 'es.'" These two items would test the rule:

1. If this word is "story," and I want to talk about more than one story, then how should the word be spelled? How did you know how to spell the plural version of "story"?

2. If this word is "berries," then how should I spell it if I want to talk about only one? How did you know how to spell the singular version of "berries"?

As with concepts, the range of examples used in testing a student's acquisition of a rule will vary, depending on how fine a discrimination you want to test. Very fine discriminations will be more difficult at earlier stages of the learning cycle. Items presented to a student who is expected to have mastered a rule would require much finer discriminations and, therefore, juxtapose more similar non-instances.

Obviously, if *strategies* are important things to teach, they are also important things to evaluate. There are three ways to do this: (1) ask, (2) use error (product) analysis, and (3) use strategy-based items.

Interview assessment usually means encouraging the student to "think aloud" (that is, work through a task slowly while she verbalizes each step). Sometimes asking a student to explain (teach) to you how to do the task will yield the same result. Teachers who listen to a student explain the process used to arrive at an answer are obtaining information about the student's knowledge of the strategy.

You also can present items that require the student to select how she would work a task. Two math examples are shown in Exhibit 6.14 (Howell et al., 2000b).

Notice that these items sample the student's knowledge of the process for finding answers and do not even ask the student for the answers.

### Guideline 7: Collect Rate Data

To make statements about learning that include time, it is sometimes necessary to collect rate data. Rate is the frequency of performance divided by time in minutes (15 products in 2.5 minutes = 6 products per minute).

All timed assessments are not rate assessments. Timing is typically added to assessments so that administration will be uniform; as a result, reliability will be inflated (it is a quick way to make a technically inadequate test look better). But the data derived from most timed assessments are still accuracy data. A rate test yields data by timing the student's response within a single domain or a series of related items. The count (number of items completed) is then divided by the time (traditionally in minutes) to obtain the rate. If one item is finished in 15 seconds, then the rate is $1/0.25 = 4$ per minute. If 80 items are completed in 5 minutes, the rate is $80/5 = 16$ per minute.

Because so few assessments are designed for collecting rate data or for use in continuous monitoring (which requires giving the same test over and over again), some of us have never seen a rate-formatted test. However, rate data are very important when curriculum-based evaluation is employed. Exhibit 5.18 was a rate-formatted CRT. Notice that there is adequate space to write the answers and that, although the items are organized diagonally by multipliers, they are randomized by difficulty. Many measures associated with curriculum-based measurement result in rate data.

### Guideline 8: Collect an Adequate Sample of Student Performance

To collect an adequate sample, an assessment must include sufficient items (test questions, observation intervals, interview prompts, or product reviews). In some cases, they must also allow for rate data, demands for repeated use, and various item formats. Here are some considerations for ensuring that an adequate sample of student knowledge and/or behavior is included in an assessment.

**Number of Items**   The number of items required on an assessment was discussed in general earlier in this section. However, there is one issue related to fluency testing that needs to be

included now. When assessments are used to collect rate data, students are often told to skip items they do not know so that their rate of response will not become distorted. For example, suppose a student was reading a selection in which the one word she did not know was the tenth word in the passage. The student might read the passage at a rate of 100 wpm up to the tenth word and then stare at it for the rest of the allowed time. Her rate would then seem to be 10 words per minute rather than the more representative 100 wpm. To avoid this problem, an adequate number of items should be provided to allow skipping (usually 50% more than the objective criterion).

The need to repeat assessments for formative evaluation also influences how an adequate sample is assured. If a test is to be used for repeated administration, enough items must be provided to avoid **ceiling effects** and prevent rote memorization of the test. A ceiling effect occurs when a student can't get a higher score because they have already responded to all of the available items. For example, suppose you were monitoring a student's progress in reading by asking her to read aloud once each week for 1 minute from a passage selected from the reading text used in her school. Over time, you would expect the student's rate of oral reading fluency to increase (if your instruction is effective). Once the student's rate of oral reading fluency becomes greater than the number of words in the passage she is reading from, she will get to the end of a passage before the minute is up.

### Guideline 9: Tests Should Use Appropriate Scoring Rules

Scoring rules were explained in Chapter 5. The key issue is that in selecting scoring rules, the metric should correspond to the smallest relevant instructional unit. As the example in Chapter 5 showed, you could score math computation items according to the number of items correctly completed or the number of correct additions made. If a student is unlikely to correctly complete entire computation problems, it makes little sense to select entire problems as a scoring unit because the student almost certainly will get scores of "0." This is not instructionally useful information. On the other hand, scoring units that focus on a finer detail of the behavior (correct additions) would be more sensitive to instruction and more likely to show growth over time.

### Guideline 10: Assessments Should Be as Complex and Interactive as Possible

In some cases it is necessary to sample small decontextualized samples of content (vowels in isolation, digits in isolation, word meanings in isolation). This isolation allows focus. However, it decreases the "authenticity" of the assessment because in the real world, skills are seldom utilized in disjunction from a context. Therefore, one must always consider the degree to which an assessment mirrors the complexity of the contexts in which it will typically be used. One must also consider with what other skills the targeted knowledge typically interacts. The goal is to produce an assessment that is as complex and interactive as possible without being insensitive to learning or misaligned with the curriculum. However, if it comes down to it, it is best to err on the side of sensitivity and alignment.

---

**The Curriculum-Based Evaluation Process**

Step 1. Define Your Purpose
Step 2. Define The Thing To Be Measured
Step 3. Devise A Way To Make The Thing In Step 2 Observable

## Step 4. Conduct Assessment
Step 5. Use The CBE Process of Inquiry
Step 6. Summarize
Step 7. Make Decisions

---

### Working with Students

There is much more to administering an assessment than reading questions from a manual. You must remember that you are interacting with a person. The child you're working with might be scared, angry, or both (Swanson & Howell, 1996). She may not have had much success in school or may not be very good at answering questions. She probably is wondering why she has to take the 65th assessment of her young life. At its best, evaluation is anxiety-producing. At its worst, it can be a devastating experience for the student as well as the examiner. So, if you don't want to be devastating, we suggest you pay close attention to this section.

### What Is the First Thing to Do When Administering an Assessment?

Get ready. Know how to give the assessment. Remember guideline 4 above: assessments should be standardized, so there will almost certainly be a set of administration and scoring procedures to follow. This is true whether you are using a test you bought from a test publisher or a curriculum-based measure you devised yourself. You should be able to administer the measure in a reasonable amount of time without any errors that would invalidate the results. To accomplish this, study the directions carefully and practice using them on as many people as possible before using it "for real" (this is what friends and their children are for!).

A word of caution before going on: most published testing procedures have been designed to be used with average students (Fuchs & Deno, 1991). The typical manual doesn't tell you what to do if a student refuses to answer a question or tells you to stuff the test up your nose (or what to do if she tries to stuff it herself). Many of the students you end up testing may be anything but "typical" in the way they respond. Here are some general rules.

### Don't Try to Commit Everything to Memory
It is perfectly legitimate to make notations in the margins of the manual, to use index tabs, or to highlight certain parts for reference during administration. (By the way, you should be doing the same with this text.) If necessary, use $3 \times 5$ cards with required information (time, directions, ceiling limits) on them. Be careful that you

make these notations in such a way that reference to them will not interrupt the flow of evaluation. There is nothing so disconcerting to both student and examiner as those long pauses when the examiner fumbles through the material trying to find out what to do next.

**Have All of the Materials Ready Before the Assessment**    This includes observation sheets, pencils, scratch paper, test booklets, manual, and a stopwatch. If you know that erasures are not permitted on a particular test, or you would like to have errors left intact for subsequent analysis, use pencils without erasers. Tear the erasers off the pencils. If the student has been conditioned to use an eraser, no matter how many times you tell her not to, she will probably keep on erasing. This behavior is easier to stop if there is no eraser on the pencil to begin with.

Have a number of pencils of assorted sizes available and let the student choose the one with which she's most comfortable. Try not to sharpen the pencils too finely. The anxious student may push down so hard when writing that she either breaks the point or tears a hole in the paper. This will only add to her anxiety. If the pencil supply is limited and there is no pencil sharpener in the room, have a pocket sharpener handy—just in case.

Provide the student with scratch paper if the assessment permits its use. Write her name or initials along with the date and any other pertinent information on *each* sheet. This is particularly important when you are testing more than one student during a given day. Staple or clip together each student's test materials, including the scratch paper, when the test is finished. Don't stuff little bits of paper inside pockets or purse and expect to remember later to whom they belong. Also, fill in pertinent data regarding the student on all forms. Do this immediately or you may forget it. If you don't know things like dates of birth or age, don't be sure the student does. On several occasions, the authors have asked students their ages and found out later they were wrong.

**Get the Materials Organized**    Place your materials (remember all of those pencils) out of reach,

or be prepared to spend the entire testing session ducking. It might be wise to place the test materials on a table behind you with the student seated across from you.

Also consider your own needs in the arrangement of materials. Try to have things easily accessible and in the proper order for use. If you don't have the table space, pile them in order of use from top to bottom.

If you are planning to use a stopwatch or tape recorder, make sure it works. If it isn't electric, remember to wind the watch even if it seems to be working. Stopwatches are notorious for stopping by themselves in the middle of timed assessments. Stay away from recorders with built-in microphones because they will pick up everything in the room you don't want to record (buzzing lights or the blowing of a nose). Use a directional microphone and tape it to the table to lessen vibration and inhibit the student from picking it up. Our experience has been that students seldom are neutral when it comes to tape recorders. Put a microphone in front of one and she'll either run and hide or begin to perform. Bring along an extra cassette in case the first one breaks or you discover at the last minute that it contains the Billy Dean concert you attended last summer. Also, make sure that the outlet in the room works. If you are using batteries, have extras available. (By the way, check on your district's view of tapes. In some jurisdictions it is legally dangerous to retain them after you have transcribed the necessary information.)

**Get the Setting Organized**    Consider which side of the student you'll sit on if you are not going to sit opposite her. For instance, if she is right-handed, you will need to be on her left side so that you can easily observe her written responses. Arrange the environment so that it is comfortable for both of you. Make sure that the lighting and the room temperature are adequate (too warm, and you'll both nod off during the test; too cold, and you'll each be distracted by the clicking of teeth). Make sure that both seats are the right size (too small, and you'll be distracted by cramped muscles; too high, and you'll have a child falling (or diving) off). Physical discomforts of any kind can invalidate a student's performance.

Noise coming either from within the room or from outside can be masked with a little gadget called a **white noise** machine. Available from specialty houses for around $50, they are worth every penny if you are required to do your testing across the hall from the gym or next to the cafeteria. If you can't afford one, tune a radio to a non-station and adjust the volume for low level static. Recorded instrumental music (especially classical) or electric room-air purifiers will also effectively mask noise, as will an electric fan (all of this advice also applies to motel rooms).

You should be aware of potential visual distractions and limit them before the student arrives. Try to have her facing in a neutral direction. She should not be facing any of the windows. As soon as she walks into the testing area, show her where you want her to sit. You sure don't want to make any adjustments afterward. This doesn't mean that you shouldn't make adjustments during the testing session as they are needed. It means that, if you do your homework, you probably won't have to. If others are to be present in the room, try to obscure any sight of movement. Post a sign on the door of the testing room that reads

---

## Testing: Do Not Disturb

---

Most people will respect your privacy. If some curious or inconsiderate souls ignore the sign, pay no attention to them and neither will your student. One last bit of trivia: Whenever possible, sit between the student and the door.

***Pay Attention to "Minor" Details***   Many of the preliminary details we have mentioned (such as chair size, room temperature, pencil points, white noise machines) may seem like so much minutiae. But if you want to get valid results and continue to remain on speaking terms with your students, it is worth your while to manage as many of these details as possible. To make sure

you don't forget any, use a checklist that includes all of the things we have talked about here.

***Modify Normed Measures***   Sometimes you may want to make changes to an assessment to assure that the students who have limited skills or physical or sensory limitations can access the test procedure. There are requirements that this be done for students who have disabilities that might prevent their display of knowledge. When making these changes, be sure to consider the distinction between accommodations and modifications. An **accommodation** is a change that compensates for the student's problems but does not alter the substance of the task. A **modification** does change the task. Therefore, a student who works on a modified assessment is working in a different curriculum (set of tasks) than other students.

Deciding to modify a task for a student is a serious undertaking. It should be made by a team, and the rationale and nature of the modification should be recorded. For example, if it is decided that a student will be allowed to stay with manuscript writing and never learn cursive, all current and future teachers must be informed of the decision. Otherwise, future teachers may penalize the student for failing to use cursive.

The distinction between an accommodation and a modification is subtle. Accommodations are supports or services provided to help a student access the curriculum and validly demonstrate learning. Modifications change the content and performance expectations for what a student should learn. The same change could fall into either category. For example, the most common accommodation for students taking tests is to allow them to have more time. However, if time is a critical part of the content, behavior, conditions, or criteria of the task, this change would represent a modification of the objective. Clearly, a student whose objective is to read 100 words correct in a minute should not be given an unlimited amount of time to read 100 words.

The primary consideration in deciding whether and how to change a test is the purpose for using the test. If the test is used on all students for accountability purposes, accommodations should be selected that will have minimum impact on scores. If the test is being used to find information that will guide in-class instructional and curriculum decisions, any accommodations or modifications that will advance that purpose should be allowed. Here are some examples of accommodations and modification that take into account instruction, curriculum, the school environment, and the learner. In situations like those described below, the *probability* that an accommodation or modification should be allowed is increased.

If you make modifications or accommodations on a standardized assessment, you may not follow all of the rules of administration exactly as

---

## Instruction

*General rule:* The stronger the instructional history, the greater the student's past opportunity to learn. Therefore, the greater the argument for a modification.

**Accommodation**

If the student has had limited instruction on writing skills needed to display knowledge of reading comprehension on this test, she may be allowed to dictate the answer.

**Modification**

If the student has been given extensive and high quality instruction on the writing skills required to display knowledge of the reading comprehension on the test, then dictation should not be allowed.

---

## Curriculum

*General rule:* Any change in the substance of the task is a modification.

**Accommodation**

*Content:* If it is a multiplication test, it cannot be changed to an addition test.

*Behavior:* If the student cannot write (because of a condition that cannot be altered through instruction), then assistive technology or oral response may be used.

*Conditions:* If it can be determined that the student cannot (or never will) work without supervision, then assistance can be allowed.

*Criteria:* If a high level of accuracy is not required for performance, then changing criteria from 95% to 80% is allowed.

**Modification**

If it is determined in a valid way that the student need not be taught or may never be taught multiplication, then the content can be changed to addition.

If writing is *always* needed to apply this skill, then the student should *not* be allowed to say the answer.

If the student is expected to do the work independently, then teacher assistance is not allowed.

If it can be determined that there is no instructional way to overcome a problem that prevents the student from reaching the necessary proficiency, then the skill should be dropped from this student's curriculum.

---

### School Environment

*General rule:* Educational decisions should be based on considerations of the student's individual needs, not on school resources.

| **Accommodation** | **Modification** |
| --- | --- |
| If the student requires a computer to finish the written expression test but a computer is not in the room, a computer should be found and provided. | If the student requires a computer to finish a word processing test but there is not a computer, then the test item cannot be given until a computer is supplied. Finding another way to do the item would not be allowed. |

---

### Learner

*General rule:* In general, if the student is younger, accommodations are more acceptable. If the student is older, modifications are more acceptable.

| **Accommodation** | **Modification** |
| --- | --- |
| If the student cannot hear, then the test directions should be written out. | If a deaf student cannot do the task, for example, because it requires him or her to listen to music, then the task should be changed or dropped. |

---

stated in the manual. However, it is bad practice to report scores derived from the nonstandard administration of a standardized test. In fact, although modifications in test administration are permissible to get behavior samples, remember that your interpretations cannot follow the standardization guidelines once the accommodation or modification has been made. We recommend that any result from nonstandard administration be accompanied by this statement: "These results were obtained through nonstandard test administration."

Changes may be made during the testing session as the need arises, but it is better to prepare for them ahead of time so that you can put together all of the materials you need (flashcards, occluders, large-print test forms, counting beads); this is where knowledge of the student's characteristics becomes so important.

If the student is a stranger, all it takes is a 10-minute question-answer session with the student's current teacher, a brief look at some student work, and a classroom observation to find out about her. While you're in the room, say hello to the student too, so she will have met you before the session. Using this information, take a look at the measure you are going to use and make any accommodations you think necessary. If accommodations are too drastic or excessive, you would probably be better off using a different test. For students in special education, these decisions about accommodations and modifications must be made by the IEP team. The 1997 reauthorization of IDEA specified that accommodations or modifications to statewide or district testing must be included on the student's IEP (Yell, 1998; Ysseldyke et al., 1994).

## Checking, Timing, and Taping

Make sure the student can't see you recording responses. If you must use a screen or a clipboard on your lap to hide your recording, explain why you are doing so. If you are sitting next to the student, sit a little back so that she can't easily look at the recording sheet.

If timing, do not leave the stopwatch where the student can see it, or she will pay more attention to the watch than to the work. Also, be sure you know how to use your stopwatch. Asking a student to reread a passage or redo a set of problems because you couldn't figure out how to turn the stopwatch on will invalidate the results and be a waste of the student's time. Also, use a stopwatch that is big enough to see at arm's length and has buttons big enough to operate with one hand. Tape the watch to your clipboard. This way you can glance quickly at the watch without moving your head or rolling up your shirt sleeves.

While you're timing, you also will need to be ready to redirect the student's attention to the test, record her responses, manage test materials, keep track of the scoring rules, and not fall off of that little tiny student chair they gave you to sit on. You get the idea. Furthermore, don't take your latest microprocessor watch into the room and let it beep at the student every half-hour, either. It's bad enough listening to them go off at the movies. While we're on that topic, if you use a pager, be sure to turn it off or put it on vibrate mode while you are testing. The same goes for your cell phone.

Some teachers report that their students get upset by stopwatches. If the student is upset by the watch, you must either time covertly (put a clock with a sweep hand where only you can see it) or desensitize the student to the watch. One teacher had some students complain that a minute was too short a time to do any work. So the teacher started the stopwatch and asked the students to raise their hands when they thought a minute had passed. Most of them had their hands up within 30 seconds. This is a good exercise for students who are nervous about running out of time.

Whenever possible, tape-record verbal responses that are lengthy or complex so that you can double check the student's work after she has gone. This technique is especially helpful with reading tests where the student is required to read aloud and you have to score responses before deciding to move on to the next level. If you feel that you missed an item or two while the student was reading, all you have to do is replay the tape. You probably won't lose her attention during this time because most students like to listen to their own voice. It is improper to have a student reread material because you didn't hear it the first time or she was moving too fast for you to score. The student may think you want her to change response(s). Besides, scoring behavior should be controlled by the student's skill at reading and not by your skill at scoring.

## Feedback

Try to limit all movement (marking or nodding) unless you are consistent. Otherwise, besides distracting the student, you may also cue correct and incorrect responses. If you need to mark test items, mark *all* of them (not just correct or incorrect ones). By seeing you mark every item, all the student knows is that the pencil moves when she responds. Because she can't see what you actually write, she doesn't know when she's correct or incorrect. Do the same thing with verbal responses. If you say "good" or "OK" for correct items and nothing for incorrect items, the student will soon know when she is right or wrong. You should say nothing at all or simply repeat the student's response. You should also be careful not to cue with tone of voice or facial expression.

Sometimes it may be necessary to encourage the student if she's reluctant to respond. Even here, try to make your encouragement as noncommittal as possible because you want to reinforce working on the test rather than on performance. Encourage with phrases such as "You're working hard," "Keep up the good work," "Let's try this one," "Do your best," "I like the way you are paying attention," and so on. Once again, the idea is to reinforce work on the test, not correct or incorrect responses.

Here is a hard one. Sometimes students will begin to give *themselves* feedback on the test. They'll say things such as "I blew that one" or "That's another one wrong." This self-defeating feedback can become a vicious circle, particularly if the feedback is incorrect. If you see such a pattern beginning, you may want to break the no-feedback rule and tell the student that she got the item correct (if she did). It is difficult to decide when this should be done. The purpose is to correct erroneous feedback, not to reinforce correct behavior. This distinction is very subtle. One clue that you can use is the student's statements. "I blew that one!" is an assertion; "I blew that one?" is a question. As a rule, you should ignore the questions and correct false assertions.

## Rapport

Every evaluation text tells you to establish rapport. Although rapport building is important, it is also difficult to teach. The keys to building rapport between student and examiner are empathy, honesty, and shared membership. Always try to put yourself in the student's place. Think about how you would feel if you were being asked to do things you weren't particularly good at in front of an adult who may be a total stranger or, worse yet, someone you know and like.

Establishing rapport simply means reducing the student's state of anxiety (or hostility) to the point where it no longer interferes with the display of knowledge. It doesn't mean you have to love each other. There are a number of general things you can do to facilitate rapport building.

- The first thing you can do to establish rapport is to ask the student questions that don't relate to school. Try to find something you and the student share. Show the student that you have a sincere interest in her as a person as well as a student. Begin with open-ended questions like "What do you have to say for yourself?" or "What's new?" If this doesn't elicit any spontaneous chatter, ask questions about what she likes to do after school, whom she plays with, or what shows she likes to watch on TV. If nothing else works, talk about pets or brothers and sisters. The talk doesn't have to be "nice"; lots of people have learned to get along during gripe sessions.
- Depending on the student, discuss what's going on and why she's being evaluated. If

she is misinformed, tell her the truth. Try to get across the idea that the assessment should help her in school. Say you expect mistakes and that this is nothing to feel bad about. Explain that if she fails to try an item because she thinks she might be wrong, you'll have less of her work to look at. Some older students may tell you that they already know what they can't do. "I can't read, I don't need to take a test to know that." Good point. Reply that you also know that she's having trouble with reading and that you are trying to help her.

- Explain each step of the procedure. Ask the student if she has any questions about anything you are doing. If she does, answer them quickly and in language she can understand. Also explain that eventually she may be exposed to test items that will be too difficult for her. Explain about discontinue rules, so that she understands why you might continue to ask questions after she's reached difficult material. Students tend to trust you more if you are open with them and encourage them to ask you questions. This emphasis on honesty can, however, promote its own problems. Some students are apt to react defensively to direct questions, and others may attempt to tailor their answers to your questions.
- After a while, you'll begin to get "feelings" about some students, and you'll act accordingly. You may end up spending an hour sitting and talking about whatever the student wanted to discuss when it is not the right time to push testing. At the end of this rapport-building session, make a date to come back, and in most cases you'll then be able to conduct the testing with no problems at all.

## Special Considerations for Working with Students

Here are some special considerations and problems you may encounter during assessment. Remember, it is as much a part of your job to work with these problems as it is to score the assessment.

## Diversity

Rapport building is especially important when there are sociocultural differences between the examiner and student (Leung, 1996; Tharp, 1989). Many students have learned to expect the worst from social institutions such as the schools, police, and child protective services. They expect to fail at all academic-related activities, including testing. Often they believe their failure is completely beyond their control; ultimately, in the assessment situation, they are correct. How do you establish rapport with a student who has learned to resent and distrust what you represent?

Initially, you need to spend a moment actually considering the problem. Because we all think we are such nice, unbiased folks, it is often surprising to run into a student who is uncooperative or even hostile. The first impulse, as is true in most cases where bias becomes an issue, is to attribute the behavior to such "visible" factors as race, gender, or language. But it is often a mistake to focus on racial and cultural differences as the cause of the problem when it may actually be the result of the things *we* (or the previous educators we represent) have done. We may be thinking "This student hates me because I am white/black/female/male/rich," when the student is thinking "You people always ask me questions I can't answer. You always ask me to do things I can't do. You're trying to make me feel dumb!"

Differences in ethnicity, sexual orientation, race, language, and gender are important (Howell & Rueda, 1996). However, the literature on evaluator-student interactions is mixed. It does indicate that evaluators of the same race or gender elicit superior performance from students. However, the critical factor does not really seem to be race or gender. The critical factor is something called shared membership.

*Shared membership* refers to the student's perception that she and the evaluator both belong to the same "club." Race and gender are simply the most immediately obvious affiliations. Time spent before the evaluation provides an opportunity for you and the student to find something else in common (in fact, this is important even if you *are* the same ethnicity, race, and/or gender). The aim of the rapport-building session should not be to become buddies. It should be to establish a common affiliation, and *any* affiliation may do. Maybe you both like dogs, enjoy the same kind of music, or even hate education. If so, you need to find this commonalty.

## Acting Out

This is everybody's nemesis, the acting-out student. She may call you names, use profanity, throw the test materials on the floor, scream, or run out of the room. She may attempt to eat the test booklet or make you eat it! This behavior may serve two functions: first, as a release for the tremendous pressure and tension she feels as a result of the testing; second, as an escape-avoidance strategy.

In the first case, assume that the assessment activity is painful for the student and then think about what you do when you get hurt. Sometimes you get mad. In fact, you may even seek revenge! If the acting-out behavior is designed to distract and/or relieve tension, you should see if you can cut out the need for the behavior by lowering the student's cost. Give her lots of verbal praise for showing up and for effort. But be careful never to tie this praise to the acting out. Make statements like "You're a good reader" only if they are true. If it isn't the truth and she knows it (and is aware that you know it), she won't trust you. So simply say "That was a good try" or "You did a good job." Start with material that the student can do (without being patronizing), then begin using "heavier" test material.

If the behavior is a learned escape technique, you have a different problem. When you are only going to be with a student for a short while, it is best to state your expectations clearly, and simply ignore it when they aren't met. If you are not the student's regular teacher, don't try to assume that role. You aren't going to make any permanent change in someone's behavior during a brief testing session, so insisting on your view of appropriate behavior is a bit presumptuous. But if the behavior cannot be ignored, then you need to control it.

A student who is asked to read out loud in class may have learned that all she has to do is scream or throw something, and most adults will make her stand in the hall. Students don't have to read when they're in the hall—so screaming is negatively reinforced. Don't make that mistake. Do not let the student's behavior lead to a payoff by removing her from the testing situation. Her behavior may be incompatible with testing, but that doesn't mean she can't stay in the room with you. If she runs away, get her and bring her back. Tell her that you will bring her back again if she runs away again. Understand that it usually gets worse before it gets better. You know you've got the student when she goes from acting out to quiet noncompliance. At this point, and not before, move down to material that has already been mastered and positively reinforce effort. If none of this works, stay the whole time and then take the student back to her room when she is calm and behaving politely toward you. Tomorrow is another day!

### Anxious

Some students either ask the same questions over and over again ("Is that the answer?" "Was I right?") or they just plain cry. They are fearful of being wrong, probably because someone has taught them that being wrong is followed by rejection and ridicule. Once again, it is unlikely that anyone can reverse this sort of pattern during the short duration of evaluation. However, this anxiety reaction often subsides once a student sees that you are not going to make fun of her every time she makes a mistake. Try to be as encouraging as you can without committing yourself as to the correctness of responses. Don't reinforce the victim role.

### Unresponsive

Students who are withdrawn can be more frustrating than acting-out students. They do not speak unless they are spoken to, seldom speak in complete sentences, and then often speak in barely audible tones. Initially avoid assessments with supply-response items. Nonverbal tests with select-response items may get them working and can be followed with supply-response items. Another good idea is to bring a friend of the withdrawn student to the session and give extra items to the friend. If a friend is not available, try using puppets (but we don't recommend that with high school students). A teacher

named Gail was once sent in to work with a student who had refused to speak to a previous evaluator. Later, when someone looked in to see how things were going he found Gail and the student chatting happily away with wooden blocks held to their ears. In response to the confused look on the observer's face Gail replied "CB radios." It seems the student was more than happy to answer questions as long as they were part of a pretend broadcast.

### Inattention

Students who lack attention skills may have difficulty following directions and remembering the test material you present to them. After asking a test question, have the student repeat it for you before asking for an answer.

### Impulsivity

Some students tend to answer questions before the examiner is finished asking them. An effective technique for dealing with such behavior is to require the student to repeat the question before she is allowed to respond. This forces her to listen to everything you say. It also clarifies the task. If you are using a select-response format, do not expose any of the choices until you've finished presenting the stimulus and the student has repeated it to your satisfaction. A modification of this technique is to expose only one of the possible answers at a time and repeat the stimulus ("Is this the letter P?") for each choice. This requires the student to stop and look at each possible choice before responding.

---

**The Curriculum-Based Evaluation Process**

Step 1. Define Your Purpose

Step 2. Define The Thing To Be Measured

Step 3. Devise A Way To Make The Thing In Step 2 Observable

Step 4. Conduct Assessment

## Step 5. Use The CBE Process of Inquiry

Step 6. Summarize

Step 7. Make Decisions

---

## What Is the CBE Inquiry Process?

We have been referring to the various aspects of curriculum-based evaluation as steps. Remember, though, as we emphasized in the last chapter, the components of the process are not necessarily sequential. For example, **defining your purpose** and **defining the things to be measured** are almost simultaneous decisions. Similarly, the **process of inquiry** we will discuss in this section actually underlies all of the other components of the CBE process.

To "inquire" is to ask questions. **Inquiry** refers to a systematic process for asking questions. Often, the term *disciplined* precedes "inquiry" to suggest a formal, rigorous questioning process such as is associated with the scientific method or legal investigations. The scientific method requires development of a hypothesis and collection of data that either refute or support the hypothesis. Legal inquiry entails development of an argument and presentation of evidence that either refutes or supports the argument. In curriculum-based evaluation, inquiry involves questions about the instructional interventions most likely to enable a student to make adequate educational progress. The process isn't finished until successful interventions have been found.

Disciplined inquiry is based on a set of underlying assumptions. In scientific inquiry, these assumptions pertain to the probability that a particular observed phenomenon might happen by chance. In legal inquiry, one underlying assumption is that an individual is innocent until proven otherwise. In CBE, we assume that if a student is not learning it is because she lacks critical prior knowledge.

Inquiry proceeds through stages. The stages of scientific inquiry include observation, development of a hypothesis, collection of data, analysis of data, and reaching a conclusion. In legal inquiries, a charge or complaint is filed, arguments based on evidence that supports the complaint are presented, arguments based on evidence that refutes the complaint are presented, and a decision is reached by an impartial third party such as a judge or jury. Inquiry associated with CBE also proceeds through stages. These stages are as follows:

Stage 1: fact finding

Stage 2: development assumed causes

Stage 3: validation

Stage 4: summative decision making

Stage 5: formative decision making

In the remainder of this chapter, we will discuss each of these stages of the CBE inquiry process. The purpose, procedures, materials, and results associated with each stage are summarized in Exhibit 6.15. A flow chart illustrating the progression through these stages is shown in Exhibit 6.16. Most of the dimensions of the inquiry process have been discussed in this and previous chapters; however, there are some aspects that will be presented in the next chapter. The questions and actions associated with each stage are indicated on the flow chart in Exhibit 6.16 by the letter and number labels used in the discussion that follows. Also, the flow chart includes references to the exhibits in Chapters 5, 6, and 7 that pertain to each stage.

## CBE Inquiry Process Stage 1: Fact Finding

The purpose of fact finding is to determine the student's general status. To do this, you first collect some information about the student, usually through a **survey-level assessment.** The purpose of fact finding is to narrow the scope of inquiry to the aspects of the student's performance that are *most likely* the cause of inadequate progress. Here are the questions and actions associated with fact finding.

### Question A: Is Survey Level Assessment Required?

Start with a clear statement of concern. The need to review, test, observe, or interview depends on your familiarity with the student relative to that concern. The less you know about the student, the more you will need to find out and the more you will need to assess. This stage is either very easy or very hard depending on your own knowledge of the curriculum and the degree to

*The goal of any assessment is to collect useful data.*

which the curriculum has already been adequately described.

### Action 1.1: Administer Survey Assessment

Survey-level assessment was discussed in the last chapter. It involves administration of a broad range of assessment tasks that are all associated with a particular domain in which a student is having difficulty. For example if a student is not making adequate progress in reading, a survey-level assessment might include decoding tasks, comprehension tasks, and vocabulary tasks. Survey procedures uncover "facts" about the stu-

dent. These facts are hardly the equivalent of universal truths. More often, they are simply lists of what the student can do, can't do, or fails to display. Survey-level assessment might just as accurately be called fishing. It is an activity of casting around for information. Usually, survey assessment is only done once, and it may not be needed at all if you are already sufficiently informed about the student's skills.

### Action 1.2: Fill Out the Status Sheet

Status sheets are used to focus your thinking, or your discussions with others, on the things the student most likely needs to know to succeed in

*Exhibit 6.15   The CBE Process of Inquiry.*

| Stage | Purpose | Procedure | Materials | Results |
|---|---|---|---|---|
| **1:**<br>**Fact finding** | To find out what the student is doing now. | Assessments are employed and information is summarized. | Wide-band/ survey assessments such as classroom work, general test, and/or status sheets. | The first part of the PLEP is determined and problem areas are identified. |
| **2:**<br>**Assumed causes for problems are developed** | To think of explanations (missing prior knowledge) for what the student is doing. | Curriculum is analyzed and, if necessary, developed. | Status sheets, tables of specifications, and/or lists of essential prior knowledge. Summaries of student work. | A list of high probability explanations are developed for the problems noted in the results of fact finding. |
| **3:**<br>**Validating** | To see if the explanations arrived at in the results of step 2 are correct. | Student work is compared with essential prior knowledge noted in the results of step 2. | Narrow band/specific-level assessment materials. | Assumed causes are accepted or rejected based on information collected during this step. |
| **4:**<br>**Summative decision making** | To select goals and objectives or to recognize the need to repeat steps 2–4. | Assumed causes that have been validated through specific assessment are listed as objectives. New assumed causes are developed as needed. | Status sheets, tables of specifications, and/or lists of essential prior knowledge. Summaries of student work. | The PLEP is completed, and the student's educational program (goals and objectives plus ideas for initial instruction) are produced. A plan for any additional evaluation is also produced. |
| **5:**<br>**Formative decision making** | To confirm that initial teaching ideas are effective and to monitor progress. | Assessments are repeated, data are visually displayed, and DBPM decision rules are applied. | Direct measures of goals and objectives and DBPM procedures. | Continuous information on the quality of the program and guidelines for making needed changes. |

*Exhibit 6.16*    **Flow Chart of the CBE Format of Inquiry.**

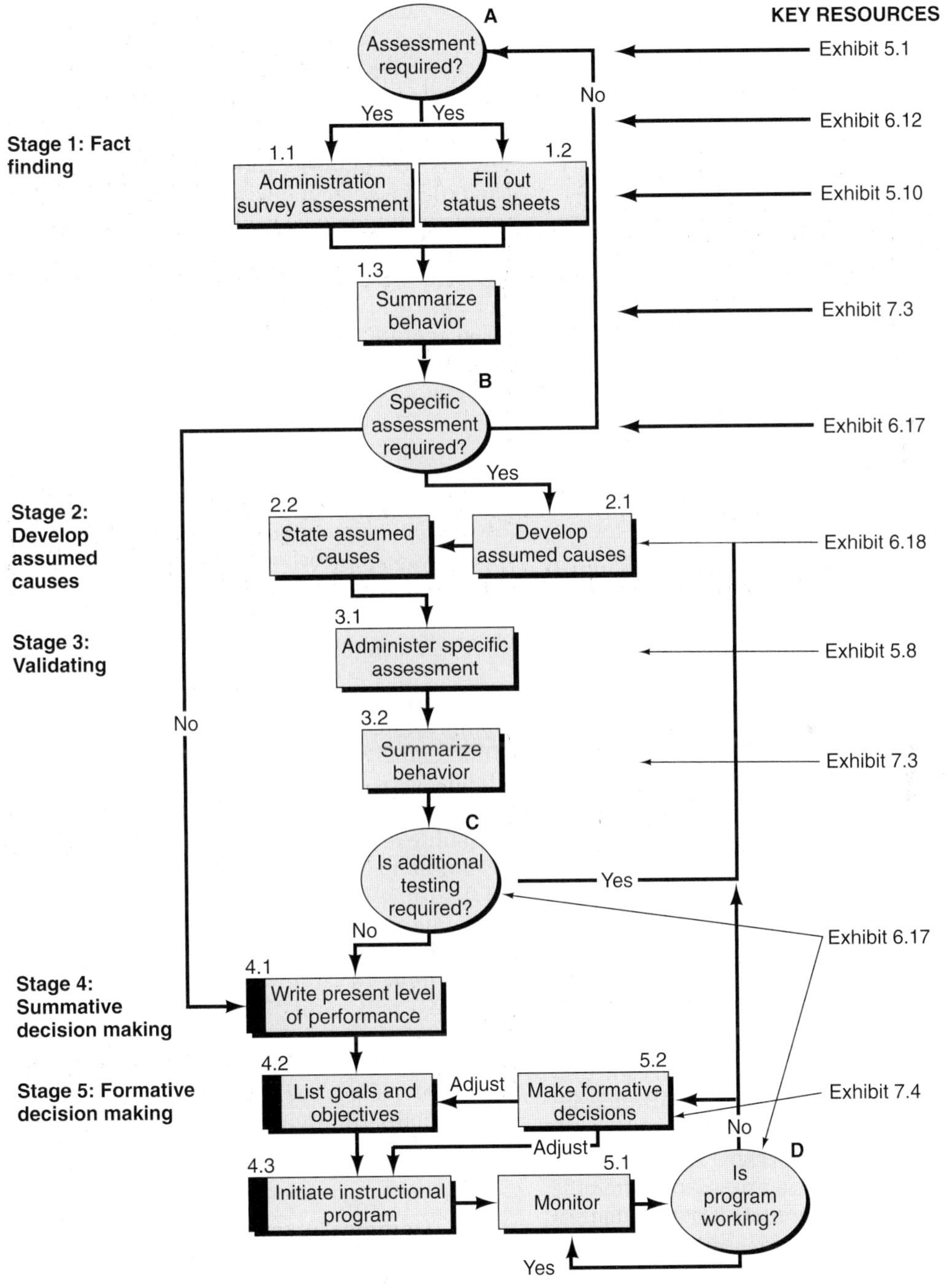

**KEY RESOURCES**

**A**
Assessment required?
→ Exhibit 5.1

Yes | Yes | No → Exhibit 6.12

**Stage 1: Fact finding**

1.1 Administration survey assessment
1.2 Fill out status sheets
→ Exhibit 5.10

1.3 Summarize behavior
→ Exhibit 7.3

**B**
Specific assessment required?
→ Exhibit 6.17

Yes

**Stage 2: Develop assumed causes**

2.2 State assumed causes
2.1 Develop assumed causes
→ Exhibit 6.18

**Stage 3: Validating**

3.1 Administer specific assessment
→ Exhibit 5.8

3.2 Summarize behavior
→ Exhibit 7.3

**C**
Is additional testing required?
Yes

No → Exhibit 6.17

**Stage 4: Summative decision making**

4.1 Write present level of performance

**Stage 5: Formative decision making**

4.2 List goals and objectives
Adjust
5.2 Make formative decisions
→ Exhibit 7.4

No

4.3 Initiate instructional program
Adjust
5.1 Monitor
**D** Is program working?

Yes

the area of concern. Go through the list of skills carefully and first mark those you are sure the student does ("yes") or does not ("no") have. If you are unsure, don't try too hard to arrive at resolution. It is better to list it as "unsure" and get more data.

### Action 1.3: Summarize Behavior

There is an entire section on summarizing behavior in Chapter 7. For now, all you need to know is that the student's performance on the status sheet or assessments must somehow be condensed so that it can be compared with her expected performance.

### Question B: Is Specific-Level Assessment Required?

The only immediate standard for making the decision about whether or not a specific-level procedure (SLP) is required is your satisfaction that you already have the insight you need into the student's knowledge to write goals and objectives. There are questions provided in Exhibit 6.17 to help you interpret the results of the survey-level assessments.

### What Is "Specific" About Specific-Level Assessment?

As we discussed in the last chapter, **specific-level assessment** entails presentation of assessment tasks that sample a narrow segment of the domain of interest. The purpose of specific-level procedures (SLPs) is to focus the evaluation process on the dimension of student performance that is *most* likely creating problems. We will provide many examples of specific-level assessment activities in the content chapters later in this text.

### CBE Inquiry Process Stage 2: Develop Assumed Causes

Once you have some information about what the student is (or isn't) doing, you pause and try to figure out why. This is done by developing explanations about what skills the student is missing. At this point, the explanations are only assumed causes, or hypotheses, to be validated or rejected through specific-level assessment.

### Action 2.1: Develop Assumed Causes

When developing assumed causes, the evaluator sits back in the chair, looks at the collected facts, and tries to figure out why these facts exist. This action is often done in consultation with other teachers or reference materials. To inform this action, the summarized information from status sheets or assessments may be used. Any missing concept, fact, or strategy component (those marked "no" or "unsure" on a status sheet) is a likely cause of student failure.

Action 2.1 probably is the most important action in the CBE format. This is where you do your best thinking. During the action, you try to evolve a clear idea about what the student can and cannot do. You then hypothesize (sounds so much nicer than "guess") about the missing prior knowledge. These guesses will determine the direction of all subsequent evaluation. The rules for developing assumed causes are presented in Exhibit 6.18. Look at them now to be sure you understand what each rule means.

### Action 2.2: State Assumed Causes

In this action, you select or produce possible behavioral objectives that you then *write down*. This written document is called an assessment plan. You will confirm the objectives later for Action 4.2.

### CBE Inquiry Process Stage 3: Validating

In the validation stage, specific-level assessment is used to verify assumptions about missing knowledge. This third stage, validating, is intended to find out if the assumptions you came up with in Action 2.2 were correct.

### Action 3.1: Administer Specific-Level Procedures (SLPs)

We've already given you advice on how to administer R.I.O.T. assessments and how to work with students.

### Action 3.2: Summarize Behavior

This is similar to Action 1.3. More information on summarizing results will be provided in Chapter 7. In Action 3.2, the student's specific-level assessment behavior is compared directly with the assumed causes written in Action 2.2.

### Question C: Is Additional Testing Required?

If the original assumed causes do not prove to be correct, you must return to Action 2.1. Take the new information you got during specific-level testing and develop new assumed causes. For example, if you suspected that a student could not comprehend a reading passage because of poor vocabulary skills, but specific-level assessment revealed that the student's vocabulary was adequate, you would have to come up with a new assumed cause for the failure.

### CBE Inquiry Process Stage 4: Summative Decision Making

In most cases, some of the assumed causes you developed will prove to have been accurate. You convert those results into the present level of educational performance (PLEP) statement and then list selected items as goals and objectives. This stage requires you to examine the student's status, determine if there is a discrepancy between where she is and where she should be, and then decide to get rid of any discrepancy that may exist. This is all part of the programming process outlined in Chapter 5. Once again, the rules in Exhibit 6.18 will be of help.

### Action 4.1: Write Present Level of Educational Performance (PLEP)

If the evaluation is being conducted for your own use in your own classroom, the *idea* of the student's PLEP is all that really matters. If it is being conducted for an IEP meeting or a school consultation team report, it will need to be stated in a formal fashion as presented in Chapter 7 (CBE Step 6).

### Action 4.2: List Goals and Objectives

This is the list of things that the student will need to be taught. You develop it by comparing the PLEP with the curriculum. This also is done by following the rules in Exhibit 6.17.

### Action 4.3: Plan and Initiate Instructional Program

Return to Exhibit 5.1 for a review of the programming process. Next apply the instructional recommendations found in Chapter 4, and the topical chapters, to the goals and objectives. Then start teaching.

### CBE Inquiry Process Stage 5: Formative Decision Making

Summative and formative decision making have been mentioned in previous chapters. They will both be explained in more detail in the next chapter and Howell et al. (2000a). For now, it is only important to understand that although every program of instruction is defined by numerous variables, the quality of the total package is only indicated by one thing: improved student progress. Therefore, you can expect that some "fine tuning" will be needed to adjust variables in the initial program for the student. The need for these adjustment decisions is illustrated through the use of formative evaluation of student progress. Formative evaluation is also used to note when a student has met an objective and requires a change to a new objective.

### Action 5.1: Monitor

Depending on the sensitivity of the measure, either survey-level or specific-level assessment may be repeated to monitor student progress. Follow the procedures explained in Chapter 7 for collecting and displaying progress data.

### Question D: Is the Program Working?

If the student is making adequate progress, then the program should be retained. If not, it should

**Exhibit 6.17    Questions to Ask Before Interpreting an Assessment.**

Before interpreting the results of any test and/or observation, ask yourself each of these questions. If the answer is no (or "unsure"), take the specified action(s).

| Question | Explanation/Example | Action |
|---|---|---|
| Are you sure you got an instructionally relevant sample of behavior? | To guide instruction, evaluation must cover the things a student is currently prepared to learn. This means mapping out *both* those things a student can do and those she cannot do. An evaluation that yields all "pass" "no-pass" is worthless. | • Continue the evaluation until you find the correct instructional level. |
| Did the student's work represent the student's skills? | Remember that a student may know something but be unable to demonstrate knowledge because of conflicts with the testing situation. Be sure the work represents the student's best efforts. Try giving a pep talk, using preferred tasks, or having a friend present during testing. | • Try to separate knowledge from display. |
| Has the student received instruction on the skills missed? | Don't be concerned when students fail at things they haven't been taught. Ask "Did you ever know how to do that?" or "Has this always been hard?" or "Is it new?" Check with teachers to see if the skill has been taught. | • Check to see if a pass is expected. |
| Have you attempted to categorize the errors? | Indicated by incorrect responses whenever particular content is involved (two-place addition, vowel sounds, on biology vocabulary). | • Look for patterns of content errors. |
| | Indicated by failure to recognize cues (borrows when it isn't necessary) and/or use vocabulary (says "reliable" when talking about "validity"). | • Look for patterns of concept errors. |
| | Indicated by predictable error patterns and/or incorrect explanation of process. | • Look for patterns of rule or strategy errors. |
| | Indicated by incorrect statements ("a = eeee" or "2 + 2 = 5"). | • Look for patterns of fact errors. |

| Question | Explanation/Example | Action |
|---|---|---|
| Does the student's skill maintain across different response formats? | If the student can't produce a correct answer, check to see if the answer can be identified. If you know something can be identified, check to see if it can be produced. | • Switch from identify to produce or from produce to identify. |
| Does the student's skill maintain across different levels of proficiency? | If the student cannot do something quickly, ask that it be done accurately. If something is done accurately ask that it be done quickly. | • Switch from fluency to accuracy or accuracy to fluency. |
| Does the student's skill maintain across different situations and context? | If a student can't do something in context (add in a word problem), check to see if it can be done in isolation. If a student can do something in isolation (add on a work sheet), check to see if it can be done in context. | • Check the effect of context. |
| Have you missed important skills? | Don't concentrate exclusively on errors. Consider the content the student avoids (if the student never tried to spell words with double consonants, you should check that area). | • Check skills *not* displayed. |
| Does the student know and understand her own skill levels? | Ask "Will this be easy for you or will it be hard?" or "Which things are you good at and which need improving?" or "Why do other kids get these problems done faster?" | • Ask the student to judge the difficulty of the task or to predict success. |
|  | Say "Pretend that you are the teacher. Tell me how to do this." | • Ask the student to explain how to do the task. |
| Do you want to make decisions about how to teach (not just about what to teach)? | Use assisted assessment. Take something the student has failed and try teaching it to her. Observe the student's learning and task-related behaviors. | • Check how the student responds to instruction. |
|  | Use instructionally sensitive repeated measures of the skill and monitor progress over time. Compare progress obtained through different instructional approaches. | • Summarize changes in the student's skill. |

**Exhibit 6.18   Rules for Developing Assumed Causes.**

| Rule | Explanation | Example Error(s) |
|---|---|---|
| 1. Don't evaluate if there isn't a problem (or if you haven't decided what the problem is). | You need to know what you are looking for before you start specific testing; vague concerns and ambiguous survey test results are useless. | • Trying to figure out why a referred students gets out of her seat when all the other students get out of their seats just as often. |
| 2. Think about your purpose. | Are you evaluating to make classification decisions? If you are interested in treatment decisions, are you trying to decide "what to teach" or "how to teach"? | • Trying to draw treatment information from a norm-referenced achievement test score.<br>• Recommending "how to teach" without any information about what treatments have already been tried. |
| 3. Think about the curriculum:<br>(a) Stay close to the main task. | Because the student's major problem is being behind in the curriculum, it is important to avoid retreating to lower levels. Don't automatically take every student back to the first grade and basic skills. | • Deciding to test a junior-high student with reading comprehension problems on her vowel sounds before testing knowledge of comprehension strategies. |
| (b) Think about what can be taught *right now*. | It is important to consider tasks within the so-called correct level of difficulty. Don't think about things that are obviously too hard (given the student's current knowledge), or things that are obviously too easy. | • Testing the vowel sound accuracy of an accurate reader.<br>• Checking to see how a student who can't add does on long division problems. |
| (c) Stick to the essential. | Don't spend time thinking about things the student doesn't need to learn. | • Roman numerals.<br>• Drawing lines between syllables in words.<br>• Educational terminology (i.e., "diagraph" or "the levels of Bloom's taxonomy"). |
| (d) Set priority. | When a student doesn't seem to know about a lot of things, you must decide which to test/teach first. | • Documenting lists of stuff a kid can't do and nothing that she can do.<br>• Ignoring what she wants to learn first.<br>• Checking on skills that have limited immediate utility. |
| 4. Don't confuse the curriculum with instruction. | What a student needs to know is determined by the curriculum—not by the way the curriculum is taught. | • Thinking that a student who fails history has to learn to read to succeed in history.<br>• Only checking for skills taught by your favorite instructional technique (remember Bob?).<br>• Giving tests for "learning style." |

| Rule | Explanation | Example Error(s) |
|------|-------------|------------------|
| 5. Don't confuse testing with evaluation. | There are many important things that are not sampled by certain tests. These must be checked. | • Ignoring a content area because it isn't sampled by the tests you happen to have available.<br>• Ignoring skill fluency because you haven't got a rate test. |
| 6. Think about *all* elements of the task. | Tasks are composed of content behavior, conditions, and criteria. You should develop assumed causes for each of these domains. | • Arranging to observe a student who gets into fights at recess during her lunch period. (You forgot about conditions!)<br>• Deciding to check the counting skills of a student who doesn't produce answers to addition facts. (You forgot to see if she could identify the answers first!) |
| 7. Consider *both* knowledge and display. | When we test and observe we only see behavior. Don't assume that all behavior indicates knowledge—or that the absence of behavior always means the absence of knowledge. | • Assuming that a student who skips the word *that* while reading a passage doesn't know how to read it.<br>• Assuming that a student who can't do addition facts quickly—because of poor handwriting—doesn't know how to add. |
| 8. Think about what can be taught. | Stick to alterable variables! Don't spend time thinking about things that can't be influenced through instruction. | • Beginning the evaluation by assuming the student's problem is the result of things like: a poor family, low IQ, or attention deficit disorder.<br>• Deciding to check task-related explanations for failure (attention, motivation, study skills) before topic specific explanations (reading skills). |
| 9. Think about something else. | Be comprehensive. Students seldom have only one missing prerequisite so it isn't safe to assume that the first thing they can't do is the only, or most important, thing they need to be taught. | • Beginning testing without sufficient analysis of the curriculum and/or survey level results.<br>• Prematurely finishing the evaluation.<br>• Failure to ask for assistance, or use reference material. |
| 10. Remember the breakout rule. | Breakout rules (White, 1984) tell a person when to ignore the rest of the rules. In this case we suggest that, if, after doing things our way three times, the student still hasn't improved significantly—try something else! | • Assuming that a student's failure to learn documents the severity of her disability, rather than the limits of your procedures. |

be changed. Step 7, in the next chapter, explains how to make timely determinations about program effectiveness. During the process of collecting formative data (Action 5.1) you will often gain useful information about how to change the program. If so, you can go directly to Step 5.2. If the program is not working and you need more information to fix it, return to Step 2.1 and reexamine the goals.

### Action 5.2: Make Formative Decisions

Data-based decision rules are discussed in Chapter 7. Decision rules pertain to the performance and/or progress indicators for a particular program. These are especially important for deciding how to teach.

### Summary

This chapter defined problem-solving evaluation, measurement, scores, reliability, and validity. Problems with existing behavior samples were listed, and requirements for good R.I.O.T. assessments were supplied. As you will see in the following chapters, it is not possible to arrive at certain conclusions, or to make certain teaching recommendations, without adequate behavior samples. The student-evaluator interaction must be carefully and thoughtfully controlled to obtain useful information in a humane and respectful fashion.

It was also pointed out that threats to data are not limited to problems with assessments. Because the problem-solving evaluation requires thought, tester/observer bias and behavior also influence scores. Therefore, as evaluators, we need to structure our inquiry and think in a productive fashion. If forced to pick one, we'd say that is the main point of this chapter. It goes without saying that to think in a productive fashion, one must see to it that her or his thinking is curriculum-based.

In addition, the CBE process of inquiry was illustrated and briefly reviewed. The process, which is the heart of problem-solving evaluation, makes use of all of the CBE steps covered in Chapters 5–7. It is outlined in Exhibit 6.15 and illustrated in Exhibit 6.16. The CBE format will be put to use throughout the chapters that follow.

## REVIEW QUESTIONS

### Item 1
Exhibit 6.3 presents a CBM oral reading fluency report card for Aurora Franklin, a third-grade student. Write a paragraph that describes Aurora's present level of performance in reading and summarizes her recent progress.

### Items 2–5
Harlan Jeffers has been having difficulty teaching some of the students in his fifth-grade class. He has asked you to help him figure out what to do. Look at the descriptions of some of Harlan's students presented here. Identify one or more assumed causes for the students' problems and tell what R.I.O.T. activities you would follow.

*Cameron*

Cameron rarely turns in his math assignments on time. His computation is generally accurate on the 3-minute CBM probes Mr. Jeffers administers once each week. Cameron doesn't seem to have problems with assignments in other content areas. Lately, Cameron has been talking out and getting out of his seat more than Mr. Jeffers is willing to tolerate.

**Assumed Causes:**

**R.I.O.T. Activities**

*Jill*

Jill often seems to be off-task. She gazes out the window, talks to the other students at her table, and frequently gets out of her seat to sharpen her pencil. Her work is generally accurate in all areas except spelling and written expression. On essays, she makes frequent errors of punctuation, grammar, and capitalization.

**Assumed Causes:**

**R.I.O.T. Activities**

*Chantelle*

Chantelle recently moved to the school from a large urban school district in the next state. Mr. Jeffers thinks she is having a hard time adjusting to the classroom. She rarely raises her hand, and when called upon in class, she often says nothing or shrugs her shoulders and says "I don't know." On recent tests in spelling and social studies, Chantelle received the lowest score in the class.

**Assumed Causes:**

**R.I.O.T. Activities**

*Mitchell*

Mitchell's handwriting is nearly illegible. He usually prints but his letters tend to be poorly formed with inadequate spacing. His papers contain many erasures and crossouts. Mitchell usually gets one of the lowest scores in the class on weekly spelling tests. His math assignments tend to be accurate but messy.

**Assumed Causes:**

**R.I.O.T. Activities**

# Chapter 7

# Problem-Solving Evaluation and Decision Making

*A trouble is a circumstance, a situation, that leaves one upset and at loose ends; one knows that things aren't going very well. It is a source of vague but persistent discomfort. A puzzle has a nice tight form, clear structure, and a neat solution. A problem, then, is what you get if you can find a puzzle form to lay on top of a trouble.*

—L. S. Shulman (1986)

In the last two chapters, we discussed the **curriculum-based evaluation** problem-solving process. At this point, you should be familiar with the various activities associated with each of the first five steps in the process. Here is a brief review of those activities.

**Step 1. Define your purpose**—Here you must decide why you are conducting an evaluation and clarify the problem you want to solve with the results.

**Step 2. Define the thing to be measured**—At this step, you must specify the content domain you will sample, the behaviors you will ask the student to display, the conditions under which you will expect those behaviors to occur, and the proficiency with which you expect the student to perform.

**Step 3. Devise a way to make the thing in step 2 observable**—At this point, you construct or select behavior-sampling processes (reviews, tests, observations).

**Step 4. Conduct assessment**—This step entails effective administration and scoring of the behavior-sampling procedures to ensure reliability and validity.

**Step 5. Use the CBE process of inquiry**—Effective and systematic inquiry underlies the entire CBE process. This problem-solving process requires you to continually question whether or not assessment is required and whether or not the trouble you are seeking to solve is being addressed. This chapter presents the remaining two steps of the CBE process.

**Step 6. Summarize**—Derive scores, make comparisons, and report results.

**Step 7. Make decisions**—Use the data to decide what and how to teach.

---

### The Curriculum-Based Evaluation Process

Step 1.   Define Your Purpose

Step 2.   Define The Thing To Be Measured

Step 3.   Devise A Way To Make The Thing In Step 2 Observable

Step 4.   Conduct Assessment

Step 5.   Use The CBE Process Of Inquiry

## Step 6.   Summarize

Step 7.   Make Decisions

---

As we discussed in Chapter 5, evaluation is undertaken for different reasons, and evaluation does not occur unless a **summary** of behavior is compared with a standard. A summary is a systematic organization of the results of an assessment that permits comparison with a reference standard. A summary also is critical to the problem-solving process because it facilitates discussion of the assessment results with others who may be involved, including the student, his parents, other teachers, administrators, or ancillary personnel such as counselors, therapists, or school psychologists.

In the context of curriculum-based evaluation, summarizing involves two dimensions: (1) the results of the assessment procedures employed (tests, observations, interviews, etc.) must be organized and compiled, and (2) these results must be compared with a reference standard.

Unfortunately, what we seem to have in education is a lot of behavior sampling but very little meaningful summary.

### *How Should I Go About Organizing and Compiling Assessment Results?*

Three ways to summarize behavior are commonly used to inform decisions about teaching. They are as follows:

Keep the actual behavior in a **portfolio;**

Write a **report** on objectives or products; or

Supply **scores.**

Each of these has advantages and disadvantages, and all three may be used simultaneously.

### *Portfolios*

Portfolios were discussed in Chapter 5. Portfolios are popular in schools because they allow teachers and students to collect and periodically examine work samples. They can be highly motivating for some students, and they can provide a way of showcasing student work. As such, portfolios may be an excellent teaching tool. However, portfolios have some major limitations as assessment tools (Nolet, 1992). For portfolios to be useful in the context of assessment, the following conditions must be met:

1. The classroom assignments are relevant to the assessment decision being made;

2. Permanent and observable products have been produced;

3. Maintenance and organization of the entire collection of a student's work is manageable; and

4. Only individual or criterion-referenced decisions are to be made.

However, portfolios can be extremely helpful during formative evaluation because products created at an earlier time can be used as *progress* standards for evaluating current work. In this way, a student or teacher can pull out the contents of the portfolio and look for evidence of improvement. They can also be helpful when screening to find areas where the student seems to be lacking skills.

### *Reports*

A student's behavior can be summarized in terms of his accomplishments by noting what things he has or has not learned and placing those notes in a report. For example, on a status sheet, one can mark the items (objectives) that are clearly adequate as "OK" and those that are

**Exhibit 7.1    Example of a Status Sheet.**

| Skill | Status | |
|---|---|---|
| | Pass | No Pass |
| Placement test<br>　Mixed division problems | | |
| Square root<br>　Square root of a number in which the answer is 0–12 | | |
| Place value<br>　Two- or more-digit number with zero<br>　Two- or more-digit number by 1, 10, 100, 1000 | | |
| Remainder and no remainder<br>　Two- or more-digit number by a one- or two-digit number | | |
| Remainder<br>　Two-digit number by a one-digit number (one- or two-digit answer) | | X |
| No remainder<br>　Two-digit number by a one-digit number (two-digit answer) | X | |
| Facts<br>　Division facts (0–10) | X | |

not as "No pass." The status sheet then becomes a report of the student's status on those skills, as shown in Exhibit 7.1.

The content on this status sheet is based on a table of specifications for division, and the **"X"** symbol represents a no-pass on a division test. Therefore, the sheet is a report of the student's status. It tells us that, on this division test, the student missed problems that required him to divide two-digit numbers by a one-digit number and get a remainder.

Reports may come in considerably more or less structured form. Sometimes they come as multiple page formal write-ups and sometimes as little yellow sticky notes. In all cases, they have the potential advantage of distilling important information and allowing interpretation. They may also have the disadvantages of being cumbersome and overblown (sometimes they tell more about the author of the report than they tell about the student).

Here is a brief excerpt from a fairly typical "formal" report written by Mark, a school psychologist. The student mentioned in the report is in high school.

*"Teri's testing showed passing at levels 2 & 3 in Math. Her basic operations were only 37% accurate with some areas dramatically weaker than others. Math application was not tested. Her reading was 42% accurate at level 3. Her achievement on the Woodcock was 5.2 for reading and 3 for math.*

*According to her WISC-III Teri's ability to solve problems using visual-motor skills are higher than her ability using verbal skills. Her Processing Speed Index was 77 (borderline range). Even routine complex tasks confuse her. She is strong in the area of grasping sequence but weak in her processing of new material. Teri's psychomotor development, as seen on the Bender and Draw-a-Person tests, is below average to weak."*

Here is part of another report on the same high school student. This report was written by Sibyl Maer, a different evaluator. She wrote this report for the same student.

*"Dear Teri,*

*Here is what I found out through the testing we did last week. First of all, you are accurate in your addition and subtraction facts which means you have not lost your math foundation. You do well with division but need to refresh your memory of multiplication facts. Like anything else (basketball, video games), the more you practice and use your knowledge the easier and more quickly the answers will flow from your mind through your pencil and on to your paper. It might help to remember that multiplication and division are, in many ways, like addition and subtraction. You are either counting forward or backward. One thing that will definitely help is for you to take your time and write as neatly as possible. In doing so you will be less likely to become confused while lining up your numbers in both long division and multiplication. Remember Teri, someday you are going to have checking and saving accounts, buy a car, or even win the lottery! For any of those situations you will need to know math."*

You can see from these excerpts that reports can be written in very different ways. When both of these examples were shown to teachers they all agreed they preferred the one written by Sibyl.

### Scores

At the survey level (fact-finding stage), scores from normative and wide-band assessment activities are regularly used to gain a perspective on the magnitude of a student's problem if one exists. Often, long-range goals also are set from these scores. However, raw scores from such measures provide relatively little information for instructional planning and usually must be transformed to some normative variant before they can be understood.

When used at the specific level, CBM scores are always direct summaries of the accuracy, rate, or quality of behavior, not derivations such as percentiles or grade equivalencies (although normative comparisons are often made with CBM). Because specific-level assessments always are built from behavioral objectives, the CAP within the objective becomes the standard. Therefore, raw scores are useful. If the CAP is 40 words per minute and the student writes 20 words per minute, then you know exactly what the student is doing and what he should be doing. No translation is needed because the score is a direct summary of a known behavior.

In reality, most educators use all three of the summary techniques mentioned here (portfolios, reports, and scores). However, scores are without a doubt the most efficient way to summarize

behavior. That is because they can reduce the material in portfolios and reports to numbers that are easily displayed and understood.

Their two disadvantages are that the scoring rules used to derive scores may be flawed. Also, many people don't like (or actually fear) anything that looks like a statistic.

### How Do I Know If I Have Summarized Something Important?

No matter how behavior is summarized, it must be compared with a standard for evaluation to occur. When this comparison indicates that there is a difference between the observed level of behavior and some expected or desired level of behavior, a discrepancy exists. This model of evaluation was illustrated as $s \overset{}{\longleftarrow}\underset{D}{\overset{}{\top}} B$. In this model, *Behavior* is compared with a *Standard* to find a *Discrepancy*. A comparison can be made by contrasting two products in a portfolio, by using words to describe the actual and expected performance in a report, or by using scores. The standard is the behavior that is expected or desired. For example, a standard could be "typical performance," indicated by normative scores; "desired rate of progress," indicated by monitoring data; or "mastery of some proportion of the objectives in a domain," indicated by criterion-referenced comparisons.

**Magnitude**  To be useful for problem-solving evaluation, a summary should supply information about both the direction and magnitude of the discrepancy. This helps us judge its significance. The magnitude of the discrepancy tells *how far* from the standard the score falls. The direction tells whether the score is above or below the standard. For example, if the standard for reading is the class average of 50 and Tom scored 45, we know the direction of his behavior change will need to be up and the magnitude is 5.

Although the raw score does represent a defined unit of behavior, the implications that score has for decision making are not always clear. To determine educational significance, a teacher must ask "How much teaching is needed to remove the discrepancy?" A small discrepancy signals the need for a small change in behavior, and therefore less teaching, than a large discrepancy.

The discrepancy between the standard and the student's performance can be described in absolute or ratio terms. An **absolute discrepancy** is determined by *subtracting* the *smaller* of the two numbers from the *larger* like this:
Behavior 1: The standard is 75, and a student obtains a score of 60.

> **Behavior 1: The standard is 75, and a student obtains a score of 60.**
>
> | Larger | – | Smaller | = Absolute discrepancy |
> |---|---|---|---|
> | Standard | – | Performance | = Absolute discrepancy |
> | 75 | – | 60 | = 15 |

Behavior 2: The standard is 75, and a student obtains a score of 90.

> **Behavior 2: The standard is 75, and a student obtains a score of 90.**
>
> | Larger | – | Smaller | = Absolute discrepancy |
> |---|---|---|---|
> | Performance | – | Standard | = Absolute discrepancy |
> | 90 | – | 75 | = 15 |

A **discrepancy ratio** is determined by dividing the larger of the two by the smaller. When decision making involves many different content areas, ratio discrepancies are superior to absolute ones. The steps to determine the magnitude of the ratio are simple:

1. Select the standard.

2. Measure the performance.

3. Divide the larger of the two by the smaller to find the ratio of magnitude.

Here are two examples.
Behavior 1: The standard is 75, and a student obtains a score of 60.

> **Behavior 1: The standard is 75, and a student obtains a score of 60.**
>
> | Larger/Smaller | = | Discrepancy ratio |
> |---|---|---|
> | Standard/Performance | = | Discrepancy ratio |
> | 75/60 | = | 1.25 |

Behavior 2: The standard is 75, and a student obtains a score of 90.

> **Behavior 2: The standard is 75, and a student obtains a score of 90.**
>
> | Larger/Smaller | = | Discrepancy ratio |
> |---|---|---|
> | Performance/Standard | = | Discrepancy ratio |
> | 90/75 | = | 1.20 |

Discrepancy ratios (Deno & Mirkin, 1977) are a good way to summarize the current performance (or progress) of a student in different areas so priorities for instruction can be set. Ratios illustrate the proportion of change a student needs to make. For example, improving from 2 to 4 and improving from 22 to 24 each require a change in magnitude of 2. However, the move from 2 to 4 requires a 100% improvement, but the change from 22 to 24 only represents a 9.6% improvement. The discrepancy ratio is the criterion-reference equivalent of a standard score such as a z-score, T-score, or percentile. For a discussion of those scores, refer to Howell et al. (2000a).

By reducing discrepancies to a common matrix, the discrepancy ratio allows you to compare the student's behavior on different objectives (which may have different CAP) to identify the area in which the most help is needed. However, magnitude of discrepancy is not the only standard for setting priority. The importance of the skill and the interests/needs of the student must also be considered. For example, being slightly behind in study skills can result in the loss of other important information. Remember our discussion of the Matthew effect?

***Direction***    Teachers are in the business of getting rid of discrepancies. The direction of change needed to remove the discrepancy is placed in front of the number. For a behavior you wish to increase, the ratio should be preceded by a plus sign (+) for absolutes or a times sign (×) for ratios. For a behavior you want to decrease, the magnitude summary is preceded by a subtract sign (−) for absolutes or a division sign (÷) for ratios. The "plus" or "times" signs mean the current performance must be *increased* to remove the discrepancy. Exhibit 7.2 shows scores summarizing Alvin's current levels of performance.

Alvin's decoding behavior is currently 35 words per minute. If it increases (is multiplied) by a factor of 2, it will be at 70 and there will be no discrepancy. Alvin's "talks-out" behavior occurs 0.2 times per minute (an average of once every 5 minutes). The typical level of talking out in his class is 0.03 times per minute. His talks-out behavior must decrease (divide) by a factor of 6.7 to be average. Therefore, it is labeled ÷6.7. Alvin is farthest "behind" in "talks out" because the proportional magnitude of the discrepancy is the greatest for that behavior. If the student's behavior is superior to his performance (better than the CAP), it is reported as "pass." You would *never* try to change superior performances.

Discrepancies can be determined for status sheets, products, observation summaries, and record reviews as well as for test scores. For example, if you know how many objectives a student is expected to have met, you can take a sequence of objectives (or items on a status sheet) and after noting the status of each skill determine the discrepancy. If the student is supposed to have met 60 objectives but, according to the status rating, has only met 25, he has a 35 objective absolute discrepancy. Similarly, if he was expected to be in school 18 days last month but was only there for 10, he has an absolute discrepancy in attendance of 8 (×1:8 in ratio terms).

Exhibit 7.3 shows a worksheet for summarizing assessment results. The processes for filling it out are noted on the sheet.

## So What Does That Mean?

Above is an example of a discrepancy described in a report. Assuming that a CRT was used and the scoring rules were appropriate, the scores above mean that, while reading out of her grade-level reader, Kris could only read at about a third of the expected rate. She has fallen way behind on her objective for fluency and will need to increase her rate to about 140 words per minute. However, her accuracy is fine. So, given that she is accurate but slow, she is ready for some fluency building lessons. She doesn't need extensive error corrections or elaborate instruction on word recognition. However, until her fluency is increased, she should be given accommodations as it would take her two-thirds longer than the typical student to read any text assignment or test item. That is quite a bit of information to get from the single score ×3.22.

---

*In 1 minute Kris read 45 words correctly and 2 words incorrectly out of her third-grade reader. She has a x3.22 discrepancy in corrects and a no discrepancy for errors.*

---

### The Curriculum-Based Evaluation Process

Step 1.   Define Your Purpose
Step 2.   Define The Thing To Be Measured
Step 3.   Devise A Way To Make The Thing In Step 2 Observable
Step 4.   Conduct Assessment
Step 5.   Use The CBE Process Of Inquiry
Step 6.   Summarize

## Step 7.    Make Decisions

---

**Exhibit 7.2**   *Summary of Alvin's Current Levels of Performance.*

| | | | Behaviors | | | |
|---|---|---|---|---|---|---|
| | Decode CVC+e Words | Add | Math Facts 0–9 Subtract | Multiply | Divide | Talk-Outs in Class |
| Standard (CAP) | 70 | 50 | 50 | 50 | 50 | 0.03 |
| Performance | 35 | 50 | 45 | 32 | 27 | 0.2 |
| Absolute discrepancy | +35 | 0 | +5 | +18 | +23 | − 0.17 |
| Discrepancy ratio | ×2 | ×1 | ×1.1 | ×1.6 | ×1.9 | ÷ 6.7 |

**Exhibit 7.3    Worksheet for Summarizing Assessment Results.**

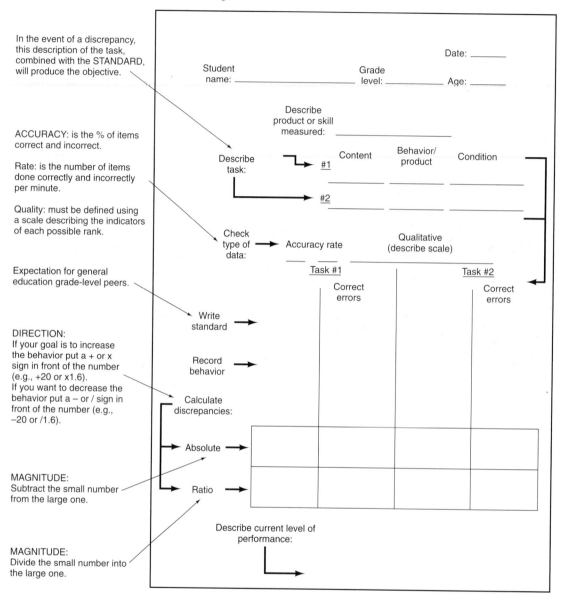

Problem-solving evaluation is a thoughtful process. As already mentioned, this is a good news/bad news situation. It is good news because it makes evaluation a professionally challenging activity that can be improved as our thinking matures. It can be bad news when someone's thinking isn't good.

## What Is "Good Thinking"?

Experts, regardless of their field, tend to work in certain characteristic ways (Laufer, 1997). As has already been pointed out, expert teachers make good use of routines, which allows them to accomplish common classroom tasks. This ten-

*Evaluation is a thoughtful process that involves decision making.*

dency to make the "small stuff" routine to save energy for the "big stuff" is one characteristic of experts. Experts also tend to see patterns, or themes, where novices may only see unrelated events (Carter et al., 1988; Sabers et al., 1991). Experts are thought to be experts because they make the best decisions or go about making decisions very well (regardless of outcome). Their work is judicious and polished. Still, experts are not always correct, as it is not possible to always be correct. This means that experts are willing to take risks and to be accountable for their actions. Experts learn from their own experience and are keenly interested in the experiences of others.

Here is an illustration. A practicum student did a lesson in front of his university supervisor, and the lesson was a disaster. Everything went wrong. After it was over, the practicum student told the supervisor, "That was terrible; I blew the lesson."

The supervisor replied, "It isn't over yet" and asked the student if he could explain what went well, what went wrong, and develop a plan for correcting the problems for the next lesson.

As it turned out, the practicum student could do all of those things and, by using what he had learned in classes and field experiences to reflect on his first lesson, he improved the second lesson. In fact the lesson was great.

### Threats to Expert Judgment

Because judgment is complex, it is easiest to produce a model for messing it up. Threats to good judgment are listed in Exhibit 7.4. These were taken largely from the work of Adams (1979),

*Exhibit 7.4   Threats to Judgment.*

| Threat | Explanation/Example |
|---|---|
| Data characterization (selective attention) | Seeing what you expect, or want to see. Two people watching the same event don't agree about what they saw. |
| Lack of the knowledge needed to make a judgment | Working on things you don't know about (that is, trying to teach about the role of minority cultures in U.S. history—when that wasn't taught to you when you were in school). |
| Stereotyping (overgeneralization) | Working with someone's label and not their characteristics (ignoring Ralph and only attending to the fact that he is labeled LD). |
| Failure to define the problem | Not knowing what it is you are trying to do (such as deciding to have students work lessons without giving them a pretest). |
| Defining the problem too trivially or narrowly | Concentrating on a trivial aspect of a larger problem (thinking about the haircut of a student who has no friends). |
| Lack of perspective | Only seeing things one way (for example, not seeing the problem from the parents' point of view). |
| Fear | Of failure, risk, notoriety, success, responsibility or nearly anything else. |
| Premature resolution | Stopping work too early—failing to be comprehensive (such as picking the first solution recommended). |
| Insensitivity to probabilities | Not considering that some things are already more or less likely to work (adopting specialized reading materials when the general education class materials haven't been tried). |
| Sample size | Drawing conclusions from too few experiences or examples (concluding student can add because he works four problems correctly). |
| Misconceptions of chance | Thinking that unrelated events can affect each other (such as believing that flipping three heads in a row somehow alters the 50/50 chance of flipping a head with a fourth coin—it doesn't). |
| Unwarranted confidence | Deciding to do something on the basis of evidence, or advocacy, that doesn't have anything to do with the problem at hand (deciding a student will have trouble in math because she is bad at reading). |
| Selective or incomplete search | Only considering one category of options (only considering the use of teaching methods advocated by your friends). |
| Mistaking a correlational relationship for cause and effect | Just because two things happen at the same time doesn't mean one causes the other (thinking that a student threw up in class for attention because everyone looked at her when she did). |
| Lack of a supportive environment | Not having a chance to observe others use good judgment or have that use encouraged (working in a school where everyone routinely makes all of these errors). |

Margolis (1987), Nisbett and Ross (1980), and Tversky and Kahneman (1973). It is reproduced as part of the problem-solving checklist in Appendix A.1.

The other portion of the problem-solving checklist found in Appendix A.1 was shown in Exhibits 2.4 and 6.18. It is a list of "rules for developing assumed causes." Assumed causes for student problems should be developed according to these rules to assure that they are functional and curriculum-based. These rules were developed by the authors as they observed IEP meetings for special education students. Eventually, these observations led to the recognition of certain patterns or themes in participant talk that bogged down or inhibited decision making. These themes were then formatted as rules and placed into the problem-solving checklist. The checklist should be used to help individuals or teams maintain productive and focused attempts at problem solving. Turn to Appendix A.1 now and examine the steps in the checklist.

The checklist can be filled out as a self-evaluation by each participant after a meeting, or it can be filled out by each observer to give participants feedback on their performance during the session. The checklist is completed by noting each error each time it occurs with a mark (for example, / or ✓).

Given that students often spend hours being evaluated, it is not unreasonable to turn our attention occasionally to our own professional efforts. However, evaluation of problem-solving processes seldom occurs, and professionals seldom are held accountable for the quality of their performance in this critical area.

***An Example of Problem-Solving Error*** Here is an example of failure to control the limitations on inference. Dr. Howell was once asked to review the individualized instruction provided in a large school. In preparation, he pulled the teaching plans on several students and noticed something interesting. While about two-thirds of the plans had various recommendations, in one-third of the cases, the teaching recommendations were all the same (therefore, they were not *individual*). Dr. Howell, being a fairly cynical sort of guy, doubted that one-third of the remedial students at this school all needed the same intervention. So, he checked the scores reported in the evaluations. The scores were *not* the same. In fact, there were only two portions of these student's plans that were similar: the teaching recommendations and the name of the person who wrote up the plans. This was getting interesting!

Suspecting major violations of the IDEA and a high level conspiracy among officials in the school, Howell sought out one of the teachers and asked, "How come all of these kids, regardless of their test scores, have the same recommendations?"

"That's easy," the teacher replied, "Bob wrote them."

"So?" Howell queried.

"Bob thinks the solution to all social behavior problems can be answered by using Dreikurs," the teacher explained, "and that all reading problems are best dealt with by using 'Big Books.' So if it's a behavior problem, he always says 'redirect,' and if it's reading he always says 'do lap reading.'"

"That doesn't seem too functional."

"Oh, we don't expect Bob to be functional. We rely on the other two evaluators to do the really hard kids."

So what is to be gained from this story? First, if you are in a program that separates its staff into "evaluators" and "teachers," you are about two decades out of date. Second, if you are a teacher who must depend on outside evaluators, you'd better hope you don't get Bob! And finally, Bob was making mistakes. He was confusing curriculum with instruction and recommending only those objectives conveniently taught with his favorite instructional approaches. Look at Exhibit 7.4 and decide which errors of judgment Bob was making. These errors in Bob's thinking altered the results of his evaluations (it made them worthless).

### A Brief Summary

The threats to good judgment in Exhibit 7.4 and the rules in Exhibit 6.15 have been adapted to educational decision making and will be referred to frequently throughout the text. Read them carefully now, and review them any time you are faced with a decision about what or how to teach a student.

We all make the errors listed in the exhibits many times a day. That's because these errors are all completely human and illustrate ways of thinking that may actually benefit us at times (Nisbett & Ross, 1980). To control these errors, we need two things. First, we need to recognize when our jobs call for work that is professional, focused, and reflective; second, we need a set of guidelines (like the ones on the checklist) to follow when we do that kind of work.

An evaluator's most sophisticated thinking should take place *before* proceeding with this final step of the CBE process. This is when the evaluator either takes the available information and converts it into interpretations or, if not feeling adequately prepared to do that yet, sets it aside and continues sampling. The move to decision making follows this sequence:

1. **Ask questions** about curriculum and about instruction;

2. **Sample behavior** to get performance data and progress data;

3. **Use systematic interpretation** by following the CBE format, avoiding the threats and following the decision rules; then

4. **Make decisions** about *what to teach* and *how to teach it.*

## How Should Teachers Decide What to Teach?

Remember, to use curriculum-based evaluation, you must clarify the curriculum. Attempting curriculum-based evaluation in the absence of a well-defined curriculum can be like assembling a piece of complicated equipment for the first time without any directions. You may know how to use all the tools but be frustrated by the need to puzzle each step out on your own. If content recognition, specification of behavior/conditions, and development of criteria have not been completed prior to the evaluation, the job of doing them falls on the person or people doing the evaluation.

Let's assume you have a clear idea of what the curriculum is. (By the way, if you have tables of specifications, status sheets, or objective sequences, these always should be on the table at problem-solving meetings.) You still need to figure out what in that curriculum a particular student already knows and what he needs to know

next. One way to decide what to teach is to use decision rules based on your expert knowledge of the curriculum and the demands it will make on the student. Exhibit 7.5 lists a set of decision rules you could use.

In Exhibit 7.5, the first question asks "Am I working on the correct objective?" If there are discrepancies between expected and actual performance, and the student has the prior knowledge required to learn the skill, select it as an objective. For example, assume that you have conducted a reading-comprehension evaluation and obtained the following results:

**Fact**—Student has poor comprehension of science book.

| Assumed Cause 1 | Test | CAP | Behavior on Test |
|---|---|---|---|
| Slow decoding | Timed reading of grade-level passage | 140 words correct 5–7 errors | 148 words correct 5 errors |

**Status**—Decoding adequate.
**Decision**—Decoding instruction isn't needed. Come up with a new assumed cause.

| Assumed Cause 2 | Test | CAP | Behavior on Test |
|---|---|---|---|
| Poor passage-dependent vocabulary | Select appropriate word definition for a given passage | 90% | 40% |

**Status**—No-pass. There is a 50% point absolute discrepancy between expected and actual performance.
**Decision**—Because the student's score of 40% is less than it should be, you will need to get rid of the discrepancy by teaching to the objective used for the CRT. In this case, the objective would be as follows: *"Given a passage with underlined words and four possible definitions per word, the student*

**Exhibit 7.5   *Decision Rules for Teaching.***

> **Directions:** Ask *each* question (more than one may be applicable to any student). Include in your considerations the kind of data (performance or progress) that is available to you *(behavior indicated by progress data listed in italics).*

| Questions | Behavior | Decisions |
|---|---|---|
| 1. Am I working on the correct objective? | Student is at or above CAP. | No instruction is required on this objective. Monitor for retention. |
| | Student is not at CAP but has the necessary prerequisites to learn the skill. | Teach this objective. |
| | Student is not at CAP but is *making some correct responses.* | Stay with current objective. |
| | Student is not at CAP and *has made no progress after several sessions.* | Confirm that the student *has the necessary prerequisites:* <br>• If yes, change instruction; <br>• If no, move back to a less complex objective. |
| 2. Should I teach this skill in content or in isolation? | Student has the necessary background information to derive meaning for the context (knows what a checkbook is and what it is used for). | Teach the skill in the context of larger tasks. Explain the relevance of the task. Make the lesson "applied" (have him do the subtraction in a checkbook). |
| | Student is lacking prior knowledge necessary to use context or is confused by context. | Teach the largest manageable portion of the objective in isolation. Use "fact" instruction. If student is accurate, employ fast-paced repetitive drill. Set daily performance aims and reinforce improvement. Put the skill in context as soon as possible. |
| 3. Should I use an acquisition or fluency format? (Application/automaticity should *always* be emphasized.) | Student is inaccurate. Typically this means that the student is making meaningful errors. Is less than 85% accurate, or is *very* slow. | Use acquisition instruction, including extensive explanations, models, demonstration, guided practice with correction, and feedback. Allow little independent work. |
| | Student is accurate (85% or better), errors are not meaningful, and/or rate is low. | Use fluency instruction. Emphasize rate. Give extensive drill and practice. Make sure accuracy is maintained. |
| 4. Am I emphasizing the correct thought processes? (Facts, concepts, and strategies are all important.) | Student's errors often reflect incorrect use of basic facts (thinks 8 + 7 = 14 or that whales breathe underwater). | Teach factual content through presentation of problems and answers. |

***Exhibit 7.5*** *Continued*

| Questions | Behavior | Decisions |
|---|---|---|
| | Students' errors often reflect incorrect understanding of the meaning of the task (thinks 8 + 7 is the same as 87, or that whales are fish). | Teach conceptual content by presenting critical attributes and requiring the student to discriminate between examples and nonexamples of the concept. |
| | Student errors, or explanations, reflect incorrect knowledge of the procedures to follow when working on an item (thinks the solution to 8 − 7 can be found by counting backwards from 8, or thinks you can tell if something is a fish simply by determining if it lives in the water). | Teach strategic content by demonstrating the processes of task completion while talking through each step. |
| 5. Am I employing the correct teacher actions when presenting the lesson? | Below CAP *but making adequate progress.* | Stay with current presentation. |
| | Below CAP but seems to have prerequisite skills. *Is making inadequate progress despite appropriate objective, emphasis, format, and incentive.* | Change setting, materials, or delivery—variables such as: <br>•Questioning <br>•Feedback <br>•Pace <br>•Explanations <br>•Length of lessons <br>•Size of group <br>•Lesson sequence <br>•Type of practice |
| 6. Should the lesson be made to seem more interesting? | Student is *improving,* seems interested in lessons, participates, and is nondisruptive. | Stay with current presentation. |
| | *Student was improving, but is now getting worse.* Student is beginning to resist lessons. Student is not participating (is bored!). | Provide meaning. Explain relevance of task. Work skills in the context of higher level skills. Begin and end lessons by explaining how the skill can be used. Allow student's input into the kind of instruction they receive. Allow them to chart their own progress. Make lessons "applied." <br><br>*or* <br><br>Change type or schedule of reinforcement. Use preferred activities or student-selected rewards. Consider increasing or decreasing the frequency of reinforcement. Change when reinforcement is delivered to make it more or less predictable. Change type of reinforcer. |
| 7. Do I need more information? | You can't answer the first six questions. | Keep evaluating! |

*will select the definition that matches the passages content, with at least 90% accuracy."*

In this example, it is clear that the student does not need to work on decoding rate but does need instruction on vocabulary. Because he is partially proficient (40%) at using passage content, it is not necessary to search for additional subskills of that task but rather to teach the student to use passage clues more efficiently to decide what words mean.

## Deciding How to Teach

By examining the status of each validated assumed cause, you will be able to make recommendations about what the student should be taught. By read-ministering specific tests for each objective, you will also be able to monitor the effectiveness of teaching by noting if the discrepancy is decreasing. This process is called data-based program modification (DBPM).

What can be done to ensure that students are learning the most material in the least amount of time? The answer lies in the application of DBPM and **assisted assessment** procedures. The collection and analysis of progress data, sometimes called formative evaluation, was discussed in Chapter 5. The term refers to decisions made on the basis of changes in behavior during instruction. Performance data, the kind collected by giving an assessment once, tell us where a student is on a skill at the time the test is given. Progress data, which are collected by monitoring a skill over a period of time, tell us how the student's behavior is changing. Because instruction is designed to produce changes in behavior, only progress data can tell us if instruction is effective. Consider this example. A teacher gives Walter and Susan a spelling test and they both get scores of 45. This means they are both performing at the same level. However, a week later when the teacher gives the test again, Susan only gets 50 whereas Walter gets 75. This means Walter is progressing faster than Susan. It also means that the instruction being used is more effective for Walter than it is for Susan.

DBPM employs the repeated administration of specific assessments to monitor the student's progress in treatments. Look again at the chart in Exhibit 5.13 as if *you* are the teacher of that student. The dots in that exhibit represent measures of a skill you want the student to learn, whereas the line represents how fast the student should be learning the skill. Would you continue to use the same treatment or would you change?

If you said you would change, you made a correct data-based program modification decision (Howell & McCollum-Gahley, 1986). DBPM requires accurate, continual measurement of important student behaviors. The resulting data can be analyzed for evidence of acceptable or unacceptable growth (progress) toward a specific objective, and, particularly if the data are visually displayed, comparisons can easily be made between a student's growth in different teaching techniques.

Exhibit 7.6 shows changes in a student's oral reading rate under two teaching approaches. Each dot represents a timed oral reading from the student's classroom reader. In this case, the student is in each treatment for 1 week. The superiority of treatment B over treatment A for this student on this task and at this time is obvious. It is obvious because there are enough data, and they are sufficiently stable, to recognize the student's learning trends.

In Exhibit 7.7a, one score is supplied. Whether the student is improving or getting worse can't be determined from this one summation of his performance. In Exhibit 7.7b, three possible posttest scores have been added. As a teacher, if you obtained posttest A, you would no doubt be pleased; posttests B and C would not cause you to celebrate.

Exhibit 7.7c contains a score as low as score **C** in Exhibit 7.7b. However, the low score in Exhibit 7.7c isn't particularly disturbing because the overall trend illustrated in that exhibit is positive. Given the data in Exhibit 7.7c, you could make decisions on the overall movement of the behavior and not worry about the single low point of datum. This is called *trend analysis*. You can do trend analysis whenever you have progress data that are so generally consolidated you can ignore any single day's performance and still draw the same trend line. In such cases, you can base decisions on trends. Howell et al. (2000a) provides more information

**Exhibit 7.6    Teaching Effect.**

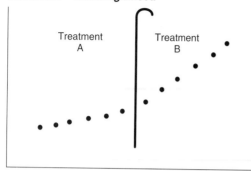

about how to collect and analyze data for use in trend analysis. You may want to look at that information (and Appendix A.1) now.

### Assisted Assessment

In DBPM, decisions are made by testing the student, teaching the student, and then interpreting the trend of scores. This teach-test, teach-test cycle is basic to all applications of formative evaluation including precision teaching (Howell & Lorson-Howell, 1990) and diagnostic teaching (Deno, 1997; Valencia & Wixson, 1991).

Assisted assessment is a procedure employed to determine the amount of aid a student must be given to learn. It is carried out by testing until the student fails on a task. The evaluator then supplies the student with carefully sequenced clues or explanations before retesting. This is done in the hope of determining the level of support the student requires for continued learning (Campione & Brown, 1985).

Conceptually, assisted assessment and DBPM are the same. Both procedures rely on repeated measures of the same skill or strategy across alterations in instruction. To do this, one must have clear curriculum sequences, and curriculum measurement overlays (Fuchs & Deno, 1991). In distinction, proponents of assisted assessment tend to accept currently available measures while focusing their attention on sequences of instructional intervention.

Exhibit 7.8 provides a summary of assisted assessment for two students designated $S^1$ and $S^2$. During initial testing on a skill sequence, both

of these students got items 1–3 correct. They both failed items 4 and 5. The evaluator then gave each student a skill-related prompt (intervention A-) and tested item 4 again. As can be seen in the exhibit, student $S^1$ failed this retest, but $S^2$ passed it. Next, the evaluator tried demonstrating how to work item 4 to $S^1$, but $S^1$ failed the second retest. Finally, after having skill 4 completely retaught, $S^1$ passed a third retest.

The results in Exhibit 7.8 are interesting. Note that on the original test—and after the entire procedure is over—both students apparently know exactly the same thing. Yet, students 1 and 2 are different. $S^1$ required considerably more assistance (levels A, B, and C) than $S^2$ ($S^2$ only required level-A assistance). Exhibit 7.8, therefore, does not simply map out what these students know, it also maps out the assistance they require to learn. That is exactly what was illustrated for a single student in Exhibit 7.6. The only difference here is that repeated measures were given during the same assessment session. Assisted-assessment procedures will be featured in several of the topical chapters that follow.

### Why Do We Need Formative Evaluation?

The key to any formative evaluation system is frequent and direct data collection. The more frequent the assessment, the more often one can make data-based decisions. The best data decisions will be made from systems that include frequent CBM because it will produce direct data that are sensitive to learning.

Formative evaluation can be particularly effective when it is combined with guidelines for systematic interpretation. These guidelines, called data decision rules, tell what to do when certain patterns in data occur. Many teachers are used to applying some set of decision-making rules to their instruction. These rules are seldom absolute, but they do provide guidance. An example of a data-based rule with which most teachers are familiar is the "three times in 3 days" rule attributed to Fernald (1943). This rule says if a student works a task correctly three times a day for 3 days in a row, he has learned the task and should move on to something new.

**Exhibit 7.7a, b, c   Determining Trend.**

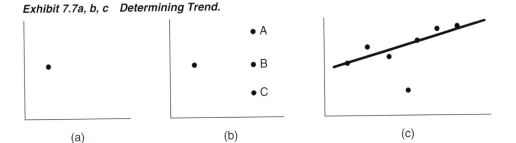

(a)                              (b)                              (c)

**Exhibit 7.8   A Summary of Assisted Behavior.**

| | | | Assistance Sequence | | | | | | |
|---|---|---|---|---|---|---|---|---|---|
| | Original Test | | A Prompt | | B Demonstrate | | C Reteach | | |
| | $S^1$ | $S^2$ | $S^1$ | $S^2$ | $S^1$ | $S^2$ | $S^1$ | | $S^2$ |
| Skill Sequence | 5NP | NP | | | | | | | |
| | 4NP | NP | NP | P | NP | | P | | |
| | 3P | P | | | | | | | |
| | 2P | P | | | | | | | |
| | 1P | P | | | | | | | |
| *P=pass; NP=no pass | | | | | | | | | |

As one might expect, the more sophisticated the data collection system, the more sophisticated the decisions that can be made with that system. Because the highest level of sophistication is characteristically reserved for the most problematic students (remember the "minimum-maximum" rule), educators may use data collection and interpretation procedures for some students that would seem needlessly complex for others. Some of the decisions described in Exhibit 7.5 depend on formative data. In cases where such data are required, the notations under the heading "Behavior" have been printed in *italics*.

**Deciding When to Make a Change**   Progress aims are important because without them a teacher may not recognize when a student is falling behind until he is so far behind that correcting the problem requires a massive interven-

tion. Monitoring can only tell us when changes are needed if we have *both* progress data and a progress standard.

It is possible to convert performance objectives into progress objectives by slicing (recalibrating) the performance objectives and adding time statements. For example, look back to objective C.1 in the Table of Specifications shown in Exhibit 3.7. It says a student will "write the answers to two-place addition problems with regrouping at the mastery level." This objective can be sliced by generating a sequence of aim dates specifying different proficiency levels. For example, ". . . rate of 5 problems a minute by November 1st," ". . . rate of 10 problems a minute by December 1st," and ". . . rate of 20 problems a minute by January 1st." To slice objectives by writing them in terms of expected progress, pick a task and set intermediate aims along a single element (content, behavior, condition, or criteria). This works best with general outcome tasks like oral reading that reflect the use of multiple skills and processes.

The idea of aim dates can be applied to any of the objective elements. Here is another example using the addition facts objective but focusing on the content dimension. "Will write answers to problems including the numbers 0–5 by November 1st" and "will write answers to problems involving the numbers 6–9 by December 1st." Additional information about developing aimlines is presented in Howell et al. (2000a).

Once a progress expectation has been developed, you can monitor the student to see if his learning is sufficient to take him to the final performance goal. The data you collect must yield a direct and sensitive representation of what the student is learning. It must also be collected frequently. Generally, it is recommended that progress data be collected at least two times a week. You should consider changing the program any time a student's performance falls below his expectation three times in a row (White, 1986). This doesn't mean you have to change. It means you should get out the rules in Exhibit 7.5 and go through each question for your student. Malott et al. (1997), who have a set of rules for performance management, state that "performance not monitored once a week turns to Jell-O" (p. 363).

How do you decide how often to collect progress data? Base your decision on your knowledge of the domain, the curriculum, the student, your instruction, and your measurement system. In other words, use your professional judgment. Your decision about how frequently to collect progress data, then, also will be informed by the amount of time you are willing to allow to elapse before you accumulate the three data points recommended above. For some behaviors, 3 weeks is a long time, and measurement more than once a week would be recommended. For other behaviors, 3 weeks might be a perfectly reasonable length of time within which to expect to see growth, and weekly data collection is appropriate.

## Collaborative Decision Making

Sometimes you will make decisions about a student on your own, and at other times you will make them through collaboration. Many of the decision rules in Exhibit 7.5 apply here; however, there are some additional considerations imposed by the act of collaboration.

1. Before any meetings take place:

Establish a structure for the meetings. This structure should be somewhat formal, and all participants should agree to follow it. This way, you won't spend time constantly renegotiating the form of the meetings.

Establish a set of value statements that reflects the group member's position on her own responsibilities and her own beliefs about education (that is, "We have more of an obligation to teach students than to keep their parents happy" or "Solutions to problems must not have the effect of reducing instructional time").

Decide on a process for determining (based upon the nature of the problem) who should or should not attend the meetings.

Determine how much authority the group will have.

2. During meetings:

Assign someone to run the meeting and hold it to the agreed-upon structure.

Assign someone to keep notes that accurately report the problems discussed, the solutions developed, and who will carry out the solutions.

Assign someone to fill out the problem-solving checklist (Appendix A.1) on each participant.

Clearly define the purpose of the meeting.

Have discussions that are aligned with the problem.

Be sure that everyone at the meeting participates.

Keep the conversation open and direct (while limiting it to the defined problem).

If other problems emerge from the discussion, write them down and then put them in order of priority. Do not allow the meeting to become so flooded by business that nothing can be accomplished.

Try to recognize things that can be solved immediately and separate them from problems requiring longer term solutions.

3. After the meeting:

Always have a brief session during which participants can comment on the strengths or weaknesses of the meeting itself. The student is not discussed at this point. This "debriefing" is to give feedback, resolve any conflicts within the group, and raise any concerns about the collaboration process (the problem-solving checklist may help here).

Follow up to assure that any solutions designed, or actions agreed upon, are implemented.

## Entitlement Decisions

Recall that in Chapter 1, we said that the only way *some* students ever receive an education that is designed to help them progress adequately in school is to be served through an **entitlement** program that provides language, remedial, or special education services. Recall, also, that we emphasized that two things must be verified about a child before he can be found eligible for an entitlement program. First, the school must determine that a child has one of the categories of eligibility specified in the law pertaining to the entitlement; second, the student must be in *need* of the entitlement program. Therefore, determining eligibility for an entitlement program requires two decisions.

The **first decision:** Is this student a member of the entitled class?

The **second decision:** Does this student need services because of low achievement or social behavior problems?

The solution to the **first decision** lies somewhere outside of this book. Excellent advice in this area can be found in Reschly et al. (1998). To make the membership decision, it must be determined that the student has a disability, meets income requirements associated with Title 1 programs, or speaks English as a second language.

You may have noticed that we have talked very little about entitlement. However, by this point, you should have a pretty good idea about how to approach the **second decision.** You would ask:

Is there a problem?

What should I do to fix the problem?

Is my solution working?

Given our discussion earlier in this chapter, you should also realize that you wouldn't just ask these questions once, but would continue to ask them over and over again until the answer to the last question *'Is my solution working?'* is "Yes." If it continues to be *"no,"* you and your colleagues might decide that special education services are warranted.

## How Do We Decide When Special Education Is Warranted?

This conclusion would be based on evidence of the student's **resistance** to a string of interventions. Such resistance would be illustrated by the development and use of *several* well-developed treatment plans as well as *documentation* of their effectiveness, or ineffectiveness, throughout the collection of curriculum-based monitoring data. The concept of "resistance" is important because it shifts our attention away from student performance and onto instructional support. By mapping out a student's resistance to interventions of varying intensity, a team can identify the amount of support required for learning to occur. The team can look to find out how to obtain the required level of support. If it can be found through general education, the student would not qualify for special education. However, if reasonable accommodations in general education would not be sufficient, special education entitlement is justified.

Consideration of resistance is necessary because it is support (in the form of the entitlement) for which we are finding the student eligible. As professionals, we are trying to recognize which interventions will be successful, which interventions will not be successful, and which may only be successful if entitlement resources are supplied.

Although the concept of *resistance to intervention* is critical, it must be applied carefully. Obviously, if the criteria for entitlement is resistance to intervention, then the quality of the intervention as well as the characteristics of the student must be considered. The following actions significantly raise the likelihood that interventions at any level of complexity will be successful (Bergan & Kratochwill, 1990; Deno, 1985; Shinn, 1989; Tilly & Flugum, 1995):

1. Establish a behavioral definition of the problem
2. Measure the behavior prior to intervention
3. Conduct an analysis of the problem
4. Set a goal
5. Prepare a step-by-step teaching plan based on sound instruction
6. Implement the intervention as planned
7. Collect formative data
8. Graph the results
9. Evaluate results of the program by using systematic decision rules and formative evaluation of program effects.

### Exactly What Goes into an Entitlement Decision?

Remember, entitlement is **not** the purpose of the evaluation and problem-solving activities described in this book. Still, it is hard to imagine a book on evaluation for remedial and special education students that does not address it in some way. The primary purpose of the problem-solving techniques in this book is to correct student difficulties. Entitlement decisions are made when the preponderance of the collected evidence consistently demonstrates performance outside of the realm of *reasonable accommodation* within a typical general education classroom. When it is documented that the resources provided within special education are required, the *need* for entitlement has been clearly established.

This determination is accomplished by comparing the student's characteristics (as revealed in the activities above) to the terms specified in the legislation that establishes the entitlement. In the case of special education, this almost always requires peer comparison.

To make entitlement decisions, the following kinds of data should be considered.

1. *Current information on the present level of performance.* Generally, two grade levels below expectancy is considered outside of typical instructional range of the classroom (obviously, this will be less for early primary students). However, this information is considered to be comparatively useless as the concept of "grade level" itself is questionable.

2. *Direct peer comparisons.* All available data (including review, interview, observation, or test data) could fall within the pool and be used to compare the target student's performance with typical peers. Comparative information from records and rating scales are also potentially useful. This comparison also could be to local CBM norms in the grade or subject area. In this case, any student scoring at or near the 10th percentile usually is viewed as outside of the typical range.

3. *Intervention outcome data.* As explained above, these can be reviewed to look at the progress of the individual compared with his entry-level behavior and to goals based on typical peer performance.

4. *Any other pertinent information.* This information may come from records, teacher interviews, permanent products assessment, and grades.

### What Is a Problem-Solving Approach to Entitlement Decisions?

Developing a preponderance of evidence that a student *needs* special education requires simultaneous documentation that the interventions that were attempted and failed were reasonably calculated to provide educational benefit (Bateman & Linden, 1997). Clearly, it would be difficult to declare a student "resistant to intervention" if the interventions that were tried were not likely to be effective.

One approach that has been tried in numerous school districts is to engage in a systematic problem-solving process (Reshely et al., 1998) not unlike the curriculum-based evaluation procedures described in this book. Generally, a student would be "referred" to a problem-solving team sometime after repeated attempts to resolve a discrepancy had failed in the context of a general education classroom *but* prior to being "formally" referred to special education. However, there are programmatic and legal considerations involved in delaying referral to an entitlement program too long, so the exact timing of the problem-solving steps described here and their integration into the CBE process described in the remainder of this book will vary according to the needs of each student. The intent of the problem-solving approach we will describe here is NOT to delay referral for help but to accelerate the development of an effective intervention through systematic and well-documented attempts to reduce a discrepancy between performance and expectations.

The problem-solving approach described here is consistent with the model used in the Heartland Education Agency (1998) in Iowa and the Student Responsive Service Delivery Model (Howell, 1997) used in the state of Washington. We will summarize the key features of these problem-solving approaches to entitlement.

For the purpose of this discussion, problem solving is a process that includes the systematic analysis of student behavior and the interventions devised to change it. Problem solving occurs within the school setting at various levels. These are listed across the top of Exhibit 7.9 and, as seen in Exhibit 7.10, become more intense as the resources needed to resolve the problem increase. Although the end result could be entitlement for special education, this should only happen after a systematic, data-based decision-making process like the one described in this chapter has clearly demonstrated the need for special education.

A key distinction between the problem-solving approach to eligibility determination and the general CBE approach to instructional planning is that the eligibility determination process almost always involves a team of teachers and other professionals. Curriculum-based evaluation can be carried out by one teacher working in the day-to-day context of her classroom (although it certainly can involve a team, too).

The problem-solving approach to entitlement involves a number of activities, each of which must be carried out across different levels of intervention. To fully understand the process, one must first understand the natures of these activities and levels. The activities associated with this entitlement approach generally include the following:

Identify the concern

Define the problem

State goals and objectives

Generate possible solutions

Evaluate the solutions

Select a solution

Write an action plan

Implement the plan

Follow up and evaluate the intervention

### Identify the Concern

Based on teacher, student, or parent concerns, derive a general description of the problem the student is having. If the student has many problems, put them in order of priority. If you can find a single behavior that accurately represents the problem, then use the "so-what" test.

### Define the Problem

Define the problem behavior in concrete, observable, measurable terms (use the "stranger" test). The description should make the behavior clear and recognizable by observers. It should include target behaviors (examples) and maladaptive behaviors (nonexamples) of the behavior of concern.

Include each of the following as part of the definition:

Data *collection.* A measurement strategy should be identified and *employed immediately.* Repeated collection of

**Exhibit 7.9    Problem Solving in School Settings.**

| Levels<br><br>Actions | Level One:<br>Consultation<br>Between<br>Teachers-Parents | Level Two:<br>Consultation With<br>Other Resources | Level Three:<br>Consultation With<br>Extended Problem-<br>Solving Team | Level Four:<br>IEP<br>Consideration |
|---|---|---|---|---|
| Identify the Concern | | | | |
| Define the problem<br>• Data Collection<br>• Problem Validation<br>• Problem Analysis<br>• Write Problem Statement<br>• Set a Progress Goal | | | | |
| Generate Solutions | | | | |
| Evaluate the Solutions | | | | |
| Select a Solution | | | | |
| Write an Action Plan | | | | |
| Implement the Plan | | | | |
| Follow-Up and Evaluate | | | | |
| Determine Eligibility | | | | |

*Source:* Howell, K. W., Zucker, S. H. & Morehead, M. K. (2000b). *Multilevel Academic Skills Inventory.* Bellingham, WA: Applied Research and Development Center. To order contact the Student Co-op Bookstore, Western Washington University. Fax (360) 650-2888. Phone (360) 650-3656. Reprinted with permission.

preintervention CBE data will be useful in future problem analysis, intervention design, and entitlement decisions.

Problem *validation*. For problem validation, and to determine the magnitude of the problem, summarize the discrepancy

**Exhibit 7.10  Resources Needed for Problem Solving.**

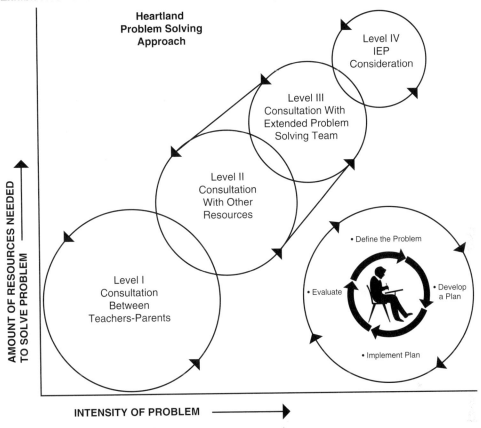

*Taken from Heartland, (1998).*

between the student's current level of performance and what he is expected to be doing.

Problem *analysis.* Formulate specific questions (for example, assumed causes) about the problem.

Write A *problem statement.* Include a quantitative and qualitative description of the dimensions of the behavior and setting.

### State Goals and Objectives

Write a progress goal that includes the conditions, behavior, and criterion (including an aim date). The goal should specify a decrease in the problem behavior and increase in the target be-

havior. The objectives should map out a path of improvement from the student's current level of performance to the goals.

### Generate Possible Instructional Solutions

Solutions are generated without discussion or comment. This step is often called brainstorming.

### Evaluate the Solutions

It is important to consider if the team can implement the instructional plan with integrity. Plans that cannot be implemented the way they were designed will not be useful. Potential solutions are judged according to the following:

Potential for success;

Alignment with the goals and objectives;

Focus on alterable variables;

Resources required (such as time, paraprofessional support, expertise, etc.); and

Intervention ease, feasibility, and acceptability.

## Select a Solution

The solution should be acceptable to everyone who is at all involved and concerned with the problem. If support cannot be arranged for the intervention, it is far less likely to succeed. Therefore, efforts to build consensus are worth the time.

## Write an Action Plan

Clearly identify procedures and instructional strategies to be utilized. *These must include the following:*

Where and when the plan will be implemented;

The materials and technical assistance needed to carry out the plan;

The persons responsible for each aspect of the plan;

Methods, schedules, conditions of data collection, and strategies to summarize the data;

A decision rule articulating the number of data points or length of time before data analysis occurs; and

A written description to be made available to <u>all</u> individuals who will be directly involved in the implementation of the plan.

## Implement the Plan

The action plan should be implemented as designed and written. Changes can be made based upon formative data analysis. This stage requires ongoing technical assistance for design, review, and troubleshooting.

## Follow-Up and Evaluation of the Intervention

Data should be systematically collected as the plan is implemented. A successful intervention may have multiple phases as changes are made on the basis of the data. The measurement strategy defined in the plan should also be utilized. Systematic decision-making rules should be applied to the data on an ongoing basis.

Possible outcomes and decisions that can be made at any level are presented in Exhibit 7.11.

## Levels

The same multistep process presented above can be carried out at varying levels. At the Heartland Education Agency in Iowa, the problem-solving activities outlined above are implemented at each of these four different levels.

### Level 1: Consultation Between Teachers and Parents

A teacher having a concern regarding a student's performance contacts the parent. Communication between the parent and the teacher is opened as general education interventions are implemented. Frequently, problems are resolved at this level by using solutions that only require the resources routinely available to teachers and parents. For example, the problem may be solved through the use of a daily report card, which is linked to home privileges.

### Level 2: Consultation with Other Resources

Many schools have created teams of school personnel to assist teachers, parents, and students. These are referred to by a variety of names such as Building Assistance Teams or Teacher Assistance Teams. These teams join the teacher and parent in the problem-solving process. They may develop solutions that still do not require additional resources but that may not have occurred to the teacher and parent. For example, the team may recommend the use of a spelling technique that is new to the teacher.

*Exhibit 7.11   Possible Outcomes and Decisions.*

| Possible Outcome | Decision |
|---|---|
| The discrepancy no longer exists. | The problem is gone and the student is no longer in need of special instructional strategies. |
| The student is making progress toward the established goal. | The current intervention should be continued to maintain the current rate of progress. |
| The student is not making progress at the expected rate. | The plan needs revision or modification to reach the progress goal. |
| The problem is not resolved. | Consider special education entitlement. |
| The intervention is successful, but the resources needed to maintain the intervention are beyond what can reasonably be continued in general education. | Consider special education entitlement. |

### Level 3: Consultation with Extended Problem-Solving Team

When a problem is not resolved at levels 1 or 2, its complex nature may require support personnel to be added to the problem-solving team. These may include school psychologists, educational consultants, school social workers, speech-language pathologists, occupational therapists, physical therapists, and/or early childhood specialists. R.I.O.T. procedures and systematic decision rules are used again to further define and analyze the problem. Example solutions such as daily monitoring or limited collaboration with the teacher about the use of a particular instructional technique may be selected. Plans to collect additional data may need to be developed to evaluate the solution's effectiveness.

### Level 4: Entitlement Consideration

When expected progress is not being made in levels 1–3 and/or resources beyond general education are needed for progress, entitlement for special education may be considered. The results of interventions at levels 1–3, and any screenings or assessments, are summarized to determine the appropriateness of those earlier interventions and services. Additional assessments may also be completed if more information is needed. If after

this information is reviewed the need for special education is identified, parental consent is obtained, and an IEP team meeting is constituted following the procedural safeguards delineated in IDEA (Bateman & Linden, 1997; Yell, 1998).

The participants in the problem-solving process will vary according to the level of the process. At all levels, efforts should be made to include personnel that have the expertise to address the presenting problem. Although the makeup of the problem-solving team will vary by level, involvement of the student's parent should remain constant at all levels. Parents should be well informed regarding all general education interventions even though special education due process rights are not available until the child is officially evaluated and staffed.

### Placement

Once a student has been found eligible for services and an instructional intervention has been planned, he will be placed into some kind of program. Such placements could range from home schooling, to a day-long self-contained special class, to a temporary support program in the general classroom. The guidelines for selecting a program are given in Exhibit 7.12.

Exhibit 7.12   Guidelines for Selecting a Placement.

| Guideline | Explanation |
|---|---|
| 1. Lessons are aligned with the goals and objectives specified in the intervention plan. | The student should be placed where someone is, or will be, teaching what he needs to learn. This is the single most important guideline. |
| 2. Use proven placements. | Select placements that incorporate the characteristics that have been shown to be successful/necessary at other levels of intervention. |
| 3. Use least obtrusive options. | Because any adaptation or accommodation must eventually be removed, it is best to select a placement that is like the student's target setting (for example, general class). |
| 4. Use least restrictive option. | To the extent possible, the student should be placed with "normal peers" in a general setting. This is only a preference. The student *must always* go where instruction is appropriate to his needs. |
| 5. Avoid control placements. | Do not place a student in a setting simply to control his inappropriate behavior. Be proactive. Assure that instruction required to teach the student is what he needs. |

## Now That We've Gotten Them In, How Do We Get Them Out?

If we searched the literature on entitlement, we'd probably find 5000 pages written on how to decide who qualifies for special services for every single page written about how to decide when someone should leave. This emphasis on the "head-hunting" aspect of entitlement evaluation raises serious questions about education's commitment to ideals like "inclusion," "reintegration," "transition," "mainstreaming," and "the least restrictive environment." The truth is, almost everyone referred goes in (Ysseldyke et al., 1983) and almost no one comes out (Flugum & Reschly, 1994; Ikeda et al., 1996; Ysseldyke et al., 1997).

With the use of progress monitoring and local peer comparison, measurement of program effectiveness and student progress can be consistently and accurately attained. Rather than waiting for the traditional 3-year reevaluation or annual review to look at progress and peer comparability, local comparison is always readily available to illustrate student performance and the relationship to typical peer performance. Essentially, if the target student's skills are comparable with peers and significant supports and services are not needed beyond what is reasonable for typical classrooms, you have to ask the question, "Why can't the target student be served through the general education setting?"

Like entitlement decisions (which consider setting demands and learner characteristics), reintegration decisions should be based on assessment information. A primary consideration should be progress toward goals. However, some comparison with typical performance is also required. This comparison should be made in relation to how regular education students perform. However, even if skill levels are sufficient for reentry, there needs also to be consideration of the supports required to maintain and generalize this skill performance. The demonstration of skills under high levels of assistance does not justify reintegration. However, it should send up the red flag alerting us to the continued need for support.

Both curricular and instructional variables should be considered because curriculum in special programs may not always be the same as that used in general education settings. Curriculum/content difference can have drastic effects on performance if the student is reintegrated without sufficient knowledge and skill of the tasks being taught in the general program. The use by all teachers of important instructional factors such as prompts, cues, frequency of feedback, instructional pace, opportunity for practice, response style, and modeling (to name but a few) should all be considered.

## *Summary*

This chapter finishes the steps of the CBE process. Many generic rules, formats, and actions you need to follow to conduct a functional teaching-oriented evaluation have been presented across the last three chapters. The focus of this particular chapter was summarizing assessment results and decision making, including entitlement.

This chapter described an alternative to traditional psycho-educational assessment for identifying students who may be entitled to remedial or special education programs. This alternative, the problem-solving approach, uses curriculum-based assessments and emphasizes the identification of alterable variables such as a student's academic skills, instructional needs, setting demands, and rate of learning. The system requires expertise in assessment, problem solving, and collaborative consultation. The problem-solving approach has the potential to provide information for the full range of educational decisions that school teams make, including screening, identification, and entitlement. You'll want to refer to this chapter while reading the remainder of the text, or when you get hung up while conducting an evaluation.

Go back to the flow chart in Exhibit 5.15. Now close your eyes and drop your finger on the page. Look at where your finger is pointing and see if you can explain the action illustrated there. If not, reread the section in the last three chapters pertaining to that action. Do this several times. There shouldn't be any circles, rectangles, or double-walled symbols on that flow chart that you haven't heard of by now. In fact, you should be knowledgeable enough to explain each symbol *and* the logic of the lines that connect them. It is important that you know this information because from this point on the text will illustrate how information presented in all of the preceding chapters (1–7) can be used within specific content domains to make quality teaching decisions.

## STUDY QUESTIONS

1. Kim obtains a score of 55 on a curriculum-based math probe. Typical performance for students in Kim's class is 85. Compute Kim's absolute discrepancy and discrepancy ratio.

2. Look at the chart illustrating Alvin's performance on page **179**. Write a short summary of Alvin's present level of performance to share with a problem-solving team. Include recommendations for prioritizing instructional interventions Alvin may need.

3. You are sitting at a problem-solving team meeting, discussing Alvin's needs. The school psychologist says the following:

It is clear that Alvin has attention-deficit disorder with hyperactivity. After all, we can see this in the profile of his scores on the published norm-referenced achievement test he took last year. I can give him an intelligence test to verify this. We don't need to worry about Alvin's problems in math. I am sure he will catch up as soon as we get his behavior under control. I worked with a student last year who had the same problem, and as soon as we instituted a token economy in the classroom, his math problems went away. I realize I have never actually taught students who have learning problems, but I think Alvin's reading will improve once you put him into a more language-based reading program. I know the students in Mrs. Herman's room over at the other elementary school liked it better when they switched to reading journals. Alvin probably is just bored with the phonics approach you have been using. I think his talk-outs are just a way to get out of boring reading work. Use the information in Exhibit 7.4 to critique the school psychologist's comments.

4.  You are trying to decide what to teach various students in your classroom to reduce the discrepancies between their present level of performance and your expectations about where they should be. What decision should you make for each of the students listed below?

| Student | Behavior |
| --- | --- |
| Sylvia | Currently below CAP. She responds correctly about 55% of the time. |
| Carlos | Has not made progress toward aim for 4 weeks. |
| Kenya | Was making adequate progress but her recent performance has leveled off. Her rate of off-task behavior during lessons has increased. |
| Brittany | Responds accurately about 90% of the time, but rate is slow. |
| Ben | Frequently fails to complete all items on tests and assignments because he skips items. Sometimes uses the wrong algorithm or procedure to solve problems. |

5.  Summarize the steps and actions associated with a problem-solving approach to entitlement decisions.

# Part Two

# THINGS TO DO

# Chapter 8

# Reading Comprehension

*The skipper remarked to one the other day, 'There are things you find nothing about in books.' I think that he got out of it very well for such a stupid man.*

—Joseph Conrad, *Typhoon*

*I took a course in speed reading, learning to read straight down the middle of the page, and was able to read* War and Peace *in twenty minutes. It's about Russia.*

—Woody Allen

## Step 1: Define Your Purpose

The purpose of this chapter, like those that follow, is to arrive at instructional objectives and teaching recommendations. This is accomplished by answering questions about the student's needs. The main questions are:

1. Does the student seem to have a comprehension problem?
2. Can the existence of the problem be confirmed?
3. Which **actions** should be taken to solve the problem?
4. Do you have adequate information to reach solutions?

5. Which enabling skills should be checked?
6. Which **teaching recommendations** should be used?

## Step 2: Define the Thing to Be Measured

Reading comprehension is an interactive process through which the reader uses code, context analysis, prior knowledge, vocabulary, and language, along with executive-control strategies, to understand text (Adams, 1990). It is a multidimensional construct and, as such, not easily observed. One way to avoid the problems of definition that come with the term comprehen-

*Reading instruction provided to low achievers often differs from that given to high achievers.*

sion is to talk about the student's *reading and re-acting,* instead of *decoding* and *comprehension* (Tindal & Marston, 1990).

Use of the term *reacting* shifts the focus from psychological processes, which cannot be observed, to behaviors and products. For example, students may react to what they read by answering questions, retelling, paraphrasing, or completing cloze passages. Each of these techniques is commonly used to illustrate a student's comprehension—but few people would agree that any of them are pure measures of comprehension.

We think that comprehension is the act of combining information in passages with prior knowledge to construct meaning. Comprehension, therefore, takes place *as* a person is reading and is composed of the set of skills that lets her find information in the text and understand it in terms of what she already knows. This process is influenced by a number of variables. The interactive nature of comprehension requires that these variables combine and at times *compensate* for each other.

Part of the complexity of comprehension comes from the certitude that many skills are used to comprehend and that they do not work independent of one another. They are *compensatory.* This means that a reader who is temporarily unable (probably because of missing prior knowledge) to distinguish relevant from irrelevant information may compensate by relying on other comprehension strategies (Rauenbusch & Bereiter, 1991), such as seeking clarification. This compensatory feature, combined with the fact that passage difficulty is actually determined by the reader's prior knowledge, makes defining and evaluating reading comprehension *really tough.*

## Comprehension Skills and Strategies

Successful readers approach passages vigorously. Unlike less efficient readers, they are energetic and almost aggressive in their pursuit of meaning (Kletzien, 1991; Paris & Oka, 1989). Successful readers are also thoughtful and reflective (Pearson et al., 1990; Stanovich, 1994). Often, they will preview the passage, formulate their own prereading questions, make comments in the margins, and underline and highlight text. In addition, these readers review what they have read and may even seek clarification if passages don't seem to make sense. Competent readers also use vocabulary, decoding, prior knowledge, and other skills to react to print. These skills *enable* comprehension. Comprehension is carried out through the application of enabling skills and comprehension strategies. The successful integration of these skills and strategies is what constitutes active reading. Here are some of the skills and strategies active readers use.

**Comprehension strategies**

1. Monitors meaning
2. Selective attention to text
3. Adjusts for task difficulty
4. Connects text to prior knowledge
5. Clarifies

**Enabling skills**

1. Decoding
2. Vocabulary
3. Syntax
4. Prior knowledge

When a teacher teaches comprehension (as opposed to its enabling skills), he teaches the four comprehension strategies (Dole et al., 1991). The content of comprehension is not factual or conceptual (those things are found in the topics being understood)—it is procedural (made up of rules and strategies). Therefore, when evaluators attempt to explain why a student is failing to react appropriately to text, they either focus on enabling skills or skill at using the comprehension strategies (Swanson and De La Paz, 1998).

Here is a brief description of the major categories of comprehension strategy knowledge and enabling skills necessary for effective reaction to text. Each category will also be found in the status sheet shown in Exhibit 8.1.

### Strategy 1: Monitor for Meaning and Self-Correct

Competent readers monitor what they are reading. Their rule is: If they find that they have lost meaning, then they do something about it. Children who don't read well don't follow the rule. Frequently, they make no effort to correct errors. For example, here is a sentence as originally written and as it was read by a student in Portland, Oregon:

**Original:** Stories of dragons are part of folktales from almost every land.

**Student reading:** Stories of danger are part of the followed from almost all the lands.

This student's errors, which generally would be categorized as "whole-word substitutions, having the correct initial sound but violating meaning," represent a common error pattern. This type of error is sometimes referred to as reading the white portions of the page (Bishop, 1992). These errors destroy the meaning of the message. Errors that do not violate meaning should generally be ignored.

Some readers don't self-monitor and, as a result, never attempt to correct their errors. These students may not even realize that errors have been made. Other students, who do self-monitor, realize when they have lost meaning and stop to try and fix it. If they have the necessary enabling skills (decoding, vocabulary, syntax, prior knowledge) and comprehension strategies to reckon out the original wording, they self-correct and regain understanding of the passage.

### Strategy 2: Selective Attention to Text

As you recall from the discussion in Chapter 2, use of selective attention is a critical part of read-

**Exhibit 8.1    *Reading Comprehension Status Sheet.***

| If the Student Makes This Error: | Then This Is the Problem Area: | And This Is the Objective: | Does the Student Have the Skills? | | |
|---|---|---|---|---|---|
| | **1. Monitors meaning** | | Yes | No | Unsure |
| Student is unaware of and continues reading when she makes errors that violate the meaning of the text. Student employs no strategies for monitoring meaning of reading. | Attends to reading and notes errors that violate meaning. | Upon request, student will explain the following meaning-monitoring tasks: self-correct when making errors that violate meaning rereading confusing portions of texts/passages making predictions regarding upcoming events identifying when additional information is needed to answer questions reading with expression. CAP 100% | ☐ | ☐ | ☐ |
| Student does not ask questions about material being read. | Self-questions. | When asked to do so the student will generate questions about up-coming events in the passage. These will be based on: ❏ Previous text ❏ Titles and subtitles ❏ Illustrations. CAP 95% | | | |
| Student reads passages at the same rate and only one time regardless of difficulty or understanding. | Rereads confusing portions of material or adjusts reading rate on difficult sections. | Given passages at [expected or intermediate curriculum levels], the student will, upon encountering difficult or confusing materials, employ one or more of the following tactics: Reread Adjust rate. CAP 90% | | | |
| Student makes random predictions without reflecting on what has happened and ignoring other cues (pictures, etc.). | Can predict upcoming events in the passage. | Given a series of passages at [the expected or intermediate levels], the student will make pre-dictions about each upcoming passage that reflect a logical extension of the previously read material. CAP 90% | | | |
| Student makes random guesses to answer questions posed about readings. | Identifies when additional infor-mation is needed, or specifically what kind of information is needed to answer questions. | Given questions related to pass-age read, student will pick out important details necessary to answer questions and report a rule or strategy for locating the information. CAP 100% | | | |
| | **2. Selective attention to text** | | Yes | No | Unsure |
| Student reading is halted and laborious. | Reads with expression and/or automation. | Given a passage at [expected or intermediate curriculum level], student will read it aloud [at automatic level]. | ☐ | ☐ | ☐ |
| Student is unaware and continues reading when she makes errors that violate the meaning of the passage. | Student corrects errors that violate meaning. | Given signals, the student will immediately locate and correct errors that violate meaning made in oral reading. The signals may be given after words, phrases, sentence, or paragraphs. CAP 95% | | | |

| If the Student Makes This Error: | Then This Is the Problem Area: | And This Is the Objective: | Does the Student Have the Skills? | | |
|---|---|---|---|---|---|
| Student reads passage as if it is independent of all previously learned information. | Connects text to prior knowledge. | Upon request, student will supply and/or explain the process of drawing from background knowledge. CAP 100% | | | |
| | **3. Adjusts for text difficulty** | | Yes | No | Unsure |
| Student reads texts/ passages as quickly as possible and for completion only. | Allocates study time according to passage difficulty. | Given a passage [at expected or intermediate curriculum level], containing difficult wording or confusing information, student will allocate additional study time necessary to employ clarification strategies. | ☐ | ☐ | ☐ |
| Student unable to identify purpose(s) for reading(s) (entertainment vs. information). | States purpose for reading. | Prior to beginning passages, student will state their purpose for reading (entertainment or information). | | | |
| Student does not realize when errors have been made that violate the meaning of passages. | Identifies and self-corrects reading errors that violate the meaning of the passage. | Given signals, the student will immediately locate and correct errors that violate meaning made in oral reading. The signals may be given after words, phrases, sentences, or paragraphs. CAP 95% | | | |
| Student reads materials at same rate regardless of text difficulty and/or importance (information vs. entertainment). | Adjusts reading rate appropriately. | Student will adjust reading rate according to difficulty and/or importance of materials. | | | |
| | **4. Connects text with prior knowledge** | | Yes | No | Unsure |
| After reading a passage/text, student supplies an unrelated or tangentially related "best title" or main idea. Student identifies supporting information as the main idea. | Answers "best title" and main ideas questions accurately. | Student will identify answers to "best title" and main idea questions for [expected or intermediate curriculum level]. CAP 100% | ☐ | ☐ | ☐ |
| Retells or paraphrases story using supporting or obscure details. Retells story word for word. | Retells story with emphasis on major points. | Given a passage [at expected or intermediate curriculum level], student will retell the content. CAP 3 | | | |
| Does not say why something was written, or gives an unlikely purpose. | Describes author's purpose for writing. | When presented with a variety of writing selections the student will provide a likely purpose for each. The purpose will be *likely* if it accurately reflects the known, and/or logically assumed, intent of the author. | | | |
| Student has to reread entire portions of the text to find answers to questions. | Can locate information in the passage that answers assigned questions. | Given passages [at appropriate level], student will locate, by scanning, answers to assigned questions. CAP 100% | | | |
| Student does not discriminate between credible and deceptive presentations. | Can accurately apply stated criteria to the story to judge its value as an information source. | When supplied with a variety of written presentations the student will sort them according to legitimacy. The student will then provide an explanation of her sorting, which will include the use of [specified critical reading rules]. CAP [determine within class]. | | | |

**Exhibit 8.1**   *Continued*

| If the Student Makes This Error: | Then This Is the Problem Area: | And This Is the Objective: | Does the Student Have the Skills? |
|---|---|---|---|
| Student does not recall information immediately after she has read it. Student reads each passage as if it is a brand new idea. | Uses information gained from reading the passage to focus on subsequent topics/information in the passage. | Given a series of passages at [expected or intermediate levels], student will identify key information/ideas to search for supported by previous passage(s). The ideas/information will reflect content that the author/teacher thinks critical. CAP 90% | |
| | **5. Clarifies** | | Yes    No    Unsure |
| Student has no clarification strategies. | Knowledge of clarification strategies. | Upon request, student will supply and explain possible clarification strategies: (CAP 100%) adjusting reading rate identifying important details strategies to determine meaning decoding self-correction asking for help. | ☐      ☐       ☐ |
| Student reads passages at the same rate and only one time regardless of difficulty or understanding. | Adjusts reading rate for material that is not understood. | Student will adjust reading rate according to difficulty and/or understanding of materials. | |
| When asked to paraphrase or retell story, student provides obscure or irrelevant details. | Is more likely to recall important passage details, not trivial ones. | Given passages at [expected or intermediate levels], student will identify [by underlining or reporting], important passage details related to one or more of the following categories: main idea relevant information characters descriptions actions conflicts resolutions. CAP 100% | |
| Student makes references to previously learned information when answering questions, even when irrelevant to the question or passage read. | Answers comprehension questions in terms of stated information in passage, not necessarily prior knowledge. | The student will provide text-dependent answers to questions drawn from reading samples. To establish that the answers are text-dependent, following production of the answer, the student will find and mark those portions of the passage that support her answer. CAP: agreement with instructor or exemplar student. | |
| Student uses a single strategy (reading text one time through) to determine the passage's meaning. | Uses multiple strategies to determine passage meaning. | Upon request, student will demonstrate metacognitive awareness of strategies for determining the meaning of the passage by supplying and/or explaining the following skills: identifying the main idea looking at the pictures rereading (current and previous passage) | |

| If the Student Makes This Error: | Then This Is the Problem Area: | And This Is the Objective: | Does the Student Have the Skills? |
|---|---|---|---|
| | | request assistance creating questions for answering defining unknown vocabulary    words. CAP 100% | |
| Student decodes words by individual letter/sound correspondences. | Uses multiple strategies to decode words. | Student will employ meaning-based strategies and decoding to read passages (at expected CAP). | |
| Student is unaware she is making reading errors that violate meaning. | Self-corrects errors that violate meaning. | Given passages at [expected or intermediate curriculum levels], the student will not make, or will spontaneously correct, errors in reading that violate meaning. CAP: no more than 5% uncorrected errors. | |
| After exhausting her strategies for clarification of word meaning, student guesses and moves on or quits. | Asks for assistance. | Whenever student has exhausted her clarification strategies, she will ask for assistance. | |

## Enabling Skills

### 1. Decoding

| | | | Yes ☐  No ☐  Unsure ☐ |
|---|---|---|---|
| Student decodes words without fluency or accuracy. | Passage reading. | Student will read passages at [specify] level with a rate of [specify] and [specify]% accuracy. | |
| Student inserts words that violate meaning and/or guesses at words. Student rereading improves passage accuracy considerably. | Reads passages with 95% accuracy. | Given passages at [expected or intermediate levels], student will read [at specified rate] with 95% accuracy. | |
| Student commonly inserts words that violate meaning and/or guesses at words. Student frequently must "sound out" words. Student misapplies decoding rules. | Reads passages at 95% accuracy. | Given passages at [expected or intermediate levels], student will read [at specified rate] with 95% accuracy. | |
| Student frequently makes errors that violate the meaning of the passage/text. | Makes few errors that violate meaning. | Given passages at [expected or intermediate curriculum levels], the student will not make, or will spontaneously correct, errors in reading that violate meaning. CAP: no more than 5% uncorrected errors. | |

### 2. Vocabulary

| | | | Yes ☐  No ☐  Unsure ☐ |
|---|---|---|---|
| Student fails to demonstrate comprehension but passes tests of decoding and prior knowledge. | Passage-dependent vocabulary. | Student will identify or produce correct definitions for terms selected from [specified] reading passages. CAP 100% | |
| Student defines words only in isolation or provides their most common definition while passage reading. | Can define words in passage. | Given passages at [expected or intermediate levels], the student will supply the correct definition for vocabulary words that are underlined or pointed to by the teacher. CAP 100% | |

**Exhibit 8.1**   *Continued*

| If the Student Makes This Error: | Then This Is the Problem Area: | And This Is the Objective: | Does the Student Have the Skills? | | |
|---|---|---|---|---|---|
| Student misses context-dependent vocabulary questions. | Can modify the definition of words in passage according to context. | Given passages at [expected or intermediate levels], the student will supply the correct definition for context-dependent vocabulary words that are underlined or pointed to by the teacher. CAP 100% | | | |
| Errors on maze or cloze exercises excessive (cloze errors > 60%; maze errors > 40%) and often syntactically correct but semantically incorrect. | Balance of errors on maze and/or cloze exercises does not show excessive semantic errors. | Given a 250-word [maze or cloze] passage at [expected or intermediate level], student answers will be [80% or 45%] semantically correct. | | | |
| Comprehension increases and errors decrease dramatically when key words are introduced prior to reading. | Comprehension does not increase dramatically and/or decoding errors do not decrease when key words are introduced prior to reading. | When provided an unfamiliar passage at [expected or intermediate curriculum level], student will read it aloud [at specified rate and with specified accuracy]. | | | |
| Student makes many non-meaningful substitutions of words or words that violate the meaning of the text/passage. | Makes few nonmeaningful substitutions. | Given passages at [expected or intermediate level], student will not make or will spontaneously correct, word substitution errors in reading that violate the meaning. CAP: not more than 5% uncorrected errors. | | | |
| Student confuses the meanings of referents contained in sentences. When retelling events in a story, student reports them in the incorrect tense. | Uses pronouns and tenses correctly. | Given passages at [expected or intermediate level], the student will supply the correct definition for referents that are underlined or pointed to by the teacher. CAP 100%. (These will include referents both near and far from the designated wording in the passage.) | | | |
| | **3. Syntax** | | Yes | No | Unsure |
| Student makes excessive syntactic errors when completing comprehension exercises. | Syntax errors during reactions to reading. | When making written or spoken reactions to passages, the student will use correct syntax 100% of the time. | ☐ | ☐ | ☐ |
| Errors on maze or cloze exercises excessive (cloze errors > 60%; maze errors > 40%) and often semantically correct but syntactically incorrect. | Balance of errors on maze does not show excessive syntactic errors. | Given a 250-word [maze or cloze] passage at [expected or intermediate level], student answers will be [80% or 45%] syntactically correct. | | | |
| Primary language is other than that of the text. | Primary language is same as texts. | Given a passage in student's primary language, student will complete a [maze or cloze] exercise with [80% or 45%] accuracy. | | | |
| Oral language contains excessive syntax errors that violate the standard of adult speech. | Oral language adequate, particularly in the use of subject-verb agreement, tense, and pronouns. | Student will produce by [imitation, with prompts, or spontaneously], sentences with subject-verb agreement, correct tense, and pronouns. CAP: adult speech or [an intermediate level]. | | | |

| If the Student Makes This Error: | Then This Is the Problem Area: | And This Is the Objective: | Does the Student Have the Skills? | | |
|---|---|---|---|---|---|
| | **4. Prior knowledge** | | Yes | No | Unsure |
| Student's performance on comprehension exercises varies considerably when student already has key prior knowledge or vocabulary before reading a passage. | Comprehension does not vary dramatically according to familiarity with the passage topic. | Given a [maze or cloze] passage at [expected or intermediate level] on an unfamiliar subject, student will [select or supply correct choices] with [80% or 45%] accuracy. | ☐ | ☐ | ☐ |
| Student provides incorrect definitions for words with context-dependent meanings. | Can correctly define words in passage. | Given passages at [expected or intermediate levels], the student will supply the correct definition for vocabulary words that are underlined or pointed to by the teacher. CAP 100% | | | |
| Performance on comprehension activities varies considerably when key concepts and ideas are previewed prior to reading. | Comprehension does not improve dramatically when a passage is previewed and unstated ideas are explained prior to reading. | Given passages at [expected or intermediate levels], student will maintain passing scores on maze/cloze tests with no assistance. CAP 100% | | | |
| During comprehension exercises, student uses only concrete information provided in the passage. | Can relate information in passage to personal experience or to other sources of information (other passages, books, authors, classes, etc.). | When supplied with questions pertaining to the theme of a passage, the student will answer the questions correctly and support the answers with information not supplied in the passage. CAP: teacher judgment or exemplar comparison. | | | |
| Student omits unstated ideas when completing comprehension activities and/or discussing the passage. | Can discuss unstated ideas accurately. | When supplied with topics pertaining to the theme of a passage, the student will discuss and/or debate the topics while including information *supplied*, and *not supplied*, in the passage. CAP: teacher judgment or exemplar comparison. | | | |

*Source:* Howell, K. W., Zucker, S. H. & Morehead, M. K. (2000b). *Multilevel Academic Skills Inventory*. Bellingham, WA: Applied Research and Development Center. To order contact the Student Co-op Bookstore, Western Washington University. Fax (360) 650-2888. Phone (360) 650-3656. Reprinted with permission.

ing comprehension. Selective attention makes use of what the student already believes or knows about the information in the text to sort portions of the message for reflection and storage. At the same time, it allows the student to disregard much of the material by sorting out portions that are not critical. Once again, as we have emphasized throughout this book, consideration of prior knowledge is critical in an-alyzing why a student is not succeeding in school.

### Strategy 3: Adjust for Text Difficulty

Any reader, regardless of skill, will eventually encounter material that is challenging. This "dif-ficulty" may be the result of a missing enabling skill such as reader prior knowledge. However, it may also be the result of lack of skill to deal with *poorly written* text. This is more of a problem as the student moves into content-specific (history, biology) texts. When use of the *comprehension-monitoring strategy* tells the student that a passage is difficult, a competent reader will make adjustments. The reader will employ tactics such as reduction in reading rate, rereading of passages, or the use of highlighting and note taking.

### Strategy 4: Connect Text with Prior Knowledge

As the student reads, she combines what she already knows about the topic with the important messages in the text. Obviously, this requires the student to make use of *strategy 2: selective attention to text,* along with prior knowledge. However, it also requires tactics for combining prior knowledge and text messages. A competent reader will not automatically throw out her prior knowledge simply because it conflicts with whatever she happens to be reading at the time (of course if people did that, it might make being a text author easier). Nor will she disregard text messages that conflict with, or contradict, what she already thinks is correct. Instead the reader will seek to resolve the apparent conflict (Carnine et al., 1997).

### Strategy 5: Clarify

When a student fails to understand what she is reading and is aware of the failure, she can attempt clarification. If she has the necessary skills to figure out the original wording, she'll self-correct and fix the mistake. If she does not have these skills, she may fall back on a general strategy like asking for help.

---

## Enabling Skills

Comprehension rules and strategies depend on competence in certain enabling skills. When these enabling skills are missing, comprehension may not occur. However, there is no reason to assume that a student who has these enabling skills will automatically comprehend anything. The following discussion explains briefly how one's reaction to print depends upon skills other than those we have identified as *"comprehension strategies."* We'll explain these enabling skills and provide keys to reaching them through other chapters, but testing approaches will not be included in this chapter (you'll have to go to Chapter 10 to find out how to confirm a vocabulary problem).

### Enabling Skill 1: Decoding

Decoding includes phonemics, phonology, phonetic generalizations, morphology, reading, fluency, and context analysis. Proficient decoding is necessary for efficient comprehension; however, comprehension instruction should not be delayed until decoding is mastered. Automaticity in decoding frees the student's working (short-term) memory so that it may focus on the meaning of the text (Adams, 1991). One indication of automaticity is the speed at which the student decodes passages through oral or silent reading (Espin & Deno, 1995).

In general, speeding up or slowing down a student will not alter the *quality* of comprehension, but it places an absolute limit on the *number of ideas* encountered during any time period. However, the biggest problem occurs when the student falls below a critical threshold of reading fluency (Carver, 1992). Then, the student must attend so closely to the task of decoding that she cannot attend to the meaning of the passage. Estimates of this critical decoding threshold vary, but 140 words per minute is probably a good minimal rate of oral reading after the third grade (Biemiller, 1978; Carnine et al., 1997; Tennenbaum, 1983).

It is impossible to set a fixed fluency aim for all reading because rate should vary according to the difficulty of the material. And, of course, difficulty depends upon the reader's own knowledge base and purpose for reading. Flexibility, having the option to speed up or slow down according to the demands of the material, is more important than simple speed. Decoding assessment will be described in Chapter 11.

### Enabling Skill 2: Semantics (Vocabulary)

If a student fails to demonstrate comprehension but passes tests of decoding (including phonics, fluency, and context analysis) as well as prior knowledge, the most likely cause of the failure is missing vocabulary. Word meaning may account for up to 70% of the variability between students who do and do not score well on published comprehension tests (Carnine et al., 1997; Rupley et al., 1999).

There are two critical elements of vocabulary knowledge that can interact with comprehension (and decoding):

- Knowledge of word definitions and
- Determination of word meaning from context.

The first of these, definitions, is totally word-based. It is the sort of knowledge one would gain from looking in a dictionary. The second has to do with the contextual nature of vocabulary (Fukkink & de Glopper, 1998). Word meaning is affected at the document level and the phrase level.

To find out if a comprehension problem is the result of poor vocabulary, an evaluator must check the student's knowledge of the meaning of the words *in the paragraph* she did not comprehend. The use of published vocabulary tests is not likely to aid in this evaluation. Such tests are composed of words that may or may not be representative of the words in the passage that is giving the student trouble. The average child enters school with a vocabulary of from 5000 to 10,000 words. By high school, the vocabulary may be 10 times that size as she adds approximately 5000 new words per year (Nagy & Scott, 1990). Given all those words to choose from, a standard vocabulary test is not likely to be relevant to any individual reading selection.

### Enabling Skill 3: Syntax (Grammar)

Assume that you have a student who was given a paragraph. Her reaction to the passage leads you to suspect that she didn't comprehend. You have tested her decoding and determined that she decodes the paragraph accurately and fluently. You have also checked her knowledge of the meaning of the words in the paragraph. You found no problems. But she still didn't comprehend! What's left?

First, a student who doesn't tell you what a passage said but (1) can decode the passage, and (2) knows the meaning of all the words in it *is rare*. But one likely explanation is a difference between the child's language and the language of the passage. Students who have oral language deficits, limited English proficiency (assuming the passage was written in English), or bilingual interference generally have difficulty understanding mainstream text (Edwards et al., 1991; Pritchard, 1990). Syntax is discussed in some detail in Chapter 10.

Any evaluation of a student's reading skills should include an evaluation of text readability (Espin & Deno, 1995). Readability should *not* be estimated with a formula of word frequency, word length, and sentence length alone. Those who want to become more conversant with text structure should read the classics: Armbruster (1984b) and MacGinitie (1984). Those who are interested in developing criteria for evaluating text should also read Anderson and Armbruster (1984) and Armbruster (1984a).

### Enabling Skill 4: Prior Knowledge

Because comprehension involves the interaction of text information with what the student already knows, the student has to know something for it to take place (Valencia et al., 1990). Prior knowledge of the passage topic is necessary for correct reaction to print. The stronger this knowledge base is, the better prepared a student is to comprehend new material about a topic (Spires & Donley, 1998; Stahl et al., 1991). A student who doesn't have some basic core of information about the topic will not be suited to comprehend the passage. Steps for evaluating the adequacy of a student's general knowledge will be presented in Chapter 14.

## A Note on Text Variables

Text structure influences the quality of the reactions we elicit from students during evaluation and contributes to, or interferes with, the way they understand text (Gerber, 1992). These structures reside in the book, therefore they are neither enabling skills nor comprehension strategies. Text variables include both general organizers and overall structure. Examples of general organizers **are** abstracts, focus questions, headings, and summaries. Overall structure is the way the ideas in the text are related to convey a message to the reader (Carnine, 1992; Duffy, 1991; Meyer & Rice, 1984). The organization of written material can signal what is relevant to a reader (Walpole, 1999). It can also provide cohesion or interrupt the flow. An illustration of this disruptive effect may have occurred earlier when you encountered the word **are** in boldface type.

## Step 3: Devise a Way to Make the Thing in Step 2 Observable

To talk about something that cannot be seen, we must rely on inference and on theories. In the case of reading comprehension, the latest reading theory often becomes that standard (Stanovich, 1991). Therefore, a student's behavior may seem either typical or atypical, depending on the theoretical view we embrace.

The prototypical "diagnostic reading inventory," for example, is made up of passages followed by questions. The student reads each passage and then answers questions about it. In these cases, the interval between reading the passage and answering the questions is 1 or 2 minutes. What if you waited 30 minutes before asking the questions? What if you waited a week? If you did wait longer, the student's score would almost certainly be different (probably lower) because what was once "comprehended" may no longer be recalled. Therefore, a student's score on post-passage questions depends not only on what she understands but on what she *remembers*. Many educators seem to accept this

confusion, though few of them would agree that memory and comprehension are synonymous.

In attempting to assess reading comprehension, an evaluator asks the student to react to printed messages. He decides that the student "comprehended" the message if the student reacts appropriately to it (Tindal & Marston, 1990). Unfortunately, different testing formats require different types of responses, depend on different enabling skills, and reflect different comprehension strategies. Therefore, as we outline the actions that should be employed during the evaluation process in the second part of this chapter, we will have to refer to a variety of testing/interview formats. Although these are explained here, they are condensed in Exhibit 8.2.

### Oral-Reading Fluency

By now, dear reader, you probably have guessed that the authors derive a certain amount of perverse pleasure in presenting something that we know many people will hate. This is one of those presentations. "Reading fluency" was listed as an enabling skill for comprehension. It is also a way people react to print. Students who react to a passage by reading it aloud quickly understand it better than students who react by reading it slowly (Carnine, 1992; Deno & Markell, 1997; Fuchs et al., 1988; Shinn, 1989; Shinn et al., 1992; Stahl et al., 1998; Tindal & Marston, 1990). Therefore, using oral-reading rate to identify students who may have a comprehension problem is a good idea. The trouble is that the oral-reading score does not give much availing information. It is an excellent way to rank order students to judge program effectiveness, make class and school comparisons, and recognize when a student has a problem, but it does not provide abundant insight into the nature of that problem. As a result, oral-reading rate has somewhat limited utility. However, fluency tests are quick to give and easily developed, scored, and summarized. Therefore, they were the only procedure in Exhibit 8.2 that can conveniently be repeated for progress monitoring. Because rate can be used to screen students and to monitor their progress, it is the preferred **general outcome measure.** If you suspect a comprehension problem because a student's reading rate is slower than expected, you should always do two things: (1) confirm the problem by following up with another survey procedure, and (2) if the problem is confirmed, check the student's decoding skills.

### Cloze or Maze

**Cloze** The cloze technique has received attention both as a comprehension measure and as a system for selecting instructional-level reading material. The basic cloze system starts with choosing a 250-word selection. The first and last sentences of the passage are left intact, whereas every fifth word in the remaining sentences is blanked out (the blanks should be of equal length regardless of the word removed or you'll end up testing the student's skill at interpreting blanks). The students are asked to read the passage orally and to say (or write) the word that goes in the blank (they do not read the unmodified passage first). Most authors require that the students supply the exact missing word. This may seem hard, but the CAP is fairly low. If a student supplies more than 45% of the missing words, the material is considered too easy for instruction. If she gets between 30% and 45% of the words correct, the material is said to be "at the instructional level." A score of below 30% is a clear no-pass (Pikulski & Pikulski, 1977). Exhibit 8.3 provides portions of two cloze passages (they are not complete, as they don't contain enough words and the first and last sentences are not intact).

Cloze is an interesting technique because it seems to challenge the student's skill at using all types of passage information. Cloze performance is closely related to the redundancy of the text as well as to the similarity between the language of the student and the language of the text. One disadvantage, therefore, is that it can't be used with passages that aren't redundant (ruling out particularly descriptive material). Also, students with language problems, or a primary language other than English, may do poorly on cloze regardless of their comprehension (of course these same students may do even worse on other assessments).

The foremost advantage of cloze is that it is easy to score (unlike the questioning, paraphrasing, and retelling techniques). Because corrects and errors are easy to recognize, cloze can also be scored reliably. The blanking out of every fifth word distributes item difficulty randomly, which permits the blanks to be treated equally and to be added together without weighting or conversion. This means the data can be analyzed and that criteria can be set.

**Maze** The maze procedure is similar to the cloze procedure, but the behavior of the student is quite different. In cloze, the student recalls and produces the correct response. In maze, the student identifies and indicates it. Again, the procedure requires the selection of a 250-word passage. The first and last sentences of the passage are left intact. Next, a group of words is inserted for every fifth word. The student is asked to select the original word (usually by circling it) from among three to five distractors. Therefore, maze is to multiple choice as cloze is to fill in the blank. Because identification of a correct word is easier than production of a correct word, the criterion for passing is higher. Sixty percent to 80% correct can be considered instructional level, with scores above 80% indicating pass and scores below 60% no pass. (This is one of the very few times it is just fine for you to use 80% as CAP.) Just as with all cutting scores (scores used as boundaries for certain decisions), the 80% maze criterion is not absolute. However, in a study conducted by the authors using 237 students of grades 2 through 8, working on the maze tests supplied in Howell et al., 2000a, the average score was 94% and the average standard deviation was 2.39 items (roughly 6%). These students were randomly selected and included both high and low achievers. This means that most of the normal and high-achieving students actually topped out on the maze passages with scores at or near 100%. Incidentally, the internal consistency, averaged across all passages and grade levels (an indicator of reliability), was 0.83.

The difficulty of maze will vary not only according to the difficulty of the passage but also according to the difficulty of the distractors

**Exhibit 8.2    Comprehension Assessment Procedures.**

| Procedure | Example | Advantages | Disadvantages | Type of Data | Criteria | Comprehension SLP (Action) | Assumed Causes for Failure |
|---|---|---|---|---|---|---|---|
| 1. Oral-reading rate | One-minute timing of passage reading | (1) Easy to give (2) Easy to score (3) Excellent screening device (4) Large sample of behavior (5) Excellent for monitoring progress | (1) Little "diagnostic" information | Rate per minute | Action 1: reading rate | See page 222 | Poor decoding accuracy and/or fluency. |
| 2. Cloze | S*: ". . . was fascinated with the _____ of war . . ." R*: ". . . was fascinated with the human aspect of war . . ." | (1) Easy to score (2) Success depends on all types of passage clues (3) Item difficulty is random (4) Large sample of behavior | (1) Does not directly test understanding of what you think is the most important part of the passage (2) Can only be used with redundant texts | Percent correct | Instructional level 30–45%; below 30% is no-pass | Action A.2: Follow qualitative interpretation guidelines for maze and cloze | Discrepancy between student language and test language  Go to Chapter 10—oral language sample |
| 3. Maze | S*: ". . . was fascinated with the _____ technical, geographic _____ human aspect . . ." R*: ". . . was fascinated with the _____ technical, geographic _____ human | (1) Easy to score (2) Success depends on all types of passage clues (3) Distractors can be used to alter the test difficulty or the focus of the test (4) Large sample of behavior | (1) Risk of poorly selected distractors | Percent correct | Instructional level is 60–80%; below 60% is no-pass | Action A.2: Follow qualitative interpretation guidelines for maze/cloze | Discrepancy between student language and text language  Go to Chapter 10—oral language sample |
| 4. Para-phrasing | S*: ". . . was fascinated with the human aspect of war . . ." R*: ". . . he wanted to know why people decide to fight . . ." | (1) Student responses aren't influenced by the way the questions are asked (2) Supplies an overall impression of the student's understanding (3) Can be used in daily lessons so has fidelity | (1) Hard to score (2) Difficult to control sudden responses without questioning, which in turn would negate advantage 1 | Percent correct | Undetermined | Action 9 & 12: prior knowledge | Poor vocabulary, lack of familiarity with procedure  Go to Chapter 10 |

| Procedure | Example | Advantages | Disadvantages | Type of Data | Criteria | Comprehension SLP | Assumed Causes for Failure |
|---|---|---|---|---|---|---|---|
| 5. Story telling | S*: ". . . was fascinated with the human aspect of war . . ." R*: ". . . was fascinated with the human aspect of war . . ." | (1) Student responses are not influenced by the way questions are asked (2) Indicates overall number of idea units the student recalls (3) Can be used as a component of daily lessons and therefore has fidelity to real life (4) Can be analyzed for match to text structure or story map | (1) Cumbersome to transcribe student responses (2) Analysis of idea units in text to enhance scoring is time consuming (3) May not sample understanding; may only tap recall | Percent correct | Undetermined | Action 7 | Lack of familiarity with procedure |
| 6. Questioning | S*: "Who was Ambrose?" R*: "A Civil War Author" | (1) The teacher can focus on information of particular interest (2) Attempts to test levels of comprehension | (1) Hard to score (2) Only a few questions can be written for each paragraph (3) Levels of comprehension may not match types of questions (or even exist) (4) Risk of poorly written questions (5) The student's answer is determined by the question asked | Percent correct | Undetermined | Action 9 or 12: prior knowledge | Lack of general knowledge Go to Chapter 14 |

selected. For example, in Exhibit 8.4, item A is easier than item B because the distractors (incorrect choices) are more clearly incorrect. Because you can choose easy or hard distractors, maze is more flexible than cloze. Of course,

this also makes it easier to produce an invalid test.

One way of controlling for the difficulty of the distractors is to have one word that is syntactically correct but semantically incorrect and to

### Exhibit 8.3   Cloze Paragraphs: Text Difficulty and Prior Knowledge.

**Passage 1**

Rayon is a synthetic _____ resembling silk and used _____ a substitute for silk. _____ is made out of _____ Spruce wood. Most _____ is manufactured in _____ different ways: the nitrocellulose _____, the cellulose-acetate process, _____ cuprammonium process and the _____ process. Of the 125,000,000 pounds _____ rayon made in America _____ year, 85 percent is _____ by the viscose process. _____ small percentage of rayon _____ made out of cotton _____, the short ends combed _____ (usually waste) when the _____ is combed away from _____ cotton seeds; but the _____ is so incidental that _____ is safe to generalize _____ the statement that rayon _____ made from spruce wood.

**Answer to Passage 1**

Rayon is a synthetic <u>fabric</u> resembling silk and used <u>as</u> a substitute for silk. <u>Rayon</u> is made out of <u>white</u> Spruce wood. Most Rayon is manufactured in <u>four</u> different ways: the nitro-cellulose <u>process</u>, the cellulose-acetate process, <u>the</u> cuprammonium process and the <u>viscose</u> process. Of the 125,000,000 pounds <u>of</u> rayon made in America <u>each</u> year, 85 percent is <u>made</u> by the viscose process. <u>A</u> small percentage of rayon is made out of cotton <u>linters</u>, the short ends combed <u>out</u> (usually waste) when the <u>cotton</u> is combed away from <u>the</u> cotton seeds; but the <u>percentage</u> is so incidental that <u>it</u> is safe to generalize <u>with</u> the statement that rayon <u>is</u> made from spruce wood.

**Passage 2**

This is a proposal _____ apply uniformity to the ___ of days in each _____, giving twenty-eight to each. _____ month and each week _____ begin on Sunday, with _____ four weeks to each _____. A new month would _____ inserted in summer, perhaps _____ June and July, thus _____ thirteen months, each month _____ twenty-eight days. Twenty-eight times _____ would give us 364 _____. An extra holiday, New _____ Day, which would not _____ in the calendar, would _____ the necessary 365 days _____ normal years. In Leap _____ a second holiday would _____ inserted. Under the new _____ system there would be _____ necessity for a separate _____ for each month.

**Answer to Passage 2**

This is a proposal <u>to</u> apply uniformity to the <u>number</u> of days in each <u>month</u>, giving twenty-eight to each. <u>Each</u> month and each week <u>would</u> begin on Sunday, with <u>exactly</u> four weeks to each <u>month</u>. A new month would <u>be</u> inserted in summer, perhaps <u>between</u> June and July, thus <u>giving</u> thirteen months, each month <u>having</u> twenty-eight days. Twenty-eight times <u>thirteen</u> would give us 364 <u>days</u>. An extra holiday, New <u>Year's</u> Day, which would not <u>appear</u> in the calendar, would <u>give</u> the necessary 365 days <u>for</u> normal years. In Leap <u>Year</u> a second holiday would <u>be</u> inserted. Under the new <u>proposed</u> system there would be <u>no</u> necessity for a separate <u>chart</u> for each month.

**Exhibit 8.4  Maze Formats with Choices of Varying Difficulty.**

| |
|---|
| Item A |
| Just as with all _____ <br> (Volkswagen, trout, cutting) <br><br> scores, the 60–80% maze _____ <br> (criterion, taco, motorcycle) <br><br> is not absolute. |
| Item B |
| Just as with all _____ <br> (reading, grade level, cutting) <br><br> scores, the 60–80% maze _____ <br> (criterion, procedure, score) <br><br> is not absolute. |

have another word that is both syntactically and semantically incorrect. A passage modified in this manner would appear as follows (the choices are categorized under the sample) (Howell et al., 2000b).

> They felt a soft wind **1.** _____(**little, pass, walk**) them by.
>
> Then standing **2.** _____(**until, little, in**) the darkness beside them, a strange little man appeared.

The distractors should be drawn from the 20 words in the passage surrounding the blank. This will control item complexity and assure that the words are taught and used at the passage's reading level (Nitko & Guo, 1996). In item 1 above, "walk" and "pass" are verbs and are syntactically correct. "Little" is a modifier and is both syntactically and semantically incorrect. Only "pass" is both syntactically and semantically correct.

Although some research has suggested that the maze format does not sample comprehension beyond sentence boundaries, the careful selection of distractors seems to influence these findings (Parker et al., 1992). It is possible to write items that require the context of a passage to be addressed correctly. For example, Nitko and Guo (1996) provide the following example:

A.  A maze item not embedded in text:
    The baby \_\_\_\_\_.

1. cried
2. laughed
3. slept
4. walked

B.  A maze item embedded in text:
    Mother and her six-month-old baby played for a long time. The baby _____. She enjoyed being tickled under the arms.

1. cried
2. laughed
3. slept
4. walked

As you can see, any of the choices could be correct for item A, but only number 2 would be correct given the context of the passage provided for item B.

Both cloze and maze formats let the evaluator sample about 40 responses in a single 250-word passage. This is certainly a larger sample than would be obtained using a question format, and this contributes to the reliability of the scores. In addition, cloze and maze seem to have superior validity for active reading comprehension because both permit readers to look ahead, as well as back, to confirm or disconfirm their choices. (Both cloze and maze are worked in much the same way that a crossword puzzle is worked. Finding one answer can cause the student to go back and change another.) The use of text look-backs and look-aheads, next to the use of phonics, is the most common self-monitoring tactic used by comprehending readers (Gunning & D'Amato, 1998). Maze, like cloze, is also easy to score (you can make a plastic overlay of the passage, mark the correct answers, and then lay the key over the student's work for quick grading).

Because the maze format lets students select a response rather than produce one, it is especially appropriate for young students and those with language-production problems or students who are acquiring a new language. Even though they may not comprehend well in the second language, the maze format permits them to demonstrate what they do understand (Bensoussan & Ramraz, 1984). This means that content teachers can maze portions of their textbooks and use the tests to determine if the student has sufficient language proficiency to comprehend the reading assignments. This is a curriculum-based, text-specific, language-competence technique.

One additional advantage of cloze and maze is that the same passage can be used to screen for both comprehension and decoding problems. Scores from these formats seem to be as useful as the graded passages found in reading inventories for selecting instructional-level material.

### Questioning

As shown in Exhibit 8.2, questioning, despite its frequent use, is one of the *worst* ways to have students react to reading. However, questioning can be used in conjunction with the cloze and maze procedures. In addition to the problems listed in the exhibit, questioning cannot really be scored (so criteria cannot be set) because the difficulty of each question depends highly on student prior knowledge of the topic. As prior knowledge varies, the difficulty of the items vary. Consequently, a score of 50% for one student could actually represent greater comprehension skill than a score of 90% for another.

However, questions can be used to focus on a topic. For example: "What would be the best title?" or "Can you tell me what the passage was about?" Such questions will not yield pass/no-pass data but will augment a technique like cloze/maze by giving some information about the student's overall understanding of the passage.

## Step 4: Conduct Assessment

## Step 5: Summarize Results

## Step 6: Make Summative and Formative Decisions

These steps will be mixed together through the remainder of the chapter. They are recursive (occurring over and over). The complete process is

illustrated in Exhibit 8.5 and outlined in the text below.

**Actions (specific level procedures [SLP]) 1** and **2** are both used to answer the question: Does the student adequately comprehend text?

### Action (SLP) 1: Reading Rate

### Directions

1. Select three 250-word passages at the student's *expected* reading level. It is important that you start at the expected level (the level at which she should be working if there was no reading problem) even if you know the student will not do well. Make a copy for yourself. You may want to use one of the reading passages provided in the supplement that accompanies this text (Howell et al., 2000a) (for primary grades 1 and 2, 100–200 words is adequate).

2. For each passage, say to the student "I want you to read part of this story out loud. Read it as quickly and carefully as you can. If you come to a word you do not know then skip it. Please begin." Time the student for 1 minute and make a bracket ( ] ) after the last word read in the 1-minute time limit. Allow the student to finish the passage unless she is having a lot of problems. If the student has missed 5 or more words in the first 10 words, discontinue, mark this level as "no-pass," and move to a lower level passage. As the student reads, mark all errors on your copy of the passage. It is not necessary to recognize different types of errors when determining rate and accuracy (that will come later in the decoding chapter).

3. To establish the student's oral-reading rate, count the number of words read correctly and the number of words read incorrectly during each minute (up to your bracket mark). Number correct and number incorrect are always reported separately (added together they will yield the total

**Exhibit 8.5** *Process of Reading Comprehension Evaluation.*

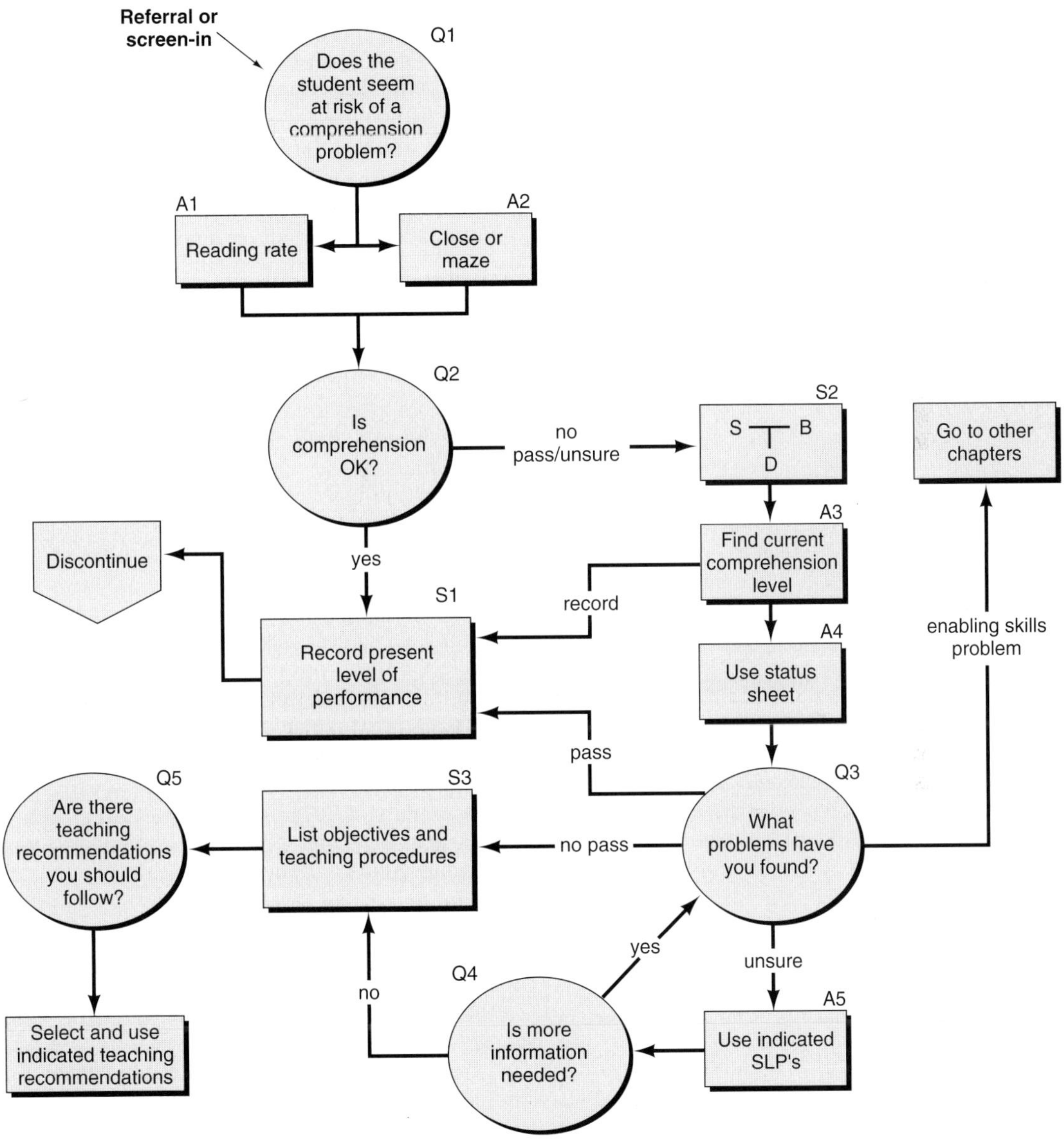

number of words read). Omissions are not errors. To obtain the student's passage accuracy, find the percentage correct on the entire passage. Divide the number of words correct by the total number of words read.

Report the median scores of the three passages.

4. The following criteria for deciding whether or not a student has a problem with reading rate are based on a set of passages

contained in the Multilevel Academic Skills Inventory (MASI), (Howell et al., 2000b). These passages were extensively researched to establish a well-calibrated scale of difficulty across grade levels. If you are using passages selected from your local curriculum material, you may want to establish criteria for deciding whether or not a student has a problem based on local norms. For example, you might administer the reading probe to five students in the middle reading group at a grade level and use the median of their performance as a standard. Procedures for establishing local norms using oral reading fluency are presented in some detail in Howell et al. (2000a).

### Oral-Reading Criteria

| Reading Fluency | | | |
|---|---|---|---|
| Grade | Pass | Unsure | No-Pass |
| Early 1st | +35 wpm | 25–35 wpm | −25 wpm |
| Late 1st | +50 wpm | 40–50 wpm | −40 wpm |
| Early 2nd | +70 wpm | 50–70 wpm | −50 wpm |
| Late 2nd | +100 wpm | 80–100 wpm | −80 wpm |
| Early 3rd | +120 wpm | 100–120 wpm | −100 wpm |
| Late 3rd and above | +140 wpm | 100–140 wpm | −100 wpm |
| Reading Accuracy | | | |
| Grade | Pass | Unsure | No-Pass |
| | +95% | 90–95% | −90% |

5. Do the cloze/maze assessment (**Action 2**) and then go to **Question 2**

### Action 2: Cloze or Maze

#### Cloze and Maze Directions

*You don't have to give both close and maze,* so select either format. Remember, maze is generally thought to be easier for younger students (k–2); both are fine for older students.

#### Cloze

1. Collect passages of varying difficulty from texts used in the classroom or from published tests. The passages should be about 250 words in length (for primary grades 1 and 2, 100–200 words is adequate). It is best to use the type of passages (expository or narrative) to which you will generalize the test results. Also, they must be roughly equivalent in topic complexity.

2. Leave the first and last sentence intact and omit every fifth word. Leave blanks of equal length for all omitted words.

3. Tell the student that you are going to have her read a passage in which some words have been omitted. Tell her to fill in each blank with the word she thinks is missing. Have her practice with a sentence such as "Twinkle, twinkle, little _____" or "Old MacDonald had a _____." Tell her that she may go back and change answers if she thinks of a better word. If she can't write or spell, fill in the blanks for her.

4. Allow 10 minutes per passage.

5. After the student has answered for each blank (remember, it is not necessary that the student write out the answer) score the cloze responses. We use "exact word only" for ease of scoring. Our criteria are based on this procedure.

6. If you haven't done so, use **Action 1.**

| Criteria | | |
|---|---|---|
| | Maze | Cloze |
| Pass | 80% or better | 45% or better |
| Unsure | 60–80% | 30–45% |
| No-pass | 60% or less | 30% or less |

## *Maze*

1. Use the set of maze tests in the supplement. If you want to prepare you own, follow the directions provided earlier.
2. Tell the student that she is going to select the correct word for each blank. Provide a practice example such as "Old MacDonald had a _____ (farm, bike, running)." Tell her that she need not do the items in sequence and may go back and change them.
3. Allow 10 minutes per passage.
4. Score responses.
5. Use the following criteria to determine the status of the student (for cloze or maze).
6. If you haven't done so, use **Action 1.**

## *Interpretation*

### *Question 2: Is Comprehension Adequate?*

Using the results from **Action 1** and **Action 2,** answer *each* of the following and then follow the recommendations.

- If the student scored PASS on both **Action 1** and **Action 2,** then go to **Summary 1** and discontinue.

- If the student scored UNSURE or NO-PASS on either **Action 1** or **Action 2,** then go to **Summary 2.**
- In addition, if the UNSURE or NO-PASS indicated that you need to assess at a lower level, go to **Action 3.**
- If there is no need to work at a lower level, go to **Action 4.**

**Summary 1**    You get to **S.1** if the student passes the survey assessments and seems to have no problems in reading comprehension. Record the student's performance (PLOP) as score and/or objectives met and discontinue.

**Summary 2**    To get here, the student's comprehension may be problematic. Before starting specific-level testing to pin down the problem, you need to set a goal. This is done by the using assessment standards and the student's behavior to summarize the discrepancy.

If the standard for oral reading *at the student's expected level* is 100 wpm and the student read 50 wpm, the discrepancy is +50 wpm or ×2 wpm. This would produce a **goal** like this: "The student will read a [insert a description of the type/level of passage you will give the student] at a rate of 100 wpm or better with at least 95% accuracy."

If the standard for maze is 80% or better and the student scored 79%, don't worry about it! These criteria are only important if they have instructional implications, and a 1% deficit does not (just checking to be sure we all understand that).

If the standard for cloze is 45% or better and the student got 30%, then the discrepancy would be +15% or (45/30 =) × 1.5. This would lead to a goal like this: "The student will fill in the blanks on a cloze passage [insert a description of the type/level of passage you will give the student] at an accuracy level of 45%."

### Action 3: Find Current Level

Sometimes you will want to move up or down in passage difficulty so you can find the student's present level of performance (PLOP). You may also need to do this to find an "instructional level" or to get a larger sample of student work.

| Comprehension Skills | Enabling Skills |
|---|---|
| 1. Monitors meaning | 1. Decoding |
| 2. Selective attention to text | 2. Vocabulary |
| 3. Adjusts for task difficulty | 3. Syntax |
| 4. Connects text to prior knowledge | 4. Prior knowledge |
| 5. Clarifies | |

The process is obvious. Give the student passages of a different type (prose, narratives, computer-operations manual) or different reading level. Employ **Actions 1** and **2** in exactly the same fashion as described above. Repeat at different levels until the student passes or you run out of levels. If the student completely bombs (less than 50% correct responses) a higher level passage, you can skip around trying to find the one with which she can succeed.

### Interpretation

When you find the current level report is using **S.1.** Then go on to **Action 4.**

### Action 4: Use Status Sheet

Here are the nine most probable assumed causes for comprehension failure. They have been lumped into two categories: Comprehension strategies and enabling skills.

Because the enabling skills are covered in some detail in other chapters, this chapter only deals with specific level procedures (SLP) for assessing comprehension strategies. That's OK, because the strategies alone provide us with the possibility of multiple ways to explain a student's failure to react appropriately to print. Any

indication of an enabling skill problem should be checked out with a survey test within that enabling domain.

The status sheet is shown in Exhibit 8.1. Fortunately, figuring out a comprehension problem is easier than explaining how to do it. Sometimes, it is possible to resolve a problem by simply reviewing products and interviewing teachers. When you, or an available colleague, think you already have plenty of information about the student but need to coordinate this information, you can start this by using a status sheet. Unfortunately, some indicators on the status sheet do not take the form of permanent products (for example, "reads with expression"). Unless you routinely make notations about such things, there often won't be any evidence of reactions that can be picked up and filed away in a portfolio. This doesn't mean that there isn't any evidence; it just means that the evidence is in a teacher's head!

Use of a status sheet is more akin to a staff meeting than to a testing session. In fact, in many instances the student won't be in attendance. The assessment involves going through the available hard evidence and professional observations. Then, this body of evidence is summarized on the status sheet in Exhibit 8.1.

### Directions

1. Ask anyone with direct knowledge of the student's skills to a meeting. Individuals who have worked on reading with the student are particularly valuable.

2. Explain that the purpose of the status sheet is to limit the field of inquiry by ruling out things we already know that the student does or doesn't do.

3. Using the status sheet in Exhibit 8.1, go through each of the primary categories and mark the appropriate status (pass, unsure, no-pass). The indicators are only there to help define the categories—*it is the category you are rating.* Therefore, you can still mark "yes" when some indicator is missing, or "no" when an indicator is present.

4. Go to **Question 3** for interpretation.

### Question 3: What Problems Have You Found?

On the status sheet, if a category is marked "pass," then it is assumed the student has this skill. No other **action** (other than monitoring for maintenance and generalization) is required. Summarize the student's performance (**S.2**) and discontinue assessment for that category.

If a category of comprehension strategies is marked NO (a clear no-pass), then the student needs instruction. This category, and its instructional objectives, should be taught. List the objectives in **Summary 3.** Go to **Question 5.**

If a category of comprehension strategies is marked "unsure," additional information is needed. Go to **Action 5** and employ the specific-level **actions** indicated for each category marked "UNSURE."

If an enabling skill is marked NO or UNSURE, go to the chapter indicated on the status sheet. If there is no problem, forget it.

### Summary 3 (S.3): List Objectives and Teaching Procedures

You get to this summary if the student has a problem and you have selected objectives. The objectives may come from the status sheet in **Action 4,** or from specific-level procedures (SLP) you will give during **Action 5. Summary 3** is a list of all of the objectives you selected, or will select, and the teaching techniques you will employ. In other words, **S.3** is an instructional plan.

### Action 5: Use Indicated SLPs

You get here if you are unsure about the student's status. The status sheet will refer you to a **specific-level procedure** (assessment action). As you go through these **SLPs** you may be asked to use others. Eventually, you will find objectives and teaching recommendations to be listed in **S.3.**

These assessment actions do not appear in the flow chart in Exhibit 8.5. They include:

**Action 6:** Assisted monitoring

**Action 7:** Retell

**Action 8:** Awareness of reading

**Action 9:** Assisted activation of prior knowledge

**Action 10:** Prediction

**Action 11a** and **11b:** Assisted search

**Action 12:** Referent knowledge

### Action 6: Assisted Monitoring

Assisted monitoring is used to verify that the student monitors the meaning of the text as she reads. The process is outlined in Exhibit 8.6. Because of the complexity of this procedure, some steps will also refer to interpretation questions.

**Directions**

### Step 1: Collect a Sample

Select a passage that the student reads inaccurately. You may want to read the survey-testing directions in Chapter 9 for information on collecting and scoring reading samples.

### Step 2: Do the Errors Violate Meaning?

This is answered by reading the passage the way the student read it and comparing the resulting message to the message of the original text.

### Step 3: Is Rate and/or Comprehension Poor?

If the errors don't violate meaning, then ask yourself if the student's reading rate and comprehension seem adequate. Refer to the results of the comprehension status sheet if you've used it. See interpretation **Questions 1** and **2.**

### Step 4: Does the Student Correct Errors That Violate Meaning?

If YES, go to Step 11.
If NO, then go to Step 5.

### Step 5: Assist the Student's Monitoring

Tell the student "Whenever you make an error, I'm going to tap the table with my pen. When I tap the table, I want you to fix the error." Have the student continue to read the passage. When she makes an error that violates meaning, immediately tap the table. Do not wait.

***Exhibit 8.6    Flow Chart for Comprehension. Action 6: Assisted Monitoring.***

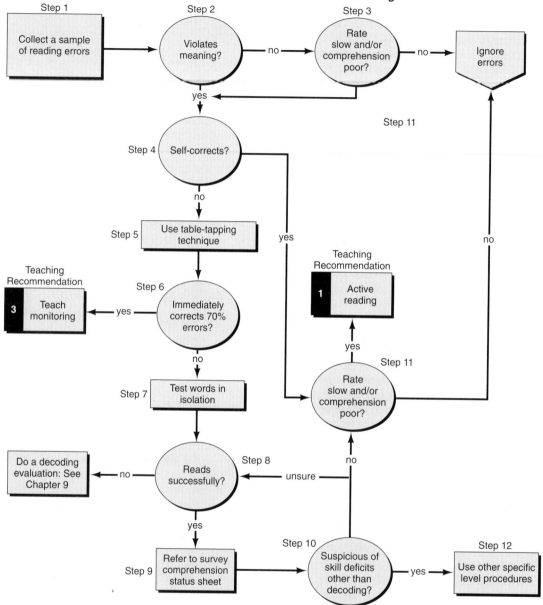

### Step 6: Decide if Assistance Leads to Immediate Error Corrections

The student should immediately self-correct most (70%) of meaning-violating errors. If the student does not correct 70% of the errors, go on to Step 7. If the student does, then use **Teaching Recommendation 3.**

### Step 7: Test Words in Isolation

Select words the student missed while reading the passage. These should only be words for which the errors violated meaning. Present the words to the student in isolation (on flash cards or paper) and ask the student to read them.

### Step 8: Were Words in Isolation Read Correctly?

If YES, then go to Step 9.

If NO, then go to Chapter 9 and check for decoding problems.

### Step 9: Review the Comprehension Status Sheet

If you have not completed the survey comprehension status sheet (Exhibit 8.1), do so now. Sit down with all the information you have collected and carefully answer the questions on the sheet. Ask yourself (or anyone else who might know) if there is evidence of problems, other than decoding. Mark the problem areas.

### Step 10: Skill Deficits Other Than Decoding?

Look at the results obtained from the comprehension status sheet. Follow the recommended actions for categories marked NO or UNSURE on the status sheet. If there aren't any problem categories (other than decoding), you may want to repeat Step 8 or go to Step 11.

### Step 11: Is Rate Very Slow (No-Pass) and/or Comprehension Poor (Unsure or No-Pass)?

If YES, then go to **Teaching Recommendation 1.**

If NO, then ignore the errors.

### Interpretation Guidelines for Assisted Monitoring

Scoring and qualitative interpretation guidelines for this procedure are included in the following interpretation questions.

### Action 7: Retell

Retell is used to verify that the student monitors the meaning of text. The retell procedure is fairly straightforward. The student reads a passage and then, upon request, tells you what she read. You score the reaction according to the thoroughness and accuracy of the student's retelling. With this technique, students are permitted to repeat exact words found in the story.

Both the development of a retell scoring procedure and the establishment of criteria are time consuming for the evaluator. Tindal and Marston (1990) have suggested a step-by-step description of how to proceed with retell. We prefer the Tindal and Marston procedure because it is the quickest to use. It uses a "scale" for judging the quality of retell (presented in the interpretation section of this **SLP**).

The way you introduce retell exercises has a great effect on the student's work (Bisanz et al., 1992). One way to standardize your directions, while clarifying the task to the student, is to go over the criteria with the student before the actual test. This will serve to define retell for the student, just as the Tindal and Marston criteria have defined it for you.

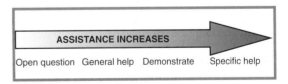

One drawback of retelling is the difficulty of judging if a student who retells a story with exact words has understood what she has read. Students may need to be asked to paraphrase and to retell a story. An advantage of the paraphrase and retell formats is that both may also be used as instructional activities to enhance comprehension.

To complete the retell procedure, you will need to have a sequence of assistance so that you can mark how much help the student needed to retell accurately. This is the sequence we recommend. Open questions provide the least assistance. If after using comprehension SLP2 (retell) you still aren't sure what the problem is, you have no choice but to begin systematically checking each area of comprehension strategy. If you don't find anything there, you will next need to check *each* domain of enabling skill listed in Exhibit 8.1. (No one said this would be easy!) Obviously, if you can again use the indicators of Exhibit 8.1 to try and narrow this search, it will be well worth your time.

**Open question** means that you just say "please tell me what the passage/story was about?" or "Please tell me what happened in the passage/story?" or "Can you tell me more?" Then, as a follow-up question, "Is there anything you left out?"

**General help** means that you encourage the student and try to clarify the task. Say things like "Please tell me what happened in the passage/story. Try hard to get all of the important parts" or "Don't forget to tell about the characters."

**Demonstrate** means that you take another passage/story and retell it for the student. Say, "I'm going to ask you to read a passage and then tell me what it was about. Here, I'll do one first to show you how."

**Specific Help** means giving the student a strategy for retell and directions to use it, demonstrating while pointing out the steps in the strat-

egy, then having the student repeat the directions. A strategy might be something like this: "Remember **W3 W2 H2**—who, when, where—what happened, what happened next—how did it end, how did they feel" (Danoff, 1993).

### Directions

1. Collect passages of varying difficulty from texts used in the classroom or from published tests. The passages should be about 250 words in length (for primary grades 1 and 2, 100–200 words is adequate).

2. Use written retell if the student has adequate skills; otherwise, set up a recorder to tape student responses.

3. Tell the student that you want her to read a passage and tell you what she has read.

4. Have the student read the passage to herself.

5. Ask the student to tell you what she has read.

6. Score responses using the scale for response quality provided below.

7. If you need to repeat the process, use the sequence of assistance discussed above and record the level needed for success.

Use the following scale to rate the retell.

There really isn't an established standard for the Tindal and Marston scale, although we have found scores 3 and above are easily produced by

| Retell Rating | |
|---|---|
| Rating    Interpretation | Tindal & Marston (1990) |
| 5 | Generalizations are made beyond the text; includes central thesis and major points, supporting details, and relevant supplemental information; exhibits coherence, completeness, and comprehensibility. |
| 4 | Includes central thesis, major points, supporting details, and relevant supplemental information; exhibits coherence, completeness, and comprehensibility. |
| 3 | Relates major ideas, includes supporting details and relevant supplemental information; exhibits adequate coherence, completeness, and comprehensibility. |
| 2 | Relates a few major ideas, supporting details, and relevant supplemental information; exhibits some coherence, completeness, and comprehensibility. |
| 1 | Relates no major ideas, and details only irrelevant supplemental information; low degree of coherence, completeness, and comprehensibility. |

*Pass:* rating of 4 or above.
*No-pass:* rating of 3, 2, or 1.

even primary students when they retell primary passages. You could develop your own (see Chapters 5 and 6), but validation would be tedious.

### Interpretation Guidelines for Retell

#### Question: Was It Possible to Score the Recall?

If YES, go to the next **question.**

If NO (errors or incoherent retell), repeat the procedure with progressively easier passages *or* progressively greater levels of assistance (described above).

If none of these produces coherent retell, go to **Action 3.**

#### Question: Did the Student Score 4 or 5?

If YES, the student monitors the meaning of text. Explore other assumed causes for the comprehension problem; start with specific procedures 3 and 7.

If NO, analyze the retell product for error patterns. Try to recognize these deficits:

- Misses main ideas
- Excludes relevant information or includes irrelevant information
- Omits references to characters, descriptions, actions, conflicts, and/or resolutions
- Constructs poor and/or incoherent retell containing major gaps
- Includes ambiguous words
- Fails to use content-specific technical vocabulary that is included in the passage

#### Question: Did Some Deficits Occur More Often?

If NO, teach Comprehension **Objective 7.**

If YES, and most errors fall into the first three categories, teach **Objectives 7, 8,** and **14** using **Teaching Recommendations 3, 4,** and **6.**

### Action 8: Awareness of Reading

This procedure is used to investigate the student's awareness of the reading process and how that process is influenced by text difficulty. It is a combined observation and interview procedure drawn directly from the work of Schmitt (1990) and Paris and Jacobs (1984). To use this procedure, you will ask the questions shown in Exhibit 8.7. Results will be recorded in Exhibit 8.8.

1. Have the student read material that she has had difficulty understanding (reacting to) in the past. As the student reads, watch for evidence of tactics listed in Exhibit 8.8.

2. Do not expect to see evidence of each tactic.

3. When you have finished observing, begin to interview the student. Tell the student that you want to ask her some questions regarding reading. Explain that your purpose is to find out what she thinks about reading, not how well she reads. Remember that different types of passages will elicit different tactics (Walpole, 1999). Therefore, you'll need to make it clear to the student when you are asking about passages read for enjoyment and those read to study. Ask the student to explain how she could go about obtaining the message of a paragraph or the sound of a word.

4. Use the interview in Exhibit 8.7. Some of these items may seem inappropriate to the student or to the sort of material she is currently reading. In that case, skip them. It may also be true that some important topic is omitted from the items in Exhibit 8.7. In that case, you will want to add tactics.

5. If at all possible, tape-record the student's responses. At the very least, take good notes on how the student answers.

6. Example responses for each item in Exhibit 8.7 are shown in parentheses. General guidelines for adequacy include answers that reflect analysis of the reading task itself or the application of specific tactics for reading. The example responses do not reflect any particular grade level; therefore, the wording your student uses may be more or less sophisticated.

7. Combine all of the information you have obtained and mark the status of each category in Exhibit 8.8.

*Exhibit 8.7    Comprehension Interview.*

Directions:

❏    Ask all questions and then, based on the answers, mark the status of categories 1–6 on the status sheet in Exhibit 8.8.

❏    In Exhibit 8.8, mark "Pass" if the student seems to correctly answer the question in a category. Mark "No-Pass" if the answers are wrong. Mark "Unsure" If you can't tell and/or think more assessment is needed.

❏    If the student's answer is short prompt her by saying "Can you tell me some more about this?" or "Are there any other things you do?"

❏    Example correct answers can be found in parentheses following each item.

❖    Remember, you are judging the categories, not the individual items (it is possible to mark a category "No-Pass" even if some items are correct).

**1. Before reading**

(Ask the questions and mark items as correct if they are answered in response to any question under this category.)

"Why do you read this text?", "What might give you a clue about what is in this story?", "How else could you try to find out about a story before you read?"

1.    Purpose (learn the information in it, for enjoyment)

2.    Title (mentions the title)

3.    Illustrations (mentions looking at the illustrations/figures)

4.    Prereading questions (mentions making up and asking questions about passage prior to reading)

5.    Predictions (try to guess what will be in the next parts of the passage)

**2. While reading**

(Ask the questions and mark items as correct if they are answered in response to any question under this category.)

"As you are reading what do you do?", "How can you tell if you are understanding while you read?", "Is there anything you try to get done while you read?"

6.    Remembers questions and predictions (answer questions, checks to see if predictions were correct)

7.    Checks to see if it makes sense (see if I know what it's saying, make sure I don't get confused or lost)

8.    Summarizes (stop and think about parts, try to sum up parts, put it in a nutshell)

9.    Keeps questioning (make up new questions, think of new predictions, decide what will happen next)

10.    Clarifies (when I get stuck I read ahead/back, I use the sentences to decide what the words mean)

**3. After reading**

(Ask the questions and mark items as correct if they are answered in response to any question under this category.)

"When you are finished reading what do you do?", "What do you do as soon as you finish reading a passage/story?"

11.    Summarize (takes time to think it over, try to sum it all up)

12.    Reviews (thinks over the questions and predictions to see if answers were found)

13.    Uses prior knowledge (try to make sense of it, checks to see if it is out of line with what is already known)

### 4. Reading awareness

Ask each question, record what student says, try to rate the answers so you can judge the overall category. Examples of correct answers are in parentheses.

14.    What's the hardest part about reading for you? (complex material, paying attention to the right stuff)

15.    What would help you become a better reader? (help from the teacher, practice)

16.    Is there anything special about the first sentence or two in a story? What do they tell you? (tells you what is important, makes the reading easier)

17.    How about the last sentence; what does it tell you? (what I should have attended to, what is important)

18.    How can you tell which sentences are the most important ones in a story? (where they are in the story, if they tell about the hardest stuff to understand)

### 5. Planning

Ask each question, record what student says, try to rate the answers so you can judge the overall category. Examples of correct answers are in parentheses.

19.    If you could only read some sentences in the story because you are in a hurry, which ones would you read? (the ones that tell about important stuff, the first or last ones)

20.    What do you try to tell someone about a story—all the words, just the ending, what the story was about, or something else? (the important stuff, what/who it was about)

21.    The other day I asked a girl to read a story and then tell me what she read. Before she started reading, though, she asked me if I wanted her to remember the story word for word or just the general meaning. Why do you think she asked me that? (because she wanted to know why she was reading the story, so she could decide what to focus on)

22.    Before you start to read a story, do you do anything special? What kinds of plans help you read better? (I try to find out why I'm reading it, I look it over before I start)

23.    If you had to read very fast and could only read some words, which ones would you try to read? (I'd look for clues, like words that are darker)

### 6. Regulation

Ask each question, record what student says, try to rate the answers so you can judge the overall category. Examples of correct answers are in parentheses.

24.    Do you ever go back and read things over? Why? (yes—because I get confused, because I want to read the stuff the teacher talked about twice, because they are the things I need to attend to)

25.    What do you do if you come to a word you don't understand? (I put another word in its place, then see if the sentence makes sense; I look it up, I ask for help)

26.    What do you do if you don't understand a whole sentence? (pay attention to it, read it over, skip it and come back later, stop and ask for help)

       What parts of a story do you skip as you read? (the stuff the teacher won't ask about, the stuff I don't think is important)

27.    What things do you read faster than others? (the easy things, the things I know about)

Questions 14–28 are based on Paris and Jacobs (1984, pp. 2085–2086): Used with permission.

*Source:* Howell, K. W., Zucker, S. H. & Morehead, M. K. (2000b). *Multilevel Academic Skills Inventory.* Bellingham, WA: Applied Research and Development Center. To order contact the Student Co-op Bookstore, Western Washington University. Fax (360) 650-2888. Phone (360) 650-3656. Reprinted with permission.

*Exhibit 8.8    Status Sheet for Awareness of the Reading Process.*

Directions:

❑    For each category in Exhibit 8.7, mark "Pass" if the student seems to correctly answer the question in a category. Mark "No-Pass" if the answers are wrong. Mark "Unsure" if you can't tell and/or think more assessment is needed.

❑    Remember, you are judging the categories, not the individual items (it is possible to mark a category "No-Pass" even if some items are correct).

| Is the category of skills OK? | Pass | No-Pass | Unsure |
|---|---|---|---|
| **Before reading** | ___ | ___ | ___ |
| 1.    Considers purpose for reading | | | |
| 2.    Considers title | | | |
| 3.    Scans illustrations/figures | | | |
| 4.    Asks questions | | | |
| 5.    Makes predictions | | | |
| **While reading** | ___ | ___ | ___ |
| 6.    Remembers predictions and questions | | | |
| 7.    Decides if passage makes sense | | | |
| 8.    Summarizes while reading | | | |
| 9.    Keeps questioning and predicting | | | |
| 10.  Seeks clarification | | | |
| **After reading** | ___ | ___ | ___ |
| 11.  Summarizes | | | |
| 12.  Reviews questions/predictions | | | |
| 13.  Fits the story to what is already known | | | |
| **Reading awareness** | ___ | ___ | ___ |
| 14.  Explains what is hard | | | |
| 15.  Knows how to get help | | | |
| 16.  Knows importance of the first sentences | | | |
| 17.  Knows importance of the last sentences | | | |
| 18.  Explains how to decide what is important | | | |
| **Planning** | ___ | ___ | ___ |
| 19.  Plans priority on parts of passage | | | |
| 20.  Focuses on important information | | | |
| 21.  Determines purpose before reading | | | |
| 22.  Plans before reading | | | |
| 23.  Looks for emphasis in passage | | | |
| **Regulation** | ___ | ___ | ___ |
| 24.  Rereads | | | |
| 25.  Clarifies vocabulary | | | |
| 26.  Deals with sentences she doesn't understand | | | |
| 27.  Skips trivial information | | | |
| 28.  Adjusts reading rate | | | |

*Source:* Howell, K. W., Zucker, S. H. & Morehead, M. K. (2000b). *Multilevel Academic Skills Inventory.* Bellingham, WA: Applied Research and Development Center. To order contact the Student Co-op Bookstore, Western Washington University. Fax (360) 650-2888. Phone (360) 650-3656. Reprinted with permission.

### Qualitative Interpretation

#### Question: Is the Status of Each Category in Exhibit 8.8 "Pass"?

If YES, then the skill does not need to be taught.

If NO, teach the skill. During instruction, use tactics the student does know to advance acquisition of knowledge from text and teach the unknown tactics. Do not emphasize knowing about the tactics—emphasize using them. Select **Objectives 5, 6,** and **9.** Use **Teaching Recommendations 1, 2,** and **6.**

If the status is "unsure," then repeat the observation and questioning by focusing directly on the categories in question.

### Action 9: Assisted Activation of Prior Knowledge

There is a difference between "providing" and "activating" knowledge. In this SLP, you will try to activate knowledge that the student already has by providing schemas, or prompts, to help the student recall the information prior to reading. If the student doesn't have the knowledge, these prompts shouldn't work. Therefore, this procedure is used to determine if the student lacks sufficient prior knowledge to comprehend a particular passage.

#### Directions

1. Select four passages from expository or narrative texts (narrative for young students) at the student's expected level. Be sure they cover four different topics.

2. Convert two of the passages into maze/cloze (whichever you used during the survey test).

3. Read each of the four passages carefully and outline their content. You may want to do this by preparing a "story grammar map" of the passage as explained in **Teaching Recommendation 3.** Recognize topics covered in the passage and any unstated information (prior knowledge) that the reader would need to understand it.

4. You are going to give each passage, but discuss the topics and information you have identified with the student prior to each passage. (Don't discuss all four and then test all four.) During the brief (5-minute) discussion, ask what the student knows and encourage her to remember it while reading. Do not "tell" the student about topics. This is important. You are trying to prime the student's recall. You are *not* trying to teach the content of the passage.

5. Discuss and administer the two cloze/maze tests in standard fashion and score them.

6. Discuss and administer the remaining two passages to get oral-reading fluency rates. Score these in standard fashion.

### Score Interpretation

1. Find the average of the scores on the two cloze/maze passages and then compute the average of the two oral-reading passages.

2. Compare the scores with those obtained during survey-level testing.

3. If the scores improve into the passing range (see criteria for oral reading on page **222** and cloze/maze on page **223**) or if they improve by at least 50%, you have confirmed that a complete lack of prior knowledge is *not* the likely cause of the survey-level failure because, if prior knowledge wasn't there, your little chat would not have raised the score. (Caution is in order here, as the low survey scores may have been because of the novelty of the survey-testing formats. In other words, the improvement you see could simply be the result of practice or the attention that came with the chat.)

### Qualitative Interpretation

#### Question: Did the Student's Work Improve into the "Pass" Range?

If *no,* employ comprehension **Actions 5** and **6.** Also consider the possibility that the student lacks a broad base of general information. This is very common among special/remedial readers and results from their limited exposure to information through reading (see the Matthew Effect). Go to Chapter 10 for information on the assessment of vocabulary and Chapter 14 for details about general information.

If YES, teach **Objective 10** and use **Teaching Recommendations 1** and **4.**

### Action 10: Make Predictions

This procedure is used to investigate how well the student uses what she already knows, along with what she has learned from the text, to make logical assumptions about upcoming material.

### Directions

1. Ask the student to begin reading from an expository passage that is appropriate for comprehension instruction (that is, she decodes it and knows what the words mean).

2. At the end of each paragraph, ask the student to predict what will be in the next paragraph. Say "What things do you think the next paragraph will tell us about?" or "What will be next?" Elicit at least two predictions for each paragraph. Do this for four paragraphs.

3. Rate each prediction as correct or incorrect by deciding if the student's prediction **follows logically from the text.** When making this determination, consider what the student knows about the topic. Criteria for judging predictions are provided later in the description of reciprocal teaching presented in **Teaching Recommendation 2. A prediction need not be true to be correct.** This means that if the student's prediction is logical, regardless of what is actually written in the next paragraph, it is correct.

### Score Interpretation

There are no established scoring conventions or standards for this test. We believe nearly all (90%) of the predictions should be correct (logical).

### Qualitative Interpretation

If the student's accuracy improves after doing a couple of passages, you may want to do a few more. Assume that the initial problem was because of the novelty of the task and interpret the student's final efforts.

### Question: Are the Student's Predictions Logical?

If YES, the student is using text and prior knowledge. Check clarification with **Action 7.**

If NO, the student cannot make predictions from text. If you believe that the student has adequate prior knowledge, use **Objective 11** and **Teaching Recommendations 2** and **6.** If you used specific-level procedure 4 and the student also failed it, consider that the student may be lacking in general knowledge. This means you should go to Chapter 14. However, it does not mean you should wait to teach prediction skills. You can begin now by carefully selecting material with which the student is familiar.

### Actions 11a and 11b: Assisted Search

These procedures are used to investigate how well the student uses what she already knows about both the topic and text structure to locate targeted information in a passage. They are particularly appropriate for students who are failing to understand topical readings (like science chapters). **Actions 11a and 11b** are designed to examine the student's skill at distinguishing relevant from irrelevant information in the passage. Both procedures attempt to answer the question by telling the student what to look for. Therefore, failure can be attributed to either poor search skills or poor text structure (Guthrie et al., 1991).

A student may have search skills but still fail to find critical information if the text or the teacher does not adequately signal emphasis.

### 11a Directions

1. Select several passages from expository texts that the student is expected to comprehend.

2. Prepare test items for each passage and have the student read a couple of the passages and take the items. If the student passes the items, then repeat with a different topic until you have found an area with which the student has trouble. (If you can't find one, she doesn't need this procedure.)

3. Now select passages the student has not read but that cover topics on which she has previously failed items. Develop prereading questions that will serve to focus the student's attention on the answers to the

questions. These questions should be related to the topics the items sample—but should not exactly duplicate the items. Here is an item for this step:

---

Prereading questions should:

a. cover irrelevant information

b. exactly match the topic of the test items

c. complement the topic of the test items

d. not address the topic of the test items

---

A good question to ask before the student reads would be "I want you to read this passage to find the answer to this question: 'What sort of prereading questions are best?'"

A bad prereading question would be "I want you to read this passage to find the answer to this question: 'Should prereading questions exactly match the topics of test items?'"

4. Give the prereading questions, ask the student to read, and then give and score the test items.

### Qualitative Interpretation

**Question: Did the Student Do Significantly Better (Pass the Test) on Test Items after Receiving Assistance?**

If YES, teach **Objective 12** using **Teaching Recommendations 2** and **4**.

If NO, go to **Action 11b**.

### 11b Directions

1. Select several passages from expository texts that the student is expected to comprehend.

2. Prepare test items for each passage and have the student read a couple of the passages and take the items. If the student passes the items, repeat with a different topic until you have found an area with which the student has trouble.

3. Now select passages the student has not read but that cover topics on which the student has previously failed items. Give the student a previously unseen question and then ask the student to read the passage and underline the words in the passage that answer the question (you may also ask the student to cross out the words that do not answer the question). For example, "I want you to read passage 3 under **Action 11a.** Underline the words that tell you what prereading questions should be like."

Develop prereading questions that will serve to focus the student's attention on the answers to the questions. These questions should be related to the topics the test items will sample, but they should not exactly duplicate the items.

### Interpretation Guidelines for Action 11b

**Question: Does the Student Underline the Correct Wording?**

If YES, teach Objective 12 (p. **237**) using Teaching Recommendations 2 and 4.

If NO, assuming you haven't already done so, give Action 3. If the student passes SLP 3, use Objectives 13, 14, and 8, along with **Teaching Recommendations 2, 3, 4,** and **5.**

### Action 12: Referent Knowledge

Common referents are words like *he, she, it, they, them,* and *those.* Referents may also include any word that has *its* meaning designated in a passage. Readers must know what these *words* mean.

For example, in the final two sentences of the last paragraph two words are italicized. The word *its* refers to, or takes the place of, "any word." *Words* in the last sentence refers to "a word that has its meaning designated in a passage." Here is another example: "Kathy took Claire for a walk and then she read her a story." In this sentence who is *she*? Who does the word *her* refer to in the same sentence?

Often, when a student loses meaning it is because she has confused referents (Greene et al., 1992).

### Directions

1. Select 250-word passages (for primary grades 1 and 2, 100–200 words is adequate)

containing common referents or words that are given designated meaning within the passage. If you know the student is having problems understanding topic-specific material (words and ideas in a history textbook), use passages from that book.

2. Have the student read the passage. Then returning to specific referents, point to them and ask "In this sentence (to whom/what) does the word ____ refer/mean?" Be careful when you judge how well the student answers these questions because they sometimes may be answered with logic or personal experience.

3. Collect responses on at least 25 referents. Try to get as much variety as you can in your selection.

### Score Interpretation

Accuracy for this SLP should approach 100%. Any errors, assuming the student decodes the material and understands most of it, are unusual.

### Qualitative Interpretation

### Question: Does the Student Correctly Determine the Meaning of Referents?

If YES, the student's failure to react appropriately is not the result of a lack of skill in referent clarification. Try SLPs (Actions) 1 or 2.

If NO, examine errors for patterns. For example, a common pattern involves referents that derive their meaning at a distance from themselves. For example, in the previous sentence, *pattern* refers to "error patterns," which was designated in another sentence. The word *their* in the same sentence refers to "referents" and was designated in that sentence. Teach Objective 15 using Teaching Recommendations 2 and 6.

## Objectives and Teaching Recommendations

This section begins by listing the objectives referenced in the interpretation sections. These, along with the objectives on the status sheets (Exhibits 8.1 and 8.8) are the objectives that, according to student need, you would put in a lesson plan and/or IEP. The objectives list is then followed by the teaching recommendations mentioned in the interpretation guidelines. The numbering of objectives and teaching recommendations is the same throughout this chapter.

### Objectives for Comprehension

Portions of the following goals/objectives have been placed in brackets ([ ]). The bracketed portions require the insertion of wording specific to the student. Whenever you see the brackets, you will need to fill in the information called for at that point. For example, many of the goals use the wording "passages at [expected or intermediate levels.]" The **expected level** is the curriculum level at which students of the same age work. Intermediate levels are those between the expected level and the present level of performance. This wording is used to indicate that the same core goal/objective (the part that isn't between brackets) may be combined with a procession of bracketed wording to establish an instructional sequence. For example, a fifth-grade student currently working at the second curriculum level could have the following sequence.

1. Given a series of passages at [the second curriculum level], the student will make predictions about each upcoming passage that reflect a logical extension of the previously read material (CAP 100%).

2. Given a series of passages at [the third curriculum level], the student will make predictions about each upcoming passage that reflect a logical extension of the previously read material (CAP 100%).

3. Given a series of passages at [the fourth curriculum level], the student will make predictions about each upcoming passage that reflect a logical extension of the previously read material (CAP 100%).

4. Given a series of passages at [the fifth curriculum level], the student will make predictions about each upcoming passage that reflect a logical extension of the previously read material (CAP 100%).

## Sample Comprehension Objectives

The objectives listed here are the ones referred to earlier in the interpretation sections.

1. Given a passage at [expected or intermediate curriculum level], the student will read it aloud at [specified rate and with specified accuracy].

2. Given a 250-word cloze passage at [the expected or intermediate curriculum level], the student will supply correct choices with at least 45% accuracy.

3. Given a 250-word maze passage at [expected curriculum level], the student will select correct choices with at least 80% accuracy.

4. Given signals, the student will immediately locate and correct errors that violate meaning made in oral reading. The signals may be given after words, phrases, sentences, or paragraphs (CAP 95%).

5. Given passages at [expected or intermediate curriculum levels], the student will not make, or will spontaneously correct, errors in reading that violate meaning (CAP no more than 5% uncorrected errors).

6. Given passages at [expected or intermediate curriculum levels], the student will, upon encountering difficult material, employ one or more of the following tactics (CAP 90%):

   ✓ Reread
   ✓ Adjust rate
   ✓ Request assistance
   ✓ Recognize what information is required

7. Given passages at [expected or intermediate curriculum levels], the student will retell the content (CAP rating of 3 or above on the Tindal & Marston scale shown on page 228).

8. Given passages at [expected or intermediate curriculum levels], the student will identify (by underlining, highlighting, or crossing out) material related to one or more of the following specified categories (CAP 100%):

   ✓ Main idea
   ✓ Relevant information
   ✓ Irrelevant information
   ✓ Characters
   ✓ Descriptions
   ✓ Actions
   ✓ Conflicts
   ✓ Resolutions

9. Upon request, the student will demonstrate metacognitive awareness of the reading process by supplying and/or explaining the following active reading tactics (CAP 100%):

   ✓ Predicting and verifying
   ✓ Previewing
   ✓ Checking purpose
   ✓ Analyzing setting
   ✓ Self-questioning
   ✓ Drawing from background knowledge
   ✓ Summarizing
   ✓ Applying fix-up tactics

10. Given passages at [expected or intermediate curriculum levels], the student will maintain passing scores on maze/cloze tests across the following sequence of conditions (CAP 100%):

    ✓ Comprehensive review of topic with teacher or peer
    ✓ Anticipatory discussion of topic prior to reading
    ✓ Reminder always to think about topic purpose prior to reading
    ✓ No assistance

11. Given a series of passages at [expected or intermediate curriculum levels], the student will make predictions about each upcoming passage that reflect a logical extension of the previously read material (CAP 95%).

12. Given passages at [the appropriate level], the student will use her knowledge of the topic and preceding passages to develop her own main-idea prereading questions. These questions will cover content that the text author or teacher thinks is critical (CAP 95%).

13. Given passages at [the appropriate level], the student will locate answers to prereading questions (CAP 100%).

14. Given specific topics, the student will identify wording in the passages that is, or is not, related to the topic (CAP 100%).

15. Given passages at [expected or intermediate curriculum levels], the student will supply the correct definitions for referents that are underlined or pointed to by the teacher (CAP 100%). (These will include referents both near and far from the designated wording in the passage.)

## Teaching Recommendations for Comprehension

The following teaching recommendations have been drawn from a review of literature on comprehension and from classroom teachers. Because the recommendations are presented in a fairly superficial way, many of them are accompanied by references to help you locate additional information. In all cases, because the content being taught is rule-governed and strategic, the information in Chapter 4 on strategy instruction applies to these techniques. Comprehension strategies include:

1. Active and reflective reading
2. Adjustment for text difficulty
3. Comprehension monitoring
4. Connection of text to prior knowledge
5. Clarification

The following suggestions are broken into two parts. First, there is a set of general suggestions that must be considered regardless of the particular comprehension objectives being taught.

## General Recommendations for Teaching Comprehension

Current practice in teaching reading comprehension, despite considerable movement in the philosophies espoused in the reading literature (Freppon & Dahl, 1998; Gaffney & Anderson, 1991), has stayed strikingly the same. For example, here are two quotes from studies examining instruction on reading comprehension:

> *There is little evidence of instruction of any kind. Teachers spend most of their time assigning activities, monitoring to be sure the pupils are on task, directing recitation sessions to assess how well children are doing and providing corrective feedback in response to pupil errors.*
>
> Seldom does one observe teaching in which *a teacher presents a skill, a strategy, or a process to pupils, shows them how to do it, provides assistance as they initiate attempts to perform the task and assures that they can be successful* (emphasis added).
>
> Duffy et al. (1980)

> Most of the teachers (11) taught reading comprehension by either reading the story aloud to the students and asking questions, or having the group take turns reading the story followed by the teacher asking questions. Observations revealed that the questions asked were largely factual and literal. In one teacher observation, the students worked in pairs and asked each other questions about the story. Of the 41 observations *there is only one record of a comprehension strategy being taught* (emphasis added) to the students. (page 220)
>
> Vaughn, et al. (1998)

These two observations, conducted years apart, describe many of today's remedial/special reading programs. Many students are never taught *how* to comprehend. Here is what these students need to learn.

### Awareness of Reading

It is important to teach the student to stop reading and think about applying problem-solving or study skills when her understanding seems inadequate. This application of self-monitoring requires the student to develop an awareness of the reading process (Walpole, 1999; McLain & Victoria, 1991). The content of this awareness was presented in Exhibit 8.8. It is taught, as are most things, through explanation, demonstration, questioning, and specific feedback. As a teacher, you may easily incorporate the Exhibit 8.8 con-

| Problem Type | Questions Students Should Ask |
|---|---|
| Missing information | Where did I get lost?<br>What kind of information would help me? Where can I find out more about this? |
| Ambiguous cues | What do the words I'm dealing with mean? What cause-and-effect relationships have been established?<br>Exactly which pieces of information pertain to which characters or concepts? |
| Missing criteria | If I understood this, what would I know (be skilled to do)?<br>What are the passage's guidelines (indicators) for understanding?<br>What is a reasonable level of understanding for this kind of passage?<br>How will I know if I have adequate understanding? |

tent into discussion and questioning during your routine reading lessons.

### Use of Prior Knowledge

It is important to impress upon the student the idea that she is bringing something to the text and not just passively receiving its message. This means that the student is continually expected to actively compare what the passage says with what she already knows.

### Use of Teacher Questions

Ask questions involving the contrast between the text and information you know the student has learned previously. Ask the student to identify events, outcomes, concepts, or operations she finds adequately or inadequately described in the text.

### Use of Self-Questioning

Self-questioning represents an excellent way to promote active understanding and reading. However, for the student to use self-questioning, she must have already developed some comprehension-monitoring skills (see Recommendation 6). Monitoring alerts a reader that a task is hard. Tasks are usually difficult because they contain missing (unstated) information, ambiguous cues, or lack distinct criteria for completion (Frederiksen, 1984). Tasks

are also hard for any student who lacks the skills needed to complete them. Students can learn to directly attack difficult portions of texts by using their existing knowledge to answer these questions.

### Encourage Prediction

Ask the student to predict upcoming events. Then have the student supply information from the text that supports the prediction. This will be explained in some detail under reciprocal teaching (Recommendation 2).

### Teach Student to Clarify Vocabulary

Vocabulary evaluation and instruction are covered in Chapters 10 and 14. Remember when you are teaching vocabulary it is important to emphasize multiple meanings and how the meaning of words is altered by context (Scott & Nagy, 1997; Rupley et al., 1999). Give examples of text where context alters meaning. Use examples with familiar words to illustrate your point. For example, "Having a shallow conversation" does not mean that the speakers are standing in a creek.

### Teach the Student to State the Unknown

Encourage the student to recognize points in the text that deserve elaboration. Teach the students to make specific, rather than general, requests for clarification. A student should say "I need to know why the problem in this passage involves the use of tax dollars, not interest payments" rather than "I need to know more about the problem."

Here is a two-step procedure for clarification.

1. First, the student is taught to identify the specific topic of concern. This is called the "unknown." The teacher promotes this skill by training the student to ask herself "What is unknown in this passage?" and to answer in a full sentence ("I don't know why the problem uses tax dollars and not interest payments").

2. Next, the student is taught how to turn the unknown statement into a question. For example, the original "...why the problem uses tax dollars and not interest payments" is attached to a stem such as "I need to know." The teacher does this by saying "Now I want you to turn your question into a statement that begins with 'I need to know.'"

The correct response would be "I need to know why the problem uses tax dollars and not interest payments."

### Teach Search Skills

Teach the student how to search for needed information. One common search technique involves summarizing a passage and examining the summary for key information. (Teaching the student to summarize preceding and subsequent discussions that can be used as links to the current passage is also a good idea.)

The student must learn to use the structure of the text, including illustrations, titles, and headings, to find information. She must also formulate questions and reread the passage for the purpose of answering the questions (Bakken et al., 1998). One system for teaching these skills is Multipass (Schumaker et al., 1982). Multipass is described in some detail by Lovitt (1991). Multipass is designed primarily for use with content-area textbooks. Here is an abstract of the Multipass content.

| Pass | Purpose | Method |
|------|---------|--------|
| Survey | Familiarization | Read chapter title, pass introduction, headings and subtitles, illustrations and captions, and summary. |
| Size-up | Gain | Find textual clues. Turn past information clues into questions. Find answers to questions. Paraphrase answer for yourself. |
| Sort-out | Self-testing | Recognize when additional past information is needed, think where to look for answers, search for the answer, and search other sections if necessary. |

### Teach the Student to Clarify Referent Structures

As explained on page **238,** referent, or *anaphoric,* words stand for something. The most common examples are pronouns or pro-verbs such as *he, she, they, it.* Consider this passage:

"Jim and Ken went out to fly *their* airplane. *It* was wet, so before *they* could do *that they* had to use a towel to dry *it.*"

In the passage, each of the referent words is italicized. A student who doesn't match the referent words with either the correct antecedents or with other key words not contained in the passage will experience comprehension difficulties (Scott & Nagy, 1997). Often, students who do not know how to determine the base for a referent will pick the closest word. This tactic, if applied to the words in the sample passage, would work fairly well for the second occurrence but not for the first.

When teaching a student to clarify a referent, the teacher presents a simple six-step tactic:

1. Recognize the unknown word ("it").
2. Picture what is happening in the passage (Jim and Ken need to dry out the airplane).
3. Relate the unknown word to the picture.
4. Select the word that is represented by the unknown ("airplane").
5. Check your answer by substituting the word you have selected for the unknown word and saying the passage out loud ("The *airplane* was wet so they had to use a towel to dry the *airplane*").
6. State the relationship ("In this sentence it refers to 'airplane'").

This procedure for clarifying anaphoric referents is explained in some detail by Carnine and colleagues (1997).

---

## Specific Teaching Recommendations

Discussions about reading practice, and comprehension in particular, often seem to be more political than empirical (Adams, 1991; Guskey & Oldham, 1997; Vaughn et al., 1998). This is because such discussions often center on controversies introduced, not by contradictory data but by contradictory interpretation and speculation. Much of this represents a classic confusion of curriculum and instruction. We are proponents of direct (hands-on) instruction because we are working in a deficit model. This text is *not* about initial instruction. The student addressed in this text has already had some sort of initial instruction—and it has failed. The goal of remedial and special education is to overcome this initial failure by changing instruction and accelerating the student through the curriculum. This may require elements of many instructional approaches (Council for Educational Development and Research, 1997). However, the goal can only be accomplished through highly focused and intentional interventions (Palincsar, 1990; Zigmond, 1997). It is up to the

teacher to arrange this focus. It is also up to the teacher to make sure the object of this focus, the curriculum, is worth the student's attention.

### Teaching Recommendation 1: Active and Reflective Reading (the Balanced Approach)

This technique is applicable to all of the sample comprehension objectives presented above.

Every reader should spend lots of time reading. And this reading should be **active reading.** The active-reading approach includes all of the other recommendations in this section. A status sheet for active reading is presented in Appendix A.2.

Many readers seem to think they are meant to be the passive recipients of an author's message, and consequently they do not interact with the passage. These students view comprehension strictly as a memory task, and their goal is to try to store the entire passage for recall. This misunderstanding is particularly fostered when the only measures, or class activities for comprehension, they see are postreading questions. A passive view of comprehension is unfortunate for two reasons: (1) It places unrealistic demands on memory, and (2) it rules out the interaction of the student with the text by elevating the text above the interests and prior knowledge of the student.

Students who are active readers approach passages with an agenda. They do something as they read; for example, they may ask questions and attempt to answer them. In short, active readers employ most of the comprehension strategies reviewed in this chapter. Students who do not read actively need to be taught to use the comprehension strategies listed in Exhibit 8.1 and referred to in the list of comprehension objectives. These objectives are taught using strategic instruction (Lebzelter & Nowacek, 1999; Mathes et al., 1997; Reid & Stone, 1991) (see Chapter 4). One such tactic teaches students to recognize that the source of answers may be in either the text or in their own prior knowledge.

Active and reflective reading, therefore, is not a term that refers to a particular methodology. It is a term that refers to the flexible application of numerous tactics. To promote active and reflective reading, an instructor must teach students two things:

1. How to use particular devices for understanding text, and
2. That it is the use of these devices (that is, the tactics), not the act of finishing pages, that constitutes reading.

This is a different view of reading than the one portrayed by many teachers and consequently transferred to many students (Rich & Pressley, 1990).

Here is an example of a procedure that promotes active and reflective reading. In a cognitive training study, Raphael and Pearson (1985) taught typical and low-achieving students to determine sources of answers using this mnemonic: The answer to my question must be—

1. *Right There,*
2. *Think and Search,* and
3. *On My Own.*

Source 1, *Right There,* meant that words used to create the question and words used for the answer are in the same sentence *"right there."* Mnemonic 2, *Think and Search,* meant that the answer is in the text, but words used to create the question and those used for an appropriate answer will only be found by looking across sentences and possibly even paragraphs. Source 3, *On My Own,* meant that the answer is not found in the text—in which case the student should say "I have to find this answer on my own."

Here is an example of Raphael and Pearson's (1985) training materials.

*"Dana sat in an old wood rocking chair. She rocked harder and harder. Suddenly she found herself sitting on the floor!"*

*Right There:* What kind of chair did Dana sit in? (old wood rocking chair)

*Think and Search:* What did Dana do while sitting in the chair? (rocked harder and harder)

*On My Own:* Why did Dana find herself sitting on the floor? (rocked so hard the chair tipped over)

## Teaching Recommendation 2: Reciprocal Teaching

This technique is particularly applicable to **Comprehension Objectives 1, 2, 3, 6, 7, 8, 9, 11, 12, and 15.**

Reciprocal teaching generally refers to the popular device of having students take on the role of teacher. It is a procedure that, like cooperative learning and peer-mediated instruction, promotes student understanding by encouraging them to reformulate the content of the lesson (Antil et al., 1998). In reciprocal teaching, the teacher gives an explanation and then asks the student to repeat the explanation as if she were the teacher. The term also has a specific meaning in relation to the topic of reading comprehension.

"Reciprocal teaching of reading comprehension" refers to a particular set of skills and instructional routines developed in part by Day (1980) and packaged for research by Palincsar and Brown (1984). The approach has been picked up by several authors and modified into a general technique (Carnine et al., 1997; Gunning, 1998; Hermann, 1988). Although the practice includes instruction on questioning, clarification, and prediction, its most interesting aspect is aggressive instruction of summarizing. Skill at summarizing what has been read seems to be a fundamental component of both understanding and comprehension monitoring (Gajria & Salvia, 1992; Thistlethwaite, 1991).

The following information about reciprocal teaching has been drawn from the literature just cited. However, we have also modified it as a result of field testing.

In early reciprocal-teaching lessons, the teacher supplies students with these rules for summarizing passages (the rules assume that the student has been taught the concept of a topic sentence).

### Step 1: Find topic sentence

1.1 Look at first sentence.

1.2 If that doesn't work, look at last sentence.

1.3 If that doesn't work, search the paragraph.

1.4 If that doesn't work, use Step 2 to invent your own.

**Step 2: If a topic sentence can't be found, invent one.**

2.1 Delete unnecessary/trivial information.

2.2 Delete redundant information.

2.3 State the "big picture" (principle point of the passage).

2.4 Say it right (the summary must be stated as a proper sentence).

Once the rules have been presented, the teacher does not repeat this initial explanation but, at the beginning of each session, asks students to supply and explain the rules. After this opening review, the teacher then selects a student to act as instructor. This student (and each other student in turn) directs the group through the following sequence.

### Read

Everyone is given the same materials to read, *one paragraph at a time* (the paragraphs are shown on an overhead projector or cut out and put on separate sheets). The selections, which are read silently, are drawn from expository texts (a history book) and should be challenging to the students (that means they have to have something in them worth comprehending).

### Summarize

After the reading, the designated instructor attempts to make a statement summarizing the selection. The teacher compares this summary with the criteria listed below and supplies feedback. In early lessons, this feedback often comes by presenting a fully demonstrated summary. Whenever the teacher demonstrates the production of a correct model, the student is asked to repeat the example.

In later lessons, the teacher prompts the use of the summary criteria by saying things like "You seem to have included the big picture and all of the relevant information, but your summary has some redundant information in it. Try again without the redundant information." Prompts such as "This paragraph tells me that _____." may also be helpful. Praise is given for applying the rules, *not* for getting the right answer (in fact, there may be many correct summaries). For ex-

ample, "The whole thing isn't perfect but you really did a great job of stating the big picture!"

Here are some guidelines for monitoring the summary statements:

A. Be sure the student:

✓ Says what she is going to do (summarize).

✓ Finds or invents a topic sentence.

B. Monitor and adjust:

✓ Don't make up your own summary and then compare the student's summary to it. Evaluate the student's summary according to the use of the rules supplied here.

✓ If possible, label errors ("That's good, but you have some unnecessary information in it." or "That's all right so far but it's not a sentence. Try to say it right.").

✓ In early lessons, provide full model corrections that expand/include the student's attempt.

✓ In later lessons, use prompts or cues (start by saying "This paragraph tells me," "Another important piece of the paragraph is," or "Can you include that in your summary?")

C. Remember the principles of strategy and rule instruction:

✓ The answer is not what the lesson is about. You are teaching the procedure for finding the answer. Talk about, prompt, give feedback, and reinforce the procedure.

✓ Assure early, active use.

✓ Make your thinking public. Demonstrate and talk aloud as you work.

Here are some other activities that may be used to teach summarizing.

1. Select main idea: Show a complex picture. Then have students pick the part that represents the main action.

2. Select main idea: Give short stories with one main event and practice picking the foremost words (actions or outcomes).

3. Select main idea: Introduce passages with redundancy and irrelevant information.

4. Select topic sentence: Define topic sentence as the author's summary of paragraph.

5. Select topic sentence: Show that topic sentences can appear anywhere in a paragraph by providing practice selecting them in varying locations.

6. Invent topic sentences: Explain that not all paragraphs have topic sentences.

7. Invent topic sentences: Have the student read paragraphs twice and remember/state the essential point of the paragraph. Be sure she states it as a sentence.

### Question

After producing an acceptable summary, the student acting as teacher attempts to convert the summary into a main-idea question. The teacher may facilitate this conversion with prompts such as "Ask a question that begins with the word *what*." In this way, a summary that says "Many Tucson citizens of that day believed the only good wolf was a dead wolf" is converted into a question like "*What* did many Tucson citizens of that day think about wolves?"

The lead student then calls on other students to answer the main-idea question. She may also call on students to ask their own questions about particular events or characters in the passage. In all cases, the teacher encourages students to "Ask the sort of questions a teacher might put on a test." Students should also be taught to:

✓ Change the same summary sentences to questions using prompts *who, how, what, when, why*, etc.

✓ Change sentences to questions without prompt.

✓ Select from three choices the question that matches a paragraph (one distractor will require information not in the paragraph and one will address trivial information).

✓ Recognize the main idea (by summarizing) and then ask a question about it.

✓ "How can you add inflection to an existing topic sentence?"

✓ "Can you invent a topic sentence and add inflection to it?"

### Clarify

In this step, the lead student calls on group members to point out items in the passage that could require clarification. Often, these will include text-dependent referents, vocabulary, and especially pronouns (Mathes et al., 1997). However, clarification may also be requested for more complex or factual references ("In the last passage, to what time period does the phrase 'of that day' refer?") (McNamara, 1990). At the least, students should be prepared to clarify:

✓ Ambiguous pronominal references

✓ Unclear protagonists

✓ Vocabulary from context (particularly technical terms)

✓ Essential vocabulary (versus words that can be ignored)

✓ Unfamiliar expressions and metaphors

### Predict

Finally, the lead student calls on several members of the group to predict what might occur in the next passage (they can't look ahead because they are only given one paragraph at a time). These predictions are judged, and feedback/corrections are given, on their logical origin in the passage—not on whether they come true.

After following this sequence, the lead student calls on another student, and the routine is repeated.

When going through these lessons, you may find that the group only finishes a few passages a session. That is fine. The point is not to finish the story but to practice use of the strategies and rules.

The procedure is often used with groups of 5–8 students; however, it has been used with whole classes. To do that, break students into groups of three and have each group come up with its own summaries. These should be written out. Then go around the class having groups read their summaries for feedback. When they are finished, follow this process with questions, clarifications, and predictions.

The groups are asked to write out their reactions so that they don't start changing them as other groups report. Students who do not decode will be able to contribute and learn from these lessons if you read the passage on the overhead aloud. One other point: the biggest problem we have run into during any reciprocal-teaching lesson is that the students get interested in the passages and want to talk about them. You want them to practice the rules. So, tell them you will save a few minutes at the end of the lesson for comments and questions about the passage.

### Teaching Recommendation 3: Story Maps and Semantic Webbing

This technique is particularly applicable to **Comprehension Objectives 1, 2, 3, 7,** and **8**.

Semantic webs are described in some detail by several authors (Ford, 1995; Grossen & Carnine, 1991; Lebzelter & Nowacek, 1999; Lovitt, 1991). Semantic webbing is an instructional technique aimed in part at developing knowledge schema (Winn, 1991). Cognitive mapping is a device used to organize what is read. "Story maps organize a story visually so specific relationships of selected story elements are highlighted" (Reutzel, 1985, p. 400). A map of a narrative story could contain the following elements: (1) setting, (2) beginning, (3) reaction, (4) attempt, (5) outcome, and (6) ending (Mandler & Johnson, 1977).

Although maps are currently extremely popular for summarizing reading and planning composition (Gunning and D'Amato, 1998; McCagg & Dansereau, 1991), you should be aware that there is little research describing exactly who will benefit from their use, or which of the several types available are best (Dunston, 1992). For additional information, refer to Grossen and Carnine (1992) and Carnine et al. (1997).

### Teaching Recommendation 4: Prereading Questioning

This technique is particularly applicable to **Comprehension Objectives 1, 2, 8, 10, 12,** and **13**.

Prereading questioning is used to develop active and reflective reading as well as recognition of central and subordinate details in a passage. The question is given before the student reads. Then she reads specifically to answer the question. As a result, passage information will be interpreted in terms of that question. This technique is particularly successful if students are taught to develop their own questions. The simplest way to implement the approach is to take all of those end-of-chapter questions authors put in textbooks and give them to the student before she starts reading. For example, if you find yourself having difficulty comprehending this text, you should look at the questions at the end of each chapter before you read the chapter.

### Teaching Recommendation 5: Critical Reading

This technique is particularly applicable to **Comprehension Objectives 1, 2, 3, 9,** and **14**.

Students need to have the skills to:

1. Identify the author's conclusions
2. Determine what evidence is presented
3. Determine the trustworthiness of the author (by judging if he is qualified or biased)
4. Identify faulty arguments (such as tradition, improper generalization, and confusion of correlation with cause)

Some time ago, experimental work by Patching et al. (1983) demonstrated that instruction in these critical reading skills improves comprehension of low-achieving students. See Carnine et al. (1997) for a thorough explanation of this critical reading technique.

### Teaching Recommendation 6: Monitoring Meaning

This technique is particularly applicable to **Comprehension Objectives 1, 2, 3, 4, 5, 8, 11, 14,** and **15**.

Comprehension monitoring refers to the student's skill at tracking her understanding of the text. This is accomplished by continual self-inquiry using the question "Do I understand what I'm reading?" It is essential that a student realize when she is failing to understand, so that she will begin to use the problem-solving techniques of adjustment and clarification. When students fail to understand what is written, readers who successfully monitor their comprehension will reread confusing passages, slow their reading rate, refer to reference materials, and even question the text author's skill. Readers who do not monitor their comprehension will either continue to read difficult passages and experience compounded confusion—or give up. Here are some ways to develop comprehension monitoring.

Table tapping is a technique that is a straightforward modification of the specific-level procedure in Action 6: *assisted monitoring.* To employ it, simply follow the directions for assisted monitoring and then systematically move to larger text units. For example, instead of tapping immediately after a meaning violating error, tap when the student reaches the end of the sentence or paragraph in which the error occurred. The explicit direction that comes with each tap is to reread that unit of text. By requiring the student to reread the unit (word, sentence, or paragraph) and self-correct the error, you encourage the student to start finding the errors on her own. To put it another way, by extending the unit size, you are fading your monitoring assistance. This requires the student to increase her own monitoring.

Other ways to promote monitoring include asking questions prior to reading and emphasizing the need to search the passage for answers. Also, ask passage-dependent vocabulary questions (Rupley et al., 1999). Allow the student to practice reading with favorite stories, predictable stories, stories chosen by the student, and stories with experiences familiar to the student. Use rereadings (see Chapter 9). Embed nonsense material in the passage (or delete some important material) and reinforce the student for recognizing it. When reading errors do occur, judge their relationships to passage meanings. If the errors jeopardize meaning, talk the student through procedures for using context to correct the error. Several of these tactics are described in the section on blending and word analysis in Chapter 9. Teach the student to make summary statements about sentences, then paragraphs, then whole passages.

### Monitoring Reading Comprehension

Once you have selected an objective and instructional technique, you will need to monitor the instruction to determine if your teaching is effective (Deno, 1997). The best monitoring techniques are those using measures that reflect what you are teaching and are sensitive to learning. In the domain of reading comprehension, such measures are difficult to find.

We recommend that reading-comprehension instruction be monitored with oral-reading fluency samples. This general outcome measure should be given and summarized (charted) during each instructional session (Deno, 1997). Procedures for using this kind of monitoring are presented in Howell et al. (2000a). Remember, the only way to determine if an instructional approach is effective is to try it, take data, and let the student tell you if it works.

## Summary

Because reading comprehension/reaction is complicated and important, this has been a long, complex chapter—in fact, it is probably the most complex chapter in Part 2. And guess what—although the chapter is over, the topic of comprehension isn't. A quick look back at Exhibit 8.1 will remind you that there are plenty of enabling skills to be explained. These enabling skills are presented in the chapters that follow. As for this chapter, it began with an attempt to define comprehension and to explain some of the problems we encounter when trying to evaluate it. From there, Chapter 8 went into considerable detail regarding techniques for measuring comprehension skills and troubleshooting comprehension problems. The chapter presented survey-level tests, specific-level tests, comprehension objectives, teaching recommendations, and monitoring procedures.

# Chapter 9

# Decoding

*Arkady waited a moment or two, until he'd gotten control of his temper, and then began to explain, slowly and reasonably how the surest way of judging a man's intelligence was his ability to handle words.*

—Bruce Chatwin, The Songlines

## Step 1: Define Your Purpose

The importance of code for students with reading problems can be summed up this simply:

- Poor readers make more reading mistakes than good readers.
- These mistakes often include errors in decoding.
- Students should be taught the things they need to know.
- Competent readers know code.
- Problem readers do not know code.

Consequently, the purpose of this chapter is to guide decision making within the domain of text decoding. There is one survey-level procedure, several specific-level procedures, and teaching recommendations. By following these procedures, one should be able to select a number of objectives and the correct teaching recommendations for decoding.

## Step 2: Define the Thing to Be Measured

There are many ways to teach reading; although they may have different rationales and present different theoretical bases, most are essentially the same. This similarity is the result of the task itself. The task of reading requires students to view print and draw information from it. All reading methods present printed material, and all are expected to teach kids to deal with printed material through a process called decoding (or word recognition).

Decoding means breaking the printed code; that is, using the relationship between print and sounds to vocalize or process words. Decoding is based upon the alphabetic principle and grapheme-phoneme correspondence. Decoding can have nothing to do with meaning at all. For example, the word *smek* has no English meaning, but you can vocalize it because you can decode it. (When you are talking to a student, don't use the word *decode*, just say *read*.)

Adams (1990) undertook an exhaustive examination of the role decoding plays in literacy. This review led to a variety of important conclusions, including this one:

> " . . . approaches in which systematic code instruction is included along with the reading of meaningful connected text result in superior reading achievement overall, for both low-readiness and better prepared students" (p. 125).

Adams' efforts support the view that decoding is important for beginning readers. However, for the most part, this text focuses on remedial readers. How important is decoding to students who have not benefited from beginning reading instruction?

Carnine and colleagues (1997) are such strong believers in code instruction that they state " . . . virtually all the reading failure in the early grades could be avoided if teachers: (1) were given well-constructed code-emphasis instructional materials, and (2) received adequate on-the-job training in how to present reading instruction to groups" (p. 56).

Code content itself is not a mystery (Adams & Henry, 1997). However, as we are sure you must already know, there is a massive, and apparently endless, debate/war about whether or not this phonetic content should be taught (Stahl et al., 1998; Stanovich, 1994). Our only addition to this wall of rhetoric follows.

It is ironic that those who are against the explicit instruction of code are supporting formats of instruction that often leave students with poor decoding skills. These students do not become proficient at using code (they lack automaticity and take longer to use the code) because it is not taught to them. The irony is that, because they lack decoding skills, they are forced to spend *more* time thinking about code.

When nonreaders attack an unknown word, they use letter cues. This may be because other cues, such as word meaning and syntax, can only be drawn by readers with some facility at decoding. Students must know letter/cluster sounds and how to blend them to decode unfamiliar material. Decoding rate is so important that the lack of it accounts for a large portion of nonreaders (Englert et al., 1998; Stahl et al., 1998). Without rapid, accurate decoding, students will not use reading to acquire large amounts of information (imagine trying to decode this book at a rate of 50 words per minute). Because the ultimate goal of reading is to construct meaning from text, students who decode slowly, even if they understand what they decode, will learn less per time unit spent reading because they take in fewer ideas per minute than students who decode fluently. Thus, evaluators need to check the rate of decoding even when students pass other measures of comprehension (Markell & Deno, 1997).

### Perceptual Processes

Many assessments are still available to measure things that aren't really word recognition but are thought to be cognitive prerequisites for it. Auditory and visual discrimination are two popular examples of these skills. There is no question that discrimination of letters and letter sounds is necessary for decoding, but there are questions about the types of discriminations that are relevant. When students are asked to discriminate between the sounds of letters, some people say they are doing an *auditory discrimination* task. We think they are *discriminating between the sounds of letters*. Don't make general statements about someone having good or bad visual discrimination (or attention, memory, motivation). Instead, make statements about *what* the student does, or does not, know how to discriminate. For example, "Rebecca doesn't know how to tell a's from o's when they are in the middle of words." This kind of statement won't encourage anyone to try to teach visual discrimination (which is outside of the curriculum), but it might encourage someone to teach Rebecca *the critical differences between a's and o's.*

A typical visual-discrimination test supplies one letter, word, or shape and then asks the student to recognize it somewhere else. In the examples below, each format tests something that is in part visual, and each requires the student to make a discrimination. However, in all tests of this kind, it is important to look at the content (what is being discriminated). Example 1 is not reading, example 2 is reading.

**Example 1**
*Directions:* "Put an X over the one that is like the one in the box."

| one | ◯ | ▭ | one | △ |

**Example 2**
*Directions:* "Put an X over the one that is like the one in the box."

| one | on | only | one | tone |

When students are asked to discriminate between animal sounds, some people will say they are doing a prereading task. We think they are discriminating between animal sounds. Tests that sample things like geometric shapes and noises are dealing with content that is far removed from the decoding curriculum. Testing them is a waste of instructional time (Lloyd et al., 1998).

**Early Reading Skills** Work by Good (1999a) and Yopp (1988) suggests that there are early reading skills that are important to reading and that are teachable (therefore, they might need to be evaluated). This skill is linked to decoding success and can be taught as a part of early decoding instruction (Griffith & Olson, 1992; Stahl et al., 1998). The skills are referred to by various names including phonological awareness, awareness of print and sound, phonemic awareness or segmentation, and orthographic awareness. These will be briefly described here and will be covered in more depth as part of decoding Action 2. A list of this content can be found in Exhibit 9.1.

Although the list in Exhibit 9.1 gives the appearance of many isolated skills, we doubt that is the case. Many enabling skills, even if discrete, are most effectively acquired in tandem with more complex tasks. Right now, we think the evidence is clear that preliminary print knowledge and enabling phonological skills interact with, and are causally or reciprocally linked to, beginning reading (M. Sprick et al., 1998). In fact, we think they should be taught to all students in kindergarten and first grade. So, we want to encourage you to test these processes with young nonreaders. At the same time, we are not aware of research indicating that older students (2nd grade or up), who are having reading problems, will benefit from instruction in these early skills. It makes sense that, if these older students can't read and lack the early reading skills, they should be taught them. We just haven't found persuasive research to support, or reject, that idea. Besides, lots of things that make sense turn out to be wrong. (Admit it, this is a lot like a philosophy text, isn't it?)

## Step 3: Devise a Way to Make the Thing in Step 2 Observable

The format for testing word or sound recognition is pretty obvious. Most of the time you show the letter, cluster (morphograph, diphthong, or digraph), word, phrase, sentence, paragraph, or passage to the student and ask him to tell you what it says. Sometimes you may show several items, and then you say the sound and ask the student to indicate the cluster, word, phrase, sentence, paragraph, or passage that makes the sound. But there are several issues raised by these simple formats (and the interpretation of student responses).

### A Note on "Reading Levels"

In a few pages, we will address the practice of selecting reading passages for students. But before we do that, we need to make some points about

*Exhibit 9.1    Early Reading Skills.*

Directions:
1. Follow directions for each skill.
2. Whenever an error occurs, write down the exact content and conditions of the test.
3. Start with production. If the student does not produce answers, move to identification.
4. Record accuracy and summarize with "pass," "no-pass," or "unsure."

Record Accuracy

| | Identification | Production | Note Conditions/ Content of test |
|---|---|---|---|
| 1. Page conventions | | | |
|    1.1  Left to right | ——— | ——— | ——— |
|    1.2  Top to bottom | ——— | ——— | ——— |
|    1.3  Book conventions | ——— | ——— | ——— |
|    1.4  Page by page | ——— | ——— | ——— |
|    1.5  Front to back | ——— | ——— | ——— |
|    1.6  Right side up | ——— | ——— | ——— |
| 2. Book length | ——— | ——— | ——— |
| 3. Word length | ——— | ——— | ——— |
| 4. Word boundaries | ——— | ——— | ——— |
| 5. Sentence boundaries | ——— | ——— | ——— |
| 6. Letter names | | | |
|    6.1  Lower-case letter names | ——— | ——— | ——— |
|    6.2  Upper-case letter names | ——— | ——— | ——— |
| 7. Environmental print and logos | ——— | ——— | ——— |
| 8. Phonology with spoken language | | | |
|    8.1  Distinguish word in speech streams | ——— | ——— | ——— |
|    8.2  Delete words | ——— | ——— | ——— |
|    8.3  Blend word parts | ——— | ——— | ——— |
|    8.4  Segment words | ——— | ——— | ——— |
|    8.5  Rhyme | ——— | ——— | ——— |
|    8.6  Blend syllables | ——— | ——— | ——— |
|    8.7  Segment syllables | ——— | ——— | ——— |
|    8.8  Delete onset/rime or phoneme | ——— | ——— | ——— |
|    8.9  Discriminate same/different phonemes | ——— | ——— | ——— |
|    8.10 Segment and blend phonemes | ——— | ——— | ——— |

the muddled nature of "readability" levels. In some reading programs, the text material is controlled, so that neighboring passages are of somewhat equal difficulty (*Read Well* by M. Sprick et al. [1998] and *Reading Mastery* by Engelmann & Bruno [1988] are examples). But this is not true in all programs, and it is certainly not true of topical textbooks (history, social studies, biology) or the books lined up on a library shelf. It is important to keep this variability in mind, as it limits the degree to which conclusions based on one passage can be generalized to other passages.

Just as it is unsafe to generalize from one passage to another in the same book, it is often dangerous to generalize from one reading series to another. In a study by Beck and McCaslin, cited in Adams (1990), the instructional sequence of eight reading programs was compared. In the first half of first grade, the researchers found that one series taught 20 single consonants, whereas another taught only 7. With that much variability introduced before the kid's first winter vacation, imagine what the differences are by the time he reaches third grade.

The concept of grade level is not useful for instructional planning and can even be misleading (Hintze & Shapiro, 1997). In the case of standardized normative measures, grade level is designated according to the way the norming population reacts to the test items. Normative tests establish grade-level scores by giving items to students and calculating the average score of sample populations selected at each grade level. The average score obtained from the fourth-grade sample then becomes "fourth-grade level." On these reading tests, the resulting grade-equivalence scores may or may not have any relationship to the actual passage difficulty of the book the student picks up in his fourth-grade classroom. Such scores are so notoriously nonfunctional that the International Reading Association (as have many other professional organizations) called for an end to their use years ago. But their use continues because scores such as "Amando reads at the third-grade, 4th-month level" seem easy to understand. Especially, when it comes time to send reports home to parents. But reporting scores is not the same as communicating. So what should you do?

Well, when we were asked to come up with a parent reporting form for a school district, we devised the one shown in Exhibit 6.3. It is a single sheet that is sent home to the parent. On one side is an actual passage the student read for the report. On that passage, errors are marked and a slash is used to indicate how far the student got in 1 minute. The parents can read the passage at the same rate and make the same errors to find out what the student's reading sounds like and how fluent it is. On the other side of the sheet is a visual display of the student's performance relative to other students at his grade level. This side also shows his change during the year and his relative position to classmates. Finally, there is a clear statement about his performance and progress at the bottom. Summary procedures like this one are easy to understand and convey real information to a parent or teacher. This system defines third-grade reading as the average rate and accuracy of third-graders on a passage. Although it would be less availing for decisions about remediation, the passage used for this sort of summary need not even be from the student's grade. If you give a fifth-grade passage to third-graders, the most skilled readers will still score better than other third-graders (although they may not do very well), and the students with the most limited scores will still be at the bottom. In other words, if your goal is simply to rank students within a grade, class, district, or state, it doesn't matter a great deal what passage you use.

Passage levels for reading inventories and textbooks are typically set through the use of *readability formulas*. Often, these formulas are based on ratios between the number of words in a sentence and other characteristics like the number of syllables or the occurrence of unfamiliar words. The formulas—and there are over 1000 of them sampling more than 250 text variables—are under constant examination and modification. Although it does seem that passages with the same readability score are equivalent in some respect (whatever is summarized by the formula), it is less clear whether these similarities are meaningful or significant. Several authors have determined that the use of such formulas may even be detrimental to reading instruction. For example, Sabers (1992) notes that some of the original standards for grade level were determined by averaging scores derived from texts available in the 1940s. This yielded average levels of sentence length and word/syllable ratios for texts in the 1940s. Unfortunately, reading-text publishers adopted these levels as ceilings and insisted that subsequent books not exceed those averages. This had the effect of removing more difficult texts from the market and, as a result, effectively *"dumbed down"* (Bowen, 1984; Hintze & Shapiro, 1997) the entire body of classroom reading texts.

### Testing to Select Texts for Instruction

Because of the *basal reader* influence, it is not uncommon for teachers to believe that the key to teaching word recognition lies in the selection of

*Independent practice can be dangerous for low achievers.*

the right book. In reading jargon, this is called the search for the "instructional level." These teachers will ask things like "What book should Amando be in?" instead of "What skill does Amando need to be taught?" Consequently, there are many techniques for finding the "best" book for each student. The assumption behind these techniques is that there **is** a best book. That is a faulty assumption, and it is especially futile in the upper grades, where texts are designed for purposes other than reading instruction.

Remedial reading teachers should not test for the purpose of placing the student into a book or series of books. They should test for the purpose of placing the student within the sequence of decoding skills—the curriculum. Then they look for a book (or books) that include opportunities for instruction and practice on the skills the student

needs. A competent teacher/evaluator compares both the student *and* the materials with the curriculum.

### Testing with Isolation, Time, and Nonsense Words

At the specific level, evaluators will sometimes test sounds in isolation, not in a word. Whenever testing a skill in isolation, remember that you are asking the student to do something successful readers seldom do—decode individual letters. Testing decoding subskills in isolation is a classic example of how evaluation procedures may, at times, differ from teaching procedures (although these differences should never be in content). Sounds are best taught within words, but if they are tested within words, the other letter sounds may obscure or transform the way the student pronounces the target letter. This can distort your conclusions. (Similarly, passage-decoding tests are timed to test for skill mastery; however, teaching with timed decoding drills is not always a good idea.)

Timing and isolation are not the only testing procedures that are different from teaching procedures. Another technique is to test with *nonsense words*. Nonsense words (nok, noke, nook) are used to sample the student's skill at sounding and blending. Often, because of their limited skills, poor readers need to be tested on short words, not polysyllabic ones. However, these same readers may already know most short words as sight words (no, nose, noon). Therefore, to test their knowledge of sounds, you must either risk confusing the results with the complexity of longer words or with the novelty of nonsense words.

The risk of using nonsense words can be diminished by taking steps to inform the student that, although the words aren't real, he should decode them as if they are. If the student reads the nonsense words, one can be sure he is doing so based on his skill at sounding and blending. Although nonsense words *make sense* for testing pure grapheme/phoneme decoding, they make no sense for teaching reading.

**Error analysis** allows an evaluator to gain insight into the thought processes of the student. It is very popular among reading evaluators and is the backbone of most of the so-called *informal reading inventories* as well as processes like "running records." It does, however have a couple of problems.

One problem with categorizing errors is that the evaluator needs some sort of error classification system. Such systems (including those in this chapter) seldom enjoy the empirical support their popularity indicates. The same can be said for efforts to categorize spelling errors. Therefore, the same error might be categorized several different ways. This variability in classification schemes confuses evaluation. (Some reading specialists don't even call the process error analysis. They prefer the term *miscue,* as they think it more accurately reflects the student's correct application of his own thought process—whereas error implies that the student has done something wrong. Therefore, one might conclude that, from a child-centered philosophy, "To error is human—but to miscue is divine.")

A second factor influencing the quality of error analysis is the thinking of individual evaluators. This is the problem of interrater agreement. Philosophical orientations aside, two different evaluators may disagree about what a student has done and, as a result, categorize the same error differently. For this reason, we recommend that you practice categorizing errors and receive feedback on your efforts.

A final problem with error analysis is that the errors a person makes depend in large part on the questions they are asked. All of the error-analysis procedures discussed in this text depend on the availability of an *appropriate error sample.* This is critical. The types of errors a student makes depends on the passage the student is reading and the directions you give. If the passage is too hard, the student will respond by making errors that reflect desperation and anxiety. If the passage is too easy, the errors will often be of little consequence, as they merely reflect attempts at efficiency. We recommend that error samples be drawn from passages the student reads with 80%–85% accuracy.

If you are making decisions about the student's relative accuracy among error types, you must count opportunities for errors as well as errors. For example, in this sentence, there are only two *probabilities* that you will <u>mis</u>read the mor-

phograph *pro,* but three chances to <u>mis</u>read *mis.* If you made a single <u>mis</u>error, you would be 67% correct for that sound. If you missed a single *pro,* your accuracy level for that sound would be 50%. Therefore, the common practice of making tally marks next to error categories and then intervening on the category with the most errors is simplistic and mistaken measurement. You must consider the opportunity for the error.

## Step 4: Conduct Assessment

## Step 5: Summarize Results

## Step 6: Make Summative and Formative Decisions

With decoding, these steps are recursive (occurring over and over). Therefore, they will be mixed together through the remainder of the chapter. The complete process is outlined in Exhibit 9.2. In this section, we are trying to make the thought processes of a skilled evaluator visible. Some of these steps that take paragraphs to describe take only seconds to accomplish.

Exhibit 9.2 illustrates the process for deciding what to teach in decoding. It's a flow chart and—once again—we recognize that these things will really annoy some readers. If you are one of those readers, take scissors and cut Exhibit 9.2 out of the book (this way you won't have to look at it, and you won't be able to resell the text!).

The decoding process illustrated in Exhibit 9.2 has seven specific-level **actions** designed to answer these questions:

✓ Is the student's reading acceptable? **Action 1**

✓ Does the student know early reading skills such as awareness of the basic concepts of print and sound? **Action 2**

✓ If the student reads accurately but slowly, is his fluency constrained by lack of experience in reading quickly? **Action 3**

✓ Is the student's reading rate, or accuracy, impeded by poor decoding skills? **Action 4**

**Exhibit 9.2    Process of Decoding Evaluation.**

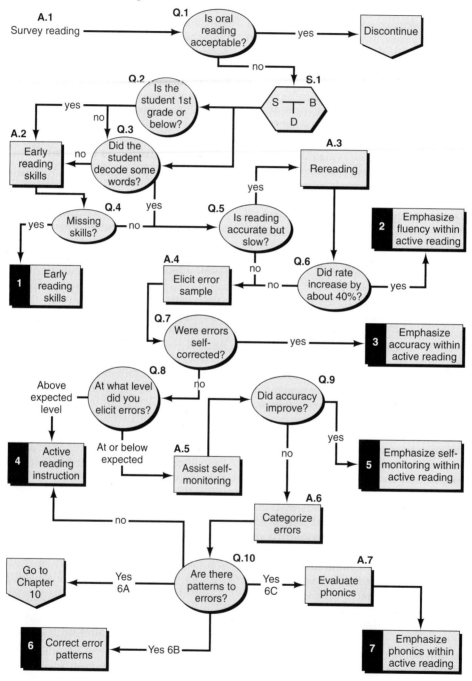

✓ Do the student's errors occur because he does not monitor his decoding or does not always make his best effort (therefore failing to consistently employ the decoding skills he has mastered)? **Action 5**

✓ Are error patterns so predictable that they indicate what sort of instruction the student should receive? **Action 6**

✓ If he needs phonics, which phonetic content should be taught? **Action 7**

### Action 1: Survey-Level Assessment of Decoding

A. **Interview** Interview the teacher using the "teacher interview/checklist" in Appendix A.3. This interview was developed by educators at the Heartland Area Education Agency 11 in Johnston, Iowa (Heartland Education Agency, 1996). The use of the interview may allow you to bypass portions of the process illustrated by the flow chart.

B. **Review** Review the materials used during reading instruction to see if they are suitable (this may be hard to tell until the evaluation has been finished).

C. **Observe** Watch the student during reading instruction. Pay particular attention to his task-related skills. Also, attend to the teacher's instruction (use the TIES II descriptors in Appendix A.13).

D. **Test** Survey testing involves oral reading of passages from the student's expected level (the level at which the student would decode if he had no decoding problem). As pointed out earlier, it's better to use multiple passages from texts the student will actually need to read than it is to trust the "levels" assigned to test passages. However, published tests with passages arranged according to levels of difficulty may also be used. The advantages of these tests (usually called reading inventories) are that they cover many levels quickly and they are often well-organized. Sometimes, they are preferable if the results are also going to be used for outside purposes (program evaluation, entitlement for a compensatory reading program).

### Directions

1. Collect at least three passages that the student would be expected to read if he had no problems in reading. Have copies for yourself and for the student. Each passage should be about 250 words long.

2. Set up a tape recorder.

3. Get a stopwatch.

4. You will need something to write with to code or score student responses. A calculator may also be useful for determining percentage scores.

5. Administer passages at the student's expected level. (Once again, this is the level at which any other student of this student's age is expected to decode. Don't decide to use a simpler passage because you think the student is a problem learner.) You may adjust the wording of these directions according to the age of the student and the type of passage. Say to the student: "I want you to read part of this story out loud. Read it as quickly and carefully as you can. If you come to a word you do not know, skip it. Please begin." Time the student for 1 minute and make a bracket after the last word decoded in the 1-minute time limit. As long as it isn't an overwhelming task, let the student finish the passage. As the student reads, mark all errors on your copy of the passage. It is not necessary to note different types of errors right now, but you should at least put a mark over them.

6. If the student pauses on a word for more than 3 seconds, mark the word and supply it to the student.

7. Any time a student clearly is unable to progress through the passage, and you perceive that the attempt is disagreeable for the student (he has tipped over in his chair and started to weep), base an estimated score on the initial effort and then discontinue and go to an easier passage.

## Score Interpretation

To establish decoding rate, count the number of words decoded correctly and the number of word errors during the first minute (up to your bracket mark). Omissions are not errors. To obtain the student's passage accuracy, divide the words correct by the total number of words decoded.

Compare the student's scores with the criteria for acceptable accuracy and fluency shown in the passage-reading summary form in Exhibit 9.3. The criteria in Exhibit 9.3 are behavioral expectations based on a review of research into functional skill levels. They are not norms. However, they are consistent with the expectations established by studies that report rates for successful students.

If the student is accurate and scores within 15% of the fluency criterion, consider readministering the test with another passage. Some students have never been asked to decode a passage at rate before.

## Qualitative Interpretation

Register if the student is accurate and fast, accurate and slow, or inaccurate. Respond to the following questions according to the student's performance and the criteria for the passage.

### Question 1

Is the student's reading acceptable?
Determine the accuracy (percentage correct) and fluency (rate).
Is it at or above the criterion for grade level?
If YES, decoding is acceptable; discontinue.
If NO, go to Summary 1.

### Summary 1

Use the directions at the bottom of Exhibit 9.3, or the general discrepancy summary in Exhibit 7.3, to determine the discrepancy. Removal of this discrepancy will be your long-range goal.
Go on to Questions 2 and 3.

### Question 2

Is the student in the 1st grade or <u>lower</u>?
If YES, then go to Action 2.
If NO, then go to Question 3.

### Question 3

Did the student read words in a way that demonstrated use of some decoding skills?
Be careful here. If the student recognized a few sight words and called them out correctly, it doesn't count for this part of the procedure. It's nice, but not what we're after right now. What you need to decide is whether the student actually used phonetic skills and sounded out words.
If YES, then go to Question 5.
If NO, test early reading skills using Action 2.

## Action 2: Early Reading

The following is a very brief description of how to assess a student on both phonological knowledge and preliminary print knowledge. You will want to attend closely to these evaluation techniques, as the same procedures are also used for instruction. In addition, a portion of a fully researched test over this content, the DIEBELS (Good, 1999), is included in Howell et al. (2000a).

### Evaluation Techniques

The assumption that a student is missing awareness of the basic reading processes is most often made for young readers. As with any assessment, and especially with the assessment of young children, the evaluator needs to be mindful of the challenge of obtaining a reliable and valid sample of the student's knowledge and skills. The procedures we describe here can be integrated into routines for group play or instruction if you have reason to think that such contexts are more likely to support a young child in displaying what he knows. (What might cause you to think that? Information that the student is unresponsive when alone or when asked to do things he considers "little kid stuff.")

If the student doesn't spontaneously produce the targeted skills, you will need to probe. This will often be accomplished by turning the assessment into an "identify" (select-response) task.

For each task, present ten or more opportunities. If the student makes an error, provide assistance by modeling the correct response before presenting the next item. The purpose of this assessment is not simply to determine if the stu-

**Exhibit 9.3    Passage Summary Sheet with Criteria for Acceptable Performance.**

**Directions:** For each passage used, record the number of corrects and errors per minute. Also record the accuracy. For each passage, check the rate and accuracy status (pass, unsure, or no-pass) for each curriculum level.

| | Expected Rate | | Obtained Rate | | | Expected Accuracy | Obtained Accuracy | Status |
|---|---|---|---|---|---|---|---|---|
| | Correct | Error | Correct | Error | Status | | | |
| 8 | 140 | 0–7 | _____ | _____ | _____ | 100–95% | _____ | _____ |
| 7 | 140 | 0–7 | _____ | _____ | _____ | 100–95% | _____ | _____ |
| 6 | 140 | 0–7 | _____ | _____ | _____ | 100–95% | _____ | _____ |
| 5 | 140 | 0–7 | _____ | _____ | _____ | 100–95% | _____ | _____ |
| 4 | 140 | 0–7 | _____ | _____ | _____ | 100–95% | _____ | _____ |
| 3 | Early 110 | 0–7 | _____ | _____ | _____ | 100–95% | _____ | _____ |
| | Late 140 | | | | | | | |
| 2 | Early 70 | 0–5 | _____ | _____ | _____ | 100–95% | _____ | _____ |
| | Late 100 | | | | | | | |
| 1 | Early 30 | 0–3 | _____ | _____ | _____ | 100–95% | _____ | _____ |
| | Late 50 | | | | | | | |

Expected level (current grade placement)

Curriculum level (highest level at which mastery criterion is met)

**Rate discrepancy at instructional level:**

Obtained rate_____Expected rate_____

Divide the largest number *by* the smallest = rate discrepancy_____

**Accuracy discrepancy at instructional level**

Obtained accuracy_____% Expected accuracy_____

Divide largest number *into* the smallest = accuracy discrepancy _____

Label discrepancies × if they should increase or ÷ if they should increase.

*Source:* Howell K. W., Zucker S. H. & Morehead M. K. (2000). *MASI-R: Remedial Screening Test.* Applied Research and Development Center, College of Education, Western Washington University, Bellingham, WA 98225-9090: Reprinted with permission.

dent has the skill. It is also to determine how much assistance/instruction the student is going to need. Preliminary print and sound knowledge can be observed in classroom contexts as well as directly assessed (Cunningham & Stanovich, 1990; Hintze & Shapiro, 1997; Nation and Hulme, 1997). Assessment can be incorporated into story-reading activities, especially the rereading of a familiar story. With students who have almost no reading skills, you may need to make use of pseudo-reading ("pretend" reading). In these cases, you sit with the student and read with him as you would with a toddler, carefully providing those segments of the task the student cannot supply. In this way, you will move through the material as the child "reads," even if the only contribution he makes is to turn the pages.

Each of the areas of content are in Exhibit 9.1. As you check each area, note the status of the student's skills. Be sure to include comments regarding the exact content (sound or print convention) of any errors.

### Action 2: Early Reading Skills

#### Directions

There are two categories of content presented: preliminary print knowledge and basic phonology. Read the explanations and carry out the assessment processes.

#### Preliminary Print Knowledge

The Greek alphabet (on which all modern western alphabets are supposed to be based) originated about 6,000 years ago. Humans first left their mark on the wall of a cave about 50,000 years ago. So it took 44,000 years to get the idea that agglutinated marks can represent sounds to go into the body of human knowledge (we aren't slighting the Sumerians, we just wanted to stick with the people who gave us words like "agglutination"). Also, it has only been within the last 100 years that anyone other than an elite few were expected to achieve "literacy."

So, it would seem that the idea that symbols represent sounds is a big one. We need to realize this when we set off to teach a student to read within 3 years.

#### Book and Page Conventions
Observe to see if the student, in "pretend" reading or in "reading with you," follows book and page conventions, especially when pretend-reading a familiar or memorized book.

Does the student consistently hold the book right-side up? start at front and go to the back? go page by page? start at the top of the page and go to the bottom? scan from left to right? When a page is skipped in a familiar story to arrive at a favorite passage or illustration, the skipping is not an error. It actually documents considerable awareness of text.

Playfulness by the evaluator may be useful (hold the book upside down, start at the back page, read the last sentence on a page first) especially if you pause, look confused, and (while holding the text sideways) ask "Now why can't I read this?"

#### Book Length
Show the student two books and ask which will take longer to read. (Try to trick the student into accepting a 90-second story time when he is accustomed to 15 minutes. When he notices, tell him that's the same as the difference between a long and a short book.)

#### Word Boundaries and Length
Ask the student to "finger-point" as you read each word (Ehri & Sweet, 1991). This process entails following the words in the book with his finger while you read. Before you ask him to try, demonstrate by using a memorized or familiar story.

#### Sentence Boundaries
Ask the student to show you the beginning of a sentence and the end. If necessary, prompt with information that "a sentence begins with a capital and ends with period" and so on. You may use a story the student has memorized or one of the student's own stories that you have transcribed.

#### Letter Names
Assess letter names in the context of story reading or by using letter cards. Ask the student to name all 52 (upper and lower) in an unordered presentation. This presentation can occur over several assessment/instructional sessions if necessary.

#### Environmental Print and Logos
When a child chants "cheeseburger, cheeseburger" four blocks from McDonald's, and all you can see is a tiny scrap of gold through a break in the billboards, you know the student has started processing symbols. Recognition of Pepsi logos, stop signs, and seat-belt warning lights are all indicators of symbolic learning. The presence of this knowledge should be noted, but if it is missing it does not need to be taught.

**Basic Concepts of Phonology**    Phonology can also be assessed in the context of group play or instructional activities. The following procedures are used with spoken language and are <u>not</u> paired to print symbols. If <u>you</u> have a speech defect, or a particularly strong regional accent that differs from the child's, get someone else to carry out these assessments for you. Summarize the results, in terms of percent right and wrong, on Exhibit 9.1.

**Distinguish Words from Other Words in Spoken Language**    Pick a familiar word to be the "word-of-the-day." If the word today is *jump*, ask the student to "raise a finger each time I say *jump*. Listen." [Pause]. "*Jump*, frog, *jump*." Check for identification with several words.

**Delete Words from Sentence**    Pick a familiar sentence. Then say "Brown bear, brown bear, what do you see?" without the word *see*. The student is expected to respond by providing the missing word. (*Brown Bear*, by Martin & Carle, 1983).

**Blend Word Parts**    Treat this task like a guessing game. Using *rainbow*, say "Today's word is /rain/-/bow/. What is our word today?" Expect the student to combine the parts and say *rainbow*. Or, "I am thinking of a word. Listen. /Help/-/ful/. What word?" Use a variety of words, including compound words and other multi-syllable words. Provide ten or more words. Continue to check during instruction until you are confident the student can blend syllables into words.

**Segment Words**    In this procedure, you want students to indicate the number of syllables in a word. Have students clap as they say words to indicate each syllable (<u>speech</u> syllable). If your student has trouble clapping, you can also use tapping, moving small blocks into a pile, or raising fingers as indicators for the syllable count. Some research suggests the use of compound words for initial assessment (rainbow: /rain/-[clap], /bow/-[clap]; football: /foot/-[clap], /ball/-[clap]). Other work indicates that using students' names is a good way to model how to

play the game. For example, "Listen—I am going to clap for the parts of my name: /Ma/-[clap], /duh/-[clap], /ka/-[clap]. Now listen while I clap for your name: /Vic/-[clap], /tor/-[clap]."

After the student learns the game, provide unprompted turns. When you speak, do not exaggerate syllable boundaries in the unprompted turns. Include one-, two-, and three-syllable words. Assess the skill over ten or more words and continue to check until you are confident the student has the idea of segmenting words.

**Rhyme**    Ask the student to indicate if words rhyme. Model with two or more pairs of words. Include at least one pair of words that do not rhyme:

> "Listen—these rhyme: mat-bat-car-far-phone-cone."

> "These do not rhyme: fall-car-boy-big."

> "Tell me if the next words I say rhyme."

Assess the student with at least ten pairs, half of which do not rhyme. Note how many the student correctly identifies.

**Blend Syllables**    Speech syllables have a beginning sound called the *onset* and an ending sound called a *rime* (Treiman, 1985). In this assessment, you want to see if a student can put the two together. The assessment for this skill parallels the procedure for blending words.

> "Listen—I am going to say parts of a word. Then I will put the word together. /Mmm/-/at/, *'mat.'* Listen again: /h/-/orse/, *'horse.'* Here is another one: /b/-/ig/, *'big.'* Your turn. I will say the parts and you put them together."

> Present ten or more and note accuracy.

**Segment Syllables**    Segmenting syllables is analogous to segmenting words. In syllable segmentation, you want to see if the student can separate the initial part of a syllable, the onset, from the final part of a syllable, the rime.

Demonstrate a "game" where you start with a syllable and then segment it. Then present the student with a syllable.

> "Listen—I can make two parts. *'Rat,'* /Rrr/-/at/; *'Sam,'* /Sss/-/am/, *'far,'* /fff/-/ar/; *'chair,'* /ch/-/air/. Now I will say one part, you make two parts."

> Teacher—*"hat"*; Student—"/hhh/-/at/."

> Teacher—*"lake"*; Student—"/lll/-/ake/."

Record accuracy and note any error patterns.

**Delete Onset/Rime or Phoneme**    In this technique, you say a word and then designate a portion (onset, rime, or phoneme) that you would like omitted. For example, the teacher says, "Say *Sam* without *am*" and the student replies *"sss."*

Be sure to ask for deletions from different portions of the word and to ask that a range of units be deleted. Note accuracy and any patterns to errors.

**Distinguishes Phoneme from Phoneme**    Using colored blocks as indicators for same and different, model the following procedures. Place two blocks of one color and two blocks of another color in front of you. Say "/mmm/, /mmm/," and then move two blocks of the same color forward and say "/mmm/ and /mmm/ are the same." Present several more two-phoneme combinations, some of which are the same and some of which are different. (When you present two that are different, move forward two different colors.) Next, ask the student to move the correctly colored blocks forward to indicate same or different when you say two sounds. After the student is successful with two sounds in isolation, increase the difficulty to words or pseudo-words with one sound that is different /mam/ (student moves two colors forward) and then three that are different /bat/ (student moves three colors forward). Record accuracy.

**Segmenting Phonemes and Blending Phonemes**    Use the procedure you employed to assess syllable blending and syllable segmentation. Break the stimulus item into phonemes rather than the onset and rime you used for the syllable task (*hat* = /h/, /a/, /t/).

### Score Interpretation

If you use the DIEBELS, there are established scoring conventions and standards for these procedures in Howell et al. (2000a). Additionally, Yopp (1992a) has noted that younger students generally are less than 70% accurate at many of the phoneme tasks. However, we have found that students *who read successfully,* even those in kindergarten, are almost always 100% accurate at these very basic skills. Therefore, we would be concerned about any error made by a school-age child. (Remember that the only reason you got to this content was that the student has failed to read simple words.)

### Qualitative Interpretation

Review the results recorded on Exhibit 9.1. Pay particular attention to the comments.

### Question 4

Are there missing concepts and/or skills?

> If NO, then go to Question 5.

> If YES, then note those concepts or skills on which the student seems to need instruction and teach them, using the objectives and techniques outlined in **Teaching Recommendation 1.**

### Question 5

Does the student decode accurately but slowly?

> Use the criteria in Exhibit 9.3 to answer. If YES, then go to Action 3.

> If NO, then go to Action 4.

### Action 3: Rereading

The purpose of this test is to determine if the student reads accurately but his fluency is constrained by a lack of experience in reading quickly. This will be true if the student's oral-decoding rate (words correct per minute) increases when he has had an opportunity to practice decoding the material. Rereading provides practice and (because the student is accurate) allows the student to learn the content of the passage during the first reading. So, he should read the same passage faster a second time.

### Directions

1. Select a new passage at which the student fails to meet the *rate* criterion but is *+90% accurate.*

2. Say to the student, "I want you to read this story aloud. Begin."

3. Note where the student is after 1 minute (]), but don't stop him. Allow him to keep reading until he has doubled the amount decoded in the first minute. Then point to the beginning of the passage and say, "Now I want you to read it aloud again as quickly and carefully as you can. Are you ready? [pause] Begin."

4. Time the student for 1 minute. Say "Thank you" to stop the reading after the minute is up.

5. Count the number of corrects-per-minute on both readings. Do the same for errors.

6. Record the rate of correct words per minute and error words per minute.

### Interpretation Guidelines

Compare the student's rate during the initial reading and his rate during the timed rereading. Compute the percentage increase by dividing the initial rate by the rereading rate and subtracting the result from 100 (assuming the second reading was faster). For example, if the original rate was 60 and the rereading rate was 80, the improvement was $60/80 = 100 - 75 = 25\%$.

### Question 6

Is the student's reading rate 35%–40% or more than it was on the first decoding?

If YES, then go to **Teaching Recommendation 2.**

If NO, then the student may be making errors and self-correcting them subvocally (so you aren't aware of it). Go to **Action 4.**

## Action 4: Elicit Error Samples

### Directions

1. Select a 250-word passage on which you estimate that the student will be about 80%–85% accurate. Use the results from the survey oral-reading test to help make your selection. You will need about 25 errors for students in grade 1; at grades 2 and above, at least 50 errors are recommended.

2. Disregard the student's decoding rate for this measure.

3. Point to the passage and say, "I want you to read these words aloud. Take your time and read them as *carefully* as you can. Try all the words. Ready? Begin."

4. If, after the first 20 words, the student is not near 80%–85% accuracy, discontinue and select another passage.

5. Continue moving up or down in passage difficulty until you find a passage on which the student is about 80%–85% accurate.

6. You may end up categorizing these errors if you get to Action 6, so you should take a look at Exhibits 9.4 and 9.5, as well as the coding directions in Action 6, now to be sure you mark errors in a way that will let you fill out Exhibit 9.4.

### Question 7

Were errors that violated the meaning of the passage self-corrected (that means without a teacher prompt)?

If YES, then go to **Teaching Recommendation 3.**

If NO, then go to **Question 8.**

### Question 8

What level of passages were required to elicit 80%–85% errors?

If *above expected*, then go to **Teaching Recommendation 4.**

If *at or below expected*, then go to **Action 5.**

**Exhibit 9.4    Categorizing Decoding Errors.**

### Action 6a: Error Category Checklist for Meaning Violations

**Directions:**

- Take a 250-word sample of student reading. The student must be very close to 80–85% accurate.
- Say "Read this passage carefully. Ready? Begin."
- Tally *each* error under the appropriate category.
- Circle the error if it is self-corrected.
- An error violates meaning if it has the *potential* to impair the student's understanding of the author's message.
- Do *not* tally mispronunciations of proper nouns.
- Determine the % of total errors for each category.

Total errors:  _____

| | Category 1<br>Violates Meaning | Category 2<br>Does Not Violate Meaning | Category 3<br>Cannot Classify |
|---|---|---|---|
| % of total errors this category | _____ | _____ | _____ |
| % of errors this category self-corrected | _____ | _____ | _____ |

### Action 6b: Error Pattern Checklist

**Directions:**

- Use a 250-word passage.
- Compare each error in the passage with the following checklist (ignore errors on proper names).
- Make a mark next to the category in which the error seems to fit.
- Come up with a total of all errors.
- Identify the categories in which most errors occur.
- List objectives, teach, and continue to monitor changes in error patterns.

| Error Categories | Tally Errors | Examples Using "We want to have . . ." |
|---|---|---|
| Mispronunciations | | |
|     Errors are substitutions of real words | ____ | (We want to have . . . ) |
|     Errors are not real words | _____ | (We hant to have  . . . ) |
|     Errors are phonetically similar to stimulus word | _____ | (We went to haven't  . . . ) |
| Insertions | | |
|     Insertions are contextually appropriate | _____ | (We still went to have  . . . ) |
|     Insertions are contextually inappropriate | _____ | (We and went to have  . . . ) |
| Omissions | | |
|     Omission affects passage meaning | _____ | (We went to  . . . ) |
|     Omission does not affect meaning | _____ | (We went have  . . . ) |
| Hesitation | _____ | (We went to have  . . . ) |
| Repetition | | |
|     Repeats a portion of target word | _____ | (We went to have  . . . ) [3 repetitions of /w/] |
|     Repeats preceding word | _____ | (We went to have  . . . ) [3 repetitions of "to" probably while trying to figure out "have"] |
|     Repeats preceding words or phrases | _____ | (We went to have  . . . ) [3 repetitions of "we went to"] |
| Punctuation | | |
|     Does not pause at punctuation | _____ | ( . . . the store. But it  . . . ). |
|     Pauses at end of lines without periods or commas. | | |
| Intonation | | |
|     Does not use appropriate intonation. | | |
| Self-corrects | | |
| Other comments/observations should be written below | _____ | (we went to haven't) |
| *Question* | | *Recommendation* |
| 1. Are there clear patterns of errors? | | If yes, correct the erroneous pattern by targeting it as an instructional objective |

**Exhibit 9.4** Continued

### Action 6c: Decoding Content Checklist

*Directions:*

- Take a 250-word sample.
- Decide what category each error is from and tally it in the "error" column.
- Count the number of opportunities for <u>each</u> type of error that occurred.
- Do not record more than two errors per word. If more than two errors were made on a word, categorize only the first two.
- Calculate the % of error per opportunity.
- List objectives, teach, and continue to monitor changes in error patterns.

|  | Opportunity | Error | % of Errors in Opportunities |
|---|---|---|---|
| Words: errors involving whole words |  |  |  |
| Polysyllabic words |  |  |  |
| • (polysyllabic) | ____ | ____ | ____ |
| Contractions |  |  |  |
| • (haven't, can't) | ____ | ____ | ____ |
| Compound words |  |  |  |
| • (into, football) | ____ | ____ | ____ |
| High-frequency words |  |  |  |
| • (do, make, yes) | ____ | ____ | ____ |
| Silent letters |  |  |  |
| • (hate, light, knit) | ____ | ____ | ____ |
| Units: errors involving combined letter units |  |  |  |
| Morphographs |  |  |  |
| • (pre, ing, im, less) | ____ | ____ | ____ |
| Beginnings (prefixes) |  |  |  |
| • (be, post, sub) | ____ | ____ | ____ |
| Endings (suffixes) |  |  |  |
| • (able, ing, ment) | ____ | ____ | ____ |
| R-controlled vowels |  |  |  |
| • (er, ir) | ____ | ____ | ____ |
| Vowel combinations (digraphs) |  |  |  |
| • (ai, ay, ee) | ____ | ____ | ____ |

| | Opportunity | Error | % of Errors in Opportunities |
|---|---|---|---|
| Consonant combinations (digraphs) | ___ | ___ | ___ |
| • (sh, kn, ph) | | | |
| CVC words | ___ | ___ | ___ |
| • (bag, pot, fed) | | | |
| Conversions: errors involving sound modification | | | |
| Double consonant words | ___ | ___ | ___ |
| • (written, butter) | | | |
| Vowel + e conversions | ___ | ___ | ___ |
| • (bite = bit, mope = mop) | | | |
| Individual letters: errors involving individual letters and sounds | | | |
| Vowels | ___ | ___ | ___ |
| Consonants | ___ | ___ | ___ |
| Capitals | ___ | ___ | ___ |
| Lower case | ___ | ___ | ___ |
| Manuscript | ___ | ___ | ___ |
| Cursive | ___ | ___ | ___ |

| Question | Recommendation |
|---|---|
| Are there identifiable problems of content? | Is yes, target it as an instructional objective. |

*Source:* Howell K. W., Zucker S. H. & Morehead M. K. (2000). *MASI-R: Remedial Screening Test.* Applied Research and Development Center, College of Education, Western Washington University, Bellingham, WA 98225-9090: Reprinted with permission.

**Exhibit 9.5   Example for Scoring a Reading Passage.**

          *pant*         *spinny*                            *Winter  c*

The yucca is a desert plant. It has long, spiny leaves. Once a year, it bears beautiful white flowers.

*These*     *loom*                        *This*        *sed*

The flowers bloom only at night or on a very dark day. The flowers produce seeds for more yucca plants.

               *the*           *parking*    *mother*     *mother*     *girls*

The yucca could not produce seeds without its partner, the yucca moth. The yucca moth has only one goal

             *pace C*    *egg*              *all*    *mother*

in life. Its goal is to find a safe place to lay its eggs. The yucca plant and the yucca moth became partners

because each one had something the other needed.

*Source:* Howell K. W., Zucker S. H. & Morehead M. K. (2000). *MASI-R: Remedial Screening Test.* Applied Research and Development Center, College of Education, Western Washington University, Bellingham, WA 98225-9090: Reprinted with permission.

### Action 5: Assisted Self-Monitoring

The procedure is designed to test the possibility that the student makes errors because he is consistently failing to employ the decoding skills he *has* mastered. The assumption here is that a student may have the skills required to decode a passage but does not use them. In some cases, this could be because the student is not monitoring his own reading. There is, however, another related explanation.

This will not sound overly theoretical, but it is our experience that students sometimes fail to decode accurately because they don't think anyone really cares if they do. The research tells us that in many classrooms, reading is unmonitored and not motivating (Baumann & Ivy, 1997). Additionally, reading assignments sometimes seem to emphasize the completion of pages over the quality of reading. Under such conditions, it is not difficult to imagine that even the most conscientious of students might occasionally decide to blow off a page or two, a book or two, or a <u>testing session</u>. Their errors, in such circumstances, would fall into the "know/display" category, and it would be a mistake to spend much time analyzing them.

**Action 5** is designed to answer this question: "Do the student's errors occur because he does not monitor his decoding or does not always make his best effort (therefore failing to consistently employ the decoding skills he has mastered)?" However, before we get to the actual test, there is an alternative procedure for answering the same question with less effort. We call it the "pep talk" technique.

Tell the student that you are interested in finding out how long it takes him to read a passage *correctly*. Tell him it is important that he do his *best* work. Emphasize the importance of *reading accurately* and your own need to get good information about his decoding skills. If you know that the student has experience with some form of reinforcement program, then you may want to offer a *reward* for his best efforts. As he reads, don't help him. The idea is to get the student to try.

If you see a 50% or better improvement in accuracy on a passage of the same difficulty as the one you used in **Action 4,** you can skip **Action 5** and go right on to **Question 9.** If not, finish this action.

**Action 5** is the same as **comprehension Action 4**. Therefore, these directions are considerably reduced. However, the interpretation guidelines are somewhat different.

### Directions

1. Select a passage that the student reads without expected accuracy.

2. Confirm that the student *does not* self-correct errors that violate passage meaning.

3. Tell the student, "I want you to read this passage. Whenever you make an error I'm going to tap the table with my pen. When I tap the table, I want you to fix the error." Have the student continue to decode the passage. When he makes an error that violates meaning, immediately tap the table with a pen or your finger. Do not wait.

### Interpretation Guidelines

### Question 9
"Were the errors immediately corrected?"

If YES, Then use **Teaching Recommendation 5.**

If NO, then go to **Action 6.**

### Action 6: Error Analysis

The purpose of this SLP is to answer the question "Are error patterns so predictable that they indicate what sort of instruction the student should receive?"

The decoding sample collected in **Action 4** (assuming the student's accuracy was between 80% and 85%) is used for these analyses. Employ *all three* of the procedures (6a, 6b, and 6c) with each student. It is permissible, and even a good idea, to categorize a single error as many ways as logic will permit (and try not to get confused by the fact that 6a, 6b, & 6c are <u>all</u> in Exhibit 9.4).

Directions

### Action 6a: Meaning Violations

This analysis is designed to answer the question "Do errors in decoding seem likely to impair the student's understanding of the text?" (errors that reflect a lack of attention to, or missing skills needed to construct meaning from, context). These errors are likely to interfere with understanding. They can be differentiated from those that are consistent with context (not likely to interfere with meaning).

1. Use the passage you found in **Action 4.** Make sure you are familiar with the passage. Reread it if necessary.

✓ Record the student's errors on your copy of the passage.

✓ Your efforts at categorization will involve the use of Exhibit 9.4, so take a look at it and be sure you can mark errors in a way that will let you fill out Exhibit 9.4. Exhibit 9.5 illustrates this system of error recording.

✓ Use a tape recorder to confirm your scoring.

✓ When the student makes a mistake, write what he said directly above the words as they appear in the passage. Circle omitted words. Indicate insertions and write in the insertion. Mark hesitations with an <u>H</u>. Underline repeated words, phrases, or portions of words <u>each</u> time they are repeated. Mark the error type and then write <u>SC</u> next to any errors the student self-corrects. Because they reflect the student's awareness of his own reading, and because they are something you should promote, it is important to register all self-corrections.

✓ Be sure to jot down whether the student reads with appropriate intonation, attends to punctuation, or makes any relevant comments about his decoding.

2. Use the meaning-violation tally sheet (6a in Exhibit 9.4).

✓ Tally all errors.

✓ If an error is self-corrected, circle the tally mark.

✓ Tally repeated errors each time they occur.

✓ Tally errors under the following categories.

**Category 1** The error has the potential to impair understanding of the author's message; that is, the error does not make semantic or syntactic sense in the context of the passage. (Judge errors in terms of the story as written—not the story as read, as the student may have misread or modified it.) Don't tally repeated mispronunciations of proper nouns as meaning violations. If, however, the student substitutes proper nouns for each other, these should be counted.

**Category 2** The error does not violate the message of the author; that is, it is appropriate or does not significantly alter the context of the story.

**Category 3** Any error you are not certain how to classify; include in this type all errors involving the first mispronunciation of proper names.

1. Divide the number of errors in each category by the total errors tallied to get a percent for that category. Also record what percent of each category the student self-corrects.

2. Compute the number of errors in each category and summarize the results by percentage (such as 50% category 1, 40% category 2, 10% category 3).

### Action 6b: Error Patterns

**Action 6b** addresses the question "Do errors in decoding seem to fall into certain patterns (for example, insertions, substitutions, omissions)?"

Directions

1. Use the information you obtained in Action 4.

2. Categorize and tally the errors according to pattern type (hesitation, mispronunciation,

insertion) by using the **Action 6b** error-patterns tally form in Exhibit 9.4.

3. Compute the number of errors in each category and summarize the results by percentage (such as 50% category 1, 40% category 2, 10% category 3).

### Action 6c. Decoding-Content Checklist

Action 6c is used to answer the question "Do errors seem to occur whenever certain code content is present in the word?"

1. Use the information you obtained by following Action 4.

2. Note the phonetic content associated with each error. Use a form like the one in Exhibit 9.4 (part 6c) to tally the errors.

3. Compute the number of errors in each category and summarize the results by percentage (such as 50% category 1, 40% category 2, 10% category 3).

4. Identify those phonetic units or strategies that seem to account for a large proportion of errors.

### Score Interpretation

There are no established scoring conventions or standards for these procedures. Because *opportunities* for each error vary, and the skills are compensatory, criteria may not even be useful. (Just as the % you just calculated is not especially informative, because you found them using total words and not total opportunities for the error.) Still, the information of most value is obtained by comparing the frequency or proportion of errors in the different categories. These sorts of coding systems are generally unreliable, so have others code the same reading by listening to your tape. (Bad things could happen if we surround the student during testing.)

### Qualitative Interpretation

The student started out as an inaccurate or slow reader at the expected curriculum level. Performance did not improve after assisted self-monitoring or rereading. After eliciting an error sample in Action 4, you tapped tables and eventually ended up using Action 6a, 6b, and 6c to see if you could find patterns in the errors the student is making. You have now collected considerable information about the student's decoding. The next challenge is figuring out what it all means.

These actions will usually lead to recommendations for most kids. Those that are left often do not represent a significant challenge for evaluators. In fact, just listening to them read will often disclose all you need to know about them. But, if it doesn't, here is what to do.

Because you can only write one thing at a time, and you can only read one thing at a time, we're now going to present a series of the questions. But they need not be sequential. In practice, an expert evaluator/teacher asks all of these questions all of the time—not one at a time. It's like a crossword puzzle. The solution to one item affects the solution to the others. But the puzzle is not finished until all questions have been asked and all the blanks have been filled in. It is possible, therefore, for a student to have error patterns *and* phonic mistakes. Don't assume that a YES on Action 6b is the same as a NO on Action 6c.

### Question 10.1 (Action 6b and/or 6c)

Are certain patterns of errors, or phonetic skill weaknesses, illustrated by 6b and/or 6c errors?

If NO, there is nothing arguing for, or against, a particular instructional emphasis. The kid needs intensified active decoding instruction. Put him in **Teaching Recommendation 4** and monitor his decoding closely.

### Question 10.2 (Action 6a)

Are there errors that violate meaning?

If NO, then go to Action 6b and/or 6c.
If YES, then go to Chapter 10.

### Question 10.3 (Action 6b)

Are there error patterns illustrated by Action 6b?

If YES, then the student needs to learn to correct these inefficient decoding habits. You'll accomplish that by using Teaching Recommendation 6.

### Question 10.4 (Action 6c)

Are there phonic errors illustrated by Action 6c?
If YES, go to Action 7.

### Action 7: Evaluate Phonics

This action is taken to answer the question "If he needs phonics, which phonetic content should be taught?" To answer this, you need to treat the information obtained through Action 4 as survey-level test results. Starting with the tallied product obtained in Exhibit 9.4, select objectives and/or conduct additional assessment to determine which phonetic content seems to be most problematic. These will become your assumed causes. They include lack of skill in:

- ✓ Letter sounds
- ✓ Words
- ✓ Sight words
- ✓ Blending and word (sound) analogy
- ✓ Testing attention to code

What follows is a brief description of the processes used to assess these different kinds of code content.

**Testing Letter Sounds** There are many hierarchies of decoding content. For an example, see the one in Exhibit 9.6 or, for early reading, M. Sprick et al. (1998). Most are essentially the same and move in a progression from single-letter sounds (vowels and consonants) to sounds associated with clusters of letters (blends and digraphs) to words (contractions and compounds). The letter and cluster sounds can be tested in words or in isolation. For example, if you are interested in finding out about the student's use of the "**a**" sounds, you can test by giving a flashcard with only that letter on it and asking, "What sounds does this letter make?" You may also test by giving a word with the letter in it: "Read this as if it is a real word: <u>ane</u>." In this case, you would score only the use of "**a**." If you present a letter in isolation, keep in mind that letters can

make more than one sound. You might say "This letter makes two sounds. Give me the two sounds this letter makes."

If you are interested in the student's skill at converting **a**'s from the long to short sound, you might give a probe such as the vowel-conversion probe shown in Exhibit 9.7. Once again, you would score only the student's response to the targeted vowel; the **t**'s and **p**'s are *carriers* that increase the validity of the sample despite the fact that real words are not used. (Some evaluators test conversions through the use of diacritical markings. Unless these markings are used in the student's decoding program, such a test will not be useful.)

**Formats for Testing Letter Sounds** Sounds can be tested with probe sheets or flashcards. Probe sheets, like the one in Exhibit 9.7, can be used for testing mastery and accuracy, whereas flashcards are only useful for accuracy. The student must give an oral response to the probe if you wish to grade it. Because the oral response is gone in an instant, you must either tape-record the behavior (you can have the student read off of a computer screen into electronic storage) or score it as the student reads. Simultaneous scoring can be simplified by having your own copy of the probe in a clear plastic binder; then you can use a transparency pen to write what the student said over each sound missed. After transferring findings, you can wipe the plastic clean. Letter-sound probes are included in the *Resources for Implementing Curriculum-Based Evaluation* (Howell et al., 2000a). Incidentally, remember to sit behind the kid so that he isn't distracted by your scoring.

The main limitation of flashcards is that they are not practical for timing because you control the student's decoding rate with the rate at which you flash the cards. The amount of time it should take a student to decode a word on a flashcard is not well-established and is difficult to identify (because it is so short). Reading a flashcard quickly is quite different from reading a line of print. It is probably more analogous to reading highway signs on a curved mountain road at night. Some commonly used measures

*Exhibit 9.6    Code Content.*

### A. Sequence for Teaching Beginning Phonics (Sprick et al., 1998)

Continuous sound: A sound that can be sustained as long as you have the breath to continue saying it.

Quick sound (stop sound): A sound that cannot be sustained unless /uh/ is added (t/not/tuh).

Quiet sound: A sound that is unvoiced.

| Sound | As In | Pronounced | Continuous or Quick | Voiced or Unvoiced |
|---|---|---|---|---|
| s, S | snake | sss | continuous | quiet |
| e, ee | emu/eel | eee | continuous | voiced |
| m, M | mouse | mmm | continuous | voiced |
| a, A | ant | aaa | continuous | voiced |
| d, D | dinosaur | d | quick | voiced |
| th | the | thth | continuous | voiced |
| n, N | nest | nnn | continuous | voiced |
| t, T | turtle | t | quick | quiet |
| w, W | wind | www | continuous | voiced |
| i | insect | iii | continuous | voiced |
| h, H | hippo | h | quick | quiet |
| c, C | crocodile | c | quick | quiet |
| r, R | rabbit | rrr | continuous | voiced |
| sh, Sh | sheep | shsh | continuous | quiet |
| k, K, ck | kangaroo | k | quick | quiet |
| oo | moon | oooo | continuous | voiced |
| ar | star | arar | continuous | voiced |
| wh, WH | whale | wh | quick | quiet |
| e, E | engine | eee | continuous | voiced |
| -y | fly | -yyy | continuous | voiced |
| l, L | lion | lll | continuous | voiced |
| o, O | otter | ooo | continuous | voiced |
| b, B | baseball | b | quick | voiced |
| g, G | gorilla | g | quick | voiced |
| f, F | frog | fff | continuous | quiet |
| u, U | umbrella | uuu | continuous | voiced |
| er | sister/brother | erer | continuous | voiced |
| y-, Y- | yarn | y | quick | voiced |

| p, P | pig | p | quick | quiet |
|------|-----|---|-------|-------|
| v, V | volcano | vvv | continuous | voiced |
| J, J | jaguar | j | quick | voiced |
| qu | queen | qu | quick | quiet |
| x, X, or | fox | ksss | continuous | quiet |
| z, Z, a-e | zebra | zzz | continuous | voiced |
| -y | story | continuous | voiced | |
| ou, ow | cloud/town | continuous | voiced | |
| ch, l-e | chicken | quick | quiet | |
| igh, o-e | flight | continuous | voiced | |

## B. Most Common Sounds of Single Letters, Letter Combinations, and Affixes (Carnine et al., 1997)

| I. Single Letters<br>Continuous sounds | II. Letter Combinations | III. Affixes |
|----------------------------------------|-------------------------|--------------|
| | ai (maid) | a (alive) |
| | ar (car) | a (formula) |
| a (fat) | au (haul) | able (enjoyable) |
| e (bet) | aw (lawn) | ac (accuse, cardiac) |
| f (fill) | ay (stay) | ad (address) |
| i (sit) | ch (chip) | age (package) |
| l (let) | ea (beat) | al (personal) |
| m (mad) | ee (need) | be (become) |
| n (nut) | er (fern) | com (compare) |
| o (not) | eu (feud) | con (confuse) |
| r (rat) | ew (shrewd) | de (defeat) |
| s (sell) | ey (honey) | dis (disappear) |
| u (cut) | igh (high) | ed (jumped, landed, hummed) |
| v (vet) | ing (sing) | en (harden) |
| w (wet) | ir (first) | ence (occurrence) |
| y (yes) | kn (know) | er (keeper) |
| z (zoo) | oa (load) | es (misses) |
| | oi (boil) | est (smallest) |
| | ol (hold) | ex (expect) |

**Exhibit 9.6**    *Continued*

| I. Single Letters Continuous sounds | II. Letter Combinations | III. Affixes |
|---|---|---|
| Stop Sounds | oo (boot) | ful (handful) |
| | or (short) | ic (heroic) |
| b (boy) | ou (cloud) | in (inside) |
| c (can) | ow (own) | ing (jumping) |
| d (did) | oy (toy) | ion (action) |
| g (got) | ph (phone) | ish (selfish) |
| h (his) | qu (quick) | ize (realize) |
| j (jet) | sh (shop) | ist (artist) |
| k (kiss) | th (thank) | ive (detective) |
| p (pet) | ue (cue) | le (handle) |
| q (quit) | ur (burn) | less (useless) |
| t (top) | wh (whale) | ly (sadly) |
| x (fox) | wr (wrap) | ment (payment) |
| | | ness (kindness) |
| | | ous (joyous) |
| | | over (overtime) |
| | | pre (preschool) |

## C. Sounds (Sprick et al., 1998)

| Sound | As In |
|---|---|
| s, S | snake |
| e, ee | emu/eel |
| m, M | mouse |
| a, A | ant |
| d, D | dinosaur |
| th | the |
| n, N | nest |
| t, T | turtle |
| w, W | wind |
| i | insect |

| Sound | As In |
|-------|-------|
| h, H | hippo |
| c, C | crocodile |
| r, R | rabbit, eat |
| sh, Sh | sheep |
| k, K, ck | kangaroo |
| oo | moon |
| ar | star |
| wh, WH | whale |
| e, E | engine |
| -y | fly |
| l, L | lion |
| o, O | otter |
| b, B | baseball |
| g, G | gorilla |
| f, F | frog |
| u, U | umbrella |
| er | sister/brother |
| y-, Y-, schwa | yarn, ago |
| p, P | pigs, say |
| v, V | volcano |
| j, J | jaguar |
| qu | queen |
| x, X, or | fox, for |
| z, ,Z, a-e | zebra, case |
| -y | story |
| ou, ow | cloud/town |
| ch, I-e | chicken, time, rain |
| igh, o-e | flight, home, first |

Note: The sequence is based on three rules: (1) separation of letter/sound relationships that sound or look alike, (2) access to sounds needed to read high frequency words, (3) access to sounds needed to write stories.

**Exhibit 9.7    *A Vowel Conversion Probe.***

|       |       |       |       |       | tip   | tipe  | tap   | tappe |
|-------|-------|-------|-------|-------|-------|-------|-------|-------|
| tip   | tupp  | tep   | topp  | tpoe  | tupe  | tape  | tepe  | tipe  |
| tap   | tipe  | tupe  | tepe  | top   | tope  | tupe  | tape  | tepe  |
| tep   | tape  | tippe | tuppe | teppe | topp  | tope  | tupe  | tape  |
| tip   | tepe  | tappe | tipp  | tupp  | tepp  | toppe | tope  | tupe  |
| top   | tipe  | teppe | tapp  | tip   | tup   | tepe  | tope  | tope  |
| tup   | tope  | tippe | tepp  | tap   | tipe  | tupe  | tep   | top   |
| tape  | tupe  | toppe | tipp  | tep   | tape  | tippe | tupe  | tepe  |
| tappe | tap   | tuppe | topp  | tip   | tepe  | tappe | tipp  | tup   |
| tap   | tippe | tuppe | tappe | tupe  | tope  | tip   | tepe  | tap   |

*Source:* Howell K. W., Zucker S. H. & Morehead M. K. (2000). *MASI-R: Remedial Screening Test.* Applied Research and Development Center, College of Education, Western Washington University, Bellingham, WA 98225-9090: Reprinted with permission.

allow students as long as 5 seconds, but a proficient reader (which is what you want the student to be) can decode a single word of nearly any length in about a half-second. As a rule, single units (letters and syllables) should be decoded with 100% accuracy at a rate of 60 per minute, whereas words in isolation should be decoded with 100% accuracy at 80 per minute.

**Testing Words**    Students will often substitute whole words or parts of words. This is sometimes called "word calling" and is typical of older *corrective* readers. These errors may include whole-word substitutions (is-at, in-to) or partial substitutions (the-them, display-discuss). Characteristically, when a partial word error is noted, the first or last few letters of the substituted word will be correct.

To gain insight into the skill deficits promoting this error pattern, take the words missed and present them in isolation (on flashcards). If the student doesn't decode the phonetically regular portions of words accurately and quickly, then he is having sound or blending problems. So test and teach those skills.

If the student reads previously missed words correctly in isolation, ask yourself if these are "sight" words. Should that be the case, move to the use of nonsense words. If the student makes errors on nonsense words, then test and teach phonics. If phonics does not seem to be a prob-

lem, recheck to see if he is making errors that affect his comprehension. If the errors do affect comprehension, have the student decode the passage while you provide assisted self-monitoring (**Action 5**). If his accuracy improves, then he needs to learn to monitor for meaning while decoding quickly. Use **decoding Teaching Recommendations 2** and **5.** If the errors don't affect his comprehension, you have found a pattern unique to oral reading. (In other words, there would be no problem were there not an oral-decoding test, so forget the errors).

**Testing Sight Words**    Evaluating sight words is somewhat like evaluating letter sounds. That is because the basic strategy involved in learning them is the recall of grapheme-phoneme correspondence. Just as "e" says /eh/ or /eee/, "boy" says /boy/. There is, however, one big difference between "e" and "boy." The difference is that boy has meaning. The domain of words/morphographs is consolidated by meaning and may even be taught, in part, through a generative approach (Westby, 1992).

Sight words become sight words after a student learns them to automaticity. There are two reasons this might happen. Words frequently used (such as "the," "and," "but," etc.) become sight words through repeated practice. Words that are phonetically irregular can also become sight words after repeated practice but not through decoding. Some are regular ("man"), whereas others are irregular ("was"). Before you get too interested in classifying words as regular or irregular, remember that as students acquire more knowledge of coding rules, more words become regular to them. If a student does not know the final **e** rule, then *mane* and *cane* are irregular for them. The way you test sight words is to show them to the student (ideally within sentences or phrases) and ask him to decode them. If he gives an immediate response (half-second for the targeted sight word), then he either knows it as a sight word or has decoded it successfully.

Theoretically, no sight word requires more energy to learn than any other, just as the sound "*b*" is not harder to learn than the sound "*n*." However, ease of learning has nothing to do with ease of usage. Some sight words are more commonly confused than others. This is particularly true of those that begin with <u>th</u> (that, those, these, them, this, that, thought, through, throw, threw). Therefore, when testing sight words at the automatic level, you will want to select a passage with a lot of these items.

High-frequency word lists are available in most reading texts or tests. There are many such lists including those developed from high-frequency words found in basal texts (in which words are often selected for their conformity to skill sequences) and high-frequency words found in children's literature. As it turns out, all of the commonly used lists contain most of the words on Adams' 1990 list of the highest-frequency words in texts.

Sight words can be tested in context, in phrases, and in isolation. If you are testing them in isolation, it is a good idea to repeat each word on the probe sheet several times. This repetition makes the student use the word more than once, which increases the validity of the test by decreasing the likelihood of lucky guesses. As a rule, only use from 10 to 20 different sight words on any test. CAPs for sight words are slightly higher than CAPs for sounds but lower than for passage decoding. A reasonable criterion is 80 correct with 0–2 errors per minute. A high-frequency sight-word probe is included in the *Resources for Implementing Curriculum-Based Evaluation* (Howell et al., 2000a).

### Testing Blending and Word (Sound) Analogy

When using phonics to decode a word, a student first segments it into units, recalls the grapheme-phoneme relationship for each unit, and then combines the sounds to say the word. These segmenting and combining activities are called *blending*. Blending is viewed as a separate task from sounding; however, blending is of primary importance to decoding (Williams, 1984; Yopp, 1992b). Some of the formats for testing blending were described in depth in Action 2. (You probably didn't read that section because it was targeted at students who are beginning readers. Guess what! The decision to emphasize phonics was a decision to treat this student as a beginning reader. So go back to Action 2 and read it now.)

A student who knows the *at* in pat can use that information in analogous words such as *fat, rat, mat,* or *bat.* A student who knows *icker* in *sticker* can use that information to decode *flicker* or *bicker.*

Word-analogy testing can be used to evaluate and teach decoding. This is particularly effective when the teacher uses morphemes as the clusters targeted for the analogy exercises. That is because morphology (Chapter 11, p. **356**) introduces meaning into the decoding task (Carnine et al., 1997). The affixes in Exhibit 9.6 are morphographs.

Decoding by word analogy requires the blending steps of unit recognition, word segmenting, sound recall, and combining. We will describe three assessment procedures that will let you analyze blending with word-analogy strategies.

**Blending Procedure 1** To see if a student blends two units, show a letter (or cluster) and supply the sounds of the units before asking for the sound of both together. Example:

| Teacher | Student |
| --- | --- |
| "This is /b/." | Pronounces the sound /b/ |
| "This is /igh/." | Pronounces the sound /igh/ |
| "What is /b/ [pause] /igh/?" | Pronounces the sound /bigh/ |

Because the sounds are supplied, this test is evaluating the blending of the *"b"* to *"igh."* Sounding of *"b"* and *"igh"* isn't being tested.

A blending test can be assembled by making up flashcards for each code unit in Exhibit 9.6. Then, put them in order, either by numbering them or affixing them to metal rings. Next, make up a record form that corresponds to the order of the cards. Then, while using the record form, you can flip through various code combinations and mark the student's performance on each.

Another technique is the use of rhyming-word teams. For example:

"This word is /bl/-/eam/."

Pronounce the word.

"What word would this be?" *"Bleam."*

The sound that was supplied (/eam/) is not being tested. Instead, the production of the /bl/ sound and the blending of /bl/ to /eam/ are being tested. Remember to change the position of the sounds because some students may be skilled enough to blend a letter in the initial position but not in the medial or final positions.

For example, to test "b" in the initial place:

This word is *"Pat."*

[Pronounce the word.]

"What word is this?" *"Bat."*

To test "b" in the final place:

"This word is *tap."*

[Pronounce the word.]

"What word would this be?" *"Tab."*

**Blending Procedure 2**    Another decoding procedure, the Glass analysis system (Glass, 1971), is ideal for testing both production and identification of blending as well as cluster sounds. It is also an excellent spelling test. In the Glass system, the whole word is shown, and the student is given the sound of the word. Next, the student is asked to indicate which letter makes each sound in the word and then what sound the letter

makes. The system requires students to find letters and clusters within the word. This task (identification of the code units) is a necessary part of blending. Remember that blending is not just putting the sounds together. First, the student must recognize code units within the word. Here is how the Glass system might be used to test segmenting, sounding, and combining subskills:

| | | Teacher | Student |
|---|---|---|---|
| Step 1 | | "This word is *bring.*" [Show and pronounce the word.] "Say it." | *"Bring"* |
| Step 2a | | "In the word *bring,* which letters make the sound /br/?" | "B-R" |
| Step 2b | | "In the word *bring,* what letters make the sound /ing/?" | "I-N-G" |
| Step 3a | | "In the word *bring,* what sound do the letters 'B-R' make?" | "/brrr/" |
| Step 3b | | "In the word *bring,* what sound do the letters 'I-N-G' make?" | "/ing/" |
| Step 4 | | "Say the word." | *"Bring"* |

You can easily modify the Glass (1971) procedure to incorporate the content already discussed. Now that you know the student knows the sounds of "br," "ing," and "bring," new words can confidently be built using them. For example:

br*ick* s*ing* br*ide*

or

f*ling* br*oke* sw*ing*

**Blending Procedure 3**    The Glass questions can also be used to obtain insight into the student's skill at combining. Let's say the student failed at working with rhyming words. You could go through the Glass (1971) technique with the words and then combine them, as shown in the following.

| Word A | | |
|---|---|---|
| | Stimulus | Response |
| Step 1 | (Show the word *drain*.) "This word is *drain*. What word is it?" | "*Drain*" |
| Step 2 | "In the word *drain*, what letters make the sound /ain/?" | "A-I-N" |
| Step 3 | "In the word *drain*, what sound do the letters 'A-I-N' make?" | "/ain/" |
| Step 4 | "Say the word *drain*." | "*Drain*" |
| Step 5 | (Show the word *train*.) "Now say this word." | "*Train*" |
| Word B | | |
| Step 1 | (Show the word *trade*.) "This word is *trade*. What word is it?" | "*Trade*" |
| Step 2 | "In the word *trade*, what letters make the sound /tr/?" | "T-R" |
| Step 3 | "In the word *trade*, what sound do the letters 'T-R' make?" | "/tr/" |
| Step 4 | "Say the word *trade*." | "*Trade*" |
| Step 5 | (Show the word *drade*.) "Now say this word." | "*Drade*" |

**Testing Attention to Code** Inattention to portions of words is often assumed when students make whole-word substitutions of words sharing initial sounds (the-their, who-what, is-if) or when they omit endings (-ed, -ing, -ion, -s). A simple procedure can be used to find out if these errors are the result of either a failure to selectively attend to the whole word or lack of skill decoding the separate word portions. (Remember, if the errors aren't affecting meaning, you don't need to worry about them.)

Select two passages of equal difficulty and underline the characteristically omitted or substituted portions of one passage in red. Time the student's reading of both passages and note ac-

curacy and rate. If, when these words are underlined, the accuracy improves considerably but rate maintains, then the student knows how to decode the endings but isn't doing so. To remedy this problem, place greater emphasis on accuracy and comprehension monitoring (Teaching Recommendations 3 and 5). If accuracy does not improve, or if it improves but rate decreases significantly (more than 20%), teach the words or units themselves. Use *Teaching Recommendation 7.*

## Teaching Recommendations

### Reading Instruction

We're going to start this section with a few comments on current reading instruction. Most of these apply equally to comprehension and word recognition. Today, nearly all students are taught to read with "basal" reading programs. These programs were out of favor in the early 1990s but are now back (they just have "literacy" somewhere in their title). They are designed to complement a mode of reading instruction not seated in skill instruction but based on the completion of daily lessons (it is not an accident that the basal readers have as many lessons as there are school days/weeks in the year).

It is also remarkable to note that, whereas many authors debate the relative merits of types of reading instruction, there is evidence that very little of it is actually occurring (Baumann & Ivey, 1988; Enghert et al., 1998). Even more disturbing is similar evidence that poor readers receive less instruction, and poorer quality instruction, than competent readers.

The reading instruction typically provided to low-performing students differs from the reading instruction provided to higher performing students. Such problems always seem compounded in the upper grades (Duffy, 1990). Perhaps the most crushing finding is that there is little relationship between student need and total time allocated to reading instruction in both special and general education class settings (Adams, 1990; Baumann & Ivy, 1997). Here are some other findings:

✓ Students are seldom taught specific reading rules or strategies.

✓ Problem readers spend more time on letters, sounds, and words in isolation.

✓ They spend less time reading words in text.

✓ They spend less time in silent reading.

✓ Problem readers spend more time doing independent and noninteractive worksheets.

✓ A greater proportion of time is spent on reading tasks in general education classrooms than in special/remedial classrooms.

✓ The more special/remedial reading programs a school has, the *fewer* minutes the average student in the school spends reading.

Disparities in instructional quality can also be seen in other ways (Vaughn et al., 1998). For example, teachers are more apt to interrupt poor readers and less likely to use semantic cues to correct their errors (Calfee & Drum, 1986). Additionally, in schools with large proportions of at-risk and problem readers, the average student reads nearly 20 minutes *less* per day than the average student in other schools (Adams, 1990). McGill-Franzen and Allington (1991) noted that, because of the overuse of individual worksheets in Chapter 1 and special education classes, many remedial readers receive as little as *2 minutes* of active reading a day.

What has gone wrong with remedial and special-reading programs? We see at least three problems.

• First, as "new corrective approaches to reading" proliferate, general education teachers lose ownership of reading instruction and decrease emphasis on it in their classes. Anyone observing a general education classroom today is likely to hear a teacher turn to a student and say something like this: "It's time for you to go down the hall to reading." The message to the student, and the one evidently accepted by the teacher, is that reading resides "down the hall" or "when the reading teacher/ instructional assistant comes in."

• Second, a peculiar model of "individualized" instruction has evolved in many remedial/ special classrooms. In this model, students collect a folder, shoe box, ice cream bucket, or notebook that is filled with worksheets. They then work on these sheets independently while the teacher circulates through the room giving feedback and/or reinforcement for the *completion of the sheets*. There is almost no explanation of the purpose of the worksheets, and the emphasis is on task completion—not learning (Zigmond, 1997).

• Finally, the stuff on many of the worksheets given to practice reading comprehension is garbage. It is drawn from a very narrow view of reading and seems to be selected for conformity with the independent-seat work mode of instruction—not the demands of literacy.

## Specific Teaching Recommendations

Some ways of teaching are better than others (Fisher et al., 1995; Lloyd et al., 1998 S. Korski et al., 1996). Seven kinds of effective reading intervention are represented in Exhibit 9.2: (1) early reading skills, (2) emphasize fluency, (3) emphasize accuracy, (4) intensified active reading instruction, (5) emphasize self-monitoring, (6) correct error patterns, and (7) emphasize phonics.

### Teaching Recommendation 1: Early Reading Skills

#### Sample Objectives: Enabling Phonology

**Segment Phonemes**  When presented with ten spoken words of three phonemes each (man, hit, sit, ram, job, etc.), the student will say the phonemic sounds in sequence with 100% accuracy on five of five trials (student says, "/mm/-/aa/-/nn/" when teacher says "man").

**Blend Phonemes**   When presented with ten spoken words segmented into phonemes (/ss/-/ii/-/t/, /mm/-/o/-/mm/, /b/-/aa/-/t/, /p/-/o/-/p/, etc.) the student will blend the sounds to make a word with 100% accuracy for five of five trials (student says "sit" when teacher says "/ss/-/ii/-/t/").

**Discriminate Same and Different Phonemes**   When presented with ten spoken words of two and three phonemes, the student will indicate which sounds are the same and which sounds are different, using colored blocks as indicators, with 100% accuracy on five of five trials (teacher says "pet" and student pushes forward three different-colored blocks; teachers says "mom" and student pushes forward two blocks of same color and one of different, /m/ = red, /o/ = white, /m/ = red).

**Segment Syllables**   When presented with ten spoken (one-syllable) words, the student will segment initial sound (onset) from remaining sound (rime) with 100% accuracy on five of five trials (teacher says "lake" and student says "/l/-/ake/"; teacher says "pat" and student says "/p/-/at/," etc.).

**Blend Syllables**   When presented with ten spoken, segmented, one-syllable words, the student will blend the parts into a whole with 100% accuracy on five of five trials (teacher says "/p/-/in/" and student says "pin"; teacher says "/r/-/am/" and student says "ram"; teacher says "/t/-/ake/" and student says "take," etc.).

**Rhyme**   When presented with ten pairs of spoken, one-syllable words, the student will identify whether the pair of words rhyme or do not rhyme with 100% accuracy on five of five trials (teacher says "pat-hat" and student says "yes"; teacher says "top-boy" and student says "no," etc.).

**Segment Words into Syllables**   When presented with words of one to three syllables, the student will indicate the number of syllables heard by clapping for each syllable with 100% accuracy for five of five trials (teacher says "football" and student claps twice; teacher says "rainbow" and student claps twice; teacher says "dog" and student claps once, etc.).

**Blend Words**   When presented with ten spoken words, of one to three syllables, segmented into syllables, the student will say the word with 100% accuracy on five of five trials (teacher says "/help/-/ful/" and student says "helpful"; teacher says "/foot/-/ball/" and student says "football"; teacher says "/Nin/-/ten/-/do/" and student says "Nintendo," etc.).

**Distinguish Word from Other Words in Spoken Language**   When presented with ten target words in ten separate sentences, the student will indicate when he hears the target word with 100% accuracy on five of five trials (target word is bark; teacher says "I heard the dog bark and bark." Student indicates hearing bark two times).

### Sample Objectives for Print Knowledge

**Letter Names**   Given all 52 letters (upper and lower case, randomly ordered in a typical print style), the student will name each with 100% accuracy on five of five trials.

**Sentence Boundaries**   When shown pre-primer or primer text with conventional sentence/paragraph format, the student will identify sentence boundaries with 100% accuracy for ten or more sentences on five of five trials.

**Word Length**   When shown five one-syllable words and five three-syllable words, the student will identify short words and long words with 100% accuracy on five of five trials.

**Word Boundaries**   Given sentences in pre-primer or primer text in conventional sentence/paragraph format, the student will identify word boundaries (space between words) with 100% accuracy.

**Book Length**   When shown five very short books and five long books (that have been previously read to the student), the student will indicate with 100% accuracy which books are short and which books are long.

### Page Conventions and Book Conventions
Given a familiar book, the student will pretend-read

✓ Holding the book upright
✓ From front to back
✓ Page by page
✓ Left to right per column
✓ Top to bottom per column

with 100% accuracy on five of five trials.

### Boundaries
[During pseudo-reading exercises with the teacher] the student will identify (point to) [sentence boundaries] with [100% accuracy].

### Logos/Signs
Student will spontaneously recognize familiar logos or signs in the environment with 100% accuracy (fast-food restaurants, grocery stores, favorite foods, restrooms); or, given 20 Polaroid pictures of familiar logos or signs in the environment, the student will name places and items the pictures represent with 100% accuracy.

These objectives may need to be modified depending on the prior knowledge of the student. Because these skills are so basic, it can be assumed that the student will need considerable teacher assistance (Mason et al., 1990). Therefore, the sequence of instruction is often more one of assistance (conditions) than content. Review the techniques you used to recognize the missing skills and then include them within the condition portion of the objectives where called upon by the brackets. For example, the content specified in "sentence boundaries" would change depending on the results noted on the status sheet. The condition "during pseudo-reading exercises" is drawn from notes taken during the testing.

The procedures for teaching early reading skills are the same as the procedures we recommended for evaluating that awareness. Rather than repeat them here, we simply refer you back to those techniques you used to decide if a particular phonological or print skill required instruction. However, we will give you some advice about teaching for awareness of print and sound.

Phonetic segmentation is an essential skill more basic than recalling sound-letter or sound-cluster correspondence (Ball & Blachman, 1991; Daneman & Stainton, 1991). With phonetic segmentation, students determine the presence, boundaries, and number of sounds (phonemes) in a word (Griffith & Olson, 1992; Hoogeveen et al., 1989). Phonemic segmentation is not syllabication. In a syllabication task, students would tell how many syllables there are in a word. In a phonemic segmentation task, they would isolate the phonemes "m-a-n" to demonstrate that they can conceptualize and manipulate phonemes. In the word "man," there is one syllable but three distinct phonemes.

You may have noticed that we included logos and signs on our content list for preliminary print knowledge. We actually wrote a procedure for assessing it but decided not to include it in the text for the following reason:

✓ There is a highly positive correlation between kids who notice that signs and logos carry messages and kids who learn to read.

✓ However, we do not think there is clear evidence that taking instructional time to teach signs will speed up learning to read (in fact we suspect the converse—that spending the time learning to read will help the student with logos).

✓ Therefore, teachers can teach that print carries meaning in a variety of ways without making up flashcards to advertise McDonald's.

Mixed results have been reported on the benefits of teaching at the phoneme level (Adams, 1990; Haskell et al., 1992). Consequently, we include the content of phoneme blending and segmentation with caution and encourage the reader to follow the research. Current research does tell us that good readers have advanced phoneme skills (Good, 1999). It doesn't tell us if teaching this awareness will turn a poor reader into a good one.

As authors, we are concerned that by including the suggestion that some students be taught "preliminary print knowledge" and "enabling phonemic knowledge," we may promote inappropriate instruction. So, here is what we don't want to see: a child in a room with no books where he is required to master choosing same and different letter sounds before anyone will read a story to him. Here is what we do want: hours of interactive reading and writing activities infused with explanations, questions, and activities designed to focus the student on preliminary print and phonological skills. These skills are best taught explicitly but within the context of reading, listening, and conversational routines (Stanovich, 1994).

Many of the techniques for teaching beginning-reading skills can take the form of games, including the learning of nursery rhymes and songs (Thompson & Majsterek, 1992). Once the student has learned a song, you can sing it together and then omit words for the student to fill in. One teacher we know uses the methods we recommended for assessing phonological knowledge to teach it. He does this across the school day on the way to recess, in the lunchroom, waiting for the bus, at the drinking fountain, as well as in the classroom. Often, these teaching activities come in the form of word games. For example, you can introduce a procedure as an integrated activity in a daily routine ("I have some secret words. Can you guess what they are? Listen: /t/-/ake/") (O'Connor, 1992). Take a look at the lesson in Exhibit 9.8 and note its game-like quality (M. Sprick et al., 1998).

### Teaching Recommendation 2: Build Fluency

#### Objective

*Given passages the student reads with 90% accuracy or better, the student will decode the passage on the first try at the rate specified for his curriculum level in Exhibit 9.3.*

The student's slow initial rate can most likely be attributed to a lack of fluency instruction and/or failure to derive context cues from passages during decoding. It could also be the result of a lack of familiarity with fluency testing. In any case, the student needs fluency building.

Students who are accurate but slow may know a particular reading strategy but not employ it efficiently because it has not been learned to fluency (Carver, 1992). Lessons designed to build fluency typically use rapid-paced drills and practice with material on which the student is at least 90% accurate. During these lessons, the student is reinforced for rapid responding and daily improvement in fluency. Errors are typically viewed as rate-induced and are ignored to the extent that error-correction procedures are not used. (Feedback may be given after the student reads the passage.)

One popular technique for building oral-decoding rate, suggested by Carnine and colleagues (1997), is summarized here:

1. Select a passage on which the student is accurate.

2. Instruct the student to read for 1 minute as quickly and as accurately as possible and then note the student's rate (60 words per minute).

3. Set a target rate for the passage that is 20% to 40% above the initial rate of the student (60 wpm × 0.40 = 24; 24 + 60 = 84 wpm).

4. Mark the target (in this example 84 wpm) in the student's book. By "mark it" we mean circle it or highlight it so that it stands out for the student. Next, have him reread the selection, just as before (step 2), as many times as necessary to reach the marked target.

5. Continue this procedure a couple of times each day, on various selections, until the student's average initial reading rate reaches the criterion for his grade level (and accuracy is maintained).

You are building fluency, not having a race, when you conduct rate-building lessons. If you look up fluency in the dictionary, you'll find that it mentions *effortless* and *laid back* as well as *speedy*. The fact is the rate criteria in Exhibit 9.3 are not all that high, and a student can easily reach them without sacrificing the smooth, flowing patterns that we associate with competent performance. Try to promote ease of reading at the same time you are promoting speed. In

**Exhibit 9.8    Blending Lesson.**

*Source:* Sprick, M., Howard, L., & Findanque, A. (1998). *Read Well: Critical Foundations in Primary Reading. Program Guide—Notebook 1* (p. 62). Longmont, CO: Sopris West.

addition to the suggestion above, Carver (1992) recommends the following:

✓ Don't worry about students "talking to themselves" (reading subvocally).

✓ Have students read every word.

✓ When students slow down, assume it is because the vocabulary or concepts are unfamiliar.

✓ Don't encourage students to skip unimportant words.

✓ Have students read relatively easy material often to practice and maintain rate.

### Teaching Recommendation 3: Emphasize Accuracy within Active Reading

#### Objective
*The student will read a [passage at a set level] aloud with 95%–100% decoding accuracy.*

The first thing to note about this recommendation is that it is carried out within the context of active reading. Also, trying to get the student to be accurate is a central part of all of the other recommendations. The only difference here is that you have a student who isn't reading at the expected level, is okay on the early reading skills, and makes mistakes while he reads *but* corrects them. So, you simply need to add four things to Teaching Recommendation 3.

**First,** you must take extra effort to produce an environment that emphasizes accuracy. A good way to do this is to insist that work be done correctly and, when there is an error, that the student corrects the error. Also, praise the self-corrections.

**Second,** teach the student to identify all errors. To do this, read Teaching Recommendation 6 and borrow whichever process seems to fit this student.

**Third,** record the student reading, then play the recording and have him follow along marking and correcting the errors (aloud) as the recording continues.

**Fourth,** set up a monitoring system and record the student's accuracy on unfamiliar pas-sages (of equal difficulty) each day. Then reinforce the student for increases in accuracy (remembering that as he approaches 95% his rate of improvement may slow; therefore, more reinforcement may be needed near the end of the task).

If there is no growth, use the other actions to check for missing skills that may be impairing his progress. Also, remember that not all errors are equal. If the student reaches a point where his rate is adequate and his comprehension is good, he can be allowed a few errors.

Finally, if this student is in the upper grades, be sure the exercises described here are carried out in content-area texts.

### Teaching Recommendation 4: Intensified Active Instruction

#### Objective
*Given passages at [the expected or an intermediate level], the student will decode them at [specify the rate] while maintaining 95%–100% accuracy.*

This recommendation is usually indicated when a student is progressing slowly through an initial, largely code-dominated, reading curriculum. The student will be decoding below an expected level. Although progress is not adequate, the pattern of errors does not seem to indicate the need to take a radically biased (all-code- or all-language-based) approach. Instead, an intensive, balanced approach is recommended, including direct instruction on phoneme-grapheme correspondence made meaningful through the periodic use of language-based exercises such as student-generated stories, teacher-student shared decoding, and teacher readings from more sophisticated texts (Cognition and Technology Group, 1990; Freppon & Dahl, 1998). Although both code strategies and context strategies are taught in an intensified but balanced approach, in the early grades the correct "balance" must favor phonics.

To balance code instruction, you will also need to focus on the student's skill at using context (titles, vocabulary, story line) to predict upcoming events and words in the story. These activities are often influenced by the size of the instructional group. That is one reason why the

Cooperative Learning (Antil et al., 1998), Classroom Wide Peer Tutoring (Fuchs et al., 1993), and Success for All (Slavin, 1998) programs are of great value. They each increase active reading by essentially decreasing the size of reading instruction groups. Students need to read, and they need to read a lot! Therefore, you need to do everything you can to increase reading activity (Cooper, Slavin, & Madden, 1998; Lloyd et al., 1998; Stanovich, 1986).

In active reading, the teacher also requires the student to take an interactive approach to reading. Explain how he can use what is being read to predict what will be read next. Show how he can confirm a prediction and how to find evidence from the passage to support both predictions and confirmations. Maximize the use of pre-reading questions. Encourage the student to "look ahead" and "look back" for context clues. Have the student close his eyes and try to visualize what occurred in a given sentence or paragraph. Encourage him to paraphrase or repeat what was just read and to always be asking "Does that make sense?"

See the **comprehension teaching recommendations** for more information about active reading.

## Teaching Recommendation 5: Teach Self-Monitoring

### Objective

*Upon receiving a passage at [specify level or type of passage on which the student makes meaning-violation errors], the student will read the passage with 95%–100% accuracy.*

If the student corrects errors when you provide monitoring assistance, you can assume that he has adequate clarifying strategies but does not automatically employ them while passage reading. Various authors have noted that successful students routinely self-correct from 30% to 50% of meaning-violating errors (Clay, 1985). We have noted that, when given a pep talk like the one described in decoding SLP 3, most kids will self-correct at least 50% of meaning-violating errors. When given SLP 3 (the table-tapping test), successful readers will correct almost every error. Therefore, if your student is not attending to errors, he is reading very differently than a suc-

cessful reader would read. Go to Chapter 8 and employ **Comprehension Teaching Recommendation 3:** Self-Monitoring.

## Teaching Recommendation 6: Correct Error Patterns

### Objective

*Given passages at [the expected or an intermediate level], the student will decode the passage fluently while making no more than 5% [specify pattern] errors.*

Error patterns are learned. Often, they result from incorrect strategies developed through attempts to shortcut the decoding task or to avoid difficult material. Sometimes they work and sometimes they don't. For example, one student may get in the habit of avoiding errors by simply omitting troublesome words, whereas another may substitute known words, and a third may mispronounce. It is just as easy for a student to generate techniques for doing something wrong as it is to generate ways for doing something correctly. Consequently, as kids practice decoding, they practice using a range of strategies, and, unless they are monitored closely, these may include "error patterns." These error patterns are actually poor decoding habits, which must be countered with direct teaching. In fact, different forms of reading instruction, by emphasizing code or meaning, frequently lead to different error patterns (Johnson & Baumann, 1984).

If you are working with a student who clearly illustrates a pattern of decoding errors, immediately implement a program to break that habit. Students whose performance shows evidence of consistent error patterns are typically beyond initial decoding instruction. These students are not *tabula rasa* (blank slates). They are employing, often automatically, strategies they have conceivably practiced for years. Sometimes they are actually skilled enough to avoid these errors. So, they don't need to learn new decoding skills, but they should learn to recognize and attack the faulty habit directly.

There are two approaches to correcting error patterns: being a highly creative pair of authors, we have labeled these type 1 and type 2:

1. Direct intervention on bad reading habits

2. Correct overreliance on one type of information

### Direct Intervention on Bad Reading Habits

1. Identify the error pattern.
2. Count the occurrence of the error pattern per 100 words and chart it. Repeat a noninstructional reading session each day to monitor decreases in the errors.
3. Be sure the student knows how to recognize and count the same error pattern (listening to a tape of his decoding is useful here).
4. Provide feedback on the occurrence of the error pattern.
5. Reinforce the student for decreasing the number of these errors or increasing self-corrections.
6. Watch the data collected during the monitoring sessions. If the student does not begin to decrease the error pattern in a few days, have him work on one of the following instructional exercises.

Have the student listen to tapes of himself decoding while you mark (or correct) errors that affect meaning. When errors violate meaning, show the student how the words before and after the error can be used to help figure it out. As the student listens to his taped decoding, show how errors do not convey the message of the text. Point out how the errors can be syntactically wrong, redundant, superfluous, or misleading. Ask the student to explain how each new error might hurt understanding of the text.

✓ Read in unison with the student or have him check the decoding of other students. Make up sentences for the student to read in which all words are very easy except for the words he typically misses.

✓ Put problematic words in short phrases on flashcards and drill the student.

✓ If the student is decoding at an appropriate level and comprehension seems adequate, tell him that it isn't necessary to read each word perfectly. Tell him to attempt the word and then use it in context to see if the attempt was correct.

✓ Accentuate punctuation marks by coloring them, or overcorrect by having the student pause a set time (a count of 5) every time there is any punctuation mark.

### Correct Overreliance on One Type of Information

When direct instruction on bad decoding habits does not seem to work, it may be that the student is actually overreliant on either code information or context information. In these cases, corrective instruction should include the following.

Recognize the kind of information (code or context) on which the student is relying. To do this, answer the following questions about the types of errors made by the student during oral decoding:

✓ Are meaning-violating errors omissions, insertions, or substitutions of real words?

✓ Do errors on portions of words sound or look dissimilar from the stimulus word?

✓ Do inserted words make sense in the sentence?

✓ Does the student omit words containing graphemes read correctly in other words?

✓ Does the student omit function words (of, the, it, a)?

✓ Does the student hesitate on short, familiar words as well as on longer ones?

✓ Does the student repeat several of the words preceding a difficult word?

✓ Does the student repeat only words and not portions of words?

✓ Does the student correct only errors that affect passage meaning?

"*Yes*" answers indicate errors that result from reliance on context information; "*no*" answers indicate errors resulting from reliance on code information. If the yes and no answers are about evenly distributed, then assume the student is not overreliant and use the type 1 error correction presented above. If overreliance is evident, then decide which skills need to be addressed to increase appropriate responses and then employ the following recommendations:

✓ Analyze the text to determine if there are adequate opportunities to use targeted patterns. Some text may contain only one or two opportunities every 200 to 300 words. To correct the pattern, more opportunities will be needed.

✓ Tell the student that he has made an error.

✓ Show how the erroneous strategy led to the error.

✓ Show how the appropriate use of the other (nondominant) kind of information would have led to correct decoding.

✓ Provide practice to make the use of the appropriate information automatic.

### Teaching Recommendation 7: Emphasize Code Content

Who needs Phonics?

✓ If a student does not seem accurate at passage decoding or if he is accurate but slow, he may be having trouble using phonics. So that is what he should be taught.

✓ Students who are slow but accurate or who omit or substitute words are sometimes compensating for weak phonics skills by slowing down or avoiding difficult words. They need phonics.

✓ Students who are very inaccurate or very slow are having trouble with phonics. They need to learn it.

✓ Consistent sound and word-recognition errors indicate that the student is not adequately employing code skills. These skills can, and should, be taught.

The student who has not adequately mastered basic grapheme-phoneme correspondence might be inaccurate at these skills, or he may not have become fluent enough to use them automatically. For this student, decoding instruction should be targeted directly on content areas indicated by high-frequency errors. When you have a corrective reading student, he will have already learned some of these skills. As a result, it is necessary to skip through the reading sequence to bypass what is already known. Once again, this student will need for you to focus on specific

grapheme or phoneme problems by teaching and correcting them. All of this requires focus on the exact facts and rules the student has missed. Highlight the target content in words, refer to it frequently, and reinforce the student for improvement.

Teaching code in context does not preclude explicit skill instruction. Explicit (hands-on) code instruction seems to be superior to implicit (generative) phonics. Phonics approaches, in which students are expected to "discover" how words are similar to "infer" phonetic rules, often require that a student know how to decode the words in the practice exercise from which the phonics rules are to be inferred. But if he knows the words, he doesn't need the instruction in the first place!

With students who are just beginning to learn to read, teach sound-symbol relationships directly. Show the letter, model the sound, and prompt the student to produce the sound (Gunning, 1998; Simmons & Kameenui, 1989). Follow the M. Sprick et al. (1998) sequence shown in Exhibit 9.6. Demonstration is essential. As Adams (1990) reminds us, "the single most important activity for building the knowledge and skills eventually required for reading appears to be *reading aloud to children regularly and interactively* (emphasis added)" (p. 124).

The need for time spent in listening to reading, and reading for enjoyment, out of texts at the correct skill level cannot be overstated. Second, this time must be augmented by periods, even if short, of intense work on skill acquisition. During these sessions insist on accuracy in decoding by urging the student to correct errors (Rosenhouse et al., 1997; Spaai et al., 1991). If necessary, prolong attention to the words by pointing to each one and not allowing the student to go on until you move your finger in response to correct decoding. Remind the student that, after sounding out a word in a story, he should remember it. Then it won't be necessary to sound it out again.

When a student has moved into passage reading you may, at first, want to reduce overuse of context clues to increase reliance on code. If that is the case, do not attack or criticize the use of context, but do select passages that aren't heavily illustrated (or tape over illustrations in the passages you have), deal with novel content, and are not redundant. This way, fewer context clues will be available. Encourage the student to attempt unknown words by applying his knowledge of code content. Employ an explicit approach to code in which essential sound-symbol relationships are directly pointed out in the words. Avoid teaching all the sounds in the world. Have the student master a core of high-utility sound-symbol relationships along with strategies for using them in new words (Baker et al., 1994). High-utility sound symbols are those that appear frequently in text and are regular (M. Sprick et al., 1998). Do not teach the student decoding terminology (digraph, blend, CVC), but do teach him sequential, code-based generalizations for word attack. Don't forget blending. Use drill and practice over passages to achieve fluency in code content. Extensive drill on words or phonemic units in isolation is generally *not* recommended, though those procedures are justified if you have tried other methods and they have failed.

In an explicit code lesson, students are taught a sound and asked to decode words that have the sound. Here is an example of explicit instruction:

**Teacher:** "The sound of this letter "s" is /sss/." "What sound will you say when you see this letter?" Hold up "s."

**Student:** "/sss/."

**Teacher:** "These new words will be in our story. Let's read them together. Remember to say /sss/ when you sound out a word with this new letter."

When explicitly teaching very specific content (such as vowel teams or word lists), be aware that you are asking the student to perform an essentially meaningless task. The promise that working on these subskills will eventually enable him to make sense of printed matter is far-removed and hollow for most special/remedial students. Therefore, be careful to supply meaning while maintaining the focus on target skills. The following recommendations may help students who need intense practice on particular skills:

✓ Be sure of the content you are teaching.

✓ Don't isolate (decontextualize) material the student has already learned.

✓ Be sure the student knows what he is trying to learn.

✓ Use the blending/analogy procedures described in Action 7 as instructional techniques.

✓ Provide short, high-intensity practice sessions that require high rates of student response.

✓ Avoid long sessions that will bore the student.

✓ Maintain a quick pace by moving to a new objective as soon as a skill has been learned.

✓ Reinforce the kid frequently but keep statements of praise or distribution of rewards brief.

✓ Tie rewards directly to acquisition of the content ("Good work! You learned the word 'not.' Great work! You're really being good.").

✓ Mix specific lessons with whole-reading experiences such as being read to.

✓ If at all possible, teach students missing similar skills in groups to derive the motivational advantage of peers and to promote vicarious learning. However, be aware that the membership of such groups should change quickly. If it doesn't, the grouping isn't working.

✓ Modify the presentation frequently, but never at the expense of focus on the content.

✓ Monitor progress and expect rapid improvement. If the student does not acquire the skills in, at most, a couple of weeks, you may wish to consider an intensified approach that emphasizes both code and context (see Teaching Recommendation 3).

## A Note on Monitoring Decoding

Once you have selected an objective, you will also need to monitor the effect of teaching to determine if your teaching is working. Monitoring procedures are discussed in *Resources for Implementing Curriculum-Based Evaluation* (Howell et al., 2000a). The best monitoring techniques are those that use measures that reflect what you are teaching and are also sensitive to learning. In the domain of decoding, this is fairly easy.

Although you can monitor a student's acquisition of a specific decoding subskill (converting vowels to the long sound when a silent e is present) unless progress is slow (it takes more than 2 weeks to teach that skill), we recommend that passage reading be used to monitor. Timed reading samples should be collected and charted during each instructional session. It doesn't matter if you time from passages the student read during the last session or from passages he has never seen before (those for the new session). It does matter that you use the same kind of passages the same way every day.

Remember, the only way to determine if an instructional approach is effective is to try it, take data, and let the student tell you if it works.

## Summary

Reading is an interactive process, and there is some validity to concerns that subdividing such a process distorts it. However, our inability to write about everything at the same time, and the considerable body of evidence demonstrating that decoding is important, have led us to separate the discussions in Chapters 8 and 9. That doesn't mean that they should be separate within instruction.

This chapter has reviewed issues relative to word recognition as a curriculum domain and presented tactics for evaluating and teaching knowledge in that domain. You will need to consider all the guidelines within this chapter and those in Chapter 8 for these tactics to be useful.

# Chapter 10

# Language

*Martin Luther King was a great man because he worked to assure freedom for all people. He used his words to do his work.*
—Chandra Clarkson, California Youth Authority, January 11, 1995

## Step 1: Define Your Purpose

This chapter provides an introduction to oral-language evaluation. It is included in the text, at this point, to serve as a bridge between reading and writing (reading being the reception of communication and writing being the expression of communication). As such, it will focus primarily on communication. It will also direct the coverage of language topics to teaching.

Language is the exclusive tool for obtaining knowledge, for communication, and for thought. As cognitive processes become both more complex and more abstract, language plays an increasingly important role in the way we learn. Consequently, children with language problems are often unable to fully benefit from school programs. Such children have difficulty gaining information from both verbal and printed messages. They may also have problems demonstrat-

ing what they know and in expressing the need for help.

There are a number of theoretical bases from which to assess language, but this chapter includes neither an in-depth discussion nor a resolution of these. Nor does it focus on the evaluation of the various processes theorists believe children use to understand and produce language (Pellegrini et al., 1997). Instead, the purpose of this chapter is to describe assessment procedures that will enable you to decide what to teach students with language problems. It will also help you decide what you should teach students with *Limited English Proficiency* (LEP).

## Step 2: Define the Thing to Be Measured

As in other domains discussed in that book, the first step in language assessment is to decide what to evaluate. The four general areas of language are:

Syntax

Semantics and morphology

Pragmatics—communication

Phonology, voice, and fluency

This chapter is limited to a discussion of syntax, semantics, and pragmatics. Because of space limitations, and the specialized techniques of evaluation and treatment, we will not cover phonology.

The major components of syntax, semantics, and pragmatics are presented in Exhibit 10.1. The exhibit is a compilation of essential language elements. Throughout this chapter, Exhibit 10.1 will serve as the primary reference—so let's take a look at it now. Exhibit 10.1 shows things that students must have the skills to do—but they are not necessarily things that students need to know about. This means that competent speakers may use the syntactic rules that govern word order but have no idea how to state the rules (for example, "Pro-verbs may stand for many events").

The content included in Exhibit 10.1 is most likely appropriate for school-age children who have moderate language problems. It would need to be extended downward to accommodate very young children and/or those with severe language problems. The sequence of the content is appropriate for children with typical language development, as well as for children with language delays. Children with typical language development would include those who are acquiring English as a second language. Most children with language delays follow a sequence of language development followed by other students; they just do it more slowly. Because it is hard to tell whether a specific set of language skills must be learned in a particular sequence, children with language delays and children with more complex language disorders may both benefit from the same instruction.

The content of Exhibit 10.1 is not necessarily arranged in prerequisite order. So don't assume that because a kid passes a higher-numbered skill she has mastered all lower-numbered skills.

In general, however, skills with higher numbers are more complex than skills with lower numbers.

The criteria for acceptable performance (CAP) is not listed within the table because information relating to the CAP for language skills is not available. There are "developmental norms/milestones" presented by many authors, but these often have standard deviations equivalent to 50% of a student's age. In addition, they are tied closely to language experience, which varies too much among children to make the norms of value. Sometimes it may be better to produce your own local milestones (Miller & Rhea, 1995). However, there *is* a standard for language use. That standard is conventional adult speech. Adult speakers of <u>Standard English</u> virtually *never* say such things as "I goed there," "Her and her are coming," "The boys is playing," "She gots a big dog," or "I out the window saw them." Therefore, even a few errors indicate a need for specific-level assessment.

The content of language, particularly that of syntax, tends to unnerve some evaluators. Evoy (1999) has suggested an analogy that may clear up some of the complexity. According to Evoy, the elements of speech and language are like the unlimited assortment of colors we see around us. These distinct shades, hues, and tones are all the result of mixing only three primary pigments—just as the messages we send through language result from a blend of semantics, syntax, and pragmatics.

### Syntax

<u>Syntax</u> is the rule system that governs word order in sentences. Some arrangements of words in English sentences are not acceptable. For example, we could say "The ball is bouncing," "Bouncing is the ball," or "Ball bouncing." However, we would not say "Ball the is bouncing." English rules of syntax do not permit this arrangement of nouns and verbs (in Exhibit 10.1 the reference for combining noun phrases and verb phrases is shown in column I, number 1–16).

Morphology is a rule system that governs how to combine units of sound or *morphemes* to make words; it is actually a subset of syntax but it depends on a particular type of semantic knowledge. Therefore, we are going to cover morphology along with semantics.

Although there is an infinite variety of ideas to express, there is a finite number of structures speakers use to produce sentences. At higher levels of language functioning, speakers expand basic sentence patterns to produce more complex sentences using syntax to modify, coordinate, substitute, and subordinate. Below, the basic sentence "The girl ran" has been expanded by John Freeman to illustrate the use of additional syntactic structures. "The girl ran" is correct. But if a 12-year-old child only communicated using such simple sentences, we would be concerned about her sophistication with language.

| Sentence | Additional Syntactic Structure |
|---|---|
| The girl ran. | |
| The *sanguine* girl ran. | Adjective |
| The sanguine girl ran *quickly*. | Adverb |
| The sanguine girl ran *up the hill* quickly. | Prepositional phrase |
| The sanguine girl, *who wore the wild shoes*, ran up the hill quickly. | Relative pronoun clause |
| The sanguine girl, who wore the wild shoes, ran up the hill quickly, *but another runner won the race*. | Conjunction coordinating two independent clauses |
| The sanguine girl, who wore the wild shoes, ran up the hill quickly, but another runner won the race *because she was in better shape*. | Relative adverb clause |

The syntactic structures listed are described in Exhibit 10.2. Few of us have committed those structures to memory, so Exhibit 10.2 can be a helpful reference.

The syntactic structures listed in Exhibit 10.2 can be combined with behavior and conditions to form tables of specifications. For example, the behaviors listed in the table of specifications for syntactic structures (Howell et al., 2000a) are (1) imitates sentences, (2) produces sentences with prompts or in controlled settings, and (3) produces spontaneous sentences. When the content and behavior are combined, they form tasks. When **pronoun** is the content and **imitates** is the behavior, the task requires the student to "**imitate** sentences that include **pronouns.**" There is evidence to support the idea that a child's skill at imitation is closely related to her current level of linguistic competence and to her comprehension of utterances. Modeling with imitation is a valuable training procedure for children with language problems (James, 1990).

Not only are the rules of syntax and morphology consistent within a language, but the chronology or sequence in which typical learners acquire these rules is predictable. For a detailed discussion of syntax and morphology, we encourage you to read Wiig et al. (1992) or James (1990).

### Semantics and Morphology

Semantics is the study of meaning within a language. It includes:

Semantic rules

Meaning of morphographs

Meaning of single words and word combinations

Multiple meaning of simple words

Figurative language

Influence of content and structure on meaning

Semantic rules include the knowledge and application of the constraints that meaning imposes on sentences. For example, English syntax permits "The book reads the child." However, semantic rules (meaning rules) preclude that word combination. Books do not read, so the ways *book* may be used in a sentence are constrained by semantics.

This chapter focuses primarily on the meaning of morphemes, words, and utterances. A list

*Exhibit 10.1    Checklist of Language Content.*

| I<br><br>Syntax | II<br>Semantics/<br>Vocabulary | III<br><br>Pragmatics |
|---|---|---|
| | **A. Basic Vocabulary** | **A. One-Way Communication** |
| 1. Noun Phrase | **1. Body Parts** | **1. Expresses Wants** |
| **2. Verb Phrase** | 2. Clothing | 2. Expresses Opinions |
| 3. Regular Plurals | **3. Classroom Objects** | **3. Expresses Feelings** |
| **4. Subject Pronouns** | 4. Action Verbs | **4. Expresses Values** |
| 5. Prepositional Phrases | **5. Animals and Insects** | **5. Follows Directions** |
| **6. Adjectives** | 6. Outdoor Words | 6. Ask Questions |
| 7. Interrogative Reversals | **7. Family Members** | **7. Narrates Event** |
| **8. Object Pronouns** | 8. Home Objects | 8. States Main Idea |
| 9. Negatives | **9. Meals** | **9. Sequences Events** |
| **10. Verb *be* Auxiliary** | 10. Food and Drink | 10. Subordinates Details |
| 11. Verb *be* Copula | **11. Colors** | **11. Summarizes** |
| **12. Infinitives** | 12. Adverbs | 12. Describes |
| 13. Determiners | **13. Occupations** | **13. Compares and Contrasts** |
| **14. Conjunction *and*** | 14. Community | 14. Gives Instructions |
| 15. Possessives | **15. Grooming Objects** | **15. Explains** |
| **16. Noun/Verb Agreement** | 16. Vehicles | **B. Two-Way Communication** |
| 17. Comparatives | **17. Money** | **1. Considers the Listener** |
| **18. *Wh-* Questions** | 18. Gender | 2. Formulates Messages |
| 19. Past Tense | **19. School** | **3. Participates in Discussions** |
| **20. Future Aspect** | 20. Playthings | 4. Uses Persuasion |
| 21. Irregular Plurals | **21. Containers** | **5. Resolves Differences** |
| **22. Forms of *do*** | 22. Days of the Week | 6. Identifies Speaker's Biases |
| 23. Auxiliaries | **23. Months** | **7. Identifies Speaker's Assumptions** |

| I<br><br>Syntax | II<br>Semantics/<br>Vocabulary | III<br><br>Pragmatics |
|---|---|---|
| **24. Derivational Endings** | 24. Emotions | 8. Formulates Conclusions |
| 25. Reflexive Pronouns | **25. Numbers** | **C. Nonverbal Communication** |
| **26. Qualifiers** | 26. Celebrations and Holidays | 1. Gestures |
| 27. Conjunctions *and, but,* | **27. Spatial Concepts** | **2. Proximity** |
| **28. or** | 28. Quantitative Concepts | 3. Position |
| 29. Conjunctions | **29. Temporal Concepts** | **4. Expression** |
| **30. Indirect and Direct** | 30. Shapes | 5. Eye Contact |
| 31. Objects | **31. Greetings and Polite Terms** | **D. Executive Function** |
| **32. Adverbs** | 32. Opposites | 1. Develops Intent |
| 33. Infinitives with Subject | **33. Materials** | **2. Plans** |
| **34. Participles** | 34. Music | 3. Monitors |
| 35. Gerunds | **35. Tools** | **4. Identifies Problems** |
| **36. Passive Voice** | 36. Categories | 5. Analyzes Problems |
| 37. Complex Verb Forms | **37. Verbs of the Senses** | **6. Recognizes Needed Assistance** |
| **38. Relative Adverb Clauses** | **B. Topical Vocabulary** | 7. Recognizes Solutions |
| 39. Relative Pronoun | **1. Reading Material** | **8. Seeks Help** |
| **40. Clauses** | 2. Content Area | 9. Adjusts Message |
| 41. Complex Conjunctions | **3. Technical** | **10. Uses Alternative Messages** |
| | 4. Idioms/Figurative Language | 11. Incorporates New Language Skills |
| | **5. Multiple Meaning of Words** | |
| | 6. Influence of Context on Meaning | **12. Attributes Events** |
| | | 13. Reflects |
| | | **14. Speculates** |
| | | 15. Regulates |
| | | **16. Repairs Communications** |

*Source:* Howell, K. W., Zucker, S. H. & Morehead, M. K. (2000b). *Multilevel Academic Skills Inventory.* Bellingham, WA: Applied Research and Development Center. To order contact the Student Co-op Bookstore, Western Washington University. Fax (360) 650-2888. Phone (360) 650-3656. Reprinted with permission.

of vocabulary categories was provided in Exhibit 10.1. Most of this listing is representative of words commonly used by children in the *early* stages of language development. In addition to basic vocabulary, there is content-specific vocabulary that is necessary for learning about particular topics (Rupley et al., 1999). These words fall into the second subdomain of vocabulary: "topical." The need to acquire vocabulary in particular content areas is discussed in Chapter 14 as part of task-related knowledge.

Semantics takes into account meaning, underlying concepts, and the relationship of words and sentences to contexts and ideas (Lascarides & Copestake, 1998). Vocabulary, the meanings of individual words, is a component of semantics. Vocabulary and semantic content are unlike the content for syntactic structures. Whereas there is a finite number of syntactic structures, the individual words and the contexts in which they are used are limitless. We even change the meaning of words. For example, the word **Fan** comes from **fanatic,** which used to refer to overindulgence in *religious* frenzy (Jeans, 1993). We also make up new words and phrases (Vanci-Osam, 1998). It has now become acceptable to say "prioritize" instead of "place things in priority" and it is not uncommon to hear "functionality" as in "that car has good functionality for off-road driving." One can continue learning and using new vocabulary and developing new meanings for previously learned words throughout life. A person's knowledge of words is so important that it has been suggested that "working memory capacity" (see Chapter 2) is really nothing more than word knowledge (Engle et al., 1990).

### Pragmatics

People use language for a reason—to communicate. Language is used to affect the behavior and attitudes of others and to regulate activities and attention. These functions are referred to as pragmatics. The goal of pragmatics instruction is to increase the child's repertoire of communication strategies for use in communication.

A critical aspect of pragmatics is code or style switching. Competent language users adjust their presentations according to the characteristics of the person to whom they are speaking (Walker, 1997). To put it simply, most people speak differently in church on Sunday morning than they do at a bar on Saturday night. Those who don't—no matter to which place they fail to adjust—are apt to be considered inappropriate. However, style switching routinely occurs across less extreme boundaries. For example, in a social gathering some individual's tone and word choice may be modified considerably by the simple presence of a wedding ring.

Pragmatics also includes the skill needed to shift between the roles of *speaker* and *listener.* These skills have verbal and nonverbal components. Some nonverbal components are physical proximity, gestures, and eye contact (Banbury & Hebert, 1992). Verbal components include turn taking, responding, and voice control. (Good speakers use their voices to influence outcomes and good listeners interpret the intent not only of words but also of intonation and volume.) In Exhibit 10.1, column 3, notice that skills associated with the role of listening and being responsive to others are summarized under part B, "two-way communication." As you will see in Chapter 13, these skills are closely related to interpersonal social skills (Walker, 1997).

### The Social Context of Language

Language has a social framework that teachers must understand if they are going to adapt instruction for individual learners (Gallas et al., 1996; Gruenewald & Pollack, 1990; Loban, 1986; Ralph, 1994). In a social framework, the function of language is to initiate and sustain interaction. Four context variables influence the use of language (Langdon, 1996; Sparks & Ganschow, 1995; Wells, 1973; Wiig & Semel, 1984):

Characteristics of participants (gender, age, status)

Setting/situation for exchange (time and place)

Topic of communication

Goal, task, or intent of speaker(s)

A child's language development depends, in part, on the extent to which the people around

*Often language samples are best taken as students interact.*

her are willing to communicate with her, to re-spond to what she says, to encourage her by their understanding, and to allow her to learn to mod-ify and expand her language. Family members, other adults, TV, and peers all play a role in the child's social linguistic environment, as do teach-ers, books, and computers (Dawkins, 1999).

### Social Rules

The child's understanding of sociolinguistic rules is another important aspect of language. Stu-dents who do not know the social rules of lan-guage usage may appear rude or insubordinate (Pellegrini et al., 1998). This applies to all ele-ments of language, not just to verbal usage. For example, when the teacher says "Would you do your spelling now?" the child who understands the sociolinguistic rules (but does not want to do the assignment) could say "Can I do it later?" or

just sharpen her pencil with great enthusiasm. A kid who does not understand sociolinguistic rules might just say "**No!**" and be considered un-responsive or rude. Some children may not par-ticipate (people surmise they are shy) when the social conditions to which they are accustomed are missing.

### Step 3: Make the Thing in Step 2 Observable

### Language Samples

Many teachers, psychologists, and speech/lan-guage pathologists believe that language assess-ment should be conducted with norm-referenced tests under conditions in which the stimulus, time, and circumstances are held constant. This is a

**Exhibit 10.2    Explanations of Syntactic Structures** (Prepared by John Freeman).

| Syntactic Structures | Purpose/Function | Example(s) | Sample Error(s) |
|---|---|---|---|
| 1. Noun/noun phrase | Identifies person, place, thing, or idea to act or be acted upon. | Girl, the girl, the wonderful girl, the girl with the wild shoes. . . . | Errors generally occur through omission. "Claire at the _____." |
| 2. Verb/verb phrase | Describes the action or state of being for the noun phrase. | runs, runs fast, runs with abandon, lightly runs over the hill. . . . | Errors generally occur through omission. "Claire at the oyster." |
| 3. Regular plural | An added -s to nouns. Indicates more than one. | Boys, girls, etc. | Many girl, three boy. |
| 4. Subject pronoun | Substitutes for nouns that act as subjects or predicate nouns. | I, you, he, she, it, we, you, they play. | It hit he. The car ran over he. |
| 5. Prepositional phrase | Consists of a preposition and a noun or pronoun object. Acts as adjectives or adverbs. | The boy went *around the bush.* The girl *in the new car.* | Girl go town. Boy sit chair. |
| 6. Adjective | Modifies nouns. Can be single words or phrases. | The *quiet* cat, the dog is *silent,* the horse *with the spots.* | The dog silent, cat quiet. |
| 7. Interrogative reversal form for question | The subject of the question; comes between the helping verb and the main verb. | Could I do that? | I could do that? |
| 8. Object pronoun | Receives the action of the verb or follows prepositions as object. | She saw *him* with *her.* | Him walked there. It's me. |
| 9. Negative | Serves to negate an action or description. | *not* green, *couldn't, never* would, nobody, *hardly.* | Double negatives: don't never, hardly nobody, no-one doesn't. |
| 10. Verb *to be* as a helping verb | am, is, are, was, were, be, been. | Has *been* seen, *is* looking, *was* peering. | She looking, boy peering. |
| 11. Verb *to be* as a linking verb | Links a predicate noun or predicate adjective to its subject. | The girl is a *genius.* The boy was *smart.* | That girl big. This boy large. |

| Syntactic Structures | Purpose/Function | Example(s) | Sample Error(s) |
|---|---|---|---|
| 12. Infinitive | *to* plus the present tense of a verb. | The boy wants *to study*. The girl likes *to learn*. | The girl wantsa learn. The boy likesoo study. |
| 13. Determiner | Precedes noun. | A, an, the, that, this, these, those. *This* type, *Those* types. | This kinds, those kinds. |
| 14. Coordinating conjunction | Joins or connects words and/or phrases. | And, but, or, nor, for, yet. | The girl boy can run jump. |
| 15. Possessive noun and pronoun | Establishes possession or ownership. | Singular possessive nouns add an *'s,* plurals add an *s'*. Possessive pronouns: my, your his, our, his, her, etc. | The *girls* shoes. The *boy* eyes. |
| 16. Noun/verb agreement | A singular subject (noun) agrees with a verb that ends in -s in the present tense. | The girl *considers*. The boy *jumps*. | There *goes* the boys. The *girl run* to the store. There*'s* is two of them. |
| 17. Comparative and superlative | Adjectives that imply comparisons add *-er* or *-est*. | Large, larger, largest, good, better, best. | She's the smartest of the two. He's more smarter. |
| 18. Question beginning with an interrogative pronoun. | *Wh–* pronouns used to set up a question. | Who, what, when, where, why, which, etc. | Subject does not use the *wh–* structure to begin questions. |
| 19. Past tense of the verb | Regular verbs add *-ed* to form the past tense. Irregular verbs take their own forms in the past tense. | Jump*ed*, look*ed*, jerk*ed*. | Yesterday, the girl look. The boy thinked she eated it. |
| 20. Future aspect | Helping verbs that indicate an action in the future. | May, can, going to, will, should. | It happen tomorrow. She do it later. |
| 21. Irregular plural | Noun that takes its own form for the plural. | Man/*men,* deer/*deer,* mouse/*mice*. | Look at the deers. |
| 22. Forms of *do* | *Do* is an irregular verb that is often misused. | *I/we/you/they/do,* he/she/it *does.* Past tense: did, have/has/had *done*. | She *done* it. He has *did* it. |
| 23. Auxiliary (helping verb) | Adds tense or intention to the action verb. | Has, have, had would, should, could, might, must, ought, will, shall. | Omission: She _____ do it if she could. |

***Exhibit 10.2***  *Continued*

| Syntactic Structures | Purpose/Function | Example(s) | Sample Error(s) |
|---|---|---|---|
| 24. Derivational ending that changes verb to noun | -or, -er, -ist, -ion when added to verbs indicates that the action is carried out by a noun. | Creat-or, operat-or, pian-*ist,* compan-*ion.* | Omission. |
| 25. Reflexive pronoun | Reflects back to and intensifies a noun in the sentence. | Myself, yourself, him-her-it-self, ourselves, yourselves, themselves. | We did it *ourself.* The girls took care of *theirselves.* The boys watched *themself.* |
| 26. Qualifier | Added to verbs to indicate to what extent or under which conditions that action is carried out. | Very, much, more, most, less, least, too, so, quite, almost, just, little, somewhat, anyway. | Omission. Overuse: So . . . So . . . So, anyway. |
| 27. Coordinating conjunction | Joins clauses or simple sentences. | And, but, or, nor, for, yet. | Omission: production of short choppy sentences. Overuse: production of run-on sentences. |
| 28. Conjunction commonly used to coordinate clauses | Relates two clauses or simple sentences. | After, before, because, if, since, so. | Omission: short, choppy sentences. Overuse: cuz . . . cuz . . . etc. |
| 29. Indirect and direct objects | The indirect object (*girl*) receives the direct object (<u>cake</u>). The direct object (<u>ball</u>) receives the action of the verb (<u>hit</u>). | He gave the *girl* the <u>cake</u>. The girl hit the <u>ball</u>. | Omission. |
| 30. Adverb | Modifies verbs, adjectives, and other adverbs. | *Sometimes* he wins. She felt *really* good. I do *much* less. | She felt *real* good. I want to go, *to.* |
| 31. Infinitive with subject | Adds a noun or pronoun to an infinitive—an infinitive phrase. | The boy wants *her to play.* | The girl wants him play. |
| 32. Participle | Formed by adding -ed or -ing to verbs. Precedes nouns and serves as adjectives. | She kept up a *running* dialog. | Omission. |
| 33. Gerund | Noun formed by adding -ing to verbs. | *Running* is fun. | Omission. |

| Syntactic Structures | Purpose/Function | Example(s) | Sample Error(s) |
|---|---|---|---|
| 34. Passive voice | Occurs when the subject/noun is acted upon by the verb. | The boy was seen in her company. | Omission. Overuse: Use of the passive voice is often discouraged in written communication. |
| 35. Complex verb form–multiple auxiliary | Usually indicates tense and intention. | He *would have been teased* if he had gone. | Omission. |
| 36. Relative adverb clause | Clause usually preceded by where, why, or when, which modifies the verb in the sentence. | The boy ran *when he was chased.* | Omission. |
| 37. Relative pronoun clause | Clause usually preceded by which, that, or who, which acts as an adjective in the sentence. | The boy, *who was chased,* ran away. | Omission or agreement problems: The boy *that.* |
| 38. Complex or subordinating conjunction | Used to set up a complex relationship between clauses in a sentence. | When, as if, where, until, before, after, etc.<br><br>While the girl lifted weights, the boy skied. | A clause beginning with a complex conjunction requires an independent clause to complete its action (make it a complex sentence). Errors often occur when the action in the complex sentence is left incomplete. While the girl was lifting weights. . . . |

*Source:* Howell, K. W., Zucker, S. H. & Morehead, M. K. (2000b). *Multilevel Academic Skills Inventory.* Bellingham, WA: Applied Research and Development Center. To order contact the Student Co-op Bookstore, Western Washington University. Fax (360) 650-2888. Phone (360) 650-3656. Reprinted with permission.

great concern when the testing is done for entitlement/eligibility determination (Dunn et al., 1996). But when trying to decide what to teach, these regulated conditions are actually contrary to what we know about language behavior. Often, tests place too great a constraint on the student's responses, making them less representative (Gerber & Bryen, 1981). The language-sampling procedure can provide information about important errors (Gavin & Giles, 1996; Oetting & Horohou, 1997). It is also the best General Outcome Measure (GOM) for screening and progress monitoring.

### Collecting the Language Sample

Directions for collecting language samples will be provided under Step 4. The more skilled you are in collecting a good language sample, the more information you will derive and the less specific level assessment you will need to do. When collecting a language sample, you must be extremely aware of the "know/display" dichotomy. Students may have trouble displaying language if you focus on a topic they don't understand. As with any assessment procedure, reliability (and hopefully validity) will tend to increase with the number of items included. We recommend collecting at least 50 utterances. However, it has also been recommended that the sample have as many as 175 complete and intelligible utterances (Gavin & Giles, 1996).

Because performance can vary depending on the nature of the cues you provide and type of sample produced (narrative, conversational), collect the language sample in at least three typical language situations. A good way to do this is to simply "cruise" by the target student and write down whatever she happens to be saying at the time. It is often useful to allow the target student to work or play in an activity area and record her language as she interacts with other children or adults. In this case, it is necessary to have a tape recorder with automatic volume control that can pick up the child's voice as she moves around. It may also be appropriate to evaluate the child's language as she interacts with a parent.

If you cannot collect a spontaneous language sample, you will have to prompt a discussion. Create an environment that will encourage the child's performance and elicit the best possible sample. When collecting a language sample, you must be willing to subordinate your interests to those of the child and to follow what the child says. This means responding to the child with vocabulary and grammatical forms she understands. However, you should respond to her message *not* the way she words it. Do not be instructive or corrective. Let your face and voice show the child that it is safe to say whatever she wants and that you are interested in what she says. It is better to go with a topic the student has brought up than to try and elicit more talk by changing the topic (Yoder & Davies, 1990, 1992).

Have objects, devices, toys, and photographs immediately available. Some children may require these tangible objects. You can present the stimulus materials one at a time as appropriate, but *do not* try to elicit responses by asking questions about the objects. Rather, simply use them to promote conversation. While trying to hold this kind of discussion, it is often a good idea to sit on the same level as the student. It is also a good idea to have a list of topics that may be of interest. These can include familiar events, school and community activities, visits the student may have made, what she likes to do after school, whom she plays with, what shows she watches on TV, current events, and brothers and sisters. With young children, one topic that has a high probability of success is the child's dog, other pets, or just animals in general. Pictures, photographs, films, and TV may also be used to stimulate discussion by asking the child to relate an episode or explain how or why something happened.

The question-answer format, which is easy to fall back on when things get uncomfortably quiet, should *be avoided* if possible. If you do use questions, be sure they are likely to elicit a whole sentence rather than a short phrase or a one-word answer. Direct questions such as "What is the boy doing?" elicit single-word responses such as "running." A language sample composed of "yes," "Tuesday," "blue," "maybe," and "Ralph" would be hard to analyze. Open-ended questions like "What happened at recess, and how did the fight get started?" may elicit more complex responses. If the child produces a high percentage of phrases or partial sentences, you may need to prompt with leads such as "Tell me more about that."

Be sure to provide an opportunity for the child to use the various structures that were listed in Exhibit 10.1. Have her discuss something a group did, or something that either happened in the past or will happen in the future to elicit plurals and past and future tense.

Puppets, if you are accomplished in their use, can provide versatility in the display of language by a young child. (The use of puppets with teenagers sometimes elicits more versatility than most of us prefer!) You may direct the child to ask the puppet something so as to elicit interrogative reversals and *wh*– questions. Having the student tell the puppet to do something will elicit prepositions, and telling the puppet not to do something will elicit negatives.

Some children will be unresponsive. It may help to have another child present on these occasions. It may also be useful to provide a game (or a classroom pet—for example, a rabbit) to promote communication between the youngsters. Record both children and transcribe the language sample for the target student only.

During oral-language sampling, intonation changes and pauses often signal sentence boundaries (Hughes et al., 1997). Make tally marks to indicate the approximate number of utterances during your conversation so that you know when you have reached the 50-utterance minimum. (That is the minimum for any individual sample. It is a good idea to collect multiple samples across multiple contexts.) After you have taken the language sample, try to decide if what the child produced was comparable with the language she usually produces. If you do not know the child well, ask someone who does to make the comparison. If you judge that the language is not typical, then add to the sample.

### Transcribing the Language Sample

Transcribing the language sample is a critical part of the assessment process and must be done with precision. After the sample is collected, it should be transcribed and analyzed immediately by the person who took it. This allows that person to analyze the sample before forgetting valuable information about inflection and voice. Because each transcribed sentence must ultimately be judged within the context of the stimulus materials and conversational circumstances in which it was collected, this context must also be recorded. For example, with the utterance "She is running up the hill," it is only possible to evaluate the use of the pronoun *she* if the evaluator knows the runner was female. Moreover, the use of the verb phrase *is running* and preposition *up* can only be evaluated by comparison with the stimulus or event being related.

Tape-record the language sample. You may also try to write down the child's utterances at the time of the sample, but this can cause problems. First, writing down a child's responses in front of her may inhibit her language performance. Second, you may not write fast enough or remember what the child actually says, and it is essential in this procedure to record *exact* utterances. Novice language evaluators tend to change what the child actually says to correspond more closely to conventional English. It is extremely difficult for adults to copy unconventional phrasing. The student may say "She running" and the evaluator will write "she's running." Therefore, compare the utterances written during the time the language sample was taken with the utterances on the tape to eliminate this type of error. Never let an uninformed person transcribe the tape of a language sample. (While conducting research, Dr. Theresa Serapiglia once recorded the language of a number of students; while typing up the sample, her unwary typist systematically corrected all of the students' errors.)

Obviously, an utterance does not need to be correct to be included in the transcription. Utterances may contain incorrect grammar, vocabulary, and/or word order. Only different utterances are counted; repetitions of utterances are not counted. If the child repeats the same thing several times, use only the first of the series. If the utterance is so garbled that it is unintelligible, it should not be included in the sample.

Most researchers require that only complete sentences be counted as utterances and scored. This may not be a reasonable expectation for some students (and we are only talking about inside-purpose assessment). Although we do not always expect children to speak in full sentences, *single-word utterances* are not to be included for analysis. However, partial sentences and one-word responses should be tallied and recorded. The number of repetitive utterances and the number of unintelligible utterances should also be noted, as well as the number of hesitations.

Decisions need to be made during the transcription process. One decision is where each utterance stops and the next one begins. The most useful indication of the beginnings and endings is the child's intonational patterns and pauses. Some children use "and" frequently to begin sentences. You should recognize that the *and* in these cases is not joining thoughts to form compound sentences but is used as a filler at the beginning of a statement. Other conjunctions such as *because* may be overused by children to start utterance. As is the case of *and,* you should not consider these words to be conjunctions joining two sentences.

A child may also produce a long, rambling sentence by stringing together several noun phrases such as "There is a boy and a truck and a dog and a ball and a tree and a flower and a cloud and the sun." In sentences like this, count only two repeated elements (you would count "boy and a" and "dog and a" but not the other occurrences of *and a*).

## Analyzing and Interpreting the Language Sample

Once the sample has been transcribed, you are ready to begin analysis. Because of the complexity of language, it is best to handle each of its domains separately. We'll briefly explain each one before providing the **Interpretation Guideline**.

### Syntax

The first step in your analysis of the sample is to identify those utterances with syntactic errors or omissions. Assuming you use Standard English (you may want to have someone else check you), read over each and then determine if the utterance sounds like something that an adult speaker with conventional usage would say. It may help to rewrite the sentence in conventional form, using information you remember about the context of the sentence. For example, if the child's utterance was "I gots three pencils," you might determine that the conventional form would have been "I have three pencils."

Next, you need to identify the type of error(s) evident in the sample. If you know the content, you can do this from memory and record it. If you haven't memorized them (we haven't), go to Exhibit 10.2 or a status sheet (an example of a specific table for syntax can be found in Howell et. al., 2000a). Also, entering the sample into a computer file will allow you to use the grammar checker in most word processing programs. Then the checker can find and label the problem.

Here is an important point: a sentence may be correct but lack desired syntactic sophistication. Because of this, you must also search the language sample for evidence of each syntactical

structure. If you find that the student has not produced a structure, mark it for later specific-level assessment. This exercise must be carried out to see if the student simply failed to display the missing structure or if she doesn't know how to use it.

Here is an example.

| What Was Said | What Should Have Been Said | Error Type Keyed to Table 10.1 (Syntax/ Morphology) |
|---|---|---|
| 1. After wash her hair what did her do? | What did she do after she washed her hair? | 4 and 18 |
| 2. I could do that Connie? (intonation indicates question) | Could I do that Connie? | 7 |
| 3. I ran. | This morning before school I went out running. | Not complex. Skills not displayed |

### Syntactic Interference

This step has some political implications (Hymowitz, 1999), which we'd rather ignore; but, they can pop up in your class. After you've identified errors, decide if they are related to interference points between other languages or dialects and English (Gorenflo, 1995; Paradis & Genessee, 1996). This will require you to become familiar with the other language or to work with someone who is familiar. We will briefly supply this information for Spanish and Black English, as they currently represent the largest language minorities in the United States. Canadians will be interested in defining the intersections of English and French as Australians may be with Aboriginal and/or Oceanic languages. Some syntactic interference points between Spanish and English are as follows.

1. The *-s* ending is often omitted in plural possessives and third-person singular verbs. Also, past-tense endings may appear to be absent. ("They *play* there yesterday.")

2. Spanish employs added words rather than suffixes to show comparatives. ("Her shirt is *more* pretty.")

3. Negative commands may be expressed by no instead of don't. ("*No* go there.")

4. Articles (the, a, an) may be absent. ("She is teacher.")

5. Spanish employs *to have* in many instances where, in English, *to be* would be used. ("I *have* hunger" or "She *has* 6 years.")

6. *Do* may be absent from questions. ("You like ice cream?")

Syntactic features of Black English that differ from Standard English are harder to identify as it varies with region. It also evolves rapidly. Here are some examples.

- The expression of possession is different. ("Joe book.")

- Negation is expressed by a double negative or *ain't.* ("I *haven't/ain't* got no car.")

- Subject-verb agreement differs. ("We *is* here.")

- The *-s* ending is omitted from third-person singular verbs. ("She laugh.")

- The word *is* is not used in present tense. ("She here.")

- *If* constructions are changed. ("I find out *do she want* to stay.")

- Past-tense *-ed* may be omitted. ("She walk.")

- Future tense of verbs may be expressed differently. ("She *gon* [going to] go.")

- *Be* expresses status. ("She *be* sick.")

### Phonological Interference

Although this chapter does not deal extensively with articulation problems, they sometimes influence semantics and syntax (Logan & LaSalle, 1999). Here are some dialect and culturally different speech codes. The major differences between Standard English and (nonstandard) Black English and the major interference points for Spanish speakers learning English have been summarized by Hopper and Naremore (1978). Phonological interference points between Spanish and English are as follows.

1. Initial and final voiceless plosives are not aspirated in Spanish. *Coat* may sound like *goat; pig* may sound like *pick.*

2. Spanish has neither voiced nor voiceless /th/, so the child may substitute /d/ for voiced /th/, giving "*dis*" instead of "*this*"; /s/ may substitute for voiceless /th/, giving "*sing*" instead of "*thing.*"

3. Spanish makes no distinction between /b/ and /v/.

4. Spanish has the /s/ sound but not the /z/, /zh/, (as in *treasure*), /sh/ (as in *shop*), and /j/ (as in *jump*) sounds.

5. /r/ and /l/ may be substituted for one another.

6. The vowel sounds in the English words *pig, fat,* and *sun* are not used in Spanish. (*Pig* may become *peeg, fat* may become *fet,* rhyming with *set,* and *sun* may sound as though rhymed with *John.*)

Phonological interference points between Black English and Standard English are as follows.

1. /r/ and /l/ may be omitted before consonants in the last sound in a word (*fort* becomes *fot*).

2. Consonant clusters at the end of words will be shorter.

3. Final consonants will be weaker (*English* becomes *Englis*).

### Semantics/Vocabulary

It is difficult to make good survey decisions about a child's functional level in vocabulary by analyzing a language sample alone. Sometimes it is obvious in the sample that a child's vocabulary skills are deficient because of her limited word choice or the use of such fillers as "that," "you know the stuff," or "thing." Other times, you come away just feeling unsure. In either case, specific-level assessment will be needed.

### Pragmatics

The language sample may also be used to determine the child's skills in communication, though an interview of teachers or family will help.

Although performance standards for communication are not precise, the child's peer group can be used as a comparison standard. Using the pragmatic content in Exhibit 10.1 or the status sheet in Howell et al. (2000a), try scanning the language sample or inquiring during the interview for evidence of successful use of each function. Here is an excerpt from a child's language sample (remember that the punctuation you see here was supplied by the evaluator during transcription of an oral sample):

> "I seen them on television. And this other guy got robbed and the other guy got mad. And she, and she, well there was a bad guy. The car was all torn up. The lady said. 'Give me the money.' They bombed the vices. They cops, do you know?"

In this sample, the child does not appear to be telling events in sequence or using subordination (placing emphasis on important parts) as an aid in organizing her material. Because she has not used subordination to decide what to feature and what to suppress, her story lacks order. You would record this information on Exhibit 10.1 as no-pass (NP) for sequence events (pragmatics part A, item 9) and subordinate details (pragmatics part A, item 10). This indicates that specific-level assessment may be needed in those areas.

The executive function of pragmatics, because it is covert, presents many measurement problems. Refer to Chapter 13 for information about the assessment of "type 2" prerequisites.

### Length Measures

A traditional method for assessing children's language development is to determine the average length of their utterances using either communication units (CU), minimal terminal units (T-units), or mean length of utterance (MLU). If complexity of utterances is a concern, use MLU. However, only a person who is very familiar with T-units and/or CU should try to collect and interpret them. The data derived from norms on all of these procedures often show ranges in scores that are as high as 50% of a student's age (Gruenwald & Pollak, 1990; Templin, 1957; Yoder et al., 1995).

So, we recommend the use of MLU (unless you are trained or want to bring in a speech/language pathologist). You can easily determine the MLU. Here is an example of calculating the MLU.

| Sentence | Repetitions and Fillers Not Counted | Number of Words per Sentence |
|---|---|---|
| 1. That . . . that dolphin has a baby. | that | 5 |
| 2. And, uh, the dolphin the fat dolphin has a big nose. | and, uh, the dolphin | 7 |
| 3. And, uh, it's the ball I liked.* | and, uh | 6 |
| 4. Pretty soon he swam uh uh away under the water. | uh, uh | 8 |
| 5. And, uh, we bought drinks and sandwiches and chips and salad. | and, uh, and, and | 7 |
| | Total Words | 33 |
| | MLU | 6.6 |

\* Count "it's" as "it is"

Count the number of words and divide by the total number of sentences. If the child repeats, count each word only once, as in the utterance, "*I I* am going to see the dolphins" or "*That that* dolphin has a baby." In this example, you would count the words *I* and *that* only once. If the child corrects her sentence, as in sentence 2, count the corrections and not the words the corrections replace. Do not count filler expressions such as "you know" or "ah, ah" as in sentence 4. Count contractions as two words. Do not count more than two *ands* plus the words that the *and* connects (as indicated by sentence 5). Do not count stereotypic starters such as those in sentences 2, 3, and 5 ("and uh").

### Quality Measures

When analyzing the language samples of children who are functioning at higher levels in language, both the mean number of words per sentence <u>and</u> the number of different kinds of structures included in the sentences should be considered simultaneously. A low number of words uttered per sentence (MLU) is a signal that the student is probably not incorporating various syntactic structures into her sentences and is not producing complex, expanded sentences (this is called a "fluency" problem). However, some caution is needed here.

Listeners are inclined to credit speakers who have a high mean length of utterance with advanced language performance, when in actuality the primary characteristic of their language is <u>verbosity</u>. Verbose speakers use stylistic devices to modify, qualify, repeat, and pad the main argument. Listeners often credit speakers like this with saying something intelligent (Labov, 1969). But, have you ever felt overwhelmed and impressed with a person's speech, only to wonder later what he really said? (Of course, we notice this phenomenon most frequently in election years.)

### Mean Utterance Rank

A final approach to categorizing utterances is similar to a technique recommended for written expression in Chapter 11. It involves collecting sample utterances and dividing them into groups by apparent (or actual) sophistication (Hughes et al., 1997).

This would involve the development of a scale of sophistication. For example, the 3-level scale by Isaacson found in Exhibit 11.6 could be used for syntax. Sentences in the language sample could be ranked as a 1, 2, or 3. The proportion of sentences at each level will then provide an image of complexity by utterance (rather than by the whole sample). An average score can be derived by summing the ranks and then dividing by the number of utterances. If a student's 50-sentence sample contained 23 ranked 1, 17 ranked 2, and 10 ranked 3, that student's average would be 23 + 34 + 30 = 87/50 = 1.74. Increases in the average should indicate decreases in utterances ranked 1 and/or increases in those ranked 2 or 3. This, in turn, should represent increased complexity (maturity) in speaking.

We want to make it clear that Hughes et al. (1997) did not recommend this procedure, but its simplicity is appealing.

### Causes of Language Difficulty

Various environmental, sensory, and psychological risk factors are related to inadequate language skill. These include insufficient stimulation, improper training, impaired hearing, excessive parental or social pressure, inadequate speech mechanisms, lack of good speech models, parental overprotection, and emotional trauma. However, the factors only increase the probability of a problem. There may be some poor kid out there with all of these risks but no language difficulty. In most cases there is no *apparent reason* for language deficits.

The cause of the problem is often of little importance to its solution. We know we've said this before, but really, if educators would spend as much time looking for solutions as they do for causes, more students would be helped. However, some causative factors such as impaired hearing, inadequate speech mechanisms, and inadequate classroom environments need to be considered before or during the assessment process. These factors need to be considered because they are related to *teaching*. This is especially true of hearing (Berry, 1992; Mauk et al., 1994).

Some indications of a hearing impairment are as follows:

Trouble with consonant sounds (which are softer and have a higher frequency than vowel sounds);

Voice production problems such as unusual pitch or quality of voice;

Unusual rhythms;

Persistent articulation errors; and

Trouble remembering and understanding long sentences.

A child may also have different hearing efficiency levels at different times. When a speech or language problem is suspected, be sure that a complete audiological evaluation is part of the assessment. New techniques make hearing evaluations of even young children short and reliable.

## Step 4    Conduct Assessment

## Step 5    Use CBE Process of Inquiry

## Step 6    Summarize

## Evaluation Procedure

The process of language evaluation is outlined in Exhibit 10.3.

### Action 1: Determine Language History

#### Directions

You are looking for two things here—limited English proficiency and language interference. These topics are discussed elsewhere in this chapter, so if you are unfamiliar with them, you may need to read ahead to get the information you need (for example, see Action 11).

Generally, the easiest way to determine language history is to interview the student and/or her family. Ask about languages spoken in the home as well as the presence of English.

#### Interpretation

Remember, the fact that a student speaks a language other than English does not automatically imply a problem with English. Bilingualism is a strength.

If there is evidence of limited English proficiency, follow the same sequence of inquiry in Exhibit 10.3, but pay particular attention to advice regarding limited proficiency and interference.

Note: If you are interested in finding out if a student can read and understand materials written in English, return to Chapter 8. Do not try to base such a decision on a "Language dominance" test. They are too far removed from the curriculum to be of any use.

### Action 2: Language Sample (Survey-Level Assessment)

#### Directions

The language sample is taken to find out if the child has a language problem in English, set a "base-line" for monitoring, and obtain guidance for additional assessment.

1. Decide on settings for conversation and assemble any stimulus materials you may need. Select these settings with the goal of eliciting a large number of natural responses. Plan to draw samples from at least three settings. *Oral narrative* is best.

2. If you plan to include other students and if you plan to sample across several settings—more than one class, recess, lunch, at home, or on the bus—then schedule appointments ahead of time.

3. Set up a tape recorder.

4. Elicit at least a 50-utterance sample (this may take a couple of days).

    a.    One-word utterances or short phrases are not counted as part of the 50-utterance minimum, but they are included in the transcription.

    b.    Sentences with incorrect grammar are counted as part of the 50-utterance minimum ("Her gonna cry?" or "Why Lee Lee barking?").

    c.    Structure the conversation to elicit plurals, past and future tense, vocabulary. Use Exhibit 10.2 to guide you.

5. Use props (pictures, comics, games, toys) and even other students to create a context for conversation. Avoid asking questions.

6. Transcribe the sample.

**Exhibit 10.3    The Process of Oral Language Evaluation.**

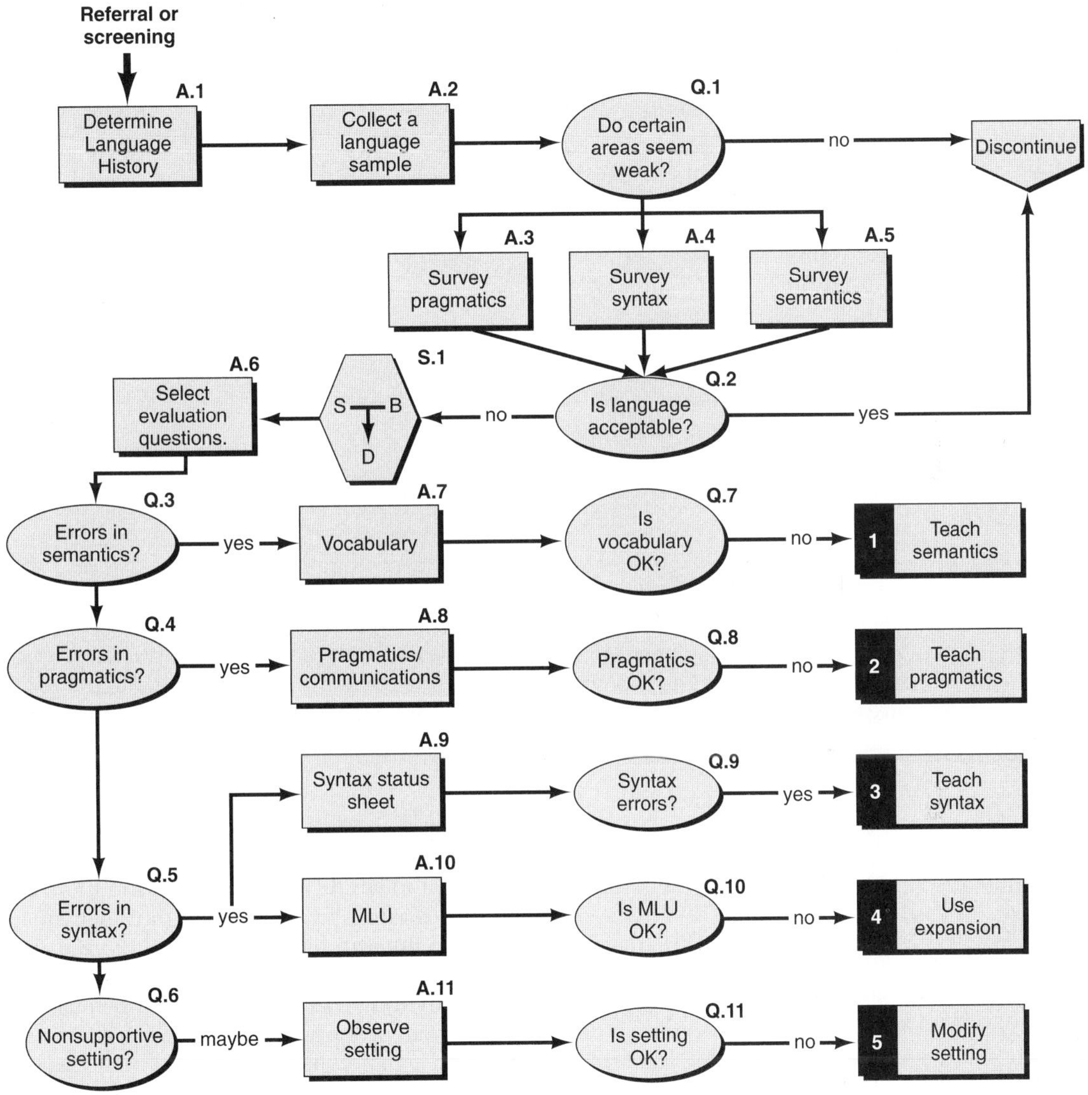

## Interpretation Guidelines
Tally errors using Exhibit 10.1.

### Question 1: Do Certain Areas Seem Weak?
If NO, then discontinue.

    If YES, for pragmatics, then go to **Action 3.**
    If YES, for syntax, then go to **Action 4.**

If YES for semantics, then go to **Action 5.**

## Actions 3–5: Use Status Sheets

Return to the language sample and fill out a status sheets for syntax and pragmatics (in Howell et al., 2000a). For semantics, use the check sheet for language content in Exhibit 10.1 (but be prepared for the student to have missed many of the topics). The CAP for all areas is either acceptable adult speech or the usage of an exemplar in the same setting.

### Question 2: Is the Student's Language Competence at Acceptable Levels?

If YES for all three areas, then cease evaluation, check referral, or repeat the survey-level procedure in another setting. You may still be interested in **Teaching Recommendations 4** and **5.**

If NO, then go to **Summary 1.** Compare the student's behavior to the standard and derive a discrepancy for *each area of concern*. This discrepancy can then be converted into an instructional goal. For example, if the standard for noun/verb agreement is 100% but the student only demonstrates agreement 80% of the time, the syntax goal would be to improve agreement by +20% (or ×1.25).

### Action 6: Select Evaluation Questions

There are three questions listed below. You must select the ones that seem to apply to your student. If you can't tell, *pick them all*. Each leads to a specific-level procedure and then to a treatment recommendation. As you select questions or carry out any operation, keep in mind that language interference and limited English proficiency are not reasons to stop the evaluation process. But they must be considered when employing teaching recommendations. Here are the questions.

### Question 3: Are There Omissions or Errors in the Student's Semantic Usage?

If YES then go to **Action 7: Probe for Vocabulary.** Also go to **Question 4.**

### Question 4: Are There Pragmatic Errors or Omissions?

If YES, then go to **Action 8: Pragmatics and Communication Status Sheet (Howell et al., 2000a).** Also go to **Question 5.**

### Question 5: Are There Syntactical Omissions or Errors Leading to a Lack of Sentence Complexity?

If YES, then go to **Action 9: Syntax/Status Sheet (Appendix A.4)** and **Action 10: Mean Length of Utterance.** Also go to **Question 6.**

### Question 6: Is the Class/School Environment Supportive of Language Learning?

If MAYBE, then go to **Action 11: Observe Setting.**

### Action 7: Probe for Vocabulary and Morphology

When you collect information about semantics, you want to find out about the student's skill at

- Knowledge of word and morphograph meaning (such as vocabulary) and

- Finding out what words mean.

If a student doesn't know what a word means, then obviously you should teach it. However, unless you are using morphographic instruction, teaching one set of words won't necessarily make it any easier to learn other words. Many students who have learning problems often have trouble figuring out the meanings of words. This is most likely because although vocabulary is best learned in a natural reading and speaking environment, often it turns out that special and remedial students don't have the skills to derive word meanings from context without direct and explicit vocabulary instruction (Brett et al., 1996; Elliot & Zhang, 1998). However, they are deprived of the opportunity to learn in this fashion by their limited reading and social skills. In addition, because of study skill and reading problems, these students often accumulate great deficits in general knowledge as they advance through school (see Chapter 13). Without adequate prior knowledge, they cannot acquire new vocabulary because they don't have the knowledge necessary to access the context (Ruddell & Hua, 1996). Therefore, explicit instruction is needed. Exhibit 10.1 presented two subdomains of semantics/vocabulary. The "basic" subdomain is composed of categories of concepts and things that typical students are familiar with before they come to school. Therefore, this domain of basic knowledge should be checked. As it turns out, this is the sort of content that is featured in published concept inventories, adaptive behavior scales, and developmental checklists. It is easiest to pick one or two of these existing devices by using the content in Exhibit 10.1 as your selection criterion.

Next, the student should be tested regarding knowledge of the vocabulary she needs to comprehend both topical instruction and/or reading material. This is called "topic-specific" (technical) vocabulary (see Chapter 13). It is recognized by reviewing the material the student needs to know and selecting words important to understanding the topic.

### Step 1: Assess Knowledge of Individual Words or Morphographs

To assess vocabulary, you need to know how to use four formats:

|  | Identify Correct Synonym or Definition | Produce (Supply) the Correct Synonym or Definition |
|---|---|---|
| Words in context | Format 3 | Format 1 |
| Words in isolation | Format 4 | Format 2 |

### Format 1: Produce Word Meaning in Context

This skill is checked by underlining important words in a passage and then asking the student to read the passage. When the student comes to an underlined word, have her stop and supply a synonym, define it, or use it in a sentence (other than the one in the passage). If the definition or sentence is in keeping with the context, she passes. Because this format relies on reading skill, don't use it with nonreaders.

### Format 2: Produce the Word in Isolation

Take the underlined words from Format 1 and present them in isolation (by dictation and/or flashcards). The student is asked to supply a definition or synonym to use the target word in a sentence. Any acceptable use is counted as correct.

### Format 3: Match the Word in Correct Context

Have the student read the passage until she reaches an underlined word. Then supply two alternative definitions, both of which match the word but only *one* of which matches the context. Ask her to pick the definition (or synonym) that makes sense in the context of the passage. Once again, this format can't be used with nonreaders.

### Format 4: Match Words in Isolation to Their Definitions

The student is shown or read words and then given age-appropriate definitions. If the student matches the word to a correct definition (regardless of context), it is correct.

### Directions for Action 7, Step 1

1. Select or develop a test to sample categories of words or morphemes that the student does not seem to know. Construct these tests using one or more of the four formats presented above. The items may be drawn from materials used in the classroom, vocabulary used for instruction, or vocabulary used for social interaction. Reference the words/morphemes to the categories presented in Exhibit 10.1. A 25-item sample is recommended.

2. Administer the tests. Say to the student "What is a _____?" for a production response. Say "Point to the _____," for an identification response. If you must give multiple tests, follow the sequence (1 through 4) presented above.

3. Score responses.

### Clarification of Results: Format 1

*Pass.* The student knows these words/morphemes. This vocabulary is not a problem.
*No-pass.* Go to **Format 2.**

### Clarification of Results: Format 2

*Pass.* The student knows word meanings but doesn't adjust them to fit context (as required in **Format 1),** so that is what needs to be taught.

This is often referred to as "multiple-meaning" instruction. Use **Teaching Recommendation 1.** *No-pass.* See **Format 3** <u>and</u> **Action 10.**

### Clarification of Results: Format 3

*Pass.* The student can identify correct definitions by using context clues but isn't sufficiently skilled to supply these definitions. Use **Teaching Recommendation 1,** but begin instruction by building from the student's existing identification skills. Start with clearly correct and incorrect choices. Then gradually fade out choices to require her to provide the definitions.
*No-pass.* Go to **Format 4** <u>and</u> **Action 11.**

### Clarification of Results: Format 4

*Pass.* The student has some knowledge of word meanings but only at the identification level. The student needs to be moved from identification to production within context. Begin by teaching production of correct definitions. See **Teaching Recommendations 1** and **4** and related information in Chapter 8 and Chapter 14.
*No-pass.* Give Step 2. You should also go to <u>*Language*</u> **Action 11.**

### Directions for Action 7, Step 2: Determining Word Meaning

This process is used to see if the student can employ context to determine the meaning of words and/or morphemes. Because this skill is critical to reading comprehension, you might want to take a look at the way the vocabulary is handled in Chapter 8.

1. Devise a pretest, or use information from other procedures, to recognize a body of words and/or morphemes (at least 20) that the student cannot define or use in sentences. These should be words and/or morphemes the student is expected to know.

2. Locate, or produce, passages containing the targeted words or morphemes. Underline these.

3. Ask the student to read or listen to the passages and then to try and define the words.

4. Ask the student how she attempts to figure out what the underlined words mean.

### Clarification of Results

If the student can define previously unknown words once they are placed in context, there isn't a problem. Recognize more unknown words/morphemes and teach them in context.

If the student cannot define the words, check (through an interview) to see if the student is aware of the following strategies for context analysis:

Comparing the word to the message that preceded it;

Comparing the word to the message that followed it;

Inserting a word that is known, and makes sense, in the place of the unknown word (assuming that the unknown word and the known word mean the same thing);

Using gender, tense, and number clues to include or rule out possible meanings;

Using syntax clues to test the appropriateness of possible synonyms;

Using reference materials such as glossaries or dictionaries; and

Asking someone what the word means.

### Interpretation Guidelines

#### Question 7: Is the Student's Vocabulary OK?

There have been several subparts of **Action 7.** You will need to answer this question for each part, and your answers may be different. Use the Clarification of Results information.

If YES, then there isn't a problem. Go to **Question 4.**

If NO, then go to **Teaching Recommendations 1** and **4.** Also, employ **Action 11.**

### Action 8: Pragmatics and Communication

Follow a procedure similar to the one used for obtaining the survey sample, except with this procedure you must structure opportunities for the student to display pragmatic skills. For example, if you want to sample "seeks help," you

*Exhibit 10.4* *Analysis of Communication.*

**Directions:** Beginning with the column on the right, judge the quality of usage for each communication skill. If use is inadequate, mark it "NO," then move to the condition(s) found to the left. Criteria should take into account the context of usage. Mark items YES, NO, or UNSURE.

| Analysis of Communication | Identify Correct Example | Produce after Model | Produce after Prompt | Produce in Familiar Content | Produce with Strangers |
|---|---|---|---|---|---|
| A. One-Way Communication | | | | | |
| 1. Expresses Wants | | | | | |
| 2. Expresses Opinions | | | | | |
| 3. Expresses Feelings | | | | | |
| 4. Expresses Values | | | | | |
| 5. Follows Directions | | | | | |
| 6. Ask Questions | | | | | |
| 7. Narrates Event | | | | | |
| 8. States Main Idea | | | | | |
| 9. Sequences Events | | | | | |
| 10. Subordinates Details | | | | | |
| 11. Summarizes | | | | | |
| 12. Describes | | | | | |
| 13. Compares and Contrasts | | | | | |
| 14. Gives Instructions | | | | | |
| 15. Explains | | | | | |
| B. Two-Way Communication | | | | | |
| 1. Considers the Listener | | | | | |
| 2. Formulates Messages | | | | | |
| 3. Participates in Discussions | | | | | |
| 4. Uses Persuasion | | | | | |
| 5. Resolves Differences | | | | | |
| 6. Identifies Speaker's Biases | | | | | |
| 7. Identifies Speaker's Assumptions | | | | | |
| 8. Formulates Conclusions | | | | | |
| C. Nonverbal Communication | | | | | |
| 1. Gestures | | | | | |
| 2. Proximity | | | | | |
| 3. Position | | | | | |
| 4. Expression | | | | | |
| 5. Eye Contact | | | | | |

*Source:* Howell, K. W., Zucker, S. H. & Morehead, M. K. (2000b). *Multilevel Academic Skills Inventory.* Bellingham, WA: Applied Research and Development Center. To order contact the Student Co-op Bookstore, Western Washington University. Fax (360) 650-2888. Phone (360) 650-3656. Reprinted with permission.

need to create a situation where the student faces a problem. This situation could be either a game or a lesson. Results can be recorded on Exhibit 10.1, the "Analysis of Communication" sheet in Exhibit 10.4, and/or the status sheet in Howell et al., 2000a.

Some of the content in the checksheet in Exhibit 10.1 is hard to observe and, even if you can initiate it, may not be displayed spontaneously. If that is the case, it is better to treat the assessment as an interview. When interviewing a parent or teacher, be sure to ask about each item of content. One of us once asked a teacher if his 10-year-old student had any communication problems. The teacher said "no." However, when asked about each item, the teacher indicated the student could actually pass only items 1 and 6 on part B of the pragmatics list.

## Directions

1. Use the Exhibit 10.4 analysis sheet to review all of the pragmatics content.

2. Record the status of each item (pass, no-pass, unsure). This sheet is best filled out by a group of individuals who are familiar with the student.

3. Follow the directions and summarize and analyze the information.

### Interpretation Guidelines

### Question 8: Are Pragmatics OK?

If YES, then go to **Question 5.**

If NO, then continue to check performance in communication following the "Analysis of Communication" assessment plan in Exhibit 10.4. When you have finished, use **Teaching Recommendation 2.**

### Action 9: Syntax Status Sheet and Probes

The goal here is to systematically assess those syntactic structures that were not produced in the language sample. Specific-level work should also be carried out for those structures about which you have conflicting or insufficient information.

A typical specific-level test in this domain is nothing more than a direct statement or question designed to prompt the use of a particular structure. Caution is necessary because students will often respond in ways that are unexpected but not necessarily incorrect. For example, "Tell me what you did yesterday" is a request designed to elicit a response that includes a verb in the past tense, such as "played." If the child responds by saying "Boyd and I like to play ball," the response is not incorrect. It is simply not the target response.

Also, bear in mind that people occasionally respond defensively to direct questions.

To determine if the child can imitate an utterance, model a sentence and then ask her to repeat it. If she is speaking in phrases, ask her to expand her response to determine if she has the skills to speak with more complex utterances (see **Teaching Recommendation 4** for an explanation of expansion). You can also ask her to "say the whole thing" or "tell me some more."

## Directions

1. Review the errors in the language sample and code them in the exhibit in Howell et al., 2000a or a syntax status sheet. Recognize structures the student used incorrectly and those the student failed to use at all. An example of a syntax status sheet can be found in Appendix A.4.

2. For each structure recognized in Step 1, if you marked the status of a skill as "pass," list it as "PLEP." If "no-pass," derive an objective from the sheet. If "unsure," continue with the directions.

3. For skills marked "unsure," you will need to develop a probe. Use the Purpose/Function column of Exhibit 10.2 as a guide. That column can be used to generate either open-ended questions or prompts. For example, here is how you can try to probe the student's knowledge of "possessive nouns and pronouns" (item 14). Pick objects owned by individuals and objects owned by groups. Then ask the student to tell you who owns them ("Who does Ms. Kelly coach?" Answer: "The girls' team."). Elicit about ten responses for each structure of concern. If the student does not produce responses, then move to an imitation format. For an "imitate" response, say to the student "Say

this, 'That is her fish.'" Again, provide about ten items for each form.

4. Record the accuracy of response in the exhibit in Howell et al., 2000a.

### Interpretation Guidelines

#### Question 9: Are There Syntactical Errors?

If NO, then go to **Action 10.**

If YES, then use the information above to select objectives and go to **Teaching Recommendation 3.**

### Action 10: Mean Length of Utterance

#### Directions

Review the steps for calculating MLU presented on page 304. Then, use the language sample to follow these steps:

1. Count the number of words in each utterance (sentence);

   a. Do not count repetitions and fillers

   b. Count contractions as two words

   c. Count self-correction, but not the words that the correction replaces

2. Count the number of words; and

3. Divide the number of words by the number of sentences.

### Interpretation Guidelines

Select one or more students with adequate oral-language fluency to serve as exemplars and collect language samples from them. Next, compare the result of Step 3 (above) to the mean length of utterance displayed by the exemplars. Use the $\underline{S}$ (exemplars), $\underline{B}$ (student), and $\underline{D}$ format to summarize any discrepancy.

#### Question 10: Is MLU OK (Is Sentence Complexity Adequate)?

If NO, then build fluency by using **Teaching Recommendation 4.**

If YES, and there were no problems identified in other areas of language, then discontinue or

return to **Action 2.** If there are other problems, go to **Action 11.**

### Action 11: Setting Observation

This action involves observing and analyzing communicative transactions within the classroom. You may want to take a look at the TIES classroom descriptors in Appendix B. The most relevant TIES components and subcategories are: Component 1 (clarity of directions, checking for student understanding), Component 2 (class climate), Component 3, Component 5, and Component 12.

The checklist in Exhibit 10.5 which is based in part on work by Rueda et al. (1993), can be used to organize your observations. The exhibit asks about teacher actions that have an impact on the flow of communication. However, remember that you are not actually attempting to examine the communicative properties of the class—only the opportunities for this particular student. Often, the language opportunities of some students are limited because of their academic skills, social skills, limited English proficiency, or other factors.

### Directions

1. If the classroom in question is your own, then attempt a self-evaluation. Also, arrange to have someone else come in and observe.

2. Review the content of the Exhibit 10.5 "Opportunity to Learn Language" checksheet and related TIES descriptors to clarify the focus of the observation.

3. Observe over several intervals and sample various times of the day.

4. Answer the questions on the checksheet.

### Interpretation Guidelines

This is a highly subjective exercise, but it deals with an extremely important factor in language competence. As you know from personal experience, your own use of language and communication, as well as your acquisition of new vocabulary, depends on the setting in which you find yourself.

*Exhibit 10.5  Setting Observation.*

| Opportunity to Learn Language | Yes | No |
|---|---|---|
| 1. Is the presentation understandable—semantics and syntactic structure at correct level? | ___ | ___ |
| 2. Is the presentation meaningful—linked to prior knowledge or interest of students? | ___ | ___ |
| 3. Is there visual support for verbal input—pictures, graphs, role playing, objects, gestures, etc.? | ___ | ___ |
| 4. Is the student given frequent opportunities to respond? | ___ | ___ |
| 5. Is there monitoring for understanding? | ___ | ___ |
| 6. Are corrections linked to critical attributes of skill and to meaningfulness? | ___ | ___ |
| 7. Are there multiple models (peers and teachers) available? | ___ | ___ |
| 8. Is the classroom structured to increase frequency of communications? | ___ | ___ |
| 9. Do peers and teacher have strategies for engaging a shy student who would remain silent if given choice? | ___ | ___ |
| 10. Are peers and teacher comfortable communicating with all students or do they look away or move away when some students initiate contact? | ___ | ___ |
| 11. If student is acquiring English as a second language, is the primary language and culture of the student valued? | ___ | ___ |
| 12. Is there collaboration with other classes, activities, and the home to ensure focus, quality, and frequency of opportunity? | ___ | ___ |
| 13. Is the teacher responsive to student contributions? | ___ | ___ |
| 14. Do class discussions typically revolve around a theme? | ___ | ___ |
| 15. Do TIES descriptors relate to this class's: | | |
|     Clarity of instructions? | ___ | ___ |
|     Checking understanding? | ___ | ___ |
|     Class climate? | ___ | ___ |
|     Teacher expectation? | ___ | ___ |
|     Motivational strategies? | ___ | ___ |
|     Student understanding? | ___ | ___ |

## Question 11: Does Your Class, or the Class You Have Observed, Seem to Provide This Particular Student with Opportunities to Learn Language?

If NO, then employ the suggestions found under **Teaching Recommendation 5.**

If YES, then return to **Action 6.**

## Teaching Recommendations

Some children do not learn language as quickly as their peers. Consequently, instruction that is appropriate for their peers may be inappropriate for them. These students must be taught language skills directly and systematically if they are to benefit from educational programming. However, certain beliefs seem to encourage educators to disregard language problems and neglect language instruction. Here are a few of them.

### Misunderstandings Leading to the Neglect of Language Instruction

### The Child Is Just Quiet and Shy

The belief that the child is just shy and will come around in time may have damaging consequences if in fact she does need instruction and that instruction is not provided. Children who have language problems but who are not behavior problems and who smile when we talk to them are frequently not identified as needing help. Therefore, they are not provided with appropriate language instruction. *Shyness* refers to a student's temperament—not to her skill in communication. When a shy child decides to say something, she should be just as skilled as any other student.

### It's OK as Long as I Know What She Means

Sometimes, teachers respond to the message the child sends and ignore the way in which she sends it. For example, the child may ask "Her coming, too?" and the teacher may respond yes.

Although it is always appropriate to respond to the message, if a child makes errors it is also important to notice the way she uses language. Sometimes teachers get used to hearing certain sentence patterns. As a result, their sensitivity to a child's language errors diminishes over time. In addition, teachers are often unaware of the degree to which they fill in the gaps for the child. For example, one teacher we know was so convinced that all children in his junior-high special class had adequate language that he recorded a conversation between himself and one of his better students just to prove it to us. When he played back the tape, the conversation went like this:

TEACHER: What is your favorite sport? pause Basketball?

STUDENT: Yes, basketball.

TEACHER: How long have you been playing basketball? pause Three or four years, hasn't it been?

STUDENT: Yes.

TEACHER: Are you glad we're going to be dismissed early today?

STUDENT: Yes.

TEACHER: Do you know why we'll be dismissed early today?

STUDENT: Mud.

TEACHER: Yes, the rain is so bad that the buses need to get children home before the roads become too muddy.

The teacher had not been aware of the extent to which he had been supplying both the questions and the answers until he listened to the tape.

### She'll Grow Out of It

Another common misconception concerning language is that children's language problems are the byproduct of immaturity. Some educators and pediatricians have been known to say "Don't worry, she'll grow out of it" to parents of a 5-year-old who still isn't talking. This may not be true. While some children do outgrow language problems, most don't.

Language tends to be discussed in *developmental* terms because almost all of it emerges when students are very young. Unfortunately, numerous educators confuse the term *develop* with the term *mature*. Although it is common to provide "developmental expectations" for language acquisition, it is a mistake to assume that these milestones are only achieved through the passage of time. A student who for some reason misses out on a critical language lesson (even because of something as innocuous as an earache) may not acquire a particular language skill by the normal age. This deficit is *not* the result of the aging process; it is the result of something that did, or didn't, happen *while the student aged.*

A corollary to the "grow out of it" misconception is that, as children are exposed to language models every day in school, they will spontaneously learn to understand and use language. Language deficiencies may be maintained throughout the elementary school years. Everyday exposure to standard language is not sufficient in itself to enable linguistically different students to learn and use language. They need instruction.

### Language Isn't Taught in School

Most children learn language without supplantive instruction at home or at school. Language is usually learned so naturally that we seldom think about it as a remarkable feat. Language development norms indicate that children in typical environments master basic language structures between 3 and 5 years of age. Three-year-olds speak in three- to four-word sentences and use speech that is 75% to 90% intelligible. Four-year-olds use more complex sentences and can give an accurate, connected account of some recent experience. Ninety percent of 4-year-old speech is intelligible. By the time children with normal language development are 5 years old, they use fully developed complex sentences of about seven to eight words and can carry on meaningful conversations with adults and children. Templin (1957) has stated that children learn to use an estimated vocabulary of about 13,000 words by age 6, 21,000 words by age 7, and 28,300 words by age 8. They also pick up another 5,000 per year while in school (Curtis et al., 1992; Nagy & Scott, 1990). However, these expectations are not true of all students and are especially inaccurate if used as English expectations when the student is learning English as a second language.

### OK, But It's the Speech/Language Clinician's Job

Yes and no. It is true that speech/language teachers have been trained to assess and teach language. It's also true that in many school districts speech/language teachers carry a heavy caseload. Often, their teacher-to-pupil ratio can be as high as 1 to 45. We know of situations where it is 1 to 95. In some cases, there is no language teacher. This scarcity of service is professionally unacceptable and often illegal. However, although we are all waiting for society to adopt more constructive patterns of school funding/staffing, someone has to teach. Given the numbers, it is unrealistic to expect language teachers to provide all language instruction.

A speech/language teacher may be able to work with a child for only 20 or 30 minutes twice a week. Yet children who need language instruction need lots of it. Besides, language instruction seems to be more successful when it is integrated into the daily school program. This requires the involvement and participation of regular and special teachers. That's you!

### But What If the Kid Speaks Another Language?

Bilingual conflicts were once cited as a cause of childhood language impairments. However, it is now recognized that this need not be the case.

Typical youngsters seem to benefit from rich multilingual environments and do not suffer from opportunities to experience and learn more than one language, as long as these various languages are appropriately presented. When children from multilingual environments have English communication disorders, bilingual interference should be considered. However, students whose first language is not English should not be considered disabled unless they exhibit indicators that would lead to that characterization for any other child.

In most English-speaking countries, the number of school-age children who have Limited English Proficiency (LEP), or who speak <u>English as a Second Language</u> (ESL) is growing rapidly. These students commonly have a primary home language other than English or a dialect that is significantly different from the language used in classroom settings. Although these students are *not* disabled, school environments that do not support their communication needs *handicap* them. Therefore, their language differences place them at risk for school failure.

We realize that by juxtaposing a discussion of students with LEP and a discussion of students with "language problems," we risk incurring the disapproval of professionals in bilingual instruction, ESL, nonstandard English, and special education. However, it is important to recognize that work in these different specialties does not demand unique evaluative techniques. Our experience indicates that (1) students who are not competent in social or academic communication are functionally incapacitated and (2) that the techniques required to correct a lack of competency do not vary by constituency (LEP, ESL, bilingual, remedial, or special). Although the *source* of difficulty for students with LEP and students in special/remedial education may not be the same, evaluation of language is. That's because the curriculum defines the technology.

When a student arrives in a classroom that uses unfamiliar language configurations, she must acquire the new language to succeed. Sometimes this is easy and sometimes it isn't. The difficulty of accommodating an unfamiliar language framework is determined, to some extent, by the <u>interference points</u> between the student's existing language and that of the class. Interference points occur when a student's prior knowledge inhibits understanding—just as some of you would have trouble understanding this text if we suddenly began to use the word *alumno* instead of *student*.

To elaborate on the concept of interference, here are some examples specific to Spanish-speaking students.

In Spanish syntax, nouns precede modifiers; this means that in Spanish "The broken chair is in the kitchen" is worded "La cilla quebrada esta en la cocina." If a student carries this syntactic structure into English, she will say "The chair broken is in the kitchen."

A teacher we know named Elana reported that one of her colleagues was very concerned that a first-grader in his class had become inexplicably fixated on the letter "L." This student was writing "L" all over her work. Our friend looked at the work and realized that, because in Spanish the "Y" sound is spelled "ll," this student was spelling words like "yoyo" as "llollo."

Such confusion is common and often very hard for teachers to deal with. In addition, this confusion isn't limited to the public schools, as the makers of Nova cars can testify. Novas never sold well in Mexico because the word means "no go" in Spanish. (The owners of Osco Drug Stores have had a similar problem, and if you don't get this joke you have just experienced language interference.)

One final point about interference: because language is the proprietor of culture, merely translating messages without an awareness of their cultural meaning is not sufficient. For example, in the United States many students grow up in a composite linguistic environment of Spanish and English. Often, these kids learn to put the Spanish gender-related "ea" on the end of English words. Therefore "line" becomes *linea*. This means that when a teacher from the same composite linguistic culture wants to use Spanish to tell the class to line up she might say "Ponganse en linea." However, teachers who learned Spanish in college are apt to use the formal Spanish translation of "line," which is fila and say "Ponganse en fila." There are two problems with this. First, some students simply don't know the word fila. Second, those who do know it may be more familiar with its slang meaning, which is "blade" or "knife."

So, what does this all mean?

1. People who speak other languages should not be considered disabled (although they may be "handicapped" by a nonsupportive classroom environment).

2. Students need to be taught the relevant language of school and society in general for them to get along.

3. Directly teaching children about classroom-relevant interaction styles will improve classroom learning.

If you have students with LEP and you are not proficient in their language(s) (some classes may have students who speak Russian, Spanish, English, and Vietnamese), there are still things you can do to help. A teacher's perception of a student's primary language and culture influences second-language acquisition (Cummins, 1986; Moeller & Scott, 1993). Think about the status of the other language in your school's society. If a student's language is not held in regard by the general population (including her peers and the staff), her communication within the classroom may be damaged. If a teacher wants a student to learn English, the best way to do it is to *honor the language the student already possesses*. Best yet, enhance the status of all languages and cultures within the classroom by demonstrating acceptance. Although language diversity is often parlayed into a rich foundation for instruction, in many classrooms that still isn't the case. Unfortunately, if history is any indicator, it will be easier to teach these students English than it will be to extinguish the bias sometimes awakened by their accents.

### A Direct Approach to Language

There are five **Teaching Recommendations** for a direct approach to syntax, semantics/morphology, and pragmatics.

1. Teach semantics.
2. Teach pragmatics and morphology.
3. Teach syntax.
4. Use expansion.
5. Modify settings to increase opportunities for communication.

Because these **Teaching Recommendations** will be covered in a very cursory manner, you may need to consult the references provided to understand them. Basic resources for teachers working with language include Moeller, A. J. & Scott, E. S. (1993) Making the Match: Middle Level Goals and Foreign Language Instruction. *Schools in the Middle*, 3(1), 35–39 as well as Hughs (1997) and Masterson & Perry (1999).

Each of the five teaching recommendations is a direct intervention. Direct teaching is rich with teacher-controlled models and meaningful opportunities for students to use "new" skills. Direct does not imply meaningless drill or absence of context. What it does mean is focused hands-on, supplantive instruction for optimal use of learning time. In a direct, hands-on intervention, you tell the student what you want her to do, show her how to do it, and provide opportunities for practice. However, there is no reason that this focus must exclude those holistic-thematic aspects of language instruction that have also been found to be effective (Wiig et al., 1992; Tompkins, 1997).

Supplantive instruction is most appropriate when the current context of communication or the student's enabling skills do not afford sufficient opportunities for generative instruction and practice in language (Tharp & Gallimore, 1989; Ragan & Smith, 1994). When this is the case, you must introduce the target skill and the necessary prompts to generate instructional opportunities. This is mandatory because the student must become an active, not passive, recipient of the language instruction. Therefore, the most important thing for you to do is to recognize a series of unambiguous models, prompts, and cues that will illustrate and activate the targeted skills.

### Error Correction

Whenever a student is making consistent errors, regardless of the content, a correction procedure should be used. It has been said that, if an error occurs in the first 30 attempts during new learning and is corrected, only a few additional corrections will be required. However, if an error goes uncorrected and is practiced (learned), it could take thousands of corrections to eradicate the error. This is especially true if opportunities to make the response occur in uninstructed situations. If there is any content area that matches that description, it is interpersonal communication. This is why early and extensive use of guided practice and error correction are so important.

Error correction needs to be immediate and frequent. Often, opportunities to make the specific errors need to be built into instruction. Corrections should be based on the cause of the error. Always consider these causes:

- Failure to see how things are different. This is called a "discrimination error."
- Failure to see how things are the same—"a generalization error."
- Missing prior knowledge.

**Discrimination errors** occur when students carry old rules into new situations. For example, a student has learned that you add /s/ to make English words plural, but that rule does not apply to all words (deer, goose, woman). The solution here is to teach the needed discrimination, For example:

TEACHER: *"We say two boys, four hats, ten pencils*—but we say six *sheep*. What do we say?"

STUDENT: "We say one sheep, two sheep, three sheep—but we say one boy, two boys, three boys."

A **generalization error** occurs when the student fails to see how two things are the same. A generalization correction should include critical information about similarities. A student who can ask for help in one classroom and not in the other needs to be taught how the ways of seeking assistance across the classes are the same.

When a student makes errors because of *missing prior knowledge* (that is, how to ask for directions), you need to provide that knowledge within the correction.

TEACHER: "The way you asked for directions was incorrect because you did not clearly state where you want to go. Remember to decide exactly where you want to go, and how to state that, before you ask."

### Teaching Recommendation 1: Teach Semantics and Morphology

#### Sample Objectives

- The student will use context to develop definitions to specified words with 95% accuracy.
- The student will supply context-specific definitions to [specified words] with ___% accuracy.
- Given words that she does not know, the student will use [specified strategies] or her enabling skills to determine and then supply [in a specified way] [morphograph] meanings. Meanings will be determined with 100% accuracy.
- The student will demonstrate language use at [a level comparable with that of other students in the setting] by increasing frequency of [specify target] [utterances and/or responses].

Even students who succeed in school require repeated exposures before learning new words. Unfortunately, few teachers or reading programs provide adequate vocabulary instruction (Council for Educational Development & Research, 1997). The traditional word list and dictionary approach to vocabulary instruction cannot begin to provide kids with the rich knowledge of vocabulary they need (Carnine et al., 1997). Effective explicit vocabulary instruction requires careful planning, a focus on context, and structured opportunities for practice (Carnine et. al., 1997). The vocabulary lesson formats we will discuss here include questions, examples, synonyms, morphemes, definitions, and semantic features. For additional information on these formats, review Carnine et al. (1997), Gruenewald and Pollak (1990), Hoover and Dwivedi (1998), Johnson (1983), and Masterson and Perry (1999).

#### Questions

Here is a sequence for questioning that can be readily adapted to instruction. The sequence involves beginning with an "open question" and then, depending on the student's response, moving to "multiple choice," "restricted alternative," and "full model" questions (Stowitschek et al., 1984). Here, the sequence is applied to vocabulary instruction.

*Open Question* "What does alacrity mean?"

If the student correctly defines the word, go to the next one. If the student incorrectly defines the word, follow up with a multiple-choice question.

*Multiple Choice* "Does alacrity mean:

> cute?
>
> travel?
>
> eagerness?
>
> anxiety?"

If the student correctly identifies the answer (eagerness), go back and ask the open question again. If the student answers the open question this time, go to the next word. If the student does not get the multiple-choice question correct, notice what word she did select and go to a "restricted alternative" question. For this example, we'll assume the student selected anxiety.

*Restricted Alternative* "Alacrity does not mean 'anxiety,' so what does it mean?"

If the student correctly identifies the answer (eagerness), go back and ask the original open question again. If the student answers the open question this time go on. If the student does not get the restricted-alternative question correct, then go to a "full model" correction.

*Full Model* "Alacrity means 'eagerness.' What does alacrity mean?"

If the student gets it right this time, go to the next word—but within a few items go back to *alacrity* and try the open question again. If the student gets it wrong this time, repeat the model.

#### Analogical Reasoning

Teach new words or morphemes by analogy when the student does not have a synonym for the word, does not know the morpheme, or lacks the vocabulary to acquire a definition. For example, concepts are frequently best defined by examples and nonexamples that focus on critical attributes (see Chapter 3). Here is an illustration: Teach the definition of *opprobrious* by showing the student that the word matches photos of Hitler, Slobodan Milosevic, and Hannibal-The-Cannibal; but not Mother Teresa, Albert Schweitzer, or Lassie. The idea is to directly teach students to apply existing knowledge to a novel situation (Masterson & Perry, 1999). The instruction must be direct so that the student does not inadvertently attach the new information to the wrong prior knowledge (Marsh et al., 1999).

### Synonyms

If a student already knows the meaning of a synonym, introduce a new word by linking it to the old. For example:

TEACHER: "*Sclerosis* [new word] means 'hardening' [known word]. What is another word for *hardening?*"

STUDENT: "Sclerosis."

TEACHER: "Yes, *sclerosis* means hardening. We sometimes say 'hardening of the arteries.' What's another way to say 'hardening of the arteries'?"

To ensure the student knows that the new word is not exclusively linked to the words used in the example, be sure to change the example. In the case of *sclerosis,* to ensure that it's not linked to arteries alone, you might practice a sentence in which you meant hardening of plant cell walls.

TEACHER: "Plants become woody when hardening of the cell walls occurs. Use your new word in this sentence. Plants become woody when _____ of the cell walls occurs."

STUDENT: "Plants become woody when sclerosis of the cell walls occurs."

### Definitions

When you're teaching definitions, do not ask students to go to the dictionary and look something up. Teach the meaning of the word by defining it

as you did when teaching morphemes. Check the learning by asking questions that verify that the student has a deep understanding of the word's meaning and recognizes critical components of the definition. An example from Carnine et al. (1997) illustrates this kind of definition teaching:

TEACHER: "*Respite* means 'short rest.' Susan worked hard all day. Then she went home and slept for 10 hours. Did she take a *respite?* Julie worked hard all morning. At twelve she stopped and ate a quick lunch and then went back to work. Did she take a *respite?* How do you know?"

### Morphemes

Morphemes are discussed in Chapters 8, 9, and 11. When units of meaning are taught and then the student is given opportunities to use that information to define new words, it is likely that she will learn more words. For example:

Teach the student that "re" means "do again."

Next, teach that "unite" means "join."

Then ask "What does *reunite* mean?" The answer: "Join again."

"Morphological word families" may also be of use when teaching semantics (Nagy et al., 1989). These are words that share semantic features (decide, decision, decided), not a simple overlapping of letters (decide, decimal, deciduous).

### Semantic Features

This is a format for enriching the meaning of new words and/or morphemes. First, students are engaged in a discussion. Old words are linked to new ones by use of defined words and analogy. Classification is used to clarify and expand a student's word knowledge. Exhibit 10.6 illustrates a semantic-features list. Semantic features can be used to augment more traditional vocabulary instruction such as examples, synonyms, morphemes, and definitions. However, do not expect students to discover the meaning of new words through semantic-feature analysis. Use the features to directly teach the meanings of new words.

*Exhibit 10.6    Semantic Features—Vehicles.*

| | | Concept: Vehicles Features | | | | | | |
|---|---|---|---|---|---|---|---|---|
| Words | Carries Things | Land | Air | Sea | Windows | Wheels | Wings | Fuel |
| Tricycle | + | + | − | − | − | + | − | − |
| Bicycle | + | + | − | − | − | + | − | − |
| Automobile | + | + | − | − | + | + | − | + |
| Truck | + | + | − | − | + | + | − | + |
| Bus | + | + | − | − | + | + | − | + |
| Train | + | + | − | − | + | + | − | + |
| Tanker | + | − | − | + | ? | − | − | + |
| Airplane | + | + | + | − | + | + | + | + |
| Helicopter | + | + | + | − | + | +/− | − | + |
| Space Shuttle | + | + | + | − | ? | + | + | + |
| Wagon | + | + | − | − | − | + | − | − |
| Rickshaw | + | + | − | − | − | + | − | − |

+     applies to concepts.

−     does not apply to concepts.

?     may apply to concepts.

+/−  sometimes applies to concepts.

Source: Adapted from D. D. Johnson, "Three Sound Strategies for Vocabulary Development." *Ginn Occasional Papers: Writing in Reading and Language Arts.* Columbus, OH: Ginn & Co., 1983.

Julkunen (1990) has identified three properties of effective vocabulary instruction. Noting the failures of traditional "definition" and "contextual" approaches, he recommended that vocabulary instruction include these three properties:

**Integration:** The new word is related to the student's prior knowledge. Relationships (including analogical), rather than facts, are stressed during the presentation of new words.

**Repetition:** Students are taught to be automatic in word usage.

**Meaningful use:** The focus of instruction is on the student using the word, not on the student defining it. This includes work with analogies and inference.

## Teaching Recommendation 2: Teach Pragmatics

### Sample Objectives

- Given a specified level of assistance (prompts, cues, or models) up to spontaneous use, the student will decrease [targeted] pragmatic errors and/or increase correct use of [targeted] pragmatic skills to the level of [other students in the specified setting].

- Given a specified communication task, the student will correctly employ the strategies (marked "No" in Exhibit 10.4 or Howell et al., 2000a) at [a level consistent with that of classroom peers].

- The student will demonstrate pragmatic usage at a level comparable with that of [exemplar students] in the setting by increasing the frequency of [specified target] utterances and/or responses.

Instruction in pragmatics requires integration of skills in syntax and semantics as well as application of knowledge of specific language functions (Bouton, 1996; House, 1996). Pragmatics is the linking of codes, or styles (James, 1990). For example, one code is used when seeking help from a friend; another code is used when seeking help from a stranger (Stephanson & Linfoot, 1996).

Role playing is a good format for teaching pragmatics and *code switching*. Students can practice a variety of roles as they learn critical information linked to a variety of communication purposes. Pick the pragmatic skills listed in Exhibit 10.1 that the student needs to learn. Lessons should include (1) information about the purpose of the skill, (2) a variety of example situations in which the student needs the skill, and, (3) critical components of the skill. During initial acquisition, lesson formats should include models, demonstrations, and guided practice. This practice should include verbal rehearsal of what the student will *think* as well as rehearsal of what she will say and do. Next, there is guided practice across settings. Finally, provide monitored independent practice (Pershey, 1997).

## Teaching Recommendation 3: Teach Syntax

### Sample Objectives

- Given a specified level of assistance (prompts, cues, or models) up to spontaneous use, student will express herself with an average MLU of "specified level."
- Given a specified level of assistance (prompts, cues, or models) up to spontaneous use, the student will decrease errors and increase correct usage of structures specified (in Exhibit 10.2) at a level equivalent to peers or [specified].

- The student will demonstrate syntax usage at a level comparable with that of [exemplar students] in the setting by increasing frequency of [specified target] utterances and/or responses.
- The student will demonstrate language usage at [a level comparable with that of other students in the setting] by increasing frequency of [specified target utterances and/or responses].

Teaching sentence structure requires knowledge of the content and allocation of instructional time. Interventions may require identification (receptive) responses or production (expressive) responses. Wiig and Semel (1984) pointed out that there are some general principles for designing syntax instruction.

1. *Unfamiliar words* and sentence-formation rules should be introduced and sequenced according to difficulty (see Exhibit 10.2).

2. The words featured in example phrases, clauses, and sentences should be highly familiar. One way to assure that this is the case is to refer to the results of **Action 2.** Another is to select words from vocabulary lists at or below the child's current performance level.

3. Sentence length should be kept to an absolute minimum. This may be achieved by limiting sentence length to 5–10 words, whereas phrase or clause length should be limited to 2–4 words.

4. Unfamiliar word- or sentence-formation rules should be introduced in at least ten illustrative examples. These rule examples should feature different words.

5. Knowledge of syntactic rules should first be established through recognition and then through production tasks.

6. The knowledge and control of rules should be established first with highly familiar concepts. It should then be extended to less familiar concepts.

7. The knowledge and use of rules should be tested in at least ten examples that feature vocabulary not previously used.

## Teaching Recommendation 4: Expansion

### Sample Objectives

- Given a specified level of assistance (prompts, cues, or models) up to spontaneous use, student will express herself with an average MLU of [specified level].

- During spontaneous speech, the student will decrease [targeted errors] and/or increase correct use of [targeted skills] to the level of other students in the [specified] setting.

The long-range goal of expansion is to increase the mean length of the child's utterances by including new language structures; the short-range objective is that the child produce sentences using specific structures. Examples of such objectives are "The child will produce sentences using prepositional phrases" or "The student will produce sentences using the relative adverb clauses."

To increase the richness and conceptual sophistication of the student's speech, it is often good practice to focus on the purpose, intent, and audience of communication (see Chapters 3 and 11). Palincsar and David (1992), for example, have found that successful students listen very differently to classroom dialogue than those who are not so successful. Unsuccessful students explain their approach to listening this way: "I stay still," "I just listen," and even "I don't know this. I'm only 7 years old!" Such passive listening strategies can be changed dramatically through dialogues in which teachers provide guided practice, extensive teacher modeling, and the systematic *expansion* of student efforts. These are principal elements of the reading comprehension technique called *reciprocal teaching* (Klinger & Vaughn, 1996).

The process of expansion is simple. Take the student's incorrect, or simple, utterance and change it into one that is closer to the student's language goal. For example,

- If a student were to say "Ask do she want a Pepsi," the correct expansion would be for the teacher to say "Ask if she wants a Pepsi."

- If a student with a semantic or advanced syntax goal were to say "Look at the bird," a good expansion might be "Look at the bird as it flies slowly across the sky."

- Similarly, a student with a pragmatic objective might start saying "I stay still" and expand this kernel into "I stay still so I can think about what I hear."

Here are some rules to remember when using expansion.

1. Expand the utterance into what the *student should have said.* This means "**I** go bathroom?" should not be expanded into "May **you** go to the bathroom?" but into "May **I** go to the bathroom?"

2. Accompany the expansion with a standard cue, such as a hand on the student's shoulder, to signal that a brief language lesson is about to occur.

3. Do not expand every utterance—the kid will quickly get sick of it and stop talking.

4. Always respond to the **message** the student is trying to convey. If you become too interested in how everything is said, and ignore the conversation, the student will stop talking to you. In other words, you say "May I go to the bathroom? *Yes, you may.*" (You don't want to fix the student's syntax but leave her with a stressed bladder.)

5. Use expansion in many different situations and times. Try to fit it into the normal course of the day and not just into language lessons.

6. Occasionally use expansion with other students so that your student of main interest does not start to feel "picked" on.

## Teaching Recommendation 5: Modify Settings to Increase Opportunities for Communication

### Sample Objectives

- The student will demonstrate language usage at a level comparable with that of other students in the setting by increasing the frequency of [specified target] utterances and/or "responses."

• Given a specified level of assistance (prompts, cues, or models) up to spontaneous use, student will express herself with an average MLU of "[specified level]."

This particular recommendation should probably be applied to every student with language or communication difficulties. Classrooms are not always the best place to learn language. As Tharp and Gallimore (1989) noted, many classrooms are characterized by teacher-dominated discourse and a lack of attention to student attempts at language usage. In addition, because students with communication difficulties sometimes have problems in the area of reading, they often miss out on the language models provided by higher-level reading lessons (see Chapter 8).

Use the results in Exhibit 10.5 to recognize needed classroom modifications. Students are most apt to develop language competence in warm and supportive classrooms where there are high expectations for communication from *all* members of the group. In settings that support all students, there is both encouragement to communicate and direct instruction (Carnine et al., 1997). Such a setting can be developed by producing the conditions listed on the setting observation in Exhibit 10.5.

In the case of second-language learners, particular care must be provided to be sure that:

1. Respect for the student's primary language is maintained by conveying the message that, while English is being added, her primary language is not being removed (Gallas et al., 1996);

2. The student receives instruction and is not simply bombarded with corrections;

3. Teaching for generalization is always primary (the goal of the instruction must reach beyond the classroom); and

4. Opportunities are provided for the student to make use of her own knowledge so that language development depends as much on the student's everyday experiences as it does on the "academic" experiences of the classroom.

Build fluency and sophistication by using **Teaching Recommendation 4** as well as **Teaching Recommendation 2.**

## Summary

This chapter defined oral language and explored some beliefs, assumptions, and misunderstandings about language acquisition. It also discussed in detail what to consider when conducting an evaluation of language. We have linked these considerations to explicit procedures for conducting survey- and specific-level tests. Many of these tests and status sheets are found in the Appendix. The specific-level procedures described match the most probable causes for language difficulties. Guidelines for interpreting test results were also linked to instruction recommendations. All that said, we want to leave you with one additional thought.

*"One of the lessons of history is that nothing is often a good thing to do and always a clever thing to say."*
—*Ariel and Will Durant*

# Chapter 11

# Written Expression

*A writer lives the sad truth just like anyone else. The only difference is—he files a report on it.*

—William S. Burroughs, Naked Lunch

*The golden alphabet, in whatever shape it chooses to reveal itself, is never spurious. From its inscrutable lettering is created man and all the towering cloudland of his dreams.*
—Loren Eiseley, The Unexpected Universe p. 146

## Step 1: Define Your Purpose

Effective writing skills, along with competence in reading, are expressions of literacy. The failure to acquire reading and writing as functional extensions of language accounts for the greatest number of referrals to special and remedial education. We (Howell & Nolet) have often pointed out that the student's knowledge, and how the student displays that knowledge, are different. Some people who know things can't seem to display them, and some people who know very little present what they know with considerable skill. Smith (1982) recognized the know/display dichotomy, which is particularly important in written communication, when he drew a distinction between the *"writer as author"* and the *"writer as secretary."* When a writer is functioning in the role of author, he is concerned primarily with content and ideas. When a writer functions in the role of secretary, he is concerned primarily with the mechanics of writing (handwriting, spelling, punctuation, etc.). Effective writers must be able to function in both roles at different times in the writing process; therefore, this chapter deals with <u>both</u> the writer as author and the writer as secretary. The purpose of the chapter is to provide tools that may be used to summarize, and then improve, student skills in both areas.

*Exhibit 11.1   Process in Writing.*

| Planning | Transcribing | Reviewing | Revising |
|---|---|---|---|
| Prewriting | Modes | Monitor | Modify to meet purpose |
| Formulate purpose | Dictation | Match of message to purpose | Style |
| Match style to purpose | Typing | Accuracy of mechanics | Content |
| Organize message | Computer keyboard | | Word selection |
| | Pen or pencil | | Sentence complexity |
| | | | Organization |
| During writing | Mechanics | | Correct errors in mechanics |
| Develop message | Handwriting, typing, etc. | | Handwriting, typing, etc. |
| Manipulate mechanics | Spelling | | Spelling |
| | Capitalization | | Capitalization |
| | Grammar | | Grammar |
| | Form-margins, heading, etc. | | Form-margins, heading, etc. |

## Step 2: Define the Thing to Be Measured

### The Writer as Author

There are three components of the author role: (1) purpose, (2) process, and (3) product (Harris & Graham, 1996a; Isaacson, 1985; Scardamalia & Bereiter, 1986).

### 1. Purpose

The purpose of writing is the author's intent. Purpose in written language is analogous to **pragmatics** in oral language. Several guides have been suggested for defining purpose (Bouton, 1996; Britton, 1978; Wiig & Semel, 1984). These guides generally take the form of lists based on categories of genre. Genre refers to kinds of writing, message type, or intent such as poetry, business letter, essay, and/or to persuade, to inform, or to entertain.

One view of purpose is that the reader must know the writer's intent to judge whether a written communication is acceptable. If the reader doesn't know what the writer intended, then she can't discern whether the writer accomplished his goal. For example, if the writer intends to ask

for a job, the writer needs to follow the formal form of business-letter writing. Another view is that purpose places the responsibility more directly on the author. Under this view, if you can't tell the intent, the writer hasn't done a very good job of expressing it. We prefer the second approach. This preference stems from the same view of communication that holds there is no greater linguistic value in **complex sentences** than in simple ones (see Chapter 10). The message is the most important aspect of communication. If the reader understands the purpose, she won't reject the message because it fails to conform to a particular style.

### 2. Process

Writing is a multistep process. Various authors disagree about whether there are three, four, six, or more stages, but generally writing involves four stages (Isaacson, 1985): planning, reviewing, revising, and transcribing. These are shown in Exhibit 11.1.

**Planning** includes a *prewriting* stage in which the writer formulates a purpose for writing, decides what to write, selects a style that is likely to accomplish the purpose, and then organizes the message. Planning also occurs *during* writing and

*Self-monitoring alerts students to the need for extra effort or the application of problem-solving strategies.*

includes ongoing planning for development of a message, as well as manipulation of mechanics. The focus of planning should be to accomplish the purpose of the communication. As writers of this text, we planned our content and how to present it to you. We also planned our format.

On large projects, like this text, allocation of time also requires planning. Some of the plans we developed for this book actually made it all the way through the process. Others, like the musical version of Chapter 6, had to be dropped. (The screenplay is still in the works.)

**Reviewing** seems to interact with planning. Good writers frequently look back over their work to check on how things are going, just as good readers look back on what they have read

to check understanding. As writers review their work, they invariably revise it. This means the stages in Exhibit 11.1 are not sequential (or even separate). They are recursive.

**Revision** may include changes in style, content, word selection, and sentence complexity to assure that the message is either as clear or vague as the writer intends (Graham, 1997; Raymond, 1989). Sometimes, most obviously in mystery writing and poetry, ambiguity is a goal. As a writing project approaches completion, the revision process tends to focus only on the secretarial aspects of the work and include corrections in spelling, punctuation, grammar, and appearance.

**Transcribing** has more to do with the secretarial function discussed below.

### 3. Product

Products are the result of purpose and process. These products are what evaluators analyze to determine how well a student has mastered writing (Isaacson, 1985). Writing products include:

- **Fluency,** the production of **simple sentences** and elaboration into compositions of gradually increasing length. Best indicated by total number of words written and ratio of correct word sequences;

- **Syntactic maturity,** the production of sentences of increasing complexity as indicated by total number of sentences by type (fragment, simple, compound), total number of **T-units** per sentences, and/or length of T-units per sentence;

- **Vocabulary or semantic maturity,** fewer repetitions of favored words and use of more sophisticated words. Semantic maturity is best indicated by the total number of unusual words, the proportion of mature words (from a word frequency list), and the proportion of nonrepeated words;

- **Content,** attention to organization of thought, originality, and style. Best indicated by text cohesion, **holistic** rating and/or analytic rating, number of words allocated to the purpose; and

- **Conventions,** mechanical aspects of writing such as margins, grammar, spelling, and punctuation. Best indicated by occurrence of errors.

Across each of these five products there is a sixth component—**quality.** Recently, quality has tended to be summarized through the use of rubrics, like the one in Exhibit 11.2.

### The Flow of Composition

As we've already pointed out, the various components of the writing process do not necessarily take place in a fixed progression. One does not finish planning, then transcribe, then review/revise, and finally hand the product to your audience. Writers do all of these things at the same time. However, there is an interactive element of composition that is important. It is a "temporal-experiential-interaction" (we love making up these terms) and it occurs as the writer's personal history is converted into the messages he is generating for the future (MacLean, 1992). During composition, the author does two things: he looks back upon his own experience and he looks forward to predict what sort of presentation will have the desired effect on the reader (Beaugrande, 1984). The writer, therefore, is attempting to govern the experience of the reader from a position between reflection and prediction. This is a very sophisticated undertaking (Harris & Graham, 1996b; Ruddell, 1997).

### The Writer as Secretary

Transcription is the process of putting a message onto paper (or computer). Transcribing requires the simultaneous integration of a number of "secretarial" skills (Flower & Hayes, 1990; Isaacson & Gleason, 1997). These skills include the mechanics and conventions of writing. Your authors (incidentally, both of us are poor spellers—it's the vowels—and use a rather primitive style of printing) consider mechanics to be less important than the process of written language. But spelling and writing are necessarily part of the curriculum. Teachers and students seem to be stuck with them, for better and worse.

Mechanics and conventions enable the display of messages developed through the processes explained above. However, despite their "secondary" role in written communication, many teachers find spelling and handwriting to be the most immediately alarming aspects of written communication. It seems that for all of the sloganeering about "meaning," many teachers still tend to judge the quality of written expression on the basis of mechanics and conventions (particularly as the students advance in grade). Actually, even if spelling and handwriting were not in the curriculum, we'd probably need to address them anyway in Chapter 14 (task-related behavior). That is because, as display skills, they account for bias in grading, which is an added hurdle that few special/remedial students need (Harris and Graham, 1994; Holbrook, 1990; Isaacson, 1992).

**Letter Formation**   Computer software and keyboarding skills can replace handwriting and spelling. However, until all students have the same access to computers that they now have to pencils (and remarkably, despite what one might conclude from the rhetoric in the popular and professional press, only a small proportion of them do) (Office of Technology Assessment, 1995), letter formation will remain a major component of transcribing.

**Spelling**   Hardly anyone ever says a kid is suffering from "dyspellia," because the only characteristic that seems to separate spellers from nonspellers is the number of words they spell correctly. However, spelling is a very difficult task. It requires exact responses based on numerous decisions that must be made without any of the contextual clues associated with reading (Fult & Stormont-Spurgin, 1995). Also, factors such as word familiarity, length of word, number of words being dealt with, and predictability of the sound-letter correspondence in the words all affect the task demands. Adding to the difficulty of learning to spell is the remarkable lack of good research into spelling acquisition. The approach of having students study weekly lists of words is ingrained in the tradition of American teaching and few people seem interested in changing. There are, however, ways out of this mess for those who are interested (Fult & Stormont-Spurgin, 1995). Both make use of clusters of letters, and one (the morphographic approach (Dixon, 1994)) adds meaning to the process.

**Punctuation and Capitalization**   For a written message to flow smoothly, its components need to be supported by an underlying framework of rules. This framework, which to a nonliterate student will seem completely arbitrary, is made up of capitalization and punctuation (Isaacson & Gleason, 1997). The content will be found in Exhibit 11.9.

### Step 3: Devise a Way to Make Things in Step 2 Observable

The writing sample is the general outcome measure for screening, comparing, and monitoring writing. There are a number of ways to obtain samples of written work (Gunning, 1998). One is to collect existing samples from class assignments. If these are not readily available, you can provide the student with a writing prompt. This writing prompt can be a picture(s) or a description of an age/content-appropriate situation. With young students (grades K–2), "story starters" are often used (for example, "what's the best and worst thing about a rainy day?"). This is also true, regardless of age, when you want the purpose to be generated by the kid. In advanced grades, the purpose of writing is commonly provided by the teacher. These prompts should focus on the kinds of writing expected in advanced grades (such as essay examination answers or report writing) as well as kinds of writing often used in jobs.

Pictures aren't great prompts as many students will simply describe what they see (therefore making originality and plot hard to judge). If you are going to use a picture prompt, try asking the student to write about "What you think will happen next." Here are three examples of story starters:

Prompts should be as free from cultural bias as possible. Consider these three prompts. In

| Prompt A | Prompt B | Prompt C |
|---|---|---|
| "What is the best thing and the worst thing about lunch?" | "Families are special people. I'd like to learn who is special in your life. Who are the members of your family? Do you have brothers and sisters? What do you like to do with your mom or dad? What do you like about your family times together?" | "A flying saucer that you suspect is filled with Martians lands near the fire hydrant in front of your house. Describe the scene and write about what happens." |

**Exhibit 11.2    Analytic Scales for Writing.**

| Narrative 5 | Story-Idea 5 | Organization-Cohesion 5 | Convention-Mechanics 5 |
|---|---|---|---|
| • Includes accurate facts and backs them up with argument or citations when necessary | • Includes characters | • Overall story is organized into a beginning, a middle, and an end | • Sentence structure generally is accurate |
| • Delineates the message and any expected response in a clear and logical fashion | • Delineates a plot | • Events are linked and cohesive | • Spelling does not hinder readability |
| • Contains ideas required to address the topic | • Contains original ideas | • Sentences are linked, often containing some transitions to help with organization (finally, then, next, etc.) | • Sometimes contain dialogue |
| • Illustrates a balance between detail and efficiency | • Contains some detail | | • Handwriting is legible |
| • Uses technical vocabulary correctly | • Word choice | | • Punctuation does not affect readability too much |
| • Contains descriptors (adverbs and adjectives) which are derivatives of the purpose and audience | • Contains descriptors (adverbs and adjectives) and colorful, infrequently used, and/or some long words | | • Word usage generally is correct • (s.v.o./homophone/s-v agreement) |
| • Cause and effect relationships as well as relative importance are clear | | | |
| **4** | **4** | **4** | **4** |
| • Includes assertions and facts that may be disputed without support | • Includes characters, but they are not original, often coming from movies | • Story has somewhat of a beginning, middle, and an end | • Sentence structure generally is accurate but not as good as 5 |
| • Messages and responses are included but may not be presented clearly and/or logically | • Delineates a plot, although it is not as clear as 5 | • Events seem somewhat random, but some organization exists | • Spelling does not hinder readability too much |
| • Sentence complexity is compatible with intent and audience | • Contains some original ideas but is fairly predictable | • Sample may contain some transitions to help with organization: finally, then, next, etc. | • Sometimes contains dialogue |
| • Is missing some important ideas, or includes some unnecessary information | • Contains some detail | • Story often contains too many events, disrupting cohesion | • Handwriting is legible |
| • Details are not always presented in an effective way | • Includes descriptors (adverbs and adjectives) | | • Punctuation does not affect readability too much |
| • Includes descriptors (adverbs and adjectives) that are repetitious or out of alignment with purpose and audience | • Word choice: contains some descriptors (adverbs and adjectives) and some colorful, infrequently used, and/or long words | | • Word usage generally is correct • (s.v.o./homophone/s-v agreement) |
| • Some omission and/or misuse of technical vocabulary | | | |

| Narrative 3 | Story-Idea 3 | Organization-Cohesion 3 | Convention-Mechanics 3 |
|---|---|---|---|
| • Presents facts that do not need to be provided (the audience already knows them) | • Characters are predictable and undeveloped | • Somewhat of a plot exists but story may still lack a beginning, middle, or an end | • Sentence structure has a few problems |
| • The information provided to support the message is insufficient and/or poorly sequenced | • Plot is somewhat haphazard | • Events are somewhat random | • Spelling is somewhat of a problem |
| • Very few ideas are included and some important ideas are missing while unimportant ideas may be included | • May or may not contain original ideas | • Often lacks transitions | • May use dialogue but does not punctuate it correctly |
| • Details are presented in a confusing way, or omitted | • Lacks detail | • Sometimes lacks referents | • Handwriting is legible |
| • Some technical terms are used incorrectly | • Word choice is somewhat predictable, only sometimes contains descriptors (adverbs and adjectives) | | • Punctuation is fair |
| • Descriptors are out of alignment with message | | | • Problems sometimes occur with word usage (s.v.o./homophone/s-v agreement) |
| 2 | 2 | 2 | 2 |
| • Few facts are present and factual errors are common | • Includes few if any characters | • Plot lacks organization into a beginning, middle and an end | • Sentence structure makes story difficult to read |
| • The message is not developed and/or its accuracy is questionable | • Plot is not developed or apparent | • Events are random, lacking in cohesion | • Spelling makes it difficult to read |
| • Ideas are trivial | • Contains virtually no original ideas | • Lacks transitions | • May use dialogue but does not punctuate it correctly |
| • Little detail is provided | • Detail is significantly absent | • Often lacks referents | • Handwriting is not very legible |
| • Technical vocabulary, while attempted, is generally used incorrectly | • Events are very predictable | • Punctuation is inconsistent and problematic | |
| • Few adverbs or adjectives are used to clarify or describe important points | • Word choice is predictable, lacking descriptors (adverbs and adjectives) | | • Word usage is problematic (s.v.o./homophone/s-v agreement) |

**Exhibit 11.2**   *Continued*

| Narrative 1 | Story-Idea 1 | Organization-Cohesion 1 | Convention-Mechanics 1 |
|---|---|---|---|
| • Factual content is filled with inaccuracies | • Includes few if any characters | • Plot is virtually nonexistent | • Sentence structure is problematic |
| • Writing distorts the message and confuses the audience; it is random ("stream of consciousness") | • Plot is nonexistent | • Events are few and random | • Spelling makes it extremely difficult to read |
| • The ideas are trivial, redundant, and/or hackneyed | • Contains no original ideas | • Lacks transitions | • Handwriting is illegible, making it extremely difficult to decode |
| • No detail | • Detail is significantly absent | • Lacks referents | • Punctuation is virtually nonexistent |
| • Technical vocabulary is missing | • Events are few and predictable | | • Word usage is problematic (s.v.o./homophone/s-v agreement) |
| • Descriptors are missing | • Lacks descriptors (adverbs and adjectives) | | |

Based on "Analyzing Student Writing to Develop Instructional Strategies," by G. Tindal and J. Hasbrouck, 1991, *Learning Disabilities Research & Practice*, 6, (4), p. 239.

prompt A, it does not matter where a student has lunch or what they have for lunch. In prompt B, however, if they do not live with both a mom and a dad and have brothers and sisters, the topic could be difficult to address. A second problem with prompt B is that it is filled with questions. This could lead to a list of "yes" and "no" responses. Prompt C is fairly typical of the sort of story starters found in published classroom programs. Its heavy dependence on imagination, while attractive, may not be good for evaluation. It is best to provide a prompt with which the student has had some personal experience. Many students would find it much easier to write about how they spent their weekend than how they would handle a visit from extraterrestrials (Harris & Graham, 1996b). Heward et al. (1991) provided a good list of writing topics and story starters including: "We searched for hours and hours and couldn't find . . . ," "If I were . . . ," and "What could you do with a deflated basketball?"

## Standards

Perhaps the greatest problem associated with samples of written communication is deciding how to score them and rate their quality (Hasbrouck et al., 1994). One reason this is such a tremendous problem is that standards for comparison often do not exist. We will recommend three techniques: a qualitative scale/rubric, a modified holistic scale, and number of correct words or word sequences.

## The Modified Tindal and Hasbrouck Scale

There are a variety of scoring rubrics for written expression in circulation. We used the one by Tindal and Hasbrouck (1991) in the last edition and found it to be as useful as anything we've seen since. We have also found that it is easy to train raters to a point of high agreement on this rubric in a short (1 hour) time (although follow-up is always required). So here it is again (in Exhibit 11.2) with modifications. The modified Analytical Scale is useful for determining the initial quality of a sample, setting long-term goals, and for recognizing problems in four areas: narrative, story/idea, organization/cohesion, and convention/mechanics. We recommend that you use the scale as an absolute standard and do not attempt to norm it. Assume that *any* student should get a 5 in *each* area regardless of the typical rankings in your class/school (allowing some consideration for grade level and genre, particularly in the domain of convention/mechanics). As students get older, they are expected to maintain the 5 rating as their work moves to more difficult tasks and different genres.

### A 6-Point Modified Holistic Scale

Because the approach to writing instruction varies so much from school to school, many teachers like to have a local standard.

If you think you need a locally derived standard (and it is probably a good idea), here is one approach. It isn't particularly easy to carry out, but once it is done it should *not* need to be repeated for some time.

The holistic scale is created by identifying a group of exemplar writings along with clusters of less expert products that can be used to anchor the ratings of writing samples.

This needs to be done for *each* grade level at the school. It might also need to be done for each school in a district, as you can expect considerable variation between schools (however, if you sampled across schools, use of the scale should eventually reduce that variability). Follow these steps:

A. Give all students a good prewriting prompt; allow 2 minutes to plan and 3 minutes to write. Collect the samples and code them to get rid of names.

B. Next, have all teachers at each grade level sort the products into six equally sized groups (if you decide not to do six groups, do four; stick to an even-numbered scale). To do this, you divide the total number of students at each grade level by 6 (for example, 60 third-grade kids/6 = 10). Each grade level team should sort the samples on the basis of their impression of the quality of the overall product. Therefore, the raters must try to balance consideration of *both* the quality of the message and the mechanics of the presentation.

C. Assuming we are still working with three teachers and 60 kids, the teachers first identify the *best* ten papers and the *ten* worst. The best are assigned a rank of 6, and the worst are ranked 1. From among the remaining papers, the teachers then select the 10 that are next to best (these will be called 5) and the 10 that are next to the bottom (called 2). Whatever is left is sorted and ranked 3 or 4. Those will be the hardest to sort because there will be relatively little difference between 3's or 4's.

D. For every grade select several typical passages at each level (1–6), photocopy or scan them, and cut portions of them out. Stick several of the cuttings on a couple of pages, and put them in a notebook. The notebook should have dividers to separate the samples by grade level and to separate the ranks within grade levels.

E. These will be used to illustrate each level so that in the future teachers can find the samples in the notebook that look most like their new kids and rate the students. Once it has been produced, the notebook becomes the standard, which means that when ranking future papers, 16.6% of them need not be ranked 1.

We recommend that teachers field test this holistic scoring procedure by reapplying it to some of the original samples. If the teachers find their standards are not stable, they should engage in a discussion to identify possible reasons for their instability and work to eliminate variability. This process of working to increase stability of teachers' judgments over time is necessary because with holistic scoring, the teachers (judges) are the criterion, and as we have talked about elsewhere in this text, standards used to make decisions about children must be reliable (free from error).

A modification of the holistic system, from Crawford (1993), is presented in *Resources for Implementing* (Howell et al., 2000a). This collection of writing standards is most useful for screening. It provides sample writings derived as explained above at levels 6 and 3. Students scoring at or below a level 3 should be considered weak in written expression and additional evaluation should be carried out. The level-6 samples are included to provide the teacher with an image of successful writing. These are the grade-level goals. Also included are scoring rubrics based on the samples.

### Number of Correct Words/Letters or Word/Letter Sequences

*The number of correct words or letters* is established by picking the skill you want to evaluate and having the student repeat the writing-sample process. Everything we will say here about words can also be applied to letters. Because this is an overlay assessment, it can be used at any age on any topic (Hasbrouck et al., 1994). You need to pick the skill you want to focus on, for example *spelling*. Then, count the correct and incorrectly spelled words (or letters) in the sample. The data are reported as rate (Total = 47 wpm: 36 correctly spelled wpm, 9 incorrectly spelled wpm).

*The number of correct words in sequence* is determined differently. With this procedure you can record numerical summaries of any writing trait you select by counting "correct word sequences." A correct word sequence is any word used correctly in a string of words. The sequence will be incorrect *if* one or more of the traits *you have selected* are used incorrectly within a word. So, you must pick what you want to measure, but the unit of measurement is *word in sequence*.

If you have selected *correctly spelled* and *semantically correct* but not *capitalized correctly* or *punctuated correctly,* only misspelling and punctuation errors are counted. Here is how a sequence is scored.

---

**Scoring Correct Word Sequence for Spelling and Semantics**

1. Collect a sample sentence (or passage) to score:

   **Claire and Felicity and Robyn last week to shell pecans**

2. Decide which traits you are going to score. You need to decide what characteristics you will be examining to decide if a word is correct.

3. Put carets *above* to indicate *correct* words counted

   ^**Claire**^**and**^**Felicity**^**and**^**Robyn last**^**week**^**to**^**shell pecons**

4. Put inverted carets *below* to indicate *errors.* (You could also use dots (.) to indicate errors because they sometimes are easier to spot later when you tally errors.)

   **Claire and Felicity and Robyn**ᵥ**last week to shell**ᵥ**pecons**^

5. So this sentence would be scored as follows.

   ^**Claire**^**and**^**Felicity**^**and**^**Robyn**ᵥ**last**^**week**^**to**^**shell**ᵥ**peacans**ᵥ

- A correct caret is placed before "Claire" to indicate a correct starting word.

- An incorrect caret is placed before "last" to indicate that "Robyn last" is not a correct semantic sequence in this sentence (*met* was probably omitted and would have been correct).

- An incorrect caret is placed before and after "peacans." Because it is misspelled, it cannot be counted as a correct sequence after "shell" nor can it be counted as a correct ending word, which the last caret would indicate.

5. Count up the carets to get the score: correct 8 = 73%, error 3 = 29%.

The resulting scores from either process, when determined for a whole class, can be used to rank-order students to find which seem to have the most problems.

Here is an example of some locally derived second-grade norms (they may *not* fit for your school). Reading is included for your interest.

include words used to describe characters, activities, events, or conclusions. The proportion of these words out of the total words would then become an indicator of the emphasis the student placed on the category. For example, the student might include many words describing actions but few describing the outcomes of actions.

| Second Grade Writing | | Fall N = 65 | Winter N = 58 | Spring N = 65 |
|---|---|---|---|---|
| Total Words Written | In Five (5) Minutes | | | |
| | Greatest: | 62 | 70 | 75 |
| | Least: | 0 | 6 | 4 |
| | Mean: | 21 | 28 | 33 |
| | Standard deviation: | 13 | 13 | 15 |
| Spelling Errors | In Five (5) Minutes | | | |
| | Greatest: | 17 | 22 | 22 |
| | Least: | 0 | 1 | 1 |
| | Mean: | 6 | 6 | 6 |
| Correct Word Sequences | In Five (5) Minutes | | | |
| | Greatest: | 41 | 42 | 50 |
| | Least: | 0 | 0 | 0 |
| | Mean: | 10 | 15 | 20 |
| | Standard deviation: | 8 | 11 | 12 |
| **Second Grade Reading** | | **Fall** N = 64 | **Winter** N = 61 | **Spring** N = 61 |
| Corrects | In One (1) Minute | | | |
| | Greatest: | 171 | 169 | 200 |
| | Least: | 2 | 3 | 9 |
| | Mean: | 47 | 71 | 83 |
| | Median: | 33 | 72 | 81 |
| | Standard deviation: | 36 | 39 | 41 |
| Errors | In One (1) Minute | | | |
| | Greatest: | 17 | 23 | 15 |
| | Least: | 0 | 0 | 9 |
| | Median: | 6 | 4 | 4 |

***Communication Complexity***   The same scoring rules can be used to score passages for complexity and communicative sophistication. All that is necessary is to come up with a trait that seems to reflect the aspect of written expression in which you are interested. For example, at a school district workshop, Jerry Tindal came up with the idea of counting the number of words per minute a student uses in selected categories. These could

### Setting Local Standards

For written expression, norms can be established using many metrics. For example:

✓ Fluency = words written per minute;

✓ Sentence maturity = proportion of fragments, simple, compound, and complex sentences;

✓ Vocabulary = proportion of words in targeted categories (technical, descriptive, more than five letters, unusual words); and

✓ Mechanics = proportion of legible words and/or letters, words spelled correctly, or correct word/letter sequences.

To finish the norming:

1. Summarize the scores obtained by time of year and grade (it is an especially good idea to have beginning-, middle-, and end-of-the-year norms for grades 1–3).

2. Find the medians and divide by 1.5 and 2.0 to get discrepancy/cutting scores for each grade level. See Chapter 6 for some examples and detailed explanations of how to develop box plots that can aid in this process.

3. Put the information in a notebook.

## Step 4: Conduct Assessment

## Step 5: Summarize Results

## Step 6: Make Summative and Formative Decisions

The process of evaluation for written communication is outlined in Exhibit 11.3. It is designed to answer the following questions:

1. Is written expression acceptable?
2. Is there evidence of a problem in expression and/or mechanics?
3. Is the writing product adequate?
4. Is the writing process adequate?
5. Are word sequences acceptable?
6. Is there a spelling, handwriting, or convention problem?
7. Are the sentences adequately complex?
8. Is the vocabulary adequate?

9. Is it a handwriting problem?
10. Is it a spelling problem?
11. Is it a conventions problem?
12. Are there patterns to the errors?
13. Do errors increase with fatigue or context?

## Survey-Level Testing

### Action 1: Collect and Rate Writing Samples

1. Collect at least two samples. One should be collected without time for review/revision, and the other should allow time for review/revision.

2. If existing samples are not available, and the student is in first or second grade, show the kid a picture and ask him to write about the topic in the illustration. If the student is older, say or write a prompt.

3. For the "no-revision" sample, tell the student that he will have 2 minutes to think about the prompt and 3 minutes to write (these times may be varied but should match those used to establish standards). Students, especially those who are younger, should be allowed to draw a picture as their approach to planning (but don't suggest it).

4. For the "revision" sample, allow the student to take whatever time he wishes to improve a previous 3-minute work.

### Score

1. If you developed one, score the student on a *6-point modified holistic* scale.

2. Also score each product using the rating form in Exhibit 11.2. When using the modified Tindal and Hasbrouck rating, select the number that most closely describes the student's work. Each indicator for a particular rank need not apply.

3. Finally, if you have developed <u>total-word or correct-word sequence</u> standards for writing

**Exhibit 11.3** *The Process of Evaluating Written Expression.*

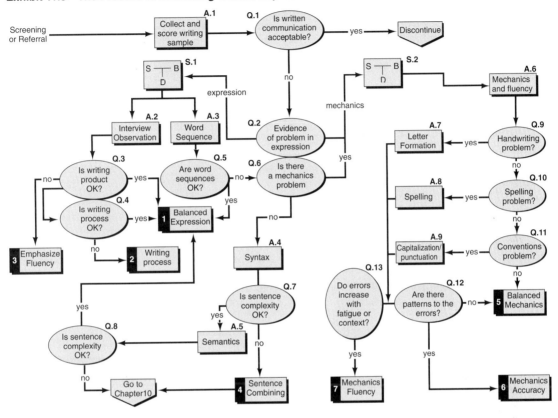

traits, convert to per minute data, then find the position of the student relative to the norm and/or behavioral criteria established from the sample.

### Score Interpretation

1. All students receiving:

✓ A rank of 1, 2, or 3 on the 6-point holistic standard; and/or

✓ A rank below 4 on the Tindal and Hasbrouck scale; and/or

✓ Low scores on a distribution of writing trait scores; and/or

✓ A score below an established behavioral criterion

should be given another story starter the next day to confirm their low rank.

2. All students still ranked low on this additional passage are considered to have inadequate skills, so they need specific-level assessment.

3. Students who might already be in a remedial/special program for written expression who score *above* the standards listed above should be reevaluated to determine if special services are no longer needed.

## Qualitative Interpretation

### Question 1: Is Written Communication Acceptable?

If YES, you can discontinue.

If NO, go to **Question 2** (Q2).

### Question 2: Is There Evidence of a Problem in Expression and/or Mechanics?

If YES, for expression (as indicated by low rating on the story idea and/or organization/cohesion subscales of the Tindal Hasbrouck scale or the 6-point holistic scale), then go to summary 1 (S1).

If YES, for convention/mechanics (as indicated by the convention/mechanics subscale of the Tindal Hasbrouck scale, or low performance on writing traits), then go to S2.

### Summary 1: Expression

Before starting specific-level testing, you need to set a goal. Summarize the standard for student behavior and discrepancy.

For example, if the standard for the 6-point holistic scale is a ranking of 4 or above and the student's work has been ranked 1, then the discrepancy is +3. This would produce a goal like this: "The student will write a [insert a description of the type of writing you will request] passage that ranks 4 or better on the 6-point holistic scale."

Now go to **Actions 2** and **3** (A2 and A3).

### Summary 2: Conventions/Mechanics

You may have reached this summary through **Question 2** or **Question 6**.

To get the PLOP, attend to the traits the student has passed as well as those he may have failed.

If the standard for the writing trait norms was a ranking of 1.5 below the **mean,** and the student's work has been ranked 2.5 below the mean, then the discrepancy is +1. This would produce a goal like this: "The student will write a [insert a description of the type of writing you will request] passage that ranks better than 1.5 below the mean on the writing trait norms."

On the modified Tindal and Hasbrouck scale, if the student got a ranking for conventions/mechanics below 2 and the standard was 4, then the

discrepancy is +2. This would produce a goal like this: "The student will write a [insert a description of the type of writing you will request] passage that ranks 4."

Now go to **Action 6** (A6).

### Action 2: Interview/Observation

Most behaviors for written communication purposes and processes are cognitive. Although you cannot directly observe these behaviors, they may become apparent through interviews with the student.

#### Directions

Observe the student during the process of writing. You may need to do this more than once. Ask the student to explain what he is doing (to pretend he is the teacher so he can explain it to you) and how he decided on the actions he is taking. Rate the student on each item in the status sheet found in Exhibit 11.4.

#### Interpretation Guidelines

Ask both **Questions 3** and **4.**

### Question 3: Is the Product OK?

If YES, then use **Teaching Recommendation 1.**

If NO, then use **Teaching Recommendation 3.**

### Question 4: Does the Student Use the Writing Process Effectively?

If YES, then consider the items marked adequate to be passed. Use **Teaching Recommendation 1.**

If NO, the skills or strategies marked "NO-PASS" or "UNSURE" become the objectives. Use **Teaching Recommendation 2.**

### Action 3: Word-Sequence Test

This procedure may be applied to letters, words, phrases, sentences, or even paragraphs. Implicit in this system is the notion that a correct sequence of words or phrases reflects fluency and syntactic maturity (Hasbrouck et al., 1994). Although correct-sequence scoring does not sample all of the components of writing, it takes very little time and correlates with a number of more time-consuming techniques.

*Exhibit 11.4   Status Sheet Interview/Observation of Writing Process and Product.*

**THE WRITING PROCESS**

| Planning | EXPLAIN | | | EMPLOY | | |
|---|---|---|---|---|---|---|
| Did the writer define a purpose or establish an intent before beginning to write? | yes | no | unsure | yes | no | unsure |
| Did the writer develop a list of content items appropriate to purpose or intent? | yes | no | unsure | yes | no | unsure |
| Did the writer formulate a drawing, model, map, or outline (plan) to structure content appropriate to purpose or intent? | yes | no | unsure | yes | no | unsure |
| Did the writer use the plan as a basis for writing the first draft? | yes | no | unsure | yes | no | unsure |

| Reviewing | EXPLAIN | | | EMPLOY | | |
|---|---|---|---|---|---|---|
| During the writing of the draft(s) does the writer go back and read what was written to check on development and structure? | yes | no | unsure | yes | no | unsure |

| Revision | EXPLAIN | | | EMPLOY | | |
|---|---|---|---|---|---|---|
| Is there evidence in the drafts to indicate that the writer made changes to accomplish purpose/obtain intent? | yes | no | unsure | yes | no | unsure |

**THE WRITING PRODUCT**

| Structure | EXPLAIN | | | EMPLOY | | |
|---|---|---|---|---|---|---|
| Is there an early sentence to focus the reader on the writer's intent or purpose? | yes | no | unsure | yes | no | unsure |
| Are the subtopics and/or events arranged in a recognizable order? | yes | no | unsure | yes | no | unsure |

| Cohesion | EXPLAIN | | | EMPLOY | | |
|---|---|---|---|---|---|---|
| Do all the sentences relate to the writer's intent or purpose? | yes | no | unsure | yes | no | unsure |
| Is there an apparent order in the presentation of the sentences? | yes | no | unsure | yes | no | unsure |
| Does the writer make use of organizing words and devices? | yes | no | unsure | yes | no | unsure |
| Does the final sentence provide an appropriate ending/conclusion? | yes | no | unsure | yes | no | unsure |
| Does the writer make use of transitional words and devices? | yes | no | unsure | yes | no | unsure |

*Source:* Howell, K. W., Zucker, S. H. & Morehead, M. K. (2000b). *Multilevel Academic Skills Inventory.* Bellingham, WA: Applied Research and Development Center. Used with permission.
To order contact the Student Co-op Bookstore, Western Washington University. FAX (360) 650-2888. Phone (360) 650-3656.

## Directions

1. Either use the samples from the survey level (**Action 1**) or obtain others. If there seems to be variability in the student's production, use more than two samples and average the scores.

2. Scoring was explained above. To score the samples, give one point for the following:

- Each word that is in correct sequence

- For appropriate beginnings and endings.

*Correct* means the word conforms to both semantic and syntactic constraints (It is correctly worded and makes sense, in that place, in that sentence).

3. Summarize data.

4. Compare with established standards. Inaccuracy in word sequence is not acceptable to most readers, so an absolute standard of 100% is advisable for revised samples. For initial drafts, compare your students' scores to scores of exemplars (students working at the expected level who are judged to be competent writers).

### Interpretation Guidelines

#### Question 5: Are Word Sequences Correct?
If YES, use **Teaching Recommendation 1**.
    If NO, then go to **Question 6**.

#### Question 6: Is There a Mechanics (Spelling, Handwriting, or Convention) Problem?
If YES, go to **S2** and **Action 6**.
    If NO, then go to **Action 4** for syntax.

### Action 4: Syntactic Maturity

Are the sentences adequately complex? As students become more proficient writers, the complexity of their writing increases. For example, they may use more clauses or compound sentences. Another way to think about it is that their writing becomes syntactically mature. One way to judge syntactic maturity is to use T-units.

A T-unit is a minimal-terminal unit, such as a main clause, plus attached subordinate clauses. In our experience, whereas numerous authors talk about the use of T-units, almost no one actually uses them. That is probably because the training and scoring time is so high. Directions on how to calculate mean T-units are included in Exhibit 11.5.

We prefer the simpler approach advocated by Isaacson (1990), as adapted from Powers and Wilgus (1983) and shown in Exhibit 11.6.

## Directions

1. Collect new samples of the student's written communication or analyze the sample obtained in the survey-level procedure.

2. Using the Isaacson (1990) guidelines in Exhibit 11.6, determine the number of sentences at *each* level and the *percent of total sentences at each level*.

### Score Interpretation
There is so much regional and school variability in this area that there are few established standards for this procedure. Standards could be established from schoolwide writing samples. Development of standards for writing proficiency should be based on the curricular sequences of writing, instruction, and the expectations of teachers in the school. In schools where writing is taught early (beginning in grades 2–3) and in an organized sequence, students would be expected to demonstrate more proficient writing in earlier grades (Harris & Graham, 1996a). On the other hand, if writing is not taught consistently until later (grades 4–5), it is unrealistic to expect students to exhibit skills they have not been taught. This last point is **particularly** important for students who have learning problems (Harris & Graham, 1996b). Obviously, it would be better to teach students how to do the things we expect them to do rather than hope they will somehow learn through osmosis. Writing instruction, like voting, is something that you should do early and often. We hope that the recent emphasis on writing in the standards-based reform movement will prompt

*Exhibit 11.5   Calculating Mean T-Unit and Rating Sentence Complexity.*

## Definition

T-unit = One group of words that will stand alone with all subordinate clauses.

### Directions

1. Count the total number of words in the sample.
2. Count the total number of T-units in the sample.
3. Divide the total number of words by the total number of T-units. The quotient will be the mean length of T-unit.
4. Rate each sentence as a fragment, simple, compound, compound run-on (more than 2 independent clauses), or complex sentence.
5. Summarize T-units and sentence types. Compare with a standard and decide if and where improvement is needed (fragments and run-on sentences would be intervention targets).

Practice: Finding T-Units
(Mark the T-Units in each sentence.)

## Score this Passage:

Howard rides his bicycle and Thad rides in a seat on the back. They wear hats to shade their eyes. They go to the park and they go down the big slide.

### Key

Howard rides his bicycle/and Thad rides in a seat on the back./They wear hats to shade their eyes./They go to the park/and they go down the big slide./

Number of words 32
Number of T-units          5

32 (words) ÷ 5 (T-units) = 6.4
(mean length of T-unit)

| Sentence | T-Units | Type of Sentence |
|---|---|---|
| Thad likes to run. | 1 | Simple sentence |
| While Thad likes to run, he also likes to swim. | 1 | Complex sentence: one independent and one dependent clause |
| Thad likes to run and he also likes to swim. | 2 | Compound sentence: 2 independent clauses |
| When Thad collects shells | 0 | Sentence fragment |
| Thad collects shells and he builds sand castles and he splashes Christopher and he also reads to Tonya. | 4 | Compound run-on sentence |

*Exhibit 11.6    A Modification of Isaacson's Syntax Scale.*

Count the number of sentences in the writing that are representative of each syntactic level. Record the number of sentences for each level in the rectangle provided. Divide the number in each rectangle by the total number of sentences and record the percentage on the line provided.

**Level 1**

Repetitive use of simple (kernel) sentences. For example:

Level 1

I like hamburgers.

I saw a dog.

The dog ate a burger.

He was sick.

_____%

**Level 2**

First expansions—kernel sentences + various phrases. For example:

The dog ran away *from McDonald's*. (prepositional phrase)

*Putting its tail between its legs*, the dog ran around the corner. (participial phrase)

The dog wants *to hide under the porch*. (infinitive phrase)

Level 2

*Lying in the cool darkness* is the cure for the dog's illness. (gerund phrase)

The writer may also use simple compound sentences. For example:

The hamburger was bad, but the dog liked the fish.

The dog felt better, and he chased the squirrel.

_____%

**Level 3**

Transformations that combine kernel sentences with relative and subordinate clauses. For example:

The fish *which was freshly caught* smelled like the sea. (relative clause)

Level 3

*While the dog slept under the porch*, the moon rose. (subordinate clause)

_____%

Total Number of Sentences:_____

frank discussions among teachers about the scope, sequence, and quality of writing instruction, particularly in early grades (Ball & Cohen, 1996; Harris & Graham, 1996a; Ysseldyke & Olsen, 1997). Obviously it is assumed that, as students advance in grade, a larger proportion of their sentences should be at levels 2 and 3. By grade 4, students should all be getting ranks of 3.

### Qualitative Interpretation

#### Question 7: Are Sentences Adequately Complex?

If YES, then go to **Action 5.**

If NO, teach specific-level skills for expanding and increasing sentence complexity using

**Teaching Recommendation 4.** Also consult Chapter 10.

### Action 5: Semantic Maturity

Is the vocabulary adequate?

**Action 5** (semantic maturity/vocabulary) is similar to the semantic **Action 4** in Chapter 10. A limitation of this approach is that most teachers tend to simply judge whether word choice is adequate. Judgment is fine with us as long as it is double-checked with a couple of other teachers. However, the following, more exacting, technique should be used with students who have problems.

**Directions:**

1.  Obtain samples of written work or analyze samples from the survey-level writing exercise.

2.  Obtain a graded list of frequently used words (for example, Carnine et al., 1997).

3.  Summarize the student's performance and compare it with locally developed standards.

## Semantic Maturity/Vocabulary

Count the number of words $= w$

Count the number of words longer than seven letters $= 7+$

Calculate the proportion of large words using this formula:

$$\frac{7+}{w} = \text{proportion/percentage of large words}$$

Count the number of words not found on a list of common, frequently used words $= Nf$

Calculate the proportion of "not found" words using the formula:

$$\frac{Nf}{w} = \text{proportion/percentage of "uncommon" words}$$

Calculate the number of repeated words $= R$

Calculated the proportion of unrepeated words using the formula:

$$1 - \left(\frac{R}{W}\right) \cdot 100 = \text{proportion/percentage of unrepeated words}$$

### Qualitative Interpretation

Once again, there are no established standards for this procedure. One indication of the semantic quality for kids K–2 is its similarity to what the student produces when talking. As the student advances to grades 3 and above, his technical writing should include vocabulary from content-area lectures and texts (so you could construct lists of words from the glossaries of those texts). Another indicator, if you developed school writing samples, is the similarity of the student's usage to exemplars (high-performing students).

### Question 8: Is the Student's Vocabulary Skill Adequate?

If YES, then use **Teaching Recommendations 1** and maybe **3.**

If NO, teach vocabulary. Refer to recommendations in Chapter 10.

### Action 6: Written Mechanics and Writing Fluency

This action takes a fair amount of writing. Read quickly through the following steps to see how much you'll need. If you do not have an adequate sample of writing from the survey testing, you will need to collect one now.

### Directions

1.  Look at Exhibit 11.7. It presents four different writing conditions. While you may not use each condition, it is best to collect at least three different samples under each of the condition(s) you chose. (Be sure to note the condition on the sample.) When scoring, mark each sample as explained below and use the *median scores* of the three samples for decision making. Although it is best to start analysis with samples taken from writing in assignments, sometimes these samples

***Exhibit 11.7   Writing Sample Summary.***

| Error Category | Type of Condition | | | |
|---|---|---|---|---|
| | Copy<br>Total Letters_____<br>Rate_____ | Dictation<br>Total Letters_____<br>Rate_____ | Story Starter<br>Total Letters_____<br>Rate_____ | Assignment<br>Total Letters_____<br>Rate_____ |
| Number<br>Letters **formed** incorrectly<br>% | | | | |
| Number<br>Letters **spelled** incorrectly<br>% | | | | |
| Number<br>Words **capitalized** incorrectly<br>% | | | | |
| Number<br>Words **punctuated** incorrectly<br>% | | | | |
| Total errors | | | | |
| Total accuracy | | | | |

cannot be analyzed (because they are so limited). If that is the case, move left in Exhibit 11.7. Stop moving left as soon as the student passes.

If the student is having spelling troubles, be sure to include a sample from dictation (poor spellers often avoid words with which they know they have trouble).

Have the student use the writing style (cursive or manuscript) being taught. Try to collect samples of at least 100 letters (for spelling and letter formation) or words (for capitalization and punctuation). A format for scoring running text was presented earlier in this chapter (see "Number of Correct Words/Letters or Word/Letter Sequences" above).

Note that spelling and letter formation are usually scored by letter, whereas capitalization and punctuation are usually scored by word. To illustrate this, the same sentence scored for spelling, capitalization, and punctuation is presented on the next page.

2. Record spelling, capitalization, and punctuation results on the summary sheet shown in Exhibit 11.7. Do this by first totaling the number of errors in each category (spelling, punctuation, capitalization). Next, divide the totals by the number of letters (for spelling) and words (for capitalization and punctuation) in the entire sample. This computation will give you a percent that summarizes the ratio of errors per letter or word for each sample. Do not score spelling of

CORRECT SENTENCE

The squirrel, or one of its band, ate Norvic's cinnamon bun.

INCORRECT SENTENCE

the squrrul or one of its band atte novics cinamon bun

| Spelling | Raw Scores: | Proportion of Corrects: |
|---|---|---|
| the squrrul or one of its band atte novics cinamon bun | *41* Correct<br>*5* Errors | 90% |
| Capitalization | | |
| the squrrul or one of its band atte novics cinamon bun | *0* Correct<br>*2* Errors | 0% |
| Punctuation | | |
| the squrrul or one of its band atte novics cinamon bun | *0* Correct<br>*4* Errors | 0% |

Scoring a writing sample.

names in lower grades. Do score capitalization of names.

3. If the student's writing seems to get worse as he writes, you may want to repeat Step 2 at intervals of 100 words to see if he has an obvious "**fatigue point**" beyond which accuracy falls off sharply.

### Interpretation Guidelines

We are going to go through all of these questions at the same time to keep the descriptions of instructional recommendations from getting mixed in with the evaluation processes.

Remember, you can use the flowchart in Exhibit 11.3 to follow a specific skill area to its conclusion.

Using the grade-by-grade holistic writing samples you have developed (see **Action 1**), or your own judgment, ask each question below.

### Question 9: Is There a Handwriting Problem?

If YES, then use **Action 7**.

If NO, then check **Question 10**.

### Question 10: Is There a Spelling Problem?

If YES, then use **Action 8**.

If NO, then check **Question 11**.

### Question 11: Is There a Punctuation and/or Capitalization Problem?

If YES, then use **Action 9**.

If NO, then use **Mechanics Teaching Recommendation 5**.

### Action 7: Letter Formation

Letter formation is important to teachers, as it accounts for most of what we think of as "legibility." Exhibit 11.8 lists ten types of formation errors.

#### Directions

1. Determine the style of writing the student is expected to be using.

2. Use a writing sample from a portfolio, **Action 6,** or a writing prompt.

**Exhibit 11.8   Letter Formation Errors.**

Student _____ Grade _____ Evaluator _____ Date _____

Task _____

TIMED/UNTIMED                    COPY(NEAR/FAR)/MEMORY                    TOTAL NO. OF LETTERS _____

| 1. Alignment | 2. Relative Size | 3. Relative Spacing | 4. Proportion of Parts | 5. Inconsistent Style | 6. Inconsistent Mode | 7. Inconsistent Slant | 8. Closed Loops | 9. Straight and Curved Lines | 10. On Line |
|---|---|---|---|---|---|---|---|---|---|
| YaK ↓ K | cαt ↑↑ Ca | ca t ⇕⇔ | bird ↑↑ rd | bird ⎵ cursive | birD ↑ cap | cat //\ | cut ↑ a | cat ↖↗ | fly ↖↖↗ |
|  |  |  |  |  |  |  |  |  |  |

Source: Howell, K. W., Zucker, S. H. & Morehead, M. K. (2000b). *Multilevel Academic Skills Inventory.* Bellingham, WA: Applied Research and Development Center. Used with permission.
To order contact the Student Co-op Bookstore, Western Washington University. FAX (360) 650-2888. Phone (360) 650-3656.

3. Try to use a sample that will be long enough to illustrate fatigue.

4. Score the writing sample. Here is a phrase that has been scored for formation by drawing arrows to each error. The number for each error is noted with the arrow pointing to it.

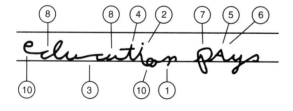

### Action 8: Spelling Accuracy

Traditionally, efforts to correct spelling problems begin with attempts to categorize errors. As with decoding, one problem with categorizing errors is that the evaluator needs some sort of error classification system. Such systems (including those in this chapter) seldom enjoy the empirical support their popularity indicates (Fuchs et al., 1990).

A complete spelling evaluation of young children and poor spellers needs to include tests of phonemic segmentation (Good, 1999a) like those explained in Chapter 9 under **Action 2.**

### Directions

1. Recognize spelling errors within the student's classroom portfolio or construct and administer a spelling test that will permit you to collect at least 75 errors (there may be more than one error per word). Be sure that the test provides an opportunity for many kinds of errors by including regular and irregular words, as well as some drawn from student lessons.

2. Score the sample using correct word sequences (as explained above).

3. Examine the errors closely to prepare yourself to answer some questions about them.

4. If appropriate, check for spelling at different ranges into compositions (50 words, 100 words, 150 words, 200 words) to see if the proportion of correct to incorrect spelling changes for the worst. That would indicate a fatigue factor.

5. Also, obtain all of the information you can about the student's instructional history.

### Action 9: Conventions (Capitalization and Punctuation)

#### Directions

1. Collect a writing sample that contains at least 50 errors (this means students who are fairly accurate will have to write more than those who are not). Try to make sure that the sample provides an opportunity for each type of punctuation/capitalization error. Use the error types shown in Exhibit 11.9.

2. Score the sample and categorize the errors by inserting an arrow and labeling the problem (this will look something like the letter-formation example in **Action 7**). Don't bother with skills the student isn't **expected** to know yet (don't score a *first-grade* student

down for *failure to use commas before conjunctions joining an independent clause*).

3. Summarize the errors by category and identify patterns of concern.

### Interpretation Guidelines

#### Question 12: Do There Seem to Be Identifiable Error Patterns?

- For letter formation:

  If NO, then go to **Teaching Recommendation 5.** You may also need to teach proofreading and text-revision skills using **Teaching Recommendation 2.** When using either teaching procedure, emphasize strategies for problem recognition and self-monitoring.

  If YES, and the student is in kindergarten or first grade, then directly teach the letters that are most troublesome. If the student is in second grade or above, then provide error-correction instruction that targets the student's patterns (as illustrated in Exhibits 11.8 and 11.9). Use **Teaching Recommendation 6.**

- For spelling:

  Use the following guidelines to make an initial attempt at selecting a spelling approach. This will be called an <u>initial</u> attempt because the only certain way to determine the best spelling approach is to put the student into one and use formative evaluation to monitor progress.

### Spelling Guidelines

| Use a Code Strategy within Mechanics Teaching Recommendation 6 | Use a Morphographic Strategy within Mechanics Teaching Recommendation 6 | Use a Balanced Approach with a Morphographic Emphasis within Mechanics Teaching Recommendation 5 |
|---|---|---|
| ✓ Student is just learning to read or spell<br>✓ Student does not seem to know letter sounds<br>✓ Spelling errors are nonphonetic (order = arif)<br>✓ Student has a long (1 year or more) history of morphographic instruction | ✓ Student has made progress in reading but has trouble spelling<br>✓ Student is fairly good at using letter sounds<br>✓ You can read student errors (order = ordr)<br>✓ Student has a long (1 year or more) history of phonetic spelling. | ✓ No particular patterns are evident<br>✓ There are numerous spelling errors<br>✓ The student has received very little spelling instruction<br>✓ The student has received poor spelling instruction |

*Exhibit 11.9   Punctuation Status Sheet.*

Directions (only do this for content where problems exist): Report the number of opportunities for each error.
✓ Report the number of errors.
✓ Report % of accuracy
✓ Report status
✓ Teach skills marked "No"
✓ Check skills marked "Unsure"

| | Opportunities | Errors | % Accuracy | Status Yes No Unsure |
|---|---|---|---|---|

**Capitalization**
First word in sentence
Name of person
Title
Days of week
Month
Street names
Towns, cities, states, countries
Personal pronoun "I"
Buildings, companies, products
Geographical names
Family relationships used for name
First word of quotation
Pronouns
Other

**Period**
End of sentence
Initials and abbreviations

**Question Mark**
End of sentence

**Exclamation point**
Exclamatory sentence
Emphasis

**Comma**
Items in a series
Month, year
Day, month
City, state

**Direct address**
After year in sentence
After state or country in sentence
After introductory word in sentence
Before conjunction joining
  independent clause
Surround appositive
Set off dependent clause
Set off adverbial clause
After greeting and closing in letters

| | Opportunities | Errors | % Accuracy | Status Yes No Unsure |
|---|---|---|---|---|

**Apostrophe**
Contraction
Possessions

**Semicolon**
Separation of series
Other

**Colon**
Salutation of letter
Expression of time
Appositives
Other

**Hyphen**
Compound word or phrase
Prefix when base
  is capitalized
Other

**Quotation Marks**
Direct quotations
Single within direct
Block quotations (no marks)
Dialogue
Titles
Words used as words
Foreign words
Special use words

**Parentheses**
Interruptions
Technical information within a text
Author comment

**Underline/Bold/Italic**
Titles
Stress

**Dash**
Interruptions

**Notation in text**
Numbers/bullets

Note: If the student has problems spelling in the context of another task, then, in addition to **Teaching Recommendation 6,** you need to teach for fluency using **Teaching Recommendation 7.**

### Question 13: Do Significantly More Errors (an Increase of at Least 35%) Occur Near the End of Longer Writing Samples?

If YES, then fatigue and/or lack of automaticity may be the problem. Teach for fluency using **Teaching Recommendation 7.**

If NO, then return to **Action 6.**

## Teaching Recommendations

Before we get into *how* writing should be taught, the question of whether it should be taught at all should probably be considered. Studies have found that, beyond the primary grades, the average student in the United States spends only about 15 minutes a week in writing instruction. Authors also report that most of the scant time spent in writing is spent copying verbatim from workbooks or teacher-prepared worksheets. Students seldom compose written messages and almost never write for an audience other than the teacher (Isaacson, 1990). Also, with the advent of word-processor access, much of the traditional focus on **writing mechanics** is becoming obsoleat (for example, if you want to know how to spell *obsoleat* correctly, click the spell checker). In some ways, it is hard to justify spending pages of the text (which you will have to pay for) on something teachers only teach about 2% of the time.

Today, tremendous emphasis is being placed on the writing process in the early grades (Du Charme et al., 1989; Englert, 1992; Harris & Graham, 1996a; Isaacson, 1992; Levy, 1996). Proponents of the literacy-based instruction seem to be reacting to what they see as an historic overemphasis on secretarial skills (Huot, 1990). These advocates worry that, by accentuating secretarial skills, teachers neglect the more complex tasks that are linked to print communication (planning, reviewing, revising). But it is hard to find this emphasis reflected in common classroom practice, and besides sometimes it takes more than one set of skills to get something done.

### Writing and Reading

Although it is safe to say that there are good readers who are not good writers, those who are good at written expression are almost always good readers (Assink et al., 1992; Tompkins, 1994). Among other explanations, this is because good writing includes reading your own text for planning and review and often reading the text of others as sources of information, inspiration, and style.

The fact that what a person reads influences his writing style can be a problem. For example, as Armbruster (1984b) pointed out some time ago, school texts are often poorly organized, obscurely written, and insensitive to their audience. Yet, this is the primary model of writing many students get.

### Teaching Recommendation 1: Balanced Expression Instruction

#### Objectives

"In response to writing prompts, the student will produce passing levels of word sequences. CAP [as specified]."

"The student will, within writing samples and revised work, produce writings reflecting adequate levels of vocabulary use. CAP [specified levels from word lists and/or ratings from **Action 5**]."

Students need time for writing (Harris & Graham, 1996a; Graham and Harris, 1988; Heward et al., 1991). They need time for both explicit instruction in the writing process (strategies for being an author) as well as explicit instruction in the mechanics of writing (skills for being a secretary) (Gunning, 1998). Without an adequate allocation of instructional time, there is little likelihood that a student's writing will improve. If you don't know how much time a student with written expression problems has to write, find out by reviewing the classroom schedule and observing what really goes on. If you are the teacher, ask someone to observe you.

It is critical in a process as complex as writing to achieve a balance between mechanical skills like handwriting, spelling, punctuation, and sentence and paragraph conventions and the broader purposes of skilled communication (Templeton & Morris, 1999). One way to assure this balance is to integrate reading and writing activities by stressing the fact that well-written books are models of authorship. Isaacson (1989b) suggested that instruction in the secretary skills of writing be separate from those of the author role when the student's secretary skills hinder fluent writing.

The roles of the teacher and the student change as the student becomes increasingly more competent at deploying writing skills (Isaacson, 1994; Isaacson & Gleason, 1997). In initial stages of acquisition, the teacher explicitly explains how to plan, review, revise, and transcribe (Graham et al., 1992; Harris & Graham, 1996b). The following strategy from Englert and colleagues (1991) illustrates the planning questions a teacher should have students repeat during initial stages of instruction:

✓ What is my topic?

✓ Who am I writing for?

✓ Why am I writing this?

✓ How can I group my ideas?

✓ How will I organize my ideas?

Whenever teaching this sort of content, the expert teacher shows and labels the correct performance. In later stages of acquisition, the teacher enlists the student as a collaborator—one who helps with the steps. At that point, the instruction is highly interactive as the teacher asks questions about the task and the student responds, having heard the teacher's thinking out loud and having seen the teacher carry out the steps. If the student's poor handwriting or spelling interferes with expression, the teacher, peers, or a cooperative work group, can take dictation (Madrid et al., 1998). With younger students, you may also allow or even encourage the use of incorrect spelling or, where available, have the student use a computer. (Even today, in the elementary grades, the keyboard becomes nothing more than a temporary novelty, and, because the student is seldom taught to use it with proficiency, its introduction actually *reduces* the stu-

dent's productivity. However, if you are really going to teach it, we think it is fine.) When teaching the writing process, select topics that are familiar to the student. This will allow him to focus on the steps in the process rather than on new topical information.

Because planning is a hard concept for younger students, you may wish to use a strategy introduced to us by a first-grader. Prior to writing, this student would draw a picture about the topic of his story and then, during composition, he'd look at the picture and describe what he had drawn.

In balanced instruction, lessons are designed to teach the student about a variety of writing forms. Today there is a bias to use only student-initiated forms of communication. However, students need instruction in forms they don't spontaneously generate (Harris et al., 1998; Isaacson, 1992), especially those they are likely to be required to use in the upper grades and in life (note taking, job applications, test responses). Student-initiated forms (stories, poems, journals) can be employed to build fluency and to increase interest, but should not be the only genre used.

As the student becomes more accurate in employing a writing process, the teacher can introduce strategies that are specific to the different writing genres. Examples and nonexamples such as informing, persuading, argumentation, and entertainment should be shown. Finally, the teacher needs to back off and let the student work on his own (Spaulding, 1995).

For a well-developed and thorough explanation of effective writing instruction, we highly recommend *Memo to Constructivists: Skills Count, Too* and *Constructivism and Students with Special Needs: Issues in the Classroom* (Harris & Graham, 1996a and 1996b).

### Teaching Recommendation 2: Teach the Writing Process

#### Objective(s)

"In response to writing cues, the student will compose [define the type of composition]. To be acceptable, a composition must conform to [you should insert appropriate indicators found in either Exhibit 11.1 or 11.2]."

A variety of strategies related to text production have been described in recent literature (Hattie & Purdie, 1996; Spires & Donley, 1998). Students may also benefit from constructing their own strategies. As with any other strategy, writing is best taught through explicit explanation and demonstration by the teacher (Gambrell & Chasen, 1991). In our experience we find that teachers explain and show models of completed work but seldom *demonstrate* the procedures—especially planning procedures—by carrying them out in view of the kids. Today, the use of maps and diagrams (like our flowcharts—we *know* you love them) has replaced the more traditional approach of planning by outline. These maps seem to represent the interactive nature of information processing. However, it should be noted that there <u>still</u> is little information on the effectiveness of different map types or on their appropriateness for students with different skill levels (Dunston, 1992).

At the least, be sure to:

✓ Teach strategies for planning, reviewing, revising, and transcribing;

✓ Teach goal-setting and self-monitoring;

✓ Teach peer collaboration strategies to enable students to interact with an audience and gain feedback on effects of communication.

*Revision* is a major part of the writing process (Raymond, 1989). However, students seldom, if ever, see revision take place. (This text has been reviewed and revised a billion times, but the endless cross-outs, margin notes, and giant red Xs don't appear in the final version (we hope).) But students need to **see** the effort and revision that goes into writing. They also need to understand that composition and revision often occur at the same time. They can only learn this through public demonstration. Only teachers who are willing to write and revise in front of their students can effectively provide this. Have your students suggest a topic and then write about the topic on an overhead projector so they can see your effort and revision (don't prepare for this; do it the way they have to). Talk your way through the writing to label strategy use for the student.

## Teaching Recommendation 3: Teach Fluency of Expression

### Objective(s)

"The student will, within writing samples and revised work, produce writings reflecting adequate levels of vocabulary use. CAP [specified levels from word lists and/or ratings from **Action 5**]."

"In response to writing prompts, the student will maintain accuracy while increasing total words written to CAP [specified according to established behavioral criteria]."

Fluency in writing means producing more ideas, and expressing them well, in a shorter period of time. This is an aspect of writing instruction for which there seems to be little empirical direction. The following ideas are ones we share, more because they make sense than because of any compelling evidence that they are useful.

Have your students:

✓ Increase the quantity of writing and reading;

✓ Write and read a variety of genre;

✓ Write for and interact with an audience;

✓ Rewrite in response to advice from peers;

✓ Assist peers in checking work for specific attributes;

✓ Assist peers in planning, reviewing, and revising for a variety of purposes;

✓ Self-monitor increases in fluency and quality for specific components/tasks that are less fluent than others; and

✓ Rewrite the same topic for different audiences or purposes.

## Teaching Recommendation 4: Sentence Combining for Expression

### Objective(s)

"The student will, [within writing samples and revised work], develop sentences reflecting syntactic maturity. CAP [specified T-unit and/or rankings on the Isaacson (1990) guidelines]."

Sentence combining consists of taking short sentences and making them into big sentences (Lawlor, 1983; Phillips, 1996; Reyes, 1990). To decide what syntactic structures to teach, review Chapter 10, look at written syntax of capable peers, or use the guidelines in Exhibit 11.6.

During sentence combining, the teacher demonstrates how to combine ideas by using conjunctions such as *and* and *but*. Short sentences with parallel ideas can be taken from the student's work to illustrate the making of bigger sentences. For example, the sentences "Thad likes to play soccer" and "Hannibal likes to swim" can be converted into "Thad likes to play soccer but Hannibal likes to swim."

In addition to combining short parallel constructions, students can be taught to combine structures that are not parallel by manipulating single sentences. For example, the declarative sentence "Claire ran upstairs after she heard the airplane," can be inverted to "After she heard the airplane, Claire ran upstairs." Once again, teacher-modeled instruction, followed by prompted and unprompted practice, should be used to teach students how to gain more control over the way they communicate their ideas.

### Teaching Recommendation 5: Balanced Mechanics Instruction

#### Objective(s)

When teaching handwriting or spelling, use the following objective: "Given [specify assignments/story starters/dictation or copy], the student will write making no more than [specify accuracy level and mechanic skill] errors per symbol, while maintaining a rate of [_____] symbols per minute."

The expectations you will place within the brackets of the objective should come from the criteria that led you to answer NO to **Questions 9, 10,** and **11.** For example:

"Given an assignment, the student will write making no more than 10% letter-formation errors while maintaining a rate of 85 letters per minute."

The recommendations for **balanced expression** instruction (#1) gave the basics for balanced

instruction. This process adds an emphasis on proofreading strategies, self-monitoring, and correcting work (Meltzer et al., 1996; Okyere & Heron, 1991). Explicit strategies for proofreading include those provided by Gleason et al. (1991) and Wong (1973, 1975). They are also found in Chapter 14. An emphasis on self-monitoring is typically provided by first using, and then gradually withdrawing, varying levels of assistance (prompts and cues).

Because writing is an active, **constructive** process, student involvement is effective. This involvement is characterized by reflection, self-evaluation, and self-management (McDougal & Brady, 1998). Even something as mechanical as handwriting can be improved with self-evaluation. Students who monitor and evaluate their work will review what they need to do, check what they have done, and judge the adequacy of their responses against a standard.

Begin by making it clear to the student that quality of production is more important than simply finishing assignments. Next, create a "strategic environment" (see Chapter 4) in the class by holding students accountable for locating and correcting their own errors. Finally, present specific proofreading strategies such as the COPS strategy (Deshler & Schumaker, 1996). COPS stands for:

C—capitalization

O—organization

P—punctuation

S—spelling

The use of this procedure is explained, along with a number of others, by Meltzer (1996) and Shannon and Polloway (1993).

There are many such strategies (and new ones coming up every day). They generally have a mnemonic "name" (COPS) that lists the essential actions. The student is then taught to employ the actions through explanation, demonstration, verbal rehearsal, practice, and the gradual removal of self-talk. Such techniques were explained back in Chapter 4. Lovitt (1995) is a good resource for finding these processes.

Students can also keep records of the kinds of mechanical errors they find as they proofread (like common spelling errors). Then they can avoid the same problems the next time they write.

### Teaching Recommendation 6: Build Mechanics Accuracy

#### Objective(s)

Any objective can be used here as long as the criteria provide an accuracy expectation. Sometimes, a string of objectives may only differ in their CAP. For example: CAP = 45 wpm, CAP = 60 wpm, CAP = 75 wpm, CAP = 90 wpm.

About 45 years ago, it was noted that "No subject in the curriculum is as neglected or as poorly taught as handwriting. And in no other subject are the results of instruction less impressive" (Cole, 1956, p. 97). The same statement applies today. Instruction on written mechanics is frequently limited to copying exercises that students complete in the absence of explanation, demonstration, or task-specific corrections.

When mechanics are taught, one of the major flaws in the instruction is that most of it occurs after the student has written. Prewriting instruction is better than postwriting instruction. Tompkins (1994) stated that because spelling is a tool used *during* writing, the *teaching* of spelling should occur *before* the writing. (The same statement is true for handwriting conventions and even keyboarding). In this way, the writing becomes a practice session for the lesson you have taught. Don't rely on feedback and error correction (which typically occurs after the error has been practiced) to offset the practice effect the student experiences when he is allowed to think through and produce an incorrect response. Accuracy is developed by carefully demonstrating strategies for correct performance. Only after the student has seen correct performance, and can explain how to carry it out, should he be given practice—and that ought to be extensive *guided* practice (Isaacson & Gleason, 1997). He should only be given *independent* practice *after* he has shown that he can perform accurately. And even then he should be given a specific purpose for the practice ("Now I want you to write in your journal and be sure to use the punctuation rules we just covered. I will be checking to see that you did.").

When a student has been allowed to practice errors, you may need to temporarily sacrifice context to employ highly targeted lessons and correction procedures. Sit down with the student and show him exactly what he is doing wrong—as well as exactly what he should be doing. Next, have the student explain it back to you. When the student can explain the correct usage, put the student in guided practice. Use lead questions and prompts to maintain accurate performance. Then gradually withdraw the prompts while emphasizing the need for accuracy.

***Letter Formation***    Even today, most students are taught manuscript and then are switched to cursive writing. However, both need not be taught. Therefore, one way to give the student who is having problems with letter formation a break is to just pick, or have him pick, a format. One argument against cursive is that the joining of letters, the increasing of their slant, the elongation, as well as the addition of loops, all serve to decrease legibility (Hildreth, 1964). Also, manuscript writing tends to vary less among people. This makes manuscript more standard and less confusing to the reader. The one thing that is clear is that success in cursive writing is not contingent upon prior instruction in manuscript (Graham, 1994; Karlsdottir, 1996).

#### Instruction

1. Begin instruction by finding errors noted during the **Action 7** process. These may be specific letters, classes of letters such as "capitals," or error patterns such as "closed loops" (as seen in Exhibit 11.8).

2. Develop an objective that states the target (desired correct) response.

3. Show the student examples and non-examples of the correct response and carefully point out the attributes that make a response incorrect.

4. Convert correct examples into errors by altering an attribute, then change errors into corrects. As you are doing this, talk out loud to the student listing the changes you have

made and explaining the effect of the changes.

5. Now have the student convert errors to corrects. If possible, have him do this on examples of his own work. The student should also talk aloud as he works.

6. Give the student feedback and correction on his talk.

7. Ask the student to write ten correct examples of the targeted response under your guidance. Give feedback and corrections, then repeat the request until ten correct examples are created.

8. Assign a writing exercise. Tell the student that his purpose for writing is to correctly make, or use, the targeted skill.

9. Ask him to check the assignment with you. Correct errors and praise corrects.

10. Repeat until the student is proficient.

**Spelling**    A number of the comments below address remedial and corrective spelling. They may not relate as well to initial spelling instruction.

Teaching spelling by having students memorize lists of words is **NOT** a good idea. Kids with spelling difficulty must be taught rules and strategies for spelling. Word lists (unless these are words derived from a set of technical vocabulary, or personal information the student must master to do well in a specialized content area, like biology) should only be used to supply material for practicing and evaluating those strategies. Therefore, explanation, demonstration, and strategy-specific feedback must always accompany lists of words (Fult and Stormont-Spurgin, 1995).

Although we do recommend the teaching of spelling rules and strategies, as opposed to words, we doubt that the world is going to change as soon as this text is published (It didn't—at least for spelling—with the last three editions). Therefore, we know a lot of you will be teaching word lists. Our advice to you is to pretest, only select words the student needs to study, and then make the studying as interactive and active as you can. Don't let students go off with lists of words but no explicit strategy for

studying them. Incidentally, as with many skills, the use of peer tutoring is highly effective with spelling and a good way to make the study sessions more active (Madrid et al., 1998).

Regardless of her philosophy about literacy, every teacher of spelling must come to grips with the alphabet. As an oversimplification, spelling can be viewed as the flip side of decoding. When you ask a student to decode, you show him letters and ask for sounds. When you ask a student to spell, you give him sounds and ask for letters. Accordingly, the predictability of the sound-letter correspondence in words is an important concern. As pointed out in Chapter 9, sound-symbol correspondence in English (especially at the level of words) is not completely predictable (Templeton & Morris, 1999). To make matters worse, for children to write, they must begin efforts at spelling before they have mastered the alphabetic principles. So their introduction to the task is typically filled with errors that can be practiced to automaticity before formal spelling instruction begins.

If a kid, like most of us, thinks the word *dropped* is pronounced *"dropt,"* he will probably write *d-r-o-p-t* in those instances where *d-r-o-p-p-e-d* would be correct. To be a good speller, a student must determine:

✓ how the word is pronounced;

✓ if it is spelled as it is sounded; and,

✓ how it is spelled if it isn't spelled as it is pronounced (Spache, 1940).

This phonetic spelling strategy is presented below in the form of objectives (Howell et al., 2000b). During assessment, you will ask the student to demonstrate competence on these objectives in the sequence presented. Use words the student has previously misspelled. If the student fails an objective, it should be listed on his instructional program. If he passes, it should be listed as PLOP.

Whenever you come across a misspelled word in the student's written work, ask him what word he was trying to write. If he mispronounces the word, you may have a speech, regional-accent, or bilingual interference problem (so you would consult Chapter 10). But, in all cases, correct the mispronunciation.

---

## Phonetic Spelling Strategy

1. Word reproduction: Given words dictated one at a time by the examiner, the student will correctly repeat each word with 100% accuracy taking no more than 5 seconds per word.

2. Word sorting: Given written words, and words dictated one at a time by the examiner, the student will correctly repeat each word and compare it with the printed version to sort the words into "Sounds like it's spelled" or "Doesn't sound like it's spelled" categories. CAP: 100% accuracy.

3. Word sorting: Given written words, and words dictated one at a time by the examiner, the student will correctly repeat each word and compare it with the printed version. He will then identify (point, circle, name letter(s)) any portions of the word that are *not* spelled as they are sounded. CAP: 100% accuracy.

4. Word sorting: Given words dictated one at a time by the examiner, the student will correctly repeat each word and sort it into "Sounds like it's spelled" or "Doesn't sound like it's spelled" categories. He will then list those words, or portions of words, for which the phonetic spelling strategy cannot be completely applied. CAP: 100% accuracy.

5. Letter isolation: Given words dictated one at a time by the examiner, the student will correctly say each word with an obvious pause between letters and/or morphemes. This will be done with 100% accuracy taking no more than 5 seconds per word.

6. Sound isolation: Given *non-morpheme* clusters/syllables, dictated one at a time, the student will correctly say each sounded phoneme with an obvious pause between sounds. This will be done with 100% accuracy taking no more than 5 seconds per cluster/syllable.

7. Sound morphograph correspondence: Given morphograph sounds (phonemes) dictated one at a time by the examiner, the student will correctly say/write the letters (graphemes) in the morphograph. This will be done with 100% accuracy taking no more than 5 seconds per sound.

8. Sound single-symbol correspondence: Given mixed (single letter or morphographs) sounds (phonemes) dictated one at a time by the examiner, the student will correctly say/write the letters (graphemes) that make each sound. This will be done with 100% accuracy taking no more than 5 seconds per sound.

9. Operational knowledge; Given the directions to do so, the student will correctly say and describe all of the steps necessary to phonetically spell unknown words. This will be done with 100% accuracy taking no more than 15 seconds. The answer is:

   ✓ Repeat words

   ✓ Recognize words that are not spelled like they sound (phonetic spelling strategy cannot be applied to all portions of the word)

   ✓ Isolate syllables in words

   ✓ Isolate sounds in syllables

   ✓ Say letters for morphograph sound

   ✓ Say letter for sound

---

One of the most important spelling skills is <u>selective attention</u> to sounds of letters, clusters/morphographs, and words (Assink et al., 1992; Dixon, 1993). The clearest prerequisite to spelling is *recalling the letters* (either single letters or clusters) *that make sounds*. Phonetic spelling is like blending, in that it requires the student to break the word down, translate it into code, and reassemble it. During the analysis ("breaking") step, it is best to attend to clusters within the word as opposed to its individual letters. That is because, when we are dealing with morphographs and letter clusters, the amount of material that must be processed is reduced. Also, the clusters are more phonically regular than words (whereas the "i," "n," and "g" sounds may vary from word to word, "ing" is always sounded the same way). In the word string, therefore, a student is better off focusing on the clusters "st" and "ring" (see Chapter 9). Sound-letter correspondence skills can be taught by selecting a decoding sequence and words that provide examples (*above, play*), then asking "In the word *above/play*, what letter(s) makes the sound /a/?" (the student should say /a/ for *above* and /ay/ for *play*).

Although we prefer sound-symbol correspondence and morphographic knowledge to the traditional "rules" of spelling, some phonetic generalizations do occur reliably enough that students may be able to use them to attack unfamiliar words. These generalizations are outlined in Exhibit 11.10. Of course, these generalizations cannot be used at the automatic or even mastery levels, but they may help a student reach accuracy. (We wouldn't stress them to the expense of other approaches such as morphographs.)

Many of the phonetic skills important to spelling seem related to phonemic segmentation (see Chapter 9). Research in phonemic segmentation indicates that it is a skill linked to both reading and spelling and that it can be taught (Good, 1999; Share, 1999; Yopp, 1988). Research has not yet confirmed whether phonemic segmentation is truly a prerequisite for spelling, an enabling skill, or part of spelling itself (Yopp, 1992).

***Morphographs***   There is a content domain within language that permits writers to geometrically increase the number of words they can spell. This is a way of using units of meaning—called morphographs—rather than individual letters. Morphographs (see Chapter 9) are the building blocks of all words. Some morphographs are words, some are affixes (the parts you use at beginnings and endings of words),

and some are bases (the parts you use with affixes to form words). In Exhibit 11.11, we list example morphographs that can be easily combined to form words. Take a few seconds to see how many words you can make by combining the morphographs in Exhibit 11.11 (or by adding a few letters to them).

Once the spelling of a morphograph has been learned, it can be used in combination with letters, or other morphographs to spell new words. Dixon (1993) suggests that if teachers teach a few phonics rules with high-utility morphographs, even very poor spellers will become successful.

Our initial bias is that all students should be taught using the morphograph approach. However, the entire approach is more complex than the space in this text allows. So here are the basics based on Dixon (1993):

✓ Teach letter sounds following the sequence presented in Chapter 9, Exhibit 9.6 (M. Sprick et al., 1998; Templeton & Morris, 1999). The rules used to produce the sequence were:

• Separation of letter-sound relationships that sound or look alike;

• Teach sounds needed to read high-frequency words; and

• Teach sounds needed to write stories.

✓ Teach the concept of morphographs.

✓ Teach the student to count the sounds (not the letters) in words (expression = ex + press + ion. Total sounds = 3).

✓ Teach the student to combine morphographs into words (<u>pro</u> + <u>spect</u> + <u>ed</u> = prospected, <u>ad</u> + <u>?</u> = advise).

✓ Teach the student commonly used morphographs.

✓ Teach the student to identify morphographs in words (replace = <u>re</u> + <u>place</u>).

✓ Teach the student exceptions (imagin<u>ary</u>/station<u>ery</u>).

✓ Teach confusing words (lose, loose, loss).

For more information about spelling, check Dixon (1993).

*Exhibit 11.10   Phonics Generalizations Applied to Spelling.*

1. Double the letters *f, l, s,* or *z* in most one-syllable words when preceded by a short vowel. Examples are *cliff, sniff, bluff, whiff, cuff, puff, fell, tell, swell, ball, spill, fill, spell, brass, press, cross, miss, fuss, pass, buzz, fizz, jazz.* Exceptions are *bus* and *gas.*

2. The silent *e* at the end of a word makes a short vowel long. Examples are *pin* and *pine, dim* and *dime, hat* and *hate, mat* and *mate, rat* and *rate, cub* and *cube, plan* and *plane, cap* and *cape, at* and *ate, mad* and *made, mop* and *mope, kit* and *kite, rod* and *rode, hid* and *hide, rip* and *ripe, fad* and *fade, cut* and *cute, tub* and *tube, can* and *cane, hop* and *hope, not* and *note,* and *fin* and *fine.*

3. When you hear *k* after a short vowel, spell it *ck;* when you hear *k* after a long vowel or consonant, spell it *k.* Examples are *neck, dusk, flank, track, hunk, slack, stuck, deck, rink, milk, check, tuck, task, fleck, lack, coke, make, rock, knock, and stink.* Use *c* at the end of polysyllabic words when you hear *ik.* Examples are *attic, plastic, metric, cosmic, classic, Atlantic, optic, frantic.*

4. When you hear *j* after a short vowel, you usually spell it *dge.* After a long vowel or consonant you use *ge.* Examples are *age, gadget, lodge, huge, strange, cage, nudge, stage, page, bridge, change, hinge, edge.*

5. When you hear *ch* after a short vowel, use *tch.* When you hear *ch* after a long vowel or consonant, use *ch. Ch* is always at the beginning of a word. Examples are *chop, bench, batch, pinch, church, witch, blotch, pitch, porch, crutch, lunch, sketch, fetch, patch.* Exceptions are *rich, which, much, such, sandwich.*

6. When you have a one-syllable word with a consonant at the end of a word that is preceded by a short vowel and the suffix begins with one vowel, double the consonant. If any one of these conditions is not met, don't double. Examples are *ship* and *shipper, ship* and *shipping, hot* and *hottest, slop* and *sloppy, mad* and *madder, rob* and *robber, star* and *starry, fat* and *fatter, fog* and *foggy, wit* and *witness, grin* and *grinning, mad* and *madly, cold* and *colder, farm* and *farming, dust* and *dusty, rant* and *ranted, boat* and *boating, weed* and *weeding, blot* and *blotter, grim* and *grimmest, rest* and *restless, flat* and *flatly, slim* and *slimmer, feed* and *feeding,* and *win* and *winning.*

7. A word ending in a silent *e* drops the *e* before adding a suffix beginning with a vowel, but does not change before an ending beginning with a consonant. Examples are *hope* and *hoping, dive* and *diving, write* and *writing, tune* and *tuneful, shine* and *shiny, time* and *timer, hope* and *hopeless, take* and *taking, sore* and *soreness, flame* and *flaming, fame* and *famous, care* and *caring, hide* and *hiding, hope* and *hoped, lone* and *lonely, use* and *useful, sure* and *surely, close* and *closely, make* and *making, life* and *lifeless, like* and *likeness, shade* and *shady, noise* and *noiseless,* and *tire* and *tiresome.*

8. Double the consonant when adding a suffix after a short vowel. Examples are *capped, caper, capping, moping, mopping, mapped, filling, filed, filing, filled, taping, tapping, taped, tapper, hopped, hoped, hopping, hoping.*

9. In word ending in *y* preceded by a consonant, the *y* changes to *i* before any ending except *-ing* or *-ist.* In words ending in *y* preceded by a vowel, keep the *y.* Examples are *cry* and *crying, rely* and *reliance, pray* and *prayer, worry* and *worrying, joy* and *joyful, enjoy* and *enjoyment, say* and *saying, sleepy* and *sleepiness, glory* and *glorious, delay* and *delayed, merry* and *merriest, study* and *studying, lonely* and *loneliness, pay* and *payable, carry* and *carried, stray* and *strayed, fly* and *flier, supply* and *supplied, healthy* and *healthier, spy* and *spying, funny* and *funniest, tiny* and *tiniest, injury* and *injurious.*

10. When adding *ble, dle, fle* to a word, consider the initial vowel sound. A long vowel or consonant simply needs *ble, dle, fle.* A short vowel sound continues to need all the help it can get. Examples are *buckle, freckle, puddle, ruffle, stable, rifle, stifle, staple.*

11. While most nouns form the plural by adding *s* to the singular, nouns ending in *s, x, sh,* and *ch* form the plural by adding *es.* A noun ending in *y* preceded by a consonant forms the plural by changing the *y* to *i* and adding *es.* Examples are *cats, dogs, kisses, boxes, fishes, churches,* and *candies.*

12. An apostrophe is used to show the omission of a letter or letters in a contraction. The possessive of a singular noun is formed by adding an apostrophe and *s.* The possessive of a plural noun ending in *s* is formed by adding an apostrophe. Examples are *cannot* and *can't, will not* and *won't, I had* and *I'd, I will* and *I'll, had not* and *hadn't, Jim's car, the dog's bone, the groups' scores.*

**Exhibit 11.11   Example of Morphographs in English.**

| Affixes | Nonword Bases | Words |
|---------|---------------|-------|
| be- | tain | born |
| de- | astro | gain |
| dis- | cant | listen |
| -ed | stance | talk |
| -ing | ject | tear |
| re- | gress | time |
| un- | lief | grade |
| -s | ceed | act |
| -ship | spect | grace |
| pro- | quire | |
| -ion | vise | |
| -ive | semble | |
| -or | sist | |
| in- | | |
| ad- | | |

### Teaching Recommendation 7: Mechanics Writing Fluency

Fluency building occurs after accuracy has been developed using one of the other teaching recommendations. Here are some example fluency objectives for writing mechanics (conventions).

#### Handwriting Objective

"Given an assignment, story starter, dictated prompt, or copy exercise, the student will make no more than ____ % [of the specified error type] while writing at a rate of 100 letters per minute."

#### Spelling Objective (for Failure to Use Generalizations in Exhibit 11.10)

"While writing answers on tests, the student will use the [specify generalization] to write the correct spelling of phonetically regular words or portions of words. CAP 100% accuracy while maintaining a rate of 25 wpm."

#### Spelling Objective (for Failure to Use the Morphographs in Exhibit 11.11)

"During the spelling test, the student will write or say the spelling of specified morphographs within phonetically regular words (or portions of words). CAP 100% accuracy while maintaining a rate of 25 wpm."

Students need frequent, meaningful opportunities to write (and they seldom get enough of this). They also need explicit instruction in the purpose, process, and products of written communication. Even after they have mastered individual components, they will probably need instruction in how to integrate these complex skills. This integration is best assured through explanation, accompanied by the demonstration of good writing by the teacher. Without this integration and considerable practice, the student will not learn to use writing automatically (Harris & Graham, 1996b; Ivarie, 1986). See **Teaching Recommendations 3** and **5** for additional guidance.

In the domain of handwriting, which is so dominated by custom, some teachers and parents are quite inflexible in their expectation that all students write in a preferred way. Yet, contrary to popular belief, there do not seem to be significant differences in writing rates between cursive and manuscript when experience and practice are comparable. Instead, handwriting rates are more closely related to the quality of instruction, the duration of practice, and the skills of the writer. Still, some will refuse to accept manuscript writing from older students. In these cases, arrange for training to change the teachers/parents, rather than have the student spend valuable time on a subjective concern about style.

First reduce the error-per-symbol ratio for later passages to the level found in earlier passages. For example, assume that the student currently misspells 12 out of every 100 letters within the first 100 words of a sample, 16 for the next 100 words, but 30 for the next 100 words. That student's first objective could read:

"Given a story starter, the student will spell no more than 16% of the letters incorrectly from any lot drawn more than 200 words into a sample."

Fluency objectives should target specific conditions for writing. If a student is 95% accurate when writing letters in isolation at a rate of 100 per minute, the objective could be:

"When writing test answers during class work, the student will maintain a rate of 100 letters per minute with 95% accuracy."

A student who has distinct problems in spelling, letter formation, or capitalization/ punctuation should be reminded of those problems prior to writing (Templeton & Morris, 1999). For example, he could be told, "While you are writing, pay particular attention to the need to capitalize the first word in each sentence." Then, the student should be required to check his own work and to summarize how he did on that skill. The summary could be on a chart, or it could be on a list that looks like this:

| What I Did | What I Should Have Done | Type of Error |
|---|---|---|
| a student who has . . . | A student who has . . . | Capitalize first word in sentence |
| A Student who has . . . | A student who has . . . | Spelling "student" |
| I saw susan at the conference . . . | I saw Susan at the conference . . . | Capitalize proper names |

Finally, slow writers with no physical condition prohibiting writing should be taught to write letters and digits with fluency. Writing slowly can limit the amount of work a student can produce and may contribute to difficulty in completing tasks. Slow writing may also impede acquisition of more complex skills if the student attends to handwriting instead of the critical attributes of problems. However, never put off other instruction while waiting for handwriting fluency to increase.

Lessons designed for building handwriting fluency use brief, intense practice sessions in which the student is encouraged to write faster while maintaining accuracy. Such fluency-building routines can be incorporated into daily lessons, and students can be taught to time each other on a free writing or a copying task. Often, several very short (10-second) timings on dictated random numbers or letters will prove to be more beneficial than one long timing.

Do not allow accuracy to fade with increased rate. After a timing, the students can check both their accuracy and rate. They should also record or chart their own progress.

## Summary

This chapter has focused on the author skills and secretarial skills required to produce and transcribe written messages. We have described techniques for evaluating these skills and provided appropriate teaching recommendations.

In parts of this chapter, expression and mechanics are separated for convenience. In practice, the process of writing should be evaluated and taught along with the conventions and mechanics of transcribing. We defined written communication as a complex system that includes purpose, process, and product. We discussed evaluation issues in writing and addressed concerns regarding the absence of writing instruction in schools. We then outlined procedures for analyzing written communication. Frequent references were made within this chapter to Chapter 10 (language).

# Chapter 12

# Math

*Too often, we ask how to measure something without asking the question of what we would do with the measurement if we had it.*

—Abraham Kaplan (1964), p. 214

*Studying mathematics in order to understand the laws of physics is not unlike learning enough of a foreign language to capture some of the special flavor and beauty of prose or poetry written in that language. In the process one may become fascinated by the language itself.*

—Robert Osserman (1995), p. 169

## Step 1: Define Your Purpose

E valuation in math centers on two broad content domains: the students' knowledge of the relationships of number and chance (the ideas expressed through math) and the students' knowledge of the language used to communicate these relationships. The value of the language resides in the need to understand and to communicate the ideas (Russell, 1999). Therefore, the purpose of this chapter is to explain the process for determining what, if anything, may be preventing a student from sending and receiving the messages conveyed through basic computational verse.

## Step 2: Define the Thing to Be Measured

Unfortunately, many people think that math is something one learns about, but they do not understand that it is a tool for learning about other things. Mathematics is a language used to describe relationships between and among various objects, events, and times (Osserman, 1995). Those fluent in the language interact appropriately with a system of symbols—just as you are interacting with alphabetic symbols, words, and punctuation marks while you read this text. It is important to remember that, without a message, any language becomes nothing more than technique (Paulos, 1988). This is often true for remedial math students.

### The Mathematics Curriculum

There have been many efforts at defining the curriculum of mathematics (Cawley & Parmar, 1992). For example, the National Council of Teachers of Mathematics (NCTM) has produced extensive "Curriculum Standards" and standards for evaluation. Portions of the NCTM curriculum standards will be presented in this chapter. A complete draft of the standards can be found on the World Wide Web at http://www.nctm.org/standards2000/.

Here are the NCTM Standards For Evaluation and Assessment as developed in 1989 and 1995. The first six apply to all grade levels:

✓ *The Mathematics Standard:* Assessment should reflect the mathematics that all students need to know and be able to do.
✓ *The Learning Standard:* Assessment should enhance mathematics learning.
✓ *The Equity Standard:* Assessment should promote equity.
✓ *The Openness Standard:* Assessment should be an open process.
✓ *The Inferences Standard:* Assessment should promote valid inferences about mathematics learning.
✓ *The Coherence Standard:* Assessment should be a coherent process.

The next ten standards have been developed specifically for the evaluation of mathematics in elementary schools:

**Standard 1: Alignment**   Methods and tasks for assessing students' learning should be aligned with the curriculum's

✓ goals, objectives, and mathematical content.

**Standard 2: Multiple Sources of Information**   Decisions concerning students' learning should be made on the basis of a conveyance of information obtained from a variety of sources. These sources should encompass tasks that

✓ demand different kinds of mathematical thinking.

**Standard 3: Appropriate Assessment Methods and Uses**   Assessment methods and instruments should be selected on the basis of

✓ the type of information sought.

**Standard 4: Mathematical Power**   The assessment of students' mathematical knowledge should yield information about their

✓ ability to apply their knowledge to solve problems within mathematics and in other disciplines.

**Standard 5: Problem Solving**   The assessment of students' ability to use mathematics in solving problems should provide evidence that they can

✓ formulate problems.

**Standard 6: Communication**   The assessment of students' ability to communicate mathematics should provide evidence that they can

✓ express mathematical ideas by speaking, writing, demonstrating, and depicting them visually.

**Standard 7: Reasoning**   The assessment of students' ability to reason mathematically should provide evidence that they can

✓ use inductive reasoning to recognize patterns and form conjectures.

**Standard 8: Mathematical Concepts**   The assessment of students' knowledge of mathematics should provide evidence that they can

✓ label, verbalize, and define concepts.

**Standard 9: Mathematical Procedures**   The assessment of students' knowledge of procedures should provide evidence that they can

✓ recognize when a procedure is appropriate.

*Special and remedial students are those who, for various reasons, have trouble moving through the curriculum at the expected rate.*

**Standard 10: Mathematical Disposition**   The assessment of students' mathematical disposition should seek information about their

✓ confidence in using mathematics to solve problems, to communicate ideas, and to reason.

### Computation and Operations

For a student to compute, she must (1) accurately and quickly substitute the various symbols for the quantities being computed, (2) arrange the symbols according to the rules for their use, and (3) know the correct messages to convey. These actions correspond to the fact, rule, strategy, and concept domains presented in Chapter 3. These domains should be taught together, although teachers may emphasize one over another depending on a student's needs.

The failure to integrate facts, rules, strategies, and concepts can best be seen through the process of error analysis. For example, a student who produces the answer "$17 + 8 = 115$" has failed to carry out a rule/strategy correctly (she has accurately used factual knowledge to add the numbers 7 and 8 together but failed to place the correct value on the 1 from 15). She has also violated the concept of addition by producing an answer that is many times larger than the numbers she started with.

*Exhibit 12.1    Basic Concepts.*

40. Cause-and-effect
39. Correlation
38. Representatives
37. Probability
36. Chance and coincidence
35. Estimation
34. Algorithms for checking problems
33. Algorithms (procedures)
32. Set up equation
31. Select operation
30. Irrelevant information
29. Missing information
28. Decimals
27. Inverse of fractions
26. Mixed numbers
25. Equivalent fractions
24. Fraction equal to "one"
23. Common denominator
22. Unity
21. Remainders
20. Distributive property
19. Multiplication/Division by 1 and 0
18. Associative property
17. Set separation
16. Union of sets
15. Sets
14. Expanded notation
13. Zero as a place holder
12. Place Value
11. Regrouping
10. Addition, subtraction, multiplication, division
9. Multidigit numbers
8. Mathematical symbols
7. Terminology and notation
6. One-to-many correspondence
5. One-to-one correspondence
4. Numeral values
3. Groups of 1's, 10's, 100's, 1000's
2. Cardinal numbers
1. Number order

## Concepts

Exhibit 12.1 lists concepts associated with different computational and problem-solving operations discussed in this chapter. A status sheet for concepts is in Howell et al., 2000a. It is based on information presented in a variety of sources (Burrill & Romberg, 1998; Hanna, 1998). The status sheet also gives examples of problems related to these concepts. Most of the concepts are basic to the successful computation of addition, subtraction, multiplication, division, and fraction problems. However, every concept is not necessary for every computation. The "common denominator," for example, isn't necessary for multiplication.

## Strategies

Mada Kay Morehead was once observing in a primary classroom. The students had been explicitly taught strategies for efficiently working with numbers. One strategy was "counting-on" from any number. (An example of *counting-on forward* would be, "Let's start with 6 and count to 10. 6, 7, 8, 9, 10." *Counting-on* <u>backwards</u> would be: "10, 9, 8, 7, 6."

In another classroom, Mada Kay observed students who had not directly been taught strategies. These students had been left to generate their own counting strategies. For example, an 8-year-old was observed counting her fingers to solve addition problems. On one problem, however, she ran out of fingers. At first she seemed to give up, but then she got out scissors, plain paper, and tape. The student then proceeded to fashion several tubes that she taped to one hand. Now, she had made more fingers! Unfortunately, although her solution was entertaining, it was inefficient. The extra fingers would not have been necessary if her teacher had shown her the counting-on strategy.

## Facts

In math, facts are simple numerical statements that must be used correctly for calculations to occur properly. For example, 2 + 2 had better equal 4 whenever a student is computing.

## Application

Application is the utilization of math. Application includes measurements of time, temperature, money, length, surface, volume, and weight. Subdomains within application are usually (1) tool use (how do you use a meter stick?), (2) content knowledge (how many centimeters in a meter?), and (3) vocabulary knowledge (what is the definition of length?).

Often, teachers allocate time for instruction in computation and operations but do not include adequate time for problem solving and application (Algozzine et al., 1987; Carpenter et al., 1984; Van de Walle, 1998). Regrettably, when computation and applications are taught separately, it is difficult to make them meaningful (Baroody & Hume, 1991).

Exhibit 12.2 illustrates what we mean by content knowledge, tool use, and vocabulary knowledge. Tables showing other application content are found in Howell et al., 2000a. The specification for time and surface in Exhibit 12.2 is not exhaustive. Other content could be included. However, do not assume that all content covered in all texts or represented on all math tests is worth instructional time. Math curricula are saturated with marginal content—the first example that comes to mind is the topic of Roman numerals. This sort of curricular residue should not be allowed to compete with things the student genuinely needs to know and use. (Dr. Nolet suggests that, if you really want to know the secret of assessing and teaching Roman numerals, you can send him $500 and he will tell you *everything* you need to know about them).

## Problem Solving

Problem solving requires the functional combination of computation knowledge *and* application knowledge. It has two steps:

1. Deciding what to do (selecting correct operations, selecting relevant information, ignoring irrelevant information, noting missing information, and estimating correct answers); and

2. Carrying out a plan (setting up equations

and judging which numbers go with which operation, working equations using procedures that result in correct answers, and checking results).

Here is a problem:

Thad and Paula are reading a story that has 38 pages. They are reading to Christopher, who is $2\frac{1}{2}$ years old. Thad has read 26 pages and Paula has read 7. How many pages are still to be read?

Carrying out the two steps above could sound something like this (if the student is "thinking out loud"):

✓ **Select relevant information** "What information do I need to solve the problem? First I need to find the thing that is 'unknown.' The problem tells me it is the number of pages left to be read! Then I'll need how many pages were read and how many pages there were altogether. Is everything I need to know there? Yes. Is there information I do not need? Yes, Christopher is $2\frac{1}{2}$."

✓ **Select correct operation(s)** "Will I add or subtract to solve the problem? I will add how many pages Thad (26) and Paula (7) read. Then I subtract that from the total (38)."

✓ **Estimate correct answer** "What do I know already? Whatever the answer is it can't be larger than 38."

✓ **Set up equation and carry out** "What are the steps? First I'll find the sum of $26 + 7$, then I'll subtract that from 38. $26 + 7 = 33$, $38 - 33 = 5$."

✓ **Check results after problem solution** "How do I know if I'm correct? I have trouble adding 7's so I'll check as I go. I'll add my solution to the sum of $26 + 7$ and see if it equals 38. $33 + 5 = 38$."

Problem solving is a neglected and misunderstood topic in the math curriculum (Cummins, 1991; Englemann et al., 1992; Morrow & Kenney, 1998; Olsen et al., 1998). The neglect is puzzling because most math teachers are as interested in the concepts of numbers as reading

*Exhibit 12.2*    ***Application Example of Subdomains.***

| Domains | Subdomains | | |
|---|---|---|---|
| | Vocabulary Knowledge | Tool Use | Content Knowledge |
| **Time** | ***Tools***—definition of function | ***Uses*** | ***Units*** |
| | clocks | Calendar | 60 seconds = minute |
| | watches | Digital clock/watch | 60 minutes = hour |
| | calendars |    Telling time | 24 hours = day |
| | |    Setting alarm | __ days = month |
| | |    Stop watch | 12 months = year |
| | ***Units***—definitions | Analog clock/watch | 10 years = decade |
| | Seconds |    Telling time | 10 decades = century |
| | Minutes |    Setting alarm | 100 years = century |
| | Hours |    Stop watch | |
| | Months | | ***Concepts*** |
| | Years | | Early |
| | Decade | | Late |
| | Century | | Duration |
| | Morning | | |
| | Night | | |
| | Fall/Autumn | | |
| | Winter | | |
| | Spring | | |
| | Summer | | |
| **Surface Measurement** | ***Terms*** | ***Kinds of Tools*** | ***Units*** |
| | Area | Ruler | Metric |
| | Perimeter | Yardstick | 10 mm = 1 cm |
| | Circumference | Meterstick | 100 cm = 1 meter |
| | Radius | Tape measure | 1000m = 1 km |
| | Angle | T-square | |
| | Line | | ***Customary*** |
| | Base | | 12 inches = foot |
| | Height | | 3 feet = yard |
| | | | 5280 feet = mile |
| | ***Shapes*** | | 43,560 sq. feet = acre |
| | Square | | |
| | Rectangle | | ***Algorithms*** |
| | Triangle | | Perimeter of a rectangle = (2)length + (2)width |
| | Circle | | Perimeter of a triangle = $\Sigma$ of sides |
| | Polygon | | Perimeter (circumference) of a circle = $2\pi r$ |
| | | | Area of a rectangle = length $\times$ width |
| | | | Area of a triangle = 1/2 base $\times$ height |
| | | | Area of a circle = $\pi r^2$ |

teachers are in recreational reading (Hanna, 1998). It may be because so many teachers confuse "problem solving" with working word ("story") problems (Howell & Barnhart, 1992). Story problems are often just computation problems stated in prose. Practicing those does little to improve problem solving. However, there can be much more to word problems than that (Xin & Jitendra, 1999).

## Task Analysis

A math problem is a task. Like any other, the nature of the task itself requires the worker to do certain things. For example, adding fractions with unlike denominators ($\frac{1}{6} + \frac{1}{4} =$ ___) requires skill at adding fractions with like denominators ($\frac{2}{12} + \frac{3}{12} =$ ___). Any missing subskill is a feasible *assumed cause* for the failure.

Everyone who computes "$\frac{1}{6} + \frac{1}{4} = \frac{5}{12}$" must do the things listed here:

5. Add fractions with like denominators.
$$\frac{2}{12} + \frac{3}{12} = \frac{5}{12}$$

4. Convert unlike-denominator fractions to like-denominator fractions.
$$\frac{1}{6} + \frac{1}{4} = \frac{2}{12} = \frac{3}{12}$$

3. Multiply fractions by a fraction equal to 1, using the factor (2 or 3) that produces a denominator equal to the lowest common denominator (12).
$$\frac{1}{6} \times \frac{2}{2} = \frac{2}{12} \quad \text{and}$$
$$\frac{1}{4} \times \frac{3}{3} = \frac{3}{12}$$

2. Find factors of the lowest common denominator.
$$12$$
$$2 \times 6$$
$$2 \times 3$$

1. Find the lowest common denominator.
$$6 = 6, \cancel{12, 18,} 20, 24$$
$$4 = 4, \cancel{8, 12,} 16, 20, 24$$

If a student does not solve $\frac{1}{6} + \frac{1}{4}$ correctly, any of the five subtasks listed above, or their sub-

tasks, could be used to explain the failure. The point is, if a kid fails at some point in the curriculum, one way to find explanations for her failure is to task-analyze the problem. In Howell et al., 2000a, computation objectives for major operations have been task-analyzed. Each objective has an identifying number and letter designation.

An alternative explanation for any error is that, although the student knows the necessary bits of task-specific prior knowledge, she does not have a strategy for combining them. As explained earlier, strategy problems can often be identified through error analysis (Miller & Carr, 1997).

## Standards

Although efforts have been made to define the content of the math curriculum (Kennedy & Tipps, 1997), the same efforts have not been employed to establish how proficient a student needs to be when working that content. Tables of specifications for computation and application are provided in Howell et al., 2000a. In these tables, objective numbers from Howell et al., 2000a are written in the squares. In some cases the CAP in Howell et al., 2000a is "undetermined." This is because those intersections cover tasks that must be used at different levels of proficiency to complete different tasks. As a result, a single statement of CAP cannot be provided yet.

The CAPs listed in Howell et al., 2000a are reasonable for students who are expected to have learned the skills. However, they are approximate. The criteria come from a variety of sources including the authors' judgment and experience. Standards for mastery were obtained by testing successful elementary students, middle school students, high school students, and adults. Among masters, there is not a terrific relationship between the CAP and grade level; a fourth-grader who has mastered addition isn't any slower, or less accurate, than a high school student who has also mastered it.

Obviously, the criteria apply only if the student has received instruction in the content. The computation rate criteria do not apply to students until they can write digits or say numbers at a rate of 100 correct per minute. If the student cannot write digits at this rate (most first- and second-graders cannot), a formula can be used to set intermediate aims. This will be explained in computation specific level **Actions 2** and **3.** Performance criteria for the domains of application and problem solving are generally set at 100% accuracy (specifying an objective that calls for a student to "make change" at anything less than that seems a bit indifferent).

## Step 3: Devise a Way to Make the Thing in Step 2 Observable

Conventional published math tests have the problems of most other published achievement tests. Specifically, these tools:

- ✓ Have standards that are irrelevant to teaching;
- ✓ Have formats and problems that don't resemble class assignments;
- ✓ Lack empirically validated skill sequences;
- ✓ Have inadequate samples of student behavior;
- ✓ Provide little insight into why errors are made; and
- ✓ Are seldom aligned with the instructional objectives.

As a teacher, don't even think about taking a student who scores at the third-grade level on such an assessment and putting that kid in a published third-grade math text. The odds that such a decision will be advantageous are less than the odds of this book being made into a movie.

Mathematics does have some important differences from curricular areas such as reading, language, and written communication. One of the biggest is that skill in math is not reflected in a general outcome measure (like oral reading, language samples, or story starters). A student may know a great deal about some aspect of math but completely bomb an assessment that doesn't cover that material. Therefore, it is necessary for an evaluator to know exactly what a stu-

dent is expected to know to conduct a functional math evaluation.

To evaluate math, we need instruments that sample computation, applications, and problem solving. These instruments need to be sensitive to short-term instructional interventions. To see if a student uses estimation or monitors her own answers, the evaluator may need to use techniques such as interviews and other less customary procedures. For example, the two test formats in Exhibit 12.3 are meant to sample a student's mastery of the algorithm for addition of a two-digit addend to a one-digit addend, with regrouping. In **format A** (an accuracy test), all the problems require regrouping. In **format B** (a fluency test), some of the problems *do not* require regrouping. **Format B** is the better test.

In **format B,** the problems that do not require regrouping are *nonexamples* (noninstances) of regrouping. The systematic and judicious use of noninstances (for example, never use a noninstance that is higher in the skill sequence than the skill you are testing) forces the student to do more than compute. To pass this test she must utilize conceptual knowledge to discriminate when regrouping is and isn't required. In fact, if you only wanted to assess that knowledge, the directions for this test could ask the student to "point to the items requiring regrouping." No items would have to be worked. (The test also includes a diagonal grid [see page 368] to help error analysis. The grid idea was originally developed by Hofmeister (1975)).

To sample problem-solving skills such as selecting the correct operation, selecting relevant information, or setting up equations, one may choose not to have the student actually work the problem but to select how she would work the problem. Examples of stimulus formats that accomplish this are illustrated for concepts 30 and 31 in the Howell et al., 2000a basic concepts status sheet.

## Interviewing

Interviews and assisted assessment can be useful for gaining insight into conceptual and strategic knowledge. The easiest interview format is

**Exhibit 12.3   Examples of Stimulus Formats.**

**Format A**

Name _____ Date _____ Grade _____ Count: correct _____ errors _____ Time: 1 min.

Addition-Double Digit with Carrying

| 48 +38 | 25 +78 | 15 +29 | 78 +13 | 16 +49 | 77 +15 | 17 +54 | 18 +49 | 14 +37 | 26 +19 |
|---|---|---|---|---|---|---|---|---|---|
| 29 +18 | 16 +18 | 17 +14 | 13 +28 | 15 +39 | 17 +43 | 19 +55 | 76 +17 | 17 +79 | 18 +19 |
| 23 +18 | 36 +15 | 48 +14 | 53 +18 | 64 +17 | 18 +69 | 68 +19 | 15 +17 | 39 +19 | 42 +19 |
| 16 +18 | 19 +18 | 18 +18 | 19 +19 | 18 +18 | 16 +16 | 68 +68 | 23 +23 | 36 +36 | 48 +48 |

**Format B**

Practice Items

| 45 +7 52 | 28 +6 34 | 95 + 8 102 | 76 +4 80 |
|---|---|---|---|

| | | | | | | | | | | | |
|---|---|---|---|---|---|---|---|---|---|---|---|
| 28 +4 32 | 53 +9 62 | 16 +8 24 | 94 +8 102 | 87 +7 94 | 63 +9 72 | 60 +8 68 | 32 +9 41 | 42 +2 44 | 51 +9 60 | | Digit count |
| 31 +5 36 | 58 +2 60 | 13 +7 20 | 26 +4 30 | 74 +7 81 | 69 +9 78 | 83 +7 90 | 49 +0 49 | 22 +8 30 | 93 +3 96 | 1s | (21) |
| 39 +9 48 | 62 +4 66 | 78 +3 81 | 43 +8 51 | 56 +5 61 | 24 +9 33 | 18 +8 26 | 73 +8 81 | 83 +5 88 | 92 +9 101 | Non-instance | (41) |
| 28 +1 29 | 49 +6 55 | 93 +6 99 | 98 +5 103 | 15 +7 22 | 85 +9 94 | 34 +6 40 | 45 +5 50 | 63 +9 72 | 71 +4 75 | 2s | (62) |
| 31 +9 40 | 97 +2 99 | 19 +5 24 | 70 +9 79 | 48 +8 56 | 65 +8 73 | 95 +6 101 | 84 +8 92 | 36 +6 42 | 83 +8 91 | Non-instance | (83) |
| 1s | Non-instance | 9s | Non-instance | 8s | 3s 5s | 6s 5s | 4s | Number added to itself | | 3s | (104) |

Howell, K. W., Zucker, S. H. & Morehead, M. K. (2000b). *Multilevel Academic Skills Inventory.* Bellingham, WA: Applied Research and Development Center.
To order contact the Student Co-op Bookstore, Western Washington University. FAX (360) 650-2888. Phone (360) 650-3656.

simply to ask the student to "be the teacher for a while" and to show you how to work problems. This promotes student talk, which makes her thought processes, like those illustrated in the Thad and Paula example above, observable.

If an open-ended request ("Be the teacher") is not sufficient, then a more structured interview should be given. Exhibit 12.4 provides a set of questions for conducting this kind of interview. The questions in Exhibit 12.4 were produced by the Assessment Alternatives in Mathematics (California Mathematics Assessment Advisory Committee, 1990) group.

### *Error Analysis*

Sometimes, more can be observed in a student's errors than in her correct answers. Basic computation (like spelling in the upper grades) is not an area where creative responses are highly prized. Because computation responses are controlled by the problem, it would seem that errors would occur by types (Stein et al., 1997). However, despite numerous efforts, no system of error categorization (including ours) seems to have gained lasting popularity.

## Step 4: Conduct Assessment

## Step 5: Summarize Results

## Step 6: Make Summative and Formative Decisions

Materials for use in evaluation of mathematics can be found in Howell et al. (2000a), which compliments this text. We will refer directly to these materials by giving the number of the test but will also provide a brief description of each in case you don't have that book or prefer to develop your own tests. One advantage of the materials we are providing is that they have been cross-referenced to the objectives supplied in Howell et al., 2000a.

The student's classwork is probably the best source of survey-level information. Other sources (such as status sheets) should sample a range of math tasks. Some math texts have chapter reviews in their appendices, and these can be used to assemble a comprehensive survey-level test. Be sure to add problems that sample strategy behavior if the test you select doesn't include them.

Before you start, here is some more advice.

✓ At first, only focus on objectives typically taught at or near the student's *expected level.*

But be ready to move up or down according to the student's responses.

✓ Encourage the student to show her work. Have scrap paper and extra pencils available for the student and a stopwatch for yourself.

✓ Remove the erasers from pencils.

✓ If necessary, allow the student to work the survey tests in separate sessions over a period of days.

✓ Use Exhibit 12.5 to guide you through the process.

✓ Keep records and copies of everything. Record summaries of the various procedures on the math summary sheet found in Howell et al. (2000a).

✓ Remember to refer to the rules for developing assumed causes, and the evaluation actions presented in Chapter 7, whenever you are interpreting the results of the various procedures. The interpretation guidelines all assume that the rules and actions have been followed.

### *Decision Making for Computation*

This process of computation evaluation is illustrated in Exhibit 12.5.

### *Action 1: Survey Facts Rate*

Slow responding to basic facts is such a frequent explanation for other difficulties in math that it warrants attention at the survey level. Because most survey tests do not sample rate of response, you will need to add this test to your materials. For the purpose of this procedure, a "fact" is any addition or subtraction problem involving a number 0–10 added to or taken from a number 0–20. For multiplication, a "fact" is any number 0–12 multiplied by any other number 0–12. For division, a "fact" is any number divided by 0–12 that yields an answer 0–12. (If you are testing a student from a lower grade, select only the items she is *expected* to know.)

## Exhibit 12.4    Asking Questions.

Asking the right question is an art to be cultivated by all educators. Low-level quizzes that ask for recall or simple computation are a dime a dozen, but a good high-level open-ended question that gives students a chance to think is a treasure!

These questions might be used as teaching or "leading" questions as well as for assessment purposes. Both questions and responses may be oral, written, or demonstrated by actions taken. The questions and their responses will contribute to a climate of thoughtful reflectiveness.

Some suggestions about assessment questioning:

✓ Prepare a list of possible questions ahead of time, but, unless the assessment is very formal, be flexible. You may learn more by asking additional or different questions.

✓ Use plenty of wait time; allow students to give thoughtful answers.

✓ For formal assessment, leading questions and feedback are not generally used, although some assessment techniques include teaching during the examination.

✓ Make a written record of your observations. A checklist may or may not be appropriate.

**Problem Comprehension**
Can students understand, define, formulate, or explain the problem or task? Can they cope with poorly defined problems?

- What is the problem about? What can you tell me about it?
- How would you interpret that?
- Would you please explain that in your own words?
- What do you know about this part?
- Do you need to define or set limits for the problem?
- Is there something that can be eliminated or that is missing?
- What assumptions do you have to make?

**Approaches and Strategies**
Do students have an organized approach to the problem or task? How do they record? Do they use tools (manipulatives, diagrams, graphs, calculators, computers, etc.) appropriately?

- Where could you find the needed information?
- What have you tried? What steps did you take?
- What did not work?
- How did you organize the information? Do you have a record?
- Did you have a system? a strategy? a design?
- Have you tried (tables, trees, lists, diagrams . . . )?
- Would it help to draw a diagram or make a sketch?
- How would it look if you used these materials?
- How would you research that?

**Relationships**
Do students see relationships and recognize the central idea? Do they relate the problem to similar problems previously done?

- What is the relationship of this to that?
- What is the same? What is different?
- Is there a pattern?
- Let's see if we can break it down. What would the parts be?
- What if you moved this part?
- Can you write another problem related to this one?

**Flexibility**
Can students vary the approach if one is not working? Do they persist? Do they try something else?

- Have you tried making a guess?
- Would another recording method work as well or better?
- What else have you tried?
- Give me another related problem. Is there an easier problem?
- Is there another way to (draw, explain, say . . . ) that?

**Communication**
Can students describe or depict the strategies they are using? Do they articulate their thought processes? Can they display or demonstrate the problem situation?

- Would you please record that in simpler terms?
- Could you explain what you think you know right now?
- How would you explain this process to a younger child?
- Could you write an explanation for next year's students (or some other audience) of how to do this?
- Which words were the most important? Why?

**Curiosity and Hypotheses**
Is there evidence of conjecturing, thinking ahead, checking back?

- Can you predict what will happen?
- What was your estimate or prediction?
- How do you feel about your answer?
- What do you think comes next?
- What else would you like to know?

**Equality and Equity**
Do all students participate to the same degree? Is the quality of participation opportunities the same?

- Did you work together? In what way?
- Have you discussed this with your group? with others?
- Where would you go for help?
- How could you help another student without telling the answer?
- Did everybody get a fair chance to talk?

**Solutions**
Do students reach a result? Do they consider other possibilities?

- Is that the only possible answer?
- How would you check the steps you have taken, or your answer?
- Other than retracing your steps, how can you determine if your answers are appropriate?
- Is there anything you have overlooked?
- Is the solution reasonable, considering the context?
- How did you know you were done?

**Exhibit 12.5    Decision Making for Computation.**

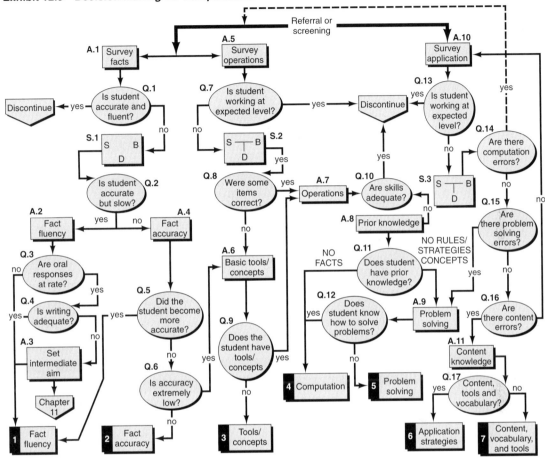

**Directions**

1. Select a fact test for each area. Computation tests 1–4 in Howell et al. (2000a) will work.

2. For each fact test, say to the student "I want you to work these items as quickly and as carefully as you can. Don't skip any problems unless you don't know how to do them. When you come to the end of a row, start at the next row. Keep working until I ask you to stop. Please begin."

   Time the student for 1 minute. When the time is up, say "Thank you." Repeat for each set of facts.

3. The answers and error-analysis grids are provided in Howell et al. (2000a).

4. To establish rate per minute, count the number of problems finished correctly and the number finished incorrectly (you may want to count digits for more complex items, but number of problems is appropriate for basic facts). Next, divide these totals by the time in minutes (in this case, 1). Omissions are not errors.

5. To determine accuracy, divide the number of items worked correctly by the total number of items worked.

6. Compare the student's scores to the 40 correct, 0 error per minute criteria suggested in Addition Objective 1m, Subtraction Objective 1m, Multiplication Objective 1m, and Division Objective 1m (Howell et al., 2000a) or to a criterion you establish.

### Interpretation Guidelines
Based on the accuracy and rate criteria, respond to the following questions.

### Question 1: Is the Student Accurate and Fluent on Basic Facts?
If YES, then discontinue testing facts (although you still need to administer survey tests for operations).

If NO, then note the current level of accuracy and fluency in **Summary 1.**

### Summary 1
Calculate the performance discrepancy by comparing the student's behavior on <u>each</u> fact test given to the criteria in Appendix A.12.3. Use this information to state long-term goals. Next, answer **Question 2.**

### Question 2: Is the Student Accurate but Slow?
If YES, then the student could be slow because she doesn't know the facts or because she doesn't write quickly enough to display her knowledge. Employ **Action 2.**

If NO (the student is inaccurate), then employ specific level **Action 4.**

### Action 2: Fact Fluency. Checking Oral Response and Handwriting

Suppose you have tested a third-grade student and found that she accurately works 22 addition fact problems in 1 minute. The CAP for fluency is 40. There are three obvious assumed causes for the student's failure to meet fluency on a written addition facts test:

1. She is slow at adding,
2. She is slow at writing digits, and
3. She is slow at adding *and* slow at writing digits.

It isn't possible to determine if assumed cause **3** is correct until assumed causes 1 and 2 have been checked. This is accomplished by having the student write digits and work problems aloud.

### Oral Response

### Directions

1. Administer basic-facts tests 1–4 (assuming the student is expected to know all four). Have the student say the answers rather than write them (a probe sheet is the best stimulus).

2. Say "Point to each problem and tell me the answer. Work as fast but as carefully as you can. Begin."

3. Time the student for **60** seconds and say "Thank you."

4. Note corrects and errors per minute. The CAP for both oral and written facts is 40 correct, 0 errors per minute (100% accuracy).

5. Record results.

### Handwriting

### Directions

1. Administer a writing-digits or a copying-digits test.

2. Say "Write/copy from 1 to 100 as quickly and carefully as you can. Please begin."

3. Time the student for 60 seconds. Say "Thank you."

4. Score the sample by counting the number of *digits* written. They are counted correct as long as they are *legible;* ideal writing is not required.

5. Record the results.

### Interpretation Guidelines

### Question 3: Are the Student's Oral Responses at Rate?
If YES, then go to **Question 4.**

If NO, then use **Teaching Recommendation 1** to teach the appropriate objective(s) (Division 1m, Multiplication 1m, Subtraction 1m, or Addition 1m).

### Question 4: Can the Student Write Fast Enough to Demonstrate Math-Fact Fluency?

Criteria for writing are 100 digits per minute starting late in the second grade. Use the results of **Actions 1** and **2** to answer this question.

If YES, then the student is accurate and slow despite sufficient writing skill. Use **Teaching Recommendation 1** to teach fact objectives.

If NO, then you will want to go to **Action 3.**

### Action 3: Set Intermediate Aim

You now know the student is accurate but slow on at least some facts. What you need to do next is set an intermediate aim.

### Directions

"Writing digits" is a "tool movement" or "basic movement cycle" (BMC), which means that other skills (in this case, displaying *written* math answers) depend upon it (White & Haring, 1982). The relationship of BMCs to larger skills has been expressed in this formula: (task $\times$ current) $\div$ 100 = intermediate.

$$\frac{\text{Task mastery rate} \times \text{Current BMC rate}}{\text{BMC mastery rate}} = \text{Intermediate aim}$$

If the student worked 22 addition problems correct with no errors per minute, and she wrote 75 digits a minute, you can compute her maximum addition rate per minute by using the formula shown here:

Mastery rate for addition facts = 40 problems per minute

BMC rate for writes-digits = 100 digits per minute

Current write-digit rate = 75 digits per minute

$$(40 \times 75) \div 100 = 30$$

The answer tells us that, even given her slow handwriting rate, the student should respond at a rate of 30 problems per minute. However, during the testing she only completed 22. This student is slow at writing digits (CAP = 100; student = 75) and is also slow at basic facts (intermediate aim = 30; student = 22). According to the formula, she has adequate writing skills to work 30 problems per minute *right now*. Therefore, 30 can be used as an *"intermediate aim."* Because the student is having trouble with *both* accuracy on facts and writing digits, teach her to write digits (go to Chapter 11 to find out about handwriting) while using **Teaching Recommendation 1** to take the student to her intermediate aim. *Do not delay math instruction while building handwriting fluency.*

Setting an intermediate aim is *not* the same as lowering the final standard for slow-writing students. However, in cases where there are physical restrictions (for example, a student has no fingers with which to hold a pencil), it is necessary to *modify* the task and use an alternative response mode (have the student say the answers or indicate them on a *communication board*).

### Action 4: Check Accuracy on Basic Facts

### Directions

1. Return to those objectives that you used in **Action 1.** Re-administer them *without* an emphasis on fluency.

2. Try to have the student complete at least 50% of the items on each appropriate probe. This is to allow you to use the error-analysis grids. Say to the student "Take your time and write the answer to each problem. Work carefully." However, if the student misses 50% or more of the first ten items, discontinue.

3. Score the responses. Compare the responses to standards you have established, or use ours (100%). Note error patterns.

4. Record the results.

## Interpretation Guidelines

### Question 5: Did the Student Become Accurate?

If YES, then the original errors were rate-induced; go to **Teaching Recommendation 1** (fact fluency).

If NO, then go to **Question 6.**

### Question 6: Is Accuracy Extremely Low (50% of Expectation or Lower)?

If YES, go to **Action 6.**

If NO (the student is better than 50% accurate), then go to **Teaching Recommendation 2** and use objectives Division 1a, Multiplication 1a, Subtraction 1a, or Addition 1a (as needed).

### Action 5: Survey Operations (Can the Student Carry Out Expected Operations?)

### Directions

The process for evaluating operations is also illustrated in Exhibit 12.5. Here is how it works.

1. Use the answer keys to make up tests 5–10 (in Howell et al., 2000a). You can also select a task (classwork) sampling a broad range of problems. The sample should include problem types the student is expected to know.

2. Say to the student: "Work each problem; take your time; show your work."

3. Score each item as correct or incorrect. In this case, count omissions as errors.

4. Answers to the problems are presented in Howell et al., 2000a. Note that on the answer key each item has two numbers in parentheses above it. The first of these numbers is the *objective number* for the content of the item and the second is the *grade level* at which we think this objective is routinely taught. You may want to replace these numbers if the expectations are different in your school. The *objective number* always refers to the objectives for the operation (addition, fractions) being assessed.

5. Compare the items correct with expectancies for the student's current level by using the computation summary sheet found in Howell et al., 2000a.

### Interpretation Guidelines

Based on the student's performance, respond to the following questions.

### Question 7: Can the Student Correctly Work Operation Items at the Expected Level?

If YES, discontinue (there isn't a problem). If you want, you can administer items beyond the expected level to determine where to begin instruction.

If NO, go to **Summary 2.**

### Summary 2

If you believe that you have obtained an adequate sample of the student's work, list objectives passed (correct) as indicators of the student's current level of performance. The objectives corresponding to items the student has missed should be listed on the student's teaching plan. Only list objectives the student is expected to know. Use the student's expected performance (as determined from the numbers above the test items) on the test as a standard and then determine the discrepancy and goal.

Next, ask **Question 8.**

### Question 8: Were Some Operation Items Correct?

If YES, employ **Action 7** to get a larger sample of work and to confirm what skills the student needs to be taught.

If NO, employ **Action 6.**

### Action 6: Basic Tools/Concepts

### Directions

Note that both **Actions 6** and **9** include interviews as assessments. Therefore, it may be convenient to do them both at the same time.

1. Make a copy of the checksheet based on Exhibit 12.1 and mark the basic tools/concepts you would expect the student to know. (If you are evaluating a student you don't know, have her teacher help you on this.) Also, note any basic tools/concepts

required for the problems the student missed on **Actions 1, 5,** and **7** (when you get to it).

2. Using the results of **Actions 1, 5,** and **7,** point to an item or write one (for example, 3 + 2 = ___). Say to the student "Tell me how you would solve this problem." If correct, say "Tell me how you are going to remember 3 + 2 = 5." If incorrect, show the right answer and ask "Tell me how you are going to remember 3 + 2 = 5."

3. Script or tape-record the student's response.

4. Examine the student's written or oral responses for evidence that she understands applicable basic tools/concepts from Exhibit 12.1. Mark the status of each basic tool/concept. Note if the student seems unaware of the material, if she has it wrong, or if she has it right.

5. Ask additional questions about those items the student may not have used or may have used incorrectly.

### Interpretation Guidelines

### Question 9: Does the Student Have the Expected Prerequisites?

If YES, then go to **Action 7.**

If NO, then teach the basic tools/concepts the student is missing by using **Teaching Recommendation 3.**

### Action 7: Checking Operations

### Directions

1. Return to the survey-operation tests and use the error-analysis forms in Howell et al., 2000a to recognize the objectives that were missed.

2. Select or construct an assessment(s) sampling only those objectives (to construct an assessment, write ten items like the ones missed at the survey level).

3. Administer the tests, encouraging the student to show all work. Several testing sessions may be required.

4. Score the tests and note error types.

### Interpretation Guidelines

### Question 10: Are Skills Adequate?

If YES, then discontinue *or* check skills at the next higher curriculum level.

If NO, then go to **Action 8.**

### Action 8: Checking Prior Knowledge

Is the student missing subskills that are distinct to the objectives (items) she has failed? And if so, can the missing knowledge be categorized by error type?

This action is accomplished by:

1. Examining the student's errors for pattern; and

2. Checking to see if the student has the required subskill knowledge.

### Directions

1. A packet of operation error-analysis materials can be found in Howell et al., 2000a. These materials cover the computation survey tests addition-decimal/ratio/percent. Each of the items on the survey-operation tests is listed along with important prerequisites and a tally grid that looks like this:

| Example of information to record From student work and Appendix A.12 | | | General Errors | | | Concept Error | Strategy/ Rule Errors | |
|---|---|---|---|---|---|---|---|---|
| Correct Problem | Student Response | Subskills | Fact | Sign | Placement | Equality | Wrong Steps | Missing Steps |
| $\frac{2}{2\overline{)4}}$ | $\frac{1}{2\overline{)4}}$ | Div 1 Mult 1a Sub 1a | 7 +5 13 | $\frac{8}{2\overline{)4}}$ | $\frac{2\overline{)4}}{2}$ | $1 \times 2 \neq 4$ | 87 +15 912 | 87 +15 92 |

The error types in this grid are explained in Exhibit 12.6.

1. Go through each item missed (that the student was expected to know) and fill out the grid. Then check the prerequisites.

2. You may need to select or create SLPs to assess some of the prerequisites.

3. For each error, try to decide if it was primarily *factual, conceptual,* or *rule/strategic* knowledge. Label the item accordingly. The same incorrect answer may contain more than one error type.

### Interpretation Guidelines

You are trying to find missing prior knowledge. This prior knowledge may be in two categories. First, it may be what we would commonly call a missing subskill (such as counting or addition facts); second, the missing knowledge may fall into a category. These categories include types of knowledge (facts, concepts, rules). There are many ways you can play around with the error-analysis task. It doesn't matter if you look for missing concepts first or missing addition fact skill. All that does matter is that you can answer **Question 11** for the items missed.

### Question 11: Which Type of Prior Knowledge Seems to Account for the Errors?

| If | Then |
|---|---|
| ✓ Missing subskill | ✓ Go to Teaching Recommendation 4 |
| ✓ Fact errors | ✓ Go to Teaching Recommendation 4 |
| ✓ Concept or strategy error | ✓ Go to Action 9 |

### Action 9: Problem-Solving Strategy

**Directions**

1. Return again to the tests you gave in **Action 7** and use them to conduct an interview.

2. Say to the student "I want to ask you how you worked some of the problems." Then use the relevant questions from Exhibit 12.4. This sort of exercise will be new to most students—so be patient. Be aware that a student's poor language skills can confound your results. Ask the student to describe what she does when she works a problem. You can ask her to construct a model to represent her answer.

3. Depending on the clarity of the student's explanation, you may need to select or construct an assessment to sample each of the following problem-solving skills:

✓ Selects correct operations

✓ Labels relevant, irrelevant, or missing information

✓ Sets up equations

✓ Estimates answers

✓ Follows algorithms

4. Exhibit 12.2 shows formats for tools and concepts. Depending on the student's skill level, you need to systematically check these across each operation ($+$, $-$, $\times$, and $\div$).

### Interpretation Guidelines

Compare the student's explanations or work with how the problems should be done. Determine if she has adequate knowledge of problem solving. (Taping a paper tube to the hand to make an additional finger probably does <u>not</u> meet the requirement for efficiency and generalization inherent in good strategy use. But it does show good conceptual knowledge.)

### Question 12: Does the Student Know How to Solve Computation Problems?

If YES, then go to **Teaching Recommendation 4.**

If NO, then use **Teaching Recommendation 5.**

## Problem Solving for Application

The process of assessing application is presented in Exhibit 12.5. The procedure is designed to answer these questions:

1. Is the student's application performance within expectations? (Q.13)
2. Does the student make errors in computation? (Q.14)
3. Does the student make errors in problem solving? (Q.15)
4. Are there errors in content? (Q.16)
5. Does the student know the content of time, temperature, money, and measurement? (Q.17)

### Action 10: Survey Application

A major problem with application is that, because it combines computation and content, it accumulates all of the variability in sequencing found in both of those domains. Therefore, it is not possible for us to give much information about the levels at which students should be skilled enough to work a particular problem. For your students, the only real solution to this dilemma is to go through the objectives found in Howell et al., 2000a. Mark the date by which your own students are expected to know how to work the items.

### Directions

Note that there is an application survey test along with directions and error-analysis procedures in Howell et al. (2000a). If you don't have that book, follow these directions.

1. Select/construct an assessment sampling a range of problem types including problems that match recognized categories of application content, problems that require several steps, and problems that require multiple operations. Refer to Howell et al., 2000a for a list of application objectives.

2. If you don't want to prepare a survey assessment, go directly to **Questions 14, 15, and 16.** Be sure to summarize the results as explained in **Summary 3** (as you will have bypassed it).

### Interpretation Guidelines
Answer the following questions.

### Question 13: Is the Student Working at about the Expected Level?
If YES, then discontinue or test at the next higher level to determine where to begin instruction.
   If NO, then go to **Summary 3.**

### Summary 3: Application

#### Directions

List the standard and behavior; then determine the discrepancy and use the increase in score required to remove the discrepancy as your goal. Go to **Questions 14, 15,** and **16.**

### Question 14: Are <u>Computation</u> Errors Indicated?
If YES, then go to computation and **Actions 1** and **5.**
   If NO, then ask **Question 15.**

### Question 15: Are <u>Problem-Solving</u> Errors Indicated?
If YES, then employ **Action 9** and **Question 12.**

### Question 16: Are <u>Content</u> Errors Indicated?
If YES, then go to **Action 11.**
   If NO, then go back to **Action 10.**

### Action 11: Content Knowledge

#### Directions

1. Select or construct an interview or test to sample the student's knowledge of vocabulary, tools, and content for the material of concern (time, temperature, money, measurement linear, surface, volume, weight). Use the objectives in Howell et al., 2000a and Exhibits 12.7 and 12.8.

*Exhibit 12.6    Computation Process Errors.*

| Computation Error | Correct Answer | Student Response | Analysis |
|---|---|---|---|
| **General Errors**<br>*Fact error*—student makes errors on specific facts or fails to respond correctly to all or most facts. | 8<br>+ 7<br>15 | 8<br>+ 7<br>16 | Thinks 8 + 7 = 16 |
| *Sign error*—student fails to use sign in selecting operation. Adds instead of subtracting, multiplies instead of adding, etc. This error type may be difficult to observe when entire page requires use of one operation. | 3<br>−2<br>1 | 3<br>−2<br>5 | Added when subtraction was called for. |
| *Placement error*—student writes digits in incorrect sequence or fails to align parts of problem correctly for required computation. | 13<br>+ 6<br>19 | 13<br>+ 6<br>91 | Added correctly but reversed digits in answer. |
|  | 6.021<br>+51.30    *6.021*<br>= *51.30*<br>   *57.321* | 6.021<br>+ 51.30<br>*111.051* | Failed to align decimals properly prior to computation. |
|  | 22<br>× 86<br>*132*<br>*176*<br>*1892* | 22<br>× 86<br>*132*<br>*176*<br>*308* | Failed to align partial products correctly. |
| **Faulty Algorithms**<br>*Wrong steps*—student uses steps which are not correct. | 22<br>+ 53<br>*75* | 22<br>+ 53<br>*12* | Added all digits together. |
|  | 24<br>+ 68<br>*92* | 24<br>+ 68<br>*11* | Added the 9 and 2 in correct answer. |

| Computation Error | Correct Answer | Student Response | Analysis |
|---|---|---|---|
| *Missing steps*—student fails to use necessary steps to complete problem. (Regrouping errors are common.) | 18<br>+ 96<br>*114* | 18<br>+ 96<br>*1014* | Added ones and tens and failed to regroup. |
| | 8942<br>− 5961<br>*2981* | 8 9⁸4 2<br>− 5 9 6 1<br>*3 1 8 1* | Borrowed in tens column but failed to borrow in hundreds and subtracted 8 from 9. |
| | 40<br>× 31<br>*40*<br>*120*<br>*360* | 40<br>× 31<br>*0*<br>*12*<br>*120* | Multiplied ones digit by ones digit and tens digit by tens digit and summed. |
| | $\frac{3}{13} + \frac{1}{3} = \frac{9}{39} + \frac{13}{39} = \frac{22}{39}$ | $\frac{3}{13} + \frac{1}{3} = \frac{3}{39} + \frac{1}{39} = \frac{4}{39}$ | Found common denominator but retained numerator, Failed to use steps to change numerator. |
| | 20 r49<br>58)1209<br>*116*<br>*49* | 2 r49<br>58)1209<br>*116*<br>*49* | Derived an answer before operation was complete, failed to calculate 49 − 58 = 0 r 49 |
| *Wrong algorithm for given operation*—student may use steps which are suitable for a different operation. | 24<br>× 3<br>*72* | '24<br>× 3<br>*32* | Multiplied in ones column and carried but failed to multiply in tens column and simply added carried number to tens. Procedure used in tens column would have been correct for an addition problem. |
| | 43<br>+ 5<br>*48* | 43  *5 + 3 = 8*<br>+ 5  *5 + 4 = 9*<br>*98* | Added ones and then added ones and tens. Order of these steps would be appropriate for multiplication. |
| | $\frac{1}{8} + \frac{3}{8} = \frac{4}{8}$ | $\frac{1}{8} + \frac{3}{8} = \frac{4}{16}$ | Added both numerator and denominator. |

*Source:* Howell, K. W., Zucker, S. H. & Morehead, M. K. (2000b). *Multilevel Academic Skills Inventory.* Bellingham, WA: Applied Research and Development Center.
To order contact the Student Co-op Bookstore, Western Washington University. FAX (360) 650-2888. Phone (360) 650-3656.

**Exhibit 12.7   Part of the Applications Content Test Summary.**

### Time

| Grade | Questions | Answers |
|---|---|---|
| 3 | 1. One minute has how many seconds? | 60 |
| 3 | 2. One hour has how many minutes? | 60 |
| 2 | 3. One day has how many hours? | 24 |
| 1 | 4. One week has how many days? | 7 |
| 4 | 5. One month has how many weeks? | 4 |
| 1 | 6. One year has how many months? | 12 |
| 4 | 7. One decade has how many years? | 10 |
| 4 | 8. One century has how many decades? | 10 |
| 4 | 9. One year has how many days? | 365 |
| 4 | 10. One year has how many weeks? | 52 |

### Money

| Grade | Questions | Answers |
|---|---|---|
| 1 | 1. How many pennies make a nickel? | 5 |
| 1 | 2. How many pennies make a dime? | 10 |
| 2 | 3. How many dimes are in a quarter? | 2 |
| 3 | 4. How many dimes are in $1? | 10 |
| 3 | 5. How many quarters are in $1? | 4 |
| 2 | 6. A quarter plus a dime are equal to how many pennies (cents)? | 35 |
| 3 | 7. A half-dollar is worth how many dimes? | 5 |
| 3 | 8. Which is worth more? Three $1 bills or one $5 bill? | one $5 bill |

### Geometry

| Grade | Target Words | Acceptable Responses |
|---|---|---|
| 3 | 1. Perimeter | the distance around the outside edge |
| 3 | 2. Area | surface measurement |
| 3 | 3. Square units | what you get when you multiply the length times the width |
| 3 | 4. Cubic units | what you get when you multiply the length times the width times the height (depth) |
| 3 | 5. Volume | capacity, how much something holds; space inside |
| 3 | 6. Circumference | the distance around a circle |

### Measurement—Customary Units

| Grade | Target Questions | Answers |
|---|---|---|
| 4 | 1. How many ounces are in a pound? | 16 |
| 4 | 2. How many pounds are in a ton? | 2,000 |
| 4 | 3. How many cups are in 1 pint? | 2 |
| 4 | 4. How many pints are in 1 quart? | 2 |
| 4 | 5. How many quarts are in 1 gallon? | 4 |
| 4 | 6. How many inches are in 1 foot? | 12 |
| 4 | 7. How many inches are in 1 yard? | 36 |
| 4 | 8. How many feet are in 1 yard? | 3 |
| 4 | 9. How many feet are in 1 mile? | 5,280 |

### Measurement—Vocabulary

| Grade | Target Words | Acceptable Responses |
|---|---|---|
| 1 | 1. heavy | having weight |
| 1 | 2. heavier | having more weight |
| 1 | 3. heaviest | having most weight |
| 1 | 4. light | having little weight |
| 1 | 5. lighter | having less weight |
| 1 | 6. lightest | having least weight |
| 1 | 7. weight | how heavy |
| 1 | 8. full | contains the maximum |
| 1 | 9. fuller | contains more |
| 1 | 10. fullest | contains the most |
| 1 | 11. empty | contains nothing |
| 1 | 12. emptier | contains less |
| 1 | 13. emptiest | contains the least |
| 1 | 14. more | a greater amount |
| 1 | 15. less | not as much |
| 1 | 16. height | tallness; how tall something is; how far up |
| 2 | 17. width | how far across; how broad something is |
| 2 | 18. depth | how far down; distance from front to back |
| 1 | 19. length | how long something is |
| 1 | 20. distance | amount of space between two things |

### Measurement—Metric Units

| Grade | Target Questions | Answers |
|---|---|---|
| 4 | 1. What does *milli* mean? | thousandths |
| 4 | 2. What does *deci* mean? | tenths |
| 4 | 3. What does *centi* mean? | hundredths |
| 4 | 4. What does *deca* mean? | ten |
| 4 | 5. What does *hecto* mean? | hundred |
| 4 | 6. What does *kilo* mean? | thousand |

### Scoring Summary

| Subtest | Total Correct | | Total Possible | Percent Correct |
|---|---|---|---|---|
| Time | _____ | ÷ | 10 | = _____ |
| Money | _____ | ÷ | 8 | = _____ |
| Geometry | _____ | ÷ | 6 | = _____ |
| Measurement—Vocabulary | _____ | ÷ | 20 | = _____ |
| Measurement—Customary Units | _____ | ÷ | 9 | = _____ |
| Measurement—Metric Units | _____ | ÷ | 6 | = _____ |

*Source:* Howell, K. W., Zucker, S. H. & Morehead, M. K. (2000b). *Multilevel Academic Skills Inventory.* Bellingham, WA: Applied Research and Development Center.
To order contact the Student Co-op Bookstore, Western Washington University. FAX (360) 650-2888. Phone (360) 650-3656.

2. Focus on vocabulary and tools as well as content. Content can be covered by having the student state equivalent units ("There are ___ inches in a foot"; "There are ___ feet in a yard"; "There are ___ centimeters in a meter") and explain algorithms ("The area of a triangle is equal to___ the base times the height"; "The area of a circle is equal to ___"). Many such tests already exist in math textbooks. It would be well worth your time to search out some of them.

3. If you have already noted computation problems (**Actions 1** and **5**), allow the student to use a calculator.

4. Score responses and summarize the results.

### Interpretation Guidelines

### Question 17: Does the Student Know Content, Tools, and Vocabulary?

If YES, then teach the student to apply this knowledge using **Teaching Recommendation 6.**

If NO, then teach the missing content knowledge, tools, and vocabulary. Use **Teaching Recommendation 7.**

## Teaching Recommendations

It is difficult to say exactly which domain of mathematics gets the least instructional attention (Battista, 1999; Burrill & Romberg, 1998). However, it is fairly common to hear that the conceptual side of math is shortchanged within schools. As Paulos (1988) points out, "A discussion of informal logic is as common in elementary mathematics courses as a discussion of Icelandic sages" (p. 74). Therefore, try to focus on concepts even when you are teaching "facts." Cross-reference the ideas in Exhibit 12.1 to your daily lessons and then integrate the concepts. Also, bear in mind that if you don't recall the reason for teaching something, it is unlikely that the student will.

One other thing before we go on to the specific teaching recommendations. We are often asked "Is it OK for the student to use a calculator?"

The answer is "**yes.**"

### Recommendation 1: Teach Fluency on Basic Facts

As we noted earlier, there are at least three explanations for accurate but slow performance on basic facts: the student does not know the facts at the automatic level, the student writes slowly, or the student does not know facts *and* is a slow writer.

### Handwriting

If assessments indicate that the student writes slowly, then set an intermediate aim for fluency on facts while you work on increasing her writing fluency. Expect the student's rate on basic facts to be about two-thirds the rate on writing numerals. For example, a child who can write numerals at a rate of 45 per minute should have a temporary criterion of about 30 facts per minute. Writing fluency was discussed in Chapter 11, **Teaching Recommendation 7.**

### Facts

Lessons designed to build fluency on facts are typically short (5–10 minutes) and use rapidly paced drill over material on which the student is at least 90% accurate. This is often accomplished with flashcards, computers, or timed practice sheets. (If you use computer software, make sure that it is sensitive to the time it takes a student to respond and that the fluency levels it requires are compatible with the CAP you use. They usually aren't.)

Reinforce the student for *rapid* responding and daily improvement in *fluency*. Errors are typically viewed as rate-induced and are ignored to the extent that error-correction procedures are not used during the timings (feedback may be given afterward). Peer-teaching groups are especially effective and time-efficient (Antil et al., 1998). Peers can use cards that contain the problem on *both* sides, without the answer, so that both students must work each fact.

Fluency instruction is intended to make the student automatic at using a skill—which means that the student will know the skill so well she can recall the fact whenever necessary. The stu-

*Exhibit 12.8    Applications Summary Checklist.*

| | | | | | | Appropriate Curriculum Level | |
|---|---|---|---|---|---|---|---|
| *Solve All Problems, Integrating Necessary Computation, Applications, and Problem-Solving Skills* | | | | | | No-Pass | Pass |
| Response Standard | | Identify Accuracy | Produce Accuracy | Mastery | Automatic | | |
| Applications-Integrate Subskills | | | | | | | |
| Measurement-Scaling | | | | | | | |
| Weight | Vocabulary Tools Content | | | | | | |
| Volume | Vocabulary Tools Content | | | | | | |
| Surface | Vocabulary Tools Content | | | | | | |
| Linear | Vocabulary Tools Content | | | | | | |
| Money | Vocabulary Tools Content | | | | | | |
| Temperature | Vocabulary Tools Content | | | | | | |
| Time | Vocabulary Tools Content | | | | | | |

dent must practice under different conditions including problems presented orally, in horizontal and vertical written formats, and ultimately on practice sheets with facts drawn from all operations (addition, subtraction, multiplication, and division mixed together). One particularly effective device for generalizing fluency instruction is to select facts that appear in a few higher-level problems. The student can then be rehearsed over this limited group of facts several times until she reaches fluency. Once that happens, the student is then allowed to work the larger problems.

## Recommendation 2: Teach Accuracy on Basic Facts

There are two approaches to teaching facts: (1) by rote (as a series of separate numerical sentences learned in a basic stimulus/response format—like flashcards) or (2) through the instruction of underlying strategies (Stein et al., 1997; Christensen & Cooper, 1991). Because the student is inaccurate, you should teach the strategies until the student is accurate and then go to **Teaching Recommendation 1** to build fluency.

When teaching facts, impress on the student the need to follow the strategy. Do this by asking questions about the use of the strategy itself. Here is an example for the problem 4 + 6 = ?

QUESTION: "What kind of problem is this? Look at the sign."

RESPONSE: "Addition."

QUESTION: "What do we know about the answers to addition problems?"

RESPONSE: "They are bigger than the numbers in the problem." (This assumes you aren't into negative numbers.)

QUESTION: "How do you solve this problem?"

RESPONSE: "I start with one number and then count on as many times as the other number tells me."

QUESTION: "What number will you start with?"

RESPONSE: "Six."

QUESTION: "Why?"

RESPONSE: "I don't have to count as many times."

QUESTION: "Good. Now solve the problem."

RESPONSE: "6 + 4 means 6-7-8-9-10 = **10**."

QUESTION: "Can you tell me the problem and the answer?"

RESPONSE: "6 + 4 = 10."

QUESTION: "Good. You followed the steps for adding."

In some cases, teachers will separate facts into subdomains like 1–5 and 6–10. If you have done that, and the student becomes accurate at the first domain, begin fluency instruction with those items while continuing to build accuracy with the next ones. Teach the strategies for subtraction and addition (or division and multiplication) at the same time.

## Recommendation 3: Teach Tools and Concepts

Teach the content identified in Exhibit 12.1 during **Action 6**.

There are a lot of prerequisites listed, so we'll show you a format for teaching them by using counting as an example. If you have a student who doesn't know counting, try teaching her to count by rote (forward and backward) from one number to another. For example:

"Count forward from 3 to 9."

"Count forward from 46 to 57."

"Count forward from 77 to 86."

"Count backward from 6 to 3."

"Count backward from 34 to 28."

"Count backward from 54 to 45."

Use directions such as "Count backward from 54 to 45. What number are you going to start on? What number are you going to stop on? Good, begin."

Also, teach the student to supply previous or next numbers in the counting sequence. Writing random numbers on a sheet and placing blanks either before or after them can do this. Tell her to fill in the blanks as quickly as possible.

Once the student can count and recognizes numbers, teach addition and subtraction through the use of objects (like blocks) or pictures of objects. Then, teach her to transfer these skills to written problems that are presented in standard form. At this point, you would also substitute operation signs (another basic tool) for the verbal directions to "add" or to "count forward."

Just because you may have targeted a prerequisite, do not assume the skill should be taught in isolation. Often, the most effective way to teach tools and concepts is within the context of real problems.

## Recommendation 4: Teach Computation

The objectives in Howell et al., 2000a are arranged in a sequence. This means that many of the lower-numbered objectives in any operation may be prerequisites for those with higher numbers. However, Howell et al., 2000a also includes a list of task-specific prior knowledge after each computation and application objective. When a student is failing to carry out an objective, you need to consult this list and check out the indicated subskills.

For example, the task-specific prerequisites for addition objective 1a are:

✓ Addition 1i,

✓ Prerequisite 5m,

✓ Prerequisite 9i,

✓ Prerequisite 7i,

✓ Prerequisite 21a, and

✓ Prerequisite 12m.

Unlike reading, most computation skills have a relatively clear succession of complexity. Recognizing the subskills of a target task will make instruction in that task far more efficient. This is why the objectives in Howell et al., 2000a are organized in a descending sequence and cross-referenced to other skills.

There are many materials available to teach computation. However, it is our opinion that these methods often fail because the student doesn't have the prior knowledge needed to learn. Our bottom-line recommendation for teaching computation is to directly teach subskills and then move up or down the hierarchy as warranted by the student's performance. This requires that the teacher cross-reference the skills to instructional techniques.

The best reference for teaching math currently available seems to be the text by Stein et al. (1997). We'd also like to note another excellent presentation on teaching arithmetic to students with learning problems. It is an article by Cawley and Parmar (1992) and can be found in the references.

## Recommendation 5: Teach Problem Solving

Students who are not accurate on facts or operations often need to develop a set of computational problem-solving strategies (Case et al., 1992). These strategies may be task-specific, such as the algorithms for adding or subtracting mixed numbers, or they may be general (Kamii, 1998). Task-specific strategies apply only to a small domain of tasks, whereas general strategies may apply across several broad domains. The task-specific strategy for adding or subtracting mixed numbers is:

✓ Recognize the problem type;
✓ Find the common denominator;
✓ Find the answer;
✓ Decide if the answer must be converted; and
✓ Convert if necessary.

The general strategy for all mathematics is to:
✓ Select the operation;
✓ Recognize the unknown quantity;
✓ Recognize relevant and irrelevant information;
✓ Set up the necessary equation(s);
✓ Estimate the answer;
✓ Follow the task-specific strategy;
✓ Check the answer against the estimation; and
✓ Correct the work if necessary.

Although it is difficult to separate problem-solving skills from other math skills, it is important to try to determine where problem solving breaks down. For example, two frequent causes of failure to solve application problems are (1) the failure to distinguish irrelevant from relevant information and (2) failure to estimate and check answers.

Once you have identified the missing (or erroneous) problem-solving component, teach the student to use the correct one within the context of real problems. De-emphasize the production of answers by asking questions about the use of the problem-solving strategy itself (an example of this technique is included in **Teaching Recommendation 2**). The following routines should help.

### Verbal and Visual Mediation

Begin demonstrating the strategy to the student by stating it aloud as you show how to carry it out. Next, have the student practice saying the strategy with you as you guide her through doing problems. Next, ask the student to work the problem while saying the strategy aloud without you. Finally, ask the student to say the strategy to herself or to draw a visual model of the solution, while working on a problem (Bryan & Tuersky, 1999).

### Questions

Questioning can be an especially powerful device for teaching problem-solving strategies. Lead questions, described in detail by Stowi-

| Strategy | Question | Desired Response |
|---|---|---|
| Select operation | "What kind of problem is this?" | "Addition." |
| Set up operation | "Where will you start adding?" | "7 plus 8." |
| Relevant vs. irrelevant information | "What does the fact that 7 + 8 = more than 10 mean?" | "I have to regroup" or "carry." |
| Follow task-specific strategy | "If 7 + 8 is 15, where will you put the 5 ones?" "Where will you put 1 ten?" | Student indicates the correct place. |

tschek et al. (1984), are used to guide a student into strategy use by focusing on one or more of the strategic elements of the task *before* asking the student to actually work the task. An example using the problem 47 + 28 is shown in the box.

This kind of questioning accounts for the fact that a problem requires a student to make *many* procedural decisions. The questions are instructional devices for focusing the student on the process *before* she must use it.

### Select Procedure

Sometimes it is effective to have a student select the correct equation for a problem rather than actually work the problem. This focuses her attention on the strategy, de-emphasizes the answer, and requires her to think through the problem from several possible directions.

For example, "Loren has 13 bicycles to fix. Four are red. Sue brings him ten more. He fixes two each day. What procedure would you use to find out how many days it will take him to fix all the bicycles?"

a. $13 \times 10$ then $130/3$

b. $13 + 4$ then $17 + 10$ then $27/2$

c. $13 + 10$ then $23/2$

d. $13/2$ then $10/2$

### Corrections

Questions can also be used to correct strategy errors without immediately giving away the answer. This shows the student that she can reason through the problem independently. An ideal sequence presented by Stowitscheck and others (1984) works this way:

1. Demonstrate the strategy.

2. Use lead questions or open questions (ask the student to work on the whole item).

3. When errors occur, change the open question to a multiple-choice question.

4. If an error still occurs, change the multiple-choice question to a restricted-alternative question.

5. If an error still occurs, repeat the demonstration and start over. Here is an example, for the problem 8 × 6:

| Student Device | Teacher | Response |
|---|---|---|
| Open question | Shows flash-card of 6 × 8. | "Fourteen." |
| Feedback and multiple choice | "The answer is <u>not</u> 14. Do you have to add or multiply in this problem?" | "Add." |
| Feedback and restricted alternative | "You don't add, so what do you have to do?" | "I don't know." |
| Demonstrate | Repeats demonstration with emphasis on operation sign. | |

### Feedback

Because you are teaching the student how to arrive at an answer, and not the answer itself, feedback should be directed at problem solving. Often, a student can arrive at a correct answer by using an incorrect strategy (guessing, cheating). If you give feedback or praise in this case, you run the risk of inadvertently reinforcing the wrong way to solve problems. To prevent this, refer to the correct strategy when giving feedback. For example, "Good for you. You must have paid attention to the sign because you multiplied" (added, subtracted, etc.).

### Recommendation 6: Teach Application Strategies

If a student has arrived at this recommendation, she has all the necessary prior knowledge to solve application problems but doesn't know how to combine this knowledge. In other words, she needs to be taught application. Because there are an unlimited number of tasks to which mathematics knowledge can be applied, this recommendation can only be stated in the simplest of terms:

✓ Decide what rule or strategy you want to teach: and

✓ Teach it using the principles of rule and strategy instruction outlined at the first of **Teaching Recommendation 5** (don't forget to demonstrate both behaviors and thought processes).

### Recommendation 7: Teach Application Content, Vocabulary, and Tools

Difficulties in applying mathematics are sometimes based on inadequate knowledge of the content rather than any lack of proficiency in computation or problem solving. Thus, application content will often be targeted for direct instruction. The list of application skills in Howell et al., 2000a includes content sequences for time and temperature, money, measurement of length, surface, volume, and weight (both metric and customary). From the appendix you can see the magnitude of the task involved in teaching content-specific information. Content-specific information is to applications and problem-solving what prior knowledge is to reading comprehension.

If it seems that the student needs to be taught this material, then instruction should be preceded by an assessment to determine targets. Such pretests may be found in many of the more structured application programs that accompany, or are included in, some math programs. Problem solving and other prior knowledge are best taught within the context of computation. Similarly, application, vocabulary, tools, and problem solving should be presented together.

## Summary

Our goal in this chapter has been to help you identify what to teach a student in computation. Chapter 12 began by discussing math. Next it described survey-level procedures, provided some examples of survey material, and listed likely causes for failure at the survey level. We also discussed error analysis, reviewed specific-level actions, and linked problems to instructional recommendations through a series of interpretation questions. In the process, we have tried to illustrate the application of a task-analytical model. We have also emphasized strategic behavior for two reasons: First, a task-analytical model permits analysis of cognitive behavior; second, math instruction in the absence of strategy and concept instruction has little utility (Fuson, 1997).

# Chapter 13

# Social Skills

*Because Thelma was educated he wanted to tell her about how he ruined his life "in that there" by beating up a variety of teachers, and carrying jack-knives. Then he asked her for another cigarette and contemplated all he had said. What he was hoping for was what he always received from people—that they would say they knew he was really good at heart, but he might have gotten off on the wrong foot. This wrong foot business was what he'd always received and what he hoped to receive again.*
— David Adams Richards, *Nights Below Station Street* (1998), p. 15

## Step 1: Define Your Purpose

Appropriate social skills are things students use to advance toward personal objectives without violating socially imposed restrictions or consuming an inordinate amount of community resources. Not everyone can do these things. Evidence of that can be found in our society's ever-increasing interest with truancy, delinquency, crime, and punishment (Gresham & Macmillan, 1997; McLellan, 1998; Office of Juvenile Justice and Delinquency Prevention, 1997). Although the entertainment industry often portrays those who act in antisocial ways as clever and cunning adversaries of law enforcement, most people with behavior problems have a very limited set of behavioral options at their disposal. Because they have few options from which to choose, they often automatically select inappropriate responses. Their social skill, and the judgment they need to go beyond personal experiences, is so poor they do not push aside the first options they recall (the inappropriate ones they have practiced so often in the past). As a result, they do not recognize and select more adaptive responses. Social-skill training is designed to address such problems through instruction.

Just as we have discussed throughout this book in the context of academic problems, social-skill problems are the result of missing prior knowledge. The purpose of this chapter is to help you figure out what to teach students who are missing critical social knowledge.

Although estimates vary, it is generally agreed that, at some time during their schooling, approximately half of all students encounter major problems with social skills. Sometimes, these problems are so intense and intractable that the student may end up in a special program, mental-health service, or prison (Malmgren et al., 1998; Sample, 1998; Walker et al., 1997). In other cases, the problems seem fairly minor.

Social-skill problems can include examples of social illiteracy that dwarf the concerns of classroom management. These problems lead to heartache for families and an incredible toll from troubled students (Israelashvili, 1997). As a group, these kids tend to have fewer friends, to be estranged from family, to get sick more often, make less money once they start work, and end up in prison. In fact, they even have a higher probability of dying earlier (Pine et al., 1999; Shaffer & Chaft, 1999; Walker et al., 1995, 1997; Walker and Stieber, 1998). Moreover, in most cases, they endure sadness and miss joy. They become hopeless (Clarizio & Payette, 1990; Zionts, 1996). These problems may occur regardless of how "bright" or advantaged a student seems. As Seligman (1991) puts it, "the notion of potential, without the notion of optimism, has very little meaning" (p. 154).

## Step 2: Define the Thing to Be Measured

### Why Is It So Hard to Define a "Social-Skills" Curriculum?

Defining social skills is a problem. Chapters 13 and 14 both deal with content that is often left out of classroom-oriented evaluation texts: social skills and task-related skills. Yet, they both have a direct relationship to literacy and its acquisition. Also, the distinction between an academic and a social skill is fairly arbitrary (Roeser & Eccles, 1998). Despite the fact that methods for the two domains are often presented in separate courses, academic skills and social skills both respond to the same sorts of interventions (Leone et al., 1991; Peacock Hill Working Group, 1991). The critical distinction between the two is found in the minds of teachers and researchers, not in the topography of learning or the nature of successful instruction (Kauffman & Wong, 1991).

In this chapter, we will address seven areas of content:

✓ Personal
✓ Interpersonal
✓ Problem solving
✓ Citizenship
✓ Classroom specific
✓ Anger and violence
✓ Other

To clarify the first six (you'll need to define the last one), you might want to look at the list of objectives in Appendix A.5 now. Obviously, this is only a partial list.

The domain being discussed (social behavior) is immense. It can be assumed to include as many skills, of as great complexity, as one would find in the entire area we call academics.

There are many confusions about social skills. Here are a few:

**Control** is something done to bring a person into alignment with the requirements of a current situation. External control is effective only as long as outside pressure is present or perceived to be present (Evans et al., 1991). The weaknesses of a control-oriented/reactive system are that:

1. All teachers do not have the same personal standards;

2. All classroom formats do not require the same social skills;

3. The behavioral requirements of classrooms are quite different from the requirements of the everyday world;

4. Simply reacting to errors is ineffective; and

5. Nondisruptive but personally debilitating problems (such as chronic sadness) often are not addressed (Pine et al., 1999; Nichols,

1992; Roeser & Midgley, 1997; Walker & Rankin, 1983; Wong et al., 1991).

**Education** also begins as an external intervention; however, its purpose is to shift control to the student by changing what and how he thinks. In this case, that means teaching the skills needed to maintain self-control. Unfortunately, many educators develop curriculum, plan lessons, and schedule instructional time for academics, but they do not do these things for social skills. Instead they wait for an inappropriate display and then react to it. **Proactive** and positive behavioral interventions are those which seek to build appropriate behaviors and to prevent the occurrence of inappropriate behaviors (Gable et al., 1999; R. Sprick et al., 1998). Teaching is giving, it isn't taking away. (Just in case you think we are naive relative to social behavior, we do recognize that it is probably superhuman to keep sight of this principle when certain classroom behaviors are out of control. Dr. Howell in particular can testify to these difficulties, having once been knocked unconscious by a student wielding a certain piece of classroom equipment. Based on this experience, he now recommends that plastic—not metal—wastebaskets be used in all classrooms.)

### Structuring the Curriculum

Obviously, curriculum-based evaluation is hard to do without a defined curriculum, and it is still difficult to find anything that looks like a widely accepted and cohesive social-skill curriculum. This failure to define expectations injects confusion and conflict into any attempt at addressing the topic of social-skill evaluation. For this chapter, we have gone about addressing the topic in two ways: by using a model of behavior to generate important domains of skill and by reviewing what is commonly taught.

### The Models

Without a curriculum, we often must compare students to models of behavior (Israelashvili, 1998). Many such models exist, but we will only look at two. We have come up with our own

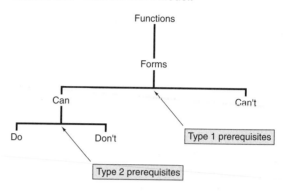

**Exhibit 13.1  Can vs. Can't Model.**

nifty models. The first is in Exhibit 13.1. This model isn't very complex, and is not even unprecedented, but it seems useful. It is called the Can versus Can't model.

As illustrated in Exhibit 13.1, **Type 1 prerequisites** consist of the skill and knowledge needed to deal with the physical/external environment; **Type 2 prerequisites** consist of internal beliefs, expectations, and perceptions that lead to the selection of an option from the group of available choices. They function within the cognitive environment.

According to the model in Exhibit 13.1, a student may be using an inappropriate form because:

- he actually can't use the appropriate form; or

- he isn't selecting to use the appropriate form even though he can use it.

Let's elaborate on these two options. You are currently reading a book (this one). If you are a student, you probably have two functions for this reading behavior: to learn and to pass tests. Regardless of your purpose, there are many forms that your reading may take. Some of you are reading this chapter 10 minutes before the test (gotcha!) and others are reading it weeks ahead of time. As you read, some of you are

*Part of learning social skills is learning how to develop a plan.*

seated in chairs, others on couches, and some are probably in bed or on the floor. None of you are sitting on the ceiling, because you *can't*. The environment (gravity) prohibits you from sitting on the ceiling, so you *can't select* that option.

When we say that a student *can't* do the appropriate thing, we mean that he lacks the skills to overcome the environmental influences that militate against that behavior. We are not saying that the student has some sort of permanent incapacity, such as brain damage, that prohibits learning the skills.

Lower in the model we find that a student *doesn't select* to do the appropriate thing. Here we mean that he has selected (from among the things he *can select*) the wrong form of behavior. Now one must be careful here; this doesn't mean the student has *consciously*, and with *intent* to irritate adults, selected an inappropriate way to behave.

Although this is sometimes true, more often selecting an inappropriate behavior is not the same as consciously deciding to behave inappropriately (Cherkes-Julkowski, 1996; Corno, 1993). People select most behaviors automatically.

If you recall the discussion of automaticity in Chapter 2, it said that automatic responses occur without the use of **working** (conscious) **memory.** So here's the question. When you started to read this chapter, did you talk to yourself about where to sit?

Unlikely.

Just as *you* are not aware of all of the choices you make, people with behavior problems are largely unaware of the ones they make and how they make them.

A student in the <u>*Can versus Can't*</u> condition cannot engage in a behavior because (1) he doesn't have the skills to do so or (2) something in the environment is inhibiting him. If either case is true, the evaluator has found an example of what we will call missing *Type 1 prerequisites,* because she has found a student who currently does not have the skill or knowledge to overcome external factors that inhibit the adaptive behavior. Obviously, the thing to do is teach him to overcome, or avoid, those barriers.

In the model (Exhibit 13.1), the Do versus Don't student can do a behavior but selects not to do it. Because different people have different learning histories, they have different ideas and beliefs about the world. As a result, they select different forms of behavior.

The selection depends upon *Type 2 prerequisites* such as beliefs, expectations, perceptions, preferences, interests, fears, and desires. All but the most primary of these are learned through experience.

### Another Model

We have lots of models. The next one is the <u>form function</u> model of behavior. This is the model that underlies **functional behavioral analysis** (Gable et al., 1999; Nelson et al., 1998; O'Neil et al., 1997). According to the model, there are many **forms** of behavior, and these forms are used by different students to do things. Functions are easiest to conceptualize as the things we want to accomplish (for example, avoid hassles, gain notoriety, watch a movie, or make a friend). The *function* of a behavior, therefore, is its purpose; the form is the way a person goes about trying to accomplish the purpose (Nelson et al., 1998). The bottom line here (and this a breakthrough bit of insight) is that human behavior is largely purposeful.

Another idea that goes with this theory is that there are no *inappropriate* functions (only human ones), but there are inappropriate ways to accomplish functions. The functions of inappropriate behavior are <u>exactly</u> the same as the functions of appropriate behavior. The so-called **behavior-disordered** student is, therefore, trying to get exactly the same things a *behavior-ordered* person is trying to get. He is simply going about it in a less socially acceptable way. There are four

primary categories of functions listed in Exhibit 13.2.

1. **To avoid external** (actions, things, or accomplishments): "I do <u>not</u> want . . ."
2. **To obtain external** (actions, things, or accomplishments): "I <u>do</u> want . . ."
3. **To avoid internal** (feelings, thoughts, emotional stress): "I do <u>not</u> want . . ."
4. **To obtain internal** (feelings, thoughts, emotional peace): "I <u>do</u> want . . ."

These categories are reflected in the construction of Exhibit 13.2, which also lists the seven principal content domains of social behavior used in this chapter. Example functions are found in the grid squares. These functions, once again, are not appropriate or inappropriate. It is the way a person goes about meeting the functions that causes problems. The distinction, between the **form** of behavior and its **function,** will become a pivotal part of the remaining discussions in this chapter.

### Looking at Common Practice

A second way to identify the curriculum for social skills is to look in classes and published materials to see what skills are currently being taught. (The weakness here is that common practice may not be the same as best practice.) The content of such a skill list has been cross-referenced to some programs. It is presented also in Howell et al., 2000a.

Based on our review, we came up with the groups of skills listed in Appendix A.7 and Howell et al., 2000a. These are the general areas in which students probably should be skilled if they are to behave appropriately across settings. This is also how we generated the categories across the top of Exhibit 13.2. This table can be used to generate specific outcomes. For example, look at grid for Type 1/Avoid/Interpersonal in Exhibit 13.2. by picking one of the functions in that grid, we can produce the following objective (minus criteria) "Gina will *avoid always doing what others* want by saying [Insert statement of appropriate behavior here, such as 'I'm sorry, I can't do that now because I am too busy']."

**Exhibit 13.2  Domains of Social Content.**

Domains of Social Content

| Categories of Functions: | A. Personal (Self Regulation and Control) | B. Interpersonal (Relations with Others) | C. Problem Solving | D. Citizenship Specific | E. Classroom | F. Anger/Violence | G. Other |
|---|---|---|---|---|---|---|---|
| **Type 1: External (actions, accomplishments, or things)** — Avoid "I do not want to . . ." | Give up preferred activities. Act impulsively. Be shocked or surprised. Be unable to decide. | Fail to explain my behavior. Make confusing statements. Criticize. Talk too much. Physically hurt others. Always be doing what the other person wants. | Deal with it now. Make mistakes. Waste my time or the time of others. Carry out other people's agenda. | Experience bias. Be accused of letting others down. Have the quality of education diminished in my local schools. Be dependent on others. Be put in jail. Fail to help those in need. | Fail to learn, do things incorrectly. Ignore the teacher or the assignments. Receive punishment. Be left out. | Be hurt. Be bullied. Be attacked. Have a friend attacked or hurt, lose things through robbery, hurt others. Fight. Be abusive and threatening. | |
| Obtain "I do want to . . ." | State why. Reward myself. Make plans. Correctly predict outcomes. List options and resources. | Make specific statements. Give compliments. Listen. Touch appropriately. Suggest alternative activities. | Get resolution. Organize my stuff. Catch mistakes before others notice them. Work efficiently. Do what I've decided to do. | Be treated as an individual. Act dependably. Contribute to an adequately supported community structure. Be responsible for my own welfare. Follow rules. Do my part to reduce suffering. | Learn. Do things correctly. Work with the teacher. Attend. Get rewards and recognition. Be a part of the group. | Go to school and move about safely. Be treated as a friend and someone who can get what he wants through intelligence and honesty. | |
| **Type 2: Internal (feelings, thoughts, emotional status)** — Avoid "I do not want to . . ." | Feel stress. Feel guilt. Be ashamed. Be afraid. Be bored. | Be isolated. Feel rejected. Be manipulated. Be disregarded. Feel ridiculed. | Worry about getting it done. Feel overwhelmed by the work, be embarrassed because I did the wrong thing. Feel like a bungler. Think I am someone else's puppet. | Feel that I am letting my community down. Want to get things through criminal activity. Be deceitful. Think I am lazy. Think I should get things I don't deserve. | Feel dumb, confused. Feel lost. Be bored. Be embarrassed. Be afraid. | Feel afraid. Feel like a victim. Feel pain. Think of ways to hurt others. Regret over what I have done. Feel that I can only get things by fighting. Feel ashamed, guilty, or embarrassed. | |
| Obtain "I do want to . . ." | Be relaxed. Have pride. Feel satisfied. Be confident. Feel excitement. | Feel related to someone. Think I am accepted. Have a sense that there is reciprocity in my life. Feel confirmation. Think I am respected. | Have a feeling of closure. Feel on top of things. Feel competent. Be confident that I am capable. Believe that I'm living the life I choose. | Think that I am a responsible member of society. Respect the laws. Be confident that I am honest with others. Feel that I work hard and hold up my part. Feel I am fair. | Feel successful. Understand. Know what to do. Be involved and interested. Feel secure and confident. | Feel secure and safe. I also want to know that my teachers, friends, and property are safe. I want to be proud of my actions and confident that others do not simply see me as a threat. | |

*Source:* Howell, K. W., Zucker, S. H. & Moorehead, M. K. (2000b). *Multilevel Academic Skills Inventory.* Bellingham, WA: Applied Research and Development Center. To order contact the Student Co-op Bookstore, Western Washington University. FAX (360) 650-2888. Phone (360) 650-3656.

### Enabling Skills

There are some important enabling skills for social skills. Although not considered social skills, many of these are linked to commonly used interventions. Here is a brief explanation of a few.

**Relaxation Techniques**    A content area commonly included in social-skills curriculum is relaxation. People who are considered successful can relax in stressful situations. This skill at relaxation allows them to function better. In addition, people can be taught to recognize when they are stressed and to respond by relaxing (Kaplan, 2000).

**Selection of Targets**    Students who are trying to control their own behavior are in the same position as teachers. They must have objectives. These targets should be picked by recognizing needs according to priority.

**Planning**    Planning is a critical part of any purposeful activity. A plan is an image of the future (Boulding, 1985). In addition, the need to plan increases with the complexity of the project (Laufer, 1997). Few would argue that social interaction is a complex domain. Therefore, the importance of teaching students planning skills is obvious. What should also be obvious is that a plan which specifies action will help to counteract the lethargy, inhibition, and depression that often accompanies problems (Roeser & Eccles, 1998).

**Initiation of Plans**    For any of us to carry out a program of self-improvement, we have to start working. We work to bring the image of the future we have captured in our plan closer to us. The most highly skilled person, even with the best plan, will not accomplish anything if she doesn't act. And, remarkably, the failure to take action accounts for many failures (Laufer, 1997). Sometimes it seems that the most chronic and disturbing problems do not prompt action because they seem to *paralyze* the person (Corno, 1993).

**Self-Monitoring**    Self-monitoring is the skill to track one's own behavior. If you have self-monitoring skills, you are in a good position to begin to control yourself. Self-monitoring may not automatically change behavior, but it allows us to be satisfied, or surprised, by the outcomes of our actions.

### How Can You Decide How Well a Student Is Supposed to Do These Things?

It is as necessary to establish criteria for social behaviors as it is for academic behaviors, but it isn't easy. That is because the appropriateness of social behavior varies with the situation (Stormont & Zentall, 1999).

The best approach to establishing CAP for social behavior is ecological (Jones, 1995; Moen, 1995). The ecological model says that a student should be expected to engage in those behaviors that are (1) available in his environment, (2) acceptable to others in the environment, and/or (3) commonly occurring in the environment. What this means is kids usually act like those around them act (just as do adults).

In the ecological model, a student's behavior is compared with the environment by asking "is this behavior acceptable in this context?" To find that out, it is necessary to attend to the environment and not just to the student (O'Neil et al., 1997; Sabornie, 1991).

One useful way to establish a social-behavior standard is to collect an ecological baseline. Suppose you think a student (Ed) "asks for help" too often. You could set up an observation form like the one in Exhibit 13.3. With this form, behavior samples are taken on Ed and a random peer. The selection must be random; therefore, devise a system for picking the other student before the signal goes off. Collect the data for 3 days and summarize by recording the median score.

Let's suppose that you collect these data and find that the median "asks for help" for Ed is seven times an hour and that it is only four times an hour for Ed's peers. This makes the standard 4, Ed's current level of performance 7, and the discrepancy 3. The goal for Ed, therefore, is to *decrease* his behavior by a factor of 1.75—or 3 every two hours.

**Exhibit 13.3    A Device for Collecting an Ecological Baseline on "Ed Asks for Help."**

### Ed's Ask for Help Behavior

|  | Hour 1 | | | | | | Subtotal | Hour 2 | | | | | | Subtotal |
|---|---|---|---|---|---|---|---|---|---|---|---|---|---|---|
| Target student (Ed) | + | 0 | 0 | 0 | + | + | 3 | 0 | 0 | 0 | 0 | + | + | 4 |
| Random peer | + | 0 | + | + | + | 0 | 2 | 0 | + | + | + | 0 | + | 2 |

Total per two hours:

+ = No request          Ed's total = 7

0 = Asks for help       Peer's total = 4

**Exhibit 13.4    Ecological Influence.**

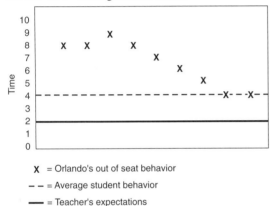

X  = Orlando's out of seat behavior

− − = Average student behavior

── = Teacher's expectations

The environmental frequency of behavior places ecological boundaries, called the **ceiling** and **floor,** on that behavior. These may not be at the same level as a teacher's expectation. For example, imagine a student named Orlando. Orlando originally "gets out of seat" in class eight times per hour. The absolute floor for this behavior would be zero times per hour. The teacher expects Orlando to be out of his seat no more than two times. However, in the class a typical student gets out of his seat an average of four times an hour. These levels are shown in Exhibit 13.4.

As you can see in Exhibit 13.4, Orlando's behavior has moved toward the teacher's expectation but has not passed the ecological floor. For this behavior, or any other social skill, the ecological floor is as far as the change should be expected to go. For Orlando, below four per hour,

the environment actually begins to work against his behavior change. A teacher can cause the student to go beyond the ecological floor by calling upon increasingly powerful interventions, yet consider what incidental lessons she would be teaching. First, she would be teaching the student to deviate from his peers—which is often the biggest problem in the first place for the student with behavior problems. Second, she would be teaching the student to disregard the primary environmental cue defining appropriate behavior—the behavior of others. Therefore, she would be decreasing the likelihood that the intervention would generalize to any other setting. If the "normal" student gets out of his seat four times in a period, it is not unreasonable to expect the student with behavior problems to do likewise.

Atypical behavior, even if it is changing in the direction in which we are most comfortable, is still *abnormal*. If a teacher wants Orlando to conform to her expectations, she should first move Orlando to the class average, and then move the whole class to a preferred level.

As a general rule, the criterion for appropriate social skill (unlike academic skills) is not the median of successful students. In North American culture, the social criterion is the norm (note that this is not CAP for academic behavior). Consequently, a teacher should not expect any student to exhibit a form of social behavior that isn't like the class average. We are not suggesting that all students should behave in the same way. We are simply stating that it is unrealistic for teachers to expect them to do otherwise.

*Exhibit 13.5   Two Kinds of Analysis.*

A. Applied Behavior Analysis of Larry's Hitting Behavior

| Antecedents $S^1$ | Behavior R | Consequences $S^2$ |
|---|---|---|
| 1. Classroom<br>2. Free time<br>3. Morning<br>4. Low structure<br>5. Peers give negative<br>    comments | Larry hits peers | Negative comments stop<br>Peers run away<br>Larry escapes comments<br>Larry loses friends |

B. Applied Cognitive Behavioral Analysis of Larry's Behavior

| Antecedents $S^1$ | Behavior R | Consequences $S^2$ |
|---|---|---|
| 1. Classroom<br>2. Free time<br>3. Morning<br>4. Low structure<br>5. Peers give negative<br>    comments | Larry thinks: *"It is better to get out of here than to punch someone and lose a friend."*<br>so<br>Larry does not<br>hit peers<br>but walks away | Negative comments continue<br>Larry escapes comments<br>Larry keeps friends |

## Step 3: Devise a Way to Make the Things in Step 2 Observable

The evaluation of social skills requires the use of multiple measurement techniques. We'll describe them all here so you can refer back to them during the process of evaluation.

One way to find the Type 1 and Type 2 prerequisites illustrated in Exhibit 13.1 is to use the **Antecedent-Behavior-Consequent** (ABC) analysis (Kaplan, 2000; Malott et al., 1997; Zirpoli & Melloy, 1997). This system is used to specify the geographic antecedents and consequences of behaviors. The assumption behind **ABC** is that an understanding of the environment is necessary to understand behavior. This is particularly true of "high-impact environments" (Bower, 1972; Stormont & Zentall, 1999) such as the school and family settings.

Behavior is interactive. So if you want to evaluate social skill, you can't just attend to the individual. You must also attend to the social en-vironment. For example, suppose Larry has the problem "hitting peers." How is his geographic environment supporting this behavior? To answer this question, the evaluator conducts an applied behavioral analysis by observing Larry and recording in the format shown in Exhibit 13.5.

Imagine that in observing Larry you find that he hits peers (1) in the classroom, (2) during free time, (3) in the mornings, (4) when there's low structure, and (5) when his peers are saying negative things about him. Next, you look around to see what happens after he hits. You find that (a) the peers decrease their abuse, (b) the peers run away, and (c) Larry escapes the negative comments, but some of his friends get scared and stay away. If the behavior is maintaining, it is assumed that the antecedents and consequences are in balance. This is assumed to be true if the antecedents and consequences are *overt* (part of the geographic environment) or *covert* (part of the cognitive environment). The cognitive/covert environment includes thoughts and feelings that, although not typically called "behaviors," are treated as behaviors in this model.

Take a second look at Larry. In the second kind of analysis shown in Exhibit 13.5 ("B"), a covert component, a thought, has been added. This shows an example of applied **cognitive-behavior analysis** (**CBA**). Applied cognitive-behavior analysis is not limited to an examination of the geographic environment of the student. This CBA shows us that Larry may think that walking away in the presence of insults is better than risking the loss of friends by hitting (we doubt if he learned that from Orlando). Because he thinks (a covert) losing these "friends" is something bad, Larry walks away (an overt). If he thought "worthwhile friends will respect my feelings and stop teasing when I ask" he might select a different response to the situation (asking the peers to stop).

Larry's beliefs comprise part of the selection tactic by which he chooses what to do. If this idea (that prior learning cultivates covert beliefs, expectations, and perceptions that in turn determine overt behavior) is correct, it follows that efforts to change behavior should include efforts to change what the student thinks. Obviously, these efforts would have to be preceded by an evaluation of the student's *cognitive environment*.

### How CBE and CBA Can Work Together

To measure coverts, or overts, we must see or hear some sort of behavior. For example, if Larry makes negative statements about himself (an overt), they can be counted. Some people may think that such statements indicate "poor self-concept" (a covert). To avoid the definitional confusion that comes with coverts, begin by targeting behaviors that can be observed.

If you pay attention to the following rules, you should have no trouble targeting behaviors.

- Try to use verbs instead of adjectives. Words like "hits," "smiles," "cries," and "talks" accommodate measurement better than "rough," "happy," "sad," or "motor-mouth."
- Avoid adverbs and adverbial phrases. For example, "talks more," "hits hard," "smiles appropriately," and "laughs at the wrong time." The secret here is to substitute, or include, the measurement rule you will use to define the adverb. Make statements like "talks four times an hour."
- Stay away from value judgments. Don't use constructs such as "lazy," "dumb," "generous," "considerate," or "conscientious."
- If you must use adverbs or make value judgments, then at least try to clarify them by supplying examples. Example instances and noninstances of maladaptive and target pinpoints can be found in Exhibit 13.8.

*Target pinpoints* should always be statements of what you want the student to do, not what you want the student to stop doing. "Ralph will not touch other people's possessions without permission" is not an acceptable target. "Ralph will ask permission before touching other people's possessions" is acceptable because it specifies what Ralph will do.

### Kind of Measurement

Once the behaviors (adaptive and maladaptive) have been specified, they need to be measured. If the behaviors are overt, they involve movement. We recommend that you measure them through direct observation. If direct observation is not possible because the behavior is covert, then you need to use the procedures for measuring covert behaviors to be described shortly.

Tips on conducting an observation were provided in Chapters 5 and 6. Remember that it is best to collect data as unobtrusively as possible. If you are the teacher, it is not a good idea to collect the data, as you will be a pivotal factor in the student's environment. In this case, design the observation system and then get an aide, or another teacher, to trade some time with you and to collect the data you need. Some general points about observation deserve to be repeated (Kaplan, 2000; Zionts, 1996).

1. The behavior must pass the stranger and so-what tests.

2. It is better to observe a behavior for several short periods than for one long one.

3. It is important to report the circumstances under which the observation occurs.

4. Use the median score from at least 3 days of observation as your best estimate of the kid's current status (obviously, if the maladaptive behavior is dangerous, you will not wait for three observations).

5. If the pinpoints never occur, then you will need to prompt them by testing. In this case, the assessments may come in forms like role-playing.

6. If the problem requires you to collect data on interactions, observe and respect the canon of confidentiality.

Once you have collected data on the student's use of the adaptive and maladaptive behaviors, examine them in terms of a standard. As you recall, the standard for social skill is the class average as determined through the collection of data on ecological boundaries. If the student's behavior is no different from that of others in the class, select a new pinpoint or devise a group intervention. There is a sample observation form, along with directions for its use, in Appendix A.6.

### Covert Behavior

Type 2 prerequisites (coverts) present particular measurement problems. Generalizations from overt behavior (talk) to covert behavior (thought or feeling) should always be made with caution (especially if you are on a date). They require the evaluator to utilize many procedures not typically associated with behavioral assessment (although they may be commonly used for academics).

### Questions

Often the simplest way to find out what someone is thinking is to ask. How reliable is it to simply ask? That depends. There are several types of questioning techniques which range in sophistication (Ralph & Coombs, 1994). You may switch from one to another according to the responses

you get (Stowitschek et al., 1984). Let's go through some using item 11 from Exhibit 13.6 (The Common Prerequisite Sheet).

### Knows Consequences of Engaging in the Adaptive Behavior

**Open Question**    This is the least constraining form of question. To use it, ask something like "What will happen to you if you get to class on time?" Because correct answers could include everything from "I'd feel good" to "Whatever the teacher wants to happen," you must be prepared to interpret the responses or to seek clarification of them.

**Multiple Choice**    This type of question limits possible responses to the choices supplied.
    "If you get to class on time, will you:

a) be sent to the office?

b) get to come to class?

c) get to take an extra 2 weeks off this summer?

d) get out of work?"

The choices may be presented verbally, in writing, or in the form of cartoons/pictures. The complexity of the item can be increased or decreased by altering either the number or wording of the alternatives. One disadvantage of multiple-choice questioning is that it doesn't allow responses that are not supplied.

**Restricted Alternatives**    If a student typically selects a certain alternative, then you can rule that one out by removing it from competition.
    "If you get to class on time, you will not get out of work; what will you get?"

**Role-Playing**    Sometimes you can use peers to role-play scenes for the student to analyze (much as you would present cartoons). At other times you may ask the student to play a part. Often, initial attempts at role-playing fail because students are uncomfortable with it. Therefore, you may need to use it routinely if you are going to use it at all. When using role-playing, keep the directions specific and the scenes short. Also be sure to specify the sort of behavior expected; for example, "show me how I want students to arrive at class." To find out more about role-playing, refer to Kaplan (1995).

***Cue Sorts***   Cue-sort techniques (Kaplan, 2000; Stephenson, 1980) are particularly useful for Type 2 behaviors. To use a cue sort, give the student several terms, cartoons, or pictures, each on a separate card. These should present the content in which you are interested and a range of plausible distracters (if you are interested in the consequence "get to come to class," you would include options like "get extra points" or "go to the office").

Once the student has the cards, you ask him to sort them according to some categorical system. For example, "Put the cards in two piles—one for what might happen if you *come to class on time* and one for what might happen if you *are late.*" You then score the responses by noting how well the sorting matches the actual consequences.

Cue sorts are uniquely suited for gaining insight into a student's beliefs and perceptions. For example, you can give a student a stack of cards with various behaviors on them and ask him to put the behaviors in order according to those his teacher would find least acceptable. Next, ask him to order the same cards according to his own idea of acceptability, and then again according to what he thinks his best friend expects him to do. Differences in the sorting reflect the student's beliefs about the behaviors as well as his perceptions of his teacher and his friend.

A sample cue sort, completed by a 6th grade student, is shown below. The student was first asked to sort the ten words according to "what you like to do" and "what your teacher likes you to do." Next, the teacher was asked to sort the cards in terms of what she wanted the student to do. Some conflicts in perceptions are apparent. These conflicts need to be "sorted" out so the student and the teacher can understand each other.

| Student's Sorting | | Teacher's Sorting |
|---|---|---|
| What Do You Like to Do? | What Does the Teacher Want You to Do in Class? | What Do You Want the Student to Do in Class? |
| Play | Be quiet | Learn |
| Be happy | Be serious | Be happy |
| Mess around | Work | Think |
| Laugh | Think | Work |
| Learn | Learn | Be serious |
| Talk | Talk | Be quiet |
| Think | Laugh | Talk |
| Work | Mess around | Laugh |
| Be quiet | Be happy | Play |
| Be serious | Play | Mess around |

***Structured Interviews***   Like cue sorts, structured interviews are often needed for coverts. The purpose of the structured interview is to get the student to talk within a defined framework, or scaffold. If this scaffold is carefully structured, the things the student says can be used to draw inferences about covert thoughts/feelings. As always, it is important to note that these inferences will not always be correct. However, if an evaluator asks a student "What is $6 \times 8$?" and the student says "48," few of us would question the inference that "the student *knows* how to multiply" (a covert status) even though the inference is based on verbal behavior. That's because this inference is supported by the structure of multiplication problems. If a similar scaffold can be developed for social skill, inferences in that area will also be easier to defend. Exhibit 13.1 presented the model that has been used throughout this chapter to structure our discussion of social skill. Having a model of this kind helps you (and the authors) to organize and clarify thinking.

***ABC***   This model asserts that how you feel is controlled by what you think. The ABC proce-

*Exhibit 13.6    Common Prerequisite Sheet.*

Directions:

1. Only use this status sheet after:
   ✓ the maladaptive behavior(s) has been specified
   ✓ the function of behavior has been specified
   ✓ the target behavior(s) has been specified
2. The sheet should be filled out through collaboration with people who know the student.
3. Each question should be answered.

Type 1 (Do Behaviors)

|  | Status: Yes-No-Unsure | |
|---|---|---|
| If a student does not engage in the target behavior, ask yourself if . . . | Odd Items | Even Items |
| 1. . . . the student can discriminate the target and maladaptive behaviors from each other and from other behaviors. | _____ | |
| 2. . . . target and maladaptive behaviors are clearly and consistently labeled and reviewed. | | _____ |
| 3. . . . the student can monitor his own behavior well enough to know he is engaging in the target or maladaptive behavior. | _____ | |
| 4. . . . the student is encouraged to reflect on his behavior and is praised for self-corrections and/or early recognition of problems. | | _____ |
| 5. . . . the student can monitor the environment well enough to recognize events that should prompt the target behavior or inhibit the maladaptive behavior. | _____ | |
| 6. . . . cause and effect relationships between events in the environment and the student's behavior are clearly explained and reviewed. | | _____ |
| 7. . . . the student knows what behavior is expected of him. | _____ | |
| 8. . . . expectations are clearly explained and/or demonstrated to the student (they are also frequently reviewed). | | _____ |
| 9. . . . the student has the skills/knowledge to engage in the target behavior | _____ | |
| 10. . . . the student is taught how to engage in the target behavior. | | _____ |
| 11. . . . the student knows the consequences of engaging in the target behavior. | _____ | |
| 12. . . . the student is taught the consequences of engaging in the target behavior. | | _____ |
| 13. . . . the student knows the consequences of engaging in the maladaptive behavior. | _____ | |
| 14. . . . the student is taught the consequences of engaging in the maladaptive behavior. | | _____ |
| 15. . . . the student understands that his behaviors cause certain consequences. | _____ | |
| 16. . . . the reasons for the reactions of others to the student's behavior are explained. | | _____ |
| 17. . . . there are no physical factors that work against the target behavior and/or promote the maladaptive behavior (such as allergies or seizures). | _____ | |

| | Status:<br>Yes-No-Unsure<br>Odd    Even<br>Items   Items |
|---|---|

18.  . . . there are environmental factors which promote the target behavior and/or work against the maladaptive behavior. For example:
  - ✓ examples of the target behaviors are commonly found in the student's environment.
  - ✓ appropriate instruction occurs in the student's classroom.
  - ✓ appropriate management techniques are used in the classroom.    _____

19.  . . . the student generates solutions to problems that include the target behavior.    _____

20.  . . . the student is taught to solve problems.    _____

21.  . . . the student knows that a target behavior may become maladaptive and that maladaptive behaviors may become targets, depending on the situation/context in which the student is functioning.    _____

22.  . . . the situational cues promoting various behaviors are identified and adequately taught to the student, along with skills for analyzing new situations.    _____

## Type 2 (Select Behaviors)

If a student does not engage in the target behavior, ask yourself if . . .

23.  . . . the student considers the consequences of engaging in the target behavior to be rewarding.    _____

24.  . . . the advantages of the target behavior are taught to the student.    _____

25.  . . . the student considers the consequences of engaging in the maladaptive behavior to be aversive.    _____

26.  . . . the disadvantages of the maladaptive behavior are taught to the student.    _____

27.  . . . the student values the target behavior more than the maladaptive behavior.    _____

28.  . . . the student is taught to consider how the target and maladaptive behaviors fit within the student's belief system.    _____

29.  . . . the student holds beliefs which are compatible with the target behavior and incompatible with the maladaptive behavior.    _____

30.  . . . the student is taught to develop beliefs through the active application of hypothesis formation, hypothesis testing, and reflection. This instruction must include public thinking by an exemplar and stress the need for beliefs to be "valid."    _____

31.  . . . the student maintains an adaptive explanatory style when attributing the causes of events.    _____

32.  . . . the student is taught to avoid permanent and persuasive attributions to external causes and/or internal abilities.    _____

33.  . . . the student avoids errors in thinking when developing and employing belief systems.    _____

34.  . . . the student is taught to avoid errors in cognition, irrational thoughts, and a helpless cognitive set.    _____

dure is based on a therapeutic device developed by Ellis (1971) and elaborated on by Kaplan (1995). **A** stands for antecedents, **B** for beliefs, and **C** for consequences (this is another way of stating the stimulus-response-stimulus model). So, if B includes thoughts and C includes feelings, then a chain can be set up that sounds like this: stimuli (A) are interpreted through beliefs (B) to produce feelings (C).

| Antecedent | Belief | Consequence |
|---|---|---|
| Both individuals have work to do but their boss has called them and told them to attend a meeting. | Joe: "I won't get my important work done." | Joe feels bad. |
| | Ken: "This is a good excuse to put off this work." | Ken feels good (until caught). |

Here, two individuals are presented with the same antecedent stimuli—the requirement that they attend a meeting. But, because they think differently about the requirement, they end up feeling differently.

To use the ABC model, you first set up a situation. For example, let's say you tell the student "you get to school without your notebook, and a friend tells you there is to be a big biology test today." Then you give him two clearly different thoughts: (1) "There's no way I can pass without my notes—I'm in trouble!" and (2) "I wrote my notes, so even if I don't have them with me I can remember what is in them—I'll make it!" Next, you ask him to describe how he might feel when thinking each thought. This takes a little practice, even for older, articulate students, so initially you shouldn't expect too much in the way of revealing responses. Also you have to remember that there aren't a lot of feelings to list. Therefore, students may supply the same responses for very different stimuli. A "first date" or a "run-over pet" might both lead a perfectly well-adjusted kid to say "I'd feel like puking."

After the student seems to have the idea of matching feelings to thoughts, you can reverse the exercise and give situations (A) and feelings (C). Now the student must come up with thoughts (B). For example, "You are walking out of the school in the afternoon. You feel nervous and uneasy; what might you be thinking?"

***Control/Investment***   You may want to put the target student with some peers because the control/investment scaffold is particularly effective when presented to a group of students. Draw two circles next to each other on the board or overhead projector. Make one of them big and label it "investment." Draw the other circle small and label it "control." Explain that the two circles represent the student's perceived control and perceived investment in a situation. The model is presented like this:

TEACHER: "Here is the *control investment* rule. Remember it. *'To the degree that our investment exceeds our control (is disproportionate to it), we may experience anxiety.'* What does the rule mean? Here is an example. When we go to a hospital for surgery, we have tremendous investment in what the surgeon will do to us, but once we're asleep we have no control over what will be done. So, we often get nervous. Why?"

STUDENTS: "The rule says if there is more investment than control we get nervous."

We are not implying that this simple model enjoys the status of biblical truth. It does, however, provide a scaffold of common experience that may allow us to gain some information about the ways the student exercises social judgment. Many of us suffer from inflated investment. It is the result of the anxiety-producing habit of adding tangential factors to an otherwise clear-cut decision. This practice can turn a trip to the grocery store into a life-and-death venture.

Have you ever started to go to the store, then realized that you have no cash? If the banks are closed, you're afraid to use your debit card without knowing your balance, and you've messed up your bank book; the anxiety you start feeling is greater than the bag of tortilla chips you were going to buy deserves. Why? You've inflated the trip to the store into a confrontation with your budget.

The other side of inflated investment is inadequate or incorrectly perceived control. Often it seems people will allow an anxiety-producing situation to go on indefinitely, when acquiring a few simple skills would help them control the situation. This is true of people who fear computers but don't learn about them, or who worry about money but won't organize a bookkeeping system. Build scaffolds by using examples the student can understand (for example, the more you know about spelling the less that you fear spelling tests).

Before shifting topics, let's run through the basics once more:

- Behavior that is **alterable** through instruction is determined by the interaction of a student's prior knowledge and the environment.
- **Behavior** may be either covert or overt.
- **Overt behaviors** are those requiring muscular movements, such as standing up or speaking. **Covert behaviors** are those involving mental activity, such as thoughts and feelings.
- **Prerequisites** are the essential skills, knowledge, beliefs, expectations, and/or perceptions that a student must have to engage in an adaptive behavior.
- The environment is "perceived" and so it can be thought of as *both* physical and cognitive.
- The **physical environment** resides in geography, and the **cognitive environment** resides in the mind (it is what the student perceives, expects, thinks, and/or feels).
- Overt behaviors directly alter the physical environment. Covert behaviors, if they do not lead to overt displays, have no effect on the physical environment (although they may modify the cognitive environment).
- The display of any behavior is influenced by the **antecedent** and **consequential** context (geographic or cognitive) in which the individual is behaving.
- **Appropriate behavior** in one context, or culture, may not be acceptable in another.
- Behavior occurs to meet a **function** (intent). Many different **forms** of behavior may be used to accomplish the same function.

- **Social skills** are purposeful. They are learned ways to carry out agendas (functions).
- Social skills can be changed through the application of various interventions, including those that fall under the headings of *instruction and behavior management.* These interventions involve modifications in the physical or cognitive antecedents and/or consequences of the behavior.
- **Instruction** alters the student's cognitive environment by teaching him to think about and to perceive the world, and himself, in a more adaptive fashion (which is the same thing it does when it is used to teach multiplication skills).
- Given a context, some behaviors are OK whereas others are not. This leads us to use terms like **maladaptive** and **adaptive.**
- To define social skills for measurement, overt behaviors should be described in terms that are not open to interpretation and are easily understood by people who are not familiar with the student or his behavior.
- Overt pinpoints are always expected to pass the **stranger test** (a test of reliability).
- Covert behaviors are not as easily observed. They must be measured by drawing inferences from overt behavior.
- Such inferences will reflect the way the evaluator (you) views things, as well as the student's covert behavior.

### A Note on Mental Illness

Many students engage in inappropriate social behavior, and it is popular—and logical—to try and figure out why (Maag, 1995). One explanation for the cause of these behaviors is **mental illness.** Such illnesses include (but are not limited to) conditions such as:

- Mood disorders (depression);
- Psychosis (incoherent thinking such as delusions and hallucinations);
- Anxiety disorders (reactive or delusional worry and stress);

- Dissociative disorders (changes in consciousness such as loss of memory);
- Substance-related disorders (dependency and withdrawal); and
- Dementia (brain dysfunction following things like trauma or Alzheimer's).

This chapter, like the others in this text, isn't about underlying pathologies, it is about the recognition and correction of skill deficits. The recognition of conditions like those just listed do not reliably tell what inappropriate behaviors a person will display. Moreover, all people with a mental illness do not need social-skill training (just as all those who need it do not have a mental illness). To use an extreme example, it seems that Ted Bundy (a serial killer) needed no instruction in interpersonal relationship skills such as *meeting others, receiving invitations and introductions, or giving compliments.*

This book is about teaching. Therefore, we cover material that we think teachers should address within their classrooms. That was true in the computation chapter, and it is true in this chapter on social skill. However, unlike computation, there are professionals besides teachers who work with social behavior (Israelashvili, 1998; Roeser & Midgley, 1997).

Obviously, mental illness is always a concern when social-behavior problems exist. So, if you are asked for the name of an outside agent, be sure he or she is an effective professional. (Develop a list of at least three good ones in the community, so you can make referrals without advocating a particular person.)

One indication of a mental-health professional's quality will be that person's willingness (given the requisite of parental permission) to obtain data from, and share data with, you (in your role as school employee). You should be particularly concerned about anyone who attempts to address problems that present themselves *in school* without routinely, and directly, contacting the school to monitor the effects of that treatment (don't get into the habit of having the parent carry messages back and forth). This is especially true when the intervention involves the use of medications.

Remember that, if there is a referral, you are not being let off the hook regarding the specific problem behaviors the student is displaying (or the desirable behaviors he is failing to display). Even when such a referral takes the student as far as a physician or psychologist, and from there to a prescription for psychoactive drugs, *teaching* will still be required (Forness et al., 1996; Howell et al., 1997). The same is true if the student's problem leads to incarceration (Robinson & Rapport, 1999; Walker et al., 1997).

It is difficult to determine when to recommend that a student's care be shared with non-school members of the mental-health profession (Kaplan, 1995), and it has been difficult for a long time (Grave, 1944). When students say or do things that you simply can't understand, even if these things aren't disruptive, you should refer the student to a qualified professional. This is particularly true when the student is considering, or participating in, either violent or suicidal behavior (take any threat of suicide or violence seriously—it is better to be fooled 100 times than to find out that, after you ignored a threat, the child is dead). This is also true if the student has been abused by others or is suffering the personal anguish of a mental illness.

Frankly, expert pecking orders aside, there is no reason to simply assume that a referral will lead the student to someone who is sufficiently skilled to provide him with the help he needs. The truth is, for an unconscionably large population of children in the United States, mental-health services are not even available (Rotheram-Borus, 1997). In these cases, you may be the only game in town. This problem is all the more immediate given the fact that the incidence of childhood problems is so highly related to later difficulties (Pine et al., 1999; Walker et al., 1997).

Attempts to alter social skills oblige us to adhere to the *highest ethical standards* and to *proceed with caution.* Some of the techniques presented later in this chapter were originally derived from the application of logic to the often less-than-logical domains of thinking, feeling, social function, and mental health. Therein lies the ultimate uncertainty of the system. A very wise psychiatrist once advised the authors that logic could only be applied successfully to things made by humans. To apply logical techniques such as task analysis to mental health, one must assume that the perceptions, expectations, and beliefs of students are human-made (having been learned during past social interactions). This assumption remains, and will remain, unproven. *As a result there should be nothing in a school procedure for securing social skill training which inhibits the consideration of a timely referral to a competent mental-health specialist.*

### Suicide

Suicide rates among children have now reached the point where suicide ranks behind accidents and homicide as the third leading cause of death among 15–24 year olds. It is the tenth leading cause of death among children under 15 (Wolfle et al., 1999). In addition, although exact data on this topic are always hard to find, it looks as if the rate for lesbian and gay students may be as much as five times higher than the rate for others (Jennings, 1999). However, whereas the wording of many school-based interventions often includes "Aggression <u>and</u> Suicide," very little seems to be done within schools regarding the problem. And what is done is not validated.

Much that is happening in schools to prevent suicide seems to be unproductive. Screening programs are ineffective, crisis hot lines don't work, and instructional programs on the topic sometimes seem to make the problem worse (Shaffer & Craft, 1999). Yet, these and many other "solutions" are commonly promoted within education (Simpson, 1999). Still, our review of this literature did convince us of at least one thing.

The lists of suicide risk factors commonly disseminated to educators are so general as to be worthless. For example, thinking about suicide (suicide ideation), while obviously frequent among those who eventually attempt to (or do) kill themselves, is so common in the general population that it is not a good predictor of the act. Other parent (divorce), school (class size), or child factors (substance abuse) listed for screening are also poor predictors of risk. Jacobs (1999) did identify one family variable to be of some predictive importance. That was low levels of parent-child communication.

The single best predictor of self-destruction is a long-term (2 years or more) psychiatric disorder. Depression is the disorder mentioned by most authors. Other mood and conduct disorders are also mentioned. Next (and probably related to the first), a past suicide attempt is the second best predictor. In their review, Shaffer and Craft (1999) found that one-third of suicide victims had made at least one past attempt. Neither of these predictors is subtle. It is hard to imagine a chronic state of depression, or an attempt at self-destruction, going unnoticed. But, apparently this is the case. There are most likely two explanations for this: poor communication between home and school and the fact that teachers fail to notice (or respond appropriately to) the appearance of depression (Maag et al., 1988; Pine et al., 1999).

Research related to teacher knowledge of, and response to, depression is surprisingly scarce. But what is available would seem to argue against reliance on teachers to recognize and manage this highest predictor of suicide (Maag et al., 1988). For example, Peterson et al. (1987) found that some teachers respond to depressed children with rejection, a reaction that would likely increase the depression. An additional finding in that study is even more disturbing. The researchers also found that, when it was explained that a student might be depressed because of stress (for example, resulting from an injury or the death of a pet), these teachers were still not accepting of the child. They apparently viewed the student as doubly unattractive because he had <u>two</u> problems: depression and stress.

Schoolwide suicide prevention programs are available, but they are not validated. (Limiting access to weapons does have support, but that may simply be changing the location of the act.) Why aren't school treatment programs more effective? It might be that it is simplistic to think that *any* broad band instructional program is going to succeed where individual therapy and medications so often fail. So what can teachers do?

They can do better than the teachers in the Peterson et al. (1987) study. They can make referrals. If you are the teacher, you should back up the immediate referral with an immediate call of concern to the parents (if they seem uninterested, find a professional way to call someone who is). A timely referral to a mental-health specialist or to special education, followed by a timely response, ought to get the student needed individualized services from the school and/or related outside agencies. Because the special education referral process already exists, it looks like the best idea is to assure that that process works effectively and in the best interest of the child (this would include "fast tracking" students with suspected psychiatric disorders or suicide attempts). Starting other identification and treatment systems seems to be redundant.

But what if a student walks up to you tomorrow and says, "I can't take this any longer—I'd rather be dead"?

None the above information means that students at risk of suicide will not benefit from the interest and proper attention of a teacher. Here are some things you can do:

✓ Observe the students;

✓ Make yourself a person that students will talk with, trust, and confide in;

✓ Take any of the signs we hear of, like dispensing of personal belongings, rapidly decreasing involvement with others, and alterations in work patterns, seriously;

✓ Take any talk (poetry, letters, jokes) about self-destruction seriously;

✓ Do not dismiss or minimize student concerns which may seem silly or "juvenile" (the loss of a boyfriend, for example, may seem like a natural part of growing up to an adult, but it can literally be the end of the world to a kid);

✓ Don't ask "What do you have to feel depressed about?", depression is not always tied to an event;

✓ Don't think that younger students are less likely to commit suicide; and,

✓ Deal with the problem:

• use established school procedures for dealing with suicide (when you find out there are none, write them up later);

• do not leave the student alone;

• contact help (call 911 if you have to); and

• stay with the student a while after the help has arrived, do not assume the next person knows the correct way to handle things. We know of a case where a principal simply badgered the student for "seeking attention" and then set him loose. He immediately went to the rest room and killed himself.

### Teaching Social Skills

Frankly, we have these concerns about presenting a cognitive-behavior approach: uncertainty about its practicality, the risk of diluting the rest of the curriculum, and fear of misapplication. Education has a long, unfortunate history of misplaced faith in ideas about unseen mental conditions and styles (Zigmond, 1997). It spent decades trying to teach hypothesized cognitive or perceptual skills (see Chapter 2). Frequently, the pursuit of the "psycholinguistic," "psychobehavioral," "psychomedical," and "psychoeducational" has led all educators far from the skills we have an ethical responsibility to teach. Why do it again by suggesting that teachers consider the cognitive skills by which kids select behaviors? One answer is that most teachers, most of the time, are already directing their attention to the covert behaviors of students. Although "education" has many meanings, it certainly implies an effort to teach students to believe, to expect, and to perceive things differently than those who are uneducated. We accept this when the task is long division; it is harder to accept when the topic is making friends, dealing with rejection, or controlling violence.

In Chapter 10, we presented an argument for respecting the first language of students and the culture from which that language evolved. Those arguments, about the value of diversity and the need to honor a student's heritage, also apply to social skills domains like friendship, sex differences, and religion (Archer, 1996; Eitzen, 1992; Etzioni, 1992). However, the call for respect in the language chapter was easy to make because different languages are more clearly linked to different heritages. Therefore, respect for Robert's use of Spanish isn't tied to Robert alone but to the linguistic culture to which he belongs. But what about Robert's own ideas? According to Coles (1990), it is a mistake to assume that students come to us without well-developed beliefs about religion, ethics, and morality. These must also be respected even if, at times, they cause problems and even when, because of these problems, something must be changed.

These are not concerns we needed to worry about in the chapter on decoding.

It would be nice to provide you with some closure relative to all of these issues, but we can't. So we'll just share your discomfort as we begin to explain the processes of social-skill evaluation.

### Step 4: Conduct Assessment

### Step 5: Use the CBE Process of Inquiry

### Step 6: Summarize

### Step 7: Make Decisions

Once again, each of these steps will occur in a recursive fashion during the processes of assessment and decision making. The entire social-skill evaluation procedure is illustrated by the flow chart in Exhibit 13.7. This flow chart is your friend, so try to get to know it.

### Evaluation Procedures

Because of the complex nature of this content, we aren't going to divide the process into "Survey" and "Specific" chunks. Instead, we will just go straight through the flow chart in Exhibit 13.7. If you look at the flow chart, you will find the following 16 questions. These are the questions that will drive your inquiry into social skills, so review them now. You may also want to take a second and review the objectives in Appendix A.5.

**Question 1:** Does the student have a maladaptive behavior?

**Question 2:** Is the behavior dangerous?

**Question 3:** Does the description of the maladaptive behavior pass the stranger test?

**Question 4:** Does the description of the maladaptive behavior pass the so-what test?

**Question 5:** Is the behavior tied to poor class management?

**Question 6:** Does the description of the target behavior pass the stranger test?

**Question 7:** Does the description of the target behavior pass the so-what test?

**Question 8:** Could you categorize the problem into one or more of the social-skill subdivisions?

**Question 9:** Can you find goals and/or objectives?

**Question 10:** Did you find subskills and/or objectives?

**Questions 11–13:** Is the problem also related to another domain such as task-related skills, academics, or language?

**Questions 14–16:** Does the student need to learn Type 1 skills, Type 2 skills, enabling skills, or a combination of the three?

### Question 1 (Q1): Does the Student Have a Maladaptive Behavior?

#### Directions

As will be the case through most of this process, the best thing you can do is assemble a team to answer the questions, conduct the assessments, and make the decisions.

Unless the student is yours, he will have come to your attention through a screening process or a request for help. To answer Q1, review the request and simply decide if a problem exists. The student need not be *causing* the problem, but a problem can still exist.

*Exhibit 13.7.*

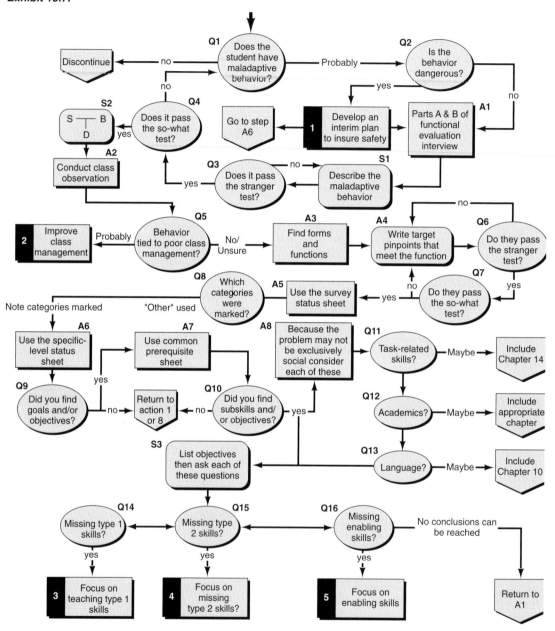

### Interpretation Guidelines

The only criterion for this decision is the impression that something of significance (including a disruption in learning) is taking place. There are no quantitative criteria.

If the answer is NO, discontinue the evaluation or ask for clarification of the referral.

If YES or PROBABLY, go to Q2.

### Question 2: Is the Behavior Dangerous?

### Directions

Be aware that labeling a child "dangerous" is a major step, but to fail to recognize danger can be worse. A group should make this decision. The only criterion for this decision is the impression that the problem is placing the student, or others, at risk of injury. This includes suicide risk (see the earlier comments on that topic).

### Interpretation Guidelines

There are no quantitative criteria.

If the answer is NO, go on to assessment **Action 1.**

If the answer is YES, go to **Teaching Recommendation 1** and **Action 6.**

### Summary 1: Describe Maladaptive Pinpoint

### Directions

If another person has referred the student, explain the idea of maladaptive and adaptive behaviors to them and show them the examples from each category presented in Exhibit 13.8.

State the maladaptive behavior as an objective. Exhibit 13.8 may help you do this.

Go to Q3.

### Question 3: Does the Objective Pass the Stranger Test?

Apply the stranger test by asking if someone who is unfamiliar with this student can, upon reading your pinpoint, recognize and count oc-

currences of the behavior. You may want to confirm your conclusion by actually asking someone to do it.

### Interpretation

If YES, go to Q4.

If NO, then return to S1.

### Question 4: Does the Objective Pass the "So-What" Test?

Apply the so-what test by asking if the behavior you have pinpointed is proactive and truly addresses the student's needs. Remember that classroom control, unless it is sought to assure a functional and therapeutic environment, is not a legitimate aim for individual students. It should be handled through classroom management (see **Q5**).

### Interpretation Guidelines

If the maladaptive behavior does not meet the so-what test, forget it or return to **Q1.**

If it does, then go on to **S2.**

### Summary 2: Summarize Discrepancy

Use the targets developed in **S1** that have passed the stranger and so-what tests.

1. Use the **RIOT** process and **PLOP** statements generated so far. If you have not already done so, collect data on the intensity, duration, frequency, and/or situational appropriateness of the maladaptive pinpoints. These data are the "**B**" in the S-B-D formula.

2. Collect information on acceptable performance for students of this age in these sorts of settings. These data represent the "**S**."

3. Determine the absolute and/or ratio discrepancy. The "**D**" supplies the number that you will use as you monitor the effectiveness of your teaching techniques.

4. Repeat this process as part of S3. You should now have some goals and objectives for teaching. Go to **Action 2.**

*Exhibit 13.8.*

| Maladaptive Pinpoints | |
| --- | --- |
| Instances | Noninstances |
| 1. Hits peers without physical provocation. | 1. Is aggressive |
| 2. Looks at ceiling. Does not have work on desk. | 2. Is off task. |
| 3. Plays with younger children during recess. | 3. Is immature. |
| 4. Calls out without raising hand. | 4. Calls out inappropriately. [What does "inappropriate" mean?] |
| 5. Hyperventilates and wrings hands. | 5. Is anxious. |
| 6. Throws work on floor. | 6. Cannot accept criticism. [What does "accept" mean?] |
| 7. Shouts answers before called upon. | 7. Is impulsive. |
| 8. Says "I don't have to" or "I don't want to" when a request is made. | 8. Uses back talk. |
| 9. Does not initiate conversations with peers at recess. | 9. Is shy. |
| 10. Wears same unwashed clothing for two or more days. | 10. Is dirty. |

| Target Pinpoints | |
| --- | --- |
| Instances | Noninstances |
| 1. Speaks In a voice audible to all parts of the room. | 1. Is considerate of others. [What does "considerate" mean?] |
| 2. Passes tests and completes assignments. | 2. Is on task. [Open to interpretation] |
| 3. Plays with children his own age during recess. | 3. Is mature. [Construct] |
| 4. Sits next to peers when talking to them. | 4. Requests permission to speak appropriately. [What does "appropriately" mean?] |
| 5. Breathes evenly and stays still. | 5. Is mellow/calm. [Compared to what?] |
| 6. Makes changes in work according to feedback. | 6. Accepts criticism. |
| 7. Uses [specified] cooling off technique. | 7. Exercises self-control. |
| 8. Complies with requests or explains why he can't. | 8. Speaks respectfully. |
| 9. Initiates conversations at median frequency of class. | 9. Talks as much as he should. |
| 10. Wears clean clothes every day. | 10. Has good hygiene. [How "good"?] |

## Action 2: Conduct Classroom Observation

### Directions

Review the information on conducting observations in Chapters 5, 6, and 10 (as well as this chapter). Then go to the class and use the *Classroom Observation* shown in Exhibit 13.9. As you will see, the form is a fairly open class observation. You may also want to make a checksheet from the TIES-II (Ysseldyke & Christenson, 1996) components dealing with teacher management. These are found in Howell et al., 2000a. You will have a more thorough instrument if you just get the whole TIES-II.

Some advice:

- Observe in several settings if the student switches class—but be sure to get the setting where the problem has been most frequently reported;
- Take several short samples rather than one long one;
- Try not to let the student know that he is the focus of your time in the class; and
- Be aware that the teacher may not be comfortable with the process.

### Question 5: Is the Behavior Tied to Poor Class Management?

#### Interpretation Guidelines

There are no quantitative criteria for the class observation (A2). Essentially, you (or your group) are trying to decide on one of three options. Here are your guidelines.

## Action 3: Determine the Function(s) of the Maladaptive Behavior

A complete set of forms and procedures for conducting this critical action can be found in Appendix A.6. These materials are from Gresham et al. (1998). They are based on the work of O'Neill et al. (1997). The O'Neill et al. text is *the* reference for conducting a functional behavioral assessment. To begin, first use the function sheet shown in Exhibit 13.10 from Gresham and Noell (1998). People who are familiar with the student should fill out this form. In fact, you may want to fill out several.

Examine the forms to recognize patterns, or "themes," that consistently seem to underpin the student's maladaptive behavior. These are the functions. They are considered to be the purpose of, or reason for engaging in, the problem behavior. Try to categorize each behavior by a purpose (for example, to *avoid* an external such as *exclusion from a discussion* or to *obtain* an internal such as a *feeling of pride*). Review the list of possible functions presented in Exhibit 13.2. Then, write down the assumed function(s)—more than one is allowed.

Don't fall into the trap of picking the most easily recalled, or stated, functions. *To get attention,* for example, has turned out to be the most common function people list. This makes it seem that attention is the primary reason anyone does anything. But, just because an act draws lots of attention does not mean that it was carried out for that purpose. Political scandals, which draw

| Option | Indicator | Answer to Q5 | Interpretation |
|---|---|---|---|
| 1. The problem is primarily the student's | • Problem seen across settings<br>• Teacher(s) responds correctly to behavior | No | Go on to assessment **A3** |
| 2. The problem is primarily the way the class (or this behavior) is managed | • Problem occurs only in certain settings<br>• The teacher(s) uses ineffective management | Probably | Go to **Teaching Recommendation 2: Improve class management** |
| 3. Both choices 1 and 2 seem like real possibilities | • No clear resolution | Unsure | Continue evaluation by going to **A3** but work to improve class management through **Teaching Recommendation 2** |

*Exhibit 13.9    Classroom Observation.*

| Date: | | Time: | | Page_____ of_____ |
|---|---|---|---|---|
| School: _____ | Teacher: _____ | | Student: _____ | |
| Interval: _____ Wh Int. | | P. Int.   MTS: ( _____sec.)   Other: _____ | | |

## ACTIVITY STRUCTURE CODES

**Student (SAS)**
lis: listen
ask: ask questions
per: perform task
ans: answer questions
cop: cooperative learning

**Teacher (TAS)**
lec: lecture
dem: demonstrate
led: lead student performance
obs: observe/supervise
ans: answer questions

**Non-Academic**
dis: discipline
hos: housekeeping
fre: free time
tran: transition

### BEHAVIOR CODES
Code    Meaning

1:1    Teacher works one to one with student ($\sqrt{}$ = event n = duration)
Seat    $\sqrt{}$ = seated   S = stand near seat   A = Away from seat
+    $\sqrt{}$ = appropriate given antecedent
Task    A = active on task   P = passive on task   O = off task

### OTHER EVENTS
Code    Meaning

PM    peer movement (n) = n of peers
PI    peer interaction
PC    physical contact
TP    teacher prompt (n) = repetitions

| # | Antecedent Events | SAS | TAS | 1:1 | Seat | + | Task | Other Events/Behaviors 1 | 2 | 3 |
|---|---|---|---|---|---|---|---|---|---|---|
| 1 | | | | | | | | | | |
| 2 | | | | | | | | | | |
| 3 | | | | | | | | | | |
| 4 | | | | | | | | | | |
| 5 | | | | | | | | | | |
| 6 | | | | | | | | | | |
| 7 | | | | | | | | | | |
| 8 | | | | | | | | | | |
| 9 | | | | | | | | | | |
| 10 | | | | | | | | | | |
| 11 | | | | | | | | | | |
| 12 | | | | | | | | | | |
| 13 | | | | | | | | | | |
| 14 | | | | | | | | | | |
| 15 | | | | | | | | | | |
| 16 | | | | | | | | | | |
| 17 | | | | | | | | | | |
| 18 | | | | | | | | | | |
| 19 | | | | | | | | | | |
| 20 | | | | | | | | | | |
| 21 | | | | | | | | | | |
| 22 | | | | | | | | | | |
| 23 | | | | | | | | | | |
| 24 | | | | | | | | | | |
| 25 | | | | | | | | | | |
| 26 | | | | | | | | | | |
| 27 | | | | | | | | | | |
| 28 | | | | | | | | | | |
| 29 | | | | | | | | | | |
| 30 | | | | | | | | | | |

*Exhibit 13.10   Function Form.*

---

### Identify the "Function" of the Undesirable Behavior(s). (What Consequences Maintain the Behavior(s)?)

Think of each of the behaviors listed and define the function(s) you believe the behavior serves for the person (for example, what does he get and/or *avoid* by doing the behavior?)

| | Behavior | What Does He Get | What Does He Avoid |
|---|---|---|---|
| 1. | | | |
| 2. | | | |
| 3. | | | |
| 4. | | | |
| 5. | | | |
| 6. | | | |
| 7. | | | |
| 8. | | | |
| 9. | | | |
| 10. | | | |

Source: From Gresham & Noell (1998) based on O'Neill et al. (1997).

---

immense attention to the participants, clearly are not carried out for that reason. The same can be said for acts of heroism or mistakes leading to tragic results.

### Action 4: Write Out Replacement Behaviors That Meet the Function

This may well be the single most important step in this entire process. It is where you decide what you are going to teach and shift your attention away from eliminating troublesome conduct. Follow these steps:

1. Develop a pool of replacement behaviors from which to select the individual pinpoints. As you work, ask yourself how students that behave appropriately in the same situation achieve the same function(s). The specific-level status sheet in Howell et al., 2000a may help.

2. Do not select replacement behaviors that seem particularly at odds with what you know about the student's temperament, beliefs, or culture.

3. Select several replacement behaviors for each function. This will allow the student to follow alternative paths to his goal. It will also allow you to "shape" the desired

outcome by moving the student through a sequence of successive approximations of the goal (Kaplan, 1995; Malott et al., 1997; Zirpoli & Melloy, 1997).

4. Write out the replacement behaviors as target pinpoints. (See the specific-level status sheet in Howell et al., 2000a and the objectives in Appendix A.5.)

### Question 6: Do the Target Pinpoints Pass the Stranger Test?

Apply the stranger test by asking if someone who is unfamiliar with this student can, upon reading your pinpoint, recognize and count occurrences of the replacement behavior. You may want to confirm your conclusion by actually asking someone to do it.

#### Interpretation
If YES, go to Q7.
If NO, then return to **A4**.

### Question 7: Does the Objective Pass the "So-What" Test?

Apply the so-what test by asking if the objectives you have selected:

- Are proactive;
- Replace the maladaptive behaviors; and
- Truly address the student's needs.

Remember that classroom control, unless it is sought to assure a functional and therapeutic environment, is not "social behavior." It should be handled through routine classroom management (see **Q5**).

### Interpretation Guidelines

If the target behaviors do not meet the so-what test, then forget it or return to **A4**.

If it does, then go on to **A5**.

### Action 5: Use Survey-Level Status Sheet

### Directions

There is so much content in the area of social skills that, rather than attempt to judge the student's status on large numbers of different behaviors, this process tries to narrow the search (in true survey tradition). Therefore, it asks you (we promise to stop saying this, but *you* should be a *team*—from now on just assume "*you*" means "*team*") to try to categorize the kind of problem using the survey status sheet in Appendix A.7. As you recall, the categories are:

- Personal (self-control) behavior;
- Interpersonal behavior;
- Problem-solving behavior;
- Citizenship behavior;
- Anger and violence alternatives; and
- Classroom-specific behavior.

Use the indicators on the sheet to judge each of the categories and then mark it.

The survey sheet is a very general assessment keyed to the specific-level status sheet in Howell et al., 2000a. Both have seven subdivisions representing the categories of social skills recognized through a review of existing published social-skill programs and research literature.

You could go directly to the specific sheet in Howell et al., 2000a, but it has 108 separate skills to be rated, whereas the survey only has six areas. So, if you can use Appendix A.7, you'll save a lot of time.

### Directions

Use the survey status sheet (found in Appendix A.7). Work with others if possible. Follow the directions on the sheet and mark the status for each of the six areas.

### Question 8: What Categories Were Marked As "No" or "Unsure"?

To move from the survey level to the specific level, note the content areas on the survey sheet that were marked "No" or "Unsure." These areas require finer analysis. However, before moving to Action 6 to conduct that analysis, record the student's status on the survey sheet so it can be used to state PLOP and to form goals.

### Action 6: Use the Specific-Level Status Sheet

### Directions

On the specific-level status sheet (found in Howell et al., 2000a), specific behaviors are listed for each of the categories on the **A5** survey-level status sheet. Find the main categories you marked "No" or "Unsure" on the survey status sheet. Find those categories on the specific-level status sheet. Within those categories, read the behaviors described under the "If the student makes this error" heading to see if one or more of them seems to match the problem behavior.

### Question 9: Did You Find Goals and Objectives?

If YES (or UNSURE), then go to **Action 7**.

If NO, then return to **Action 1**.

### Action 7: Common Prerequisite Status Sheet

In the task-analytical model, a maladaptive behavior is assumed to occur because something is keeping the adaptive behavior from replacing it. Therefore, the operational question is not "Why is the kid screwing up?" but "Why isn't the kid doing it right?" As with any other task, it is assumed that the student is failing to employ adaptive social tasks because of a missing prior knowledge.

Obviously, social tasks vary from one another as much as academic tasks. However, most social skills do share the common set of prerequisites illustrated in the common prerequisite status sheet found in Exhibit 13.6 and Howell et al. (2000a). This list is based in part on the work of Kaplan (2000). The list contains two categories of items. The first category is defined by the content of the items (Type 1 and Type 2 prerequisites); the second category is defined by the focus of the item (the student or the environment). On the status sheet, the first 22 items relate to Type 1 content, and items 23 to 34 relate to Type 2 content. Even-numbered items pertain to the student's skills, whereas odd-numbered items indicate instructional actions.

### Directions

1. Fill out the common prerequisite status sheet found in Exhibit 13.6 and Howell et al. (2000a) as directed.

2. Using the sheet, decide if any generic prerequisites listed there apply. If they don't, cross them out. If there are other prerequisites, add them to the list. Don't forget environmental prerequisites.

3. Get everyone together who knows the student and mark the status of each prerequisite. Remember that an environmental prerequisite may be "yes" for one setting but "no" for another. If people report situational differences, record this information because it will be important for decision making.

4. If item 31 or 33 was marked "No" or "Unsure," use the thinking error summary in Appendix A.8.

5. Decide which prerequisites the student does or does not have (don't forget the results of Appendix A.8 if you used it). Also note those about which you are unsure. These are the assumed causes for failure on the objective. They may need to be verified before becoming objectives.

6. Additional specific-level testing may be necessary to validate the rating or to test causes listed as "No" or "Unsure." This usually means developing specific probes, as few "knows the consequences of engaging in the adaptive behavior" tests already exist. Exhibit 13.11 provides brief descriptions of specific-level tests for each of the common student prerequisites (the odd-numbered items) found on the common prerequisite status sheet. Most of these involve the use of direct questions or structured interviews, although role-playing and cue sorts may also be used.

### Question 10: Did You Find Goals and Objectives?

If YES, then note which objectives were in the following categories:

- Missing Type 1 student prerequisites?
- Missing Type 1 environment prerequisites?
- Missing Type 2 student prerequisites?
- Missing Type 2 environment prerequisites?

You will need this information for questions 14–16. Next, go to **Action 8.**

If NO, there are three possible explanations: (1) you missed something and need to start over with **Action 1,** (2) you did everything right but *we* missed something so you need to get additional direction, or (3) the student does not have

*Exhibit 13.11    Example Assessments.*

| Prerequisites | Specific-Level Probes |
|---|---|
| | Type 1 (Do Behaviors) |
| 1. . . . the student can discriminate the target and maladaptive behaviors from each other and from other behaviors. | Give the student a list of behaviors, a series of pictures, or role-playing examples and ask him to indicate the target and maladaptive behavior. |
| 3. . . . the student can monitor his own behavior well enough to know when he is engaging in the target or maladaptive behavior. | Ask the student to record his own behavior or to think back and state whether or not he engaged in two specific behaviors. |
| 5. . . . the student can monitor the environment well enough to recognize events that should prompt the target behavior or inhibit the maladaptive behavior. | Ask the student how he can tell what to do or give the student statements of the behavior and various scenes (through pictures, descriptions, or role-playing) and ask him to match scenes to behaviors. |
| 7. . . . the student knows what behavior is expected. | Ask him. Say "What do I want you to do?" or "What should you be doing?" If the student is unable to produce the desired response, give some choices and ask him to identify which one is correct. Say, "Should you be in your seat, or should you be out of your seat?" Use cue sorts. |
| 9. . . . the student has the skills/knowledge to engage in the target behavior successfully. | Conduct an assessment using criterion-referenced measures to check necessary skills. Task analyze the behavior first if it is fairly complex. |
| 11. . . . the student knows the consequences of engaging in the target behavior. | Ask him. Say, "What happens to you when you . . . ?" If he is unable to produce the desired response, give some choices and ask him to identify which one is correct. Say, "Do you get to go to recess?" or "Do you get to read?" |
| 13. . . . the student knows the consequences of engaging in the maladaptive behavior. | Ask him. Say, "What happens to you when you?" If he is unable to produce the desired response, give some choices and ask him to identify which one is correct. Say, "Do you miss recess?" or "Do you have to stay after school?" |
| 15. . . . the student understands that his behaviors cause certain consequences. | Ask the student to explain the reactions of others to his behaviors. Note if he attributes these reactions to beliefs and preferences of others, or if he simply knows what the reactions will be. |
| 17. . . . there are no physical factors which militate against the target behavior and/or promote the maladaptive behavior (such as allergies or seizures). | Look for any evidence of personal or environmental factors that might trigger the maladaptive behavior or prevent the student from engaging in the target behavior. |
| 19. . . . the student generates solutions to problems that include the target behavior. | Supply the student with various restatements of the problem, involving other people. Ask, "What could they do to get what they want?" Use a forced-choice questioning format, such as "Which would you rather have [the problem solved] or [the resource required to solve it]? |
| 21. . . . the student knows that a target behavior may become maladaptive and that maladaptive behaviors may become targets, depending on the situation/context in which the student is functioning. | Supply a picture or role-play of a situation and several behavioral options. Ask the student to select the best, or worst, behavior. Note if the student adjusts his answers according to the situation. |

| Type 2 (Select Behaviors) | |
| --- | --- |
| 23. . . . the student considers the consequences of engaging in the target behavior to be rewarding. | Give him a list of rewards including ones you have used in the past and are presently using with him and ask him to sort them according to value (which he likes the most to the least). Use the ABC technique to determine thoughts about receiving various rewards. |
| 25. . . . the student considers the consequences of engaging in the maladaptive behavior to be aversive. | Give him a list of punishers, including ones you have used in the past and are presently using with him, and ask him to sort them according to value (which he finds the most aversive to the least). Use the ABC technique to determine thoughts about receiving various punishers. |
| 27. . . . the student values the target behavior more than the maladaptive behavior. | Give him a list of behaviors (including the target behavior) and have him sort them according to their importance to him. If he cannot complete this; type of exercise, ask a series of restricted alternative questions such as, "Which would you rather do, work by yourself or with a group?" |
| 29. . . . the student holds beliefs which are compatible with the target behavior and incompatible with the maladaptive behavior. | Use the control investment technique or other forms of structured interview. |
| 31. . . . the student maintains an adaptive explanatory style when attributing the causes of events. | Refer to Appendix A.13. |
| 33. . . . the student avoids errors in thinking when developing and employing belief systems. | Refer to Appendix A.13. |

Howell, K. W., Zucker, S. R & Morehead, M. K. (2000b). *Multilevel Academic Skills Inventory.* Bellingham, WA: Applied Research and Development Center.

To order contact the Student Co-op Bookstore, Western Washington University. FAX (360) 650-2888. Phone (360) 650-3656.

the sort of problem these procedures were developed to address. Go through **Action 8.** Consider the possibility that the difficulty may actually be academic in nature, language-based, or task-related.

### Action 8: Consider the Following Questions

The purpose of **Action 8** is to find out if other domains may contribute to the social problem. Remember, things like academic problems are highly related to school behavioral problems.

### Directions

The directions are simple. Ask **Questions 11–13.**

### Question 11: Does the Problem Seem to Be Task-Related?

If YES (or even MAYBE), particularly if the student is failing to display knowledge or complete assignments, then go to Chapter 14.

### Question 12: Does the Target Pinpoint Seem Related to an Academic Skill Problem?

If MAYBE, particularly if the student is not complying with instruction, or the problems occur during lessons, include a screening in the topical areas involved. Then go to the appropriate chapter (8–14).

## Question 13: Does the Target Pinpoint Seem Related to Language?

If MAYBE, particularly if the student seems to be having interpersonal problems, include a language screening in your evaluation by going to Chapter 10.

## Summary 3: List Objectives

This is your last major step (you have permission to be relieved). Line up your objectives and review the status of each. Now ask *each* of these questions (you may end up saying "yes" to more than one).

## Question 14: Missing Type 1 Skills?

If YES, then use **Teaching Recommendation 3.**
    If NO, then ask **Questions 15 and 16.**

## Question 15: Missing Type 2 Skills?

If YES, then use **Teaching Recommendation 4.**
    If NO, then ask **Questions 14 and 16.**

## Question 16: Enabling Skills Missing?

If YES, then use **Teaching Recommendation 5.**

    If NO, then we have problems. There is nothing to do but go back to **Action 1.**

## Summary 4: Decision Making

## Teaching Recommendations

Because of the size of the topic we are dealing with, these recommendations will have to be brief. The topic of behavioral change is simply too large to approach in the span of one chapter. That is why there are classes on social behavior and texts that tell how to teach it. We will provide a couple of mechanisms for making this portion of the text more helpful. First, Appendix A.5 contains a list of the content found in some social-skills programs (please note the limitations of these programs presented below). That list is cross-referenced to the programs. This alignment should allow you to go from the objectives you found with the specific-level status sheet directly to lessons within those published programs. The "other" column is for you to include new programs.

Educators commonly, and justifiably, complain that things (such as computer literacy, child abuse prevention, and AIDS awareness) are added to the curriculum without any addition of resources. Teaching social skills, particularly those involving metacognitive operations, is not easy (Kauffman & Wong, 1991; Mathur et al., 1998; Walker et al., 1995), and it is time consuming. How then is it justifiable to recommend adding social skills to the teaching load?

The answer is that several decades of teacher effectiveness and time-on-task literature have demonstrated that more time in the school day (roughly 55% of it) is spent managing students than is spent teaching them (Doyle, 1986; Price & Nelson, 1999). Consequently, the argument that one does not have time for social-skills training is not persuasive as the time is already being spent. Second, social problems in school are often causally related to academic problems. So you may find that the solution to a social behavior problem is to return to academics. Finally, social skills are probably best taught within the context of other lessons, not as an added class. This means that the adoption of particular social-skills programs may not be the correct action for teachers and schools to take. Besides, there is a major problem with the rapidly growing batch of such programs. We don't know if they work!

To date, the use of broad-based programs of instruction on social skills has not found tremendous support in the empirical literature (Kavale et al., 1997; Mathur et al., 1998). As we read these studies, we've noted at least four problems you might want to watch for in the future literature:

1. The outcome measures used to judge success often focus on the reduction of inappropriate behavior, whereas truly instructional programs focus on the development of appropriate behaviors;

2. The interventions often don't incorporate efforts to make sure change will maintain and generalize. Typically, the studies are *very* short, regularly allocating less time to teach students to *cooperate*, for example, than is typically allocated to teach them to *add*;

3. Some types of social skills may need to be taught, at least initially, one-to-one. Arnold and Hughes (1999) think this is particularly true to correct overt behaviors such as aggression. Yet, most published programs make exclusive use of group (small) formats; and

4. Few of the currently available social-skills programs contain preinstruction placement tests to see if the student even needs the program. If the wrong behavior (for example, one the student cannot currently learn because of missing prior knowledge) is selected, *any* intervention is useless.

Without denying the importance of the research (Mathur et al., 1998), there are some reasons for our continuing to recommend the teaching of social skills.

- First, we are *not* recommending the use of broad-based social-skills *programs,* we are (as always) recommending the use of narrow band interventions exclusively selected according to the needs of individual students; and

- Many of the separate interventions, which are a part of social-skills programs, *have* been validated. These include self-monitoring, relaxation training, interpersonal skill building, attributions retraining, and empathy/perspective taking (Goldstein, 1988; Walker et al., 1995).

We also want to echo two other things mentioned above. First, the topic of social skills is *not* the same as the topic of classroom management (which is addressed under **Teaching Recommendation 2**). Second, effective instruction in social skills requires tremendous work. Our students will have already learned, through experience, a set of social skills. That means we have to get

them to abandon, at least in some situations, what they already know and believe. This requires the use of instructional techniques that actively involve the student in reflection, hypotheses testing, and validation (see Chapter 2) (McDaniel & Schlager, 1990). Often, one of the most difficult parts of social-skills instruction is getting students to think and think in a social (interdependent and cooperative) way. This means getting the student to understand that the validation of social "truth" does not necessarily come through personal experience (which has been the test for personal truth all of the kid's life). What one experiences in a social context is *not* completely personal.

### A Note on Medications

Despite controversy related to the practice, the reality is that more children and adolescents are being prescribed stimulant medication (STM) for attention or behavior-related difficulties at school. At the same time, the research suggests that a large number of these children and adolescents do not take these medications as prescribed (this is commonly referred to as "noncompliance"). This is a problem because the effectiveness of medication (if any) will not simply result from the *prescription* of STMs. Any long-term impact (either positive or negative) of medication use will result from how it is understood by the student and handled by teachers, parents, and physicians (Howell et al., 1997). The step between prescription and correct usage can be a big one. Here are some guidelines for correct application of treatment by stimulant medication.

### Try to Assure That the Decision to Use Medication Is Made Appropriately   The explicit assumption underlying each of the following actions is that the use of STMs is appropriate for the student involved. This means that the less intrusive alternatives of behavioral management and/or instructional modification must have been employed correctly, and without success, prior to the move to medication (DuPaul et al., 1991; Walker et al., 1995). If this is not the case, argue that behavioral and instructional interventions should be used first.

**Establish Direct Communication Among All Parties**   Arrange for direct communication among parents, teachers, physicians, school psychologists, school nurses, administrators, and, of course, the child (Forness et al., 1996; Hansen et al., 1992).

The involvement of the teacher(s) in the initial development of a medication regimen is critical if long-term educational benefits are to be achieved. The teacher's knowledge of education is crucial in the development of an appropriate educational plan that is based on the needs of the classroom as well as those of the student. The plan should target academic and social behaviors as well as having the long-term aim of getting the students off the prescribed STMs. The early development of clearly understood lines of communication, and procedures for conflict resolution, are essential.

**Plan Who Will Administer the Medications and How It Will Be Done**   The need for a clear plan is all the more compelling when medication is being used on a child or on someone who is not considered sufficiently competent to consent to the treatment. That is why, even though it may be the child who is taking the pill, everyone involved has a stake in the process. We offer the following minimal actions for teachers:

- Find out what laws and school policy require you to do before you *do* anything;

- Make sure that you are not liable for errors or negative outcomes;

- Don't administer the medications yourself;

- Make a written report of any violations of the policy regarding the administration of medications; then send the report to your supervisor (keep a copy); and

- Never store medications in your classroom.

**Internalize Responsibility**   It is important for students to believe that their academic and/or behavioral problems can be corrected and that the solutions to these problems are under the student's direct control (Dweck, 1986). This means that the student must be taught to separate the symptoms from the person.

- Give the problem (or symptom) a face or at least a name. Even older students should have a name for the problem that the whole family, and fellow students, understand and can use. For want of better names, we tend to refer to the symptoms by terms like "attention thieves."

- Explain to the student that the problem, despite the unfortunate connotation of terms like "attention deficit," is not a lack of ability or attention but the lack of control over the attention one possesses. In other words, that with work and training, the child will have enough control to stop those pesky "attention thieves" without the medications.

- Separate the child from the symptom.

- The need for medication should always be explained in terms that will lead the student to believe that, although the problem may effect him, it is not synonymous with him.

**Never Do This!**   When the kid is acting up, never ask "have you taken your medication this morning?" Such questions reinforce the misunderstanding that the child's behavior is under the control of the drug. If you really need to know, check later with the person responsible. If the medication hasn't been taken, deal with the lapse by prompting ("Justin, did you finish all of the things you need to do before going to lunch?").

**Alert the Student to Possible Changes**   When students go on STMs they may experience loss of appetite, weight loss, dry mouth, stomachaches, and/or irritability (to name a few). In addition, it is a good idea to prepare the student for the possibility that *nothing* may happen at all. DiTraglia (1991) found that 43% of students on medication did not seem to benefit from STM use.

**Help Children Tell Others about the Pills**   Children, especially older ones, often hate taking STMs. Sometimes they think it makes them seem strange. As children needing medications often do have difficulties in peer relationships, their concern is well founded. Preparing children to explain the medications will only improve compliance with the medication regimen. The best way to prepare children is to role-play with them, even if it initially seems strange to them or their parents. If the child has understood the externalizing of the symptom, a typical rehearsal might go like this:

*Parent plays child taking pill, child or other parent/adult plays a classmate. Child pretends to take medication.*

CLASSMATE: "What are you doing?"

CHILD: "Taking my pills."

CLASSMATE: "Can I have one then?"

CHILD: "Sorry, I can't give my pills to people. Besides, these pills won't work for you; they are made to work for me."

It is important not to underestimate children's concern about their peers' response to the medication.

**Use Reminders Appropriately**   Everybody has trouble remembering to take daily medications, so set up a reminder system. It is best to link the medication with a regularly occurring event and to record the taking of the medication on a calendar or chart. (Don't, as we saw in one school, stamp the kid's hand with ink.) Avoid including the taking of the medication with a list of chores ("Justin, complete your math assignment, clear your desk, and don't forget to take your pill"). Instead, associate it with a time, a location, and a pleasant event, such as going to lunch.

**Before You Start, Decide How to Stop**   One of the first questions children will have, though they may not ask it directly, is when they will get off the medication. This is a fair question, and criteria for stopping should be negotiated with all parties before medication is commenced. All parties need to know what will guarantee stopping the medication and what will lead to the medication being reinstated.

**Teach!**   It is incorrect to assume that STMs, even if they reduce inappropriate behavior or increase attention, will automatically improve relationships and academics (Pelham, 1993). Any appropriate STM program needs to include effective instructional plans for addressing targeted academic and social behaviors. Nonoccurring desired behaviors must be taught directly and systematically.

**Monitor**   Fischer et al. (1991) reviewed students placed on Ritalin. Careful monitoring of the 161 students found that 57% required dosage changes. Thirty-four percent of the students had to be taken off the medications because of side-effects or the absence of results. Sensitive monitoring showed that the initial prescription was *incorrect* for over 90% of the students.

Monitoring plans should be developed for at least four domains: academic behavior, classroom behavior, social interactions, and adverse side-effects (DuPaul et al., 1991).

When preparing these plans, remember that systems which only focus on negative behaviors may give false impressions of improvement (Kaplan, 1995). If "making reading errors" were the only behavior monitored, a student could improve by going to sleep.

Developing monitoring procedures that are adequate and efficient is as important as any other part of the medication regimen. Some excellent guidance for the development of such monitoring procedures can be found in Fischer et al. (1991), Deno (1997), Kaplan (1995), and Sugai and Pruitt (1993).

### Teaching Recommendation 1: Planning and Working with Violent and/or Aggressive Behavior

At Western Washington University, where we both work, there are a lot of deer on campus. There are also, occasionally, cougars. These are not mascots; they are the wild ones. They come to eat deer. However, even though attacks on humans are *very* rare (none have ever taken place at Western, so you can feel free to come visit or study), the presence of large carnivores on campus does make some people nervous. So, we have cougar warning signs. There is also a list of things to do if you see a cougar.

Karna Nelson, of Price and Nelson (1999), observed that the recommendations for dealing with a cougar are very similar to those for dealing with an aggressive student. They include:

✓ Never ignore the problem

✓ Stay calm

✓ Speak with a relaxed but loud, voice

✓ Try to look physically powerful but do not act aggressively (the cougar directions actually advise making yourself "look bigger"; we don't know if that applies to kids)

✓ Avoid physical contact

✓ Do not turn your back

The similarity between this list and those provided for teachers who may need to deal with aggressive students is interesting. And it may tell us that knowledge of aggression, not just the person or animal doing the aggression, is important. So once again it seems that knowledge of the task itself is always necessary if a teacher is going to be effective.

### Aggression

This is an enormously important topic to educators confronted with school violence. Effective efforts to prevent and react to violence should include a schoolwide program and also provide for one-to-one work with problematic students (Arnold & Hughes, 1999). Schools and teachers who plan to work effectively with aggressive students use, or develop, programs containing these components.

1. Preaggression

✓ Teacher training

✓ Training of peer negotiators

✓ Promotion of a peaceful environment

✓ Establishing student commitment/ investment/ownership of the school

✓ Fostering student "resilience"

✓ Get in the habit of scanning for trouble and planning how you would handle it if it occurred (just as many pilots continually scan for places to land if their plane malfunctions)

✓ Have fight drills (like fire drills) to teach students how to protect themselves if a violent event occurs.

2. During aggression

✓ Follow the cougar rules listed above

✓ Send a student for help

✓ Clear the area of all other students

✓ Establish strong but nonthreatening body language

✓ As a rule never directly intervene alone (however, know that sometimes teachers have had to intervene to save children from harm)

✓ If the problem is a fight:

- Give a professional but strong command telling the student(s) to "STOP"

- Remember that the longer two people fight the more tired they will be and the easier to handle (assuming there are no weapons)

- Scan for any indication that the fight may spread to other students who want to take sides—command these students to separate (tell them and *point* to where you want them to go)

- Try a trick we heard from Eugene Edgar. It is the "pick the wimp" technique. Decide which student is losing the fight (Les) and command "Les! I want you to come over here right now!" Odds are Les will want to come because he is losing, and whoever he is fighting with will let him go in the mistaken belief you have decided the fight is Les's fault.

3. After aggression

✓ Do not let an aggressive act, or threat, go by without a serious, but educational, response

✓ Don't allow the aggressive person to get rewarded for his act (that includes approval from peers)

✓ Don't allow the student to be physically punished (no swats)

✓ Talk with the participants; use good judgment and a calm voice so that you don't rekindle the aggression

✓ Try to recognize the function of the act and then discuss the advantages of other ways to accomplish that function

✓ Talk with others who saw the fight; don't try to smooth things over or put a positive spin on the action; model the way you desire nonfighting students to respond

✓ Have participants work with you to develop a plan for avoiding a recurrence

✓ If the situation warrants it, call the police (there should be a school policy on this; it would have been set as part of component 1).

We recommend you read:

Crawford, D. & Bodine, R. (1996) Conflict resolution education: A guide to implementing programs in schools, youth-serving organizations, and community and juvenile justice settings. United States Department of Justice, Office of Juvenile Justice and Delinquency Prevention. Office of Elementary and Secondary Education. Washington, D. C. (it's on the web).

Two more things:. First, for your own mental health, understand that at times violence is brought into the school. It has little to do with how the school is organized or with the quality of your efforts at prevention. In these cases, you will be forced into reaction and containment. Do what you have to do.

Second, if it is a bear, not a cougar, you should only fight or act aggressive with black bears. Do not act aggressively with brown (grizzly) bears. (There *really* is a lot of valuable information in this text.)

### Teaching Recommendation 2: Improving Classroom Management

There are plenty of good sources for information on classroom management, so we will only provide a list of recommended actions and a brief explanation as given by Ysseldyke and Christenson (1996). The full TIES-II list is in Appendix A.13.

1. A small number of important rules (for example, talking, out of seat) are selected and reinforced.

2. Expected behavior in the classroom is communicated through discussion of rules and *routines.*

3. Behavior that will and will not be tolerated is clearly communicated to the student.

4. Both examples and nonexamples of rules and procedures are used.

5. Classroom rules and *routines* are introduced at the beginning of the year.

6. There is a system to involve the student in the management of his behavior.

7. The teacher continuously keeps good eye contact on the student.

8. Reminders about expected behavior are given in advance of an activity (for example, transition, field trip, assembly).

9. Noncompliance or disruptive behavior is handled immediately.

10. Inappropriate behavior is used as an opportunity to reteach or reinforce behavioral expectations.

11. Nonverbal signals are used to redirect the student while teaching other students.

12. Praise is specific and administered continently.

13. The student's compliance with rules is continuously monitored.

14. The student understands the consequences of misbehavior.

15. The student understands the classroom rules and *routines.*

Routines are mentioned several times in this list and are an important aspect of good class management. However, whereas most readers will already be familiar with the principles and techniques of behavior management, some of you may not be familiar with the importance and use of classroom routines, so see Price and Nelson (1999), Udvari-Solner (1996), and Chapter 4.

## Teaching Recommendation 3: Focus on Type 1 Skills

The first step is to consult the common prerequisite form and attempt to recognize objectives and teaching actions.

The common Type 1 objectives and teaching actions are listed here using numbering from Exhibit 13.6:

Each of the objectives listed can be converted into a full instructional objective by inserting the student's own behavior and the criteria. For example, item 7 might be changed to read "The student will demonstrate that he knows the consequences of engaging in [the specified adaptive behavior] by listing the consequences in response to a question. [CAP 100%]." Objectives

| Type 1 Objectives | Type 1 Teaching Actions |
|---|---|
| 1. . . . the student can discriminate the target and maladaptive behaviors from each other and from other behaviors. | 2. . . . target and maladaptive behaviors are clearly and consistently labeled and reviewed. |
| 3. . . . the student can monitor his own behavior well enough to know he is engaging in the target or maladaptive behavior. | 4. . . . the student is encouraged to reflect on his behavior and is praised for self-corrections and/or early recognition of problems. |
| 5. . . . the student can monitor the environment well enough to recognize events that should prompt the target behavior or inhibit the maladaptive behavior. | 6. . . . cause and effect relationships between events in the environment and the student's behavior are clearly explained and reviewed. |
| 7. . . . the student knows what behavior is expected of him. | 8. . . . expectations are clearly explained and/or demonstrated to the student (they are also frequently reviewed). |
| 9. . . . the student has the skills/knowledge to engage in the target behavior successfully. | 10. . . . the student is taught how to engage in the target behavior. |
| 11. . . . the student knows the consequences of engaging in the target behavior. | 12. . . . the student is taught the consequences of engaging in the target behavior. |
| 13. . . . the student knows the consequences of engaging in the maladaptive behavior. | 14. . . . the student is taught the consequences of engaging in the maladaptive behavior. |
| 15. . . . the student understands that his behaviors cause certain consequences. | 16. . . . the reasons for the reactions of others to the student's behavior are explained. |
| 19. . . . the student generates solutions to problems that include the target behavior. | 20. . . . the student is taught to solve problems. |
| 21. . . . the student knows that a target behavior may become maladaptive and that maladaptive behaviors may become targets, depending on the situation/context in which the student is functioning. | 22. . . . the situational cues promoting various behaviors are identified and adequately taught to the student, along with skills for analyzing new situations. |

can also be drawn from the specific-level status sheet.

Instruction on Type 1 skills is the same for the domain of social behavior as it is for any academic domain. Therefore, the information in Chapter 4, particularly that covering concepts and strategies, applies. What may be different is the *idea* of teaching this material. As many teachers do not use explicit instruction to teach social skills, the students may be confused when you start. Initially, this is best handled by declaring a fixed period of time to cover the content (eventually you will expand this time by applying the lessons to the whole day). Although you might think there isn't enough time in your busy day to include social-skills training, remember that most teachers already are spending more time on student management than instruction. Even problems that are comparatively lightweight for an individual can represent a major loss of time. Larson (1989b) has concluded that in a typical middle school of 2,000 students, as many as 14,681 classroom removals for problem behavior can occur in a year. At that rate, a conservative allowance of 15 minutes of class/teacher time for each disruption yields a total of 3,670 hours lost. This does not even come close to matching the time forfeited to more routine classroom disruptions. It would be better to spend those hours teaching the students how to behave.

Some published programs are listed in Howell et al., 2000a, and you can get an idea of the content they cover by reviewing that information. You may also wish to update it as you run across the many new programs coming out. This will allow you, after the evaluation, to pick portions of programs applicable to individuals.

### Teaching Recommendation 4: Focus on Missing Type 2 Skills

Sometimes, when working with a student, an obviously unrealistic Type 2 expectation or inaccurate perception will pop out. In these cases, it seems clear that the inappropriate expectation/perception should be changed. Often, the best change technique is to promote (through teaching and demonstration) cognitive behaviors

that are incompatible with the inappropriate ones. The first step in this effort is to demonstrate these adaptive alternatives.

Cognitive changes are not always monumental readjustments of personal philosophy. More often, they are simple corrections of an inaccurate expectation. Karna Nelson (who thinks making herself look big will take care of cougars) used the process in this chapter with a teacher who had a new student. After being given assignments, the kid frequently just put them away saying "I'll do it tomorrow." Although this was more of a class behavior problem than a social one, the teacher was puzzled. When Karna task-analyzed "immediately begins work," the prerequisite "thinks work should be done immediately" emerged. As a test, the teacher asked "How long do you think you have to do an assignment?" to which the student replied "A week." Baffled, the teacher asked "Why do you think that?" and the kid explained "In my last school we had assignment contracts, and it didn't matter when we worked as long as the contract was met in a week."

This simple explanation took the two teachers some time to find, but they didn't find it at all until they sat down and analyzed the adaptive behavior. The intervention took only a few minutes and involved explaining the differences between the new class and the old one. In this case, the student was behaving *inappropriately*, not because of complex missing skills, entrenched beliefs, or mysterious emotional peculiarities. He was behaving inappropriately because he held the *"irrational"* expectation that two classroom teachers would have the same rules.

Type 2 behaviors are covert. They include thoughts, beliefs, feelings, perceptions, and expectations. The first step in teaching them is to consult the common prerequisite form (Exhibit 13.6) and attempt to recognize objectives and teaching actions. These are listed on the next page.

You can convert any missing Type 2 student prerequisite into an instructional objective. For example, item 31 states "The student will use an adaptive explanatory style when attributing the causes of [specify the target behavior]." The general teaching action for this behavior is to teach the student to ". . . avoid permanent and

| Type 2 Objectives | Type 2 Teaching Actions |
|---|---|
| 23. . . . the student considers the consequences of engaging in the target behavior to be rewarding. | 24. . . . the advantages of the target behavior are taught to the student. |
| 25. . . . the student considers the consequences of engaging in the maladaptive behavior to be aversive. | 26. . . . the disadvantages of the maladaptive behavior are taught to the student. |
| 27. . . . the student values the target behavior more than the maladaptive behavior. | 28. . . . the student is taught to consider how the target and maladaptive behaviors fit within the student's belief system. |
| 29. . . . the student holds beliefs which are compatible with the target behavior and incompatible with the maladaptive behavior. | 30. . . . the student is taught to develop beliefs through the active application of hypothesis formation, hypothesis testing, and reflection. This instruction must include public thinking by an exemplar and stress the need for beliefs to be "valid." |
| 31. . . . the student maintains an adaptive explanatory style when attributing the causes of events. | 32. . . . the student is taught to avoid permanent and persuasive attributions to external causes and/or internal abilities. |
| 33. . . . the student avoids errors in thinking when developing and employing belief systems. | 34. . . . the student is taught to avoid errors in cognition, irrational thoughts, and a helpless cognitive set. |

persuasive attributions to external causes and/or internal abilities." (There will be a full discussion of attribution in Chapter 14.)

The natural focus of **Teaching Recommendation 4** is student thought. This includes a category of thought we commonly refer to as belief. A belief is an idea an individual takes as fact regardless of situational information which contradicts the belief. What a person believes is as real to him as what he is seeing and hearing at any given moment. Therefore, two individuals in the same situation may behave differently because they hold different beliefs. These beliefs have been raised to factual status by the experiences of the individual. They can be thought of as rules the person applies to all situations. A delinquent may believe, for example, that "cops can't be trusted" and hold that belief at *all* times. To others, that belief may seem appropriate in some situations and inappropriate in others.

Here is another example. If the student seems to always produce the same solutions, regardless of the problem, these responses could be the result of a belief that overshadows his current perceptions about what is going on. Such inflexible beliefs often limit the student's options because they mask them. Once again, the stereotyped "delinquent" beliefs that authority is bad and that force is the most effective solution to conflict are the easiest for teachers to spot. Nevertheless, other beliefs such as "I should be taken care of" or "The others are better than I" are just as common and show up frequently in ABC exchanges. Prejudices are examples of beliefs. They are acquired through unbefitting learning and, like other beliefs, can be diminished by teaching.

**Irrational Thoughts**   Some thoughts are irrational and easily recognized. Kaplan (1995, 2000) has listed irrational beliefs that will influence a student's **social competence;** these include:

✓ I must be good at everything I do.
✓ Everyone should treat me fairly.

✓ Anyone who walks away from a fight is a punk.

✓ School is dumb.

The rest of Kaplan's list is included under "Thinking Errors" in the Thinking Error Summary (Appendix A.8). In the cognitive-behavioral approach, it is assumed that these beliefs can be converted into adaptive beliefs ("Everyone should treat me fairly" is converted to "No one gets fair treatment all of the time"). Here are some sample objectives:

1. "Given lists of rational and irrational statements, including statements commonly made by the student, the student will label them accurately. CAP 100%."

2. "Given lists of irrational statements, the student will supply a rational counter-thought for each. CAP 100%."

3. "The student will decrease spontaneous use of irrational statements (relative to his current frequency) and increase the use of rational statements."

When attempting to work with irrational statements, keep in mind that the stated expression is not the focus of this intervention. That focus is the irrational *belief* that we assume generated the statement (although it may also be true that if you tell yourself something long enough you will believe it). Therefore, the intervention should be directed at the *thought*. In other words, don't just tell the student to stop making the statement—teach the student rational thinking skills. Some excellent procedures for doing this are found in Kaplan (2000), Olsen (1997), and Zionts (1996).

Sometimes, it also seems that irrational statements are the product of communicative confusion. For example, statements that seem to have little relationship to the current situation may be the result of:

✓ Lack of knowledge

✓ Misinterpretation

✓ Personal agenda (socially competent individuals do not insist on turning every conversation to a topic about which they are particularly concerned).

If out-of-context statements, as well as those that seem irrational, seem to be a problem for the student, use this objective (material in brackets will vary with student):

"Given [commonly encountered social situations], the student will analyze and interpret the context in accordance with the material learned [through a selected social-skills program] and will decrease the use of out-of-context statements to [the level of peers in the adaptive setting]."

For teaching recommendations relative to out-of-context statements, consult the literature on pragmatics (see Chapter 12).

***Cognitive Set***   A nonadaptive cognitive set can interfere with decision making and limit the student's interpretation of current situations. Appendix A.8 contains a list of indicators for identifying the "helpless" nonadaptive set. The topic of learned helplessness is tied to attribution and will be covered in Chapter 14.

A typical procedure for dealing with irrational thoughts and nonadaptive attributions will include these steps in teaching the student to:

1. Identify and sort adaptive from nonadaptive thoughts;

2. Monitor the occurrence of the thoughts;

3. React to the occurrence by using a thought-stopping response such as saying "Stop!" to himself, or snapping a rubber band worn around his wrist; and

4. Substitute an adaptive thought in place of the nonadaptive thought.

When following these steps with an individual student, you need to identify personally important pairs of rational and nonrational thoughts. Kaplan (2000) provides the examples upon which this list was based. Examples of Kaplan's assessment procedures can be found in Howell et al. (2000a).

Some of these thoughts represent more than one thinking error. For example, "No one likes me. I'll never have any friends" contains the permanent ("never"), pervasive ("no one" and

| Irrational Thought | Counter Thought |
|---|---|
| I must be good at everything I do. | No one is good at *everything* they do. I just need to be sure I'm doing my *best*. |
| No one likes me. I'll never have any friends. | There are people who like me, if I want more I'll need to work hard to do the things people like. |
| Only bad people do bad things and bad people must be punished. | There aren't *bad people*, but there are plenty of people who do *bad things*. It is easier to deal with the thing that happened than it is to change a whole person into someone else. Besides, even if punishment is called for, it isn't necessarily my job to carry it out. |
| I should be treated fairly by *everyone all of the time.* | I need to get real! *I* don't even treat everyone fairly all of the time, and even if I wanted to I wouldn't know how. It's irrational for me to expect that, or to be disappointed/angry when it doesn't happen. |

"have any"), and personal ("me" and "I'll") elements that should alarm you (Pine et al., 1999). The use of irrational, pervasive, permanent, and personal statements is associated with depression and hopelessness. Such statements need to be countered directly (Israelashvili, 1998; Kaplan, 1995). For example, "Walter likes you, so what you are telling yourself is wrong." and "People don't just 'have' friends, they make them by doing the things we have been talking about and practicing. As you get better at these skills, you'll make and keep more friends" (by the way, don't say "I like you," use a friend or family member).

### Teaching Recommendation 5: Enabling Skills

Sometimes, students will make social-skills errors, or be blocked from obtaining better social skills, by the absence of enabling skills. These are skills that may also be considered academic, task-related, or social. It depends on why the kid needs them.

**Judgment and Decision Making**    Judgment and decision making were discussed in Chapters 1 and 2. They are probably the pivotal domains

for a social-skills curriculum (see Appendix A.8). Although problem-solving and thinking-skills training has been widely discussed (Derry & Murphy, 1986), some main points need to be summarized.

Students who have difficulty in social skills don't solve problems well (Schumaker et al., 1983). Given problems, they generate fewer solutions (meaning they literally have less freedom to act); given solutions, they pick those that are ineffective and sometimes dangerous (often picking options with which they are familiar over those that are more effective).

Therefore, teaching students to generate and select options becomes an important area of content for social-skills training. For more information, see Chapter 14, R. Sprick et al. (1998), and McCagg and Dansereau (1991).

**Use of Change Techniques**    Students need to be aware of behavioral and cognitive change techniques if they are to control their own behavior (Kaplan, 2000). They need to know a few simple principles of reinforcement, punishment, extinction, and positive self-talk to use these techniques on themselves. Once students have intervention skills, they must also use their *self-*

*monitoring and evaluation* skills to recognize adaptive thoughts, feelings, and behaviors that need to be changed. This includes recognizing what is appropriate and what is not appropriate, given different situations. Kaplan (1995) is a good resource.

**Empathy**    Skill at understanding the position, and feelings, of others is generally recognized as an essential part of getting along with them (Goldstein, 1988). Students who do not establish empathetic links to others are often considered to be rude, unfeeling, or even "sociopathic." They are prime candidates for becoming victims and/or committing crimes against others. In fact, classes on subjects such as victim awareness are common in many adult and juvenile prisons.

For more on empathy training, take a look at Waters (1997).

**Language**    Although this material was covered in Chapter 10, it is important to recall that the child's understanding of social rules and the range of his familiarity with different social contexts are important aspects of communication and literacy. Students who do not know the social rules may seem rude or insubordinate (Iglesias, 1985; Larson & Gerber, 1987; Martens & Witt, 1988; Saville-Troike, 1976).

Children often communicate poorly in classes or social situations because the cultural and linguistic conditions to which they are accustomed are missing (Padilla & Medina, 1996; Philips, 1970). These conditions occur when the kid is raised in a subgroup that differs significantly in communication style from the style used in the class or work setting. This may occur at the family level or larger cultural level (for example, by groups such as economic status, gender, language, or race).

There are **sociolinguistic rules** for turn-taking, for following directions, and for the structure of discourse. When a child's discourse style is different from the majority, he may have trouble understanding both oral and written messages (Moreland, 1996). Research indicates that directly teaching children about different class

room interaction styles will improve learning (see Chapter 10) (Kawakami & Hupei Au, 1986).

**Problem Solving**    Remember, students with social-skill problems want the same things anyone else wants, and they make the same kinds of mistakes trying to get them (they just make more mistakes, and some are spectacular).

Problem-solving interventions might be general or specific. If the student seems to have only one particular block to effective problem solving (Fitzgerald, 1989), you may choose to go after it directly. Here is an example objective for general problem solving; material in brackets should be worded to match the student's individual needs.

"The student will demonstrate flexible thinking by supplying multiple solutions to [problems and interpretations of events] (including empathetic descriptions of peers). [These problems and events] will include items drawn from [situations that are personally relevant to the student]. The number and form of the responses the student supplies will be consistent with [the instructional program used to teach the skill]."

If the student seems to have a more general difficulty with problem solving, we recommend the unit on that topic in *The Prepared Curriculum* by Goldstein (1988).

We're going to leave the topic of social behavior with a final thought. For any academic, social, or cognitive behavior, once you have selected a pinpoint and started an intervention, you must monitor the effect of the intervention (Deno, 1997). When dealing with cognitive pinpoints, poor teachers and therapists will often persist with an intervention that conforms to their idea of mental health but does not produce healthy change in the client. Sometimes, this persistence will even produce damage (Arnold & Hughes, 1999). If a teacher cannot document positive change in the client, then it's time for the teacher to change. (Incidentally, that is the same recommendation we make regarding the use of drug **therapy** to address learning or behavior problems.) Additionally, if a private mental-health professional is working on a school-related problem and hasn't developed a mechanism for collecting data in the schools, you shouldn't cooperate with the treatment until she does.

## *Summary*

This chapter has been different from those that preceded it because it deals with the global domain of social skill. Some of the major points presented were as follows.

Social skill and academic behavior are not that different.

✓ Efforts to develop social-skills curriculum are needed.

✓ Social skills should be taught and not simply controlled.

✓ Attempts to deal with social skills must address covert as well as overt behaviors.

In addition to these points, we covered a variety of specific procedures and provided some examples. We intentionally moved extensive discussions of data collection, observation, and charting out of this chapter. That was because we think those topics are just as important for academics as social skills. Throughout the chapter, we attempted to illustrate the application of a curriculum-based, task-analytical approach to social skills and to caution against its misapplication.

A popular saying tells us that "Children are a message that we send to the future." It is not a bad saying to recall when considering social skills. Sometimes, programs in this area may run into objections from people who say "Why spend time and money on 'bad' kids?" (Howell, 1995). The answer, of course, is that by choosing to help these students we also choose to help our own children and ourselves. As Boulding put it:

"Every normal human being is constantly making judgments about good and bad, better and worse. These judgments of good and bad, better and worse, are not only subjects of reflection or conversation, they are also absolutely necessary in any process of decision. A decision essentially involves a choice among different images of the future that we conceive to be within our power to achieve."

K. E. Boulding (1985)

# Chapter 14

# Task-Related Behaviors

*Excellence is a range of differences, not a spot. Each location on the range can be occupied by an excellent or an inadequate representative—and we must struggle for excellence at each of these varied locations.*
—Stephen Jay Gould, *Full House* (1996), p. 229

*I can explain it to you again, but I can't understand it for you.*
—Mary Doria Russell, *The Sparrow* (1996), p. 245

Ken Howell once had a student, Jennifer, come in to complain about her student teaching placement. It seemed that the cooperating teacher in the schools had given his fourth-grade social studies students an assignment to write a paper about a particular state. But after the first draft he had complained loudly about the quality of the papers and the students, in front of the class and other teachers at lunch.

"Why did he complain?" Howell asked.

"Because most of the first drafts were really bad," Jennifer replied.

"So?"

"He was saying how poor the class was and how *stupid* some of the kids were."

"But you did say they had done a poor job."

"Yes," Jennifer responded. "But he never taught them how to write a major paper."

"Of course not," Howell, a little slow to catch on, reminded her. "It was a social studies class."

"But he called them *dumb* and gave them low grades because they couldn't do something that he didn't teach." Jennifer was exasperated.

"Well," Howell recalled, "I've asked you to write papers for classes and I don't teach that content either."

"But for your classes that's a reasonable expectation."

Because this was one of the few times anyone had ever associated one of his classes with the word "reasonable," Howell thought about it. "Okay, he is clearly behaving in an

*Strategy instruction teaches procedures for using previously learned skills.*

unprofessional manner when he calls kids dumb for failing to do what they have never been taught. But, there is another issue here. One accepts that he *is* unreasonable in his expectation of fourth-graders, and I am *not* in my expectations for university seniors—where is the boundary that separates us?"

What do you think? When is it reasonable to expect students to have the skills to display their knowledge in the form of a paper? Were you ever taught an explicit strategy for writing a class paper? And, were you taught that strategy in or before fourth grade?

Today, most adults in higher education have been taught how to write papers (typically in grade 7 or above), but few were taught that skill in or before fourth grade (and some report they were never taught it.)

Was Jennifer right to be upset? Or, to put it another way, "Is it fair to expect students to display their knowledge in ways that they have never learned?"

## Step 1: Define the Purpose

Knowing how to acquire, process, and display knowledge are all examples of task-related skills (TR). Students who don't seem to learn without the benefit of highly tailored instruction may be missing these skills. Although their failures to learn are regularly attributed to unalterable variables such as being "dumb," that is not the case. These students fail to learn because they lack necessary knowledge about learning in typical classrooms (Deshler et al., 1996). The purpose of this chapter is to guide decision making within the domain of task-related behavior. By following the procedures, one should be able to select objectives, and the correct teaching recommendations, for this important area.

## Step 2: Define the Thing to Be Measured

Task-related skills embody a wide range of skills that lead to school success (Deshler et al., 1996; Gorden, 1994; Liborowski, 1995; Mercer et al., 1996). These include following directions, completing tasks, attending, accepting authority, having an adaptive attitude about work, and maintaining positive beliefs about the value of tasks. TR skills are not peripheral to schooling; they are essential for learning the curriculum. The exact content of TR behavior remains unclear, and there are almost no published devices for evaluating it. However, many educators have come to realize that it is often easier (and almost always more productive) to teach a student how to learn from the same instruction that is working with most other students, than it is to arrange completely personalized instruction for the majority of students with learning problems (Mercer et al., 1996).

Exhibit 14.1 is a list of TR skills. The exhibit has seven major subdivisions. These have been set up to facilitate our explanation of the content and the evaluation processes. In actuality, they are highly interdependent. Problems in any or all of these areas may be used as an assumed cause for a student's failure in a conventional academic area (such as reading or social studies).

### Class Support

Often, learning failure occurs because of a mismatch between the student's needs and what is being provided in the class (as a student you probably experienced such a mismatch). The purpose of evaluating class support is to find out if there is a mismatch and if reasonable accommodations in instruction, and/or modifications in curriculum or materials, can be made so that the student will learn. An operational definition of class support has yet to evolve from the considerable discussion—but fairly limited research—on the topic. However, one logical position has been taken by Göncü and Rogoff (1998). They viewed support as effective if students learned more with it than they would without it. That would also be the current authors' position (it is not a hard idea to accept). In other words, an action taken by a teacher is considered supportive if it enhances student learning. Therefore, although actions are undertaken by teachers, they are defined as supportive by their students.

Considerable information about the delivery of instruction was presented in Chapter 4 and Appendix 13. We recognize that all teachers don't run lessons the same way. Therefore, students must acquire systems for learning that will generalize across content and teachers. Students must learn to "individualize" for teachers. However, just as students must be flexible, instructors are expected to make reasonable accommodations, and even modifications, for students. Accommodations are made in teaching (such as providing the student with an outline of every lecture), whereas modifications are made in curriculum and/or materials (such as deciding that a student does not need to be taught cursive). The distinction between accommodations and modifications was discussed in Chapter 6.

Accommodations should be nothing more than adjustments, or "fine tuning," of the effective practices outlined in Chapter 4. Modifications of the learning expectations are serious. They are adjustments of the curriculum or material attributes described in Chapter 3 (for example, the content, conditions, behavior, and CAP changes on page **54–57**). Although the evaluation of class support is difficult, it is required for a thorough evaluation (Warner et al., 1996). If changes are required that are unreasonable for a general classroom teacher to make, then a request for support services may be needed.

### Prior Knowledge

A student's prior knowledge of a topic is generally the best predictor of success in any lesson. Chapters 9–13 of this text deal with topical knowledge from the domains of literacy and social skills. These domains were selected because they are pivotal to success in so many endeavors and, as a result, are the source of so many referrals for support services. However, there are other domains of knowledge in which students may be deficient. These include the various subjects in the arts, science, social studies, transition, technology, and the humanities.

### Study and Test-Taking Skills

The quality of the study and test-taking skills a student uses influences how much he will learn (Deshler et al., 1996). Study skills are those things that allow the student to make use of instruction. Test-taking skills are those things that allow a student to display what she has learned (Antes, 1989; Elliot et al., 1998). The skills apply differently to each form of instruction and testing. As you can imagine, if one teacher lectures and gives multiple-choice tests while another assigns readings and gives essay exams, some students may do better in one class than in the other.

Exhibit 14.1 lists content for study skills and test taking. Much of this content was drawn from the work of Gleason et al. (1991) and Deshler et al., (1996). However, it is consistent with skill sequences originally produced by Schumaker et al.

*Exhibit 14.1    Content of Task-Related Knowledge.*

Part A: Class Support

*The Student Has the Skill and Knowledge*
*Needed to Learn in this Setting:*
Descriptors:
> Instructional presentation
> Classroom environment
> Teaching expectations
> Cognitive emphasis
> Motivational strategies
> Relevant practice
> Academic engaged time
> Informal feedback
> Adaptive instruction
> Progress evaluation
> Instructional Planning
> Checks for student understanding

Part B: Prior Knowledge

*The Student Has Required Prior Knowledge:*
Descriptors:
> Has taken prerequisite classes
> Received acceptable grades in prerequisite classes
> Understands text and presentations
> Knows topical vocabulary
> Is familiar with related topics

Part C: Study and Test-Taking Skills

*Study and Test-taking Skills Are Adequate:*
*Before Class:*
Descriptors:
> Arrives on time
> Enters in a pleasant manner
> Brings materials to class
> Gets ready for learning

*During Class:*
Descriptors:
> Follows classroom rules
> Listens carefully
> Works during class
> Asks for assistance
> Moves quickly to new activity

*After Class:*
Descriptors:
> Takes materials home
> Completes homework
> Brings homework back

Part D: Self-Monitoring and Evaluation

*The Student Monitors and Evaluates Work:*
Descriptors:
> Self-monitors
> Recognizes errors
> Judges quality of work given criteria
> Judges quality of work on own

Part E: Problem Solving

*The Student's Problem Solving/Self-Monitoring*
*Is Adequate:*
Descriptors:
> Defines problems
> Identifies goals
> Identifies obstacles
> Recognizes types of problems
> Anticipates problems

*The Student Recognizes Types of Problems:*
Descriptors:
> Identifies open system
> Identifies closed system

*The Student Recognizes Solution:*
Descriptors:
> Generates options
> Considers resources
> Anticipates outcomes
> Selects solutions

*The Student Plans:*
Descriptors:
> Thinks before acting
> Explains what will happen
> Has immediate goals
> Allocates time

*The Student Works:*
Descriptors:
> Follows plan
> Follows schedule

Part F: Academic Motivation

*The Student Holds and Expresses These Beliefs:*
Descriptors:
> My goals are important, my learning
> Depends on what I do
> I'm a success as long as I improve
> My goals are interesting
> If I make a mistake I need to work hard to fix it

*Organization:*
Descriptors:
  Organization of materials (e.g., use of
  Notebook or folders)
  Organization of time (e.g., use of calendar,
  Scheduling work)
  Organization of content on paper (e.g.,
  heading, margins)

*Gaining Information:*
Descriptors:
  Reading expository material
  Reading narrative material
  Gaining information from verbal
  presentations (lectures, demonstrations)

*Demonstrating Knowledge or Skills:*
Descriptors:
  Completing daily assignments
  Answering written questions
  Writing narrative and expository products
  Preparing for and taking tests
  I am an important member of my class
  and my school

Part G: Basic Learning Skills
*The Student Uses Selective Attention:*
Descriptors:
  Focuses on relevant cues
  Ignores irrelevant cues
  Uses effective techniques to focus and
  maintain attention

*The Student Uses Recall/Memory:*
Descriptors:
  Recalls information
  Uses effective techniques to store and recall
  material

*The Student Uses Motivation:*
Descriptors:
  Perseveres in the face of difficulty
  Perceives value of task
  Maintains an adaptive explanatory style (i.e.,
  Is not "learned helplessness")
  Indicates feelings of control
  Uses effective techniques to maintain
  motivation

(1985). Those authors noted that, in later grades, students were expected to:

1. Work independently with little feedback;
2. Gain information from grade-level texts;
3. Gain information from lectures and discussions;
4. Demonstrate command of knowledge through tests; and
5. Express knowledge through writing.

The recognition of these classroom demands has led to the development of a copious body of "learning strategies" (see *Teaching Exceptional Children,* July/August, 1998, 30:6).

### Self-Monitoring and Evaluation

Because both problem solving and self-evaluation are so topic-specific, many procedures for evaluating them have already been placed in the topical chapters (see Chapters 10 and 13). Problem recognition is particularly important, as this is an area in which mildly disabled students, as a group, experience difficulty (Lloyd et al., 1991).

Self-monitoring is not the same thing as self-evaluation. Evaluation implies a comparison of one's own behavior to a standard. Self-monitoring is simply a student's awareness of what she is doing and what is going on nearby. Therefore, a student who is self-monitoring may have the skill to tell you that she is confused or angry without knowing if those things are even problems. As such, self-monitoring may not seem like a big deal, but all self-evaluation—and subsequent problem solving—depends upon it.

### Problem Solving

Most students with learning problems are in general education classrooms where all students need to follow directions, complete tasks, pay attention, accept authority, and maintain a positive attitude about learning. Numerous researchers have noted that students who experience academic or social-skill difficulties in school are poor at problem solving (see Chapter 2). The theme and content of problem solving has been mentioned many times throughout this text. Here is a set of general problem-solving steps that, when followed correctly, can help students succeed in many areas (the asterisks will be explained shortly):

- Recognize Problem
  1. Compare performance to expectations*
  2. Compare support to needs
- Identify Problem Type
  1. Open system
  2. Closed system
- Identify or Develop Solutions
  1. Generate potential solutions*
  2. Find solutions
- Select Solutions
  1. Consider resources
  2. Anticipate outcomes*
- Plan
  1. Develop a project design*
  2. Set a timeline
- Work
  1. Carry out plan
- Monitor and Adjust
  1. Self-monitor progress toward goal*
  2. Self-monitor implementation of plan
  3. Adjust plan if it isn't working*
  4. Ask for help when needed

Although this problem-solving strategy does not take the place of task-specific strategies (such as applying the steps for editing a first draft), it can provide students with a way to deal with most problems.

One of the steps is identification of problem type. Identification of problem type is critical, as some types of problems are solved differently than others. There are two types of generally rec-

ognized problems: *"open system"* and *"closed system"* (McCagg & Dansereau, 1991). Closed-system problems, which tend to have distinct and predictable boundaries, are solved through task-specific strategies called *algorithms* (dividing 6 by 2.3 or location of a phone number). Open-system problems have vague boundaries (selection of a friend or recognizing when to apologize) and are approached through **heuristics**.

When rating a student's problem solving, you must consider the situation in which she is working. "Recognizing when an assignment is complete" could involve distinct boundaries in one teacher's classroom and vague boundaries in another teacher's classroom. Therefore, the same problem-solving step can be open or closed depending on the context in which it occurs. Because the characteristic which distinguishes an open from a closed problem is the clarity of boundaries, certain steps in the problem-solving sequence will be especially hard. These are marked with an asterisk on the list above. Note that most require comparison. Obviously, comparison is difficult if one of the things being contrasted is unclear. In a case like this, efforts should first be made to define the thing (i.e., to specify the critical attributes of friendship). If that doesn't work, another system of problem solving, which does not require clear definition, may need to be used (this is not usually a problem within the academic areas). Some examples of heuristics that might be used to pick a solution are availability of the solution, familiarity with a solution, trial and error, copying from a mentor, or even guessing.

### Academic Motivation

Although there is evidence that students with learning problems are often deficient in basic learning, it is important to recognize that the content of *basic learning skills* (covered below and in Action 9) is often far removed from the curriculum students are expected to learn. Therefore, spending time on them is risky because it takes time away for the curriculum. They are also hard to assess in any instructionally relevant fashion. In most cases, we believe that it is easier to build attention, memory, and motivation through effective instruction than to attempt to measure and remediate any of these very dynamic aspects of learning.

Academic motivation, as opposed to the motivation skills required for all activities, can be functionally defined as perseverance on classroom learning tasks—even in the face of difficulty (Dweck, 1986). Some of the strongest effects found in the literature on poor academic performance fall into this area of academic motivation (Ames, 1992; Wigfield et al. 1998). Yet, as Ford (1995) points out, motivation is barely mentioned in many discussions of learning problems and their interventions.

Here is a set of key beliefs that the literature would seem to indicate are related to motivation.

---

### Key Beliefs: Related to Motivation

**1. Goals:**
My academic goals should be clear and important to me.

**2. Internal Effort Attributions:**
Achievement of my academic goals depends on what I do.

**3. Success:**
I am successful as long as I am learning and progressing toward academic goals.

**4. Interest:**
I am interested in learning my academic goals.

**5. Response to Errors:**
To learn best I must always keep working and look for other ways to study.

**6. School Partnership:**
I know that I am a part of this class, and belong in this school, because my teachers and administrators agree with me about points 1–5. I can tell by the things they say and the way they support me.

---

There are several important concepts embedded in this set of beliefs. Briefly, they are:

- That learning is goal oriented;

- That learning is change, not an accomplishment (an accomplishment is a result of learning but it is not learning);

- That success and failure should be defined by progress (or the lack of progress);

- That task difficulty changes with increases in skill; therefore, task difficulty, like intelligence, is not fixed;

- That the student is responsible for his or her own successes and failures (but this responsibility is for putting out needed effort; it is the result of alterable things like deciding when to adopt a new approach or intensity of work and perseverance at tasks; it is not the result of unalterable personal limitations, like low capacity); and

- That schools and teachers should work (through instruction) to have students personally adopt the goals of the curriculum; educators should also talk and act in ways that compliment the key beliefs and, as a result, help the student feel as if she belongs in the schools.

### Basic Learning Skills

Basic learning skills include the general phenomena we recognize as attention, memory, and motivation. This part deals primarily with attention and memory, and motivation. The discussion will draw heavily from content presented in Chapter 2. If you haven't read that chapter, or need to be refreshed relative to its content, it would be a good idea to do that right now. This discussion of more basic learning skills will come from a broader range of literature, and the recommendations should work in both classroom and non-classroom settings (such as at the dinner table).

Things like attention, memory, and motivation exist within executive control (see Chapter 2). They are complex and interactive sets of skills that predispose students to sort relevant from irrelevant cues, recall prior learning, and work hard (even in the face of failure). They are not, and cannot be, separated. Additionally, they cannot be detached from the various tasks that demand their use. This means that "attention" does not exist without something to which one can attend. It is appropriate, therefore, to say "The student does not attend to initial sounds." It is not appropriate to say "The student does not attend." No one, regardless of the impression conveyed by terms like "attention deficit disorder," lacks attention. Similarly, no one lacks memory or motivation. However, many students fail to effectively focus on specific cues, recall information about certain topics, and/or persevere in the face of failure.

## Step 3: Devise a Way to Make It Observable

The topics found on the sheet in Exhibit 14.1 do not, for the most part, appear within school curriculum guides. These are the things students are expected to know before they arrive in class (as illustrated by the Jennifer story). Unfortunately, because they are not in the curriculum, no one teaches them to those students that have not learned the TR skills. Similarly, this content has been generally ignored by evaluators. It is unlikely that any of you have ever heard someone say "Larry attends to lectures at the fourth-grade, third-month level" or "Dick scored at the 27th percentile in completing daily assignments." That's because traditional evaluation procedures and devices are not designed, or intended, for the assessment of task-related behavior. In fact, most evaluators and teachers scrupulously try to avoid making lessons and measures that are sensitive to it. A reading test score that reflects too much "careful listening" will be considered invalid. Similarly, a teacher who spends as much time preparing students to receive information as he does delivering information may be accused of "spoon feeding" the class. Yet, many teachers will grade on things like "organization" or "effort."

TR are sometimes called the "hidden" curriculum. And of course things that are hidden are hard to observe. Therefore, **Step 3** requires some innovative sampling processes. Often, you will need to find out about the student and the classroom through collaborative discussions, observation, structured interviewing, and assisted assessment.

## Steps 4–7: Assessment, CBE Inquiry, Summary, and Decision Making

Exhibit 14.2 summarizes the following directions and interpretations. The actions in Exhibit 14.2 are taken to answer the following questions.

1. Is the student failing to learn?
2. Does the problem pass the stranger test?
3. Does the problem pass the so-what test?
4. Can you specify problem areas?
5. Is the quality of instructional environment okay?
6. Does the student have the prior knowledge needed to learn this topic?
7. Does the student have adequate study and test-taking skills?
8. Does the student have adequate monitoring and problem-solving skills?
9. Does the student have adaptive academic motivation skills?
10. Does the student have adaptive basic learning skills?

The process of evaluation for task-related behaviors is presented in Exhibit 14.2. The first question in the exhibit asks "Is the student failing to learn?"

### Action 1: Screen for Inadequate Progress

The closest things to TR measures are grades, point totals, and class rankings. However, none of these are sensitive to short instructional efforts, but you can review them and talk with the teacher (if you are the teacher, just talk with yourself). Ideally, all students will be screened periodically, and students with learning problems will continuously be monitored.

### Interpretation

### Question 1: Is the Student Failing to Learn from Current Class Instruction?
If YES, then go to **Action 2**.
If NO, then discontinue.

*Exhibit 14.2* **The Process of Evaluating Task-Related Behavior.**

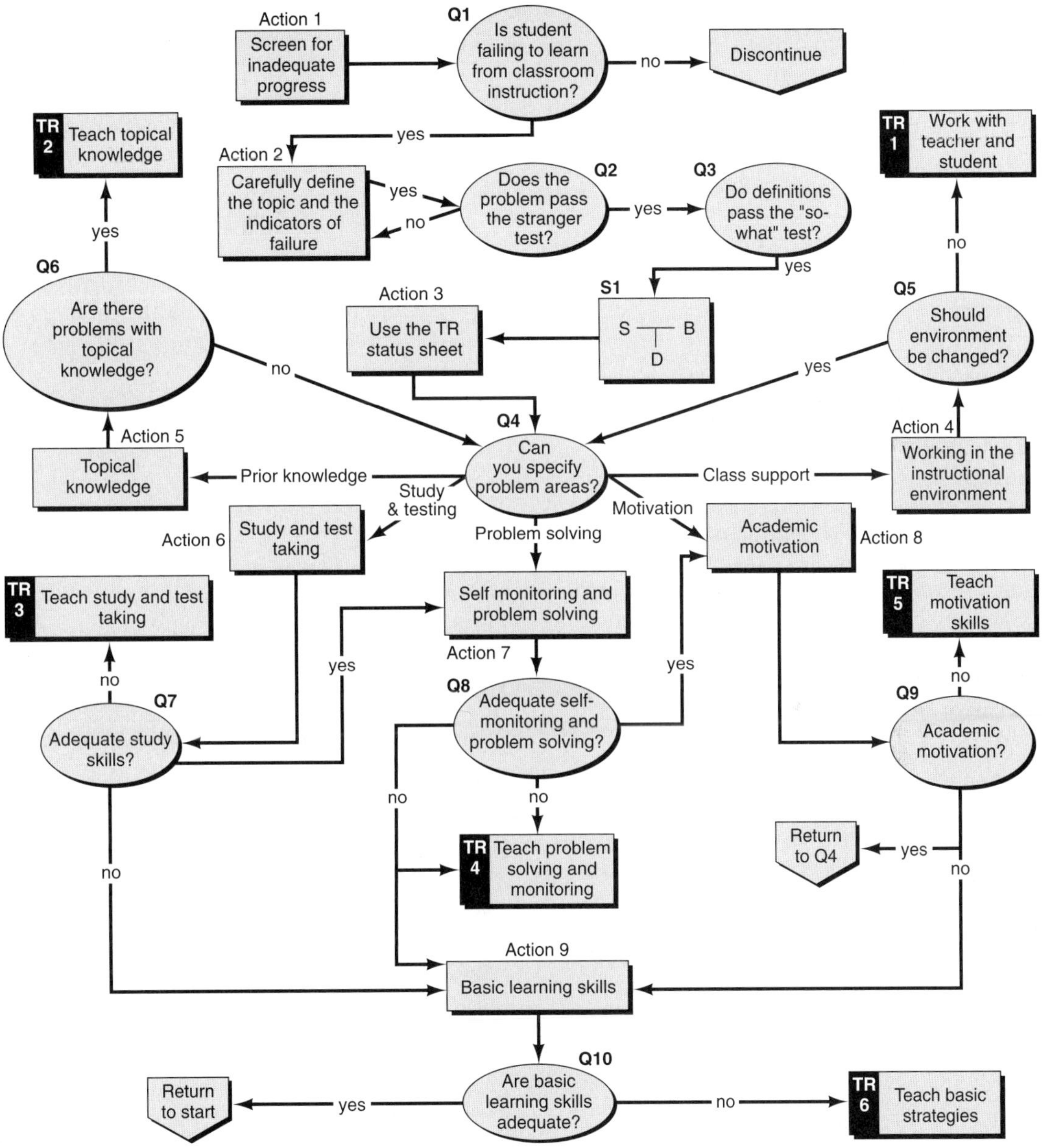

## Action 2: Carefully Define the Topic and the Indicators of Failure

Problems with task-related behaviors are indicated when a student fails to work efficiently, learn effectively, or to display knowledge adequately. This step is necessary because of the situational variability in instruction and the varying demands different topics place on prior knowledge. Don't merely state that the student is having trouble in social studies; try to identify the exact topics and activities that are problematic.

### Directions

Carefully define the topic and setting of suspected failure. Select topics, classes, and activities in which the student is having trouble. Be sure that you know exactly where, when, and under which conditions the student is experiencing difficulty. During this definition process, be sure to include information about the nature of the tasks (interactive/independent, long/short, directions clear or ambiguous), the composition of the work groups (large/small, skill-grouped or heterogeneous), and format of instruction (hands-on/hands-off, lecture/reading, process for delivering information, types of activities, how questions are asked, and how the student gets feedback and correction).

Once again, indicators of trouble may include things like low class grades, assignments done incorrectly, questions answered incorrectly, or items answered incorrectly on tests. Another option is to ask the teacher to rate the student's overall progress on this scale (but before you do that have a discussion on the meaning of "expected rate"):

1 = getting worse

2 = no improvement

3 = improving at only 1/4 of expected rate

4 = improving at 1/2 of expected rate

5 = improving at 3/4 of expected rate

6 = improving at or above expected rate.

## Question 2: Do Definitions Pass the Stranger Test?

### Directions

If you forgot it, look up the "stranger test" in the glossary. The depiction of the problem should be so accurate that another professional, upon reading it, would be able to identify the same problem you are working to correct.

### Interpretation

If YES, ask **Question 3**.
If NO, go back to **Action 2** and try again.

## Question 3: Do Definitions Pass the So-What Test?

### Directions

Once again, if you forgot it look it up in the glossary. The problem must be important enough to work on. Allocating instructional time to it, and fixing it, should have a positive impact on student learning.

### Interpretation

If NO, then don't worry about a task-related problem—apparently there isn't one.

If YES, then summarize the discrepancy as a score in **Summary 1**. The score will tell the difference between what the student is doing and what the student should be doing (for example, out of a total of 200 test items given so far, the student correctly answered 75 when 180 was expected (a discrepancy of +105).

If you are using the 6-point scale presented above, 6 would be the standard, the teacher rating would be the behavior, and the discrepancy would be the difference (that is, if the rating is 3, the ratio discrepancy would be ×2).

Go to Action 3.

### Action 3: TR Status Sheet

#### Question 4: Can You Specify Problem Areas?

#### Directions

Fill out the status sheet shown in Appendix A.9. Follow the directions on the sheet. We will describe each part of the sheet in sequence. However, you can go directly to those you have marked as NO or UNSURE.

#### Interpretation

The main purpose of the status sheet is to narrow the field of concern. This is a complex area (just look at that flow chart!), so use the status sheet to form an opinion about the student's success within each of the seven primary categories listed on the status sheet and then mark the appropriate box. This opinion should be based on the indicators under each category, and the confidence you have in judging them. Items marked NO become objectives, those marked YES are the student's PLEP, and those marked UNSURE need clarification through specific-level assessments.

If you think there are no problems in an area, ignore it (for now). If you are unsure, remember that you have the UNSURE option. Also, remember that a student may have problems in more than one category. From here on, you should follow the flow chart in Exhibit 14.2 and the interpretations attached to each procedure.

If class support seems low, then go to **Action 4**.

If prior topical knowledge seems low, then go to **Action 5**.

If study and test-taking skills seem weak, then go to **Action 6**.

If problem solving seems weak, then go to **Action 7**.

If motivation seems weak, then go to **Action 8**.

### Action 4: Class Support

It is necessary to gain information about the sort of instruction, curriculum, and materials em-ployed in the setting where the kid is failing. To finish this action, you will need to do structured interviews, observations, and/or reviews of materials and documents. So, you might want to read the earlier material on conducting observations and interviews.

#### Question 5: Does the Class Environment Support the Student's Learning?

#### Directions

#### Teaching

1. Conduct a series of short observations in the class (or instructional setting) at different times of day over several days.

    If you aren't the teacher, and you can't do the observations, try interviewing the teacher. If you are the teacher, a self-evaluation is possible, but we recommend getting someone else to come in and observe.

2. Summarize your observations according to the descriptors of effective classes found in Appendix A.13.

    Howell et al., 2000a contains TIES-II (Ysseldyke & Christenson, 1996) descriptors of effective instruction that have been categorized according to the schema presented in Chapter 4. These descriptors are cross-referenced to the original TIES-II components as summarized in Howell et al., 2000a. You might want to take a look at Howell et al., 2000a now.

    There are four ways to link a class observation to the descriptors:

1. Read the component descriptors and, using them as a holistic standard (an image of an exemplar), judge the quality of the environment; this is the fastest option.

2. Using the descriptors in Appendix A.13 as a check sheet, rate the instructional environment; then, use Exhibit 14.3 as a summary form to record the results.

3. Buy the TIES-II and use it. This should produce the most accurate information, as

*Exhibit 14.3   Summary Form for Student Knowledge.*

Student Name _____

Topic_____

Date _____

Evaluator Name _____

Directions:

1. List key ideas.
2. Mark conditions; test, essay, interview.
3. Mark the student's status using this key:
   C = answers correct
   CP = answers correct with prompts
   EP = error made with prompts
   E = error

| Key Idea(s) | Facts | Concepts | Principles/Rules | Note Incorrectly Used Terms Here |
|---|---|---|---|---|
| 1. | | | | |
| 2. | | | | |
| 3. | | | | |
| 4. | | | | |
| 5. | | | | |
| 6. | | | | |
| 7. | | | | |
| 8. | | | | |
| 9. | | | | |
| 10. | | | | |

the procedures have been standardized and observation techniques have been clarified; student interviews are also included.

4. Combine b and c by using the TIES-II to collect the data and then convert the results (using the cross-reference in Howell et al., 2000a) to the model of instruction in Exhibit 14.3. The use of Exhibit 14.3 has the advantage of producing results that are conceptually keyed to the presentation of instruction in Chapter 4. Due to the complexity of this topic, we are breaking this interpretation into several questions.

### Interpretation. Ask each question (5.1–5.4).

#### Question 5.1: Is the Quality of the Teaching OK?

If YES, then return to Q4.

If NO, then go to **Teaching Recommendation 1**.

#### Question 5.2: Is the Curriculum OK?

Remember that, for students in special education, the curriculum is defined by the IEP. However, there is also a requirement in special education law that the student's progress in the general education curriculum be monitored (which is a good idea). When decisions about curriculum are being made, it is important to consider the following:

✓ Accommodations (use of alternative acquisition modes, content enhancements, alternative response models)

✓ Modifications (use of less material, different material, different products)

✓ Differential expectations (use of separate expectations for different groups of students)

✓ Alternative acquisition modes (use of videotape, audiotape, computer, reading, interpreters such as Braille, etc.)

✓ Content enhancements (use of visual displays, study guides, mnemonic devices, peer-mediated instruction, computer-assisted instruction)

✓ Alternative response modes (use of oral responding, untimed responding, computer/word processing, scribes)

✓ Differing evaluation procedures (use of alternative objectives, display formats, and standards)

### Directions: Judging Quality of Curriculum

Review the curriculum requirements for clarity, sequence, and importance (as described in Chapter 3). Use that information to inform your judgement.

### Question 5.2: Is the Curriculum Inadequate?

### Interpretation

If NO, then note discrepancies in curriculum, materials, and activities; then go to **Teaching Recommendation 1**.

If YES, then go to back to **Question 4**.

### Question 5.3: Are the Materials/Activities OK?

### Directions

1. Look over sample materials and review activities the student has been using and will be using in the next month.

2. Carefully review the TIES-II descriptors for relevant practice, especially the sections on task relevance and instructional material (these are found in Howell et al., 2000a). Remember that the primary requirement for any material, or activity, is alignment with currently relevant goals and objectives.

3. Using the TIES-II descriptors as a checklist, mark those areas that may not apply to the materials and/or activities the student uses.

### Interpretation

If you are using the full TIES-II you can obtain scores. Otherwise, there aren't any scoring conventions.

### Question 5.3: Are the Materials Adequate?

If NO, then note discrepancies and go to **Teaching Recommendation 1**.

If YES, then go back to **Question 4**.

### Question 5.4. Does the Student Have Access to Instruction and Materials?

This procedure is designed to find out if the student has the skills needed to access the materials. It is written as if the materials in question are text books. However, the same process can be applied to the directions and wording on worksheets or even to transcriptions of lectures. Also, remember that all access problems are not based on the student's academic skills. It is possible that, because of a physical or sensory impairment, the student will not have access. Additionally, when a process requires that the student work with peers, it is a good idea to consider interpersonal skills (Chapter 13) as part of access.

### Directions

1. Check the reading level of material against the student's skills by having her read them to you. Use the procedures and standards in Chapters 8 and 9.

2. Check the language demands against the student's skills by following procedures in Chapter 10.

3. Check to see if the teacher has adequate redundancy in his planning. Has he planned ways to teach the same skills so there is a back-up if a student has problems with certain materials or activities?

### Interpretation

Does the student have trouble accessing the materials and activities?

If NO, then go to Teaching Recommendation 1.

If YES, then go to Question 4.

### Action 5: Topical Knowledge

The importance of prior knowledge has been stressed throughout this text. However, the range of topical content taught in schools is simply too large for complete coverage in one book (we are talking about all human knowledge!). Still, there are a couple of fairly simple overlay techniques that can be applied to see if a student has adequate prior knowledge to benefit from lessons on a topic. The two parts of **Action 5** are topic-specific vocabulary and prior knowledge. Both should be given.

### Topic-Specific Vocabulary

### Directions

1. Select three passages, or lessons, that the student is about to read or be taught. Carefully analyze these current lessons and identify examples of prerequisite vocabulary knowledge. In highly organized topical domains, and with highly structured texts or teachers, this is fairly easy. If the material is not well-organized, try to find tests used in preceding units or classes. Then take the topic-specific terms from there.

2. To check key vocabulary, make up or use a test that follows the formats shown in Chapter 10 on page **309.** An example multiple-choice vocabulary test is shown in Exhibit 14.4. This test, along with others in math/science, social studies, language/ music, and everyday living, can be found in

Howell et al. (2000a). They were developed by selecting terms, at different curriculum levels, from the glossaries of published materials (see Chapter 6).

### Interpretation

For vocabulary, assuming the terms are critical, the criterion for each item is 100%. However, for a sample of 20 or more items, the expected criteria seem to be about 90%.

### Question 6.1: Did the Student Have Problems with Terminology?

If NO, then go back to **Question 4**.

If YES, then develop a list of topic-specific vocabulary. Teach this vocabulary with **Teaching Recommendation 2**.

### Background Information

The process of finding out about a student's background information is no different that the processes of testing, questioning, or requiring essays that teachers use every day. The only difference is the focus.

### Directions

There are many ways to go about this. Here are five (you only need one).

1. Ask for a summary. For example, say "You are about to read a set of passages dealing with the types, sources, and uses of energy." Then ask the student to tell you what she *already* knows about the topic and—this is important—what she expects to find in the passages (or lectures) when she reads (or hears) them.

2. Another way to check is to use the same technique employed to examine the quality of materials in **Action 4**. The process described there can be applied to the texts, directions, and wording on worksheets or even to transcriptions of lectures. It goes like this:

• Select three samples of at least 250 words from that portion of the text/lecture which the student will be expected to use next. If a text is not used in the class, find a text

*Exhibit 14.4   Multiple-Choice Vocabulary Test.*

1. Abyss
   a. infected cyst
   b. bottomless pit
   c. road equipment

2. Axis
   a. being able to reach something
   b. to keep changing one's mind
   c. straight line about which things revolve

3. Condense
   a. to make more compact
   b. change from solid to liquid
   c. a general agreement

4. Epicenter
   a. part of a continuing story
   b. earth's surface above the center of an earthquake
   c. inside concentric circle of a geometric form

5. Diatom
   a. unicellular algae
   b. four-sided figure
   c. combination of proton and electron

6. Saturation
   a. holding up to ridicule
   b. make a strong promise
   c. maximum concentration

7. Solstice
   a. point of greatest distance from sun
   b. point of closest distance from sun
   c. electromagnetic switch

8. Species
   a. one of a kind
   b. biological classification below genus
   c. a scale of values

9. Blood pressure
   a. pressure exerted by the blood
   b. pressure at which the veins burst
   c. hemoglobin count

10. Convex
    a. curved in
    b. curved out
    c. violent shaking

11. Pasteurization
    a. soft, pale colors
    b. branching out from the center
    c. partial sterilization by heat

12. Reflex
    a. related to the subject of the sentence
    b. type of blood vessel
    c. an inborn act

13. Algorithm
    a. step-by-step procedures
    b. letters representing numbers
    c. musical composition

14. Arc
    a. a scenic representation
    b. line from center of circle to perimeter
    c. curved line between two points

15. Ellipse
    a. partial blocking of the sun
    b. a glowing fragment
    c. oval shape

16. Equilateral
    a. having all angles equal
    b. having all sides equal
    c. many sided figure

17. Exponent
    a. symbol indicating power of a number
    b. an integral part
    c. a structural form

18. Median
    a. average score
    b. fortune teller
    c. middle score

19. Pi
    a. 6.28
    b. 3.14
    c. 1/2 of 3.14

20. Rational number
    a. number used only in equations
    b. divisible by a finite number of times
    c. computer related

*Source:* Howell, K. W., Zucker, S. H. & Morehead, M. K. (2000b). *Multilevel Academic Skills Inventory.* Bellingham, WA: Applied Research and Development Center.

To order contact the Student Co-op Bookstore, Western Washington University. FAX (360) 650-2888. Phone (360) 650-3656. Reprinted with permission.

covering the same content or transcribe lectures.

- Using these samples, develop either maze or cloze tests as explained in Chapter 8. The use of maze is probably superior in this case, as the words generated by blanking out every fifth word can be used as a bank of topic-related distracters. Words from all three passages may be put in a distracter pool from which the two incorrect choices for each item can be selected.

- Administer and score the tests as explained in Chapter 8.

3. To more directly target information about key ideas, use texts, materials, or lectures to pick out critical *facts*, *concepts*, and *principles and rules* related directly to that idea. List the key idea, along with the facts, concepts, and principles on the interview form in Exhibit 14.3.

4. The form in Exhibit 14.3 can be used as an assessment summary. To test, ask the student to supply examples of each category of knowledge for the key ideas listed. Or, you could ask the student to write an essay on the idea and then scan for the examples and record what you find by using Exhibit 14.3 as a summary sheet.

5. You may wish to interview the student by asking questions like "Tell me what you know about [insert key idea]," and again use Exhibit 14.3 as a summary sheet. Or, you could ask a direct question about each <u>fact</u> (that is, "How many [insert fact] were there?"), <u>concept</u> ("Do you think the novels of William Kennedy might be considered an example of [insert concept]?"), or <u>principle</u> ("In general, how might you use what you know about [insert principle] to predict what will happen next in this story?"). Score the student's reaction to your questions.

This all may seem very complex, but actually, once you have identified the key ideas, and the facts, concepts, and principles that go with them, it is easy to do the rest. This is something a teacher of the topic ought to be able to do quickly. If for some reason you have been put in the position of evaluating a student to find out why she is failing in a class you don't teach, then the referring teacher will have to cooperate and supply the information.

### Interpretation

If the information identified is critical, the criteria are 100%.

This standard may be lowered if the expectation for all students is lower. However, an absolute criteria cannot be determined. Certainly for any key fact, concept, or principle, the expectation should be that a student knows it. In addition, even though the emphasis in many texts and lectures is on facts, misunderstanding of any important concept or principle should outweigh knowledge of numerous facts.

### Question 6.2: Is the Student Missing the Background Information Needed to Learn This Topic?

If NO, assume the student has adequate prior knowledge but be prepared to repeat this process on other topics.

If YES, use the summary sheet to analyze what information is missing so that you can tailor the student's instruction to her needs. Also, you might want to repeat the process on material that should have been taught in earlier lessons. This is done in an attempt to locate the student's current level of knowledge regarding the topic.

### Action 6: Study Skills and Test-Taking Skills

Study and test-taking skills were outlined in Part C of Exhibit 14.1. Each of these skills is most appropriately examined through observation and interview techniques. Because they can be expected to occur with varying levels of success within different teaching environments, it is important to clearly define the situations in which you observe the student.

### Directions

1. Review the status sheet in Appendix A.9 and note the categories under Part C in which the student seems to be having trouble.

2. Using the checklist in Exhibit 14.5, begin at the right-hand side and observe for the appropriate and spontaneous use of each skill. You may need to observe for several sessions and provide opportunities for this use to occur. If it does not occur spontaneously, provide assistance in the form of prompts or instruction to see if you can get the student to employ the skill. On the checklist, be sure to note the kind of assistance you provide.

3. If the use of a particular study or test-taking skill cannot be observed, ask the student to explain it. If the student doesn't do that, see if she can identify examples of spontaneous use, or through role-playing.

### Interpretation

### Question 7: Did the Student Appropriately and Spontaneously Employ Each of the Study Skills and Test-Taking Skills Listed in Exhibits 14.1 and 14.5?

If YES, then go to **Action 7**.

If NO, then go to **Action 9** and use **Teaching Recommendation 3**. Teach the missing skills by starting at the level of current functioning and specifying objectives across the know/apply axis of 14.5. For example, the "during class" content was used to produce the following sequence of objectives.

4. The student will spontaneously move quickly to a new activity when the teacher signals to the class that it is time. CAP: 90%.

3. Given the support of additional prompts and/or signals, the student will move quickly to a new activity. CAP: 100%.

2. When asked, the student will explain the process, and reason for, moving quickly to a new activity. [The explanation will conform to the material the student has been taught regarding classroom transitions.] CAP: 100%.

1. When shown items representing examples and nonexamples of students moving

quickly to a new activity, the student will correctly categorize the items. CAP: 100%.

The criteria for these objectives, because they are generic, may not be good for every skill. These sorts of objectives can be addressed with **Teaching Recommendation 3**.

### Action 7: Problem Solving and Self-Monitoring

This content was explained in depth in Chapter 2. **Action 7** includes two related sets of skills. It also uses three tools: Parts D and E of the status sheet in Appendix A.9 (you may as well fill out both parts at once) and the table in the following text.

### Directions: Part D—Self-Monitoring

Fill out Part D of the status sheet presented in Exhibit 14.1. To fill out the status sheet, meet with others who are familiar with the student's work in the classroom. If at all possible, fill one out with the student.

### Interpretation

### Question 8 (for Part D): Is the Status of Self-Monitoring OK?

If YES, then go on to Part E of the status sheet and **Actions 8 and 9**.

If NO, then go to **Teaching Recommendation 4** and Part E.

### Objectives

The student should spontaneously employ each of the skills listed in Part D and Appendix A.9. If that doesn't happen, she should be taught to do so by starting at the level of current functioning and specifying objectives across the know/apply axis. For example, the monitoring content was used to produce the following sequence of objectives.

4. The student will spontaneously recognize problems [in a specified domain] which have the potential of interfering with work. This recognition will be indicated by a

*Exhibit 14.5    Checklist for Study/Test Taking and Problem Solving/Self-Monitoring.*

Directions:

    1. Start on the right and move left if skill is not passed.
    2. Designate skills as passed (P) or no-pass (NP).
    3. Judge each heading by summarizing the status of the majority of descriptors under that heading.

| | Know | | Apply | |
|---|---|---|---|---|
| | Recognize | Explain | With prompts | Spontaneously |
| **Study and Test Taking** | | | | |
| **Before Class:** | ____ | ____ | ____ | ____ |
| Arrives on time | | | | |
| Enters in a pleasant manner | | | | |
| Brings materials to class | | | | |
| Gets ready for learning | | | | |
| **During Class:** | ____ | ____ | ____ | ____ |
| Follows classroom rules | | | | |
| Listens carefully | | | | |
| Works during class | | | | |
| Asks for assistance | | | | |
| Moves quickly to new activity | | | | |
| **After Class:** | ____ | ____ | ____ | ____ |
| Takes materials home | | | | |
| Completes homework | | | | |
| Brings homework back | | | | |
| **Organization:** | ____ | ____ | ____ | ____ |
| Organization of materials (use of notebook or folders) | | | | |
| Organization of time (use of calendar, scheduling work) | | | | |
| Organization of content on paper (heading, margins) | | | | |
| **Gaining Information:** | ____ | ____ | ____ | ____ |
| Reading expository material | | | | |
| Reading narrative material | | | | |
| Gaining information from verbal presentations (lectures, demonstrations) | | | | |
| **Demonstrating Knowledge or Skills:** | ____ | ____ | ____ | ____ |
| Completing daily assignments | | | | |
| Answering written questions | | | | |
| Writing narrative and expository products | | | | |
| Preparing for and taking tests | | | | |

| | Know | | Apply | |
|---|---|---|---|---|
| | Recognize | Explain | With prompts | Spontaneously |
| Problem Solving | | | | |
| **Recognizes Problem:** <br> Defines problems <br> Identifies goals <br> Identifies obstacles <br> Recognizes types of problems <br> Anticipates problems | ____ | ____ | ____ | ____ |
| **Identify Problem Type:** <br> Open system <br> Closed system <br> Identify or develop solutions | ____ | ____ | ____ | ____ |
| **Select Solutions:** <br> Generates options <br> Considers resources <br> Anticipates outcomes <br> Selects solutions | ____ | ____ | ____ | ____ |
| **Plans:** <br> Thinks before acting <br> Explains what will happen <br> Has immediate goals <br> Allocates time | ____ | ____ | ____ | ____ |
| **Works:** <br> Follows plan <br> Follows schedule | ____ | ____ | ____ | ____ |

labeling statement ("Oops, I think I've got a problem") or by beginning efforts at problem resolution/avoidance. CAP: 85%.

3. Given the support of prompts and/or signals, the student will recognize problems [in the specified domain]. Recognition will be indicated by labeling. CAP: 100%.

2. When asked, the student will explain the process of self-evaluation. The explanation will conform to the material which the student has been taught regarding monitoring. CAP: 100%.

1. When shown items (cartoon or role-play) representing examples and nonexamples of monitoring [in the specified domain], the

student will correctly categorize the items. CAP: 100%.

This set of objectives could be used across many content areas (such as social skills, computation, written expression). The wording "[in the specified domain]" is inserted to allow the objectives to be modified. The criteria for these objectives, because they are generic, may not be good for every skill.

### Directions: Part E—Problem Solving

Fill out Part E of the status sheet presented in Appendix A.9. The following table should help to clarify some of the content in that part of the status sheet. The "appropriate examples" in this table should also help you select objectives.

| Indicators of Problem-Solving Skill | Appropriate Example | Inappropriate Example |
|---|---|---|
| Is a self starter. | Immediately recognizes when to start work. | Requires prompts and reminders to start work. |
| Behaves differently on different tasks. | Adjusts study time and working strategy according to task demands. | Spends the same amount of time on tasks (regardless of difficulty) and often approaches new tasks by using strategies which worked on previous ones. |
| Knows the requirements of different tasks. | Can compare the salient demands of different tasks. | When asked to compare tasks, misses some features which would determine how to do each task. |
| Recognizes errors. | Recognizes when an error has been made. | Fails to recognize when an error has been made. |
| Attends to the way his/her behavior alters outcomes. | Notes which specific actions lead to improvement or to errors. | Does not identify actions that led to errors or successes on specific tasks. |
| Uses "means-end" analysis. between | Compares progress to goals and adjusts work if progress is inadequate. | Cannot state if the difference actual and desired performance is getting greater or smaller. |
| Changes with feedback. | When (s)he recognizes that progress toward goal is inadequate, (s)he tries harder or uses a different approach. | When (s)he recognizes that progress is inadequate, (s)he continues using the same approach or changes to a less effective approach. |

Each of these skills is most appropriately examined through observation and interview techniques and can be expected to occur with varying levels of success within different teaching environments.

1. Using the checklist in Exhibit 14.5, begin at the right-hand side and observe for the spontaneous use of each problem-solving skill. You may need to spend several sessions to provide opportunities for this use to occur. If it does not occur spontaneously, then provide assistance in the form of prompts, lead questions, or instruction to see if you can get the student to appropriately employ the skill. On Exhibit 14.5, be sure to note the kind of assistance you provided.

2. If the use of a particular skill cannot be observed, ask the student to explain it. If the student can't explain, see if she can identify examples of problem solving used by other students or in role playing.

### Interpretation

#### Question 8 (14.1 for Part E): Is Problem Solving OK?

If YES, go to **Action 8**.

If NO, go to **Teaching Recommendation 4** and **Action 9**.

The student should spontaneously employ each of the skills listed in Exhibit 14.1 (Part E) and presented in the box above. If that doesn't happen, she should be taught to do so by starting at the level of current functioning and specifying objectives across the know/apply axis. The problem-solving content of Exhibit 14.1 was used to produce the following sequence of objectives.

5. The student will spontaneously solve problems [in the specified domain] which have the potential of interfering with work. These solutions should follow the procedures taught in class (CAP: 90%), and they should actually lead to a successful resolution whenever possible.

4. When asked what would happen if a certain step were left out of one of the strategies used in Objective 3, the student will correctly anticipate the effect. CAP: 95%.

3. Given the support of prompts and/or signals, the student will solve problems [in the specified domain]. These solutions should follow the procedures taught in class. CAP: 100%.

2. When asked, the student will explain the process of solving problems [in the specified domain] supplied by the teacher. The student will correctly explain a solution which will adequately solve the problem. CAP: 100%.

1. When shown items (cartoon or role play) representing examples and nonexamples of correct problem solving [in the specified domain], the student will correctly categorize the items. CAP: 100%.

This set of objects could be used across many content domains (such as social skills, computation, written expression). The criteria for these objectives, because they are generic, may not be good for every skill.

Problem solving can be taught using **Teaching Recommendation 4**.

### Action 8: Academic Motivation

Academic motivation skills were outlined in Part F of Exhibit 14.1. Each of these beliefs is most appropriately illustrated through testing and structured interview techniques. They can be expected to occur with varying levels of success within different teaching environments because motivation is highly related to context.

There are two parts to this Action: a test and an interview. However, they can be administered and interpreted in tandem. They are both referenced to the Key Beliefs listed in Exhibit 14.1, Part F.

1. Give the test shown in Exhibit 14.6 (it is also in Howell et al. (2000a) and Appendix A.10). Don't show the answer key. The test should be worked by the student; however, if she can't read it, you should read it to her while she follows along. Stop after each item and ask her to mark her answer. Try hard not to cue your preferred answer and do not give feedback on the quality of her work.

2. Follow the test with the interview in Exhibit 14.7 (it is also in Howell et al. (2000a) and in Appendix A.11). Define terms that may be unfamiliar to the kid (for example, "expectations," "vague," or "belong"). Ask the questions. Take notes on the answers. If the student does not talk or gives unclear answers, you should give lead questions and other prompts (but note their use).

3. If you have taken **Action 5**, review the student's work to see if there was evidence of avoidance behavior or comments indicating a dislike for the task.

4. Score the test and summarize the interview using the test key and interview keys in Appendix A.10 and Appendix A.11. Summarize performance by category to see if you can recognize a pattern to the responses. For example, if the student gave inappropriate responses to most of the "partnership" items while giving appropriate answers to most of the others, this could mean her perception of partnership is low.

### Question 9: Is Academic Motivation OK?

#### Interpretation

If YES, go back to **Question 4**.

If NO, the student's academic motivation seems to be low. Go to **Action 9** and use **Teaching Recommendation 5**.

Use the presenting indicators from Part F of the status sheet (or from particular concerns you and/or a referring teacher may have had) to find a specific behavior for the objective. Then, add in

*Exhibit 14.6   Motivation.*

Answer "yes" or "no" to the following questions:

1.  I work best when I know what I am trying to learn.
2.  If I fail it is most likely because the task is too hard.
3.  I don't need to get the best score in class, I just need to do better than I have before.
4.  I don't find most school work to be interesting.
5.  If I make mistakes it means I should think about changing the way I am studying.
6.  During class my teacher sometimes compares my work to others.
7.  I only study what the teacher wants me to know.
8.  If I fail it is my job to fix the problem.
9.  I like to pick simple things to do so I'll get a good grade.
10. I find most school work interesting.
11. If I'm doing well I don't need to study as much.
12. The teacher knows my goals and helps me reach them.
13. It is hard for me to learn when I don't know exactly what I'm supposed to know by the end of the lesson.
14. I often get high grades because I am very smart.
15. I like to pick hard things to do because I feel good when I learn something challenging.
16. If I could pick stuff to learn it wouldn't be what we have to study.
17. When I am having trouble learning something it means I must work harder.
18. Sometimes it seems like my teacher is more interested in my finishing the work than in my learning.
19. Knowing that I must reach a certain target makes the lesson scary and/or unpleasant.
20. My teacher doesn't give me grades, I earn them.
21. It doesn't matter if I get a higher score than last time; all that matters is that I get a good score.
22. The things I am learning in class are the things I would like to be learning anyhow.
23. If I make mistakes I should stop working because I've run into something I can't do.
24. In our school there are as many rewards for improvement in classes as there are for attendance and sports.

*Exhibit 14.7   Interview Questions.*

(Talk about classes in which student is having trouble)

1.1 When you do school work in [name subject of class] do you like to know exactly what is expected of you, or would you rather the expectations were open or vague?

**Follow-up**

1.2 Why?

1.3 Does your [name subject of class] teacher usually supply vague expectations or clear expectations?

2.1 Who is mainly responsible for you meeting goals in [name subject of class], you or your teacher?

**Follow-up**

2.2 Why?

2.3 What does your [name subject of class] teacher say to let you know if he or she is mainly responsible for your learning or if you are responsible?

3.1 Do you feel most successful in [name subject of class] when you think you've learned a lot or when you get a high grade?

**Follow-up**

3.2 Why?

3.3 What does your [name subject of class] teacher do to let you know if he or she thinks high grades or learning is most important?

4.1 If something seems uninteresting to you do you study it anyhow, try to get interested in it, or avoid studying it?

5.1 In [name subject of class] when you run into something that seems hard to do, do you usually stop working or try working harder?

**Follow-up**

5.2 Why?

5.3 When you run into something that seems hard what does your [name subject of class] teacher do?

6.1 Do you feel like you are a part of this school and that you belong here?

**Follow-up**

6.2 Why?

6.3 What does your [name subject of class] teacher do that might help make you feel you don't belong, or that you do belong?

wording for the categories of motivation to complete the objective. For example, suppose you have a student who has, upon failure, been tearing up work and throwing it at other students. How would this be for an alternative? "Upon experiencing failure at a task the student will, without [a defined] outburst, illustrate perseverance by continuing to work, noting the problem for later and/or appropriately asking for help." As will be explained in **Teaching Recommendation 5**, such objectives are not always addressed head on.

### Action 9: Basic Learning

The basic learning skills emphasized in this section are general motivation (as opposed to academic-specific motivation), selective attention, and recall. These were all described in Chapter 2.

Although many tests of "attention," "self-concept," and "memory" exist, they often have little if any classroom utility. There are two reasons for this: first, this content is a long way from the curricula; second, the nature of these constructs simply prohibits the production of any single test that is aligned with all of the various demands of individual tasks and classes. Yet, everyone knows that knowledge of basic learning skills is important for classroom success.

The problem is that to have a measure of attention that is relevant to reading, for example, it has to have reading content on it. This is because attention to reading cues can be unrelated to attention to computation cues. Similarly, attention to Dr. Kelley's lectures may require different skills than attention to Dr. Bigelow's lectures. The secret to evaluating basic learning skills, therefore, does not lie in the development of attention tests. It lies in the development of academic tests highly sensitive to learning. In case you don't recognize where this is going, we're talking about assisted assessment (see Chapters 3 and 7).

In Chapter 8, we told you the way to find out if a student isn't self-evaluating is to provide monitoring assistance to the student and observe its effect. This is the format we recommend using whenever hypotheses about basic learning strategies are developed. Assisted assessment involves repeated measures taken across time to reflect the impact of various levels of assistance. The repeated measures must employ learning-sensitive curriculum-based samples. To aid interpretation, the assistance should be provided within a *defined sequence* so that conclusions about its impact can be formed.

The sequence of assistance we suggest for basic learning strategies is illustrated in Exhibit 14.8. There are four levels of assistance: prompts, directions, practice, and lessons. Prompts are used to activate skills the student has already learned. They are conveniently thought of as reminders. Directions are explicit calls for the use of a skill. Practice is designed to promote proficiency on existing skills. Lessons are designed to teach a skill that is not known. Exhibit 14.8 provides brief examples of teacher actions that might be employed at each level of assistance to promote attention, memory, and motivation. To understand these actions, you may need to review material in Chapters 2 and 4.

## Directions

1. Fill out Part G of the status sheet (Appendix A.9).
2. Select an academic area in which the student has problems.
3. Assess the student's status in the area using tests, observations, or assignments. These must yield scores that are sensitive to instruction (words read per minute, items worked correctly). A GOM is best. Refer to the monitoring procedures recommended in the chapters. Additional information on formative evaluation can be found in Howell et al. (2000a).
4. Provide assistance by using the techniques presented for the first level of assistance (prompts). A digest of sample teacher actions for each basic skill area can be found in Howell et al., 2000a (you might want to look at those now).
5. Repeat the monitoring test or assignment given in Step 3 and note any improvement. Be aware that, if you need to move toward higher levels of assistance (levels 3 and 4), more sessions will be needed to produce an effect great enough to actually influence the scores on the monitoring. Summarize the effect of assistance by recording pre- and postassistance scores.
6. Repeat steps 1–5 until the required level of assistance has been found, or all levels of assistance have been exhausted.

### Question 10: Are Basic Learning Skills OK?

### Interpretation

There are no scoring rules for this procedure. However, the scoring rules and interpretation guidelines for the tasks used to monitor may be found in the topical chapter covering that task. Also, the techniques for data display and analysis presented in Howell et al. (2000a) should be employed to recognize and illustrate trends in progress resulting from the assistance.

**Exhibit 14.8   Basic Learning Skills and a Sequence of Assistance.**

Directions:

1. Take sensitive measure(s) of skill.
2. Provide first level of assistance.
3. Retest and note improvement.
4. Repeat until sufficient improvement is achieved.

|  | 1 | 2 | 3 | 4 |
|---|---|---|---|---|
|  | Prompt | Direction | Practice | Lesson |
| Attention | Use novelty to change and surprise. | Direct the student to stop and think before working. | Have the student identify critical attributes at rate. | Explain and demonstrate ways of recognizing critical attributes. |
| Memory | Tell the student to preview the lesson and link it to previous lessons. | Tell the student to use a technique like note taking, or a key word strategy. | Teach skills to high levels of proficiency if the student must recall them. | Help students develop realistic ideas about their memory skill—teach them to recognize difficult material. |
| Motivation | Be personally interested in, and enthusiastic about, the task. | Relate the task to its context. | Place greater value on overcoming a problem than on initial success. Show the student evidence of her progress. | Teach tasks in the context of higher level tasks. Explain that success is the result of student effort. |

If YES, then you are at the bottom of the flow chart. Once again, this is a problem! If you worked your way down here you may need to start over with **Action 1**. Or, try reviewing the flow chart to see if, now that you have collected more information, another area looks like a possible concern.

If NO, then go to **Teaching Recommendation 6**.

## Teaching Recommendations

### Teaching Recommendation 1: Work with Teacher and Student

It should be obvious by now that task-related skills represent a considerable range of content. They also require a wide variety of interventions. Some of these have already been covered in other chapters. But, there are some bits of advice that we can give. So here they are.

We begin with the assumption that the current circumstances of instruction and evaluation are not complementing the student's current knowledge in receiving, processing, and displaying knowledge. Therefore, the instruction needs to change. If the materials and/or activities are not relevant, or if they are poorly designed, they should be replaced. There are two key considerations when judging instructional materials and class activities. One is student *access*. The other is the quality of the activities and their *alignment* with the objectives being taught.

Although alignment probably can't be stressed enough, it is unlikely that you could have gotten this far in the text without reading the author's harping on the topic. So we'll be brief. You pick materials because they cover what needs to be taught, not because of colorful covers, charismatic sales people, or even price.

For a student to have *access* to materials, the student must have the skills required to acquire the information in the materials. The simplest example is a nonreading student being told to "... read Chapter 7 in the history text for next Tuesday's test." How could a nonreader gain access to the information? Well, you could get a history text the student can read (change the materials) or accommodate the student by letting someone read the text to her. (The option, teaching the kid to read, is not rational within the time constraint of "next Tuesday.") For some excellent advice on this particular problem, read Ciborowski (1995) and Lebzelter and Nowacek (1999).

There are cases where a mismatch between the student and an activity or resource is more subtle. In such cases, rather than try to pinpoint the interference, it is often most efficient to just change materials and see if the student's learning improves.

The use of materials and activities should always be somewhat flexible. Therefore, making a change should not be a big deal. In some cases, when materials are too hard to come by, or only a particular set has the alignment you need, then accommodations are called for. The TIES-II descriptions, especially the sections on task relevance and instructional material (these are found in Howell et al., 2000) should help you make decisions about the appropriateness of materials.

After examining the instructional environment and answering questions Q5.1–Q5.3. you may have identified changes that need to be made in teaching, the curricula, or materials/activities. However, making changes often requires support *to the teacher*. So you should decide if it is reasonable to expect the current teacher to make the changes you think the kid needs on her own. This decision is best made by a group. The standard should be "Is it reasonable to expect a typical teacher, with this teacher's current resources and class composition, to make this change on her own?" Remember, we all want each teacher to get all the help he can, but the resources needed for

support services are limited. There is no reason to expend those resources to prop up teachers who, due to missing prior knowledge of their own, can't go to a workshop or read a book to raise their skills to the typical level.

Ask this additional question: Does the teacher need outside support? If YES, ask for the support prior to implementing the teaching recommendations.

Teaching was covered in Chapter 4 and within the teaching recommendations found at the end of each content chapter. The first step in any move toward accommodation is to see to it that those techniques are being used. If not, a more systematic analysis of the instructional environment using a tool such as the TIES-II (Ysseldyke & Christenson, 1990) is called for.

What are the reasonable accommodations a teacher can be expected to make? The answer to that question depends on a variety of factors. For example, class size, the age of the students, the content being taught, how far behind the student needing the accommodation has fallen, and how much outside support is available to the teacher. It is because of the range of such variables that decisions about accommodation are often made by groups of educators.

Accommodations, because they do not change the substance of the learning task, are generally simple undertakings. But, what is simple depends on the teacher's knowledge of the intervention. Some common accommodations are peer tutoring, cooperative learning (Antil et al., 1998), extended instructional time, shifts to different materials, adjustments in size of instructional groups, adjustment in the composition of instructional groups, skill (not ability) grouping, instruction in study and test-taking skills, supplying a volunteer tutor, supplying a reader, giving the student a textbook in which another student has underlined critical information, and implementing a behavior management program. The research support for best practice is presented in Exhibit 14.9.

It is always a good idea to begin accommodations by using "natural supports" in the classroom (Grigal, 1998). Natural supports are broadly defined to include all supportive elements that already exist within a school (for example, time,

*Exhibit 14.9  Effective Methods.*

| Peacock Hill Working Group (1991) | Fisher et al. (1995) | King-Sears & Cummings (1996) | Lloyd et al. (1998) |
|---|---|---|---|
| ✓ Systemic, data-based interventions<br>✓ Continuous monitoring of progress<br>✓ Provision of practice for new skills<br>✓ Treatment matched to problem<br>✓ Multicomponent treatment<br>✓ Programming for transfer and maintenance<br>✓ Commitment to sustained intervention | ✓ Peer tutoring<br>✓ Cooperative learning<br>✓ Organizers/study guides<br>✓ Content enhancement routines<br>✓ Curriculum revision<br>✓ Strategies instruction | ✓ Curriculum-based assessment<br>✓ Cooperative learning<br>✓ Self-management<br>✓ Classwide peer tutoring<br>✓ Strategy instruction<br>✓ Direct instruction<br>✓ Goal setting | ✓ Early intervention<br>✓ Formative (curriculum based) evaluation<br>✓ Direct instruction<br>✓ Behavior modification<br>✓ Reading comprehension<br>✓ Mnemonic training |

curriculum, instruction, space, peers, all personnel, parents, and instructional materials). But this has its own strengths and weaknesses. Primary among the weaknesses is that, by accommodating the student, you may be making her more dependent (Giangreco et al., 1997; Landfried, 1987). Therefore, the support *must* be withdrawn as the student becomes more competent.

The implementation of any teaching accommodation is always a leap of faith. That is why accommodations must be monitored to see if the faith is justified. Remember that the student got to this point because she has fallen behind. She cannot afford to spend more time in an ineffective program.

### Modifying Curriculum and/or Instruction

Once again, the distinction between an accommodation and a modification is important. When you modify the curriculum, you are changing the definition of a student's education. Modifications often take the form of throwing out a skill, cutting

down criteria, or allowing atypical levels of support. Because of this, they are extremely serious. They are best made by a group that should include current teachers and the parents. If the student is getting special education services, modification decisions *must* be made in IEP meetings.

If a student is failing to progress to the point that modifications are being considered, then a more thorough examination of the curriculum is called for. What if it contains time-consuming objectives of limited importance to the student? What if it is poorly sequenced and/or unorganized? Just as good teaching is the baseline for making teaching accommodations, a good curriculum must be the baseline for curricular modifications. To further examine the quality of the curriculum, consider using the procedures described by Warner et al. (1996).

It is a good idea to remember that modifications do not just affect the student, they also affect future teachers who may have been expecting the student to know the things you have decided to modify. Therefore, it is important to record modification decisions and to see to it that no teacher asserts the expectation that the student know that skill in the future. For example, if it has been decided that a student will not be taught cursive but will stay with manuscript, it would be a professional violation (or in the case of a student on an IEP, a legal violation) for a future teacher to insist on cursive in his class. This is heavy stuff.

In our opinion, it is generally better to completely exclude a topic of study than to reduce the criteria. You could classify this under the fear that "a little knowledge is a dangerous thing." However, our main concern is that a student with a problem so great that it calls for modifications should not be wasting valuable instructional time learning skills to levels which are so low that they are not functional. It seems better to spend the time teaching useful substitute skills. For example, assume it has been determined that, given individual priorities, it is not worth the time it will take to teach a student to manage money. Then in place of those skills we would like to see the student taught how to go to a bank and arrange for direct deposit of pay and bank payment of bills. The student should also be told directly, and taught to understand, that she does <u>not</u> have the skills required to manage money.

A good test to use when considering modifications is the "rational relationship test." If a student has an unalterable limitation that can be rationally expected to limit the student in a particular activity, then teaching skills related to that activity *might* be a poor use of time. This could, for example, include modifying the graduation requirements for high school so that a deaf student is not required to take a music appreciation course. Or it might mean modifying the expectation that a nonreader use the internet without assistance. But even with these two examples, you should be able to imagine accommodations and variations which could allow the student access to the content (one can read about the history and qualities of music). The question, therefore, as always remains "Is it worth the cost—in student time, energy, and other learning?" If not, modify the curriculum.

## Teaching Recommendation 2: Build Topic-Specific Vocabulary

You may be surprised to find the vocabulary words in Exhibit 14.4 are from early grades. Many teachers have told us that they are considerably more sophisticated than the words found in reading books (particularly remedial readers) for those grades. However, these words *were* taken from lessons taught in the early grades. It is a mistake to assume that the vocabulary students need in classes is the same as the vocabulary in their reading book (Walpole, 1999). Besides, it is actually harder for a student to learn to read a word if it is not *already* in her speaking vocabulary. This means that it is better if the sophistication of vocabulary coming from other sources is higher than that in readers.

But then where does content-specific vocabulary come from? One good place to look is in the glossary of the materials used to teach content like science, art, or health.

Once the terms have been identified, there are several ways to teach them. Some of these are presented in Chapters 8 and 10. Others include the time honored, and apparently very effective, use of drill. A good way to conduct such drills is to pair two students who need to learn the definitions and give them a set of flash cards with the word on both sides (no definition). Also, give them a list of all the words, with definitions, in a folder. One of the students begins to flash the cards to the other and decides if the response is correct. If there is disagreement the two can refer to the supplemental word list. By having the two take turns showing the cards and judging the answers, each is required to identify and produce correct definitions. Fluency can be added to the exercise by only allowing a count of five, or three, before a word is judged to be wrong. Words that are thought to be missed can be placed in a separate pile to be looked up after the whole set has been shown (so if the checker is wrong and a correct definition was given, it will be discovered). In using this technique, we have found that students are more apt to call a correct definition "incorrect" than to call an incorrect definition "correct."

Rauenbusch and Bereiter (1991) have another procedure for teaching technical terminology. Here are the steps:

1. Students note problematic terms as they read.

2. They then select one or more of the following strategies and apply it to the word:

- Summarizing: sum up what you know so far about the word

- Reading ahead: read ahead to see if you can find out about the word

- Backtracking: go back to the point where you started to get confused

- Think of what kind of word it is most likely to be

3. Then, after coming up with a tentative definition, the student reads the sentence and inserts the definition in place of the word to see if it fits.

For more information on teaching vocabulary, try Gunning, T. G. (1998) *Assessing and Correcting Reading and Writing Difficulties.* Needham, MA: Allyn & Bacon.

### Prerequisite Content

We can only provide general recommendations in this text for students who lack the fundamental knowledge to approach lessons on a particular topic. Missing prerequisite knowledge, particularly that knowledge which we think of as conceptual and procedural, can be supplied by repeating lessons on content from earlier portions of the curriculum. Of course, this must be done by using instruction tailored to the student's individual needs. Chapter 4 and Appendix B (TIES-II) provide extensive summaries of effective instruction, and the rest of this book is about targeting needed knowledge; so, even though we would love to write the book again, we'll need to refer you to other chapters. If the content in question is not in this text, then find another resource or use the procedures presented in Chapter 3 to clarify the curriculum.

### Teaching Recommendation 3: Study and Test-Taking Skills

Thomas (1993) looked at the study habits of middle school students and found, among other things, that they don't study much. This raises some interesting questions about the utility of searching for, and teaching, the perfect studying technique. What if your student knows all sorts of great study approaches but doesn't use them? If that is the case, the best study intervention might be to make studying worthwhile by attending to motivation as covered in **Teaching Recommendation 6**. Gorden (1994) indicates that the two most important factors in study may have little to do with the actual techniques employed. Instead, *consistency of study* (setting a schedule and allocating time) and *active study* (*really* using some sort of strategy) may be the details in greatest need of teacher emphasis.

However, there is the probability that many students don't study because they don't know how. In that case, teaching study approaches would be a good idea. And, even if almost no one in your class is studying, that logic still holds up. That is because, in most schools, teachers can't be sure that study skills have ever been taught. In these cases, the school needs to specify who should be teaching which TR (Riehl & Sipple, 1996). Additionally, everyone should know *when* it is taught so that others will know when to expect competence. Otherwise, there is really no way to tell the difference between a system problem or a student problem (although both need to be fixed, the process will be different). As it is now, some upper grade teachers think that lower grade teachers are setting students up for failure through the omission of TR from the curriculum (Roeser et al., 1996). This isn't an individual student or teacher issue, it is a schoolwide curriculum issue ( See Chapter 3).

Regardless of the cause, many students are "nonstrategic" in their efforts to study. They don't seem to pick rigorous study approaches, organize, or change what they are doing according to the nature of the task. However, simply raising the stakes of studying (telling students their next test score will determine all of their future access to the internet), although it may increase total study time, will not improve the quality of the studying (Thomas, 1993). What is needed is good instruction of effective study strategies. The results of specific study-skill training are clearly positive (Archer & Gleason, 1996; Bryan & Sullivan-Burstein, 1998; Gunning, 1998; Jitendra et al., 1999; Mastropieri & Scruggs, 1998; McDougall & Brady, 1998; Swaggart, 1998).

There are, however, some cautions regarding study-skill instruction that we want to pass on. First, given that different tasks place different demands on learners (Marx & Walsh, 1988), a student may learn strategies but find no place to use them. Second, make sure the approaches to studying and test taking you decide to teach are appropriate to the places where your student is going to work. Be particularly aware that those tactics that seem useful at lower grades, or in the special/remedial classrooms, may not work in upper grades. Third, be careful to keep study and test-taking content simple. Sometimes complex strategies, or accommodations such as unnecessary study guides and advanced organizers, may actually distract students. They may also reduce demands by *modifying* performance to the point that it no longer reflects the true nature of the targeted task (Thomas, 1993). Finally, be aware that, if the study skill procedures are too complex, they may actually take longer to learn than the original objective.

We think that most of the study and test-taking content is strategic in nature. Therefore, the instructional procedures outlined in Chapter 4 apply. Exhibit 14.1 (which is presented in its entirety in Howell et al., 2000a) includes a list of commonly recognized study skills.

### Teaching Recommendation 4: Self-Monitoring and Problem Solving

### Self-Monitoring

The terms self-monitoring and self-evaluation are used differently within the profession. For example Lenox and Wolfe (1984) define it as ". . . the extent to which people regulate their self-

presentation by tailoring their actions in accordance with immediate situational cues" (p. 1349). This definition, like most of those found in the literature, seems more directly linked to social competence than academic competence. However, if self-evaluation is simply knowing what you are doing, and if it is the correct thing to do, then the skills required are probably similar for social and academic objectives. Here are indications shown on page **450**.
The student:

Is a self starter;

Behaves differently on different tasks;

Knows the requirements of different tasks;

Recognizes errors;

Attends to the way his/her behavior alters outcome;

Uses "means-end" analysis; and

Changes with feedback.

Some of these skills do not require much explanation, but there are a few that do. For example, the term "means-end" analysis may be unfamiliar. It is the process of checking to see if you are progressing toward your goal (the end) and, if not, deciding what changes need to be made in your approach (the means). Whenever we work, we should be checking to see if we are getting closer to our objectives, as this is the only way to know if the approach we are using is effective. It is this act of comparison that changes self-monitoring into self-evaluation.

Recognition of an ineffective approach should signal a student to change either the effort or technique she is using. If the student has been correctly attending to the requirements of the task, and noting how the things she does alter the product, she should be in a good position to make a sound adjustment in approach. For example, if she knows that the strategy she is using is the correct strategy, but she is making limited progress, then she should decide to work harder or change the way she is working by carefully monitoring the impact of each step she takes.

### Self-Monitoring

Self-monitoring is to self-evaluation what assessment is to evaluation. The first step of teaching self-evaluation is to teach monitoring. Monitoring is the collection of data about one's status. There are various ways it can be taught. For example, Howell et al. (1983), who all have aged remarkably well, conducted a study with a group of students with severe impairments. This approach would be a good start for similar students or those who are young. First, we taught the kids to play musical chairs. Then we gave each student a card with two drawings separated by a line. On one side of the line was a drawing of a student sitting in a chair. On the other side was a drawing of a student standing next to a chair. The kids in the study were then told to play the game and, after the music stopped and they had scrambled for a seat, to mark the drawing on the card which corresponded to their status (sitting or standing). All of the students quickly became accurate at this monitoring task.

The next step was to transfer the musical chair monitoring to other tasks and/or behaviors. This was accomplished by taping cards on each student's desk. The cards contained what are commonly called "countoons" (Kaplan, 1995). These are pictures of student-specific inappropriate and/or appropriate behaviors (ideally drawn by the student or photos of the student engaging in each behavior) separated by a line. When the student is signaled, she is to mark her status.

Once the student is accurate at using the countoon, it can then be modified in a variety of ways. For example, under each drawing you can write in numbers and then put a red circle around the number that represents criteria for the behavior. For example, if you want the student to "ask for assistance" when she is confused a total of ten times during the day, circle the digit 10. And, if you are going to reward the student for reaching 10, have her draw a picture of the reward (such as a token that can be exchanged for free time) at the bottom of the countoon. Now the student can look at the countoon to see what she is supposed to do and what she is not supposed to do. She can mark what she actually is doing when a signal is given. She can also see her progress to the goal as she marks the numerals leading to the circled 10. And, she can see what she'll get if she reaches 10.

### Self-Evaluation

The student's observation of her progress toward the goal allows for the comparison of behavior to a standard. This converts the monitoring exercise to an evaluation. It also sets up the conditions needed for means-end analysis. Therefore, the steps to teaching self-evaluation (which could be the basis for objectives in the area) are:

6. Comparison of current status on appropriate and inappropriate behaviors to the standard;

5. Recognition of a standard for acceptable performance;

4. Summary of current status on appropriate and inappropriate behaviors;

3. Self-recording of engagement in appropriate and inappropriate behaviors;

2. Labeling of appropriate and inappropriate behaviors; and

1. Discrimination between displays of appropriate and inappropriate behaviors.

These skills are essentially the same as the ones you would follow as you establish a measurement system for any evaluation. Keeping that in mind, consider that almost everything you have learned about assessment and evaluation can be taught to your students. However, there are cautions that go with that idea. First, just because something can be taught does not mean it needs to be taught. So do a thorough evaluation to determine need. Second, don't teach terminology. Countoons can be used without ever mentioning terms like "record," "interval sample," or "CAP."

Still, it is a good idea to have students do what you do. Of course, the best way to do that is to talk through your own work to demonstrate how you solve problems and monitor. This can teach, or bolster, self-evaluation. For example, suppose you are working with an older student on a fairly abstract problem (picking the *best* solution, talking *appropriately* at lunch). (Sometimes it is better to go to these constructs with older students because you can avoid their attempts to discover ways to circumvent precise lists of behaviors. Of course the move to constructs means that you must shift to the use of *concept instruction* as outlined in Chapter 4.) A good way to define the construct is to go with the student to another room where you can both observe other kids at work. Set up your recording instruments and take data. When you disagree, the two of you can negotiate until you arrive at a clear understanding of what each of you means by "the best solution."

As another variation, you can ask a student who is having problems in some area to observe and take data on a student that is successful in the area. Then, have the successful student observe the one with problems and let the two negotiate and problem solve. Of course, with any of these suggestions you, as the teacher, should be linking the students' actions to the six skills listed above. You will also need to remove your support to get the student to take care of herself (McDougall & Brady, 1998).

### Teach Problem Solving

General problem-solving instruction is becoming more common; however, there is still little consensus about how to teach it. The two primary sources we recommend for classroom-specific guidance are R. Sprick et al. (1998) and Goldstein (1988). The Goldstein source is most applicable to social skills.

Any successful approach to problem solving must include elements of problem recognition, problem analysis, resource analysis, planning, and monitoring. These functions may be addressed in classroom settings; however, they must ultimately be transported out of the classroom. One way to do this is to use "routine" language and steps for each function regardless of the setting. For example, the words *choose* and *plan* can be used consistently to debrief errors:

"What happened?"

"What did you *choose* to do?"

"What happened because of *your choice*?"

"What else might you have *chosen* to do?"

"If you had *chosen* to do that, what do you think would have happened?"

"It looks to me as if you need a *plan* for solving this sort of problem in the future."

"How do *you plan* on recognizing this sort of problem in the future?"

"What is *your plan for choosing* the best things to do?"

There are plenty of sequences like this one. Some of them have three steps while others have a dozen. In our review, we were unable to find compelling evidence that any of the various schemes was more or less effective. We have concluded, however, that none of them will work unless they are taught in ways that promote generalization.

The sort of problem analysis just illustrated can be applied across situations and tasks. Remember, it isn't sufficient for the student to simply recognize problems and plans; she must also use them in a variety of settings. This means problem-solving skills must be raised to automaticity through extensive practice and ongoing maintenance procedures.

Some techniques currently available to teachers in the form of published programs do not provide sufficient depth for this sort of learning. Using these programs, teachers often have students repeat rules but don't have them carry out the rules in actual practice.

Here are some useful resource materials:

Goldstein, A. P. (1988) *The Prepare Curriculum*. Champaign, IL: Research Press. (ISBN#0-87822-295-2)

Larson, K. A. (1989) Task-related and interpersonal problem-solving training for increasing school success in high-risk young adolescents. *Remedial and Special Education*, 10(5), 32-42.

McCleary, J. A., and Tindal, G. A. (1999). Teaching the scientific method to at-risk students and students with learning disabilities through concept anchoring and explicit instruction. *Remedial and Special Education*, 20(1), 7-18.

## Teaching Recommendation 5: Academic Motivation

Motivation has been covered in some detail earlier in this chapter and in Chapter 2. Before going on with this part of that discussion, it may be helpful to remind you of some common misconceptions about motivation.

- Motivation is not a character issue—it is a skill.
- No one lacks motivation, but they may employ it inappropriately.
- Motivation is not the same thing as "self-esteem." It is not built through exercises designed to get students to feel good about themselves (or about school).
- Motivation is not a generalized construct—a person may seem motivated to do one thing but not motivated to do another.
- Inappropriate motivational behaviors may be exhibited by high-performing, as well as low-performing, students.

Motivation can be taught like any other skill. The instruction can be roughly divided into preteaching, during teaching, and post-teaching actions (understanding that these phases are recursive and may occur many times during any lesson).

### Preteaching

The more a student understands about motivation, the better off she will be when trying to use it appropriately. For example, the distinction between the **learning** and **performance** orientations, as explained on pages 24 and 25 (in Chapter 2), is critical. Sometimes, you may wish to precede a lesson that you think will be challenging with a brief presentation, or review, on the motivation basics. This is not some sort of pregame pep talk. It is a "lead lesson" given in anticipation of motivational errors. If done correctly, it can prevent students from practicing bad motivational habits.

Occasionally go over the operational definition of academic motivation with students. That definition is perseverance at a task, particularly in the face of difficulty (such as errors). Also, periodically go over the six key ideas that they should hold to understand and use appropriate academic motivation. Those ideas are listed on page **439.**

There were several important concepts listed after that set of beliefs. Explain that these ideas are not easy to understand and, in some cases, seem at odds with everyday experience. You may also want to explain the ideas to parents (or have them read this whole section) as children tend to explain things to themselves the way parents explain things to them.

### During Teaching

There are two ways to approach motivation during the act of teaching. Both make use of similar processes, and they both fall under the heading of Attribution Retraining (a good topic on which to do a literature review).

In an attribution retraining lesson, the teacher uses content that is challenging for the student to actually promote errors. The retraining occurs as the teacher uses adaptive motivational statements to explain the errors and then elicits similar statements from the students. This process is nicely explained in Lovitt (1995). Additional information can be located in Green-Emrich and Altmaiser, (1991) and Susskind et al. (1999). The advantage of this sort of arranged lesson is that it allows the teacher to prepare responses.

The second choice is to react to errors which occur throughout the day (including those in the hall or at lunch). It involves adopting an overlay program for correcting attribution errors. This approach is harder (although we think it is more effective) because the errors cannot be anticipated; therefore, the teacher must think "on his feet." The steps of this program are to:

1. Listen to the student
2. Identify the content of the error statement
3. Identify the type of attribution "error" the student is making
4. Use the student's original statement and expand it into an adaptive reply

*Exhibit 14.10   Attribution Error Correction.*

| Attribution Retraining: General Correction Guidelines |
| --- |

1. Listen to the student;
2. Identify the <u>content</u> of the statement;
3. Identify the type of **attribution "error"** the student is making;
4. Use the student's original statement and expand it into an adaptive reply;
5. Be sure you portray the situation/problem accurately (teaching adaptive attributions does not mean teaching students to distort the way things really are).

| Attribution Type | Example "Error" | Example Correction |
| --- | --- | --- |
| **Internal unalterable** (change to **internal alterable**) | "I am too **dumb** to do this <u>problem</u>." | "You can't do the <u>problem</u> yet because you haven't **learned the skills to do it.**" |
| **External unalterable** (change to **external alterable**) | "The <u>test</u> was too **hard**." | "**You need to study** the things on the <u>test,</u> then it will be easier." |
| **External alterable** (change <u>content</u> and shift to **internal alterable**) | "My <u>desk</u> is too **messy** to study." | "To study you need to **organize** your <u>desk</u>." |
| **Performance/accomplishment** (change to **progress/learning**) | "Great! I **passed** the <u>assignment</u>." | "Great! Your work on the <u>assignment</u> shows how much you **improved**." |
| **Personal effacing** (change to **personal supportive**) | "**I am no good** at <u>math</u>." | "**You** can learn <u>math</u>." |
| **Pervasive negative** (change to **situation-specific negative** (if negative is accurate)) | "I missed another <u>subtraction problem</u>. I'm just **no good at math**." | "You are having trouble with <u>subtraction</u>, **not all math**." |
| **Permanent** (change to **temporary**) | "I don't have any <u>friends</u> and I **never will**." | "**You can** have <u>friends</u> once you learn how to make them." |

5. Be sure you portray the situation/problem accurately (teaching adaptive attributions does <u>not</u> mean teaching students to distort the way things really are).

This entire process, along with examples, is shown in Exhibit 14.10.

### Post-Teaching

It is what the teacher (or parent) does after a student engages in a correct or incorrect behavior that is often most important. These actions include the use of feedback, reinforcement, and punishment. When a student lacks interest in a topic, or her interest begins to fade (as often oc-

curs during adolescence—possibly because of the less gratifying teaching techniques employed in the upper grades), incentives and rewards can be used (Wigfield et al., 1998). Because these incentives and rewards are sometimes delivered to the student in the absence of information about attribution, the student is allowed to infer what they mean—and frequently what she infers is wrong.

You need to be careful about what you say during the process of giving rewards (including praise). In an attempt to be "proactive" and "positive," most teachers prefer to use rewards to build desired behaviors. However, the use of rewards can be used inappropriately, particularly if the student does not see a direct relationship between the reward and progress on the targeted task (Malott et al., 1997). Additionally, if the student perceives that the rewards are given differentially (some students get them while others don't), she may attribute the giving of rewards to nonsalient characteristics such as a student's race or the teacher's partiality.

To cut off incorrect conjecture by the student, link behavioral contingencies to explanations about those contingencies. There are a couple of general rules for doing this.

1. Be very clear about the aspects of the student's behavior to which you are responding. (Don't say "Here, I've decided to give you 5 extra minutes of recess." Do say *"Because you have worked hard* to correct your spelling errors you have earned 5 minutes of extra recess.")

2. Be sure that reinforcement and punishment are directed at things that the student includes as one of *her* personal goals. If the student does not want to make the behavior change you are working on, the consequences you deliver can backfire. This means that you must teach the student to *want* the behavior before you can reinforce it (Ford, 1995).

3. Don't accompany consequences with talk which can encourage nonadaptive motivational beliefs. (Don't say "Great job, you finished all of your work!" Do say "Great job, you practiced all of the skills we had covered!")

The product-oriented talk illustrated by the *don't say* in number 3 is too common and can foster an accomplishment definition of success (which is nonadaptive). You want to promote the idea that success comes with perseverance and that it is defined as learning, *not* finishing stuff.

One other point. You may need to be loud enough for others to hear so that they don't develop inaccurate perceptions. Here are some other actions you can take. For some good advice about building adaptive motivational skills, see Prawat (1998), Schunk (1996), Thomas (1993), and Urdan et al. (1998).

## Teaching Recommendation 6: Basic Learning Strategies

This is not a teaching recommendation that can easily be carried out with precision. Frankly, the various suggestions ought to be commonly used by most teachers most of the time. However, if you can focus on a particular student's needs, you may be able to select some combination of these recommendations for a targeted skill. First read the material on learning strategies in Chapter 2. Then review the evaluation to try and find the level of assistance the student requires on the task of interest. Once these have been recognized, select the most self-evident instructional recommendations from the examples below. Then be prepared to monitor their effects and adjust your instruction if needed. A more complete set of recommendations can be found in Howell et al., 2000a.

Function

1. Secure attention
2. Direct attention
3. Teach attention skills

Memory

1. Promote storage
2. Promote storage and recall
3. Promote recall
4. Teaching memory skills

Motivation

1. Supply meaning
2. Raise perceived value
3. Convey a sense of control
4. Promote feelings of success
5. Alter consequences

It is logical to wonder why, if these suggestions for assistance are so great, we wouldn't simply use all of them in all cases. Good question! For basic learning strategies, we begin by establishing the student's position along the sequence of assistance in Exhibit 14.8. Objectives can then be specified leading from that position toward independent functioning. For example, if the student needs lessons on memory skills to learn the

## Key Beliefs—Teacher Actions

Take the following actions to support each key belief:

**1. Goals:**
- Make learning goals clear and concrete.
- Describe goals as behaviors or products (will sort mushrooms into piles) not as constructs (will know and understand types of mushrooms).
- Ask the student to repeat the goal and describe what she will do to meet it.
- Give direct feedback and reinforcement by including the *goal* in your statement ("nice work; you selected all of the *mushrooms with free gills*").
- Give frequent feedback and earned reinforcement.
- Evaluate the student on progress toward the goal and on goal attainment.
- Conference with the student about the selection of new goals (but always maintain curriculum alignment).

**2. Internal Effort Attribution:**
- Always make it clear that tasks are only difficult when one doesn't know how to work them, or one lacks a needed resource.
- Always make it clear that errors are signals for the need to learn or to obtain resources.
- Always make it clear that learning is accomplished through perseverance and work.
- Never blame errors on fixed ability deficits ("you made that error because you have a learning disability").
- Only blame errors on external factors if it is the truth. Even then, explain how the student must work hard to learn to deal with the external factor.
- Use the correction process in Exhibit 14.10 when a student makes an attribution error.
- You need to believe that each of these recommendations is correct so that you don't make your own attribution errors in front of the student.

**3. Success:**
- Define success in terms of learning/progress.
- Get used to talking about, giving feedback on, and reinforcing progress/learning.
- Never emphasize task completion over learning (say "I want you to learn how to tell a mushroom with free gills from those with attached gills before recess," <u>not</u> "I want you to get the mushroom sorting done by recess").
- Provide tasks which are challenging.
- Fight the temptation to lower standards.
- Show progress through charting or reviews of work products. During these reviews stress tangible evidence of improvement.

**4. Interest:**
- Explain how the skill will be used.
- Show the skill being used.
- Work with the student doing the parts she can't do yet while she does the parts she can.
- Explain what problem the skill is meant to solve.
- Be enthusiastic about teaching the task.
- Use reinforcement (whatever needed) to get initial effort. Gradually remove the reinforcement as competence improves.
- Let the student work on the skill with a friend.
- Teach the skill in context.

**5. Response to Errors:**
- See the items pertaining to errors in the section on Internal Effort Attribution.
- See the error correction procedure in Exhibit 14.10.
- When a student makes an error explain that it is probably due to missing prior knowledge and that once the knowledge is acquired (through perseverance) the item can be done correctly.
- Remind the student of tasks which were difficult until she learned how to do them ("Addition was once hard for you but now it is easy—you'll find that, if you work hard, the same will be true of multiplication").
- Make it clear that errors are not failures. The only failure would be to give up. Errors simply indicate when it is time to work harder or to try working in a different way.

chemical elements in the human body, her sequence of learning objectives might look like this:

5. Given a list of [insert new content], the student will learn the content without teacher assistance related to memory strategies and will list the content accurately.

4. Given assistance in the form of prompts for use of memory strategies, the student will correctly list [insert new content].

3. Given assistance in the form of explicit directions to use memory strategies, the student will correctly list [insert new content].

2. Given assistance in the form of practice on memory strategies, the student will correctly list [insert new content].

1. Given assistance in the form of memory strategy lessons, the student will correctly list [insert new content].

If you aren't trying to move the student toward independent use of basic learning strategies and really want the student to learn something right away, then employ all levels of assistance and polish off the learning.

For additional information on basic learning strategies in the classroom, see:
DuPaul, G. J. et al. (1991) Interventions for attention problems. In G. Stoner et al. (Eds.), *Interventions for Achievement and Behavioral Problems* (pp. 685–714). Silver Spring, MD: National Association of School Psychologists.

## Summary

This chapter has covered task-related knowledge by referring to several extremely broad categories of information. These categories ranged from basic learning strategies to note taking. We believe this is an important chapter and hope that its position in the text does not somehow lead you to conclude that it isn't. It may very well be that support in this domain will have greater cumulative benefits than instruction in more "academic" content. While we are mentioning the end of things, we'd like to note that this is the end of the last chapter. It has been a long trip, but we hope it has been useful. Thank you all for your attention. See you in school tomorrow!!

# *Appendix*

## APPENDIX A.1   PROBLEM-SOLVING CHECKLIST

### Part 1 *Be Sure You Have Used Good Educational Judgment.*

| Status | | Guidelines |
|---|---|---|
| Yes | No | 1. I worked with others to define the problem. |
| Yes | No | 2. We decided if the problem is a priority. |
| Yes | No | 3. From now on we will focus on solutions not problems. |
| Yes | No | 4. From now on we will focus on alterable variables and the curriculum. |
| Yes | No | 5. We have specified the specific behaviors the student will be displaying once the solution has been learned. |
| Yes | No | 6. We have isolated the parts of the tasks the student must be taught. |
| Yes | No | 7. We have selected simple solutions. |
| Yes | No | 8. We are acting quickly. |
| Yes | No | 9. We have reconfigured the problem to be sure all aspects have been covered. |
| Yes | No | 10. I will monitor for decreases in problem and increases in behaviors specified for the outcome. |

### Part 2 *Be Sure You Selected and Constructed Good Assessments.*

| Status | | Guidelines |
|---|---|---|
| Yes | No | 1. The assessments are aligned with the curriculum. |
| Yes | No | 2. The assessments are easy to use. |
| Yes | No | 3. The assessments have clearly defined purposes. |
| Yes | No | 4. The assessments are standardized. |
| Yes | No | 5. The assessment sample clearly defined content domains. |
| Yes | No | 6. The assessments sample relevant types of knowledge. |
| Yes | No | 7. Some of the assessments collect rate data. |
| Yes | No | 8. All of the assessments collect an adequate sample. |
| Yes | No | 9. All of the assessments use appropriate scoring rules. |

### Part 3 *Review the Quality of Your Decisions.*

| Status | | Guidelines |
|---|---|---|
| Yes | No | 1. The correct objective should have been selected. |
| Yes | No | 2. You have decided if you should teach this skill in content or in isolation. |
| Yes | No | 3. You have decided if you should use an acquisition or fluency format (application/automaticity should *always* be emphasized). |

| Yes | No | 4. The plan places emphasis on the correct thought processes (facts, concepts, rules, and/or strategies are all important). |
|-----|-----|----|
| Yes | No | 5. I am employing the correct teacher actions when presenting the lesson. |
| Yes | No | 6. The lesson is made sufficiently interesting. |
| Yes | No | 7. I have all of the information needed to accurately fill out this Check Sheet. |

# APPENDIX A.2   STATUS SHEET FOR ACTIVE READING

| If the Student Makes This Error | Then This Is the Problem | And These Are the Goals | Does the Student Have the Skills? | | |
|---|---|---|---|---|---|
| Student is unaware of and continues reading when she makes errors that violate the meaning of the text. Student employs no strategies for monitoring meaning of reading. | **1. Monitors meaning** | • Attends to reading and notes errors which violate meaning<br>• Self-questions<br>• Rereads confusing portions of material, or adjusts reading rate on difficult sections<br>• Can predict upcoming events in the passage<br>• Identifies when additional information is needed, or specifically what kind of information is needed to answer questions | Yes ☐ | No ☐ | Unsure ☐ |
| Student makes random guesses to answer questions posed about readings. | **2. Selective attention to text** | • Reads with expression and/or automation<br>• Student corrects errors which violate meaning<br>• Connects text to prior knowledge | Yes ☐ | No ☐ | Unsure ☐ |
| Student reads texts/passages as quickly as possible and for completion only. | **3. Adjusts for text difficulty** | • Allocates study time according to passage difficulty<br>• States purpose for reading<br>• Identifies and self-corrects reading errors which violate the meaning of the passage<br>• Adjusts reading rate appropriately | Yes ☐ | No ☐ | Unsure ☐ |

| If the Student Makes This Error | Then This Is the Problem | And These Are the Goals | Does the Student Have the Skills? | | |
|---|---|---|---|---|---|
| After reading a passage/text, student supplies an unrelated or tangentially related "best title" or main idea. Student identifies supporting information as the main idea. | **4. Connects text with prior knowledge** | • Answers "best title" and main ideas questions accurately<br>• Retells story with emphasis on major points<br>• Describes author's purpose for writing<br>• Can locate information in the passage which answers assigned questions<br>• Can accurately apply stated criteria to the story to judge its value as an information source<br>• Uses information gained from reading the passage to focus on subsequent topics/information in the passage | Yes ☐ | No ☐ | Unsure ☐ |
| Student has no clarification strategies. | **5. Clarifies** | • Adjusts reading rate for material which is not understood<br>• Is more likely to recall important passage details, not trivial ones<br>• Answers comprehension questions in terms of stated information in passage, not necessarily prior knowledge<br>• Uses multiple strategies to determine passage meaning<br>• Uses multiple strategies to decode words<br>• Self-corrects errors which violate meaning<br>• Asks for assistance | Yes ☐ | No ☐ | Unsure ☐ |

# APPENDIX A.3   TEACHER INTERVIEW/CHECKLIST

*Reading*

Student _____   Date _____

School _____   Grade _____

Teacher _____   Interviewer _____

Please consider each of the following components of reading. Indicate if it is a skill that has been taught, if you expect the student to be able to use the skill, and then indicate if you consider this a problem area for the student.

| Reading Component | Has the Skill Been Taught? | | Is the Student Expected to Use This Skill? | | Considered a Problem for This Student? (If Yes, please describe) | |
|---|---|---|---|---|---|---|
| **Concepts of Print** (e.g., page/book conventions, book/word length, word/sentence boundaries, letter names) | No | Yes | No | Yes | No | Yes |
| **Phonemic/Sound Awareness** (blending, segmentation, deletion) | No | Yes | No | Yes | No | Yes |
| **Decoding Skills** (Phonics) | No | Yes | No | Yes | No | Yes |
| **Reading for Meaning** (Comprehension) | No | Yes | No | Yes | No | Yes |
| **Vocabulary** | No | Yes | No | Yes | No | Yes |
| **Sight Words** | No | Yes | No | Yes | No | Yes |
| **Summarizing** | No | Yes | No | Yes | No | Yes |
| **Clarifying** | No | Yes | No | Yes | No | Yes |
| **Reading for Information** (scanning, skimming) | No | Yes | No | Yes | No | Yes |
| **Other** _____ | No | Yes | No | Yes | No | Yes |

1. Briefly describe typical instructional procedures and the types of reading activities the student is engaged in on a regular basis. *Include curriculum materials used, contingencies for accuracy and completion, types of assignments given, and setting demands.*

2. What interventions have been tried to address concerns and what were the results?

3. Do problems occur consistently or occasionally? *If occasionally, describe conditions when problems occur and conditions when they do not.*

4. Other concerns regarding reading:

*Source:* Heartland Education Agency (1996). Program Model for Special Education. Used with permission.

# APPENDIX A.4: STATUS SHEET FOR SYNTACTIC STRUCTURES

**Directions:**
1. Use this status sheet with a group of people who have worked with the student.
2. Carefully describe the settings and task you are thinking about while you fill out the sheet.
3. Filling out the sheet begins with the recognition of error (i.e., maladaptive) behavior. If the student makes an error, he/she doesn't have the skill so mark the category "NO." If the student doesn't make the error mark "YES." If you can't decide about the status of the category mark it "unsure."
4. Skills marked "YES" are considered PLOP. Those marked "NO" must be corrected, so teach the corresponding objective. For behaviors marked "UNSURE" employ a recommended **SLP** to get more information.

| If the Student Makes This Error | Then This Is the Problem | And This Is the Objective (without criteria) | Does the Student Have the Skills? | | |
|---|---|---|---|---|---|
| | | | Yes | No | Unsure |
| Student omits noun/noun phrases or verb/verb phrases *or* student consistently fails to produce above. | 1. Noun/noun phrase | Student will produce (*by imitation, with prompts, or spontaneously*) sentences containing nouns/noun phases. | ☐ | ☐ | ☐ |
| | 2. Verb/verb phrase | Student will produce (*by imitation, with prompts, or spontaneously*) sentences containing verb/verb phrases. | | | |
| Student incorrectly uses quantity phrases or numbers to indicate more then one. *Ex.: Many girl, three boy.* | 3. Regular plurals | Student will produce (*by imitation, with prompts, or spontaneously*) sentences containing regular plurals | Yes ☐ | No ☐ | Unsure ☐ |
| Student incorrectly uses nouns as predicate nouns or subjects. *Ex.: It hit he. The car ran over he.* | 4. Subject pronouns | Student will produce (*by imitation, with prompts or spontaneously*) sentences containing subject pronouns | Yes ☐ | No ☐ | Unsure ☐ |
| Student omits preposition and/or noun or pronoun object. *Ex.: Girl go town. Boy sit chair.* | 5. Prepositional phrases | Student will produce (*by imitation, with prompts, or spontaneously*) sentences containing prepositional phrases. | Yes ☐ | No ☐ | Unsure ☐ |
| Student vocabulary lacks descriptors and detail, no modifiers for nouns. *Ex.: The dog silent. The cat.* | 6. Adjectives | Student will produce (*by imitation, with prompts, or spontaneously*) sentences containing adjectives | Yes ☐ | No ☐ | Unsure ☐ |

| If the Student Makes This Error | Then This Is the Problem | And This Is the Objective (without criteria) | Does the Student Have the Skills? | | |
|---|---|---|---|---|---|
| | | | Yes | No | Unsure |
| Student places the subject of the question before the helping verb. *Ex.: I could do that?* | 7. Interrogative reversal form for questions | Student will produce (*by imitation, with prompts, or spontaneously*) questions containing interrogative forms. | ☐ | ☐ | ☐ |
| Student omits pronouns that receive the action of the verb or follow prepositions as objects. *Ex.: Him walked there. It's me.* | 8. Object pronouns | Student will produce (*by imitation, with prompts, or spontaneously*) sentences containing object pronouns. | ☐ | ☐ | ☐ |
| Student uses double negatives to show negation of an action or description. *Ex.: Don't never, hardly nobody, isn't never.* | 9. Negatives | Student will produce (*by imitation, with prompts, or spontaneously*) sentences containing proper negatives. | ☐ | ☐ | ☐ |
| Omits or incorrectly uses *am, is, are, was, where, be, been. Ex.: She looking. Boy peering.* | 10. Verb *to be* as a helping verb | Student will produce (*by imitation, with prompts, or spontaneously*) sentences using *to be* as a helping verb. | ☐ | ☐ | ☐ |
| Student omits *to be* in sentences with predicate nouns or predicate adjectives and subjects. *Ex.: That girl big. That boy large.* | 11. Verb *to be* as a linking verb | Student will produce (*by imitation, with prompts, or spontaneously*) sentences using *to be* as a linking verb. | ☐ | ☐ | ☐ |
| When using the present tense of a verb as a noun, adjective, or adverb in a sentence, the student omits the word *to. Ex.: The girl wansa study. The boy wants ride bike.* | 12. Infinitives | Student will produce (*by imitation, with prompts, or spontaneously*) sentences containing infinitives. | ☐ | ☐ | ☐ |
| Student uses incorrect form, or omits determiners (*a, an, the, that, this, these,* and *those*) in sentence. *Ex.: This kinds are bad.* | 13. Determiners | Student will produce (*by imitation, with prompts, or spontaneously*) sentences containing determiners. | ☐ | ☐ | ☐ |
| Student omits words that join or connect words and/or phrases. *Ex.: The girl (and) boy run (and) jump.* | 14. Coordinating conjunctions | Student will produce (*by imitation, with prompts, or spontaneously*) sentences containing coordinating conjunctions. | ☐ | ☐ | ☐ |

| If the Student Makes This Error | Then This Is the Problem | And This Is the Objective (without criteria) | Does the Student Have the Skills? | | |
|---|---|---|---|---|---|
| | | | Yes | No | Unsure |
| Student uses improper forms of words to establish possession or ownership. *Ex.: The girls shoes. The boy eyes.* | 15. Possessive nouns and pronouns | Student will produce (*by imitation, with prompts, or spontaneously*) sentences containing possessive nouns and pronouns. | ☐ | ☐ | ☐ |
| Noun and verb tense do not agree in phrases. *Ex.: There goes the boys. The girl run to the store. There's is two of them.* | 16. Noun/verb agreement | Student will produce (*by imitation, with prompts, or spontaneously*) sentences with noun/verb agreement. | ☐ | ☐ | ☐ |
| When making comparisons with adjectives, student omits or uses the incorrect suffix ('er or 'est). *Ex.: She's the smartest of the two. He's more smart.* | 17. Comparatives and superlatives | Student will produce (*by imitation, with prompts, or spontaneously*) sentences using comparatives and/or superlatives. | ☐ | ☐ | ☐ |
| Student does not use the *wh*- structure to begin questions. *Ex.: At the store you need?* | 18. Questions beginning with an interrogative pronoun. | Student will produce (*by imitation, with prompts, or spontaneously*) questions beginning with an interrogative pronoun. | ☐ | ☐ | ☐ |
| Student omits -*ed* from regular verbs to signify past tense. Student uses improper form for irregular verbs in past tense. *Ex.: Yesterday the girl look. The boy thinked she eated it.* | 19. Past tense of the verb | Student will produce (*by imitation, with prompts, or spontaneously*) sentences containing the correct past tense forms of verbs. | ☐ | ☐ | ☐ |
| When describing something taking place in the future, student omits helping verbs (*may, can, going to, will, should*). *Ex.: It happen tomorrow. She do it later.* | 20. Future aspect | When describing events of the future, student will produce (*by imitation, with prompts, or spontaneously*) sentences using future aspect helping verbs. | ☐ | ☐ | ☐ |
| Student adds *s* to all nouns to signify plurality. *Ex.: Mans, mouses, deers.* | 21. Irregular plurals | Student will produce (*by imitation, with prompts, or spontaneously*) sentences using correct forms of irregular plurals. | ☐ | ☐ | ☐ |
| Student uses incorrect form of do (*I/we/you/they do; he/she/it does; past tense did; have/has/had done*). *Ex.: She do it. We does it. He has did it.* | 22. Forms of do | Student will produce (*by imitation, with prompts, or spontaneously*) sentences containing the correct form of do. | ☐ | ☐ | ☐ |

| If the Student Makes This Error | Then This Is the Problem | And This Is the Objective (without criteria) | Does the Student Have the Skills? | | |
|---|---|---|---|---|---|
| Student omits helping verbs that add tense or intention to the action verb (*has, have, had, would, should, could, might, must, ought, will, shall*). *Ex.: She __ do it if she could.* | 23. Auxiliaries (helping verbs) | Student will produce (*by imitation, with prompts, or spontaneously*) sentences using the auxiliaries. | Yes ☐ | No ☐ | Unsure ☐ |
| Student omits derivational endings (*-or, -er, -ist, -ian*) when changing verbs to nouns. *Ex.: I am the paint of this picture.* | 24. Derivational endings which change verbs to nouns | Student will produce (*by imitation, with prompts, or spontaneously*) nouns from verbs by using derivational endings. | Yes ☐ | No ☐ | Unsure ☐ |
| Student uses incorrect form of reflexive pronouns when reflecting back on nouns. *Ex.: We did it ourself.* | 25. Reflexive pronouns | Student will produce (*by imitation, with prompts, or spontaneously*) sentences containing the correct form of reflexive pronouns. | Yes ☐ | No ☐ | Unsure ☐ |
| Student omits or overuses qualifiers (*very, much, more, most, less, least, too, so,* etc.) to indicate when/why an action is carried out. *Ex.: So then . . . so then . . . so anyway . . .* | 26. Qualifiers | Student will produce (*by imitation, with prompts, or spontaneously*) sentences correctly using qualifiers. | Yes ☐ | No ☐ | Unsure ☐ |
| Student omits or overuses coordinating conjunctions (*and, but, or, nor, for, yet*) to join clauses or simple sentences. *Ex.: The fair was fun. The rides were fun. This summer we went to the zoo, and the beach, and the fair, and the pool and the park.* | 27. Coordinating conjunctions | Student will produce (*by imitation, with prompts, or spontaneously*) sentences, from simple sentences or clauses, using coordinating conjunctions. | Yes ☐ | No ☐ | Unsure ☐ |

| If the Student Makes This Error | Then This Is the Problem | And This Is the Objective (without criteria) | Does the Student Have the Skills? | | |
|---|---|---|---|---|---|
| | | | Yes | No | Unsure |
| Student omits (causing short, choppy sentences) or overuses (causing run-on sentences) conjunctions to relate clauses or simple sentences *(after, before, because, if, since, so).* *Ex.: We went for a run. Then we went to a movie. Then we went to eat. cuz . . . cuz . . . cuz . . .* | 28. Conjunctions commonly used to coordinate clauses | Student will produce (*by imitation, with prompts, or spontaneously*) complex sentences using conjunctions. | ☐ | ☐ | ☐ |
| Student omits direct and indirect objects from sentences. *Ex.: He gave (the girl) the cake.* | 29. Indirect and direct objects | Student will produce sentences (*by imitation, with prompts, or spontaneously*) using indirect and direct objects. | ☐ | ☐ | ☐ |
| Student uses the incorrect forms of adverbs to modify verbs, adjectives, and other adverbs. *Ex.: She felt real good. I want to go, to.* | 30. Adverbs | Student will produce (*by imitation, with prompts, or spontaneously*) sentences using correct forms of adverbs to modify verbs, adjectives, and other adverbs. | ☐ | ☐ | ☐ |
| Student omits *to* in infinitive phrases with subjects. *Ex.: The girl wants him (to) play.* | 31. Infinitives with subjects | Student will produce (*by imitation, with prompts, or spontaneously*) sentences containing all parts of an infinitive phrases. | ☐ | ☐ | ☐ |
| Student omits *-ed* or *-ing* on verbs preceding nouns used as adjectives. *Ex.: She felt better after run laps.* | 32. Participles | Student will include (*by imitation, with prompts, or spontaneously*) correct forms of participles in sentences. | ☐ | ☐ | ☐ |
| Student omits *-ing* from verbs used as nouns. *Ex.: Walk is a healthy exercise* | 33. Gerunds | Student will produce (*by imitation, with prompts, or spontaneously*) gerunds in sentences. | ☐ | ☐ | ☐ |

| If the Student Makes This Error | Then This Is the Problem | And This Is the Objective (without criteria) | Does the Student Have the Skills? | | |
|---|---|---|---|---|---|
| Student overuses (in written communication) or omits passivity in communication. *Ex.: The boy was saw in her company.* | 34. Passive voice | Student will produce (*by imitation, with prompts, or spontaneously*) sentences in the passive voice. | Yes ☐ | No ☐ | Unsure ☐ |
| Student omits phrases, which indicate tense and intention. *Ex.: They (have been) studying diligently.* | 35. Complex verb forms—multiple auxiliaries | Student will produce (*by imitation, with prompts, or spontaneously*) sentences which are indicative of tense and intention. | Yes ☐ | No ☐ | Unsure ☐ |
| Student omits relative adverb clauses (clauses preceded by *where, when,* or *why*) which modify the verb in the sentence. *Ex.: The boy ran (when he was chased)* | 36. Relative adverb clauses | Student will produce (*by imitation, with prompts, or spontaneously*) sentences containing relative adverb clauses. | Yes ☐ | No ☐ | Unsure ☐ |
| Student omits clauses (clauses preceded by *which, that,* or *who*) which act as adjectives in sentences. Student creates agreement problems when using relative pronoun clauses. *Ex.: The boy (who was chased) ran away. The boy, that was chased, ran away.* | 37. Relative pronoun clauses | Student will produce (*by imitation, with prompts, or spontaneously*) sentences, in agreement, containing relative pronoun clauses. | Yes ☐ | No ☐ | Unsure ☐ |
| Student leaves action in a complex sentence incomplete or no conjunctions are used. *Ex.: While the girl was lifting weights. The girl was lifting weights, the boy skied.* | 38. Complex or subordinating conjunctions | Student will produce (*by imitation, with prompts, or spontaneously*) complete sentences using complex or subordinating conjunctions. | Yes ☐ | No ☐ | Unsure ☐ |

# APPENDIX A.5   SOCIAL SKILL CURRICULUM OBJECTIVES

## Personal (self control)

1. Knows own feelings
   - √  In role play, student will recognize and state his/her feelings associated with different external events.

2. Understands own feelings
   - √  When shown pictures depicting emotions, student will identify them. Student may use verbal/nonverbal means to express their feelings.

3. Deals with conflicting feelings
   - √  When encountering a situation which leads to conflicting feelings, the student will react by selecting options that are best in the long run and which reduce the conflict.

4. Recognizes changing feelings due to maturation
   - √  When confronted with a situation in which past feelings no longer exist or have changed, student will identify possible reasons.

5. Recognizes another's feelings
   - √  Shown a photograph or in a role play, student will correctly label feelings of others.

6. Shows understanding of another's feelings
   - √  Shown a photograph or in a role play, student will make statements in accordance to other's feelings.

7. Rewards self
   - √  During role play, student will make positive remarks regarding achievements.
   - √  Student will reward self following achievements.

8. Uses self-control strategies
   - √  Will employ [specified strategy] when presented with stressful situations.

9. Accepts consequences
   - √  In a role-play situation student will identify appropriate consequences for actions.
   - √  Student will accept consequences related to their actions.

10. Deals with boredom
    - √  Student will choose and engage in an activity of individual choice when faced with a boredom situation.

11. Deals with losing
    - √  Following activities involving competition, student will congratulate the (those) individual(s) who win.

12. Deals with being left out
    - √  Student will ask to be included in activities of choice and will identify variable alternatives to said activities.

13. Deals with embarrassment
    - √  Student will respond to embarrassing situations by using one of several reactions he/she has generated and had approved by the teacher.

14. Deals with failure
    - √  Student will accept assistance and continue to work after experiencing a failure.

15. Accepts "NO"
    √ After hearing "NO," student will discontinue his/her present behavior.
16. Understands reasons for being told "NO"
    √ Student will identify and/or reiterate reasons for being told "NO."
    √ Student will explain rationale behind being told "NO."
17. Eats well
    √ Student identifies rationale for eating healthy.
    √ Student identifies sources of appropriate nutrition.
    √ Student plans and follows a nutritious diet.
18. Exercises
    √ Student identifies rationale for exercising.
    √ Student plans and incorporates physical activity into each day's routine.
19. Manages time
    √ Student will prepare and follow a daily schedule—incorporating all important activities of his/her day.
20. Relaxes
    a) Muscle relaxation (tightening and relaxing muscles)
    b) Deep breathing (belly breathing)
    c) Counting backwards (from a preselected number)
    d) Positive imagery
    e) Meditation

In a group setting, student will use the following relaxation techniques:
    a) Muscle relaxation
    b) Counting backwards
    c) Positive imagery
    d) Meditation

When faced with an identified stressor, student will utilize relaxation techniques.

21. Eliminates distorted thinking
    a) Identify feelings triggered by distorted thoughts
    b) Identify distorted thoughts
    c) Refute distorted thoughts
    d) Stop distorted thoughts
22. Maintains supportive environment
    √ In a role play, student will identify characteristics of friends.
    √ Student will identify people in his/her life they can turn to for support.
23. Maintains a support group
    √ When faced with a negative situation during role play, student will appropriately solicit assistance/advice.
    √ Student will choose a peer buddy each day.

## Interpersonal

1. Introduces self
    √ In role play, student will introduce him-/herself to unknown individuals.
2. Makes clear statements
    √ Student will plan and make clear, concise statements.

3. Uses "I" messages
   √ In role play, student will use "I" messages in conversation (i.e. "I feel sad when I don't pass my spelling tests.")

4. Begins a conversation
   √ Student will initiate conversations with peers across settings.

5. Pauses in conversation
   √ In role play, student will pause speaking to allow listeners to speak.

6. Ends a conversation
   √ In role play, student will conclude conversations.

7. Turn taking in conversation
   √ Student will wait for pauses by speaker before speaking.

8. Joins in
   √ Student will ask to join in activities of interest.

9. Plays a game
   √ Student will accept invitations to play games of interest.

10. Asks for a favor
    √ During role play, student will politely (i.e., saying please/thank-you) ask for assistance with tasks.

11. Offers help to a classmate
    √ During role play, student will recognize peer's need for help and offer assistance.

12. Gives a compliment
    √ Student will make positive statements about the qualities and accomplishments of others.

13. Accepts a compliment
    √ In role play, student will acknowledge and accept compliments.

14. Says "Thank-You"
    √ Student will appropriately (i.e., voice tone, facial expression) thank individuals for their assistance.

15. Suggests an activity
    √ In role play, student will identify activities which he/she enjoys doing.
    √ Student will suggest activities to play to peers.

16. Shares
    √ When asked appropriately to share by a peer/adult, student will do so.

17. Apologizes
    √ In role play, student will apologize to others after hurting them (with words or actions).
    √ In role play, student will identify when others' feelings have been hurt.

18. Interrupts politely
    √ In role play, student will wait for pauses in conversations or activities, then say "excuse me" to get attention.

19. Gets ready for a difficult conversation
    √ After viewing interactions which failed (messages from speaker to listener not understood) student will identify possible reasons why and rewrite/plan alternatives.

20. Deals with contradictory messages
    √ While viewing a video, student will identify contradictions between verbal and nonverbal messages.

21. Deals with accusations
    √ In role play, student will deal constructively with accusations.

22. Answers a complaint
    √ In role play, student will correct behaviors identified in complaints.

23. Says "NO"
    √ In role play, student will refuse unreasonable or unaccomplishible requests of another politely.

24. Deals with wanting something that isn't his or hers.
    √ In role play, student will ask permission to borrow things from others.
    √ In role play, student will identify reasons for being denied access to others' things.

25. Recognizes and expresses feelings
    √ In role-play conversations, student will describe his or her feelings verbally.

26. Solves arguments
    √ In role play, student will identify and employ problem solving techniques to constructively solve arguments.

27. Recognizes and deals with intentional and accidental actions
    √ Student will define the terms accidental and intentional.
    √ In role play or after watching a video, student will identify intentional and accidental actions.

28. Expresses concern for another
    √ Student will illustrate [acceptable] interest in others.
    √ Student will express [designated reaction] to others experiencing notable harm or good fortune.

29. Expresses affection
    √ In role play, student will display affectionate behaviors (i.e. smiling, hugging, shaking hands) towards another.

30. Has empathy
    √ After watching a video, student will pretend he/she is in the character's position, identify what they were feeling, and the reasons why.

31. Responds emotionally to another person
    √ In a role play, student will recognize the emotions of another and respond to them in an empathetic way.

32. Knows ways to enhance empathy
    √ In a role play, student will pay attention to and read emotions from facial expressions, body language, voice tone, and verbal content.

33. Respects other people's feelings
    √ Student will identify several possible emotions related to the same situation.

34. Respects differences in wants and likes
    √ Student will identify differences in wants and likes between him-/herself and those close to him/her.

35. Asks permission
    √ Student will appropriately obtain permission for activities requiring it.

36. Asking permission
    √ During role play, student will utilize socially acceptable means (i.e., "may I please") to gain permission for activities.

37. Recognizes interpersonal expectations
    √ Given situations, the student will correctly label the expectations of other individuals.
38. Maintains interpersonal relationships
    √ Student will use various devices (phone, mail, personal contact) to maintain contact and put effort in working through conflicts that threaten relationships.

## Problem Solving

1. Identifies problem
   √ During role-play scenarios, the student will identify problems in terms of environmental variables and emotional factors.
2. Generates several solutions
   √ After identifying problems, student will brainstorm a list of possible solutions and their consequences.
3. Decides what caused a problem
   √ In role plays, student will identify the cause and effect relationship in problems.
4. Avoids labels and stereotyping
   √ In role play, student will use objective language during problem solving.
5. Chooses solutions
   √ After assessing possible solutions for effectiveness, student will choose one.
6. Evaluates solutions for effectiveness
   √ After implementing a solution, student will evaluate it for effectiveness (is the problem solved?) and return to problem solving as necessary.

## Citizenship

1. Employs moral reasoning
   a. understands morality
   b. understands social systems
   c. understands conscience
   d. understands individualism
   e. understands social contracts
   f. understands individual rights

   √ Student demonstrates knowledge and use of the following:
       (a) understands morality
       (b) understands social systems
       (c) understands conscience
       (d) understands individualism
       (e) understands social contracts
       (f) understands individual rights
2. Negotiates
   √ In mock conflict situations with other's, student will identify and offer ways to compromise.
3. Stands up for rights
4. Stands up for a friend
5. Deals with group pressure
   √ In role play, student will refuse pressures to engage in actions known to be wrong.

6. Is honest
   √ In role play, student will accept consequences $(+/-)$
   √ When asked questions, student will tell the truth.
7. Takes people's perspectives
   √ In role play, student will identify possible reasons for differing points of views.
8. Is fair
   √ Student will identify and employ consistent consequences for actions by others.
9. Respects rights and equality of others
10. Is caring and helping
   √ After viewing videos of others in need, student will identify ways in which he/she can assist them.

## Classroom Specific

1. Enters quietly
   √ Student will enter classroom without disruption.
2. Puts things away
   √ Student will place materials/personal effects in proper location.
3. Sits in seat
   √ Student will remain in seat during times specified by instructor.
4. Starts work immediately
   √ Student will begin work immediately upon request by teacher.
5. Listens
   √ During role-play conversations, student will employ active listening techniques.
6. Asks for help
   √ Student will request task-related assistance when needed.
7. Offers help
   √ Student will politely offer assistance to peers having difficulty with classroom tasks.
8. Brings materials to class
   √ Student will enter classroom with necessary materials.
9. Follows instructions
   √ Student will behave congruent to all instructions given by school adults.
10. Completes assignments on time
   √ Student will turn in completed assignment on time.
11. Contributes to discussions
   √ During role play, student will make remarks related to discussions.
   √ Student will offer relevant contributions to classroom discussions.
12. Asks questions
   √ Student will raise hand and ask questions related to presentation information.
13. Ignores distractions
   √ Student will remain focused on classroom tasks.
14. Makes corrections
   √ Student will check for and correct all detected errors on assigned work before turning it in.
15. Sets goals
   √ The student will select or produce realistic, yet challenging goals.

16. Asks permission
    √ Student will obtain permission for activities.

17. Continues activities (on task)
    √ Student will remain on task throughout the school day.

### Anger/Violence

1. Knows physiological indicators of anger
   √ During role play, student will identify physiological indicators of his anger.

2. Recognizes external and internal triggers
   √ During role play, student will identify situations and/or behaviors that contribute to his anger.

3. Uses anger reducers and relaxation
   a. uses self-statements in pressure situations
   b. uses self-evaluation in pressure situations
   c. anticipates
      √ short and long term
      √ most and least probable
      √ internal and external
   √ Student will use following techniques to reduce anger:
      (a) uses self-statements in pressure situations
      (b) uses self-evaluation in pressure situations
      (c) anticipates
         √ short and long term
         √ most and least probable
         √ internal and external

4. Knows angry behavior cycle
   √ Student will describe how anger occurs and what may signal its onset.

5. Changes own provoking behavior
   √ Student will identify behaviors in his repertoire that anger others.

6. Deals with own anger
   √ During role play, student will accept ownership for his/her feelings of anger.

7. Deals with another's anger
   √ Student will identify indicators of anger in others.

8. Deals with fear
   √ In role play, student will identify indicators of fear.
   √ In role play, student will identify the similarities and differences between anger and fear.

9. Avoids trouble
   √ In role play, student will identify situations of individuals which preceded trouble.
   √ Student will avoid environments that cause them trouble.

10. Stays out of fights
    √ When faced with conflict, student will utilize nonaggressive problem solving techniques.

11. Controls impulses
    √ In role play, student will identify possible consequences before taking action.

12. Employs non-violent alternative solutions

    During role play, student will identify nonviolent solutions to possible conflicts and/or problems.

# APPENDIX A.6  FUNCTIONAL ASSESSMENT INTERVIEW FORM

Name of Student _____ Age _____ Date _____

Interviewer _____ Respondent _____

## A. Describe the Behavior(s)

1. What are the behaviors of concern? For each behavior, define the topography (how it is performed), frequency (how often it occurs per day, week, month), duration (how long it lasts when it occurs), and the intensity (what is the magnitude of the behaviors: low, medium, or high). Does it cause harm to others or the student?

| Behavior | Topography | Frequency | Duration | Intensity |
|----------|------------|-----------|----------|-----------|
|          |            |           |          |           |
|          |            |           |          |           |
|          |            |           |          |           |
|          |            |           |          |           |
|          |            |           |          |           |
|          |            |           |          |           |
|          |            |           |          |           |
|          |            |           |          |           |

2. Which of the behaviors above occur together (e.g., occur at the same time, occur in a predictable "chain," occur in the same situation)?

## B. Define Ecological Events That May Affect Behavior(s)

1. What medications is the student taking (if any) and how do you believe these may affect behavior?

2. What medical complications (if any) does the student have that may affect his or her behavior (e.g., asthma, allergies, seizures)?

3. Describe the extent to which you believe activities that occur during the day are *predictable* for the person. To what extent does the student know the activities that will occur (e.g., reading, lunch, recess, group time)?

4. About how often does the student get to make choices about activities, reinforcers, etc.? In what areas does the student get to make choices (academic activity, play activity, type of task)?

5. How many other people are in the classroom setting? Do you believe that the density of people or interactions with other individuals affect the target behaviors?

6. What is the staffing pattern? To what extent do you believe the number of staff, training of staff, quality or social contact with staff, etc., affect the target behavior?

7. Are the tasks/activities presented during the day boring or unpleasant for the student, or do they lead to results that are preferred or valued?

8. What outcomes are monitored regularly by you and/or your aide (frequency of behaviors, skills learned, activity patterns)?

### C. Define Events and Situations That Predict Occurrences of Target Behaviors

1. **Time of Day:** When are the behaviors most likely? Least likely?

   Most likely _____

   Least likely _____

2. **Settings:** Where are the behaviors most likely? Least likely?

   Most likely _____

   Least likely _____

3. **Social Control:** With whom are the behaviors most likely? Least likely?

   Most likely _____

   Least likely _____

4. **Activity:** What activity is most likely to produce the behavior? Least likely?

   Most likely _____

   Least likely _____

5. Are there particular situations, events, etc., that are not listed above that "set off" the behaviors that cause concern (particular demands, interruptions, transitions, delays, being ignored, etc.)?

6. What would be the one thing that you could do that would be the most likely to make the undesirable behavior(s) occur?

### D. Identify the "Function" of the Undesirable Behavior(s). What Consequences Maintain the Behavior(s)?

1. Use Exhibit 13.2 to guide your thinking about the functions of behavior. The template for that Exhibit is shown on page 488.

Domains of Social Content

| Categories of Functions | | A. Personal (Self Regulation and Control) | B. Interpersonal (Relations with Others) | C. Problem Solving | D. Citizenship | E. Classroom Specific | F. Anger/ Violence | G. Other |
|---|---|---|---|---|---|---|---|---|
| Type 1: External (actions, accomplishments, or things) | *Avoid* "I do *not* want to . . ." | | | | | | | |
| | *Obtain* "I *do* want to . . ." | | | | | | | |
| Type 2: Internal (feelings, thoughts, emotional status) | *Avoid* "I do *not* want to . . ." | | | | | | | |
| | *Obtain* "I *do* want to . . ." | | | | | | | |

2. Think of each of the behaviors listed in Section A and define the function(s) you believe the behavior serves for the student (i.e., what does he/she get and/or avoid by doing the behavior)?

| Behavior | What Does He/She Get? | What Does He/She Avoid? |
|---|---|---|
| | | |
| | | |
| | | |
| | | |
| | | |
| | | |
| | | |
| | | |
| | | |
| | | |

3. Describe the student's most typical response to the following situations:

   a. Are the above behaviors more likely, less likely, or unaffected if you present him or her with a difficult task?

   b. Are the above behaviors more likely, less likely, or unaffected if you interrupt a desired event (e.g., talking with a peer, reading a book, etc.)?

   c. Are the above behavior(s) more likely, less likely, or unaffected if you deliver a "stern" request/command/reprimand?

   d. Are the above behaviors more likely, less likely, or unaffected by changes in routine?

   e. Are the above behaviors more likely, less likely, or unaffected if something the student wants is present, but he/she cannot get it (i.e., a desired object that is visible but out of reach)?

   f. Are the above behaviors more likely, less likely, or unaffected if you are present, but do not interact with (ignore) the student for 15 minutes?

   g. Are the above behaviors more likely, less likely, or unaffected if the student is alone (no one else is present)?

### E. Define the Efficiency of the Undesirable Behaviors

1. What amount of physical effort is involved in the behaviors (e.g., prolonged, intense tantrums vs. simple verbal outburst, etc.)?

2. Does engaging in the behaviors result in "payoff" (getting attention, avoiding work) every time? Almost every time? Once in awhile?

3. How much of a delay is there between the time the student engages in the behavior and receives the "payoff"? Is it immediate, a few seconds, longer?

### F. What Events, Actions, and Objects Are Perceived as Positive by the Student?

1. In general, what are things (events/activities/objects/people) that appear to be reinforcing or enjoyable for the student?

### G. What "Functional Alternative" Behaviors Are Known by the Student?

1. What socially appropriate behaviors/skills does the student perform that may be ways of achieving the same "function(s)" as the behaviors of concern?

2. What things can you do to improve the likelihood that a teaching session will occur smoothly?

3. What things can you do that would interfere with or disrupt a teaching session?

H.  Provide a History of the Undesirable Behaviors and the Programs That Have Been Attempted

| Behavior | How Long Has This Been a Problem? | Programs | Effect |
|---|---|---|---|
| | | | |
| | | | |
| | | | |
| | | | |
| | | | |
| | | | |
| | | | |
| | | | |

# APPENDIX A.7  SURVEY LEVEL STATUS SHEET

**Directions:**

1. Use this status sheet with a group of people who have worked with the student.
2. Carefully describe the settings and task you are thinking about while you fill out the sheet.
3. Fill out the sheet by reviewing the indicators and then marking the content areas of concern. If an area seems OK mark "yes." If the student has trouble in an area mark it "no." If you can't decide about the content mark it "unsure."
4. Remember you are judging the whole content area, not each indicator. So some indicators may be missing even though you have marked the area "yes."
5. Areas marked "yes" provide the students PLOP. Content marked "no" needs to be taught and may require additional testing. Content marked "unsure" definitely needs additional assessment.

| Social Skill Content Areas | Indicators | Does the Student Have the Skills? | | |
|---|---|---|---|---|
| | | Yes | No | Unsure |
| Personal (self-control) | 1) Knows Own Feelings | ☐ | ☐ | ☐ |
| | 2) Understands Own Feeling | | | |
| | 3) Deals with Conflicting Feelings | | | |
| | 4) Recognizes Changing Feelings Due to Maturation | | | |
| | 5) Recognizes Another's Feelings | | | |
| | 6) Shows Understanding of Another's Feelings | | | |
| | 7) Rewards Self | | | |
| | 8) Uses Self-Control Strategies | | | |
| | 9) Accepts Consequences | | | |
| | 10) Deals with Boredom | | | |
| | 11) Deals with Losing | | | |
| | 12) Deals with Being Left Out | | | |
| | 13) Deals with Embarrassment | | | |
| | 14) Deals with Failure | | | |
| | 15) Accepts NO | | | |
| | 16) Understands Reasons for Being Told NO | | | |
| | 17) Eats Well | | | |
| | 18) Exercises | | | |
| | 19) Manages Time | | | |
| | 20) Relaxes | | | |
| |    a) Muscle Relaxation *(tightening and relaxing muscles)* | | | |
| |    b) Deep Breathing *(belly breathing)* | | | |
| |    c) Counting Backwards *(from a preselected number)* | | | |
| |    d) Positive Imagery | | | |
| |    e) Meditation | | | |
| | 21) Eliminates Distorted Thinking | | | |
| |    a) Identify Feelings Triggered by Distorted Thoughts | | | |
| |    b) Identify Distorted Thoughts | | | |
| |    c) Refute Distorted Thoughts | | | |
| |    d) Stop Distorted Thoughts | | | |
| | 22) Maintains Supportive Environment | | | |
| | 23) Maintains a Support Group | | | |

| Interpersonal | | Yes | No | Unsure |
|---|---|:---:|:---:|:---:|
| | 1) Introduces Self | | | |
| | 2) Makes Clear Statements | ☐ | ☐ | ☐ |
| | 3) Uses "I" Messages | | | |
| | 4) Begins a Conversation | | | |
| | 5) Pauses in Conversations | | | |
| | 6) Ends a Conversation | | | |
| | 7) Turn Taking in Conversation | | | |
| | 8) Joins in | | | |
| | 9) Plays a Game | | | |
| | 10) Asks a Favor | | | |
| | 11) Offers Help to a Classmate | | | |
| | 12) Gives a Compliment | | | |
| | 13) Accepts a Compliment | | | |
| | 14) Says Thank-You | | | |
| | 15) Suggests an Activity | | | |
| | 16) Shares | | | |
| | 17) Apologizes | | | |
| | 18) Interrupts Politely | | | |
| | 19) Gets Ready for a Difficult Conversation | | | |
| | 20) Deals with Contradictory Messages | | | |
| | 21) Deals with Accusations | | | |
| | 22) Answers a Complaint | | | |
| | 23) Says NO | | | |
| | 24) Deals with Wanting Something That Isn't Yours | | | |
| | 25) Recognizes and Expresses Feelings | | | |
| | 26) Solves Arguments | | | |
| | 27) Recognizes and Deals with Intentional and Accidental Actions | | | |
| | 28) Expresses Concern for Another | | | |
| | 29) Expresses Affection | | | |
| | 30) Has Empathy | | | |
| | 31) Responds Emotionally to Another Person | | | |
| | 32) Knows Ways to Enhance Empathy | | | |
| | 33) Respects Other People's Feelings | | | |
| | 34) Respects Differences in Wants and Likes | | | |
| | 35) Asks Permission | | | |
| | 36) Recognizes Interpersonal Expectations | | | |
| | 37) Maintains Interpersonal Relationships | | | |
| **Problem Solving** | | Yes | No | Unsure |
| | 1) Identifies Problem | | | |
| | 2) Generates Several Solutions | ☐ | ☐ | ☐ |
| | 3) Decides What Caused a Problem | | | |
| | 4) Avoids Labels and Stereotyping | | | |
| | 5) Chooses Solutions | | | |
| | 6) Evaluates Solutions for Effectiveness | | | |
| **Citizenship** | | Yes | No | Unsure |
| | 1) Employs Moral Reasoning | | | |
| |    a) Understands Morality | ☐ | ☐ | ☐ |
| |    b) Understands Social Systems | | | |
| |    c) Understands Conscience | | | |
| |    d) Understands Individualism | | | |
| |    e) Understands Social Contracts | | | |
| |    f) Understands Individual Rights | | | |
| | 2) Negotiates | | | |
| | 3) Stands Up for Rights | | | |

| | | | | |
|---|---|---|---|---|
| | 4) Stands Up for a Friend<br>5) Deals with Group Pressure<br>6) Is Honest<br>7) Takes People's Perspectives<br>8) Is Fair<br>9) Respects Rights and Equality of Others<br>10) Is Caring and Helping | | | |
| Classroom Specific | 1) Enters Quietly<br>2) Puts Things Away<br>3) Sits in Seat<br>4) Starts Work Immediately<br>5) Listens<br>6) Asks for Help<br>7) Offers Help<br>8) Brings Materials to Class<br>9) Follows Instructions<br>10) Completes Assignments on Time<br>11) Contributes to Discussions<br>12) Asks Questions<br>13) Ignores Distractions<br>14) Makes Corrections<br>15) Sets Goals<br>16) Asks Permission<br>17) Continues Activities (on task) | Yes<br>☐ | No<br>☐ | Unsure<br>☐ |
| Anger/Violence | 1) Knows Physiological Indicators of Anger<br>2) Recognizes External and Internal Triggers<br>3) Uses Anger Reducers and Relaxation<br>    a) Uses Self-Statements in Pressure Situations<br>    b) Uses Self-Evaluation in Pressure Situations<br>    c) Anticipates Consequences Which Are:<br>       √ Short and Long Term<br>       √ Most and Least Probable<br>       √ Internal and External<br>4) Knows Angry Behavior Cycle<br>5) Changes Own Provoking Behavior<br>6) Deals with Own Anger<br>7) Deals with Another's Anger<br>8) Deals with Fear<br>9) Avoids Trouble<br>10) Stays Out of Fights<br>11) Controls Impulses<br>12) Employs Nonviolent Alternative Solutions | Yes<br>☐ | No<br>☐ | Unsure<br>☐ |

# APPENDIX A.8 THINKING ERRORS

## Directions

1. During interviews or specific level testing for Type 2 prerequisites make a list of statements which seem to reflect errors in thinking.
2. Rate the errors under both the Explanatory Style and Cognitive Error categories.
3. Under the Explanatory style heading review the list of statements and select those which seem to relate to a positive or negative experience. Also list "absolute" statements.
4. Under the heading "Thinking Errors" you may categorize the same error several ways (e.g. 1h, 2a, 2d).

### Explanatory Style

List statements made by the student and then mark the appropriate description(s).

| List Statements | Mark Errors | | | | |
|---|---|---|---|---|---|
| | Negative | Performance Oriented | Permanent | Pervasive | Personal |
| a. ______________________ | ☐ | ☐ | ☐ | ☐ | ☐ |
| b. ______________________ | ☐ | ☐ | ☐ | ☐ | ☐ |
| c. ______________________ | ☐ | ☐ | ☐ | ☐ | ☐ |
| d. ______________________ | ☐ | ☐ | ☐ | ☐ | ☐ |
| e. ______________________ | ☐ | ☐ | ☐ | ☐ | ☐ |

### Thinking Errors

| List Statements | Label the Statements with the Appropriate Descriptors (e.g., 3a, 2d, 1g) |
|---|---|
| a. ______________ | ______________________________ |
| b. ______________ | ______________________________ |
| c. ______________ | ______________________________ |
| d. ______________ | ______________________________ |
| e. ______________ | ______________________________ |
| f. ______________ | ______________________________ |

1. Errors in Problem Solving
   a) Lack of knowledge
   b) Stereotyping
   c) Failure to define problem
   d) Defining problem too narrowly
   e) Lack of perspective
   f) Fear
   g) Premature resolution
   h) Insensitivity to probabilities
2. Irrational Thoughts
   a) I must be good at everything I do and it's terrible if I'm not.
   b) Everybody I meet must like me and it's awful if they don't.
   c) If people do things to me that I don't like, they must be rotten.
3. Helpless Cognitive Set
   a) Something must be completed correctly in order for me to be a success.
   b) I should only pick easy things to do.
   c) If I fail it is because I am dumb.
   d) If I fail it is because the task is too hard.

i) Sample size
j) Misconceptions of chance
k) Unwarranted confidence
l) Selective or incomplete search
m) Mistaking correlation for cause
n) Lack of supportive environment

d) You can't trust (anyone over thirty).
e) When things don't go my way, it's awful.
f) Everyone should treat me fairly and it's awful if they don't.
g) I have no control over what happens to me in my life.
h) I shouldn't have to wait for anything I want.
i) When something bad happens to me, I should [think about it all the time].
j) Anyone who walks away from a fight is a punk.
k) I must be stupid if I make mistakes.
l) I always have to win and it's terrible if I don't.
m) People should not have to do anything they don't want to do.
n) School is dumb.
o) You don't need to go to school.

e) If I fail I should stop working because it means I have encountered a task that is too hard for me.

# APPENDIX A.9    STATUS SHEET FOR TASK-RELATED KNOWLEDGE

**Directions:**

1. Use this status sheet with a group of people who work with the student.
2. Carefully describe the settings and tasks on which the status designations are based.
3. Give an overall designation for each of the principal skill areas by marking the appropriate box.
4. Check or circle all those descriptors which seem to apply to the student or setting.
5. Employ the indicated actions.

Part A: Class Support

| | Yes | No | Unsure | Additional Testing Action 4 |
|---|---|---|---|---|
| The Student Has the Skill and Knowledge Needed to Learn in this Setting: | | | | |
| Descriptors: | ☐ | ☐ | ☐ | |
| Instructional presentation | | | | |
| Classroom environment | | | | |
| Teaching expectations | | | | |
| Cognitive emphasis | | | | |
| Motivational strategies | | | | |
| Relevant practice | | | | |
| Academic engaged time | | | | |
| Informal feedback | | | | |
| Adaptive instruction | | | | |
| Progress evaluation | | | | |
| Instructional planning | | | | |
| Checks for student understanding | | | | |

Part B: Prior Knowledge of Topic

| | Yes | No | Unsure | Additional Testing Action 5 |
|---|---|---|---|---|
| The Student Has Required Prior Knowledge: | | | | |
| Descriptors: | ☐ | ☐ | ☐ | |
| Has taken prerequisite classes | | | | |
| Received acceptable grades in prerequisite classes | | | | |
| Understands text and presentations | | | | |
| Knows topical vocabulary | | | | |
| Is familiar with related topics | | | | |

Part C: Study and Test-Taking Skills

| | Yes | No | Unsure | Additional Testing Action 6 |
|---|---|---|---|---|
| Study and Test-Taking Skills Are Adequate: | | | | |
| *Before Class:* | ☐ | ☐ | ☐ | |
| Descriptors:<br>    Arrives on time<br>    Enters in a pleasant manner<br>    Brings materials to class<br>    Gets ready for learning | | | | |
| *During Class:* | ☐ | ☐ | ☐ | |
| Descriptors:<br>    Follows classroom rules<br>    Listens carefully<br>    Works during class<br>    Asks for assistance<br>    Moves quickly to new activity | | | | |
| *After Class:* | ☐ | ☐ | ☐ | |
| Descriptors:<br>    Takes materials home<br>    Completes homework<br>    Brings homework back | | | | |
| *Organization:* | ☐ | ☐ | ☐ | |
| Descriptors:<br>    Organization of materials (use of notebook or folders)<br>    Organization of time (use of calendar, scheduling work)<br>    Organization of content on paper (heading, margins) | | | | |
| *Gaining Information:* | ☐ | ☐ | ☐ | |
| Descriptors:<br>    Reading expository material<br>    Reading narrative material<br>    Gaining information from verbal presentations (lectures, demonstrations) | | | | |
| *Demonstrating Knowledge or Skills:* | ☐ | ☐ | ☐ | |
| Descriptors:<br>    Completing daily assignments<br>    Answering written questions<br>    Writing narrative and expository products<br>    Preparing for and taking tests | | | | |

## Part D: Self-Monitoring and Evaluation

|  | Yes | No | Unsure | Additional Testing Action 7 |
|---|---|---|---|---|
| The Student Monitors and Evaluates Work: | ☐ | ☐ | ☐ | |

Descriptors:
  Self-monitors
  Recognizes errors
  Judges quality of work given criteria
  Judges quality of work on own

## Part E: Problem Solving

|  | Yes | No | Unsure | Additional Testing Action 7 |
|---|---|---|---|---|
| The Student's Problem Solving/Self-Monitoring Is Adequate: | | | | |
| *The student recognizes problems:* | ☐ | ☐ | ☐ | |

Descriptors:
  Defines problems
  Identifies goals
  Identifies obstacles
  Recognizes types of problems
  Anticipates problems

*The student recognizes types of problems:* ☐ ☐ ☐

Descriptors:
  Identifies open system
  Identifies closed system

*The student recognizes solution:* ☐ ☐ ☐

Descriptors:
  Generates options
  Considers resources
  Anticipates outcomes
  Selects solutions

*The student plans:* ☐ ☐ ☐

Descriptors:
  Thinks before acting
  Explains what will happen
  Has immediate goals
  Allocates time

*The student works:* ☐ ☐ ☐

Descriptors:
  Follows plan
  Follows schedule

Part F: Academic Motivation

|  | Yes | No | Unsure | Additional Testing Action 8 |
|---|---|---|---|---|
| Descriptors (The Student Holds and Expresses These Beliefs):<br>  My goals are important<br>  My learning depends on what I do<br>  I'm a success as long as I improve<br>  My goals are interesting<br>  If I make a mistake I need to work hard to fix it<br>  I am an important member of my class and my school | ☐ | ☐ | ☐ | |

Part G: Basic Learning Skills

|  | Yes | No | Unsure | Additional Testing Action 9 |
|---|---|---|---|---|
| The Student Uses Selective Attention: | ☐ | ☐ | ☐ | |
| Descriptors:<br>  Focuses on relevant cues<br>  Ignores irrelevant cues<br>  Uses effective techniques to focus and maintain attention | | | | |
| The Student Uses Recall/Memory: | ☐ | ☐ | ☐ | |
| Descriptors:<br>  Recalls information<br>  Uses effective techniques to store and recall material | | | | |
| The Student Uses Motivation: | ☐ | ☐ | ☐ | |
| Descriptors:<br>  Perseveres in the face of difficulty<br>  Perceives value of task<br>  Maintains an adaptive explanatory style (is not "learned helplessness")<br>  Indicates feelings of control<br>  Uses effective techniques to maintain motivation | | | | |

# APPENDIX A.10   MOTIVATION TEST AND KEY

|  |  | Key Ideas | | | | | |
|---|---|---|---|---|---|---|---|
|  |  | 1 | 2 | 3 | 4 | 5 | 6 |
|  |  | Goal | Internal | Success | Interest | Persevere | Partnership |
| Correct | YES | 1, 13 | 8, 20 | 3, 15 | 10, 22 | 5, 17 | 12, 24 |
| Answers | NO | 7, 19 | 2, 14 | 9, 21 | 4, 16 | 11, 23 | 6, 18 |

Answer "yes" or "no" to the following questions:

1. I work best when I know what I am trying to learn.
2. If I fail it is most likely because the task is too hard.
3. I don't need to get the best score in class, I just need to do better than I have before.
4. I don't find most schoolwork to be interesting.
5. If I make mistakes it means I should think about changing the way I am studying.
6. During class my teacher sometimes compares our work.
7. I only study what the teacher wants me to know.
8. If I fail it is my job to fix the problem.
9. I like to pick simple things to do so I know I'll get a good grade.
10. I find most schoolwork interesting.
11. If I'm doing well I don't need to study as much.
12. The teacher knows my goals and helps me reach them.
13. It is hard for me to learn when I don't know exactly what I'm suppose to do by the end of the lesson.
14. I often get high grades because I am very smart.
15. I like to pick hard things to do because I feel good when I learn something challenging.
16. If I could pick stuff to learn it wouldn't be what we have to study.
17. When I am having trouble learning something it means I must work harder.
18. Sometimes it seems like my teacher is more interested in my finishing the work than in my learning.
19. Knowing that I must reach a certain target makes the lesson scary and/or unpleasant.
20. My teacher doesn't give me grades, I earn them.
21. It doesn't matter if I get a higher score than last time, all that matters is that I get a good score.
22. The things I am learning in class are the things I would like to be learning anyhow.
23. If I make mistakes I should stop working because I've run into something I can't do.
24. In our school there are as many rewards for improvement in classes as there are for attendance and sports.

# APPENDIX A.11   MOTIVATION INTERVIEW QUESTIONS

*(Focus on classes in which student is having trouble.)*

1. When you do schoolwork in [name subject of class] do you like to know exactly what is expected of you, or would you rather the expectations were open or vague?

   **Follow-up**

   Why?

   Does your [name subject of class] teacher usually supply vague expectations or clear expectations?

2. Who is mainly responsible for you meeting goals in [name subject of class], you or your teacher?

   **Follow-up**

   Why?

   What does your [name subject of class] teacher say to let you know if he or she is mainly responsible for your learning or if you are responsible?

3. Do you feel most successful in [name subject of class] when you think you've learned a lot or when you get a high grade?

   **Follow-up**

   Why?

   What does your [name subject of class] teacher do to let you know if he or she thinks high grades or learning is most important?

   If something seems uninteresting to you do you study it anyhow, try to get interested in it, or avoid studying it?

4. In [name subject of class] when you run into something that seems hard to do, do you usually stop working or try working harder?

   **Follow-up**

   Why?

   When you run into something that seems hard what does your [name subject of class] teacher do?

5. Do you feel like you are a part of this school and that you belong here?

   **Follow-up**

   Why?

   What does your [name subject of class] teacher do that might help make you feel you don't belong, or that you do belong?

# APPENDIX A.12   SUMMARY FORM FOR MOTIVATION

Student Name _____

Topic _____

Date _____

Evaluator
Name _____

**Directions:**

1) List key ideas.
2) Mark conditions: test, essay, interview.
3) Mark the student's status using this key:
   C  = answers correct
   CP = answers correct with prompts
   EP = error made with prompts
   E  = Error

| Key Idea(s) | Facts | Concepts | Principles | Note Incorrectly Used Terms Here. |
|---|---|---|---|---|
| 1. | | | | |
| 2. | | | | |
| 3. | | | | |
| 4. | | | | |
| 5. | | | | |
| 6. | | | | |
| 7. | | | | |
| 8. | | | | |
| 9. | | | | |
| 10. | | | | |

# APPENDIX A.13  DESCRIPTORS OF TIES COMPONENTS

The material in this appendix is taken, with permission, from Ysseldyke, J.E., & Christenson, S.L. (1996). *TIES II: The Instructional Environment System-II.* Longmont, CO: Sopris West. There are three separate sections.

1. Descriptors of TIES Components (Ysseldyke and Christenson, 1987)
2. Two Cross-Reference of TIES Indicators of Effective Instruction to Teacher Actions in Exhibit 4.3.

A template for classroom observations.

## TIES Descriptors for Component 1
### Instructional Presentation

Instructional Presentation, a primary component of effective instruction, includes factors related to lesson development, clarity of directions, and checking for student understanding. Lesson Development refers to the presence of an adequate overview; the manner in which the lesson is explained, structured, and sequenced; the variety and richness of teaching examples; the clarity with which the lesson content is presented; the adequacy of guided practice opportunities and degree of teacher-student interaction; the kind of feedback used; and the appropriateness of task directions; kind and amount of examples used; and degree to which task directions are repeated. Checking for Student Understanding refers to the method used to check the student's understanding, the timing of the checking, the degree to which cues and prompts (error correction procedures) are used to promote accurate responses, and the way in which the teacher interprets student inattentiveness. Refer to Howell et al., 2000a for a listing of the TIES indicators that define effective teaching for this component.

## TIES Descriptors for Component 2
### Classroom Environment

An effective classroom environment is influenced by the extent to which classroom management procedures reduce disciplinary concerns; the extent to which instructional routines maximize productive use of time in the classroom; and the affective tone or climate in the classroom. Classroom Management refers to the kind of rules established to maintain appropriate behavior; how the rules are communicated; the system word to maintain appropriate behavior; and the emphasis placed on student accountability. Productive Time-Use refers to the extent to which noninstructional routines are established and class time is used to increase academic activities. Class Climate refers to the extent to which the classroom atmosphere is characterized by cooperation, a pleasant atmosphere, and acceptance of individual differences. Refer to Howell et al., 2000a for a listing of the TIES indicators that define effective teaching for this component.

## *TIES Descriptors for Component 3*
## Teacher Expectations

Establishing high, yet realistic, expectations for student performance, including task completion, quality of work, and use of time in the classroom, is an important characteristic of effective instruction. Teacher Expectations refers to the kind of expectations set for student performance; the communication of the expectations; and the extent to which the student understands the expectations. Refer to Howell et al., 2000a for a listing of the TIES indicators that define effective teaching for this component.

## *TIES Descriptors for Component 4*
## Cognitive Emphasis

Effective instruction emphasizes the development of thinking skills. Cognitive Emphasis refers to the extent to which varied lessons are planned for the purpose of teaching recall, reasoning, evaluating, and application skills; the extent to which thinking skills necessary to accurately complete a task or master a skill are modeled for the student; and the extent to which learning strategies are directly taught. Refer to Howell et al., 2000a for a listing of the TIES indicators that define effective teaching for this component.

## *TIES Descriptors for Component 5*
## Motivational Strategies

Encouraging student motivation is an important component of effective instruction. Teachers understand the importance of motivation for learning and consequently use varied techniques to increase student motivation. Motivational Strategies refers to the enthusiasm with which the lesson is presented; the extent to which the lesson is interesting and varied; the kind of motivational strategy (extrinsic vs. intrinsic orientation) used; and the student's sense of self-efficacy. Refer to Howell et al., 2000a for a listing of the TIES indicators that define effective teaching for this component.

## *TIES Descriptors for Component 6*
## Relevant Practice

Students spend approximately 70% of their school day engaged in seatwork practice activities. In order for this time to be effective in promoting positive academic outcomes for a student, the student must engage in relevant practice. Relevant Practice includes the amount of practice opportunity on relevant tasks with appropriate instructional materials. Practice Opportunity refers to the amount and kind of practice. Task Relevance refers to the extent to which the practice activities are related to the lesson presented and are important for attaining the instructional goal in addition to the student's success rate. Instructional Material refers to the academic and effective appropriateness of the assigned materials for the target student to attain the instructional goal. Refer to Howell et al., 2000a for a listing of the TIES indicators that define effective teaching for this component.

## *TIES Descriptors for Component 7*
## Academic Engaged Time

In order to achieve optimally, students must be engaged and actively involved in completing academic tasks and responding to oral and written questions. Both the amount of opportunity to engage in academic work and the rate of student engaged time during completion of the work influence achievement levels. Student Involvement refers to the opportunities the student has to respond and the extent to which the student actively participates in academic activities. Contextual factors may influence student involvement. Maintenance of Student Engagement refers to the extent to which varied teacher behaviors or systems are used to facilitate time on task. Refer to Howell et al., 2000a for a listing of the TIES indicators that define effective teaching for this component.

## *TIES Descriptors for Component 8*
## Informed Feedback

Informed Feedback includes feedback and alternative, corrective procedures. The provision of specific, informative feedback and corrective procedures is a necessary step in successfully instructing students. Feedback refers to several characteristics of effective feedback, the type of feedback, and the student's understanding of the feedback. Corrective Procedures refers to the kind of alternative teaching strategies employed, the amount of supervised practice and monitoring provided, and the extent to which student accountability is stressed. Refer to Howell et al., 2000a for a listing of the TIES indicators that define effective teaching for this component.

## *TIES Descriptors for Component 9*
## Adaptive Instruction

Instruction needs to be modified to accommodate individual needs and differences. Adaptive Instruction refers to the extent to which there is a systematic effort to modify instruction, the options available for modifying instruction, and the degree to which the effectiveness of the modifications is communicated to the student. Refer to Howell et al., 2000a for a listing of the TIES indicators that define effective teaching for this component.

## *TIES Descriptors for Component 10*
## Progress Evaluation

Effective instruction includes continuous monitoring and systematic follow-up planning for a student. Monitoring Student Progress refers to the kind of student performance data collected, the frequency with which the student's performance is monitored, and the system used for record keeping and communicating to the student. Contextual factors may influence the amount of monitoring for an individual student. Follow-Up Planning refers to the basis for making subsequent instructional decisions for a student and the extent to which reviews are planned systematically. Refer to Howell et al., 2000a for a listing of the TIES indicators that define effective teaching for this component.

## *TIES Descriptors for Component 11*
## Instructional Planning

Systematic Instructional Planning includes two functions: diagnosis and prescription. Instructional Diagnosis refers to the extent to which student characteristics (e.g., skill level, motivation), task characteristics (e.g., sequence, cognitive demands) and classroom characteristics (e.g., instructional groupings, materials) have been accurately assessed. Instructional Prescription refers to the match between the student's instructional needs and instruction delivered. Student success rate and amount of content covered characterize the degree of task appropriateness for a student. Several factors influence the extent to which instructional planning is optimal for a student's academic progress. Refer to Howell et al., 2000a for a listing of the TIES indicators that define effective teaching for this component.

# APPENDIX A.14   OBSERVATION OF INSTRUCTION

1. Read TIES-II descriptions in Appendix A.13.
2. Observe instruction over several time intervals across subjects and days.
3. Place an X in the square that best summarizes the instructional practice you have observed.

Indicators

| TIES Components: | NONE | FEW | SOME | MOST | ALL |
|---|---|---|---|---|---|
| 1. *Instructional Presentation* | | | | | |
| 2. Classroom Environment | | | | | |
| 3. *Teacher Expectations* | | | | | |
| 4. Cognitive Emphasis | | | | | |
| 5. *Motivational Strategies* | | | | | |
| 6. *Relevant Practice* | | | | | |
| 7. *Academic Engaged Time* | | | | | |
| 8. Informed Feedback | | | | | |
| 9. *Adaptive Instruction* | | | | | |
| 10. *Progress Evaluation* | | | | | |
| 11. *Instructional Planning* | | | | | |

# Glossary

**Ability**   See *potential*.

**Ability training**   Treatment that attempts to change cognitive or perceptual characteristics of the student. See *aptitude treatment interaction*.

**Academic learning time**   See *time*.

**Acoustically similar**   Sounding almost like (b/p/d/t, f/v, k/p/g).

**Active participation**   When a student is overtly (with muscle activity) or covertly (through thought) involved in doing a task and/or carrying out a lesson. See *time*.

**Active reading**   Use and integration of a variety of skills and information sources to derive meaning from text. Active readers use relevant prior knowledge, decoding skills, language knowledge, and context to understand what they read. They monitor their own understanding and problem solve when they fail to understand.

**Aggression**   Action (verbal or physical) taken against another person. Aggressive acts may be violent or merely provocative (although the term is routinely reserved for extreme and even physical action).

**Aim (target)**   An objective expressed in terms of expected performance and the date by which the performance level will be reached.

**Algorithm**   A step-by-step process for finding the solution to a problem. Usually used in relation to Math. See *strategy*.

**Alignment**   Goals, objectives, instructional procedures, and assessments are all commensurate with the student's needs and each other. See *table of specifications*.

**Alterable variables**   In this text the only things that are referred to as alterable are those student characteristics that teachers can change through instruction. Alterable variables, therefore, include the student's skills, knowledge, and use of executive control strategies. See *proximal and unalterable variables*. Also see *fixed ability*.

**ALT (Academic Learning Time)**   See *time*.

**Annual goal**   The expected outcome of one year's instruction. Annual goals for special education students are set in the IEP meeting.

**Aptitude treatment interaction (ATI)**   The belief that individuals with certain abilities will behave differently in certain treatments than individuals with different abilities. Efforts to use ability measures to select treatments are commonplace and generally ineffective. See *LSI*.

**Assertiveness**   As used in popular psychology, assertiveness refers to the strong but nonaggressive declaration of opinion or need. In this context, being assertive is a positive and healthy activity. It does not mean "pushy," rude, or aggressive.

**Assessment**   The process of collecting information for use in evaluation. Assessment can be carried out by reviewing products, interviewing, observing, and/or testing. See *RIOT*.

**Assisted assessment**   Assisted assessment involves the development of a sequence of instructional involvement that is systematically employed in combination with formative evaluation to recognize the degree of support a student must have to succeed on a task.

**Assumed cause**   Hypothesized explanations for student failure. Different assumed causes may be developed by different evaluators resulting in different conclusions. In this text, assumed causes are curriculum-based and deal exclusively with the student's prior knowledge.

**Attributes**   Characteristics of a person or thing. See *critical attribute*.

**Authentic assessment**   Evaluation that makes use of real-life tasks rather than contrived test items. Technical concerns aside, the main issue surrounding the idea of authentic assessment is "Who gets to define *real-life*"?

*Automaticity* An accurate response performed at a high rate with distractions present. Automatic responses are often thought to occur without use of short-term memory. Automaticity is generally considered to be the highest level of proficiency.

*Awareness of print* Knowledge of the concepts and conventions of reading. See *DIBELS*.

*Basic learning strategies* Strategies applied to the fundamental information-processing functions of self-monitoring, attention, memory, and motivation.

*Basic skills* Sometimes referred to as tool skills, basic skills include elementary reading, mathematics, and social and communication tasks. They are the skills one must use repeatedly to carry out complex tasks.

*Behavior* In a classical sense, behavior refers to some kind of muscular activity or movement. However, in this text, there are two categories of behavior: overt and covert. Overt behavior involves movement that can be detected and confirmed reliably by observers without the use of specialized equipment. Covert behavior may be self-reported or detected by inference from overt behaviors (such as biofeedback recordings or psychological test scores). Covert behaviors include thoughts and feelings. When special educators use the term behavior, they are often referring exclusively to social behavior, as in the explanation "She has a behavior problem." This gives the erroneous impression that academic and social behaviors are somehow different when, in fact, both respond to the same learning processes.

*Behavior disordered* A label applied to individuals who engage in any of a variety of inappropriate or deviant behaviors. The term behavior disordered has gained wide acceptance as an alternative to emotionally disturbed. Many special educators are uncomfortable with the speculation and inference necessary to work with so-called "emotions" and prefer the accent that behavior disorders places on observable or overt behaviors. The term is used almost exclu-

sively to describe social, addictive, or idiosyncratic behaviors. It is almost never used to describe behavior related to academic, physical, or language skills.

*Behavior modification* Although the term could apply to any effort to change any behavior, it is used almost exclusively to describe the use of contingency management programs arranged by educators to address specific student behaviors. See *contingency*.

*Behavioral model* See *medical model*.

*Best-fit line* A line drawn through a set of charted data that best represents both the central tendency of the data and changes in trend (data pattern).

*Blending* A decoding strategy in which the reader isolates letters and/or clusters within words, recalls the sounds they make, and combines them to say the word (in the word *sister*, a student might isolate *SIS* and *TER*, then combine the sounds to say *SISTER*).

*Bound morphograph* Unit of meaning that cannot stand alone (affixes like *re, de, ing,* and *er* do not stand alone).

*Box plot* A graphic display used for showing the performance of a group. Box plots show the 10th, 25th, 50th, 75th, and 90th percentile ranks. Guidelines for interpreting and using box plots can be found in Howell et al. (2000a).

*Calibrate* To adjust size. In educational evaluation, calibration often involves slicing tasks into smaller ones or combining them to others to produce more complex ones.

*CAP* See *criteria*.

*Capacity* See *potential*.

*Categorical funding* Money made available (through entitlement) by federal or state governments for use with certain "types" of students. Categorical funding policies necessitate the time-consuming, expensive, almost meaningless and sometimes damaging process of labeling. (In case you are not a perceptive person—the authors don't like it). See *purpose*.

*CEC* See *Council for Exceptional Children*.

*'Celeration* A general term for changes (acceleration or deceleration) in behavior. On a graph,

it may be represented by a line drawn through the data.

**Child-study team**   A group of professionals assembled to review information about a student and to solve problems related to his or her academic and/or social behavior. The term also has certain regulatory meanings when used in conjunction with special education and IEP's.

**Classification**   The evaluative process of labeling or naming things to facilitate communication and understanding. In special education, the term may refer to a label placed on a student (MR or LD). See *entitlement*.

**Cloze**   A highly useful procedure used to sample reading comprehension. The student is asked to fill in the blanks in a passage where every –nth word has been deleted. Students who understand what they read are able to make good guesses about what the omitted word should be. Cloze is also a procedure used with oral language to check language comprehension.

**Cluster**   Group of letters that can be sounded together to make one sound (in *sister, er* is a cluster of letters that can be sounded together).

**Code emphasis**   An approach to reading instruction that focuses on skills for decoding words. See *decoding*.

**Cognition**   Activity of the mind—thinking.

**Compensatory**   The capability of one skill to balance the effect of another skill that is weaker.

**Comprehension**   See *reading comprehension*.

**Comprehension monitoring**   Self-checking for understanding (during reading, students might say to themselves, "What does this mean? Do I need to reread, should I slow down?"). The term can be applied to any domain.

**Comprehensive evaluation**   The evaluation required by *IDEA* prior to a child-study team meeting. It typically includes estimates of skill and ability along with a developmental history and behavioral observations.

**Computation operations**   Rote skills, procedures, and concepts students use to (1) add, (2) subtract, (3) multiply, (4) divide, and (5) calculate fractions, decimals, ratios, and percents.

**Concept analysis**   Process through which defining characteristics are identified. Defining characteristics include critical and noncritical attributes (in the letter "b," the critical attributes are its shape and orientation. Noncritical attributes include size and typeface).

**Consolidated**   A term used to refer to groups of objectives that share common rule and strategic or conceptual characteristics.

**Constructive**   A type of instruction through which the teacher actively arranges the environment to increase the probability that a student will generate knowledge. The teacher does not directly supply the targeted information because it is believed that the student's learning experience will be qualitatively superior if she extracts the information on her own. See *generative*.

**Context**   The circumstances, either physical or cognitive, in which something exists.

**Contingency**   The arrangement between a behavior and its consequences. The contingency is the thing that links a behavior to the stimulus that follows it. It is the contingency that raises (in the case of an expected reward) or lowers (in the case of an expected punisher) the probability of someone doing something.

**Corrective**   Interventions designed to fix problems. A "corrective reader," therefore, would be a student who needs help.

**Correlation**   The relationship between two measures (not necessarily a causative relationship).

**Correlation coefficient**   A fraction falling between $+1$ and $-1$, usually labeled $r$. The significance of the correlation depends on many things such as the size and composition of the population used to obtain it. The seriousness of the decision being made should be the primary determinant of any ideal level. However, levels above .85 are usually demanded for measures used to make treatment decisions for individuals.

**Council for Exceptional Children (CEC)**   The largest organization of special educators. The council has state branches and a large national structure. Its annual conventions have been attended by as many as 10,000 people. The organization promotes several publications and lobbies on behalf of special education at the state and national levels. The address of CEC is 1920 Association Drive, Reston, Virginia 22091. It has a

Web page for easy access to information about teaching students with learning problems.

*Covert behavior*   Unseen behavior such as thinking/feeling.

*Criteria (criteria for acceptable performance, or CAP)*   The standards in an objective. The criteria tell how well (accurately, frequently, or to what quality) a behavior should be carried out by a student who has finished instruction on a task.

*Criterion-referenced testing*   Evaluation that compares an individual's behavior to a performance standard or criterion.

*Critical attribute*   A defining characteristic of a task, product, or concept. Some critical attributes must be present for the thing to exist, whereas others must be absent (straight lines are needed for a square, curved lines must always be absent).

*Critical effect*   The result of a behavior.

*Critical thinking skills*   Sometimes referred to as problem-solving skills, they are largely ill-defined. Critical thinking skills are supposed to be needed when working tasks that require inference, synthesis, or creative solutions. Teachers often refer to critical thinking skills as those that exceed rote recall or literal understanding. Their use implies the active application of strategies for solution, understanding, or memory. Individuals with these skills are supposedly better prepared to control their own learning and to achieve more sophisticated understanding of content.

*Current level of performance*   Sometimes thought of as the "instructional" level, this is the position of the student's skills within the curriculum. The current level is mapped out by identifying both skills the student does not have and those she has acquired. See *present level of performance.*

*Curriculum*   The content and behaviors (objectives) taught in a class. It is not synonymous with the published materials used in a class or the teacher's approach to delivery of instruction.

*Curriculum level*   The grade at which an objective is typically taught. The term is not synonymous with "grade level," which is a normative concept referring to the average test score of students at a grade level.

*Data-based program modification (DBPM)*   An evaluative system that summarizes changes in performance over time through direct and daily measurement of behaviors. DBPM refers directly to a behavioral teaching procedure based on repeated measures of the objective behavior, charting, and standardized instruction. It is used in general to describe a variety of formative evaluation (data-based program modification) systems. The basic idea of DBPM is that trends in objective learning can be summarized, and the trends of learning under different instructional conditions can be interpreted to select the most efficient instruction.

*Data decision rules*   The use of empirically validated guidelines (rules) that can be used to aid in the interpretation of data. The rules are linked to patterns of data and are employed at some fixed interval (often every 2 weeks).

*Date-determined 'celeration*   'Celeration calculated by a line drawn from the student's PLOP to the intersection of an aim rate and aim date. See *aim.*

*Decision making*   In this text, it refers to conclusions drawn about the entitlement or teaching of students. Teaching decisions deal with the selection of objectives and the delivery of instruction. See *purpose.*

*Decoding*   The sounding and blending of letters and words. Decoding and comprehension are the two primary subdivisions of reading. "Translating printed words into a representation similar to oral language, e.g., reading 'I am hot' for the words 'I am hot'."

*Decoding rules*   A rule that when applied should assist a reader in figuring out a word (when a word ends in "e," the vowel says its name and the "e" is silent. "Rope." "O" says its name and "e" is silent). Some rules are better than others, and they are not all related to phonics. There are many meaning-based rules for decoding.

*Development*   The result of aging in a particular environment. It is not the same as maturation, which is simply aging. Two people of the same age may develop differently because of the different environments in which they have lived (or their different interpretations of the same environment).

*Diagnosis*   In special education, diagnosis may have any of several meanings. It may refer to a statement of the student's physical or psychological status, or it may refer to the category of handicapping condition into which the student is placed. Diagnosis may also refer to a statement of what and how the student should be taught. The three definitions do not necessarily relate to each other.

*DIBELS*    The Dynamic Indicators of Basic Early Literacy Skills (DIBELS) are used to measure very early reading skills. The various subscales of the measure are particularly powerful predictors of a student's later success, or difficulty, at reading tasks (Good, 1999a).

*Direct evaluation*    Evaluation that measures the performance of students in the materials that they are using or on the tasks they are learning. Direct evaluation is not possible without curriculum-test alignment.

*Direct instruction*    The term originally referred to instruction limited to content (concepts, skills, discriminations) that is linked in a causative way to an objective. In that sense, direct instruction involved teaching only the target task or its immediate subtasks. Direct instruction has also come to mean the use of various behavioral techniques during instruction. These include the consistent use of scripts, prompts, cues, correction procedures, and teacher responses. A third definition emphasizes the relationship of tasks to each other and emphasizes concept analysis and curriculum design.

*Disability*    The condition in which a person's functioning, relative to some criteria, is inferior. Disabilities are said to reside within the person and may have no consequences unless the person enters an environment that will only accommodate higher levels of function. In that case, the person becomes "handicapped" by the nonsupportive environment.

*Discrepancy*    Difference. A discrepancy may be either positive (above expectation) or negative (below expectation). Recognition of important discrepancies is fundamental to identification of annual goals and short-term objectives.

*Discrimination*    Recognizing how things are different.

*Distractions*    Noncritical information embedded in a test or lesson to see if the student can automatically distinguish what is and is not important.

*Distributed practice*    Several short and intense practice sessions are used instead of one long session. See *practice*.

*DISTAR Direct Instruction System For Teaching And Remediation*    Materials developed by Bereiter and Engelmann in the late 1960s as part of the effort to give students a head start in school. The materials have evolved over the years and expanded to cover most basic skills. The format and structure of DISTAR have come to define what many think of as Direct Instruction. See Adams & Engelmann (1996).

*Domain*    A set of skills or ideas defined by some sort of unifying boundaries or common rules. See *consolidated*.

*Down's syndrome*    A genetic condition associated with mental retardation. The syndrome accounts for a tremendous proportion of those considered to be mentally retarded for whom a known pathology exists.

*Dumbing down*    The process, usually applied to reading texts, of reducing complexity in an effort to facilitate student use.

*Dynamic data*    Data that describe progress over a period of time. See *formative evaluation*.

*Dyslexia*    Dyslexia is used to describe individuals who have difficulty dealing with symbols. In special education, it is associated very closely with learning disabilities and nonreading. Originally a medical/psychological term, its transition into education resulted in extensive overuse. Today it is not a particularly useful term.

*Efficacy*    In social service and particularly special education, this term refers to the "goodness" of a program. If the program is effective and cost-efficient, it has efficacy. The term also refers to one's view of his or her self. Those who have "good self efficacy" are thought to think well of themselves.

*Eligibility decisions*    Decisions that determine whether or not a student qualifies for a particular program. Eligibility decisions often seem to be unrelated to student need. See *labeling*, *purpose*, *categorical funding*, and *entitlement*.

*Embedded strategy instruction* Instruction through which general and/or specific strategies for a pinpointed task are explicitly taught along with the rest of the task. In embedded instruction the strategies are not isolated and are not taught separately.

*Emotional disturbance (ED)* See *behavior disordered*. Sometimes called emotional handicap (EH).

*Enabling skill* The skills needed to employ a strategy.

*Entitlement* The process of finding a student eligible for a categorically funded support program. See *eligibility decisions*.

*Envelope* Best-fit lines drawn to incorporate the variability in data.

*EPS* Errors per symbol in handwriting. The average number of errors in a sample of handwriting.

*Error analysis* The investigation of errors to recognize patterns of missing factual, conceptual, or strategic knowledge.

*Error correction* A strategy employed to increase a student's accuracy.

*Evaluation* The process by which investigators come to understand things and by which they attach relative value to things. Evaluation cannot take place without comparison of behavior to a standard.

*Examples* In concept analysis, examples are positive instances of the concept.

*Exemplar* A product, or person, used as a benchmark of quality. Exemplars are selected to illustrate expected outcomes and are particularly important when using holistic measurement and generative instruction. It is important for teachers to find exemplars in their classes. This will help them develop and standardize expectations.

*Expectation* See *criteria*.

*Expected level* The level of curriculum or proficiency at which a student is supposed to be working. It is the level at which general education students at the same grade work.

*Extrinsic* The term is used to refer to something coming from the outside. In education, it is used to label information, such as knowledge provided through instruction or consequences (reinforcement or punishment), supplied by a teacher. *Extrinsic* information comes from "outside" of the student, whereas *intrinsic* information is thought to come from inside of the student. This is a really difficult categorization system to defend because the source of the quality being discussed may change with time. For example, the term "intrinsic motivation" might be applied to a student who perseveres because s/he was previously taught how to do that by a teacher.

*F-A-C-T (model)* A process for completing the evaluation. It is described in detail in Chapter 5.

*Fatigue point* The point at which a reduction in physical stamina is reflected in a skill (tired hand, poor handwriting).

*Feedback* Feedback comes after a student has done something. It is the information that tells her if what she did was wrong or right. Whereas this information may also be reinforcing and even instructional, reinforcement, correction, and feedback are not necessarily the same.

*Fidelity* The degree to which a task or test item corresponds to real life. See *authentic assessment*.

*Fixed ability* This refers to the idea that a student's learning is capped by her capacity, or potential, for learning. The idea is probably correct at some extremely high level but dangerous to entertain with respect to particular students because:

✓ There isn't a tool that can measure it (despite frequent claims);

✓ It is unlikely that the tasks we are talking about in this book require much in the way of capacity;

✓ When an educator thinks a student isn't learning because she has reached the limits of her ability, the educator thinks there is nothing he can do. So, he writes the kid off.

*Fluency* Fluency is a proficiency dimension defined by the rate of student response. (See *mastery*.) Fluency may also refer to the type of instruction used to raise a student from accuracy to mastery.

**Form**   The observable expression of a behavior. See *function*.

**Formative evaluation**   Evaluation that occurs as skills are being developed. Formative data are called "dynamic" because they show movement. See *progress data*.

**Formats**   The arrangement or style of a test or test item. Example formats include multiple choice, production, and fluency.

**Free morphograph**   Unit of meaning that can stand alone; a word (courage, male, tent).

**Frequency data**   The number of times a behavior occurs during a time interval (usually minutes).

**Frequent evaluation**   Ongoing or continual assessment (daily if at all possible).

**Function**   The goal of a behavior. See *form*.

**Functional evaluation**   Functional evaluation is most commonly associated with the domain of social performance. This term increasingly refers to a specific set of evaluation actions. The idea behind it is not simply to do an evaluation that is useful/functional (although that is always nice). Rather, the "function" being referred to here is the *purpose*, or goal, of the behavior. The assumption behind functional evaluation is that, by recognizing *why* a student is, or is not, engaging in a behavior, educators can design programs to teach the student the skills required to meet that goal in an appropriate fashion.

**General outcome measure (GOM)**   General outcome measures are procedures, or measurement rules, that reflect growth in the central aspects of a task. A GOM should be the largest, most interactive task you can find that is sensitive to instruction and still aligned with the goal. GOMs are of particular value for screening, summarizing performance discrepancies, and monitoring progress. Oral reading is a good GOM as, to carry it out, the student must make use of most of the salient skills of reading.

**Generalization**   A skill learned in one environment or under one condition is used under new conditions or in a new environment.

**Generalize**   In special education, this term is usually used in a behavioral sense. A behavior is said to generalize if it transfers (switches) from one situation (set of stimuli) to another. Students with a disability are often characterized as those who do not generalize—meaning that they learn to do something for one teacher in one class but can't do it anywhere else. Generalization is harder if the two settings in question are very different. This is why special evaluation procedures should be similar to classrooms if their results are to be generalized to instruction. (Classrooms should be similar to the real world.)

**Generative**   Instruction in which the student induces, or generates, the outcome. See *constructive*.

**Geographic environment**   The physical context in which a behavior occurs.

**Handicap**   A debilitating condition imposed on a person by a hostile and/or nonsupportive environment. See *disability*.

**Hands-off instruction**   Instruction in which the teacher is nondirective and may even be inactive.

**Hands-on instruction**   Instruction in which the teacher is aligned and actively involved in promoting a targeted outcome. See *supplantive* and *direct instruction*.

**Holistic**   In evaluation, this term refers to comparisons and judgments based on consideration of an entire behavior or product, rather than on an analysis of its components.

**Hyperactive**   The term refers to abnormally frequent movement. It also is used to describe highly distractible or inattentive behavior. The term is associated with learning disabilities and has been widely misused. Today, it has little descriptive power.

**IDEA**   The Individual with Disabilities Education Act of 1997 (PL105-17) reauthorized the intent and procedures of PL 94-142. (PL stands for public law; 94 refers to the Ninety-Fourth Congress, and 142 means it was the one-hundred forty-second law that Congress passed). The rules and regulations associated with IDEA spell out appropriate treatment for entitled students.

The public laws mentioned here are explained in the introduction to almost every special-ed text written since 1974. The original (PL 94-142) said students with disabilities should be given an education. Beyond that, it is difficult to say what it meant because of the various regulations it has spawned and court decisions it has led to. Special educators have probably erred by overstating the impact of the laws to secure resources and respect for the field. It may have been better to say "It is correct and practical to educate children with disabilities" rather than to say "It is the law." Laws can disappear through funding cuts, legislation, or litigation.

*Idiosyncratic* A type of standard that is used to determine if a student's skills have improved relative to her previous performance. Unlike norms or CAP, the idiosyncratic standard compares the student with herself and is useful for determining progress or change in student's performance over time. Progress data are not necessarily positive, as a student can "progress" away from an expected outcome.

*IEP (individual education plan)* The control component of IDEA; the plan is required for all special-ed students and contains a complete outline of the services they are provided. The IEP contains annual goals, specific short-term objectives, statements of current educational performance, statements describing the resources to be used to meet the goals and objectives, and dates for initiation and review of the program. Cost, or school policy, can not be used to select the student's program. The only consideration should be the student's needs. The IEP is written in conjunction with parents, teachers, the school administration, and, in some cases, the student. Any party who disagrees with the plan may appeal it to a review board or to the courts. The plan is not a contract for service. See *child-study team.*

*Individualized instruction* Making decisions about student instruction on a one-to-one basis. Individualized instruction implies tailored lessons on specifically selected objectives. It does not mean one-to-one instruction. (A teacher may employ individualized instruction by deciding to teach a student in a group.)

*Information processing* The activity of a person's mind.

*Instructional aim* An objective that also includes an expected date of completion.

*Interactive process* Activity that functions through the relating of multiple variables. Interactive processes are compensatory, as they may be successfully applied even when one of the variables is failing by adjusting for the failing skill with another.

*Intermediate aim* A reference point on the way to an aim. For example, if the aim (criteria) is to have a student be 100% accurate in 6 weeks, an intermediate aim could be to have her 50% accurate in 3 weeks.

*Interpreter* The function of information processing that attributes and explains events for the mind. This component within the information-processing model explains and attributes data. These explanations vary among people because the interpretations are based on categories of prior knowledge that develop differently according to a person's personal history.

*Interrogative* A question.

*IQ* The "intelligence quotient" is conceptualized as a summary of student potential. Under old psychology, it was assumed that intelligence was fixed; therefore, tests designed to measure it were constructed to be insensitive to instruction.

*Judgment* The set of knowledge and beliefs that focuses attention and leads to decisions. Good judgment increases the probability of successful decision making. Good judgment is learned.

*Labeling* A classification process. Not useful in treatment.

*Language sample* The recorded transcription of oral communication. Often used in survey-level assessment of language.

*Learning* Relatively permanent modifications in thought or behavior that result from environmental events (instruction) but not from things like pathology, maturation, or fatigue. Learning is operationally defined (indicated by) a change in behavior over time.

*Learning disabled* The single most frequently redefined term in special education, learning disabled usually refers to someone who doesn't learn when no one can tell why. The explanations for this failure range from brain damage to bad teaching. Learning disabilities represent the largest (in terms of clients) category of educational disability. It is a mild designation and is definitionally linked to the lack of curricular progress in school.

*Learning mode (modality, channel)* Mode or modality refers to the medium of presentation. It could be useful to refer to lecture, tutoring, or self-instruction; however, in education it tends to relate to so-called stimulus-response categories. The categories are sometimes called channels, particularly by those who believe in processing deficits. The common styles referred to by teachers are the auditory and visual channels. Some educators believe that learners have stable styles and attempt to make use of these preferences during instruction. This idea has questionable utility. Learning is more clearly influenced by the structure, organization, presentation, and grouping practices of the teacher.

*Least restrictive environment* A term from IDEA, it refers to the placement of students. Given two equally productive settings, the student should be placed in the one that is "least restrictive." This means the placement most like the placement to which the treatment is to generalize (usually the regular classroom).

*Literacy* The concept of literacy includes attributes of communication, planning, and accommodation of context. In this text, the term is not necessarily associated with the rules of communication but with social competence.

*LSI* Learning Style Instruction. (see *Aptitude Treatment Interaction.*)

*Maintenance* Continued mastery of a skill after instruction has ended.

*Mastery* See *rate* and *fluency*. Mastery is a proficiency dimension. Mastery criteria go beyond accuracy in that they require the student to work correctly and quickly. Rate statements, usually in terms of a rate per minute, are used in mastery objectives. Percent statements are used in accuracy objectives.

*Mastery learning* The idea that learning is accelerated if the student is instructed to sufficient proficiency on prerequisite skills. See *prior knowledge*.

*Matthew effect* The idea that students who have good skills will have a better educational experience, learn more, and leave the students with poor skills further and further behind.

*Maze* A procedure used to check reading comprehension. Students are asked to select correct words in passages in which words have been omitted. Like cloze, every –nth word is omitted. Unlike cloze, the correct word and several incorrect words are presented above or below the blank where the word was omitted.

*Mean* The average score; a measure of central tendency.

*Measurement* The assignment of numerals to objects or events according to rules (Campbell, 1940).

*Median* The middlemost score; a measure of central tendency.

*Medical model* The medical model assumes that causes of behavior problems reside within the client—that is to say, the client is sick. In contrast, the so-called behavioral model used in most social services assumes that behavior grows out of the interaction of the person and the environment. In the medical model, therapy is directed at the internal "cause" of the problem (surgery and medication are examples of this treatment). Teachers do not administer that kind of treatment. They attempt to alter people's behavior by manipulating the environment through instruction.

*Metacognitive* The student's awareness of and control over her own thinking.

*Minimum 'celeration* The minimal amount of change considered acceptable; calculated by comparing current progress rate to the aim rate.

*Minimum/maximum rule* Students with the least skills should get the greatest interventions.

*Mode* The most frequent score; a measure of central tendency.

*Morphograph* Smallest unit of meaning in the English language (born is a morphograph, it has meaning; *orn* is not a morphograph because it does not have meaning; *ed* is a morphograph as it has meaning; *e* is not).

*Morphology* Rule system for combining units of meaning to make words. We can add *ed* to *talk* to indicate that someone spoke in the past.

*Neurologic (neurologically impaired)* The neurologic system comprises the brain and nerves. People who have injured their brains or nerves may have trouble with behavior or learning; however, not all problem learners have damaged neurologic systems.

*Node* A node is a mass of something. Usually, this mass is bound into a single unit by some sort of adhesive agent. In this text, the term node is most often used in association with knowledge *schema*. Under learning theory, separate points of an array (schema) are thought to be bound by a theme composed of prior knowledge. Information is stored within, and defined by, the arrays (patterns) created from the association of the informational nodes. Because these nodes are tied together by learned links, the recognition of several nodes may trigger the recall of the entire web of knowledge. In this way, all united information about a topic can become immediately accessible to the thinker. See *schema*.

*Nonexamples* Illustrations that do not demonstrate the attributes of a given concept. A porcupine would be a nonexample of something soft.

*Norm* Scores generated from the behavior of a group.

*Objective* Objectives are statements of the expected behavioral outcomes that will result from instruction. They contain behavioral descriptors, conditions for the behavior, content descriptions, and criteria.

*Off-task* A general term implying that the student isn't doing what she is supposed to be doing. A student could be "off" one task by being "on" another. The appropriate task is usually defined by the observer or teacher.

*On-task* See *off-task*.

*Overachievement* A term often applied to students that do *better* than someone has predicted. It is a silly term that shows how far educators and psychologists will go to maintain the idea that all outcomes (good or bad) can be attributed to some sort of internal student variable. The alternative explanation for a student doing better than predictions based on ability, for example, is

that the expert was wrong when he made the prediction.

*Overlay* In evaluation, an overlay technique is a set of assessment rules and strategies which can be used on any set of materials, individuals or settings. The rules for collecting a language sample, for example, can be applied to a student of any age, in any setting, speaking any language.

*Pace* Pace has two meanings. It may refer to the actual speed of presentation or to the speed of movement from one objective to another. Speed of presentation includes the rate at which the teacher talks or uses other instructional techniques. Additionally, a class in which the students master and move to new objectives quickly may be called a fast-paced classroom.

*Paraphrasing* A procedure used to sample reading comprehension. Students read a passage and tell what was read in their own words.

*Peer tutoring* The use of students to deliver instruction to other students.

*Percentage* Number correct divided by the total possible correct.

*Performance* A measure of behavior taken on one occasion.

*Personal* See *idiosyncratic*.

*Phoneme* The smallest sound unit that can be used to distinguish one utterance from another.

*Phonetic generalizations* Rules about the way combinations of letters are sounded.

*Phonetic misspelling* Misspelling of a word that can be read (*ordr* for *order*).

*Phonetic segmentation* Isolating sounds within a word (for example, man—*mmm aaa nnn*). A subtask of blending. See *blending* and *DIBELS*.

*Phonics* Sound-symbol relationships in words. See *decoding*.

*Pinpoint* A measurement target that has been identified in behavioral terms. An objective.

*PLEP or PLOP* See *present level of educational performance*.

*Portfolio assessment*  Measurement of skills and knowledge displayed in examples of daily assignments rather than tests.

*Potential*  The hypothesized limit of a person's learning. Because potential is not an alterable variable, its measurement is of little value to teachers. Deciding that a student's failure is due to a lack of potential is a major block to effective problem solving.

*Practice*  There are two elements of practice. The first is to practice deciding what to do and the second is to practice doing it. For example, if students are given a math problem, they must decide what kind of problem it is and they must work it. Most teachers only have students "practice" by doing things (the second element) and do not allow sufficient practice at deciding what to do.

*Pragmatics*  A term that refers to the purposes or functions of language (for example, to inform or control).

*Present level of educational performance (PLEP)*  A statement describing what the student can and cannot do. The statement must be based on sound evaluation. The *E* (educational) in PLEP includes transition, social, and task-related outcomes (some states and agencies use PLOP instead of PLEP).

*Prior knowledge*  The best single predictor of learning success. Prior knowledge is what a person knows about a task, or its prerequisites, before the lesson begins. When an evaluator summarizes a student's current level of performance, he is reporting the student's relevant prior knowledge.

*Probe*  A criterion-referenced assessment.

*Problem solving*  See *strategy* and *critical thinking skills*.

*Process of written communication*  There are at least four components: planning, transcribing, reviewing, and revising.

*Process remediation (process deficit)*  Information processing takes place within the individual. If a person who is poked in the finger with a needle withdraws the finger and says "ouch," a process of the kind we are discussing has taken place. Even today, the term process remediation is used under the assumption that learning takes place through certain neurologic, psychological, or perceptual modalities, and that if one of these processes is damaged (or impaired), learning will not take place. Process remediation is directed at repairing the impaired process. These learning processes are hypothetical, and their remediation is based on theories of learning. Different theories produce different processes and different remediation activities. Process remediation directed at various so-called learning modalities was very popular in special ed during the 1960s and early 1970s. The theoretical basis and remedial utility of process remediation remains invalidated.

*Proficiency*  Criterion level necessary for student to satisfactorily perform next skill in skill sequence.

*Prognosis*  Prediction.

*Progress*  Improved performance or increased rate of learning.

*Progress data*  Information obtained by taking repeated measures of a behavior across time. Progress data are typically used in formative evaluation and in conjunction with data decision rules.

*Proximal variables*  Teacher actions, or other environmental factors which influence learning and are "close" to it. For example, quality of teacher directions or time spent studying. Proximal variables are the easiest for teachers to control. They are also the most important to learning. These are the variables listed in Appendix B.

*Pseudo-reading*  Asking a student to engage in such reading-related behaviors as turning pages or sounding nonsense words.

*Psychoeducational evaluation*  Assessment of processing abilities (also referred to as psychomedical evaluation).

*Public*  Observable. During strategy instruction, a teacher should make his thought processes public.

*Purpose*  In evaluation, the purpose (reason for doing it) must always be determined prior to assessment. Two general categories of purpose are mentioned throughout this text:

✓ Outside purposes are those involved with concerns other than instruction of individual students (such as school accountability testing);

✓ Inside purposes are those which apply to and are useful for informing the teaching decisions made for individual students within your classroom.

**Purpose of written communication** Why we write; the functions of written language (expressive, poetic, transactive).

**Qualitative interpretation** The aspect of behavior analysis that is not predicated on the quantitative examination of scores. For example, if two teams are playing basketball and one gets 112 points while the other gets 113, the difference of a single point is not statistically significant and probably does not represent any real difference in team performance. But qualitatively, the team with 113 feels a lot better.

**Rate** The number of responses divided by the time the behavior is observed. Rate is a form of data, or behavior summary, that takes into account the frequency with which a behavior occurs and the length of time during which it occurs (usually in minutes). The formula for rate is count ÷ time in minutes. Other types of data include accuracy (percent), duration, and intensity. See *criteria*.

**Raw score** The number of responses.

**Reacting** The way a person responds to what she has read. A more behavioral way to refer to reading comprehension.

**Reading** An interactive process in which the reader brings what she knows about the world to the printed page. What is known is used to decode the symbolic message and to construct meaning from what is written. See *reading comprehension*.

**Reading comprehension** Understanding text. Students combine what they know with what is printed to construct meaning. It occurs as a student reads. Students draw upon decoding skills, vocabulary knowledge, language, and prior knowledge of the topic to make sense of what is written. See *reacting*.

**Reading method** An instructional approach, not a program that is a published series.

**Reading program** A published series rather than a method.

**Reductionist** An approach to curriculum development that involves the recognition of elements of the task to be taught. See *task analysis*.

**Referral** A teacher's request for additional resources when dealing with a particular student.

**Reflective reading** The active use of reading comprehension strategies and metacognition while reading.

**Reform (reformulate)** To incorporate information into one's own knowledge base. Students reformulate during peer tutoring and cooperative learning as well as when asked to explain an idea in their own words.

**Reliability** How consistently a test measures the same thing. The stranger test.

**Remedial** A term applied to curriculum and occasionally to the students placed in that curriculum. Remedial instruction presents students with curriculum that typical students received at a younger age. It usually follows the same sequence but at a later time. See *corrective*.

**Repeated measure** An assessment that is given the same way over time to note trends in learning. See *slope* and *data-based program modification*.

**Resource (instruction or room)** Resource programs are designed to supplement regular class instruction, not to substitute for it. In a typical resource program, a student leaves the regular class for an hour a day for concentrated tutoring in areas of curricular weakness; therefore, the students in resource programs have two or more teachers, and it is necessary for the special education resource room teacher to communicate and schedule with the other teachers. Often, the scheduling and communication/consultation role of the resource teacher requires more time and energy than instruction.

*Response type*   The way a student is expected to display knowledge during a test or observation. For example, the student may say the answer, write it, or act it out.

*Retelling*   A procedure used to sample reading comprehension. A student reads a passage and says what she read. Unlike paraphrasing, where a student must use her own words, a student may simply restate what she read.

*RIOT*   RIOT stands for the primary modalities of assessment. These are *Review, Interview, Observe,* and *Test.* Each of these four can be used to collect information about student knowledge.

*Routines*   Commonly employed procedures learned and used to accomplish trivial tasks. Routines free our short-term memory so we can attend to important things.

*Rule*   A rule is an if/then relationship. For example, "If the student hasn't learned, Then the teacher hasn't taught." Rules are considered to be one of the four types of knowledge. Those are facts, rules, strategies, and concepts. The four types are often assessed and taught differently.

*Scaffolding*   The process of using a student's understanding of one topic to support learning of new information. The scaffold functions as a bridge between the prior knowledge from which it is constructed and the content of the new lesson.

*Schema*   A pattern of knowledge composed of several nodes of information linked by a unifying theme. According to learning theory, information is stored in long-term memory within these schemata, and once activated by addressing a critical combination of the nodes, an entire schema can be recalled. When this happens, the information-processing system has immediate access to all of the stored information. Recall by theme is therefore much more efficient than recall by a single stimulus. This is thought to be why efforts by the teacher to consolidate information by concept or strategy results in superior storage and recall. See *node.*

*Self-monitoring*   The critical prerequisite for all problem solving is recognition that one has a problem. Effective learners constantly monitor their performance and their learning just as effective teachers are always aware of the status of their students.

*Semantic maturity*   Skill in selecting individual words for a particular message.

*Semantics*   A term that refers to the study of meaning within language. It includes (1) meaning of single words and word combinations, (2) multiple meaning of words, (3) figurative language, and (4) the influence of content and structure on language.

*Sentence fragment*   Incomplete idea (*My grandchildren are*).

*Sentence types*   Sentence types include:

✓ Complex sentence—A complete idea that includes one independent (*Kim writes well*) and one dependent clause (*when she plans, reviews, and revises her work*).

✓ Compound sentence—Two complete ideas joined by a connecting word (*Kim composes music and she enjoys playing the piano*).

✓ Compound run-on sentence—More than two complete ideas joined by a connecting word (*Eddie runs fast and Eddie drives fast and Eddie talks fast and Eddie likes cars*).

✓ Simple sentence—Complete idea that consists of a single subject and a single predicate (*Eddie runs fast. Eddie* is the subject and *runs fast* is the predicate).

*Short-term memory*   Working memory. The function within the information processing model that allows for conscious attention to a task. Short-term memory is very limited.

*Situational behavior*   Behavior triggered by specific environmental conditions.

*Slope (trend)*   Slope refers to the trend in the student's learning as seen on a chart, with time on one axis and content or skill on the other. Slope is another term for progress, trends, or learning. The student with the greatest positive slope is progressing the fastest and learning the most. She is covering the most content in the least amount of time.

*So-What Test.*   The test of validity. Something passes the so-what test if it is worth working on.

*Social behavior* Social behavior includes those things that are done in response to, or in consideration of, others. It includes almost everything except self-stimulating behavior and addiction (although these may have social components, also). For some reason, social behavior is usually separated from academic behavior during teacher training.

*Social competence* Using the skills required to advance both personal and community agendas without interfering with others and without expending an inordinate amount of resources.

*Sociolinguistic rules* Cultural guidelines for communication. Knowledge of what can be said, to whom, and in what context.

*Sound analogy strategy* Refers to strategy where a student uses known sounds to decode new words. (*If I can decode rich, I can use that information to decode the similar word which.*) This is sometimes referred to as a rhyming strategy.

*Speech* Mechanical aspects of language (phonology, voice, and fluency).

*Staffing* See *child-study team.*

*Standard error of measurement* A boundary of confidence that can be placed around a test score. Standard error is calculated from the standard deviation and reliability of the test.

*Standardization of criterion-referenced tests* Process of testing agemates who possess the skill to establish successful behavior (the criterion).

*Standards* Expectations. See *criteria.*

*Static data* Data that describe performance at only one time.

*Structured instruction* See *direct instruction.*

*Status sheet* A list of the skills a student needs to succeed at a task. The list is typically developed through a task analysis, and the sheet is used to summarize what is known about the student's proficiency on each skill. Status sheets are usually employed in place of survey-level testing or during the development of assumed causes for a student's problem.

*Story map* A technique used to assist readers in understanding what they read. Often, a map is a diagram that illustrates how events are sequenced, how ideas are related, and what aspects of characters are important. It is a graphic representation of events and concepts in a story. See *schema.*

*Strategy* A learned (although not necessarily consciously employed) procedure for dealing with a situation or problem. The term refers to any of a variety of activities employed to aid one's own attention, memory, academic production, or social competence. See *task.*

*Subskill* See *task analysis* and *subtask.*

*Subtask* An essential component of a task that, when mastered, enables the learner to successfully perform the task.

*Summarizing* Summarizing is one way a student can react to print. Summarizing can be taught and involves the development of a statement that relates the central message of a passage without redundancy or trivial information.

*Summative evaluation* Evaluation that takes place at the end of a unit or section of instruction. Summative and formative evaluation can be contrasted like this: summative evaluation takes place at the end of a lesson or project and tells the evaluator what has happened. Formative evaluation takes place during the lesson or project and tells the evaluator what is happening. Summative evaluation "sums up" the learning. It is after the fact, like end-of-the-year testing. Formative evaluation is ongoing and yields information that can be used to modify the program prior to its termination.

*Supplantive* An approach to teaching through which the teacher actively adds to the student's knowledge through direct instruction. Supplantive instruction is hands-on instruction.

*Syntactic interference* The influence of the syntax of one known language or dialect on the use of another language or dialect.

*Syntax* Rule system that governs the order of words in a sentence.

*Syntax maturity* Skill in combining words to convey a message.

*Table of specifications* Tables of specifications are used to organize the display of task elements for the purpose of generating objectives, planning tests, and planning lessons. Therefore, they are useful tools for assuring alignment. A table is created by selecting objective elements (typically content and behavior) and subdividing them into their essential components. These components are then sequenced and placed along the two axes of a grid. As a result, the intersections within the grid form squares that contain content/behavior expectations (these can then be converted into objectives, viewed as material to be covered by a test or taken as the outcomes for lessons). See *alignment*.

**Task**    The things we teach are sometimes called concepts or tasks. It is hard to separate these clearly. Superficially, a task is a thing and a concept is an idea; however, we only know the concept has been learned if the task can be completed and, if designed properly, the task can't be completed without knowing the concept. Therefore, a task could be just about anything. Before a task can be dealt with, it must be made "behavioral" by stating it in the form of a performance objective. Several objectives form a curriculum. In education, the objective is typically called a task. All tasks are composed of two things: essential subtasks and a task strategy. Essential subtasks are simply the other tasks a person must be able to complete in order to complete the main task. In a cumulative sense, a task is "harder" than its subtasks (although an individual subtask may have taken longer to learn). A subtask is essential if the task cannot be done without it. A task may have several subtasks (the number depends on how finely the task is calibrated). The task strategy is the procedure by which these subtasks are combined to produce the task. If a student is skilled at all essential subtasks but does not know the strategy needed to combine them, she cannot do the task. Effective teacher decision making is guided by task analysis.

**Task analysis**    Task analysis is the process of clarifying the task, recognizing its essential subtasks, recognizing the task strategy, and sequencing the elements for instruction. Teachers use task analysis to avoid attempting to teach things students cannot learn (owing to a missing subtask) or things they already know.

**Task related**    Skills that allow a student to succeed at learning a task which are not specific to that task. Task-related skills include note taking, listening, studying, and test taking.

**Teacher action**    Things teachers can do. Effective teachers engage in different sets of teacher actions than do preservice and ineffective teachers. See *teacher thought processes* and *proximal variables*.

**Teacher expectations**    What the teacher thinks the student will learn. High teacher expectations are related to high student learning.

**Teacher thought processes**    Effective teachers think differently than teachers who are not effective. It is these different thoughts that cause them to use different teacher actions. The categories of teacher thought that seem related to effectiveness are (1) thoughts about the task, (2) thoughts about instruction, (3) thoughts about the student, and (4) thoughts about the nature of learning. See *teacher expectations*.

**Technical Vocabulary**    Terms specific to a topic. For example, in this text, terms like calibrate, trend, and scaffold all have slightly different meanings than they might in a book on construction. See *Topical Knowledge*.

**Test format**    The way the test stimuli are presented (multiple choice, fill in the blank, matching, etc.).

**Testing**    A process to determine how a child functions in reality by asking her to perform a selected sample of behaviors.

**Text structure**    The organization of written material; the way ideas are interrelated to convey a message. Some text structures interfere with a reader's comprehension, whereas other text structures facilitate comprehension. Headings, transition statements, alerting statements, and summaries are often used by writers to organize a message so that it is easily understood.

**Text variables**    The features of written material that contribute to or interfere with a reader's comprehension. Text variables include organizers such as headings, introductory comments, and summary statements. They also include vocabulary complexity and sentence length. See *text structure*.

**Therapy**    Therapy is not control. Control is the process by which you work to get the students to conform to the situation they are in. Therapy is what you do to prepare clients for situations outside of that situation. It goes beyond the rules and considerations of the moment. Therapy is analogous to teaching someone how to do something, whereas control is like doing it for her. Control is necessary before therapy can take place, but it is not sufficient.

*TIES* The instructional environment scale is a device used to assess teaching environments. It serves as the basis for content listed in Appendix B.

*Time* Time can be defined as follows:

✓ *Total/available time* is the amount of time in a day the student is at school (and therefore could be taught).

✓ *Engaged time* is the time a student is actually involved in a lesson. It does not refer to passive activities such as waiting for a turn or for help. Active participation may be covert or overt. Covert participation refers to thinking about the objective; overt participation refers to doing something pertaining to the objective. The higher the active participation on an objective, the higher the learning.

✓ *Academic learning time (ALT)* is the amount, or proportion, of available time the student is engaged in something that is resulting in learning. For example, two students may both be engaged in reading but only one may be reading from a text at the correct level of difficulty. Therefore, although both are engaged, only one is learning.

*Tool skills* Skills that are essential subtasks of many basic skills. For example, "saying sounds" is a tool skill necessary for all oral language tasks, and "writing digits" is a tool necessary to write out a phone number or balance a checkbook.

*Topical knowledge* Knowledge of a curricular domain. In this text, the term refers to material presented in Chapters 8 and 14.

*Topical Vocabulary* See *Technical Vocabulary* and *Topical Knowledge.*

*Treatment modality* See *learning mode.*

*Trend* See *slope.*

*T-unit* A group of words that can stand alone and make sense. T-units are used in analysis of sentence complexity. The number of units that can stand alone within a sentence is one indicator of sentence complexity.

*Unalterable variables* Conditions that cannot be altered within a reasonable time through the act of teaching. See *alterable variables.*

*Validity* How well a test describes reality. Does the test measure what it's supposed to measure? The so-what test.

*Variable* A characteristic, trait, skill, or condition of the student.

*Verbal mediator* Once the students are able to verbalize the procedure, they are able to literally "talk" their way through a situation to its solution. In the literature, this is sometimes called verbal mediation.

*Visually similar* Look alike (b/d/p/q/g, m/n/u/h, v/w, n/r) (Carnine & Silbert, 1979, p. 73).

*Working memory* See *short-term memory.*

*Writing mechanics* Grammar, punctuation, capitalization, handwriting, and spelling.

*Writing-process approach* A teaching focus that emphasizes writing as a communication act. Proponents suggest that currently there is too much emphasis on skill instruction and not enough on planning, transcribing, reviewing, and revising.

*Written communication* Written language, written expression.

# References

Aarnoutse, C. A. J., Van Den Bos, K. P. & Brand-Gruwel, S. (1998) Effects of listening comprehension training on listening and reading. *Journal of Special Education, 32* (2), 115–126.

Adams, D. R. (1997) *Nights Below Station Street.* Toronto, Ontario: McClelland & Stewart.

Adams, G. L. & Engelmann, S. (1996) *Research on Direct Instruction: 20 Years Beyond DISTAR.* Seattle: Educational Achievement Systems.

Adams, J. L. (1979) *Conceptual Blockbusting.* 2nd Ed. San Francisco: W. H. Freeman.

Adams, M. J. (1990) *Beginning to Read: Thinking and Learning About Print.* Urbana-Champaign, IL: University of Illinois, Center for the Study of Reading.

Adams, M. J. (1991) Beginning to read: A critique by literacy professionals and a response by Marilyn Jager Adams. *Reading Teacher, 44* (6), 370–395.

Adams, P. E. (1995) Teaching Romeo and Juliet in the non-tracked English classroom. *Journal of Reading, 38* (6), 424–432.

Adams, R. J., Wilson, M. & Wu, M. (1997) Multi-level item response models: An approach to errors in variables regression. *Journal of Educational and Behavioral Statistics, 22* (1), 74–76.

Algozzine, B., O'Shea, D. J., Crews, W. B. & Stoddard, K. (1987) Analysis of mathematics competence of learning disabled adolescents. *The Journal of Special Education, 21* (2), 97–107.

Ames, C. (1992) Classrooms: Goals, structures, and student motivation. *Journal of Educational Psychology, 84* (3), 261–271.

Anderman, E. M., Griesinger, T. & Westerfield, G. (1998) Motivation and cheating during early adolescence. *Journal of Educational Psychology, 90* (1), 84–93.

Anderson, J. R., Reder, L. M. & Simmon, H. A. (1996) Situated learning and education. *Educational Researcher, 24* (4), 5–11.

Anderson, L. M. (1982) *Student Responses to Seatwork: Implications for the Study of Students' Cognitive Processing (Research Series No. 102).* East Lansing: Michigan State University, IRT Publications.

Anderson, L. M. (1984) The environment of instruction: The function of seatwork in a commercially developed curriculum. In G. G. Duffy, L. R. Roehler & J. Mason (Eds.), *Comprehension Instruction: Perspectives and Suggestions* (pp. 93–103). New York: Longman.

Anderson, L. M. (1985) What are students doing when they do all that seatwork? In C. W. Fisher & D. C. Berliner (Eds.), *Perspectives on Instructional Time* (pp. 189–202). New York: Longman.

Anderson, R. C. & Armbruster, B. (1984) Content area textbooks. In R. C. Anderson, J. Osborn & R. Tierney (Eds.), *Learning to Read in American Schools* (pp. 217–226). Hillsdale, NJ: Erlbaum.

Antes, R. L. (1989) *Preparing Students for Taking Tests. Fastback 291.* Bloomington, In: Phi Delta Kappa Educational Foundation.

Antil, L., Jenkins, J., Wayne, S. K. & Vadasky, P. F. (1998) Cooperative learning: Prevalence, conceptualizations, and the relation between research and practice. *American Educational Research Journal, 35* (3), 419–454.

Archer, A. & Gleason, M. (1996) Advanced skills for school success. *Intervention in School and Clinic, 32,* 119–123.

Archer, J. (1996) Sex differences in social behavior: Are the social role and evolutionary explanations compatible? *American Psychologist, 51* (9), 909–917.

Arkes, H. R. & Hammond, K. R. (Eds.) (1986) *Judgement and Decision Making: An Interdisciplinary Reader.* New York: Cambridge University Press.

Armbruster, B. (1984a) The problem of "inconsiderate text." In G. G. Duffy, L. R. Roehler & J. Mason (Eds.), *Comprehension Instruction Perspectives and Suggestions.* New York: Longman.

Armbruster, B. (1984b) Commentary. In R. J. Tierney & M. Leys (Eds.), *What is the value of connecting reading and writing? Reading Education Report No. 55.* Urbana-Champaign, IL: University of Illinois.

Arnold, M. E. & Hughes, J. N. (1999) First do no harm: Adverse effects of grouping deviant youth for skills training. *Journal of School Psychology, 37* (1), 99–115.

Arter, J. A. & Jenkins, J. R. (1979) Differential diagnosis prescriptive teaching: A critical appraisal. *Review of Educational Research, 49,* 517–555.

Assink, E. M. H., Kattenberg, G. & Wortmann, C. (1992) *Reading Ability and the Use of Sublexical Units in*

*Word Identification.* Paper presented at the annual meeting of the American Educational Research Association, San Francisco, CA.

Aster, A. A., Meyer, H. A. & Behre, W. J. (1999) Unowned places and times: Maps and interviews about violence in high schools. *American Educational Research Journal, 36* (1), 3–42.

Baker, J. M. & Zigmond, N. (1990) Are regular education classes equipped to accommodate students with learning disabilities? *Exceptional Children, 56* (6), 515–526.

Bakken, J. P., Mastropieri, M. A. & Scruggs, T. E. (1998) Reading comprehension of expository science material and students with learning disabilities: A comparison of strategies. *Journal of Special Education, 31* (3), 300–324.

Ball, D. L. & Cohen, D. K. (1996) Reform by the book: What is—or might be—the role of curriculum materials in teacher learning and instructional reform? *Educational Researcher, 25* (9), 6–8.

Ball, E. & Blachman, B. (1991) Does phoneme awareness training in kindergarten make a difference in early word recognition and developmental spelling? *Reading Research Quarterly, 26* (1), 49–66.

Banbury, M. M. & Hebert, C. R. (1992) Do you see what I mean? Body language in classroom interactions. *Teaching Exceptional Children, 24* (2), 34–39.

Barnwell, D. (1987) *Syntactic and Morphological Errors of English Speakers on the Spanish Past Tenses.* ERIC: ED281369.

Baroody, A. J. & Hume, J. (1991) Meaningful mathematics instruction: The case of fractions. *Remedial and Special Education, 12* (3), 54–68.

Bassuk, E. L., Browne, A. & Buckner, J. C. (1996) Single mothers and welfare. *Scientific American, 275* (4), 60–67.

Bast, J. & Reitsma, P. (1997) Matthew effects in reading: A comparison of latent growth curve models and simplex models with structured means. *Multivariate Behavioral Research, 32* (2), 135–167.

Bateman, B. D. (1998) *Legal Research on What Constitutes "Specially Designed Instruction" and Quality Technology, Media, and Materials for Students with Disabilities (Tech. Rep.).* Eugene, OR: University of Oregon, National Center to Improve the Tools of Educators.

Bateman, B. D. & Linden, M. A. (1997) *Better IEPs.* Reston, VA: Council for Exceptional Children.

Battista, M. (1999) The mathematical mis-education of America's youth. *Phi Delta Kappan, 80* (6), 424–433.

Baumann, J. (1988) Direct instruction reconsidered. *Journal of Reading, 31* (8), 712–718.

Baumann, J. F. & Ivy, G. (1997) Delicate balances: Striving for curricular and instructional equilibrium in a second grade literature/strategy based classroom. *Reading Research Quarterly, 32* (3), 244–275

Beck, I., Perfetti, C. & McKeown, M. (1982) Effects of long-term vocabulary instruction on lexical access and reading comprehension. *Journal of Educational Psychology, 74,* 506–521.

Beck, I., McKeown, M. & McCaslin, E. (1983) Vocabulary development: All contexts are not created equal. *The Elementary School Journal, 83,* 178–181.

Bennett, N. & Desforges, C. (1988) Matching classroom tasks to students' attainments. *The Elementary School Journal, 88,* 221–234.

Bennett, S. N., Roth, E. & Dunn, R. (1987) Task processes in mixed and single age classes. *Education, 15,* 43–50.

Bennett, T., DeLuca, D. & Bruns, D. (1997) Putting inclusion into practice: Perspectives of teachers and parents. *Exceptional Children, 64* (1), 115–131.

Bensoussan, M. & Ramraz, R. (1984) Testing EFL reading comprehension using a multiple-choice rational cloze. *The Modern Language Journal, 68,* 230–239.

Bergan, J. R. & Kratochwell, T. R. (1990) *Behavioral Consultation and Therapy.* New York: Plenum Press.

Berk, L. & Winsler, A. (1995) Scaffolding children's learning: Vygotsky and early childhood education. *NAEYC Research Into Practice. Vol. 7.* Washington DC: Author.

Berliner, D. C. (1984) The half-full glass: A review of research on teaching. In P. L. Hosford (Ed.), *Using What We Know About Teaching.* Alexandria, VA: Association for Supervision and Curriculum Development.

Berliner, D. (1987) *Effective Classroom Teaching.* Paper presented at the fourth annual School Effectiveness Workshop, Phoenix, AZ, January 1987.

Berliner, D. (1989) *The Place of Process-Product Research in Developing the Agenda for Research on Teacher Thinking.* Paper presented at the meetings of the American Educational Research Association, Boston, MA.

Berliner, D. C. (1993) Mythology and the American system of education. *Phi Delta Kappan 74* (8), 634–640.

Bernard, B. (1993) Fostering resiliency in kids. *Educational Leadership, 51* (3), 44–45.

Berry, V. (1992) Communication priorities and strategies for the mainstreamed child with hearing loss. *Volta Review, 94* (1), 29–36.

Biemiller, A. (1978) Relationships between oral reading rates for letters, words, and simple text in the development of reading achievement. *Reading Research Quarterly, 13,* 223–253.

Bisanz, G. L., Das, J. P., Varnhagen, C. K. & Henderson, H. R. (1992) Structural components of reading time and recall for sentences in narratives: Exploring changes with age and reading ability. *Journal of Educational Psychology, 84* (1), 103–114.

Bishop, G. (1992) *Personal Communication.* Tigard, OR.

Bloom, B. S. (1976) *Human Characteristics and School Learning.* New York: McGraw-Hill.

Bloom, B. S. (1980) The new direction in education research: Alterable variables. *Phi Delta Kappan, 61,* 382–385.

Bloom, B. S., Engelhart, M. D., Furst, E. J., Hill, W. H. & Krathwohl, D. R. (1956) *Taxonomy of Educational Objectives: Cognitive Domain.* New York: Longman.

Bloom, B. S., Madaus, G. F. & Hastings, J. T. (1981) *Evaluation to Improve Learning.* New York: McGraw-Hill.

Boorstin, D. J. (1983) *The Discoverers.* New York: Random House.

Borg, W. R. (1980) Time and school learning. In C. Denham & A. Liberman (Eds.), *Time to Learn.* Washington, DC: National Institute of Learning.

Borko, H., Livingston, C. & Shavelson, R. J. (1990) Teachers' thinking about instruction. *Remedial and Special Education, 11* (6), 40–49.

Boulding, K. E. (1972) The schooling industry as a possible pathological section of the American economy. *Review of Educational Research, 42,* 129–143.

Boulding, K. E. (1985) *Human Betterment.* Beverly Hills, CA: Sage Publications.

Bouton, L. F. (Ed.) (1996) Pragmatics and language learning. *Monograph Series, 7,* 1–20.

Bowen, E. (1984) A debate over dumbing down. *Time, 124,* 68. December 3, 1984.

Bower, E. M. (1972) Education as a humanizing process and its relationship to other humanizing processes. In S. E. Golann and C. Eisdorfer (Eds.), *Handbook of Community Mental Health.* Englewood Cliffs, NJ: Prentice-Hall.

Bracht, G. H. (1970) Experimental factors relating to aptitude treatment interactions. *Review of Educational Research, 40,* 627–645.

Braungart-Bloom, D. S. (1986) *Assessing Holistic Rater's Perceptions of Writing Qualities: An Examination of a Hierarchical Framework Following Pre-Post Training and Live Readings.* Paper presented at the Annual Meeting of the American Educational Research Association, San Francisco, CA.

Brehmer, B. (1986) In one word: Not from experience. In H. R. Arkes, K. R. Arkes & K. R. Hammond (Eds.) *Judgement and Decision Making.* New York: Cambridge University Press.

Brett, A., Rothlein, L. & Hurley, M. (1996) Vocabulary acquisition from listening to stories and explanations of target words. *Elementary School Journal, 96* (4), 415–422.

Britton, J. (1978) The composing process and the functions of writing. In C. R. Cooper & L. Odell (Eds.), *Research on Composing: Points of Departure* (pp. 13–28). Urbana, IL: National Council of Teachers of English.

Brown, V. (1978) Independent study behaviors: A framework for curriculum development. *Learning Disability Quarterly, 1* (2), 78–84.

Brown, A. L. (1987) Metacognition, executive control, self-regulation and other even more mysterious mechanisms. In R. H. Kluwe and F. E. Weinert (Eds.), *Metacognition, Motivation, and Learning.* Hillsdale, NJ: Erlbaum.

Brown, J. S. & Duguid, P. (1996) Stolen knowledge. In H. McLellan, (Ed.), *Situated Learning Perspectives.* Englewood Cliffs, NJ: Educational Technology Publications.

Bryan, T. & Sullivan-Burstein, K. (1997) Homework how-to's. *Teaching Exceptional Children, 29* (6), 32–37.

Bryant, D. J. & Tversky, B. (1999) Mental representations of perspective and spatial relations from diagrams and models. *Journal of Experimental Psychology, Learning, Memory, and Cognition, 25* (1), 137–156.

Burrill, G. & Romberg, T. (1998) Statistics and probability for the middle grades: Examples from mathematics in context. In *Reflections on Statistics: Learning, Teaching and Assessment in Grades K–12* (pp. 33–62). Mahwah, NJ: Lawerence Earlbaum Associates.

Burstein, L., McDonnell, M., Van Winkle, J., Ormseth, T., Mirocha, J. & Guiton, G. (1995) *Validating National Curriculum Indicators.* Santa Monica, CA: RAND.

Cadwell, J. & Jenkins, J. (1986) Teacher's judgements about their students: The effect of cognitive simplification strategies on the rating process. *American Educational Research Journal, 23,* 460–475.

Cain, K. M. & Dweck, C. S. (1995) The relation between motivational patterns and achievement cognitions through the elementary school years. *Merrill-Palmer Quarterly, 41* (1), 25–52.

Calfee, R. & Drum, P. (1986) Research on teaching reading. In M. C. Wittrock (Ed.), *Handbook of Research on Teaching.* 3rd Ed. (pp. 804–849). New York: Macmillan.

Campbell, N. R. (1940) *Final Report, Committee of the British Association for Advancement of Science on the Problem of Measurement.* London: British Association.

Campione, J. C. & Brown, A. L. (1985) *Dynamic Assessment: One Approach and Some Initial Data (Tech. Report No. 361).* Urbana: University of Illinois, Center for the Study of Reading.

Carbo, M. (1992) Giving unequal learners an equal chance: A reply to a biased critique of learning styles. *Remedial and Special Education, 13* (1), 19–39.

Carnine, D. W. (1990) New research on the brain: Implications for instruction. *Phi Delta Kappan, 71,* 372–377.

Carnine, D. W. (1992) Introduction. In D. Carnine & E. J. Kameenui (Eds.), *Higher-Order Thinking: Designing Curriculum for Mainstreamed Students* (pp. 1–22). Austin, TX: Pro-Ed.

Carnine, D., Silbert, J. & Kameenui, E. (1997) *Direct Instruction Reading*. 3rd Ed. NJ: Prentice-Hall.

Carpenter, T. P., Matthews, W., Lindquist, M. M. & Silver, E. A. (1984) Achievement in mathematics: Results from the national assessment. *The Elementary School Journal, 84,* 475–495.

Carter, M. & Kemp, C. R. (1996) Strategies for task analysis in special education. *Educational Psychology, 16* (2), 155–170.

Carter, J. & Sugai, G. (1989) Survey on pre-referral practices: Responses from state departments of education. *Exceptional Children, 55,* 298–302.

Carter, K., Cushing, K., Sabers, D., Stein, P. & Berliner, D.C. (1988) Expert-novice differences in perceiving and processing visual classroom information. *Journal of Teacher Education, 39,* 25–31.

Carver, R. P. (1992) What do standardized tests of reading comprehension measure in terms of efficiency, accuracy, and rate? *Reading Research Quarterly, 27* (4), 346–359.

Case, L. P., Harris, D. R. & Graham, S. (1992) Improving the mathematical problem-solving skills of students with learning disabilities: Self-regulated strategy development. *The Journal of Special Education, 26* (1), 1–19.

Cawley, J. F. & Palmer, R. S. (1992) Arithmetic programming for students with disabilities: An alternative. *Remedial and Special Education, 13* (3), 6–18.

Chan, L. K. (1996) Combined attributional training for seventh grade average and poor readers. *Journal of Research in Reading, 19* (2), 111–127.

Cherkes-Julkowski, M. (1996) The child as a self-organizing system: The case against instruction as we know it. *Learning Disabilities: A Multidisciplinary Journal, 7* (1), 19–27.

Chow, S. H. (1981) *A Study of Academic Learning Time for Mainstream Learning-Disabled Students. Final Report.* San Francisco, CA: Far West Laboratory for Educational Research and Development.

Christensen, C. A. & Cooper, T. J. (1991) The effectiveness of instruction in cognitive strategies in developing proficiency in single digit addition. *Cognition and Instruction, 8* (4), 363–371.

Ciborowski, J. (1995) Using textbooks with students who cannot read them. *Remedial and Special Education, 16* (2), 90–101.

Cipani, E. (1998) *Classroom Management for All Teachers: 11 Effective Plans.* NJ: Merrill.

Clarizio, H. F. & Payette, K. (1990) A survey of school psychologists' perspectives and practices with childhood depression. *Psychology in the Schools, 27,* 57–63.

Clark, C. M. (1987) The Carroll model. In M. J. Dunkin (Ed.), *The International Encyclopedia of Teaching and Teacher Education.* Oxford: Pergamon.

Clark, C. M. & Peterson, P. L. (1986) Teachers' thought processes. In M. C. Wittrock (Ed.), *Handbook of Research on Teaching.* 3rd Ed. (pp. 255–296). New York: Macmillan.

Clay, M. M. (1985) *Reading: The Patterning of Complex Behavior.* 2nd Ed. (pp. 200–204). Auckland, New Zealand: Heinemann.

Cognition and Technology Group at Vanderbilt University. (1991) Technology and design of generative learning environments. *Educational Technology, 34–40,* vol. 31 (5).

Cohen, A. S. (1987) Instructional alignment: Searching for a magic bullet. *Educational Researcher, 57,* 16–20.

Cohen, D. K. (1996) Standards-based reforms: Policy, practice, and performance. In H. F. Ladd (Ed.), *Holding Schools Accountable: Performance-Based Reform in Education.* Washington DC: Brookings.

Cole, L. (1956) Reflections on the teaching of handwriting. *Elementary School Journal, 57,* 95–99.

Coles, R. (1990) *Spiritual Life of Children.* Boston, MA: Houghton Mifflin.

Committee for Children (1992) *Second Step: A Violence Prevention Curriculum.* Seattle, WA.: Author.

Cooper, R., Slavin, R. E. & Madden, N. A. (1998) Success for all: improving the quality of implementation of whole-school change through the use of a national reform network. *Education and Urban Society, 30*(3), 385–408.

Corno, L. (1993) The best laid plans: Modern conceptions of volition and educational research. *Educational Research, 22* (2), 14–22.

Council of Chief State School Officers (CCSSO) (1996) *State Student Assessment Programs Data-base.* Oak Brook, IL: North Central Regional Educational Laboratory.

Council for Educational Development and Research (1997) *What We Know about Reading, Teaching, and Learning: EdTalk.* Washington, DC (Eric Document Reproduction Service No. ED410553).

Crawford, D. & Bodine, R. (1996) *Conflict Resolution Education: A Guide to Implementing Programs in Schools, Youth-Serving Organizations, and Community and Juvenile Justice Settings.* Washington, DC: United States Department of Justice, Office of Juvenile Justice and Delinquency Prevention, Office of Elementary and Secondary Education.

Crawford, W. (1993) *Standards of performance: Evaluating Grading Standards and Their Role in Student*

*Revision Research Processes.* Paper presented at the Annual Meeting of the Conference on College Composition and Communication, San Diego, CA. April, 1993.

Cronbach, L. J. (1957) The two disciplines of scientific psychology. *American Psychologist, 12,* 671–684.

Cummins, D. D. (1991) Children's interpretations of arithmetic word problems. *Cognition and Instruction, 8* (3), 261–289.

Cummins, J. (1986) Empowering minority students: A framework for interaction. *Harvard Educational Review, 56,* 18–36.

Cunningham, A. E. & Stanovich, K. E. (1990) Assessing print exposure and orthographic processing skill in children: A quick measure of reading experience. *Journal of Educational Psychology, 82* (4), 733–740.

Curtis, M. & McCart, L. (1992) Fun ways to promote poor readers' word recognition. *Journal of Reading, 35* (5), 398–399.

Czarbecki, E., Rosko, D. & Fine, E. (1998) How to call up notetaking skills. *Teaching Exceptional Children, 30* (6), 14–19.

Daneman, M. & Stainton, M. (1991) Phonological recoding in silent reading. *Journal of Experimental Psychology: Learning, Memory, and Cognition, 17* (4), 618–632.

Danoff, B. (1993) Incorporating strategy instruction within the writing process in the regular classroom: Effects on the writing of students with and without learning disabilities. *Journal of Reading Behavior, 25* (3), 295–322.

DaPaepe, P. A., Shores, R. E., Jack, S. L. & Denny, R. K. (1996) Effects of task difficulty on the disruptive and on-task behavior of students with severe behavior disorders. *Behavioral Disorders, 21,* 216–225.

Darling-Hammond, L. (1996) The right to learn and the advancement of teaching: Research, policy, and practice for democratic education. *Educational Researcher, 25* (6), 5–17.

Dawkins, R. (1999) The selfish meme. *Time, 153*(15), 52–53.

Day, J. D. (1980) *Teaching Summarization Skills.* Unpublished doctoral dissertation, University of Illinois.

de Beaugrande, R. (1984) *Text Production: Toward a Science of Composition.* Norwood, NJ: Ablex.

de Bettencourt, L. (1987) Strategy training: A need for clarification. *Exceptional Children, 54* (1), 24–30.

De La Paz, S. & Graham, S. (1997) Strategy instruction in planning: Effects on the writing performance and behavior of students with learning difficulties. *Exceptional Children, 63* (2), 167–181.

Deno, S. L. (1985) Curriculum-based measurement: The emerging alternative. *Exceptional Children, 52,* 219–232.

Deno, S. L. (1986) Formative evaluation of individual student programs: A new role for school psychologists. *School Psychology Review, 15* (3), 358–374.

Deno, S. L. (1997) Whether thou goest . . . Perspectives on progress monitoring. In J. W. Lloyd, E. J. Kameenui & D. Chard (Eds.), *Issues in Educating Students with Disabilities.* Mahwah, NJ: Lawrence Erlbaum.

Deno, S. L. & Espin, C. A. (1991) Evaluation strategies for preventing and remediating basic skill deficits. In G. Stoner, M. Shinn & H. Walker (Eds.), *Interventions for Achievement and Behavior Problems* (pp. 79–97). Silver Springs, MD: National Association of School Psychologists.

Deno, S. L. & Markell, M. A. (1997) Effects of increasing oral reading: Generalization across reading tasks. *Journal of Special Education, 31* (2), 233–250.

Deno, S. L. & Mirkin, P. K. (1977) *Data-Based Program Modification: A Manual.* Reston, VA: The Council for Exceptional Children.

Derry, S. J. & Murphy, D. A. (1986) Designing systems that train learning ability: From theory to practice. *Review of Educational Research, 56,* 1–39.

Deshler, D. D., Ellis, E. S. & Lentz, B. K. (1996a) *Teaching Adolescents with Language Disorders: Strategies and Methods.* 2nd Ed. Dencer: Love Publishing.

Deshler, D., Schumaker, J. & Fisher, J. (1996b) *The Effects of an Interactive Multimedia Program on Teachers' Understanding and Implementation of an Instructional Innovation (technical report).* Lawrence: Kansas University, Dole Center for Human Development.

Dev, P. (1997) Intrinsic motivation and academic achievement: What does their relationship imply for the teacher? *Remedial and Special Education, 18* (1), 12–19.

Dick, W. & Hagerty, N. (1971) *Topics in Measurement: Reliability and Validity.* New York: McGraw-Hill.

DiTraglia, J. (1991) Methylphenidate protocol: Feasibility in a pediatric practice. *Clinical Pediatrics, 30* (12), 656–660.

Dixon, F. (1993a) Literacy seminars for gifted and talented students. *Gifted Children Today, 16* (4), 15–19.

Dixon, R. C. (1993b) *The Surefire Way to Better Spelling.* New York: St. Martin's Press.

Dole, J. A., Duffy, G. G., Roehler, L. R. & Pearson, P. D. (1991) Moving from the old to the new: Research on reading comprehension instruction. *Review of Educational Research, 61* (2), 239–264.

Doyle, W. (1983) Academic work. *Review of Educational Research, 53,* 159–199.

Doyle, W. (1986) Classroom organization and management. In M. C. Wittrock (Ed.), *Handbook of Research on Teaching.* 3rd Ed. (pp. 392–431). New York: Macmillan.

Doyle, W. & Carter, K. (1987) Choosing the means of instruction. In V. Richardson-Koehler (Ed.), *Education Handbook*. White Plains, NY: Longman.

Du Charme, C., Earl, J. & Poplin, M. S. (1989) The author model: The constructivist view of the writing process. *Learning Disability Quarterly, 12* (3), 237–242.

Duffy, E. & Mowery, D. (1989) The power of language to efface and desensitize. *Rhetoric Society Quarterly, 19* (4), 163.

Duffy, G. G. (1991) *Reading in the Middle School*. 2nd Ed. Newark, DE: International Reading Association.

Duffy, G. G. & McIntyre (1982) A naturalistic study of instructional assistance in primary-grade reading. *Elementary School Journal, 83*(1), 15–23.

Duffy, M. & Zeidler, D. L. (1996) *The Effects of Grouping and Instructional Strategies on Conceptual Understanding and Critical Thinking Skills in the Secondary Biology Classroom*. Presentation at the Annual Meeting of the National Association for Research in Science Teaching. St. Louis, MO, April 2, 1996.

Duffy, G., Dole, J., Roehler, L. & Pearson, P. (1991) Moving from the old to the new: Research on reading comprehension. *Review of Educational Research, 61* (2), 239.

Dunn, M., Flax, J., Sliwinski, M. & Aram, D. (1996) The use of spontaneous language measures as criteria for identifying children with specific language impairment: An attempt to reconcile clinical and research incongruence. *Journal of Speech and Hearing Research, 40* (1), 62–74.

Dunn, R. (1983) Learning style and its relation to exceptionality at both ends of the spectrum. *Exceptional Children, 49*, 496–506.

Dunn, R., Dunn, K. & Price, G. E. (1981) Learning styles: Research vs. opinion. *Phi Delta Kappan, 62*, 645–646.

Dunston, P. J. (1992) A critique of graphic organizer research. *Reading Research Instruction, 32* (2), 57–65.

DuPaul, G. J., Stoner, G., Putman, D. & Tilly, W. D. (1991) Interventions for attention problems. In G. Stoner, M. Shinn & H. Walker (Eds.), *Interventions for Achievement and Behavioral Problems* (pp. 685–714). Silver Springs, MD: National Association of School Psychologists.

DuRant, R. H., Krowchuck, D. P., Kreiter, S. Sinal, S. & Woods, C. R. (1999). The relationship between early age of outset of initial substance abuse and engaging in multiple health risk behaviors among young adolescents. *Archives of Pediatrics and Adolescent Medicine, 153* (1), 21.

Dweck, C. (1986) Motivational processes affecting learning. *American Psychologist, 41* (10), 1040–1048.

Eckert, T. L., Hintze, J. M. & Shapiro, E. S. (1997) School psychologists' acceptability of behavioral and traditional assessment procedures for externalizing problem behaviors. *School Psychology Quarterly, 12* (2), 150–169.

Editors (1999) Demanding results. *Education Week, 18* (17), 5.

Edmunds, A. L. (1999) Cognitive credit cards: Acquiring learning strategies. *Teaching Exceptional Children, 31* (4), 68–73.

Edwards, W. J. & Newman, R. J. (1986) Multiattribute evaluation. In H. R. Arkes & K. R. Hammond (Eds.), *Judgement and Decision Making: An Interdisciplinary Reader*. New York: Cambridge University Press.

Edwards, P. A., Beasley, K. & Thompson, J. (1991) Teachers in transition: Accommodating reading curriculum to cultural diversity. *The Reading Teacher, 44*, 436–437.

Ehri, L. C. & Sweet, J. (1991) Fingerpoint reading of memorized text: What enables beginners to process the print? *Reading Research Quarterly, 26* (4), 442–462.

Eisner, E. W. (1982) *Cognition and Curriculum*. New York: Longman.

Eitzen, S. D. (1992) Problem students: The sociocultural roots. *Phi Delta Kappan, 73* (73), 584–590.

Elbaum, B., Vaughn, S., Hughes, M. & Moody, S. W. (1999) Grouping practices and reading outcomes for students with disabilities. *Exceptional Children, 65* (3), 339–415.

Elliott, R. T. & Zhang, Q (1998) Interference in learning context-dependent words. *Educational Psychology, 18*(1), 5–25.

Ellis, A. (Ed.) (1971) *Growth Through Reason: Verbatim Cases in Rational-Emotive Therapy*. Palo Alto, CA: Science and Behavior.

Ellis, E. S. (1997) Watering up the curriculum for adolescents with learning disabilities: Goals of the knowledge dimension. *Remedial and Special Education, 18* (6), 326–346.

Ellis, E. S. (1998) Watering up the curriculum for adolescents with learning disabilities: Part 2. Goals of the affective dimension. *Remedial and Special Education, 19* (2), 91–105.

Ellis, E. S. & Lenz, B. K. (1990) Techniques for mediating content-area learning: Issues and research. *Focus on Exceptional Children, 22* (9), 1–15.

Elmore, R. E. (1995) Structural reform in educational practice. *Educational Researcher, 24* (9), 23–26.

Engle, R. W., Nations, J. K. & Cantor, J. (1990) Is "working memory capacity" just another name for word knowledge? *Journal of Educational Psychology, 82*, 799–804.

Englemann, S. (1997) Theory of mastery and acceleration. In J. W. Lloyd, E. J. Kameenui & D. Chard

(Eds.), *Issues in Educating Students with Disabilities*. Mahwah, NJ: Lawrence Erlbaum.

Englemann, S., Carnine, D. & Steely, D. G. (1992) Making connections in mathematics. In D. Carnine & E. J. Kameenui (Eds.), *Higher-Order Thinking: Designing Curriculum for Mainstreamed Students* (pp. 75–106). Austin, TX: Pro-Ed.

Englert, C. S. (1992) Writing instruction from a so-cio-cultural perspective: The holistic, dialogic, and social enterprise of writing. *Journal of Learning Disabilities, 25* (3), 153–172.

Englert, C. S. & Marriage, T. V. (1996) A sociocultural perspective: Teaching ways-of-thinking and ways-of-talking in a literacy community. *Learning Disabilities Research and Practice, 11* (3), 157–167.

Englert, C. S., Marriage, T. V., Garmon, M. A. & Tarrant, K. L. (1998) Accelerating reading progress in early literacy project classrooms. *Remedial and Special Education, 19* (3), 142–159.

Englert, C. S., Raphaet, T. E., Anderson, L. M., Anthony, H. M. & Stevens, D. D. (1991) Making strategies and self-talk visible: Writing instruction in regular and special education classrooms. *American Education Research Journal, 28*, 337–372.

Ensminger, E. & Dangel, H. L. (1992) The Foxfire pedagogy: A confluence of best practices for special education. *Focus on Exceptional Children, 24* (7), 1–16.

Espin, C. A. & Deno, S. L. (1995) Curriculum-based measures for secondary students. *Diagnostic, 20* (1–4), 121–142.

Espin, C. A. & Foegen, A. (1996) Validity of general outcome measures for predicting secondary student's performance on content-area tasks. *Exceptional Children, 62* (6), 497–514.

Etzioni, A. (1992) Education for intimacy. *Educational Leadership, 54* (8), 20–23.

Evans, W. H., Evans, S. S., Gable, R. A. & Kehlhem, M. A. (1991) Assertive discipline and behavior disorders: Is this a marriage made in heaven? *Beyond Behavior, 2*, 13–16.

Evoy, A. (1999) *Personal communication*. January, Vancouver, B.C.

Fernald, G. M. (1943) *Remedial Techniques in Basic School Subjects*. New York: McGraw-Hill.

Fischer, M., Roman, M. A. & Newby, R. F. (1991) Parent training for families of children with ADHD. *School Psychology Review, 20* (2), 252–265.

Fisher, C. W. & Hiebert, E. H. (1990) Characteristics of tasks in two approaches to literacy instruction. *The Elementary School Journal, 91* (1), 3–18.

Fisher, C., Berliner, D., Filby, N., Marliave, R., Cahen, L. & Dishaw, M. (1980) Teaching behaviors, aca-demic learning time, and student achievement. In C. Denham & A. Liberman (Eds.), *Time to Learn*. Washington, DC: National Institute of Learning.

Fisher, J. B., Schumaker, J. B. & Deshler, D. D. (1995) Searching for validated inclusive practices: A review of literature. *Focus on Exceptional Children, 28* (4), 1–20.

Fister, S., Conrad, D. & Kemp, K. (1998) *Cool Kids*. Longmont, CO: Sopris West.

Fitzgerald, F. S. (1989) In J. E. Russo & Schoemaker (Eds.), *Decision Traps*. New York: Doubleday.

Flower, L. S. & Hayes, J. R. (1990) The dynamics of composing: Making plans and juggling constraints. In L. W. Gregg & E. R. Steinberg (Eds.), *Cognitive Process in Writing* (pp. 31–50). Hillsdale, NJ: Erlbaum.

Flugum, K. R. & Reschley, D. J. (1994) Pre-referral interventions: Quality indices and outcomes. *Journal of School Psychology, 32*, 1–14.

Ford, J. A. (1995) *Content vocabulary, graphic aids, and comprehension in science and related literature*. Master's thesis, Kean College of New Jersey, New Jersey.

Forness, S. R., Kavale, K. A. (1987) Substance over style: Assessing the efficacy of modality testing and teaching. *Exceptional Children, 54*, 228–239.

Forness, S. K., Kavale, K. A., MacMillan, D. L. & Asarnow, J. R. (1996) Early detection and prevention of emotional or behavioral disorders: Developmental aspects of systems of care. *Behavioral Disorders, 21* (3), 226–240.

Fox, N. E. & Ysseldyke, J. E. (1997) Implementing inclusion at the middle school level: Lessons from a negative example. *Exceptional Children, 64* (1), 81–98.

Frederiksen, N. (1984) Implications of cognitive theory for instruction in problem solving. *Review of Educational Research, 54*, 363–407.

Frederiksen, N. (1986) Toward a broader concept of human intelligence. *American Psychologist, 41*, 445–452.

Freire, P. (1993) *Pedagogy of the City*. New York: Continuum.

Freppon, P. A. & Dahl, K. L. (1998) Balanced instruction: Insights and considerations (theory and research into practice) *Reading Research Quarterly, 33* (2), 240–257.

Fuchs, D., Fuchs, L. S., Benowitz, S. & Barringer, K. (1987) Norm-referenced tests: Are they valid for use with handicapped students? *Exceptional Children, 54*, 263–271.

Fuchs, D., Fuchs, L. S., Dailey, A. M. & Power, M. H. (1985a) The effect of examiner's personal familiarity and professional experience on handicapped children's test performance. *Journal of Educational Research, 78*, 141–146.

Fuchs, L. S. & Deno, S. L. (1991) Paradigmatic distinctions between instructionally relevant measurement models. *Exceptional Children, 57*, 488–500.

Fuchs, L. S. & Fuchs, D. (1986) Linking assessment to instructional interventions: An overview. *School Psychology Review, 15* (3), 318–323.

Fuchs, L. S., Deno, S. L. & Mirkin, P. K. (1985b) Data-based program modification: A continuous evaluation system with computer software to facilitate instruction. *Journal of Special Education, 6,* 50–57.

Fuchs, L. S., Fuchs, D. & Maxwell, L. (1988) The validity of informal reading comprehension measures. *Remedial and Special Education, 9* (2), 20–28.

Fuchs, L. S., Allinder, R. M., Hamlett, C. L., & Fuchs, D. (1990) An analysis of spelling curricula and teachers' skills in identifying error types. *Remedial and Special Education, 11* (1), 42–52.

Fuchs, L. S., Fuchs, D., Hamlett, C. L. & Ferguson, C. (1992) Effects of expert system consultation within curriculum-based measurement using a reading maze task. *Exceptional Children, 58* (5), 436–450.

Fuchs, L. S., Fuchs, D., Hamlett, C. L., Phillips, N., Karns, K. & Dutka, S. (1997) Enhancing students' helping behavior during peer-mediated instruction with conceptual mathematics explanations. *Elementary School Journal, 97,* 223–250.

Fukkink, R. G. & deGlopper, K. (1998) Effects of instruction on deriving word meaning from context: A meta-analysis. *Review of Educational Research, 68* (4), 450–469.

Fult, B. M. & Stormont-Spurgin, M. (1995) Spelling interventions for students with disabilities: A review. *The Journal of Special Education, 28* (4), 488–513.

Fuson, K. (1997) Children's conceptual structures for multi-digit numbers and methods of multi-digit addition and subtraction. *Journal for Research in Mathematics Education, 28* (2), 130–162.

Gable, R. A., Quinn, M. M., Rutherford, R. B., Nelson, C. M. & Howell, K. W. (1999) *Addressing Student Problem Behavior: An IEP Team's Introduction to Functional Behavior Assessment and Behavior Intervention Plans.* Washington, DC: American Institute for Research, Center for Effective Collaboration.

Gaffney, J. S. & Anderson, R. C. (1991) Two-tiered scaffolding: Congruent processes of teaching and learning. In E. H. Hiebert (Ed.), *Literacy for a Diverse Society: Perspectives, Programs and Policies.* New York: Teachers College Press.

Gagne, R. M., Briggs, L. J. & Warner, W. W. (1988) *Principles of Instructional Design.* 3rd Ed. New York: Holt, Rinehart, and Winston.

Gajria, M. & Salvia, J. (1992) The effects of summarization instruction on text comprehension of students with learning disabilities. *Exceptional Children, 58* (6), 508–516.

Gallis, K., Anton-Oldenburg, M., Ballenger, C. & Beseler, C. (1996) Talking the talk and walking the walk: Researching oral language in the classroom. *Language Arts, 73*(8), 608–617.

Gambrell, L. B. & Chasen, S. P. (1991) Explicit story structure instruction and the narrative writing of fourth- and fifth-grade below-average readers. *Reading Research and Instruction, 31* (1), 54–62.

Gavin, W. & Giles, L. (1996) Sample size effects on temporal reliability of language measures of preschool children. *Journal of Speech and Hearing Research, 39* (6), 1258–1262.

Gazzaniga, M. S. (1989) Organization of the human brain. *Science, 24,* 947–952.

Geary, D. (1995) Reflections of evolution and culture in children's cognition. *American Psychologist, 50,* 1–38.

Gerber, A. & Bryen, D. N. (1981) *Language and Learning Disabilities.* Baltimore, MD: University Park.

Gerber, M. M. (1987) Application of cognitive-behavioral training methods to teaching basic skills to mildly handicapped elementary school students. In M. C. Wang, M. C. Reynolds & H. J. Walberg (Eds.), *Handbook of Special Education: Research and Practice.* Vol. 1 (pp. 167–86). New York: Pergamon.

Gerber, P. J. (1992) Being learning disabled and a beginning teacher and teaching students with learning disabilities. *Exceptionality: A Research Journal, 3* (4), 213–231.

Gersten, R. (1990) Enemies real and imagined: Implications of "teachers' thinking about instruction" for collaboration between special and general education. *Remedial and Special Education, 11* (6), 50–53.

Gersten, R. (1992) Passion and precision: Response to "Curriculum-based assessment and direct instruction: Critical reflections on fundamental assumptions." *Exceptional Children, 58* (5), 464–466.

Gersten, R. & Brengelman, S. U. (1996) The quest to translate research into classroom practice: The emerging knowledge base. *Remedial and Special Education, 17* (2), 67–74.

Gersten, R. & Dimino, J. (1993) Visions and revisions: A special education perspective on the whole language controversy. *Remedial and Special Education, 14* (4), 5–13.

Gersten, R., Woodward, J. & Darch, C. (1986) Direct instruction: A research-based approach to curriculum design and teaching. *Exceptional Children, 53,* 17–31.

Giangreco, M. F., Edelman, S. W., Luiselle, T. E. & MacFarland, S. Z. C. (1997) Helping or hovering? Effects of instructional assistant proximity on students with disabilities. *Exceptional Children, 64* (1), 7–18.

Gilbert, T. F. (1978) *Human Competence: Engineering worthy performance.* New York: McGraw-Hill.

Gillespie, C. (1991) Questions about student-generated questions. *The Journal of Reading, 34,* 250–257.

Glass, G. G. (1971) Perceptual conditioning for decoding: Rationale and method. In B. B. Bateman (Ed.), *Learning Disorders* Vol. 4. Seattle, WA: Special Child Publications.

Glass, G. V (1983) Effectiveness of special education. *Policy Studies Review, 2,* 65–78.

Gleason, M. M., Colvin, G. & Archer, A. L. (1991) Interventions for improving study skills. In G. Stoner, M. Shinn & H. Walker (Eds.), *Interventions for Achievement and Behavior Problems* (pp. 130–167). Silver Springs, MD: National Association of School Psychologists.

Gleason, M. M., Colvin, G. & Archer, A. L. (1991) Interventions for improving study skills. In G. Stoner, M. Shinn, H. Walker (Eds.), *Interventions for Achievement and Behavior Problems* (pp. 137–160). Washington, DC: National Association of School Psychologists.

Goldstein, A. P. (1988) *The Prepare Curriculum.* Champaign, IL: Research Press.

Goldstein, A. P. (1997) *Skillstreaming the Adolescent.* Revised Edition. Champaign, IL: Research Press.

Göncü, A. (1998) *Children's Engagement in the World: A Sociocultural Perspective.* New York: Cambridge.

Good, R. H. (1999a) *Dynamic Indicators of Basic Early Literacy Skills (DIEBLS).* Eugene OR: University of Oregon, school psychology program.

Good, R. H. (1999b) *Personal Communication.* Eugene, OR.

Good, T. L. & Brophy, J. E. (1986) School effects. In M. C. Wittrock (Ed.), *Handbook of Research on Teaching.* 3rd Ed. New York: Macmillan.

Good, T. L. & Brophy, J. E. (1994) *Looking in Classrooms.* 6th Ed. New York: HarperCollins.

Gorden, R. A. (1994) The effect of perceived resource availability on the revision of written assignments. *Journal of Psychology, 134* (1), 41–45.

Gorenflo, C. W., Gorenflo, D. W. & George, P. (1995) An intervention for educating child care personnel on language milestones. *Early Child Development and Care, 105,* 13–19.

Graham, S. (1994) Are slanted manuscript alphabets superior to the traditional manuscript alphabet? *Childhood Education, 70* (2), 91–95.

Graham, S. (1997) Executive control in the revising of students with learning and writing difficulties. *Journal of Educational Psychology, 89* (2), 223–234.

Graham, S. & Harris, K. R. (1988) Instructional recommendations for teaching writing to exceptional students. *Exceptional Children, 54,* 506–512.

Graham, S. & Harris, K. R. (1994) The role of development of self-regulation in the writing process. In D. Schunk & B. Zimmerman (Eds.), *Self-Regulation of Learning and Performance: Issues and Educational Applications* (pp. 203–228). New York: Lawrence Erlbaum.

Graham, S., MacArthur, C., Schwartz, S. & Page-Voth, V. (1992) Improving the compositions of students with learning disabilities using a strategy involving product and process goal setting. *Exceptional Children, 58* (4), 322–334.

Grave, C. E. (1944) The psychotherapeutic value of a remedial education program. *The Nervous Child, 3,* 343–349.

Green-Emrich, A. & Altmaier, E. M. (1991) Attribution retraining as a structured group intervention. *Journal of Counseling and Development, 69*(4), 351–355.

Greene, S. B., McKoon, G. & Ratcliff, R. (1992) Pronoun resolution and discourse models. *Journal of Experimental Psychology: Learning, Memory, and Cognition, 18* (2), 266–283.

Greenwood, C. R. (1991) Longitudinal analysis of time, engagement and achievement in at-risk versus non-risk students. *Exceptional Children, 57,* 521–535.

Gresham, F. M. & Elliot, S. N. (1993) Social skills intervention guide: Systematic approaches to social skill training. *Special Services in the Schools, 8* (1), 137–158.

Gresham, F. M., Elliot, S. N. & Evans-Fernandez, S. E. (1993) Student self-concept scale. *Journal of Psychoeducational Assessment, 16* (2), 181–186.

Gresham, F. M. & MacMillan, D. (1997) Social competence and affective characteristics of students with mild disabilities. *Review of Educational Research, 67* (4), 377–415.

Gresham, F. M. & Noell, G. H. (1998) Functional analysis assessment as a cornerstone for noncategorical special education. In D. J. Reschly, W. D. Tilly III & J. P. Grimes (Eds.), *Functional and Noncategorical Identification and Intervention in Special Education,* Iowa Department of Education. Adapted from O'Neill, Horner, Albin, Sprague, Storey & Newton O'Neill, R. E. (1997) *Functional Assessment of Problem Behavior: A Practical Assessment Guide,* 2nd Ed. Pacific Grove: Brooks/Cole.

Gresham, F. M., Duhon, G. & Noell, G. H. (1998) Fundamental agreements and epistemological differences in differentiating what was said from what was done in behavioral consultation. *School Psychology Review, 13* (1), 81.

Griffith, P. L. & Olson, M. W. (1992) Phonemic awareness helps beginning readers break the code. *The Reading Teacher, 45* (7), 516–523.

Grigal, M. (1997) An evaluation of transition components of individual education plans. *Exceptional Children, 63* (3), 357–372.

Grigorenko, E. A. & Sternberg, R. J. (1997) Styles of thinking, abilities, and academic performance. *Exceptional Children, 63* (3), 295–312.

Gronlund, N. E. (1973) *Preparing Criterion-Referenced Tests for Classroom Instruction.* New York: Macmillan.

Grossen, B. & Carnine, D. (1991) Strategies for maximizing reading success in the regular classroom. In G. Stoner, M. Shinn & H. Walker (Eds.), *Interventions for Achievement and Behavioral Problems* (pp. 333–356). Silver Springs, MD: National Association of School Psychologists.

Grossen, B. & Carnine, D. (1992) Translating research on text structure into classroom practice. *Teaching Exceptional Children, 24* (4), 48–53.

Gruenewald, L. J. & Pollak, S. A. (1990) *Language Interaction in Curriculum and Instruction.* 2nd Ed. Austin, TX: Pro. Ed.

Gunning, T. G. (1998) *Assessing and Correcting Reading and Writing Difficulties.* Needham, MA: Allyn and Bacon.

Guskey, T. R. & Oldham, B. R. (1997) Despite the best intentions: Inconsistencies among components in Kentucky's systemic reform. *Education Policy, 11* (4), 426–442.

Guthrie, J. T., Britten, T. & Baker, K. G. (1991) Roles of document structure, cognitive strategy, and awareness of searching for information. *Reading Research Quarterly, 26* (3), 300–324.

Hall, T. & Tindal, G. (1991) *The Portfolio Concept with Applications in Curriculum-Based Measurement: Resource Consultant Training Program (Research Report No. 13).* Eugene: University of Oregon.

Hammond (Eds.) *Judgement and Decision Making.* New York: Cambridge University Press.

Hansen, F. J., Stanilla, J. K., Ross, J. I. & Sinvani, C. (1992) Integrating child psychiatry and family systems approaches. *Journal of Family Psychotherapy, 3*(3), 13–16.

Hanley-Maxwell, C. & Collet-Klingenberg, L. (1995) *Research Synthesis on Design of Effective Curricular Practices in Transition from School to the Community (Technical Report No. 9)* Eugene, OR: National Center to Improve the Tools of Educators.

Hanna, G. (1998) *How Do Students' Notions of Proof Explanation and Justification Develop Over Time? A Discussion of Selected Research Studies.* White Paper prepared for the National Council of teachers of Mathematics, Reston, VA.

Hansen, F. J., Stanilla, J. K., Ross, J. I. & Sinvani, C. (1992) Integrating child psychiatry and family system approaches. *Journal of Family Psychotherapy, 3* (3), 13–16.

Harris, K. R. & Graham, S. (1994) Constructivism: Principles, paradigms, and integration. *Journal of Special Education, 28* (3), 233–247.

Harris, K. R. & Graham, S. (1996a) Memo to constructivists: Skills count, too. *Educational Leadership, 53* (5), 26–29.

Harris, K. R. & Graham, S. (1996b) Constructivism and students with special needs: Issues in the classroom. *Learning Disabilities Research and Practice, 11* (3), 134–137.

Harris, K. R. J. & Pressley, M. (1991) The nature of cognitive strategy instruction. *Exceptional Children, 57,* 392–404.

Harris, K. R., Graham, S. & Deschler, D. (1998) *Teaching Every Child Every Day: Learning in Diverse Schools and Classrooms.* Advances in Teaching and Learning Series. Cambridge, MA: Brookline Books.

Hasbrouck, J. E., Tindal, G. & Parker, R. I. (Winter 1994) Objective procedures for scoring student's writing. *Teaching Exceptional Children, 26*(2), 18–22.

Haskell, D. W., Foorman, B. R. & Swank, P. R. (1992) Effects of three orthographic/phonological units on first-grade reading. *Remedial and Special Education, 13* (2), 40–49.

Haynes, M. C. & Jenkins, J. R. (1986) Reading instruction in special education resource rooms. *American Educational Research Journal, 23,* 161–190.

Heartland Education Agency 11 (1996) *Program Manual for Special Education.* Johnston, IA: Author.

Heartland Education Agency 11 (1998) *Technical Manual: Academic and Social/Behavior Problem Decision Making.* Johnston, IA: Author.

Hemingway, Z., Hemingway, P., Hutchinson, N. L. & Kuhns N. A. (1987) Effects of student characteristics on teachers' decisions and teachers' awareness of these effects. *Journal of Special Education, 11,* 313–326.

Herrmann, B. A. (1988) Two approaches for helping poor readers become more strategic. *Reading Teacher, 42* (1), 24–28.

Heward, W. L., Heron, T. E., Gardner, R. & Prayzer, R. (1991) Two strategies for improving students' writing skills. In G. Stoner, M. Shinn & H. Walker (Eds.), *Interventions for Achievement and Behavioral Problems* (pp. 379–398). Silver Springs, MD: National Association of School Psychologists.

Hildreth, G. (1964) Manuscript writing after sixty years. In V. D. Anderson et al. (Eds.), *Readings in the Language Arts.* New York: Macmillan.

Hoeg, P. (1994) *Borderliners.* New York: Farrar, Straus & Giroux.

Hofmeister, A. (1975) Integrating criterion-referenced testing and instruction. In W. Hively & M. Reynolds (Eds.), *Domain-Referenced Testing in Special*

*Education* (pp. 77–87). Reston, VA: Council for Exceptional Children.

Holbrook, A. P. (1990) Handwriting legibility. In H. J. Walberg & G. D. Heartel (Eds.), *The International Encyclopedia of Educational Evaluation* (pp. 146–155) New York: Pergamon.

Holdaway, D. (1979) *The Foundations of Literacy.* Portsmouth, NH: Heinemann Educational Books.

Hoogeveen, R. R., Birkhoff, A. E., Smeets, P. M., Lancioni, G. E. & Boelens, H. H. (1989) Establishing phonemic segmentation in moderately retarded children. *Remedial and Special Education, 10* (3), 47–53.

Hoover, J. J. & Collier, C. (1991) Meeting the needs of culturally and linguistically diverse exceptional learners: Prereferral to mainstreaming. *Teacher Education and Special Education, 14* (1), 30–36.

Hoover, M. L. & Dwivedi, V. D. (1998) Syntactic processing by skilled bilinguals. *Language Learning, 48*(1), 1–29.

Hopper, R. & Naremore, R. C. (1978) *Children's Speech: A Practical Introduction to Communication Development.* 2nd Ed. New York: Harper & Row.

House, J. D. (1996) *College Persistence and Grade Outcomes: Noncognitive Variables as Predictors for African-American, Asian-American, Hispanic, Native American, and White Students.* Paper presented at the Annual Forum of the Association for Institutional Research, Albuquerque, NM.

Howe, K. R. (1994) Standards, assessment, and equality of educational opportunity. *Educational Researcher, 23* (8), 27–32.

Howell, K. W. (1983) Task analysis and the characteristics of tasks. *Journal of Special Education Technology, 5,* 5–14.

Howell, K. W. (1986) Direct assessment of academic performance. *School Psychology Review, 15* (3), 324–335.

Howell, K. W. (1995) Special education: Merit? Eligibility? Need? *Beyond Behavior, 6* (3), 11–17.

Howell, K. W. (1997) *Student Responsive Service Delivery: A Model of Intervention Driven and Special Education Eligibility Procedures for the State of Washington.* Olympia WA: Washington Superintendent of Public Instruction.

Howell K. W. & Davidson, M. J. (1997) Programming: Aligning teacher thought processes with the curriculum. In J. W. Lloyd, E. J. Kameenui & D. Chard (Eds.) *Issues in Educating Students with Disabilities.* Mahwah, NJ: Lawrence Erlbaum.

Howell, K. W. & Evans, D. G. (1995) A comment on "Must instructionally useful performance assessment be based in the curriculum?" *Exceptional Children, 64* (4), 394–396.

Howell, K. W., Evans, D. & Gardiner, J. (1997) Medications in the classroom: A hard pill to swallow? *Teaching Exceptional Children, 29* (6), 58.

Howell, K. W., Fox, S. L., Zucker S. H. & Moorehead, M. K. (2000a) *Resources for Implementing Curriculum-Based Evaluation.* Atlanta, GA: Wadsworth.

Howell, K. W., Kaplan, J. S. & O'Connell, C. Y. (1979) *Evaluating Exceptional Children: A Task Analysis.* Columbus, OH: Merrill.

Howell, K. W. & Lorson-Howell, K. (1990) What's the hurry? Fluency in the classroom. *Teaching Exceptional Children, 22* (3), 20–23.

Howell, K. W. & McCollum-Gahley, J. (1986) Monitoring instruction. *Teaching Exceptional Children, 19,* 47–49.

Howell, K. W. & Rueda, R. (1996) Achievement testing with culturally and linguistically diverse students. In L. A. Suzuki, P. J. Meller & J. G. Ponterotto (Eds.), *Handbook of Multicultural Assessment: Clinical, Psychological, and Educational Applications* (pp. 253–290). San Francisco, CA: Jossey-Bass.

Howell, K. W., Zucker S. H. & Moorehead, M. K. (2000b) *Multilevel Academic Skills Inventory.* Western Washington University, Bellingham, WA: Applied Research and Development Center.

Howell, K. W., Rueda, R. & Rutherford, R. B. (1983) A procedure for teaching self-recording to moderately retarded students. *Psychology in the Schools, 4,* 202–209.

Howell, S. C. & Barnhart, R. S. (1992) Teaching word problem solving at the primary level. *Teaching Exceptional Children, 24* (2), 44–46.

Hughes, D. L. (1997) *Guide to Narrative Language: Procedures for Assessment.* Eau Claire, WI: Thinking Publications.

Huot, B. (1990) The literature of direct writing assessment: Major concerns and prevailing trends. *Review of Educational Research, 60* (2), 237–264.

Hymowitz, K. A. (1999) Multicultural illiteracy. *Public Interest, 135,* 124–128.

Iglesias, A. (1985) Communication in the home and classroom: Match or mismatch? *Topics in Language Disorders, 6,* 29–41.

Ikeda, M. J., Till, W. D. III & Allison, R. (1996) Agency-wide implementation of problem solving consultation: Foundations, current implementation, and future directions. *School Psychology Quarterly, 11* (3), 228–243.

Isaacson, S. (1985) Assessing written language. In C. S. Simon (Ed.), *Communication Skills and Classroom Success: Assessment Methodologies for Language-Learning Disabled Students.* San Diego, CA: College Hill.

Isaacson, S. (1989a) Role of secretary vs. author: Resolving the conflict in writing instruction. *Learning Disability Quarterly, 12* (3), 209–217.

Isaacson, S. (1989b) Confused dichotomies: A response to Du Charme, Earl, and Poplin. *Learning Disability Quarterly, 12* (3), 243–247.

Isaacson, S. (1990) Written language. In P. J. Schloss, M. A. Smith & C. N. Schloss (Eds.), *Instructional Methods for Secondary Students with Learning and Behavior Problems* (pp. 202–228). Boston: Allyn & Bacon.

Isaacson, S. & Gleason, M. M. (1997) Mechanical obstacles to writing: What can teachers do to help students with learning problems? *Learning Disabilities Research and Practice, 12* (3), 188–194.

Isaacson, S. L. (1992) Volleyball and other analogies: A response to Englert. *Journal of Learning Disabilities, 25* (3), 173–177.

Isaacson, S. L. (1994) Integrating process, product, and purpose: The role of instruction. *Reading and Writing Quarterly: Overcoming Learning Disabilities, 10* (1), 39–62.

Israelashvili, M. (1997) Situational determinants of school students' feelings of injustice. *Elementary School Guidance and Counseling, 31* (4), 283–292.

Israelashvili, M. (1998) Preventative school counseling: A stress inoculation perspective. *Professional School Counseling, 1* (5), 21–25.

Ivarie, J. J. (1986) Effects of proficiency rates on later performance of a recall and writing behavior. *Remedial and Special Education, 7*, 25–30.

Jacobs, D. G. (1999) Depression screening as an intervention against suicide. *The Journal of Clinical Psychiatry, 60*, 42–45.

James, S. L. (1990) *Normal Language Acquisition.* Austin, TX: Pro-Ed.

Jeans, P. (1993) *My Word: Digressions on Language, Literacy, and Life.* Perth, Western Australia: St. George Books.

Jenkins, J. R. & Jenkins, L. M. (1988) *Cross-Age and Peer Tutoring: Help for Children with Learning Problems.* Reston, VA: The Council for Exceptional Children.

Jenkins, J. R. & Leicester, N. (1992) Specialized instruction within general education: A case study of one elementary school. *Exceptional Children, 58*, 555–563.

Jennings, K. (March 4, 1999) Gay youths face hostility in schools [Letter to the editor]. *Wall Street Journal,* p. 15.

Jitendra, A., Nolet, V. W., Xin, Y. P., Gomez, O., Renouf, K. & Lubov, I. (2000) Geography: Curriculum evaluation and modification for students with learning problems. *Reading and Writing Quarterly.*

Johnson, D. D. (1983) *Three Sound Strategies for Vocabulary Development.* Ginn Occasional Papers: Writings in Reading and Language Arts, Number 8. Columbus, OH: Ginn.

Johnson, D. D. & Baumann, J. F. (1984) Word identification. In P. D. Pearson (Ed.), *Handbook of Reading Research, Part 3.* New York: Longman.

Johnson, J. & Immerwahr, J. (1994) *First Things First: What Americans Want from the Public Schools.* New York: Public Agenda Forum.

Johnson, L. R. & Johnson, C. E. (1999) Teaching students to regulate their own behavior. *Teaching Exceptional Children, 31* (4), 6–10.

Johnson, L. J. & Pugach, M. C. (1991) Peer collaboration: Accommodating students with mild learning and behavioral problems. *Exceptional Children, 57*, 454–461.

Johnson, M. (1967) Definitions and models in curriculum theory. *Educational Theory, 7*, 127–140.

Jones, E. D., Southern, W. T. & Bringham, F. J. (1998) Curriculum-based assessment: Testing what is taught and teaching what is tested. *Intervention in School and Clinic, 33* (4), 239–249.

Jones, R. A. (1995) *The Child-School Interface: Environment and Behavior.* Children, Teachers and Learning Series. Herndon, VA: Cassell Books.

Joram, E., Subrahmanyam, K. & Gelman, R. (1998) Measurement estimation: Learning to map the route from number to quantity and back. *Review of Educational Research, 68* (4), 413–449.

Julkunen, K. (April 1990) *Affective Properties of Open and Closed Vocabulary Tasks in Individualistic and Cooperative Learning Situations.* ERIC Document Reproduction Service No. ED322752.

Kameenui, E. & Carnine, D. (1998) *Effective Teaching Strategies That Accommodate Diverse Learners.* Upper Saddle River NJ: Merrill/Prentice Hall.

Kamii, C. (1998) The harmful effects of algorithms in grades 1–4. In *Teaching and Learning of Algorithms in School Mathematics.* Reston, VA: National Council of Teachers of Mathematics.

Kane, M. (1994) Validating the performance standards associated with passing scores. *Review of Educational Research, 64* (3), 425–461

Kaplan, A. (1964) *The Conduct of Inquiry: Methodology for Behavioral Science.* San Francisco, CA: Chandler.

Kaplan, D. S. (1994) Structural relations model of self rejection, disposition to deviance and academic failure. *Journal of Educational Research, 87* (3), 166–173.

Kaplan, J. S. (1972) *A Comparison of the Effects of Giving versus Receiving Instruction on the Oral Reading of Low Achievers.* Unpublished doctoral dissertation, University of Oregon.

Kaplan, J. S. (1995) *Beyond Behavior Modification.* 3rd Ed. Austin, TX: Pro-Ed.

Kaplan, J. S. (2000) *Beyond Functional Assessment: A Social-Cognitive Approach to the Evaluation of Behavior Problems in Children and Youth.* Austin, TX: Pro-Ed.

Karlsdottir, R. (1996) Print manuscript as initial handwriting style II: Effects on the development of reading and spelling. *Scandinavian Journal of Education Research, 40* (3), 255–262.

Katzell, R. A. & Thompson, D. E. (1990) Work motivation: Theory and practice. *American Psychologist, 45,* 144–153.

Kauffman, J. M. & Hallahan, D. P. (1997) A diversity of restrictive environments: Placement as a problem of social ecology. In J. W. Lloyd, E. J. Kameenui & D. Chard (Eds.), *Issues in Educating Students with Disabilities.* Mahwah, NJ: Lawrence Erlbaum.

Kauffman, J. M. & Wong, K. L. (1991) Effective teachers of students with behavioral disorders: Are generic teaching skills enough? *Behavior Disorders, 16,* 225–237.

Kavale, K. (1981) Functions of the Illinois Test of Psycholinguistic Abilities (ITPA): Are they trainable? *Exceptional Children, 47,* 496–510.

Kavale, K. A. & Forness, S. R. (1987) Substance over style: Assessing the efficacy of modality testing and teaching. *Exceptional Children, 54,* 228–239.

Kavale, K. A., Mathur, S. R., Forness, S. R., Rutherford, R. B. & Quinn, M. M. (1997) Effectiveness of social skills training for students with behavior disorders: A meta-analysis. In T. E. Scruggs & M. A. Mastropieri (Eds.), *Advances in Learning and Behavioral Disabilities, 11* (1), 1–26.

Kawakami, A. J. & Hupei Au, K. (1986) Encouraging reading and language development in cultural minority children. *Topics in Language Disorders, 6,* 71–80.

Kelly, K. (1994) *Out of Control.* Reading, MA: Perseus Books.

Kennedy, L. M. & Tipps, S. (1997) *Guiding Children's Learning of Math.* 8th Ed. Belmont, CA: Wadsworth Publishing.

Kerka, S. (1995) *Prison Literacy Programs* (ERIC Document Reproduction Service No. ED 383859). http://ericae.net/db/edo/ed383859.htm.

Kerr, M. M. & Nelson, C. M. (1998) *Strategies for Managing Behavior Problems in the Classroom.* New Jersey: Merrill.

King-Sears, M. E. (1998) Best academic practices for inclusive classrooms. In E. O. Meyen, G. A. Vergason & R. J. Whelen (Eds.), *Educating Students with Mild Disabilities: Strategies and Methods.* Denver CO: Love Publishing.

King-Sears, M. E. & Cummings, C. S. (1996) Inclusive practices of classroom teachers. *Remedial and Special Education, 17* (4), 217–225.

Kletzien, S. B. (1991) Strategy use by good and poor comprehenders reading expository text of differing levels. *Reading Research Quarterly, 26* (1), 67–86.

Klinger, J. K. & Vaughn, S. (1996) Reciprocal teaching of reading comprehension strategies. *Elementary School Journal, 96*(3), 275–282.

Kotovsky, K. & Simon, H. A. (1990) What makes some problems really hard: Explorations in the problem space of difficulty. *Cognitive Psychology, 22* (2), 43–83.

Krathwohl, D. R. (1994) Reflections on the taxonomy: It's past, present and future. In L. A. Anderson & L. A. Sosniak (Eds.), *Bloom's Taxonomy: A Forty Year Retrospective.* Chicago, IL: University of Chicago Press.

Kucan, L. & Beck, I. L. (1997) Thinking aloud and reading comprehension research: Inquiry, instruction and social interaction. *Review of Educational Research, 67* (3), 271–299.

Kulik, J. A., Kulik, C. C. & Bangert-Drowns, R. L. (1990) Is there better evidence on mastery learning? A response to Slavin. *Review of Educational Research, 60* (2), 303–307.

Labov, W. (1969) The logic of nonstandard English. In J. E. Alates (Ed.), *Monograph Series on Language and Linguistics.* No. 22. Washington, DC: Georgetown University Press.

Lakin, K. C. (1983) A response to Gene V Glass. *Policy Studies Review, 2,* 233–239.

Landfried, S. E. (1989) "Enabling" undermines responsibility in students. *Educational Leadership, 47* (3), 79–83.

Langdon, H. (1996) English language learning by immigrant Spanish speakers: A United States perspective. *Topics in Language Disorders, 16* (4), 38–53.

Langer, J. A. (1991) Literacy and schooling: A socio-cognitive perspective. In E. H. Hiebert (Ed.), *Literacy for a Diverse Society* (pp. 9–27). New York: Teachers College Press.

Larson, K. A. (1989a) Problem-solving training and parole adjustment in high-risk young adult offenders. *The Yearbook of Correctional Education,* 279–299.

Larson, K. A. (1989b) Task-related and interpersonal problem-solving training for increasing school success in high-risk young adolescents. *Remedial and Special Education, 10* (5), 32–42.

Larson, K. A. & Gerber, M. M. (1987) Effects of social metacognitive training for enhancing overt behavior in learning disabled and low achieving delinquents. *Exceptional Children, 54* (3), 201–211.

Lascarides, A. & Copestake, A. (1998) Pragmatics and word meaning. *Journal of Linguistics, 34*(2), 387–414.

Laufer, A. (1997) *Simultaneous Management: Managing Projects in a Dynamic Environment.* New York: American Management Association.

Laufer, B. & Paribakht, T. S. (1998) The relationship between passive and active vocabularies: Effects of language learning context. *Language Learning, 48* (3), 365–387.

Lawlor, J. (1983) Sentence combining: A sequence for instruction. *Elementary School Journal, 84* (1), 53–62.

Leader, C.A. (1983) The talent for judgment. *Proceedings,* 49–53.

Lebzelter, S. & Nowacek, E. J. (1999) Reading strategies for secondary students with mild disabilities. *Intervention in School and Clinic, 34* (4), 212–219.

Legters, N. & McDill, E. L. (1995) *Rising to the Challenge: Emerging Strategies for Educating Youth at Risk.* Urban Monograph Series. ERIC doc. No. ED397202. http://ericae.net/db/riecije/ed397202.htm.

Leinhardt, G. & Greeno, J. C. (1986) The cognitive skill of teaching. *Journal of Educational Psychology, 78,* 75–95.

Lennox, R. D. & Wolfe, R. N. (1984) Revision of the self-monitoring scale. *Journal of Personality and Social Psychology, 46,* 1349–1364.

Leone, P. E. (1994) Education services for youth with disabilities in a state-operated juvenile correctional system: Case study and analysis. *Journal of Special Education, 28* (1), 43–58.

Leone, P. E., Rutherford, R. B. & Nelson, C. M. (1991) Juvenile corrections and the exceptional student. (ERIC document Reproduction Service No. ED340153). http://ericae.net/db/digs/ed340153.htm.

Leung, B. P. (1996) Quality assessment practices in a diverse society. *Teaching Exceptional Children, 28* (3), 42–45.

Levy, N. R. (1996) Teaching analytical writing: Help for general education middle school teachers. *Intervention in School and Clinic, 32* (2), 95–103.

Lewis, T. J. & Sugai, G. (1999) Effective behavior support: A systems approach to proactive schoolwide management. *Focus on Exceptional Children, 31* (6), 2–24.

Liberty, K. A., Haring, N. G. & White, O. R. (1980) Rules for data-based strategy decisions in instructional programs: Current research and instructional implications. In W. Sailor, B. Wilcox & L. Brown (Eds.), *Methods of Instruction for Severely Handicapped Students.* Baltimore, MD: Paul H. Brookes.

Linn, R. L. & Baker, E. L. (1996) Can performance-based student assessments be psychometrically sound? In J. B. Baron & D. P. Wolf (Eds.), *Performance-based student assessment: Challenges and possibilities* (pp. 84–103). Chicago: The National Society for the Study of Education.

Lipman, P. (1997) Restructuring in context: A case study of teacher participation and the dynamics of ideology, race, and power. *American Educational Research Journal, 34* (1), 3–38.

Lloyd, J. W. (1984) How shall we individualize instruction—Or should we? *Remedial and Special Education, 5,* 7–15.

Lloyd, J. & Kameenui, E. (1994) Academic instruction. *Learning Disability Quarterly, 27* (3), 166–168.

Lloyd, J. W. & Loper, A. B. (1986) Measurement and evaluation of task related learning behaviors: Attention to Task and Metacognition. *School Psychology Review, 15* (3), 336–346.

Lloyd, J. W., Landrum, T. J. & Hallahan, D. P. (1991) Self-monitoring applications for classroom intervention. In G. Stoner, M. Shinn & H. Walker (Eds.), *Interventions for Achievement and Behavior Problems* (pp. 201–214). Silver Springs, MD: National Associations of School Psychologists.

Lloyd, J., Forness, S. & Kavale, K. (1998) Some methods are more effective than others. *Intervention in School and Clinic, 33* (4), 195–200.

Loban, W. (1996) Research currents: The somewhat stingy story of research into children's language. *Language Arts, 63*(6), 608–616.

Lockwood, A. T. (1996) *Tracking: Conflicts and Resolutions. Controversial Issues in Education.* ERIC document reproduction service No. ED400604. http://ericae.net/db/riecije/ed.400604.htm.

Logan, K. J. & LaSalle, L. R. (1999) Grammatical characteristics of children's conversational utterances that contain disfluency clusters. *Journal of Speech, Language and Hearing Research 42*(1), 80–91.

Logan, K. R., Bakeman, R. & Keefe, E. B. (1997) Effects of instructional variables on engaged behavior of students with learning disabilities in general classrooms. *Exceptional Children, 63* (4), 481–497.

Lovett, S. & Pillow, B. H. (1995) Development of the ability to distinguish between comprehension and memory: Evidence from strategy selection tasks. *Journal of Educational Psychology, 87* (4), 523–536.

Lovitt, T. C. (1991) *Preventing School Dropouts.* Austin, TX: Pro-Ed.

Lovitt, T. C. (1995) *Tactics for Teaching.* 2nd Ed. Columbus, OH: Merrill.

Lovitt, T. C., Fister, S., Freston, J. L., Kemp, K., Moore, R. C., Schroeder, B. & Bauerschmidt, M. (1990) Using precision teaching techniques: Translating research. *Teaching Exceptional Children, 22* (3), 16–19.

Maag, J. W. (1995) Social and behavioral predictors of popular, rejected and average children. *Educational and Psychological Measurement, 55* (2), 196–205.

Maag, J. W., Rutherford, R. B. & Parks, B. T. (1988) Secondary school professionals' ability to identify depression in adolescents. *Adolescence, 23* (89), 73–83.

MacGinitie, W. H. (1984) Readability as a solution adds to the problem. In R. C. Anderson, J. Osborn &

R. Tierney (Eds.), *Learning to Read in American Schools* (pp. 141–51). Hillsdale, NJ: Erlbaum.

MacLean, R. (1992) Innovations and reforms in schooling in Asia's developing countries. *Prospects, 22* (3), 336–378.

Madrid, D., Terry, B., Greenwood, C., Whaley, M. & Webber, N. (1998) Active vs. passive peer-tutoring: Teaching spelling to at-risk students. *Journal of Research and Development in Education, 31* (4), 236–244.

Mahoney, M. (1977) Reflections on the cognitive-learning trend in psychotherapy. *American Psychologist, 32* (1), 5–13.

Malmgren, K., Edgar, E. & Neel, R. S. (1998) Postschool status of youths with behavioral disorders. *Behavioral Disorders, 23* (4), 257–263.

Malott, R., Whaley, D. & Mallott, M. (1997) *Elementary Principles of Behavior*. 3rd Ed. Upper Saddle River, NJ: Prentice Hall.

Mandler, J. M. & Johnson, N. S. (1977) Remembrance of things passed: Story structure and recall. *Cognitive Psychology, 9*, 111–151.

Margolis, H. (1987) *Patterns, Thinking, and Cognition.* Chicago: University of Chicago Press.

Markel, S. M. (1975) They teach concepts don't they? *Educational Researcher, 4*, 3–9.

Markell, M. A. & Deno, S. L. (1997) Effects of increasing oral reading: Generalization across reading tasks. *Journal of Special Education, 31* (2), 233–250.

Marsh, R. L., Ward, T. B. & Landau, J. D. (1999) The inadvertent use of prior knowledge in a generative cognitive task. *Memory and Cognition, 27* (1), 94–105.

Martens, B. K. & Witt, J. C. (1988) On the ecological validity of behavior modification. In J. C. Witt, S. N. Elliott & F. M. Gresham (Eds.), *Handbook of Behavior Therapy and Education* (pp. 115–139). New York: Plenum.

Martin, B., Jr. & Carle, E. (1983) *Brown Bear, Brown Bear, What Do You See?* New York: Henry Holt.

Martin, G. & Pear, J. (1996) *Behavior Modification: What It Is and How to Do It.* 5th Ed. Upper Saddle River, NJ: Merrill Prentice Hall.

Marx, R. W. & Walsh, J. (1988) Learning from academic tasks. *Elementary School Journal, 88* (3), 207–219.

Marzano, R. J., Brandt, R. S., Hughes, C. S., Jones, B. F., Presseisen, B. Z., Rankin, S. C. & Suhor, C. (1988) *Dimensions Of Thinking*. Alexandria, VA: Association for Supervision and Curriculum Development.

Mason, J. M., Herman, P. A. & Au, K. A. (1990) *Children's Developing Knowledge of Words* (Tech. Report No. 513). Urbana-Champaign: University of Illinois, Center for the Study of Reading.

Masterson, J. J. & Perrey, C. D. (1999) Training analogical reasoning skills in children with language disorders. *American Journal of Speech-Language Pathology, 8*, 53–61.

Mastropieri, M. A. & Scruggs, T. E. (1996) Promoting thinking skills of students with learning disabilities: Effects on recall and comprehension of expository prose. *Exceptionality, 6* (1), 1–11.

Mastropieri, M. & Scruggs, T. (1998) Enhancing School Success with Mnemonic Strategies. *Intervention in School and Clinic, 33* (4), 201–208.

Mathes, P. G., Fuchs, D. & Fuchs, L. S. (1997) Cooperative story mapping. *Remedial and Special Education, 18* (1), 20–27.

Mathur, S. R., Kavale, K. A., Quinn, M. & Forness, S. R. (1998) Social skills interventions with students with emotional and behavior problems: A quantitative synthesis of single-subject research. *Behavioral Disorders, 23* (3), 193–208.

Mauk, G. W. (1994) Suicide postvention with adolescents: School consultation practices and issues. *Education and Treatment of Children, 17* (4), 468–483.

McCagg, E. C. & Dansereau, D. F. (1991) A convergent paradigm for examining knowledge mapping as a learning strategy. *Journal of Educational Research, 84* (6), 317–324.

McCleery, J. A. & Tindal, G. A. (1999) Teaching the scientific method to at-risk students with learning disabilities through concept anchoring and explicit instruction. *Remedial and Special Education, 20* (1), 7–18.

McConaughy, S. H. (1996) The interview process. In M. J. Breen & C. R. Fiedler (Eds.), *Behavior Approach to Assessment of Youth with Emotional/Behavioral Disorders* (pp. 225–242). Austin, TX: Pro-Ed.

McDaniel, M. A. & Schlager, (1990) Discovery learning and transfer of problem-solving skills. *Cognition and Instruction, 7* (2), 129–159.

McDonnell, L. M. & McLaughlin, M. J. & Morrison, P. (Eds.) (1997) *Educating One and All.* Washington, DC: National Academy Press.

McDougall, D. & Brady, M. P. (1998) Initiating and fading self-management interventions to increase math fluency in general education classes. *Exceptional Children, 64* (2), 151–166.

McGee, L. M. & Lomax, R. G. (1990) On combining apples and oranges: A response to Stahl and Miller. *Review of Educational Research, 60* (1), 133–140.

McGill-Franzen, A. & Allington, R. L. (1991) The gridlock of low reading achievement: Perspectives on practice and policy. *Remedial and Special Education, 12,* 20–30.

McGinnis, E. (1997) *Skillstreaming the Elementary School Child,* Revised Ed. Champaign, IL: Research Press.

McIntyre, D. J., Copenhaver, R. W., Byrd, D. M. & Norris, W. R. (1983) A study of engaged student behavior within classroom activities during mathematics class. *Journal of Educational Research, 27*, 55–59.

McKeachie, W. J. (1987a) Cognitive skills and their transfer: Discussion. *International Journal of Educational Research, 11* (6), 707–712.

McKeachie, W. J. (1987b) The new look in instructional psychology: Teaching strategies for learning and thinking. In E. De Corte, H. Lodewijks, R. Parmentier & P. Span (Eds.), *Learning and Instruction: European Research in an International Context.* Vol. I. pp. 443–456.

McLain, K. & Victoria, M. (November 1991) *Effects of Two Comprehension-Monitoring Strategies on the Metacognitive Awareness and Reading Achievement of Third- and Fifth-Grade Students.* Paper presented at the Annual Meeting of the National Reading Conference, Miami, FL, November, 1991.

McLellan, A. (July 7, 1998) Best youth justice is neither tough nor lenient, but effective. *The Vancouver Sun,* p. A11.

McNamara, T. C. (1990) *Training Students to Take Better Control of Their Learning by Framing Questions in Multiple-Choice Format.* Paper presented at the Annual Meeting of the American Educational Research Association, Boston MA.

Metzler, L., Roditi, B., Haynes, D. & Biddle, M. S. (1996) *Strategies for Success: Classroom Teaching Techniques for Students with Learning Problems.* Austin, TX: Pro-Ed.

Mercer, C. D., Lane, H. B., Jordan, L, Allsopp D. H. & Eisele, M. R. (1996) Empowering teachers and students with instructional choices in inclusive settings. *Remedial and Special Education, 17* (4), 226–236.

Mergendoller, J. R., Marchman, V. A., Mitman, A. L. & Parker, M. J. (1988) Task demands and accountability in middle-grade science classes. *The Elementary School Journal, 8,* 251–265.

Messick, S. (1995) Validity of psychological assessment. *American Psychologist, 50* (9), 741–749.

Meyer, B. & Rice, G. E. (1984) The structure of text. In D. Pearson, R. Barr, M. Kamil & P. Mosenthal (Eds.), *Handbook of Reading Research.* New York: Longman.

Miller, G. & Carr, A. (1997) Information and training needs of agricultural faculty related to distance education. *Journal of Applied Communication, 81* (1), 1–9.

Miller, J. & Rhea, P. (1995) *The Clinical Assessment of Language Comprehension.* Baltimore, MD: Paul H. Brookes Publishing.

Miller, M., Brownell, M. & Smith, S. (1999) Factors that predict teachers staying in, leaving, or transferring from the special education classroom. *Exceptional Children, 65* (2), 201–218.

Miller, W. G., Snowman, J. & O'Hara, T. (1979) Application of alternative statistical techniques to examine the hierarchical ordering in Bloom's taxonomy. *American Educational Research Journal, 16* (4), 241–248.

Miller-Jones, D. (1989) Culture and testing. *American Psychologist, 44* (2), 360–366.

Moeller, A. J. & Scott, E. S. (1993) Making the match: Middle level goals and foreign language instruction. *Schools in the Middle, 3* (1), 35–39.

Moen, P. (Ed.) (1995) *Examining Lives in Context: Perspectives on the Ecology of Human Development.* Technical Report. Hyattsville, MD: American Psychological Association.

Moody, S. W., Vaughn, S. & Schumm, J. S. (1997) Instructional grouping for reading: Teachers' views. *Remedial and Special Education, 18* (6), 347–356.

Moos, R. H. (1973) Conceptualizations of human environments. *American Psychologist, 28,* 652–655.

Moreland, K. L. (1996) Persistent issues in multicultural assessment of social and emotional functioning. In L. A. Suzuki, P. J. Meller & J. G. Ponterotto (Eds.), *Handbook of Multicultural Assessment: Clinical, Psychological, and Educational Applications* (pp. 51–76). San Francisco, CA: Jossey-Bass.

Morrow, L. J. & Kenney, M. J. (Eds.) (1998) *The Teaching and Learning of Algorithms in School Mathematics: 1998 Yearbook.* Reston, VA: National Council of Teachers of Mathematics, Inc.

Murphy, J., Weill, M. & McGreal, T. L. (1986) The basic practice model of instruction. *The Elementary School Journal, 87,* 83–183.

Muyskens, P. & Ysseldyke, J. E. (1998) Student academic responding time as a function of classroom ecology and time of day. *Journal of Special Education, 31* (4), 411–424.

Nagy, W. E. & Scott, J. A. (1990) Word schemas: Expectations about the form and meaning of new words. *Cognition and Instruction, 7,* 105–157.

Nagy, W., Anderson, R. C., Schommer, M., Scott, J. A. & Stallman, A. C. (1989) Morphological families in the internal lexicon. *Reading Research Quarterly, 24* (3), 262–282.

Nation, K. & Hulme, C. (1997) Phonemic segmentation, not onset-rime segmentation, predicts early reading and spelling skills. *Reading Research Quarterly, 32* (2), 154–167.

Nelson, J. R., Roberts, M. L., Mathur, S. R. & Rutherford, R. B. (1998) Has public policy exceeded our knowledge base? A review of the functional behavioral assessment literature. *Behavioral Disorders, 24* (2), 169–179.

Nelson, R. Arndt, A., Smith, D. & Dodd, J. (1994) Do children classified as learning disabled understand the critical dimensions of different types of uncontested and contested knowledge? *Learning Disabilities Research and Practice, 9* (1), 24–32.

Nichols, P. (1992) The curriculum of control: Twelve reasons for it, some arguments against it. *Beyond Behavior, 3* (2), 5–11.

Nisbett, R. & Ross, L. (1980) *Human Inference: Strategies and Shortcomings of Social Judgement.* Englewood Cliffs: Prentice-Hall.

Nitko, A. J. (1995) Is the curriculum a reasonable basis for assessment reform? *Educational Measurement: Issues and Practice, 14* (3), 5–10.

Nitko, A. J. & Guo, F. (1996) Graduate programs that prepare educational measurement specialists. *Educational Measurement, Issues, and Practice, 15* (4), 28.

Noble, A. & Smith, M. L. (1994) Old and new beliefs about measurement-driven reform: "Build it and they will come." *Educational Policy 8* (2) 111–136.

Nolet, V. W. (1992) Classroom-based measurement and portfolio assessment. *Diagnostique, 18* (1), 5–26.

Nolet, V. W. (1999) Working together in the 21st century high school. In S. Graham, K. Harris & M. Pressley (Eds.), *Working Together.* Cambridge, MA: Brookline.

Nolet, V. & Tindal, G. (1994) Curriculum-based collaboration. *Focus on Exceptional Children, 27* (3), 1–12.

Nolet, V. W. & Tindal, G. R. (1995) Essays as valid measures of learning in middle school science classes. *Learning Disabilities Quarterly, 18* (4), 311–324.

Nolet, V., Tindal, G. & Howell, K. W. (1992) *Teacher Assistance Team (TAT) Models.* Monograph No. 4. Eugene: University of Oregon, Resource Training Program.

Nowacek, E. J. (1992) Professionals talk about teaching together: Interviews with five collaborating teachers. *Intervention in School and Clinic, 27* (5), 262–276.

Nowacek, E. J., McKinney, J. D. & Hallahan, D. P. (1990) Instructional behaviors of more and less effective regular and special educators. *Exceptional Children, 57*, 140–149.

O'Connor, R. (April 20, 1992) *Personal Communication.* Washington Research Institute.

Oetting, J. B. & Horohov, J. E. (1997) Past-tense marking by children with and without specific language impairment. *Journal of Speech, Language, and Hearing Research, 40* (1), 62–74.

Office of Juvenile Justice and Delinquency Prevention. (1997) *Balanced and Restorative Justice for Juveniles.* University of Minnesota, St. Paul: Center for Restorative Justice and Mediation.

Office of Technology Assessment. (1995) *Teachers and Technology: Making the Connection.* Washington DC: Author.

Okyere, B. A. & Heron, T. E. (1991) Use of self-correction to improve spelling in regular education classrooms. In G. Stoner, M. Shinn & H. Walker (Eds.), *Interventions for Achievement and Behavioral Problems* (pp. 399–414). Silver Springs, MD: National Association of School Psychologists.

Olsen, J. ( 1997) *Managing Classroom Gambits: Working with Difficult Classes in School.* Canberra ACT, Australia: Goanna Print.

Olson, M., Sakshaug, L. & Olson, J. (1998) How many sandwiches? *Teaching Children Mathematics, 4* (7), 402–403.

O'Neil, R. E., Horner, R. H., Albin, R. W., Storey, K. T. & Sprague, J. (1989) *Functional Analysis: A Practical Assessment Guide.* Eugene: University of Oregon.

O'Neil, R., Horner, R., Sprague, R., Storey, K. & Newton, J. (1997) *Functional Assessment of Problem Behavior: A Practical Guide.* 2nd Ed. Pacific Grove, CA: Brooks/Cole.

O'Shea, L. J. & O'Shea, D. J. (1994) A component analysis of metacognition in reading comprehension: The contributions of awareness and self-regulation. *International Journal of Disability, Development and Education, 41* (1), 15–32.

Osserman, R. (1995) *Poetry of the Universe.* New York: Anchor Books.

Padilla, A. M. & Medina, A. (1996) Cross-culturally sensitivity in assessment. In L. A. Suzuki, P. J. Meller & J. G. Ponterotto (Eds.), *Handbook of Multicultural Assessment: Clinical, Psychological, and Educational Applications* (pp. 3–28). San Francisco, CA: Jossey-Bass.

Palincsar, A. S. (1990) Reaction: Providing the context for intentional learning. *Remedial and Special Education, 11* (6), 36–39.

Palincsar, A. S. & Brown, A. L. (1984) Reciprocal teaching of comprehension-fostering and comprehension-monitoring activities. *Cognition and Instruction, 1*, 117–175.

Palincsar, A. S. & Brown, A. L. (1987) Advances in improving the cognitive performance of handicapped students. In M. C. Wang, M. C. Reynolds & H. J. Walberg (Eds.), *Handbook of Special Education: Research and Practice.* New York: Pergamon.

Palincsar, A. S. & David, Y. M. (1992) Promoting literacy through classroom dialogue. In E. Hiebert (Ed.), *Literacy for a Diverse Society: Perspectives, Programs, and Policies.* New York: Teachers College Press.

Paradis, J. & Genessee, F. (1996) Syntactic acquisition in bilingual children: Autonomous or independent? *Studies in Second Language Acquisition, 18* (1), 1–25.

Paris, S. G. & Jacobs, J. E. (1984) The benefits of informed instruction for children's reading awareness and comprehension skills. *Child Development, 55*, 2083–2093.

Paris, S. G. & Oka, E. R. (1989) Strategies for comprehending text and coping with reading difficulties. *Learning Disabilities Quarterly, 12,* 32–42.

Paris, S. G. & Winograd, P. (1990) Promoting metacognition and motivation of exceptional children. *Remedial and Special Education, 11* (6), 7–15.

Parker, R. I., Tindal, G. & Hasbrouck, J. (1991) Progress monitoring with objective measures of writing performance for students with mild disabilities. *Exceptional Children, 58* (1), 61–73.

Parker, R., Hasbrouck, J. & Tindal, G. (1992) The maze as a classroom-based reading measure: Construction methods, reliability, and validity. *The Journal of Special Education, 26* (2), 195–218.

Parmar, R. S., Cawley, J. F. & Frazita, R. R. (1996) Word problem-solving by students with and without mild disabilities. *Exceptional Children, 62* (5), 415–429.

Patching, W., Kameenui, E., Carnine, D., Gersten, R. & Colvin, G. (1983) Direct instruction in critical reading skills. *Reading Research Quarterly, 18,* 361–365.

Paulos, J. A. (1988) *Innumeracy: Mathematical Illiteracy and its Consequences.* New York: Hill and Wang.

Peacock Hill Working Group. (1991) Problems and promises in special education and related services for children and youth with emotional or behavioral disorders. *Behavioral Disorders, 16* (4), 299–313.

Pearson, J. W. & Santa, C. M. (1995) Students as researchers of their own learning. *Journal of Reading, 38* (6), 462–469.

Pearson, D. P., Roehler, L. R., Dole, J. A. & Duffy, G. G. (1990) *Developing Expertise in Reading Comprehension: What Should Be Taught?* (Tech. Report No. 512). Urbana-Champaign: University of Illinois, Center for the Study of Reading.

Pelham, W. (1993) Pharmocotherapy for Children with Attention-Deficit Hyperactivity Disorder. *School Psychology Review, 22* (2), 199–227.

Pellegrini, A. D., Galda, L., Bartini, M. & Charak, D. (1998) Oral language and literacy learning in context: The role of social relationships. *Merrill-Palmer Quarterly, 44* (1), 38–54.

Pershey, M. (1997) Teaching pragmatic language awareness as an integral aspect of reading and language arts instruction. *Reading Horizons, 37* (4), 299–314.

Peterson, L., Wonderlich, S. A., Reaven N. M. & Mullins, L. L. (1987) Adult educators' response to depression and stress in children. *Journal of Social and Clinical Psychology, 3* (1), 51–58.

Peterson, P. L., Fennema, E., Carpenter, T. P. & Loef, M. (1989) Teachers' pedagogical content beliefs in mathematics. *Cognition and Instruction, 6,* 1–40.

Philips, S. (1970) *Acquisition of roles in appropriate speech usage.* Monograph Series on Language and Linguistics, No. 23. Washington, DC: Georgetown University Press.

Phillips, S. E. (1996) *Sentence combining: A literature review.* Information Analysis. (ERIC Document Reproduction Service No. ED398589).

Pikulski, J. J. & Pikulski, E. C. (1977) Cloze, maze, and teacher judgment. *The Reading Teacher, 30,* 776–770.

Pine, D. S., Cohen, E., Cohen, P. & Brook, J. (1999) Adolescent depressive symptoms as predictors of adult depression: Moodiness or mood disorder? *American Journal of Psychiatry, 156* (1), 133–135.

Pirsig R. M. (1974) *Zen and the Art of Motorcycle Maintenance: An Inquiry into Values.* New York: Morrow.

Polansky, H. B. (1995) Homogenous vs. Heterogeneous: Is tracking a barrier to equity? *School Business Affairs, 61* (8), 30–33.

Postman, N. & Weingartner, C. (1969) *Teaching as a Subversive Activity.* New York: Dell.

Powers, A. R. & Wilgus, S. (1983) Linguistic complexity in written language of hearing impaired children. *Volta Review, 85,* 201–210.

Prawat, R. S. (1998) Current self-regulation views of learning and motivation viewed through a Deweyan lens: The problems with dualism. *American Educational Research Journal, 35* (2), 199–224.

Pressley, M. (1995) The comprehension instruction that students need: Instruction fostering constructively responsive reading. *Learning Disabilities Research and Practice, 10* (4), 215–224.

Pressley, M. (1996) The challenges of instructional scaffolding: The challenges of instruction that supports student thinking. *Learning Disabilities Research and Practice, 11* (3) 138–146.

Price, K. & Nelson, K. (1999) *Daily Planning for Today's Classroom: A Guide for Writing Lesson and Activity Plans.* Belmont, CA: Wadsworth.

Pritchard, R. (1990) The effects of cultural schemata on reading processing strategies. *Reading Research Quarterly, 25* (4), 273–295.

Pugach, M. C. & Johnson, L. J. (1988) Rethinking the relationship between consultation and collaborative problem solving. *Focus on Exceptional Children, 21,* 1–8.

Puntambekar, S. (1995) Helping students learn "how to learn" from texts: Towards an ITS for developing metacognition. *Instructional Science, 23* (1–3), 163–182.

Puntambekar, S. & DeBoulay, B. (1997) Design and development of MIST: A system to help students develop metacognition. *Journal of Educational Computing Research, 16* (1), 1–35.

Purdie, N. & Hattie, J. (1996) Cultural differences in the use of strategies for self-regulated learning. *American Educational Research Journal, 33* (4), 845–871.

Ragan, T. & Smith, P. (1994) *Opening the Black Box: Instructional Strategies Examined.* Conference paper presented at the National Convention of the Association for Educational Communications and Technology, Nashville, TN, February 16–20, 1994.

Ralph, A. & Coombs, V. (1994) Assessing social competence of adolescents using the verbal interaction analysis system. *Diagnostique, 19* (2–3), 41–58.

Raphael, T. E. & Pearson, D. P. (1985) Increasing students' awareness of sources of information for answering questions. *American Research Journal, 22,* 217–235.

Rauenbusch, F. & Bereiter, C. (1991) Making reading more difficult: A degraded text microworld for teaching reading comprehension strategies. *Cognition and Instruction, 8* (2), 181–206.

Raymond, R. C. (1989) Teaching students to revise: Theories and practice. *Teaching English in the Two-Year College, 16* (1), 49–58.

Reid, D. K. & Stone, C. A. (1991) Why is cognitive instruction effective? Underlying learning mechanisms. *Remedial and Special Education, 12,* 8–19.

Reid, S. K. (1992) *Cognition.* 3rd Ed. Pacific Grove, CA: Brooks/Cole.

Reif, L. (1990) Finding the value in evaluation: Self-assessment in a middle school classroom. *Educational Leadership, 47* (6), 24–29.

Reschly, D. J., Genshaft, J. & Binder, M. S. (1986) *The 1986 NASP Survey: Comparison of Practitioners, NASP Leadership, and University Faculty on Key Issues* (pp. 1–58). Silver Springs, MD: National Association of School Psychologists.

Reschly, D. J., Tilly, W. D. & Grimes, J. P. (1998) *Functional And Non-categorical Identification And Intervention In Special Education.* Des Moines, IA: Iowa Department of Education.

Reutzel, R. (1985) Story maps to improve comprehension. *The Reading Teacher, 38,* 400–404.

Reyes, M. (1990) *Comparison of L1 and L2 Pre and Post Writing Samples of Bilingual Students.* Paper presented at the Annual Meeting of the American Educational Research Association Conference, Boston, MA, April 1990.

Reynolds, R. D. & Anderson, R. C. (1982) Influence of questions on the allocation of attention during reading. *Journal of Educational Psychology, 74* (5), 623–632.

Rich, S. & Pressley, M. (1990) Teacher acceptance of reading comprehension strategy instruction. *The Elementary School Journal, 91* (1), 43–64.

Richardson, J. (1994) Common, delinquent and special: On the formalization of common schooling in the American states. *American Educational Research Journal, 31* (4), 695–723.

Riehl, C. & Sipple, J. (1996) Making the most of time and talent: Secondary school organizational climates, teaching task environments, and teacher commitment. *American Educational Research Journal, 33* (4), 873–901.

Rigney, J. W. (1980) Cognitive learning strategies and dualities in information processing. In R. Snow, P. A. Federico & W. Motaguel (Eds.), *Aptitude, Learning and Instruction.* Vol. 1. Hillsdale, NJ: Erlbaum.

Robinson, T. R. & Rapport, M. J. (1999) Providing special education in the juvenile justice system. *Remedial and Special Education, 20* (1), 19–26.

Roeser, R. W. & Eccles, J. S. (1998) Adolescents' perceptions of middle school: Relation to longitudinal changes in academic and psychological adjustment. *Journal of Research on Adolescence, 8* (1), 123–158.

Roeser, R. W. & Midgley, C. (1997) Teacher's views of issues involving students' mental health. *Elementary School Journal, 98* (2), 115–133.

Roeser, R. W., Midgley, C. & Urdan, T. C. (1996) Perceptions in the school psychological environment and early adolescents' psychological and behavioral functioning in school: The mediating role of goals and belonging. *Journal of Educational Psychology, 88* (3), 408–409.

Rogoff, B. (1978) Spot observation: An introduction and examination. *Quarterly Newsletter of the Institute for Comparative Human Development, 2,* 21–26.

Rosenhouse, J., Feitelson, D., Kita, B. & Goldstein, Z. (1997) Interactive reading aloud to Israeli first graders: Its contribution to literacy development. *Reading Research Quarterly, 32* (2), 168–183.

Rosenshine, B. (1997) Advances in research on instruction. In J. W. Lloyd, E. J. Kameenui & D. Chard (Eds.), *Issues in Educating Students with Disabilities.* Mahwah, NJ: Lawrence Erlbaum.

Rosenshine, B. V. & Stevens, R. (1986) Teaching functions. In M. C. Wittrock (Ed.), *Handbook on Research and Teaching.* 3rd Ed. New York: Macmillan.

Rotheram-Borus, M. (1997) Mental health services for children and adolescents. In *Establishing Preventive Services, Healthy Children 2010.* Vol. 9. Issues in Children's and Families' Lives.

Rotter, J. B. (1982) *The Development and Application of Social Learning Theory: Selected Papers.* New York: Praeger.

Rudell, A. P. & Han, J. (1997) The recognition potential, word difficulty, and individual reading ability: On using even-related porentials to study perception. *Journal of Experimental Psychology, 23*(4), 1170–1195.

Ruddell, M. R. (1997) *Teaching Content Reading and Writing.* 2nd Ed. Des Moines, IA: Allyn & Bacon.

Rueda, R., Goldenberg, C. & Gallimore, R. (1993) *A Manual for the Use of the Instructional Conversion Rating Scale: National Center on Cultural Diversity*. Second Language Learning and Center for Applied Linguistics. Santa Cruz, CA: University of California.

Rupley, W. H., Logan, J. W. & Nichols, W. D. (1999) Vocabulary instruction in a balanced reading program. *The Reading Teacher, 52* (4), 336–342.

Russell, S. (1999) Mathematical reasoning in the elementary grades. In *National Council of Teachers of Mathematics Yearbook*. Reston, VA.

Ryder, R. J. (1991) The directed questioning activity for X subject matter text. *Journal of Reading, 34*, 606–612.

Sabers, D. (1992) *Personal Communication*. Tucson, AZ.

Sabers, D., Cushing, K. S. & Berliner, D. C. (1991) Differences among teachers in a task characterized by simultaneity, multidimensionality and immediacy. *American Educational Research Journal, 28*, 63–88.

Sabornie, E. J. (1991) Measuring and teaching social skills in the mainstream. In G. Stoner, M. Shinn & H. Walker (Eds.), *Intervention for Achievement and Behavior Problems* (pp. 161–178). Silver Springs, MD: National Association of School Psychologists.

Sample, P. L. (1998) Postschool outcomes for students with significant emotional disturbance following best-practice transition services. *Behavioral Disorders, 23* (4), 231–242.

Sands, D. J., Adams, L. & Stout, D. M. (1995) A statewide exploration of the use of curriculum in special education. *Exceptional Children, 62* (1), 68–83.

Sargent, L. R. (1998) *Social Skills for School and Community Systematic Instruction for Children and Youth with Cognitive Delays*. Reston, VA: Division on Mental Retardation and Developmental Delay of the Council for Exceptional Children.

Saville-Troike, M. (1976) *Foundation for Teaching English as a Second Language: Theory and Method for Multi-Cultural Education*. Englewood Cliffs, NJ: Prentice-Hall.

Scardamalia, M. & Berieter, C. (1986) Research on written composition. In M. C. Wittrock (Ed.), *Handbook of Research on Teaching* (pp. 778–803). New York: Macmillan.

Schickedanz, J. A. (1990) The jury is still out on the effects of whole language and language experience approaches for beginning reading. *Review of Educational Research, 60* (1), 127–132.

Schmitt, M. G. (1990) A questionnaire to measure children's awareness of strategic reading processes. *The Reading Teacher, 43*, 454–461.

Schumaker, J. B., Deshler, D. D., Alley, G. R., Warner, M. W. & Denton, P. H. (1982) Multipass: A learning strategy for improving reading comprehension. *Learning Disability Quarterly, 5*, 295–304.

Schumaker, J. B., Pederson, C. S., Hazel, J. S. & Meyer, E. L. (1983) Social skills curriculum for mildly handicapped adolescents: A review. *Focus on Exceptional Children, 4*, 1–16.

Schumaker, J. B., Nolan, S. M. & Deshler, D. D. (1985) *Learning Strategies Curriculum: The Error-Monitoring Strategy*. Lawrence: University of Kansas.

Schumaker, J. B., Deshler, D. D. & McKnight, P. C. (1991) Teaching routines for content areas at the secondary level. In G. Stoner, M. Shinn & H. Walker (Eds.), *Intervention for Achievement and Behavioral Problems* (pp. 473–494). Silver Springs, MD: National Association of School Psychologists.

Schunk, D. H. (1996) Goal and self-evaluative influence during children's cognitive skill learning. *American Educational Research Journal, 24* (2), 359–382.

Scott, J. A. & Nagy, W. E. (1997) Understanding the definitions of unfamiliar verbs. *Reading Research Quarterly. 32* (2), 184–200.

Seligman, M. (1990) A gifted ninth grader tells it like it is today. *Gifted Child Today 13* (4), 9–11.

Seligman, M. E. P. (1991) *Learned Optimism*. New York: Knopf.

Sfard, A. (1998) On two metaphors for learning and the dangers of choosing just one. *Educational Researcher 27* (2), 4–13.

Shaffer, D. & Craft, L. (1999) Methods of adolescent suicide prevention. *The Journal of Clinical Psychiatry, 60*, 70–74.

Shannon, T. R. & Polloway, E. A. (1993) Promoting error and monitoring in middle school students with L.D. *Intervention in School and Clinic, 28* (3), 160–164.

Share, D. L. (1999) Phonological recoding and orthographic learning: A direct test of the self-teaching hypothesis. *Journal of Experimental Psychology, 72*, 95–129.

Shavelson, R. J. (1983) Review of research on teachers' pedagogical judgements, plans, and decisions. *Elementary School Journal, 83*, 392–413.

Shavelson, R. J. & Stern P. (1981) Research on teachers' pedagogical thoughts, judgements, decisions, and behavior. *Review of Educational Research, 51*, 455–498.

Shepard, L. A., Flexer, R. J., Hiebert, E. H., Marion, S. F., Mayfield, V. & Weston, T. J. (1995) *Effects Of Introducing Classroom Performance Assessment On Student Learning*. CSE Technical Report 394. Los Angeles CA: National Center for Research on Evaluation, Standards, and Student Testing (CRESST).

Sheridan, S. M. (1995) *Tough Kid Social Skills*. Longmont, CO: Sopris West.

Shinn, M. R. (1989) *Curriculum-Based Measurement: Assessing Special Children.* New York: Guilford.

Shinn, M. R. & Hubbard, D. D. (1992) Curriculum-based measurement and problem-solving assessment: Basic procedures and outcomes. *Focus on Exceptional Children, 24* (5), 1–20.

Shinn, M. R., Good, R. H., III, Knutson, N., Tilly, D. W., III & Collins, V. L. (1992) Curriculum-based measurement of reading fluency: A confirmatory analysis of its relationship to reading. *School Psychology Review, 21* (3), 485–478.

Shrum, L. (1996) Psychological processes underlying cultivation effects: Further tests of construct accessibility. *Human Communication Research, 22* (4), 482–509.

Shu, H., Anderson, R. C. & Zhang, H. (1995) Incidental learning of word meanings while reading: A Chinese and American cross-cultural study. *Reading Research Quarterly, 30* (1), 76–95.

Shuell, T. J. (1990) Phases of meaningful learning. *Review of Educational Research, 60* (4), 531–547.

Shulman, L. S. (1986) Paradigms and research programs in the study of teaching: A contemporary perspective. In M. C. Wittrock (Ed.), *Handbook of Research on Teaching.* 3rd Ed. New York: Macmillan.

Siegler, R. S. (1983) How knowledge influences learning. *American Scientist, 71,* 631–638.

Sikorski, M. F., Niemiec, R. P. & Walberg, H. J. (1996) A classroom checkup: Best teaching practices methods. *Teaching Exceptional Children, 29* (1), 27–29.

Silbert, J., Carnine, D. & Stein, M. (1990) *Direct Instruction Mathematics.* 2nd Ed. Columbus, OH: Merrill.

Simmons, D. C. & Kameenui, E. J. (1989) Direct instruction of decoding skills and strategies. *LD Forum, 15* (1), 35–38.

Simmons, D. C. & Kameenui, E. J. (1990) The effect of task alternatives on vocabulary knowledge: A comparison of students with and without learning disabilities. *Journal of Learning Disabilities, 23* (5), 291–297.

Simmons, D. C. & Kameenui, E. J. (1998) A focus on curriculum design: When children fail. In E. O. Meyen, G. A. Vergason & R. J. Whelen (Eds.), *Educating Students with Mild Disabilities: Strategies and Methods.* Denver, CO: Love Publishing.

Simpson, M. L. (1995) Talk throughs: A strategy for encouraging active learning across the content areas. *Journal of Reading, 38* (4), 296–304.

Simpson, R. L. (1998) Behavior modification for children and youth with exceptionalities: Application of best practice methods. *Intervention in School and Clinic, 33* (4), 219–226.

Simpson, M. D. (1999) Suicide prevention: What you can do. *NEA Today, 17* (5), 25.

Slavin, R. E. (1998) Can education reduce social inequality? *Educational Leadership, 55*(4), 6–10.

Smith, F. (1982) *Writing and the Writer.* New York: Holt, Rinehart & Winston.

Smith, P. L. (1992) *A Model for Selection from Supplantive and Generative Instructional Strategies for Problem-Solving Instruction.* Paper presented at the conference of the American Educational Research Association, San Francisco, CA. April, 1992.

Snider, V. E. (1992) Learning styles and learning to read. *Remedial and Special Education, 13* (1), 6–18.

Snow, R. E. & Lohman, D. F. (1984) Toward a theory of cognitive aptitude for learning from instruction. *Journal of Educational Psychology, 76* (3), 347–376.

Spaai, G. W., Ellermann, H. H. & Reitsma, P. (1991) Effects of segmented and whole-word sound feedback on learning to read single words. *Journal of Educational Research, 84* (4), 204–213.

Spache, G. D. (1940) Characteristic errors of good and poor spellers. *Journal of Educational Research, 34,* 182–189.

Spady, W. G. (1988) Organizing for results: The basis of authentic restructuring and reform. *Educational Leadership, 46,* 4–8.

Sparks, R. & Ganschow, L. (1995) Parent perceptions in the screening performance in foreign language courses. *Foreign Language Annals, 28* (3), 371–391.

Spaulding, C. L. (1995) Teacher's psychological presence on student's writing-task engagement. *The Journal of Educational Research, 88* (4), 210–219.

Spires, H. A. & Donley, J. (1998) Prior knowledge activation: Inducing engagement with informal texts. *Journal of Educational Psychology, 90* (2), 249–260.

Spiro, R. J., Coulson, R. C., Feltovich, P. & Anderson, D. K. (1988) *Cognitive Flexibility Theory: Advanced Knowledge Acquisition in Ill-Structured Domains* (Tech. Report No. 441). Urbana-Champaign: University of Illinois, Center for the Study of Reading.

Sprick, M., Howard, L. & Fidanque, A. (1998) *Read Well: Critical Foundations in Primary Reading.* Longmont, CO: Sopris West.

Sprick, R., Garrison, M. & Howard, L. (1998) *Champs: A Proactive and Positive Approach to Classroom Management for Grades K–9.* Longmont, CO: Sopris West.

Stahl, S. A. (1990) Riding the pendulum: A rejoinder to Schickedanz and McGee and Lomax. *Review of Educational Research, 60* (1), 141–151.

Stahl, S. A. & Kuhn, M. R. (1995) Does whole language instruction matched to learning styles help children learn to read? *School Psychology Review, 24,* 393–404.

Stahl, S. A., Jacobson, M. G., Davis, C. E. & Davis, R. L. (1991) Prior knowledge and difficult vocabulary in the comprehension of unfamiliar text. *Reading Research Quarterly, 26* (1), 27–43.

Stahl, S. A., Duffy-Hester, A. M. & Dougherty-Stahl, K. A. (1998) Everything you wanted to know about phonics (but were afraid to ask). *Reading Research Quarterly, 33* (3), 338–355.

Stallings, J. A. (1995) Ensuring teaching and learning in the 21st century. *Educational Researcher, 24* (6), 4–8.

Stanovich, K. E. (1986) Matthew effects in reading: Some consequences of individual differences in the acquisition of literacy. *Reading Research Quarterly, 21* (4), 360–407.

Stanovich, K. E. (1991) Discrepancy definitions of reading disability: Has intelligence led us astray? *Reading Research Quarterly, 26* (1), 7–29.

Stanovich, K. E. (1994) Romance and reality. *The Reading Teacher, 47* (4), 280–290.

Starlin, C. M. (1982) *Iowa Monograph: On Reading and Writing.* Des Moines, IA: Department of Public Instruction.

Stein, M., Silbert, J. & Carnine, D. (1997) *Designing Effective Mathematical Instruction.* Englewood Cliffs, NJ: Prentice-Hall.

Stein, M., Carnine, D. & Dixon, R. (1998) Direct instruction: Integrating curriculum and effective teaching practice. *Intervention in School and Clinic, 33* (4), 227–234.

Stephanson, J. & Linfoot, K. (1996) Intentional communication and graphic symbol use by students with severe intellectual disability. *International Journal of Disability, Development, and Education, 43* (2), 147–165.

Stephenson, W. (1980) Newton's fifth rule and Q methodology application to educational psychology. *American Psychologist, 35,* 882–889.

Stevens, R. J. & Salisbury, J. D. (1997) Accommodating student heterogeneity in mainstreamed elementary classrooms through cooperative learning. In J. W. Lloyd, E. J. Kameenui & D. Chard (Eds.), *Issues in Educating Students with Disabilities.* Mahwah, NJ: Lawrence Erlbaum.

Stodolsky, S. S. & Grossman, P. L. (1995) The impact of subject matter on curricular activity: An analysis of five academic subjects. *American Educational Research Journal, 32* (2), 227–249.

Stone, J. E. (1996) Developmentalism: An obscure but pervasive restriction on educational improvement. *Educational Policy Analysis Archives, 4* (8), http://seamonkey.ed.asu.edu/epaa/.

Stormont, M. & Zentall, S. S. (1999) Assessment of setting in the behavioral ratings of preschoolers with and without high levels of activity. *Psychology in the Schools, 36* (2), 109–115.

Stough, L. M. & Baker, L. (1999) Identifying depression in students with mental retardation. *Teaching Exceptional Children, 31* (4), 62–66.

Stowitschek, J. J., Stowitschek, C. E., Hendrickson, J. M. & Day, R. M (1984) *Direct Teaching Tactics for Exceptional Children.* Rockville, MD: Aspen.

Strickland, B. & Turnbull, A. (1990) *Developing and Implementing Individualized Education Programs* 3rd Ed. Columbus, OH: Merrill.

Sugai, G. (1997) Using flowcharts to plan teaching strategies. *Teaching Exceptional Children, 29* (3), 37–42.

Sugai, G. & Pruitt, R. (1993) *Phases, Steps, and Guidelines for Building School Wide Behavior Management Programs.* Eugene, OR: Behavior Disorders Program.

Sulzer-Azaroff, B. & Mayer, R. (1991) *Behavior Analysis for Lasting Change.* New York: Holt, Rinehart & Winston.

Susskind, J., Maurer, K., Thakkar, V., Hamilton, D. L. & Sherman, J. W. (1999) Perceiving individuals and groups: Expectancies, dispositional inferences, and causal attributions. *Journal of Personality and Social Psycholoy, 76*(2), 181–191.

Swaggart, B. (1998) Implementing a cognitive behavior management program. *Intervention in School and Clinic, 33* (4), 235–238.

Swanson, P.N. & DeLaPaz, S. (1998) Teaching effective comprehension strategies to students with learning and reading disabilities. *Intervention in School and Clinic, 33* (4), 209–218.

Swanson, H. & Hoskyn, M. (1998) Experimental intervention research on students with learning disabilities: A meta-analysis of treatment outcomes. *Review of Educational Research 68* (3), 277–321.

Swanson, S. & Howell, C. (1996) Test anxiety in adolescents with learning disabilities and behavior disorders. *Exceptional Children, 62* (5), 389–398.

Sweller, J. (1990) On the limited evidence for the effectiveness of teaching general problem-solving strategies. *Journal for Research in Mathematics Education, 21* (5), 411–415.

Tateyama-Sniezek, K. M. (1990) Cooperative learning: Does it improve the academic achievement of students with handicaps? *Exceptional Children, 56* (5), 425–437.

Teddlie, C., Kirby, P.C. & Stringfield, S. (1989) Effective versus ineffective schools: Observable differences in the classroom. *American Journal of Education, 97,* 221–236.

Telzrow, C. F. (1999) IDEA amendments of 1997: Promise or pitfall for special education reform? *Journal of School Psychology, 32* (1), 7–28.

Templeton, S. & Morris, D. (1999) Questions teachers ask about spelling. *Reading Research Quarterly, 34* (1), 102–112.

Templin, M. C. (1957) *Certain Language Skills in Children: Their Development and Interrelationships.* Minneapolis: University of Minnesota Press.

Tennenbaum, H. A. (1983) Effects of oral reading rate and inflection on comprehension and its maintenance. Doctoral Dissertation, University of Florida. *Dissertation Abstracts International, 45,* 1086A.

Terwilliger, J. S. (1998) Rejoinder: Response to Wiggins and Neumann. *Educational Researcher 27* (6), 22–33.

Tharp, R. (1989) Psycho-cultural variables and constant: Effects on teaching and learning in schools. *American Psychologist, 44,* 349–359.

Tharp, R. & Gallimore, R. (1989) Rousing schools to life. *American Education, 13* (2), 20–25.

Thistlethwaite, L. L. (1991) Summarizing: It's more than finding the main idea. *Intervention in School and Clinic, 27,* 25–30.

Thomas, J. W. (1993) Promoting independent learning in the middle grades: The role of instructional support practices. *Elementary School Journal, 93* (5), 575–591.

Thompson, L. & Majsterek, D. J. (1992) *Classroom Procedures for Increasing Phonological Awareness of Preschool Children: Justification and Preliminary Support.* Paper presented at the Annual Meeting of the American Education Research Association, San Francisco, CA. April 20, 1992.

Thorndike, R. L. & Hagan, E. (1969) *Measurement and Evaluation in Psychology and Education.* 3rd Ed. New York: Wiley.

Thornton, N. E., Bohlmeyer, E. M., Dickson, L. A. & Kulhavy, R. W. (1990) Spontaneous and imposed study tactics in learning prose. *Journal of Experimental Education, 58* (2), 111–124.

Thurlow, M. L. & Ysseldyke, J. (1997) Large-scale assessment participation and reporting issues: Implications for local decisions. *Diagnostique, 22* (4), 225–236.

Tilly, D. W. & Flugum, K. R. (1995) Best practices in ensuring quality interventions. In A. Thomas & J. Grimes (Eds.), *Best Practices in School Psychology.* Vol. 3. Washington, DC: NASP Publications.

Tindal, G. A. & Hasbrouck, J. (1991) Analyzing student writing to develop instructional strategies. *Learning Disabilities Research and Practice, 6,* 237–245.

Tindal, G. A. & Marston, D. B. (1990) *Classroom-Based Assessment.* Columbus, OH: Merrill.

Tindal, G. & Nolet, V. W. (1996) Serving students with learning disabilities in middle school content classes: A heuristic study of critical variables linking instruction and assessment. *Journal of Special Education, 29* (4), 414–432.

Tobias, S. (1994) Interest, prior knowledge, and learning. *Review of Educational Research, 64* (1), 37–54.

Tomlinson, C. A., Callahan, C. M., Tomchin, E. M., Eiss, N., Imbeau, M. & Landrum, M. (1997) Becoming architects of communities of learning: Addressing academic diversity in contemporary classrooms. *Exceptional Children, 63* (2), 269–282.

Tompkins, G. (1994) *Teaching Writing: Balancing Process and Product.* Englewood Cliffs, NJ: MacMillan.

Tompkins, G. (1997) *Literacy for the Twenty-First Century: A Balanced Approach.* Des Moines, IA: Merrill-Prentice Hall.

Torgesen, J. & Kail, R. J. (1980) Memory processes in exceptional children. In B. K. Keogh (Ed.), *Advances in Special Education: Basic Constructs and Theoretical Orientations.* Vol. 1. Greenwich, CT: JAI Press.

Treiman, R. (1985) Onsets and rims as units of spoken syllabus: Evidence from children. *Journal of Experimental Child Psychology, 39,* 161–181.

Tversky, A. & Kahneman, D. (1973) Availability: A heuristic for judging frequency and probability. *Cognitive Psychology, 5,* 207–232.

Tversky, A. & Kahneman, D. (1988) Judgement under uncertainty: Heuristics and biases. In H. R. Arkes & K. R. Hammond (Eds.), *Judgement and Decision Making.* New York: Cambridge University.

Tversky, A. & Koehler, D. J. (1994) Support theory: A non-extensional representation of subjective probability. *Psychological Review, 101* (4), 547–567.

Udvari-Solner, A. (1996) Examining teacher thinking: Constructing a process to designing curricular adaptations. *Remedial and Special Education 17* (4), 245–254.

Ulman, J. D. & Rosenberg, M. S. (1986) Science and superstition in special education. *Exceptional Children, 52,* 459–460.

Valencia, S. (1990) A portfolio approach to classroom reading assessment: The whys, whats, and hows (assessment). *Reading Teacher, 43* (4), 338–340.

Valencia, S. W. & Wixson, K. K. (1991) Diagnostic teaching. *The Reading Teacher, 44* (6), 420–422.

Valencia, S. W., Stallmann, A. C., Commeyras, M., Pearson, D. P. & Hartman, D. D. (1990) *Four Measures of Topical Knowledge: A Study of Construct Validity* (Tech. Report No. 501). Urbana-Champaign: University of Illinois, Center for the Study of Reading.

Valencia, S., McGinley, W. L. & Pearson, D. P. (1992) Assessing literacy in the middle school. In G. Duffy (Ed.), *Reading in the Middle School.* 2nd Ed. Newark, DE: International Reading Association.

Valli, L., Cooper, D. & Frankes, L. (1997) Professional development schools and equity. In M. W. Apple (Ed.), *Review of Research in Education.* Vol. 22, pp. 251–304. Washington: American Educational Research Association.

Vanci-Osam, U. (1998) May you be shot with greasy bullets: Curse utterances in Turkish. *Asian Folklore Studies, 57*(1), 71–86.

Van de Walle, J. A. (1998) *Elementary and Middle School Mathematics: Teaching Developmentally* 3rd Ed. Reading, MA: Addison-Wesley Longman, Inc.

Vaughn, S., Moody, S. W. & Schumm, T. S. (1998) Broken promises: Reading instruction in the resource room. *Exceptional Children, 64* (2), 211–225.

Vernarec, E. (1998) The high cost of hidden conditions. *Business and Health, 16* (1), 19–23.

Wade, S. E., Trathen, W. & Schraw, G. (1990) An analysis of spontaneous study strategies. *Reading Research Quarterly, 25* (2), 147–166.

Wagner, R. K. & Sternberg, R. J. (1984) Alternative conceptions of intelligence and their implications for education. *Review of Educational Research, 54,* 179–223.

Walberg, H. J. (1988) Synthesis of research on time and learning. *Educational Leadership, 45,* 76–85.

Walker, H. M. & Rankin, R. (1983) Assessing the behavioral expectations and demand of less restrictive settings. *School Psychology Review, 12,* 274–284.

Walker, H. M. & Stieber, S. (1998) Teacher ratings of social skills as longitudinal predictors of long-term arrest status in sample of at-risk males. *Behavioral Disorders, 23* (4), 222–230.

Walker, H. M., Colvin, G. & Ramsey, E. (1995) *Antisocial Behavior in School: Strategies and Best Practices.* Pacific Grove, CA: Brooks/Cole.

Walker, H. M., Stieber, S. & Bullis, M. (1997) Longitudinal correlates of arrest status among at-risk males. *Journal of Child and Family Studies, 6* (3), 289–309.

Walling, M. D. & Martinek, T. J. (1995) Learned helplessness: A case study of a middle school student. *Journal of Teaching in Physical Education, 14* (4), 54–66.

Walpole, S. (1999) Changing texts, changing thinking: Comprehension demands of new science textbooks. *The Reading Teacher, 52* (4), 358–359.

Wang, M. C. & Peverly, S. T. (1987) The role of the learner: An individual difference variable in school learning and functioning. In M. C. Wang, M. C. Reynolds & H. J. Walberg (Eds.), *Handbook of Special Education: Research and Practice.* Vol. 1. New York: Pergamon.

Wang, M. C., Haertel, G. D. & Walberg, H. J. (1990) What influences learning? A content analysis of review literature. *Journal of Educational Research, 84,* 30–43.

Warner, C. L. (1992) *Peer Tutoring: When Working Together Is Better Than Working Alone.* Research and Resources No. 30. ERIC/OSEP Special Project. Reston, VA: The Council for Exceptional Children.

Warner, M. M., Cheney, C. O. & Pienkowski, D. M. (1996) Guidelines for developing and evaluating programs for secondary students with mild disabilities. *Intervention in School and Clinic, 31* (5), 276–284.

Wassermann, S. (1999) Shazam! You're a Teacher. *Phi Delta Kappan, 80* (6), 464–468.

Waters, J. V. (1997) Staff training: Taking the child's perspective. *Young Children, 52* (3), 38–41.

Waugh, R. P. (1975) The I.T.P.A.: Ballast or bonanza for the school psychologist? *Journal of School Psychology, 13,* 201–208.

Webber, J., Anderson, T. & Otey, L. (1991) Teacher mindsets for surviving in BD classrooms. *Intervention in School and Clinic, 26* (5), 288–292.

Weed, K., Ryan, E. B. & Day, J. (1990) Metamemory and attributions as mediators of strategy use and recall. *Journal of Educational Psychology, 82* (4), 849–855.

Weinstein, C. E. & Mayer, R. E. (1983) The teaching of learning strategies. *Innovation Abstracts, 5* (32).

Wells, G. (1973) *Coding Manual of the Description of Child Speech.* Bristol, England: University of Bristol School of Education.

Westby, C. (1992) Whole language and learners with mild handicaps. *Focus on Exceptional Children, 24* (8), 1–16.

White, O. R. (1986) Precision teaching—Precision learning. *Exceptional Children, 52,* 522–534.

White, O. R. & Haring, N. G. (1982) *Exceptional Teaching.* 2nd Ed. Columbus, OH: Merrill.

Wigfield, A., Eccles, J. & Rodriguez, D. (1998) The development of children's motivation in school context. *Review of Research in Education, 23,* 73–118.

Wiig, E. H. & Semel, E. (1984) *Language Assessment and Intervention for the Learning Disabled.* 2nd Ed. Columbus, OH: Merrill.

Wiig, E. H., Freedman, E. & Secord, W. (1992) Developing words and concepts in the classroom: A holistic-thematic approach. *Intervention in School Clinic, 27* (5), 278–285.

Williams, J. P. (1984) Phonemic analysis and how it relates to reading. *Annual Review of Learning Disabilities, 2,* 91–96.

Williams, R. G. & Haladyna, T. M. (1982) Logical operations for generating intended questions (LOGIQ): A typology for higher order level test items. In G. H. Roid & T. M. Haladyna (Eds.), *A Technology for Test-item Writing* (pp. 161–186). New York: Academic Press.

Willis, G. W. (1985) Successive and simultaneous processing: A note on interpretation. *Journal of Psychoeducational Assessment, 4,* 343–346.

Winn, W. (1991) Learning from maps and diagrams. *Educational Psychology Review, 3* (3), 211–247.

Wisker, G. & Brown, S. (1996) Enabling students learning, systems & strategies. In *Staff & Educational Development Series.* London, England.

Wolery, M., Bailey, D. B., Jr. & Sugai, G. M. (1989) *Effective Teaching: Applied Behavior Analysis with Exceptional Students.* Boston: Allyn & Bacon.

Wolfe, J. A., Mertler, C. A. & Hoffman, J. S. (1998) Do increasing adolescent suicide rates result in increasing prevention/postvention programs in Ohio schools?: A survey. *Education, 118* (3), 426–439.

Wong, S. (1973) What are we doing about proofreading? *Journal of Business Education, 49* (3), 122–124.

Wong, B. Y. L. (1991a) *Learning about Learning Disabilities.* San Diego: Academic Press.

Wong, B. Y. L. (1991b) The relevance of metacognition to learning disabilities. In B. Y. L. Wong (Ed.), *Learning About Learning Disabilities.* San Diego: Academic Press.

Wong, K. L. H., Kauffman, J. M. & Lloyd, J. W. (1991) Choices for integration: Selecting teachers for mainstreamed students with emotional and behavioral disorders. *Intervention in School and Clinic, 27,* 108–115.

Wong, S. (1975) Proofreading pitfalls. *Business Education Forum, 29* (8), 16–17.

Woodward, J. (1999) Redoing the numbers: Secondary math for a postsecondary work world. *Teaching Exceptional Children, 31* (4), 74–79.

Woolery, M. & Schuster, J. W. (1997) Instructional methods with students who have significant disabilities. *Journal of Special Education, 31* (1), 61–79.

Wraga, W. (1999) Extracting sun-beams out of cucumbers: The retreat from practice in reconceptualized curriculum studies. *Educational Researcher, 28* (1), 4–13.

Yavorsky, D. K. (1977) *Discrepancy Evaluation: A Practitioner's Guide.* Charlottesville, VA: University of Virginia, Evaluation Research Center.

Yell, M. (1998) *The Law and Special Education.* Columbus, OH: Merrill/Prentice Hall.

Yoder, P. & Davies, B. (1990) Do parental questions and topic continuations elicit replies from developmentally delayed children? A sequential analysis. *Journal of Speech and Hearing Research, 33* (3), 563–573.

Yoder, P. & Davies, B. (1992) Do children with developmental delays use more frequent and diverse language in verbal routines? *American Journal on Mental Retardation, 97* (2), 197–208.

Yoder, P. J., Spruytenburg, H., Edwards, A. & Davies, B. (1995) Effects of verbal routine contexts and expansions on gains in the mean length of utterance in children with developmental delays. *Journal of Language, Speech, and Hearing Services in Schools, 26* (1), 21–32.

Yopp, H. K. (1988) The validity and reliability of phonemic awareness tests. *Reading Research Quarterly, 23,* 159–177.

Yopp, H. K. (1992a) Developing phonemic awareness in young children. *The Reading Teacher, 45* (9), 696–703.

Yopp, H. K. (1992b) *A Longitudinal Study of Phonological Awareness and Its Relationship to Reading Achievement.* Paper presented at the Annual Meeting of the American Educational Research Association, San Francisco, CA.

Ysseldyke, J. E. (1987) The impact of screening and referral practices in early childhood special education: Policy consideration and research directions. *Journal of Special Education, 21* (2), 85–96.

Ysseldyke, J. E. & Christenson, S. L. (1987) *TIES: The Instructional Environment Scale.* Austin, TX: Pro-Ed.

Ysseldyke, J. E. & Christenson, S. L. (1996) *TIES II: The Instructional Environment System-II.* Longmont, Co: Sopris West.

Ysseldyke, J. E. & Olsen, K. (1997) *Putting Alternate Assessments into Practice: What to Measure and Possible Sources of Measurement* (Data Synthesis Report No. 28). ERIC Document Reproduction Service No. ED 416605. Minneapolis, MN: National Association of State Directors of Special Education.

Ysseldyke, J. E., Thurlow, M., Graden, J., Wesson, C., Algozzine, B. & Deno, S. (1983) Generalizations from five years of research on assessment and decision making: The University of Minnesota Institute. *Exceptional Education Quarterly, 4* (1), 75–93.

Ysseldyke, J. E., Algozzine, B. J. & Thurlow, M. L. (Eds.) (1992) *Critical Issues in Special Education.* Dallas, TX: Houghton Mifflin.

Ysseldyke, J. E., Thurlow, M. L., McGrew, K. & Vanderwood, M. (1994) *Making Decisions about the Inclusion of Students with Disabilities in Large Scale Assessments* (Synthesis Report 13). Minneapolis, MN: University of Minnesota and National Center on Educational Outcomes.

Ysseldyke, J. E., Vanderwood, M. L. & Shriner, J. (1997) Changes over the past decade in special education referral to placement probability: An incredibly reliable practice. *Diagnostique 23* (1), 193–202.

Zephr, H. (1990) *Changing Lenses.* Scottsdale, PA: Herald Press.

Zigmond, N. (1997) Educating students with disabilities: The future of special education. In J. W. Lloyd, E. J. Kameenui & D. Chard (Eds.), *Issues in Educating with Disabilities.* New Jersey: Lawrence Erlbaum Associates.

Zionts, P. (1996) *Teaching Disturbed and Disturbing Students: An Integrative Approach.* 2nd Ed. Austin, TX: Pro-Ed.

Zirpoli, T. J. & Melloy, K. J. (1997) *Behavior Management: Applications for Teachers and Parents.* Columbus, OH: Merrill.

# Photo Credits

Page 1: Mimi Forsyth/Monkmeyer; page 8: Sybil Shelton/Monkmeyer; page 19: Frank Siteman/Monkmeyer; page 43: Will Hart/Photo Edit; page 85: Mary Kay Denny/Tony Stone Images; page 116: Robert Kalman/The Image Works; page 163: Elizabeth Crews/The Image Works; page 181: Miriam Reinhart/Photo Researchers; page 201: Barbara Rios/Photo Researchers; page 204: Myrleen Ferguson/Photo Edit; page 252: Mimi Forsyth/Monkmeyer; page 295: Nancy Sheehan/Photo Edit; page 327: Zigy Kaluzny/Tony Stone Images; page 362: Michael Newman/Photo Edit; page 391: Jonathan Meyers/Monkmeyer; page 432: Kathy McLaughlin/The Image Works.

# Name Index

# Subject Index